Catholicity Challenging Ethnicity

European University Studies

Europäische Hochschulschriften

Publications Universitaires Européennes

Series XXIII	**Theology**
Reihe XXIII	Theologie
Série XXIII	Théologie

Volume/Band **954**

Erik Berggren

Catholicity Challenging Ethnicity

An Ecclesiological Study of Congregations and Churches in Post-apartheid South Africa

Bibliographic Information published by the Deutsche Nationalbibliothek
The Deutsche Nationalbibliothek lists this publication in the Deutsche Nationalbibliografie;
detailed bibliographic data is available in the internet at http://dnb.d-nb.de.

ISSN 0721-3409
ISBN 978-3-631-66055-3 (Print)
E-ISBN 978-3-653-05387-6 (E-Book)
DOI 10.3726/978-3-653-05387-6

© Peter Lang GmbH
Internationaler Verlag der Wissenschaften
Frankfurt am Main 2016
All rights reserved.
PL Academic Research is an Imprint of Peter Lang GmbH.
Peter Lang – Frankfurt am Main · Bern · Bruxelles · New York · Oxford · Warszawa · Wien

All parts of this publication are protected by copyright. Any utilisation outside
the strict limits of the copyright law, without the permission of the publisher,
is forbidden and liable to prosecution. This applies in particular to reproductions,
translations, microfilming, and storage and processing in electronic retrieval systems.

This publication has been peer reviewed.

www.peterlang.com

To Helena, Gabriel and Elise.

Contents

Acknowledgements 15

Part I

Chapter One: Introduction 19
1.1 General Outline of the Thesis 22
1.2 An Abductive Reasoning Approach 22
1.3 'Catholicity' as an analytical tool to study Congregations
 and Churches 24
1.4 Limitations 26
1.5 Material 28
1.6 Previous Research 29
1.7 Terminology and Definitions 32
1.8 Differentiation of People 38
1.9 Disposition 45

Chapter Two: Church Rejecting Division 47
2.1 Declarations, Conferences and Consultations before
 Democratisation 47
 'Message to the People of South Africa' and the Kairos Document 48
 The Rustenburg Conference and Declaration 49
 The Cape Town Consultation and Statement 51
2.2 Consultations after Democratisation 53
 Vanderbijlpark Consultation and Statement 53
 Johannesburg Consultation 55
2.3 The TRC's Faith Communities Hearing 56
 Institutional Hearings 57
 Roman Catholic Church 58

7

	Church of the Province of Southern Africa (Anglican Church of Southern Africa)	59
	The Methodist Church of Southern Africa	60
	Apostolic Faith Mission of South Africa	61
	ELCSA, ELCSA N-T and ELCSA-Cape	63
	The TRC's Final Report	64
	The TRC's Recommendations to the Faith Communities	66
2.4	Conclusion	67

Chapter Three: Catholicity of the Church 69

3.1	Catholicity in Faith & Order and the WCC	70
	Church as Catholic, described as the Body of Christ	73
	Catholicity in Christology and Pneumatology	76
	Baptism as incorporation in the Body of Christ	77
	The Role of the Eucharist in Catholicity	79
	Koinonia in Catholicity	80
	The Church as Local and Catholic	82
	Catholicity Makes the Church a Sharing Community	83
	The Catholicity of the Church: An *in via* Perspective	85
	Catholicity in Apostolicity	86
	Catholicity as Inclusion and Exclusion	87
3.2	Catholicity as an Analytical Tool for Studying Ethnicity	89
	The Christian Communion Transcends the Local Congregation	90
	Ethnicity Transcends Division	95
	Reconciliation of Ethnic Division is part of the Church's Ministry	97
	Languages Contribute to the Church's Diversity	99
	Poverty Eradication Eliminates Ethnic Boundaries	101
3.3	Conclusions	103

Chapter Four: Ecclesiology in Practice 105

4.1	'New Ecclesiology' and 'Modern Ecclesiology'	105
4.2	Ecclesiology and Ethnography	107

4.3	Ecclesiologies Revealed	109
	Practices	111
	Ecclesial Practices	113
	South African Churches and their Operative Ecclesiology	115
4.4	Case Study Design	115
	Researcher's Background	116
	Choice of Churches	116
	Choice of Congregations	117
	Choice of Churches' Leaders and Resource Persons	118
	Research Ethics	119
4.5	Case Study Approach	120
	Interviews	121
	Individual Interviews	122
	Group Interviews	123
	Observations	125
	Collected Printed Material, Websites, DVD	125
4.6	Conclusions	126

Part II

Chapter Five: Congregations and Churches on South African Soil 131

5.1	The Churches in South Africa	131
	Roman Catholic Church	131
	Anglican Church	132
	Methodist Church	133
	Lutheran Churches	134
	Apostolic Faith Mission of South Africa	137
5.2	Congregations on the Ground	138
	Johannesburg – the Place of Gold	138
	St Peter Claver, Pimville – Roman Catholic Church	140

St Thomas' Anglican Church, Linden – Anglican Church of Southern Africa.. 144

Cape Town, the Mother City.. 147

Athlone Methodist Church – Methodist Church of Southern Africa 149

Lutheran Church Bellville – Evangelical Lutheran Church in Southern Africa Cape Church 151

Durban or eThekwini... 157

City Harvest Ministries, Ntuzuma – Apostolic Faith Mission of South Africa 159

St Michael's Evangelical Lutheran Church – Evangelical Lutheran Church in Southern Africa.. 163

5.3   Conclusions 170

Chapter Six: Reconciliation as Part of the Church's Ministry........... 173

6.1   Congregations as Communities for Reconciliation 173

St Peter Claver in Pimville – Roman Catholic Church................................. 174

St Thomas' in Linden – Anglican Church of Southern Africa 176

Athlone Methodist Church – Methodist Church of Southern Africa 179

Lutheran Church in Bellville – Evangelical Lutheran Church in Southern Africa Cape Church 181

City Harvest Ministries in Ntuzuma – Apostolic Faith Mission of South Africa 183

St Michael's Evangelical Lutheran Church – Evangelical Lutheran Church in Southern Africa.. 186

6.2   Church Leaders' views of Reconciliation.. 190

6.3   Commissioners of the TRC's views of Reconciliation 201

6.4   Conclusions 205

Chapter Seven: Ethnicity and the Christian Communion................. 209

7.1   Congregations Affected by Division 209

St Peter Claver in Pimville – Roman Catholic Church................................. 210

St Thomas' in Linden – Anglican Church of Southern Africa 213

Athlone Methodist Church – Methodist Church of Southern Africa 217

	Lutheran Church in Bellville – Evangelical Lutheran Church in Southern Africa Cape Church 223
	City Harvest Ministries in Ntuzuma – Apostolic Faith Mission of South Africa 226
	St Michael's Evangelical Lutheran Church – Evangelical Lutheran Church in Southern Africa 229
7.2	Ethnic Diversity or Division 231
	Roman Catholic Church 231
	Anglican Church 235
	Methodist Church 239
	Apostolic Faith Mission 243
	Lutheran Churches 247
7.3	Conclusions 252

Chapter Eight: Church Services Gathering Christian Communion or Ethnic Groups 257

8.1	Similarities and Differences 258
	St Peter Claver in Pimville – Roman Catholic Church 258
	St Thomas' in Linden – Anglican Church of Southern Africa 261
	Athlone Methodist Church – Methodist Church of Southern Africa 268
	Lutheran Church in Bellville – Evangelical Lutheran Church in Southern Africa Cape Church 271
	City Harvest Ministries in Ntuzuma – Apostolic Faith Mission of South Africa 275
	St Michael's Evangelical Lutheran Church – Evangelical Lutheran Church in Southern Africa 279
8.2	Diversity as an Obstacle for Communities 285
	Diverse Church Services 286
	Liturgy and Hymns 289
	The Residence of Worshipers and their Attendance at Services 293
	Eucharistic Celebration 295
	Diversity in Duration of Services 297
	Cultural Diversity 298

Prayers and Intercessions in Church Services 299
Confessing Catholicity 300
8.3   Conclusions 302

Chapter Nine: Tower of Babel or Day of Pentecost? 305

9.1   Congregations' Accommodation of Languages 305
St Peter Claver in Pimville – Roman Catholic Church 305
St Thomas' in Linden – Anglican Church of Southern Africa 307
Athlone Methodist Church – Methodist Church of Southern Africa 311
Lutheran Church in Bellville – Evangelical Lutheran Church in Southern Africa Cape Church 313
City Harvest Ministries in Ntuzuma – Apostolic Faith Mission of South Africa 319
St Michael's Evangelical Lutheran Church – Evangelical Lutheran Church in Southern Africa 320

9.2   Language Change in the Churches 323
9.3   Conclusions 328

Chapter Ten: Congregations' Relationships with Other Congregations and Churches 335

St Peter Claver in Pimville – Roman Catholic Church 335
St Thomas' in Linden – Anglican Church of Southern Africa 337
Athlone Methodist Church – Methodist Church of Southern Africa 340
Lutheran Church in Bellville – Evangelical Lutheran Church in Southern Africa – Cape Church 342
City Harvest Ministries in Ntuzuma – Apostolic Faith Mission of South Africa 345
St Michael's Evangelical Lutheran Church – Evangelical Lutheran Church in Southern Africa 348
Conclusions 353

Chapter Eleven: Congregations' and Churches' Ministries and Work towards Poverty Eradication 357

11.1   Local Engagement Serving Community and Society 357

St Peter Claver in Pimville – Roman Catholic Church 357
St Thomas' in Linden – Anglican Church of Southern Africa 359
Athlone Methodist Church – Methodist Church of Southern Africa 363
Lutheran Church in Bellville – Evangelical Lutheran Church in
Southern Africa Cape Church 368
City Harvest Ministries in Ntuzuma – Apostolic Faith Mission of
South Africa 371
St Michael's Evangelical Lutheran Church – Evangelical Lutheran
Church in Southern Africa 374

11.2 Difficulties in Making an Impact on Democratic Society 380

11.3 Conclusions 386

Part III

Chapter Twelve: The Church in an Ethnically-diverse Society 391

12.1 Theoretical Background, Analytical Tool, and Methodology 392

12.2 The Churches before Democratisation 395

12.3 The Churches' Visions for a New Society 396

12.4 Reconciliation as a Practice of Catholicity 397

12.5 Ethnicity and Socio-economic Conditions Challenge
     Congregations and Churches 399
     Church Organisations Serving Catholicity 402
     Sharing as an Instrument to Change Society and the Church 406
     Language as a Means to Communicate 408

12.6 Denominational Belonging Influences a Realised Catholicity 410

12.7 Final Comments 413

References 415

Abbreviations 447

Acknowledgements

During my time as a student at the Graduate School of Ecumenical Studies in Bossey, Geneva, I realised that differences of ethnic background had a vast effect on the student community. Living and working in South Africa was another experience where ethnic background affected how people related to one another, even in the church. My research is a result of such issues, which have intrigued me for many years.

Professor Sven-Erik Brodd came for an exchange visit to the University of Cape Town, encouraged me to become a doctoral student at Uppsala. Sven-Erik Brodd and my co-supervisor, Professor Kajsa Ahlstrand, have guided and accompanied me on my journey, giving me many challenges and much freedom. They have given me insights and new perspectives, and helped me with improvements. Their broad knowledge of Ecclesiology and World Christianity has inspired me in my research. I appreciate Sven-Erik's British kind of humour and Kajsa's many stories from diverse parts of the world.

I am honoured that the Faculty of Theology at Uppsala appointed me as a postgraduate with research and teaching. I have also had the opportunity to attend several training courses for university teachers that have increased my didactic competence. I was also granted a generous contribution from the university from the Sederholms scholarship for travel abroad. This made it possible to carry out the case studies in South Africa during the spring semester of 2011. I also received contributions from the Nathan Söderblom Memorial Foundation, Lund's Mission Society, and the Clergy Support Foundation.

I am grateful that the theological faculty at the University of Stellenbosch invited me to be a guest researcher during my stay in South Africa. Special thanks go to the International Office at the university, and in particular to Lidia du Plessis, who arranged the stay for the whole family. Few universities have such an excellent international office, and Lidia is brilliant.

Special thanks to church councils, congregations, church leaders, former TRC commissioners, and university academics in South Africa who gave me time for interviews, meetings, and discussions. Congregations allowed me to carry out my observations, and I receive several documents and a range of materials that were important for my research. The meetings became very important to me, and were special moments in my research. I also want to thank ELCSA, Cape Orange Diocese, and Bishop Andreas Fortuin, who originally invited me to work as a hospital chaplain in Kimberley 1999–2003. Without that invitation I would never have done this kind of research about South Africa.

Besides my supervisors, several people have, at different stages, examined parts of the thesis and provided valuable advice: Jan-Åke Alvarsson, Ninna Edgardh, Hans Engdahl, Sune Fahlgren, Ove Gustavsson, Anders Göranzon, Jonas Ideström, Mattias Martinson, and Herbert Moyo. The research seminar in ecclesiology has been an important and stimulating environment over the years, and I have made many new friends. The seminar has given me constructive criticism and feedback and offered many good post-seminars. I have also been invited to research seminars at the University of Western Cape and the University of KwaZulu-Natal, where I have presented papers and received valuable advice and comments.

Professor Dirk Smit from Stellenbosch came to Uppsala for a short but valuable visit to be my opponent at my final seminar. From him I received valuable and constructive advice to improve the whole thesis.

Barbro Engdahl has providing me with articles from South African libraries that were difficult for me to access from Sweden. Karin and Johannes Oljelund assisted me with materials from the Department of Government Communication and Information System in Pretoria. Viera Larsson has contributed the illustrations as part of the thesis' visual communication. Enid Nelson has at different stages helped me to choose the right vocabulary. My dissertation has profited greatly from Mike McCoy's corrections regarding language. He does not only speak English and Afrikaans, but also knows some isiXhosa and other languages, which has been valuable for this thesis. I appreciate his help very much.

I am grateful that the Faculty of Theology at Uppsala, the Segelbergska Foundation for Liturgical Research, and the CSM's Foundation for Mission Research have given financial support for the printing of the thesis.

My parents, Sven and Else-Britt, took me as a child to live in North and West Africa, broadening my horizons and forming me to be open to diverse forms of life. They have always supported and believed in me. My children Gabriel and Elise have reminded me that life is so much more than books and a computer. They have waited for the thesis to be finished. It is finally a book, and I hope now to have much time for them.

My wife Helena shares my passion for Africa and its people. She has given me support and encouragement throughout the whole process of completing the thesis. There are no words to express my love for you. This thesis is dedicated to you.

Uppsala November 2015
Erik Berggren

Part I

Chapter One: Introduction

South Africa is probably one of the most diverse countries in the world. Some people have even described South Africa as a continent in a country because of its enormous diversities. There are seas and deserts, mountains and fields, poverty and wealth, peace and violence, and people from many parts of the world. South Africa must have been one of the first multi-ethnic places in the world, but with a complex history that has produced a society full of contrasts. The extremes make the country very interesting but, at the same time, very challenging.

South Africa was colonised early in the European colonial period, and people were segregated according to background from the start. Its origins may be found in the first efforts of different people to live peacefully together, and in particular in the British attempts to systematise government and reconcile contrary interests.[1] When the National Party came to power in 1948 and began to implement its racially discriminatory policies, it legalised what had been going on for a long time. After the election of 1948 a more explicit path to a discriminatory society appeared in South Africa, and the term 'apartheid' was coined. No single area of society was exempt from the influence of discriminatory policies. Even the religious life was supposed to be included, but protests from the churches meant that this was never applied to the text of the law.[2] One of the central apartheid laws established certain territories and places of residence for each 'race' group, resulting in the compulsory relocation of certain parts of the population. The Group Areas Act of 1950 and the establishment of 'homelands', which earlier had been called 'reservations', separated the different groups in South African society almost completely.[3]

Apartheid in South Africa was one experiment among many others during the colonial era that were devised as an attempt to handle diversity, and to enable the colonial power to govern. The idea of creating apartheid was to handle ethnic diversity, but also to provide a basis for exploiting and oppressing the majority of the population. The whole society, including the churches, was affected by apartheid.

For a long time, South Africa's apartheid legislation permeated the whole society, and even churches became divided on 'racial' lines. The struggle against apartheid also induced many churches and religious groups to unite in action against the government. Because of international pressure, and wise leadership, South

---

1 Grundlingh, Albert, 1989, pp. 19–27.
2 South Africa & Apartheid, 1971, p. 17.
3 Thompson, Leonard, 2001, p. 194.

Africa overcame violence and political uprisings and succeeded with a peaceful democratisation process, leading to the first democratic elections in 1994.[4] Reconciliation became a key word, and influenced the transformation process as well as the development of the country when the new democratic government came to power. Inequalities, racism and divisions between people were supposed to be eliminated in order to unite the people of South Africa into one nation. It was also natural that diversity was accommodated to counter possible threats to national unity when the new constitution was drafted.[5]

Many years have passed since democratisation, but the society is still divided on the basis of peoples' backgrounds. Congregations and churches in South Africa are no exception: they too are divided. Studies of churches and diversity could have been undertaken in Sydney, Rio de Janeiro, New York, or London with similar patterns emerging. South Africa, however, is unique in its divisions because of its very specific history of a government policy that divided people into diverse ethnic groups.

Churches around the world have often avoided dealing with ethnic diversity. Various solutions for handling ethnic diversity within the churches have been adopted, both by churches themselves and by societies; but they are seldom studied and investigated. Some churches, for example, have tried to integrate people of different backgrounds within the same worshipping community, with varying degrees of success. Others have accepted the existence of different worshipping communities. They have understood that Church unity is to be found within the church as an organisation as dioceses or districts, but with diverse ethnic communities. Some churches have a divided organisation and divided worship communities according to ethnic background, and emphasise the unity of the church as a spiritual and eschatological reality.[6]

Unity in the Church in the face of human diversity is a challenge. The Church claims that baptised members are one single community, the body of Christ. At the same time, ethnic diversity often divides the human community into specific groups.[7] The South African churches are, from this point of view, uniquely

---

4   Thompson, Leonard, 2001, pp. 262–264.
5   De Beer, Frik C., 1989, pp. 32–39.
6   See for example: Polish mission among Roman Catholics: Pacyga, Dominic A., 1991, p. 132; German immigrants in America: Butler, Jon, 2008, pp. 74–78. When I use the term 'organisation' in the thesis I mean a church with congregation, parishes, deaneries, circuits, dioceses, districts, provinces etc. on local, regional and central levels.
7   Called to One Hope – The Gospel in Diverse Cultures, 1998, pp. 45–48.

placed to understand the relationship between catholicity and ethnicity because of the challenge of their history.[8]

In this thesis, I will investigate the relationship between the catholicity of the Church and ethnic diversity. The purpose of the thesis is twofold. Firstly, I want to develop the notion of 'catholicity' as an analytical tool, using key documents from the Faith & Order (F&O) movement and the World Council of Churches (WCC).[9] Secondly, using that analytical tool, I want to investigate how South African congregations and churches have been dealing with ethnic diversity two decades after democratisation.

To achieve my twofold purpose, I have analysed documents and texts from the beginnings of the international ecumenical movement to develop an analytical tool concerning the Church's catholicity. I have also conducted a case study of six congregations in South Africa and the denominations they belong to, two decades after the advent of democracy. Through interviews, observations, and printed material, I have established a body of source material that I will analyse through the lens of catholicity. When I use the term 'analytical tool' I mean that I have chosen specific issues from the ecumenical documents concerning the catholicity of the Church. These issues are adopted as a pattern to analyse the empirical material.

---

8   I have chosen to use ethnicity as my lens in studying the churches in South Africa. This determines the approach of the thesis. It would have been possible to develop other considerations to highlight the complexity of the South African context. I could, for example, have investigated the South African churches from the perspectives of inequality, power, class, economic privileges, 'White' peoples' supremacy, etc. The South African scholar Sampie Terreblanche, for example, has reinterpreted the South African history. He starts by describing the exploitation of the indigenous people by Europeans settlers until the end of apartheid. Terreblanche, Sampie, 2002. Ethnicity helps us to investigate important issues; but there are of course other issues that are not brought into focus by using ethnicity. Different issues of diversity in the South African society are nevertheless related to ethnicity, and are also evident in the thesis. I am fully aware that ethnicity is but one aspect, and that the picture is much bigger than a focus on ethnicity would suggest.

9   The Faith & Order movement and the Life & Work movement agreed to form the WCC in 1948. The International Missionary Council (IMC) merged with the WCC in 1961 and became the Commission on World Mission and Evangelism (CWME). The Roman Catholic Church is a member of Faith & Order (F&O) and the CWME, and the Pentecostal churches are members of the CWME. My decision to use only F&O documents might mean that I will not cover every aspect of the entire international ecumenical movement. I have, however, included statements and reports from the WCC's World Assemblies, which cover several areas of the international ecumenical movement.

Before I go on to describe the theory, method, research questions, and material, I will first explain the general outline of how I have chosen to structure the thesis.

1.1 General Outline of the Thesis

The thesis is divided into three parts, and I have chosen to place background, theory, and method in specific chapters rather than in the introductory chapter. The reason for this structure is that I do not want to produce an oversized chapter right at the beginning. A fuller disposition of the thesis will come at the end of this chapter.

Part I consists of a general introduction, history, theory, method, and material. A large part of the introductory chapter will explain how I am going to use specific terms in the thesis.

Part II will present the empirical material derived from the South African congregations and churches. Every chapter in this part examines diverse themes related to ethnicity, and all are productive to examine.

Part III will present the conclusions of the thesis, and I will discuss the theory and method that I have used.

In the sections that follow, I will offer a general introduction to the theory, method, and material and to the research questions. A more detailed elaboration will be presented in Chapters Three and Four.

1.2 An Abductive Reasoning Approach

I have adopted an abductive reasoning approach, which is most common in research that is based on case and field studies. Abductive reasoning can be characterised as a combination of inductive and deductive approaches; but it is not simply a mixture of inductive and deductive reasoning. It is a kind of interaction between empirical material and theory. During the process of abductive reasoning the theory is adjusted and refined.

The abductive approach can be criticised for not having a definite view point from the start of the study, and for allowing the theory to be adapted to the empirical material.[10]

The inductive approach has its own weaknesses: it does not always take into account the underlying structures or situations that have to be considered. It is based on a variety of individual cases, and claims that there is a correlation in

---

10 Alvesson, Mats, & Sköldberg, Kaj, 2008, pp. 41–46, 54–56.

the observed material that is generally valid. Generalisations are easily made on the basis of observed external connections. The deductive approach also suffers from the weakness of easily presupposing what is to be explained: it starts from a general rule, and confirms what is to be explained.[11]

My original intention, when I started my research, was to construct a theory of Catholicity based on the documents of the Truth and Reconciliation Commission (TRC), and especially the Faith Communities Hearing in East London in 1997. I would then have applied this material to the empirical material from the South African congregations and churches. I discussed my research design with several scholars in Europe and South Africa before I began my field study. Soon after I had begun to undertake the interviews, however, I realised that few interviewees indicated that the TRC had had any effect on them or their churches. Hardly any follow-up processes to the TRC were evident in the churches. There was also limited awareness of the Faith Communities Hearing and particularly of the TRC's final recommendations to the faith communities.

The knowledge that I thus acquired led me, in accordance with abductive reasoning, to change the theoretical foundation. I decided instead to use the key documents, statements, and papers of F&O and the WCC as the foundation for developing 'catholicity' as an analytical tool. However, it is essential to state that F&O and the WCC have not produced an extensive document on the Church's catholicity. I have instead analysed the key documents of F&O and the WCC from 1927 to 2011. I decided to stop in 2011 because my case study was conducted in 2011. I have analysed the documents concerning ethnicity, and have developed 'catholicity' as an analytical tool for studying the catholicity of the congregations and churches in South Africa. As a consequence of using this theoretical framework, I can also make statements about the congregations' and churches' catholicity. The analytical tool has been developed in dialogue with the empirical material, becoming refined during the process as part of the abductive approach. I will come back to this analytical tool in Chapter Three, where I will develop my theoretical framework.

I found it interesting that the ecumenical documents are very disparate. There is little continuity between the different meetings, assemblies, and studies. A subject has been discussed in one meeting, and another issue has drawn attention in the next meeting. One example is 'catholicity': it was highlighted during the Fourth World Conference on Faith and Order in Montreal in 1963. The issue was brought to the attention at the Fourth World Assembly of the WCC in

---

11 Alvesson, Mats, & Sköldberg, Kaj, 2008, pp. 41–46, 54–56.

Uppsala in 1968, but at the next World Assembly 'conciliar fellowship' was discussed instead. The Seventh World Assembly of the WCC in Canberra in 1991 dealt with the Holy Spirit, and the Fifth World Conference on Faith and Order in Santiago de Compostela in 1993 discussed the *koinonia* of the church. It is possible, however, to find clear statements about the Church's catholicity in the ecumenical texts and documents, despite the fact that the organisation has dealt with disparate issues concerning the Church.

1.3 'Catholicity' as an analytical tool to study Congregations and Churches

Ecumenical documents have been produced since the emergence of the modern ecumenical movement in the early twentieth century. The F&O and WCC documents contain material on the catholicity of the Church, both explicitly in the form of statements, but also implicitly in several documents.[12] I have used the F&O and the WCC's key documents as the foundation for creating an analytical tool about catholicity that is focused on ethnicity. This analytical tool has been applied to the empirical material in order to study the congregations' and churches' understanding of ethnicity. This means that there are three intentions. Firstly, the F&O and WCC documents make statements about the catholicity of the Church. Secondly, I am creating an analytical tool based on the ecumenical documents. Thirdly, the congregations' and churches' understanding of ethnicity can be revealed by using the analytical tool.[13] The analytical tool will, as mentioned earlier, be described in Chapter Three.

I have established an ecclesiology focused on ethnicity in the congregations and churches, based on the case study material mainly derived from interviews, but also based on observations, documents, statements, and various printed materials. My approach is based on the assumption that ecclesiology is made visible through ecclesiastical practices and also through congregations' and churches' statements, documents, resolutions, creeds, etc. I will apply an operative ecclesiology to both practices and doctrines in order to establish an ecclesiology of the South African

---

12 The Fourth World Assembly of the WCC at Uppsala, for example, had one section that exclusively dealt with the Catholicity of the Church. The Uppsala Report 1968, 1968, pp. 11–20. An example of a document that implicitly deals with the Church's catholicity is Baptism, Eucharist and Ministry. Baptism, Eucharist and Ministry, 1982, pp. 2–32.

13 The tool can also be seen as an evaluating tool to measure how well the congregations and churches have been dealing with ethnicity, and whether they are acting in accordance with the documents of the international ecumenical movement.

churches and congregations. The operative ecclesiology that I have used derives from the work of the French theologian Yves Congar, as later developed by other theologians. I argue that, according to Congar, it is possible to reveal a church's ecclesiology by examining both the doctrines and the practices of the church being studied.[14]

I will use the concept of 'realised catholicity' in the thesis. This expression will mean that the teaching of the Church about being 'catholic' is related to and interlinked with actions that are carried out in the Church. When the catholicity of the Church is lived, created, and practised, the catholicity of the Church is realised. The Church's practices cannot be isolated from the teaching about the Church as catholic. Realised catholicity appears when a church enacts catholicity through its practices.[15]

The Scottish philosopher Alasdair MacIntyre has described practices in society as important because they are part of a narrative history and create communal frames for groups of people.[16] Several theologians have used MacIntyre's social definition of practices, and have transferred the concept by studying ecclesial practices. Dorothy Bass and Craig Dykstra from the USA, for example, have identified church services, sacraments, hospitality, forgiveness, prayers, etc. as ecclesial practices that deal with needs in life and are cooperative human activities.[17] According to this method, an ecclesiology can be revealed by examining ecclesial practices in the congregation and churches, as well as through statements, documents, resolutions, creeds, etc.

In my thesis, I will use the analytical tool to examine the selected South African congregations and churches by studying their practices through interviews, observations, and collected material. In Chapter Four I will develop the foundation for my method of studying an operative ecclesiology.

---

14 Congar, Yves M.-J., 1966, pp. 242–246, 251–254, 261–262, 268.
15 Jakob Tronêt has defined 'realised catholicity' in his thesis thus: "*Realised Catholicity* signifies that the *Catholic Practices* are practiced and that they can be mutually recognised by the divided Churches. Furthermore, the term Realised Catholicity comprises a distinction between two ways of bringing about this realization: *Applied Catholicity* and *Created Catholicity*. *Applied Catholicity* means that catholicity is realised when a Catholic Church does what is catholic, while *Created Catholicity* expresses this realization in the opposite direction: by doing what is *Catholic* a Church becomes *Catholic*". Tronêt, Jakob, 2014, p. 258.
16 MacIntyre, Alasdair, 1984, pp. 62–78, 187, 251.
17 Bass, Dorothy & Dykstra, Craig, 2010, pp. 170, 204.

Through the description of my ecclesiological approach, my research questions have emerged. It will be productive to investigate how the South African congregations and churches have been dealing with issues concerning ethnicity two decades after democratisation, and what determines ethnic integration. It is interesting, furthermore, to examine whether there are differences between the congregations' and churches' practices concerning ethnicity, tested against the notion of the Church's catholicity as found in the ecumenical documents. Congregations and churches belong to different denominations, and it is useful to analyse different possibilities of a realised catholicity. The concept 'realised catholicity' will be developed later. My task of exploring the South African congregations and churches will be developed in Chapter Four.

1.4 Limitations

I have studied the five largest historical mainline churches in South Africa by membership – that is, those that had more than one million members according to the latest national census reflecting religious affiliation. These are the Roman Catholic, Anglican, Methodist, Lutheran, and Pentecostal/Charismatic churches. The Apostolic Faith Mission (AFM) was selected to represent the Pentecostal/Charismatic churches because it is the largest and oldest Pentecostal church in South Africa.

All of these churches are present in South Africa, but some also have congregations, dioceses or districts in other southern African countries. This study will consider the churches' activity within the borders of South Africa. I decided from the beginning not to include the Reformed churches in the study, even though they are the largest church family by membership among the mainline churches. The Reformed churches mainly supported the previous government's policy, and many scholars have already carried out much research on these churches.[18]

I am aware that not the whole Dutch Reformed Church supported apartheid, and that several theologians opposed apartheid. Some of them even used the Church's catholicity as an ecclesiological foundation against divisions in the Christian communion.[19]

---

18 Nicol, Willem, 2004, pp. 115–120.
19 Several books and articles have been written by South African scholars about the churches' catholicity and human divisions in the Church. J.J.F. Durand, for example, has written about the Church's catholicity related to pluralism in the Church from an ecumenical perspective. Durand, J.J.F., 1961. Nico Smith has analysed the ecclesiological implication of the establishment of separate churches for the non-white population in South

I have to admit that it would have been interesting to include the Nederduitse Gereformeerde Kerk (NGK), but then I would also have needed to include the Uniting Reformed Church in Southern Africa (URCSA). I suggest that these churches need to be studied separately.

The case studies were located in the three largest municipalities in South Africa. The selection of congregations in urban areas was made in order to obtain a large range of the ethnic diversity found in South African society – a range that is not attainable in rural areas. It was also important that the selected congregations did not include a cathedral or a similarly important church building, for at least two reasons. The first is that such congregations have always included people of diverse backgrounds. The second is that these congregations mostly represent a diocese, district, or region; and not all the denominations have such buildings and congregations in the cities. Further limitations will be presented in Chapter Four when the research design will be described, and I will explain my choice and selection of congregations, church leaders, and material.

The ecclesiology that has developed in Sub-Saharan Africa during the twentieth century emphasises, for example, the Church as 'the family of God' or as an 'ancestral *koinonia*'. I will not, however, use African ecclesiology, even though it makes many significant contributions to the understanding of the Church. I have chosen an international ecumenical approach that includes a perspective that could be applied in any context, not just in Africa. The ecumenical documents have been developed in an environment with people from different backgrounds. The international ecumenical approach, furthermore, creates a helpful distance between the language of analysis and the empirical material. Using African ecclesiology would involve a different kind of research task.[20]

Africa. Smith, Nico, 1972. Willie Jonker has written an article entitled *Catholicity, Unity, and Truth* in which he describes the development of the concept 'Catholicity' in the reformed tradition, and states that from its beginning, the reformed tradition regarded the unity and the catholicity of the Church highly. Calvin even used in a certain sense the concept of catholicity for the Church. Jonker, Willie D., 1992, pp. 16–27. In his book *Die ekklesia as kosmies-eskatologiese teken*, P.F. Theron argues that there is a cosmic and eschatological character to the unity of the Church. The church is a sign of the kingdom of God, and the unity that the Church proclaims is an interim sign of the eschatological salvation of the cosmos. Catholicity is a concern for the whole cosmos. Theron, P.F., 1978. He has also described the unity of the church in other books and articles. See for example: Theron, P.F., 1979, 1986. David Bosch has opposed apartheid division in the Church, and has labeled the ideology a heresy. Bosch, David, 1993.

20 For examples of African ecclesiology, see: Post-synodal apostolic exhortation Ecclesia in Africa of the Holy Father John Paul II to the bishops, priests and deacons, men and

1.5 Material

As described earlier, I aim to develop a concept of catholicity derived from documents on the Church's catholicity from the World Conferences on F&O from 1927 onwards, and from the World Assemblies of the WCC from 1948 onwards, together with F&O and WCC Central Committee documents regarding ethnicity, until 2011. I will refer to these documents in Chapter Three.

To establish the nature of a particular ecclesiology, I will primarily use interviews, supplemented by observations, statements, texts, and information documents from the congregations and churches. The congregations were selected according to a combination of convenience sampling and snowball sampling in the three largest municipalities in South Africa. The church leaders who were interviewed were the respective churches' general secretaries or equivalent persons. The interviews with the congregations' leadership were conducted with the local decision-making body, to which for convenience I have given the generic name 'church council'. A description of the case study design will be given in Chapter Four.

The material from the case studies of the congregations and churches has been thematically divided into different chapters. The first theme in Part II, for example, is an examination of reconciliation, the second is about ethnicity, and the third is about church services, etc. The material could, of course, have been classified differently. Initially I tried to use a geographic structure for the material, but this created obstacles to effective analysis.

I therefore found that using a thematic structure would be the most constructive way of presenting the findings. The themes have been selected in accordance with issues that became evident in the material and that were productive to study in relation to ethnicity.

Dealing specifically with ethnicity is important, because this issue is central to the thesis. The question of ethnicity determined the material that I use in the thesis. Describing the liturgy or church services was important, because they can be seen as a significant ecclesial practice. It is the place where the members of the Church congregate. The services can be seen as an expression of the nature of the Church when the congregation gathers as a corporate communion.[21] Language diversity was brought to my attention in the interviews, as well as the

---

women religious and all the church in Africa and its evangelizing mission towards the year 2000, 1995, p. 65; Orobator, Agbonkhianmeghe E., 2005, pp. 76–77.

21 An example of emphasising the church service as an important church practice is found in the work of Yves Congar. He states that the Church's liturgy is an expression of the

congregations' relationships with other congregations. The ministry of the congregations and churches and poverty eradication were other issues that were discussed during the interviews. I will come back to all of these themes: they will be discussed and analysed in the different chapters in Part II of the thesis.

1.6 Previous Research

Several books and theses have been written about South Africa, the ecumenical movement, catholicity, and ethnicity. However, I will only present research that is linked to my thesis. Since the establishment of the Faith and Order movement with the aim of achieving visible unity, the organisation has battled with issues of 'Church and World'. These kinds of studies have been significant not only because of divisions within and among churches, but also because of divisions within the human community.

Faith and Order began a major study of 'Church and World' after a meeting in 1990, and it also agreed that the study should explore issues of ethnic and national identity in relation to the unity of the Church. After a meeting in 1997, a project was initiated called *Ethnic Identity, National Identity, and the Unity of the Church* – also called ETHNAT. The project supported various case studies in different contexts, and ended almost ten years later in 2006, with the publication of *Participating in God's Mission of Reconciliation: A resource for Churches in Situations of Conflict*. There was no consensus about the text among the member churches, and there was, it seems, no further support for the continuation of the project. The project might have been controversial, and the focus shifted from an ecclesiological problem to the challenge of ethnicity. My ecclesiological study of congregations and churches in South Africa can be linked to the ecclesiological study project ETHNAT by examining one context with diverse ethnicities.[22]

The South African theologian Doris Thembeka Mufamadi has written a thesis entitled *The World Council of Churches and its Programme to Combat Racism*. Mufamadi showed through her research that there was a discrepancy in the early ecumenical movement. She argued that the discrepancy was that, although there were several statements against apartheid, at the same time the WCC's members did not put the anti-apartheid policy into practice. Unity-building among churches was a more important issue, and it was not until the Sharpeville massacre on 21 March 1960 that the movement's engagement with the South African

---

nature of the Church. "[…] la liturgie exprimant et manifestant au plus haut point la nature authentique de la véritable Église […]" Congar, Yves M.-J. 1966, p. 268.

22 Williams, Catrin, 2005, 217–222; Van der Borght, E. A. J. G., 2012, pp. 318–320.

situation changed. A programme to combat racism was launched after the fourth WCC General Assembly. The programme changed the approach of the WCC, and apartheid was challenged. Some questioned the programme, and even accused the WCC of aiding political revolution; but the programme received continued support. Mufamadi stated, however, that it was only during the final years before South Africa achieved democracy that the WCC was most effective in challenging apartheid. Her thesis offers the historical background to the WCC's work, and finds that policy and practice were not always consistent, thus showing that doctrine and practice are not always the same thing.[23] My own research analyses an ecumenical understanding of catholicity derived from F&O and the WCC, and how this relates to congregations' and churches' practices in contemporary South Africa.

A related body of research about the ecumenical movement and the South African situation was undertaken by the South African theologian Wesley Mabuza. I use a comparable method to that of Mabuza: I also relate ecumenical documents to the present situation. Mabuza, in his thesis *Kairos Revisited*, used both an ecumenical South African document and ethnographic methods. He investigated whether issues raised in the Kairos Document are relevant to the Church today. He examined whether the Kairos Document remains applicable, even though it was written before democratisation. Mabuza used qualitative methods, conducting interviews and using questionnaires among people who had been involved with the Kairos Document to capture their views about significant issues in the document that might still be relevant. The chosen and revisited issues were examined in relation to the contemporary context. He found that while the context had changed, the Church could still find itself in a similar situation to that of the Reformed Church under apartheid. He argued that the Church needed to work in cooperation with other religions to struggle with contemporary issues of inequality.[24]

Another South African theologian, Cas Wepener, used ethnographic methods in the book *From Fast to Feast*, a study of reconciliation as practised in South African congregations. First he investigated Christian reconciliation rituals in history, in biblical images, and then in South African reconciliation liturgies. He studied earlier images of reconciliation and the reconciliation liturgies of three congregations of 'White', 'Black', and 'Coloured' ethnicity respectively. His purpose was to

---

23 Mufamadi, Thembeka Doris, 2011, pp. 250–262.
24 Mabuza, Wesley Madonda, 2009, pp. 76–77, 180, 269–273.

investigate the Church's rituals for reconciliation, and how, in his view, the rituals could be improved.[25]

Another book that deals with church and ethnicity is *Medium or Message?*, written by the Australian linguist and researcher Anya Woods. She focused on language use among ethnic churches in Australia. Woods gave examples from sixteen congregations she studied, representing different periods of migrant history in the country with diverse language, cultural, and church backgrounds. She described the relationship between language and religion, and how that affects society. She argued that language has different roles in different churches, and that it can either unite people, or divide and fragment them. Churches that look to the future are those that are flexible in their language use and are willing to lose the link between a particular language and religious faith. Woods studied the Australian context, but hoped for more international research. My thesis does not specifically look into language alone, but my studies could be regarded as one piece emerging from the South African context.[26]

Ethnographic research about churches is common, and there is also a special network of theologians, journals, and books presenting theological approaches to qualitative research on the Church.[27] Recent studies of ethnicity/race and the Church have mostly been done in the USA. The concept of 'race', rather than 'ethnicity', is the term that is mostly used in the USA. Korie Edwards, for example, examined interracial churches in the USA, in which mixed-race churches remain faithful to 'White' norms. She showed that 'Blacks' must adjust their way of being the Church to accommodate 'White' members.[28]

Michael Emerson and Christian Smith did a similar study in *Divided by Faith*. They described how religion and race have played a significant role in the history of the USA. They examined the country's history by showing how religion was used both to justify and to abolish slavery, to justify segregation and also to advocate for integration. They gave as an example the fact that Evangelical Christians in the USA today support equality, but at the same time continue indirectly to support racial division. In a follow-up study, *United by Faith*, a team of sociologists argued that the Church is in a key position to resolve the situation of a society divided by race.[29]

---

25 Wepener, Cas, 2009, pp. 115–202.
26 Woods, Anya, 2004, pp. 26–40, 175–178. Her surname was later changed to Lloyd-Smith.
27 Ward, Peter, ed., 2012. pp. 1–10; Ecclesial Practices, 2014, pp. 1–4.
28 Edwards, Korie L., 2008.
29 Emerson, Michael O. & Smith, Christian, 2000; DeYoung, Curtiss, et al., 2003.

The anthology *This Side of Heaven* also described the responses and challenges of ethnic and racial diversity among North American churches. In it, many theologians showed an awareness of the ethnically diverse reality, and described how at the same time church-owned universities, seminaries, and churches struggled to reflect the reality of American society. Scholars from different ethnic backgrounds in American society described the ethnic contexts and historical backgrounds that have affected the churches in USA. The aim of the book was to inspire people to discover how change could be possible and to achieve integration.[30]

In 2003 I carried out a case study in Kimberley, South Africa, and wrote the article 'Pieces in the Puzzle: A Local Study of Denominationalism and Ethnicity towards Unity in South Africa'. This study showed that there was a strong desire among the members of church councils in the case congregations to have closer relations with other ethnic groups, and that many also expressed a willingness to cooperate ecumenically. Some congregational members of particular denominations had a stronger attachment to ethnicity, while members of other congregations belonging to particular denominations had a stronger affiliation to the denomination rather than to ethnicity.[31] The present thesis can be regarded as building on this article.

The overview of previous research shows that several scholars have been dealing with ethnicity in relationship to the Church from both a sociological and an ecclesiological perspective. There are, however, no studies that have used texts and documents from F&O and the WCC to interpret the catholicity of the Church. There have also been studies of South African congregations and churches, but no research has been done using church practices to discern their ecclesiology. My study can thus help to develop both theory and methods to provide new knowledge through similar studies of the Church's catholicity and the practices of congregation and churches. I hope that my research will especially stimulate South African scholars to investigate ecclesiologies in a context where a narrative theology is profoundly developed but rarely recorded. The thesis will also contribute to the development of research concerning ecclesial practices.

1.7 Terminology and Definitions

I have chosen to set out my use of terms, and their definitions, in this introductory chapter. I have found this necessary because I will use these terms from the start of the thesis and throughout the chapters that follow. There are several terms that

---

30 Priest, Robert J. & Nieves, Alvaro L., eds, 2007.
31 Berggren, Erik, 2005, pp. 87–113.

are used in the area of my research. Not all of them are frequently used in the thesis or form part of my analytical tool. However, they need to be defined because they might have diverse meanings in the area of my research, and because I will refer to these terms in my discussion. The terms have been grouped into different clusters because some of them belong under similar subjects. Some terms will be defined later in the thesis, when they are used in specific chapters. I have chosen to separate my discussion about how people can be differentiated. This is inevitable, because various arguments have to be developed more thoroughly.

Culture and Nation

I am using a broad definition of 'culture': it can be understood as all aspects of a society with learned patterns and behaviour that are shared by members of a group. Culture enables collaboration and communication between people, and the common frames are passed on to other members and new generations.[32] One issue group at the Sixth World Assembly of the WCC at Vancouver in 1983 produced a definition of culture, which I share. It stated: "Culture is what holds a community together, giving a common framework of meaning. It is preserved in language, thought patterns, ways of life, attitudes, symbols and presuppositions, and is celebrated in art, music, drama, literature and the like. It constitutes the collective memory of the people and the collective heritage which will be handed down to generations still to come. [...]".[33] Culture thus includes, for example, communications, patterns of behaviour, beliefs, shared symbols and thinking. This definition does not mean that individuals are restricted to being part of only one particular culture. Culture is fluid, and individuals can sympathise with or be affiliated to several cultures. This definition is important, so that people are not seen as limited to belonging to only a specific culture.

'Nation' can represent the political borders of a culture. It is a construction of a group of people who form a political community, but it can also coincide with a cultural community. Common language, traditions, religion, myths, and symbols are shared, and others are not part of this community. A nation can also be a political community without a shared ethnic foundation. Other features – a

---

32 Culture is defined in the *Cambridge Encyclopaedia*: "The way of life of a group of people, consisting of learned patterns of behaviour and thought passed on from generation to the next. The notion includes the group's belief, values, language, political organization, and economic activity, as well as its equipment, techniques, and art forms (referred to as material culture)". The Cambridge Encyclopedia, 1994, pp. 312–313.
33 Gathered for Life, 1983, p. 32.

national anthem, flag, or symbols – unite the citizens' common elements and are negotiable. 'Nation' as a term will not be used in this thesis, but South Africa will be regarded as a nation in which there are several ethnicities, resulting in a huge diversity that forms a political community with common features.[34]

Exclusion and Inclusion

The term 'exclusion' is used when individuals or groups are prevented from participation, or are rejected and are not part of a community. 'Inclusion' is the opposite: it is when somebody is incorporated into a community and embraced by others. 'Inclusive' is when a community incorporates groups or individuals irrespective of their background or origin.[35]

'Racism' will be defined as a widespread form of prejudice that is related to physical distinctions. Racism means that there are some who perceive themselves as superior to other individuals or groups. There is also institutional racism, when a society internalises racism, and its policies favour certain groups and discriminate against other groups in the same society. Apartheid can be described as a form of institutional racism.[36]

There are several definitions of 'segregation'. The term describes what happens when individuals or groups live apart, separated by socioeconomic conditions, skin colour, religion, sex, ethnic belonging, etc. Segregation entails limited or no contact between individuals or groups, and can result in discriminatory treatment

---

34 Hylland Eriksen, Thomas, 2010, pp. 115–116, 110–112, 100–102. There are various discussions about whether South Africa should try to become one nation with shared common symbols, national holidays, festivals, events, etc., or a country founded on working for human dignity and human rights, pluralism, etc. The football World Cup in 2010, for example, was an event that united the people in the country as a nation. An example of what divides the people is national festival days that are celebrated with diverse meanings. Johan Degenaar wrote an article before democratisation entitled *Nation and Nationalism*, in which he stresses that the vision for a divided country should rather be to attain tolerance, respect, human rights, etc. Degenaar, Johan J., 1990. The ecumenical movement met in Vanderbijlpark in 1995, and understood that they were contributing to building a nation by supporting reconstruction, development, and educational programmes. The ecumenical movement took it for granted that the churches in South Africa should support the South African nation. It might be asked whether the Church as 'catholic' should support nation-building or emphasise global community. The relationship between catholicity and nation-states needs to be further investigated. Being the Church in South Africa Today, 1995, pp. 170–172.
35 Munck, Ronaldo, 2005, pp. 22–26, 34–37.
36 Giddens, Anthony, & Sutton, Philip W., 2013, p. 682.

and exploitation of other people. Apartheid can be described as an extreme form of segregation in which, because of skin colour, people were deprived of their civil rights, exploited, and forced to live in specific areas.[37]

The term 'diversity' is interpreted as something positive, and represents the different characteristics of individuals or groups in the human community. Diversity should be understood as something that can be shared and received, and that enriches communities. Division should be understood as something negative, when there is separation within the human community: people are kept apart, and boundaries are created between communities, societies, or churches.[38]

'Integration' has various meanings depending on the context. In this thesis, it means the social processes that lead individuals or groups to unite into larger communities, based on equal conditions that lead to increased interaction. Integration is a mutual process aimed at social cohesion, respect for the dignity of each individual, and giving equal opportunities regardless of background.[39]

Stratification

'Social stratification' is used to describe inequalities between individuals or groups within a society. A society can be studied according to the stratification, for example, of gender, age, religion, language, wealth, or education. The stratum is hierarchical, with the more favoured on the higher levels and the less privileged on the lower levels. Wealthy people can be ranked as better than the poor, males can be ranked as better than women, and 'White' can be ranked as better than 'Black'. So cial stratification is a construction, and it has changed throughout history. Social mobility refers to either 'vertical mobility', which means that individuals or groups move upwards or downwards between social strata, or 'lateral mobility', which includes, for example, geographic movements from rural to urban areas, from townships to suburbs, or movements within a country or region. A combination of vertical and lateral mobility is often applied.[40]

'Suburb' is often used in South Africa to describe a residential area in the former 'White' areas before democratisation. These areas often have better conditions of housing, water, sewerage, waste collection, communication, etc. 'Township' or

---

37 Cantle, Ted, 2012, pp. 112–140.
38 See, for example, the Third World Conference on Faith and Order, 1953, pp. 23–24. cf. 239; The Evanston Report, 1955, p. 87; The Fourth World Conference on Faith and Order, 1964, p. 70.
39 Cantle, Ted, 2012, pp. 112–140.
40 Giddens, Anthony, & Sutton, Philip W., 2013, pp. 480–481, 511.

'location' are often used of an underdeveloped urban residential area on the periphery of a city. They were often built under apartheid for the 'Black' population. There are, however, areas within townships – such as Soweto – where living conditions are similar to those of 'White' suburbs. An example of how naming areas identifies their social status is that of Sandton, which is defined as a 'suburb', while Soweto is identified as a 'township'.[41]

South Africa has eleven official languages, but the Constitution also promotes and ensures respect for sign language and for specific languages used in special communities. I will name English and Afrikaans, but mostly use the term 'indigenous languages' for Sepedi, Sesotho, Setswana, siSwati, Tshivenda, Xitsonga, isiNdebele, isiXhosa, and isiZulu. Community languages include German, Greek, Hindi, Portuguese, Arabic, and Hebrew.[42]

Ecclesiological Terms

When references are made to the 'ecumenical movement', it refers to the World Council of Churches (WCC), the Faith & Order Commission (F&O), and in South Africa, to the South African Council of Churches (SACC). I am aware that there are several other ecumenical networks, organisations, and communities that also belong to similar ecumenical movements. The WCC and its related organisations are the largest organised ecumenical organisation, bringing together the mainstream churches globally. All the churches studied in this thesis are related in one way or another with the WCC, F&O, and the SACC.

The Greek term *koinonia* is sometimes translated *communio* in Latin, which in English becomes 'communion' or 'community'. *Communio* is similar to *koinonia*, but there are also etymological differences. When the English terms 'communion' or 'community' are used, they refer to the same content as the Greek word *koinonia*. 'Community' in the South African context often exclusively means 'Black' people. This South African meaning will not be applied. When the term refers to the South African context, it will have an additional description – for example, the 'White' community or the 'Black' community.

The terms 'church' or 'denomination' are often used to describe a particular community within the Christian faith with a common name, tradition, confession, and identity. The churches or denominations that I study are the Roman Catholic, Anglican, Methodist and Lutheran churches, and the Apostolic Faith

---

41 See for example: Staff, Grant, 1994, pp. 377–391.
42 The Constitution of the Republic of South Africa, 1996 - Chapter 1: Founding Provisions, 6. Languages.

Mission. I mostly use 'church' (with a lower-case initial letter) or 'denomination' to describe these ecclesiastical organisations. When I use 'Church' (with an initial capital letter), I refer to the whole body of Christian believers in the world. The same word with a lower-case initial letter will imply a specific church, such as the Anglican or Methodist churches. The term 'church' (lower case) can also mean a building or congregation, but the context will explain the meaning of the word. On a few occasions, 'church' will also have the same meaning as 'congregation'. The context will clarify the meaning of 'church' in such cases.

The term 'congregation' will be used to describe the local Christian community in one place where people gather and come to worship. It is a limited territorial area with a place of worship, such as a church building, where members come together. Some churches prefer to use 'parish', 'church' or 'assembly', and these terms are occasionally used in the text.

Several terms describe the local decision-making body of the local Christian community as a congregation. Churches use terms like 'parish council', 'church council', 'assembly council' or 'congregation council', 'parochial church council' (PCC), etc. I will use the term 'church council' as a generic term for the local decision-making body in a congregation.

Congregations often belong to a community consisting of a small group of congregations forming a district. These could be named 'deanery', 'circuit', or 'area', and the terms used here will follow the churches' or the denominations' use of the terminology.

There are many terms to describe a person specially ordained to work in the Church. These persons can be named 'clergy', 'minister', 'priest', 'pastor', 'dominee', or 'predikant'. In this thesis the term 'minister' is used because it is the title used in the texts of F&O and the WCC. In some cases when the term 'minister' is used to describe people who are not ordained but who have a particular ministry in the church, the term used is 'lay minister'. An ordained minister's salary is called different things in the churches or denominations because of tradition, and sometimes because of countries' tax legislation. It can be called 'stipend', 'wages', 'pay', etc. Some churches also have non-stipendiary ministers. This term means that the minister is ordained but does not receive a salary from the church. These are fully-recognised ministers in the churches, but their role is voluntary, and they receive their income from other jobs or other sources.[43]

The title for the highest administrative staff person in the churches or denominations is 'general secretary'. This is the chief officer of a church or denomination

---

43 Baptism, Eucharist and Ministry, 1982, pp. 20–27.

on the central level, distinct from the ministerial leadership. Some churches that I studied did not have a general secretary: the Anglican Church, for example, has a Provincial Executive Officer, and ELCSA N-T and ELCSA Cape do not have general secretaries but have bishops with the same function. I will use 'general secretary' or 'church leaders' as a common term for all churches or denominations, but when a specific church is described I will use its own title.

The sacred meal in the church service is called 'Eucharist', 'Holy Communion', 'Lord's Supper', or 'Nagmaal'. The term 'eucharist' will be applied as a generic term. I acknowledge that there are theological differences behind the different terms for the meal, but that is not significant in my description of the meal in the church service.[44]

The Lutheran Church family has been divided into three churches, coinciding with the previous government's division of people before democratisation. These churches are named ELCSA, ELCSA-Cape, and ELCSA N-T. ELCSA-Cape and ELCSA N-T were founded by German immigrants and the descendants of missionaries, and are organised like German Landeskirchen. These two Lutheran churches have predominantly 'White' members. ELCSA, without any additional identifier, was founded through mission work from northern Europe and the USA, and has predominantly 'Black' and 'Coloured' members. The term 'Lutheran churches' is used to describe all three Lutheran churches collectively.

1.8 Differentiation of People

The differentiation of people into specific groups is not easy, and there is no good terminological schema to describe diversities in the human community. Any form of differentiating people into groups risks making distinctions that are based on prejudice. All such terms arise from a variety of constructions, and they can be deprived of their power if they are named. South Africa segregated people into specific race groups during apartheid, and the term 'race' is still used in public life and political debates. There are other terms, such as 'population group', that have in some sectors replaced the term 'race'; but there is no consensus or common definition of the meaning of 'population group'. A different term may be used, but it has the same meaning as 'race' in the past.[45]

---

44 Baptism, Eucharist and Ministry, 1982, pp. 10–15.
45 Politicians still use 'race' as a term in debates. See for example: Mtyala, Quinton, & Serrao, Angelique, & Davis, Gaye & Williams, Murray, 2011, p. 1. Statistics South Africa uses 'population group' instead in the latest Census 2011 questionnaire. The term has in reality only replaced the term 'race'. See: Census 2011, Census in Brief,

I could have used 'race' or 'population group', but I have instead chosen 'ethnicity'. I acknowledge that the term is not good for differentiating people in the human community either. The language of 'ethnicity' and its cognates is not widely used in South Africa, and there is no common definition among scholars. Many times 'ethnicity' refers only to the Zulu, Xhosa, or Tswana people, for example, and does not include all those who make up the South African society. Ethnicity also risks being another term for 'race' without any further discussion. I prefer, however, to use 'ethnicity' because the term derives from a 'pure' construction: it does not have biological connotations, it recognises a wider shared identity, and it is fluid, not fixed.[46]

However, using ethnicity as the point of departure for my thesis is not without its problems and complications. I am aware that using the term 'ethnic' also contributes to the construct of ethnicity in South Africa. Focusing only on ethnicity can also be a way of avoiding dealing with other issues that contribute to causing division, such as inequality, power relations, poverty, exclusion, politics, gender, and class. I have tried to take an intersectional approach to ethnicity, but future studies will need to examine other approaches to the catholicity of the Church in South Africa.

The word 'ethnicity' is relatively new: sociologists began to use it in the 1950s. Ethnicity and its cognates such as the word 'ethnic' have their roots in the Greek word *ethnos* (ἔθνος), 'nation' or 'people', which is related to *ethnikos* (ἐθνικως) with the meaning 'heathen', referring to people who are not Christian or Jews.[47] The word 'ethnic' had this meaning in the English language from the middle of the fourteenth century until the middle of the nineteenth century, when the word gradually started to take on racial connotations. 'Ethnic' began, for example, to indicate subordinate groups in the USA in distinction from the dominant population of British heritage. People with the 'ethnic' label tended to be defined by the majority, but there were also exceptions. During apartheid in South Africa, for example, 'ethnic' was applied by the 'White' minority to other groups in the

---

2012, pp. 21–27, 41–46, 53–54; Household Questionnaire A, Demographics, Census 2011, 2010, p. 2.
46 There are several scholars who use the term 'race' without further discussion. James L. Gibson, for example, has studied the South African reconciliation process, but he does not critically discuss the development of 'race' or how the concept is applied to the human community. See: Gibson, James L., 2004, pp. 24–27.
47 New keywords, 2005, p. 12.

society. Even today, 'ethnic' is often used in vernacular language to define the 'Black' majority population.⁴⁸

The word 'ethnicity' can be questioned because of its early etymological heritage and because it makes it possible to define certain similarities or even to interpret the divisions between groups of people. There has never been consensus about the term among scholars, and so 'ethnicity' has been given diverse definitions. The word has, nevertheless, developed scientifically, and is used constructively by defining, for example, indigenous peoples' rights or acknowledging groups of peoples' traditions or language. 'Ethnicity' has a different kind of emphasis from that of 'race', because it is thoroughly social by nature. It is a non-biological communal identifier that includes language, religion, and culture, and that is a construction for categorising and classifying people. The use of the discourse attached to 'ethnicity' to look for demarcations in society will, of course, also contribute to the further definition of the concept. The notion of ethnicity can be used positively; but it can also be a negative term when it is used to exclude. Words in the 'ethnicity' group are commonly used today in debates, publications, and the media, and they have been developed in the late twentieth century, especially in academic writings.⁴⁹

It is important to state that demarcations are not always sharply defined, and can change over time. If there is no understanding of the differences associated with a perception of 'us' and 'them', there can be no ethnicity. Ethnicity in this sense is thoroughly constructed through social contacts, and becomes especially important when identities are threatened.⁵⁰ In South Africa there are so-called Afrikaners and Coloureds who predominantly speak Afrikaans, sometimes voting for the same political party and living in the same parts of the country. They are nevertheless – according to the country's history – often seen as being different from each other on the basis of their histories or dialects of language. In

---

48 Hylland Eriksen, Thomas, 2010, p. 4; Banks, Marcus, 1996, p. 149; New keywords, 2005, p. 12. A hairdresser in South Africa, for example, could have a sign in the window saying "No ethnic hair cut", meaning that they were not qualified to cut the hair of 'Black' people.
49 Hylland Eriksen, Thomas, 2010, pp. 2, 60–61.
50 Hylland Eriksen, Thomas, 2010, pp. 12–13, 73, 88. Simon van der Stel, for example, was the last commander and first governor of the Cape Colony. Because of his background he would certainly not have held this prominent position if he had lived during National Party rule. Ironically, the towns Stellenbosh and Simonstown are named after him; and yet a person such as van der Stel would not have been allowed to live in these places during the apartheid era.

the South African context, ethnicity includes aspects of social relations between people who understand themselves apart from other groups in the society. This differentiation is either chosen or forced: some want to maintain old structures, while others have no interest in prolonging earlier distinctions. Developing stereotypes of one's own group or of other groups is part of creating demarcations. The stereotypes do not need to be true; and because they are constructed, they are also fluid.[51]

The notion of ethnicity has been used instead of 'race' by several South African scholars, especially sociologists, anthropologists, linguists, and jurists. The term 'race' has been perceived as inadequate in the democratic South Africa. Nkonko M. Kamwangamalu et al., for example, have used ethnicity as a concept to move away from earlier fixed apartheid boundaries, and instead have argued that there are several ethnicities, and that it is possible for individuals to embrace new ethnicities. Roelof D. Coertze argues against the concept of biological and social 'race'. He states that ethnicity should replace earlier concepts in order to avoid racism, but that the term 'ethnicity' needs to be developed and defined.[52]

I agree with scholars who advocate a change of terminology. The term 'ethnicity' is more constructive because it is not attached to biology, is more fluid, and acknowledges that people can belong to several ethnicities simultaneously. Furthermore, South Africa would gain from replacing racial terminology with the language of ethnicity. But the term must be defined and developed so that 'ethnicity' does not simply replace 'race' and carry the same meaning.

In this thesis, I will use the language of 'ethnicity', not 'race', as my analytic language to describe South Africa's diverse society.

The word 'race' is often used in South Africa to categorise people as a legacy of the former colonial power and the apartheid state. The concept has also continued to be used as a vernacular term by the public and the media, and is still applied, for example, in work places, political debates, and education. The continued use of 'race' may have specific purposes – for example, to correct unequal conditions in the society – but it simultaneously reinforces 'racial' categories and keeps them alive.

There is no longer legislation or a legal process that 'boxes' people into diverse groups; but there are bodies or people that choose to use 'race' or 'population group'. The situation becomes uncertain when government officials continue to

---

51 Hylland Eriksen, Thomas, 2010, pp. 12–13, 24–25.
52 Kamwangamalu, Nkonko M., 2000, pp. 1–6, 7–17, 51–68, 137–138; Coertze, Roelof D., 2007, pp. 13–15, 18.

define people according to the apartheid-era concepts of 'race' or 'population group' as their principal method of attaining equality and the reversal of apartheid's damage. Continuing to use the old apartheid demarcations can be questioned, furthermore, because there are no criteria for such classification.[53]

In many contexts – and especially since the late eighteenth century – the term 'race' has often been used to describe groups of people who show similarities, often with a biological connotation. In South Africa, and in many other countries, skin colour has been a source of division between people, and the result has been the naming of separate 'races'. The word 'race' became a biological identification that was imposed by the former rulers.

The concept has continued to exist as a cultural classification, even though scientists have abandoned 'race' theories. Some scholars, organisations, countries, and groups still use the word 'race' without analysing its complexity, while others use 'race' sociologically as a social construction in order to study how the concept influences people's actions. There are also scholars who use the word in order to show the absurdity of the concept of different 'races', by deliberately making plain the damage the concept has caused throughout history, and continues to cause.[54]

The concept of 'race' is questionable because humanity is always a mixture of different 'groups'. Ethnic boundaries are constructions and are fluid, unstable, and not fixed. Sections of the population do not constitute clearly divided units; instead there is variety within populations. The apartheid government, for example,

---

53 See for example: Employment Equity Act, No. 55 Of 1998, 1998; Census 2011, Census in Brief, 2012, pp. 21–22, 25–27, 41–42, 46.

54 Hylland Eriksen, Thomas, 2010, pp. 5–9. One example of a scholar who uses the word 'race' to show the irrationality of the concept is Kimber Buell, Denise, 2005, pp. 2–4. United Nations Universal Declaration of Human Rights 1948, Article 2, 1948, unfortunately uses the word 'race', which was adopted in a number of later texts, conventions, and documents – for example, The European Convention for the Protection of Human Rights and Fundamental Freedoms, Article 14 and the United Nations' Convention on the Rights of the Child, Article 2. This has excused and even increased the usage of the word 'race' without further reflection. I am aware that 'race' is not always intended to be related to biology, and furthermore that the term has different meanings in various languages. It is, though, difficult not to relate it to biology when 'race' is used, especially when the term is not defined. Professor of English literature Patrick Brantlinger has stressed how, during colonisation, Europeans saw the African people as different and as 'the other', which meant that 'race' became important. Africa was described as the 'the dark continent' that was supposed to become civilised. Brantlinger, Patrick, 1985, pp. 166–172, 186–193.

allowed a person of light complexion to apply to be transferred to another 'racial' classification. A person of darker complexion could be forced to change 'racial' category. This shows that a change of identity was possible, but only after several generations – proving that 'race' classification even in the apartheid state was fluid.[55]

Hereditary physiological characteristics also know no borders: variation is independent of any form of categorisation. A certain population may have some similarities, but the amount of variation within the 'group' may be greater than the similarities they have with other 'groups'. In any case, differentiating people according to certain characteristics is a construction: skin colour, for example, might be regarded as an important distinguishing factor, while hair or eye colour, or left- or right-handedness have minor or even no importance. Racism is built on the belief that a person's personality is attached to biological, hereditary, or physical characteristics that govern a person's actions and make it possible to judge certain behaviours. Furthermore, distinctions between people are an important element in maintaining power and perpetuating injustice within a society.[56]

I have used the categories 'Black' or 'Black African', 'Coloured', 'Indian or Asian', and 'White' in my thesis at the risk of being accused of reinforcing these categories. Colour blindness is honourable, but it can also prevent people from recognising inequality and discrimination. I use these categories because they are still used in South Africa, and because they provide a tool to analyse South African congregations and churches.

The term 'race' has also been deliberately placed between inverted commas to emphasise that the term is part of apartheid's legacy. I have likewise used inverted commas for 'Black', 'Coloured', 'Indian or Asian', and 'White' to stress that these categories are linked to a construction.[57] I have used 'ethnicity' and its cognates as an analytical term to study social integration in South African two decades after democratisation.

My main focus in the thesis is to investigate how ethnic diversities have affected congregations and churches. Nevertheless, it is impossible not to acknowledge other power constructions in society, and an intersectional perspective regarding gender and class will sometimes be considered. Intersectionality is a theoretical perspective that reveals how different historical and situational power relations at

---

55 Encyclopedia of Race, Ethnicity, and Society, 2008, p. 83.
56 Hylland Eriksen, Thomas, 2010, p. 5.
57 I discussed the use of inverted commas in the research seminar in ecclesiology at Uppsala University. Some scholars claim that its use is disturbing, while others state that it helps to make it clear that the terms are constructions. I prefer to use inverted commas.

the same time have an effect on gender, class, and ethnicity. Intersectionality reveals interconnections that are constructed for the exercise of power and the preservation of inequality.[58] One example of an intersectional power relation is that of a South African 'Black' women domestic worker employed in a former 'White' suburb. The women are subordinate because of their gender, but also because of ethnicity and class; and these structures are interrelated.[59]

South Africa had a population of 51 770 560 according to Census 2011, which divided the South African population into five groups.[60] 'Black African' is the largest population in South Africa: 79.2 per cent identified themselves as 'Black African'. The group is very heterogeneous, with the diversity of, for example, Zulu, Xhosa, Sotho, Pedi, Venda, and Tswana people. Since democratisation it has become important to emphasise ethnic groups within the 'Black' population. Most 'Black Africans' use diverse 'indigenous' languages as their first language.[61]

So-called 'White' South Africans are considered to be ethnically descended from European settlers who came mostly from the former colonial powers of Holland and Britain, but also from Germany and France. There were 8.9 per cent who identified themselves as 'White' in Census 2011. They mostly use Afrikaans or English as their first language, and the majority live in the Western Cape and Gauteng provinces.[62]

Identifying people as 'Coloured' is an exclusively South African classification, created by the apartheid state to classify people who are not 'White' or 'Black', but have a mixed ancestry. 'Coloured' people come from diverse backgrounds, originating in the Khoikhoi and San people, slaves from the Indian Ocean region, European settlers, African people, and so on. 'Coloured' is reconstructed in the democratic South Africa in relation to other identities and interactions in the public space. The 'Coloured' ethnic group questions the whole concept of ethnic or 'racial' identities in the democratic South Africa. Racist legislation has been

---

58 Fish, Jennifer N., 2006, pp. 112–114; De los Reyes, Paulina, & Mulinari, Diana, 2005, p. 24.
59 De los Reyes, Paulina & Mulinari, Diana, 2005, pp. 7–9, 12–18. See also, for example, the article "Class, Race and Gender: Domestic Workers in South Africa" for a discussion of 'Black' women's working conditions. Gaitskell, Deborah, et. al., 1983.
60 Census 2011, Census in Brief, 2012, pp. 21–22.
61 Thompson, Leonard, 2001, pp. 190–196; Census 2011, Census in Brief, 2012, pp. 18, 21. In the Population Registration Act No 30 the 'Black' population was only referred to as 'natives'. Population Registration Act No 30 of 1950, 1950. See for example paragraph 1 (iii).
62 Thompson, Leonard, 2001, pp. 33–40, 52–58; Census 2011, Census in Brief, 2012, p. 21.

abolished, but social identity continues to be built around the shared trauma of forced removals. There were 8.9 per cent people who identified themselves as 'Coloured' in Census 2011; this group mainly uses English or Afrikaans as their first language, and they predominantly live in the Western and Northern Cape provinces.[63]

The 'Indian or Asian' group is mainly of Indian descent, from guest workers who came to the British Colony of Natal in the nineteenth century to work in the sugar, vegetable, and fruit fields and as tailors and servants. There were 2.5 per cent who identified themselves as 'Indian or Asian' according to Census 2011. The 'Indian or Asian' population mainly lives in the KwaZulu-Natal and Gauteng provinces, and they mostly use English as their first language.[64]

The last group that is identified in Census 2011 is 'Other', which could be regarded as an unspecified group of people who did not see themselves as belonging to one of the other groups. Only 0.5 per cent identified themselves as 'Other'.

Census 2011 also recognised that there were 22.7 per cent with IsiZulu as their first language, 16 per cent with IsiXhosa, 13.5 per cent with Afrikaans, 9.6 per cent with English, 9.1 per cent with Spedi, 8.0 per cent with Setswana, 7.6 per cent with Sesotho, 4.5 per cent with Xitsonga, 2.5 per cent with SiSwati, 2.4 per cent with Tshivenda, 0.5 per cent with Sign language, and 1.6 per cent Other languages. Most South Africans are at least bilingual, and many speak more than two languages. English has become a dominating language since democratisation; a majority of the population can speak it, even though it is not the first language among most of the population.[65]

1.9 Disposition

Chapters 2 to 4 are a continuation of Part I of the thesis, and will focus on the South African churches' rejection of apartheid, and on theory and method. Chapter 2 describes how the international and South African ecumenical movements reacted towards segregated communities during apartheid and democratisation. Several documents, conferences, and consultations from the early twentieth century until the democratisation of South Africa have questioned apartheid. Chapter 2 describes what the churches and the ecumenical movement have declared about integration and democratisation.

---

63 Adhikari, Mohamed, 2009, pp. viii–xi, xii; Ruiters, Michele, 2009, pp. 104–107, 109; Census 2011, Census in Brief, 2012, p. 21.
64 Thompson, Leonard, 2001, p. 100; Census 2011, Census in Brief, 2012, p. 21.
65 Census 2011, Census in Brief, 2012, pp. 18, 21, 27.

Chapter 3 describes a theory of catholicity that emerges from documents and texts from Faith & Order and the World Council of Churches. It also presents specific issues concerning ethnicity that are especially interesting and productive to use in the South African context. These issues will be my analytical tool when I examine the case study congregations and churches.

The methodology that I have used to examine the congregations and churches two decades after democratisation is described in Chapter 4. It is an operative ecclesiology originating from the theologian Yves Congar. Operative ecclesiology is a way of studying congregations and churches through the teaching of the Church in the form of documents, statements, resolutions, creeds, and so on, but also through different practices in the Church. I will define how ecclesial practices could determine an ecclesiology, and also describe how the case study of the South African congregations and churches was conducted.

Chapters 5 to 11 constitute Part II of the thesis, where the South African congregations and churches that make up the case study are described. They will be tested against the catholicity of the Church. Chapter 5 describes the chosen churches' and congregations' history and background, and the chapters that follow focus on diverse themes that are relevant and productive to examine. Chapter 6 explores how congregations and churches have been dealing with reconciliation, and Chapter 7 investigates the congregations' and churches' ethnic composition and how they perceive ethnic diversity. Chapter 8 focuses on church services as a major ecclesial practice, while Chapter 9 focuses on language as a significant form of diversity that creates division in a worshipping community. Chapter 10 investigates the congregations' contacts with other worshipping communities. Chapter 11 discusses the final theme of activities in the congregations and churches in relation to poverty eradication to overcome divisions in the community.

The thesis concludes with Part III, where Chapter 12 offers conclusions and a summary. Here, the theory and method that I have used in my research will be discussed.

Chapter Two: Church Rejecting Division

In several documents, conferences, and consultations from the early twentieth century, South African churches and the ecumenical movement have questioned ethnic divisions in the Church. In this chapter I will portray how the churches and the ecumenical movement have reacted to the separation of the human community, and outline their approach to a just Church and society. This chapter should be regarded as background to understanding the South African context before and after democratisation.

Firstly, I will examine the ecumenical movement's rejection of apartheid before democratisation. It is primarily based on documentation from ecumenical conferences and consultations held in South Africa before democratisation. Secondly, I will examine ecumenical consultations and the TRC's Faith Communities Hearing held after democratisation. In this part I have mainly made use of documentation from the TRC, churches' submissions, and audiovisual materials and transcripts from the Faith Communities Hearing in East London in 1997. A large part will look at the churches' submissions to and responses at this hearing. The churches' submissions and responses are central because they illustrate the churches' positions when the society was segregated, and how they regarded the future.

2.1 Declarations, Conferences and Consultations before Democratisation

Discrimination against people who were not 'White' had been going on since colonisation, and also in the two Boer republics and the two British colonies.[1] The situation did not change after the negotiations between the Boer republics and the British parliament, when the Union of South Africa was created in 1910. The disqualification of 'Black' people from access to political decision-making bodies aroused strong reactions. The African Native National Congress, later renamed the African National Congress (ANC), was formed in 1912 to unite the 'Black' people for their political and land rights.[2]

Discrimination because of 'race' was also on the agenda among churches at the First World Assembly of the WCC at Amsterdam in 1948. The assembly rejected

---

1   The Orange Free State and Transvaal were the two Boer republics. The British had the Cape Colony and Natal.
2   Thompson, Leonard, 2001, pp. 154–157.

47

all forms of racism or 'racial' segregation in the Christian community. The Second World Assembly of the WCC at Evanston in 1954 also took strong stands against several countries such as the USA, Rhodesia, Kenya, and South Africa, all of which had laws calling for 'racial' segregation that were seen as contrary to the gospel. Any discrimination according to 'race' could not be approved by the Church of Christ.[3] A special consultation was later held in Cottesloe, Johannesburg in 1960, arranged by the WCC to negotiate with the South African churches over apartheid. The South African Reformed churches left the WCC as a consequence of the consultation. Their withdrawal from the WCC was also a result of governmental interference in church policy. The WCC initiated the Programme to Combat Racism (PCR) after the Fourth World Assembly of the WCC at Uppsala 1968; the PCR would monitor the Council's work against racism, and particularly against apartheid.[4]

'Message to the People of South Africa' and the Kairos Document

In 1968 the SACC addressed the South African churches in the *Message to the People of South Africa*. The message questioned apartheid, and declared that separate development was against the gospel. The SACC received massive attention, and the Message provoked reactions even from the South African Prime Minister.[5] *The Kairos Document* of 1985 was another important document, published by a group of South African theologians. It was a critique of state and church theology, and appealed for a prophetic theology. 'State theology' was questioned because it would not change the society's racist patterns; and 'church theology'

---

3 The First Assembly of the World Council of Churches, 1949, p. 56; The Evanston Report, 1955, p. 156.
4 De Gruchy, John & de Gruchy, Steve, 2005, pp. 62–66. After the massacre at Sharpeville in 1960, the Anglican archbishop of Cape Town insisted that the WCC should have expelled the Cape and Transvaal NGK synods and NHKA as members of the Council. The WCC responded by organising a consultation with its member churches in South Africa in Cottesloe, Johannesburg, in December 1960. All the delegates, including NGK representatives but excluding NHKA representatives, reached agreement and rejected segregation in the churches. They affirmed that all were eligible for citizenship, rejected the government's policy prohibiting racially mixed marriages, the migratory labour system, the policy that prevented black people from owning land, etc. Prime Minister Hendrik Verwoerd, together with conservative NGK church leaders, rejected the outcome of the Cottesloe consultation. The NGK synods, together with the NHKA, withdrew from their membership of the WCC. McCullum, Hugh, 2004, pp. 345–353.
5 De Gruchy, John & de Gruchy, Steve, 2005, pp. 114–118; Mufamadi, Thembeka Doris, 2011, pp. 93–97.

because it did not question apartheid. The document introduced instead the notion of 'prophetic theology' – a theology that was contextual. Prophetic theology used interpretations of the Bible to question existing inequalities in the society.[6] The document received much attention both nationally and internationally.

The Rustenburg Conference and Declaration

One of the first official signs that South Africa had begun to dismantle apartheid and had started on the road towards democratisation came when President F.W. de Klerk made his Christmas address to the nation in December 1989. He called on the churches to find a strategy for negotiation, reconciliation and democratisations in South Africa.[7] Almost a year later, around 230 church leaders from 97 denominations and 40 church associations and ecumenical agencies came together for a five-day conference in Rustenburg, from 5 to 9 November 1990. They represented more than 90 per cent of the Christian community, or about 70 per cent of the total population of South Africa. The theme for the conference was 'Towards a united Christian witness in a changing South Africa'. The meeting was unique because it was the first time that church leaders from different ethnic and confessional backgrounds had come together. The meeting was an important step in the churches' – but also the whole society's – journey towards democratisation. Desmond Tutu said in his opening sermon that nobody would have believed two years before that this kind of national conference could have taken place, and that the conference was already a miracle.[8]

The reason for organising the conference was to build a common foundation to develop a united Christian witness in a changing South Africa.[9] Many of the addresses could be characterised as rather euphoric, because of their sense that an historic moment was approaching, with democratisation and radical changes taking place in the society despite the prevailing instability, violence, and insecurity. Several of the speakers were hopeful, and acknowledged the importance of the churches as being a major force in society for transformation. Prof. Willie Jonker of the University of Stellenbosch, for example, addressed the conference by saying: "It is very encouraging that a process of reorientation has begun to take place. The present climate in our country makes it possible to discuss these things in a

---

6   The Kairos Document, 1985, pp. 3–27.
7   Walshe, Peter, 1995, p. 78.
8   Chikane, Frank & Alberts, Louw, 1991, pp. 9–11; Tutu, Desmond, 1991, p. 20.
9   Chikane, Frank & Alberts, Louw, 1991, pp. 10–15.

meaningful way".[10] It was also remarkable that a representative from the Dutch Reformed church, Prof. Koos Vorster, addressed the delegates by saying:

> This Conference of Churches in South Africa has justifiably been described as the most important meeting in the history of the Church in this part of the world. Bearing in mind the deep-rooted differences that developed between Churches on the issue of apartheid, this meeting can be seen as quite an achievement. It promises a new dimension in Church relations in South Africa for the future. There is new hope for Christians and Christianity in the 'new South Africa' which is inevitably on its way.[11]

The conference can be characterised as an attempt to unite the churches against apartheid, as the WCC had tried to do in 1954 and at Cottesloe in 1961. Several of the speakers explained why apartheid had been able to become dominant in the South African churches. There were appeals to the churches to confess their guilt and undergo a thorough change.[12] Only a few women were represented at the conference, and only one woman had been part of the steering committee. Prof. John de Gruchy mentioned in his message, for example, that there had been division in the churches, not just between the races, but also between those who believed that scripture required males to be in charge, and those who believed that scripture required a church where all were equal in Christ. He also pointed out that while most of the active churches members were women, the leadership of the churches were male.[13] The problem that churches were organised on a racial basis was also identified in the conference. The Afrikaans-speaking churches rejected racism, even though they still organised their churches on a racial basis; and those churches that claimed to be multiracial or non-racial were in fact divided by racism.[14]

The conference resulted in *The Rustenburg Declaration*. In it, participants declared that they had achieved rapprochement and had discovered a broad

---

10 Jonker, Willie, 1991, p. 90.
11 Vorster, Koos, 1991, p. 62.
12 See for example messages delivered by John de Gruchy and David Bosch. De Gruchy, John, 1991, p. 120; Bosch, David J. 1991, pp. 129–138. The conference can be seen as breaking through the former theological positions in South Africa that stressed segregation based on a practical ecclesiology, built on a God-given pluriformity. In his thesis, Hans Engdahl has investigated two South African theologians, B. J. Marais and F. J. M. Potgieter, and showed that they had conflicting ecclesiologies. They were both defending apartheid. Potgieter had an ecclesiological entry: 'A life system', and Marais had an ecclesiological entry: 'The Ecumenical Church'. Engdahl, Hans S. A., 2006, pp. 133–136, 232–235, 289–296.
13 De Gruchy, John, 1991, p. 115.
14 Vorster, Koos, 1991, p. 63; De Gruchy, John, 1991, p. 113.

consensus through the different parts of the process in the conference. The participants unequivocally agreed to reject apartheid, and declared that apartheid was a sin. They condemned, for example, the escalating violence, acknowledged the extensive alienation among young 'Blacks', and expressed their concern about unemployment, which had reached critical proportions. They also confessed that men had often disregarded the human dignity of women, and had ignored sexism in the Church. They called for an end to racial inequalities between ministers in the churches, and stated that ministers should be appointed without regard to colour or social status. They called for an end to discrimination within the Church on the basis of sex or race.[15]

The Cape Town Consultation and Statement

Almost a year after the Rustenburg conference, another ecumenical conference was organised by the WCC and the SACC, and took place in Cape Town in October 1991. The conference's theme was 'Towards an Ecumenical Agenda for a Changing South Africa'. The conference has sometimes been called 'Cottesloe II' as a way of connecting it with the previous consultation of South African member churches of the WCC in Johannesburg in 1960. The general secretary of the SACC, Frank Chikane, invited the general secretary of the WCC, Emilio Castro, to South Africa to indicate a change in the relationship between the WCC and South Africa. The visit was an attempt to revive and improve the ecumenical climate, to strengthen the SACC's position, and to take further steps following the Rustenburg conference. The conference brought together a broad spectrum of South African church leaders, together with WCC staff, SACC staff, and international participants.[16]

The statement issued by the Cape Town conference begun by referring to the previous WCC and SACC conference in South Africa, which stated that apartheid was contrary to the gospel. They welcomed the release of political leaders, the unbanning of political organisations, and the rescinding of some apartheid laws. They emphasised that, even if the apartheid laws were removed, the legacy of apartheid would continue. The participants reported that the task was: "To expose and eradicate all forms of apartheid which persist in the economic, social, cultural and political structures of South African society. It is also to uncover and fight against all forms of exploitation that threaten to carry apartheid into a new society

---

15 The Rustenburg Declaration, 1990, pp. 275, 279–280, Preamble, par. 2.8, 3.1.
16 De Gruchy, John, 1997, pp. 162, 171; Mutambirwa, James, 1991, pp. 7–9; List of Participants of the Cape Town Consultation, 1991, pp. 109–112.

in disguised forms".[17] The delegates also committed themselves to participate in the reconstruction of the society, to address new life-threatening issues, to be in solidarity with those who were suffering, and to be engaged in global struggles for justice, peace and the integrity of creation. The delegates said about the churches' own structures: "While fighting against racism, sexism and other injustices, we may have left unchallenged the structures in our own churches that continue to promote these evils".[18] The statement suggested that the churches would become counterproductive in the society if they were not themselves transformed.

The statement indicated several areas for particular attention by describing the country's situation of endemic violence, the need for reconciliation, the revival of the church, and other themes such as AIDS, the youth, and the political economy. The situation of women was given special attention by stressing the importance of equal opportunities in Church and society.[19] The representation of women at the consultation was low, but the statement did not fail to challenge the churches about equality between men and women, and to raise particular awareness of the situation of black women. The statement also highlighted the churches' situation:

> The church has a special obligation to teach mutual cultural and ethnic respect in the quest of a non-racial, non-sexist, pluralistic society. The pluralism of God's creation is to celebrate a basis for the larger unity of all people – not as a basis for suspicion and chauvinistic division. Affirming the biblical and African ethos which teaches that we are only completely human in community with others, we recognise that different ethnic and cultural groups only come to completion in a transcendent humanness given us in God's creation and redemption.[20]

The statement affirmed the importance of unity in one single community by referring both to celebrating unity among God's people and to the African tradition of being together as humans. The Cape Town consultation ended with a proposal for action based on issues in the official Cape Town Statement. The proposal for action was in many ways something new for the South African ecumenical movement. The delegates at the consultation condemned others during apartheid, but by proposing a plan for action, the statement became self-critical – and participants in the consultation also made a commitment to act. The proposal for action became an aid to the churches in implementing the statement. Strengthening the inner life

---

17 Statement issued by the Cape Town Consultation, 1991, p. 89.
18 Statement issued by the Cape Town Consultation, 1991, p. 89.
19 Statement issued by the Cape Town Consultation, 1991, pp. 99–100.
20 Statement issued by the Cape Town Consultation, 1991, p. 101.

of the churches, ecumenical action, violence, sanctions, and youth were some of the subjects mentioned in the proposal for action.[21]

The action plan identified that there was a need for reconciliation between the churches and within each church, given the divisions of the human community caused by apartheid. The Dutch Reformed family received particular attention: the 'White' Dutch Reformed Church was challenged to be united with the other churches in the Reformed family, and to become one church. The challenge was also addressed to other SACC member churches because they too had not yet achieved a non-racial fellowship.[22]

Women received special attention through, for example, the suggestion to develop and use language that acknowledged women and youth, and to ensure the full participation of women in the programmes and structures of the churches on an equal basis with men. Women should also be part of the decision-making processes; resources should be given for women's empowerment; and the leadership of women in church and society needed to be developed.[23]

2.2 Consultations after Democratisation

The political transition was rapid, and after protracted negotiations, the first democratic elections took place in April 1994. Nelson Mandela was installed as president, and the country had a new government. The situation also changed for the churches and the ecumenical movement in a democratic society. New issues had to be tackled, and the legacy from the past had to be recognised.

Vanderbijlpark Consultation and Statement

Two-and-a-half years after the Cape Town consultation, the SACC and the WCC organised a second consultation, this time in Vanderbijlpark, south of Johannesburg, in March 1995. Its theme was 'South Africa in Regional and Global Context: Being the Church Today', and it dealt with issues and problems in the new democratic South Africa. The consultation gathered leaders, pastors, lay people, theologians, community workers, and politicians from both South Africa and southern Africa.[24]

---

21 Cape Town Consultation Proposal for Action, 1991, p. 105.
22 Cape Town Consultation Proposal for Action, 1991, p. 105.
23 Cape Town Consultation Proposal for Action, 1991, pp. 107–108.
24 Pityana, Barney N., & Villa-Vicencio, 1995, pp. *ix*, 164.

Because of the new political situation, the content of the consultation was very different from that of the Cape Town consultation. The first democratic elections on 27 April 1994, the new democratic government, and Nelson Mandela as president produced an entirely new scene. The focus switched to the position of the South African churches and the South African ecumenical community as part of the nation-building and national reconstruction process in South Africa. Compared with the Cape Town consultation, the Vanderbijlpark consultation was much more focused on Africa and on the global situation. Subjects such as the world economy, the arms industry, AIDS, poverty, and violence were frequently mentioned. The presenters put the churches' involvement and mission in the context of, for example, economic justice, the RDP, the TRC, education, health, land, etc.[25] Many of the speakers tried to articulate the question about how to be in critical solidarity with the new government.[26]

It is important to note that there was a shift in the argument about church unity at the Vanderbijlpark Consultation, compared with the Rustenburg Conference and the Cape Town Consultation. The discussions among speakers at the previous meetings were mainly concerned with the churches' own perspective and structures as being part of the apartheid system, while the Vanderbijlpark Consultation mainly dealt with the unity of the church as a contribution to social stability in South Africa. This change was natural, owing to the emergence of the new democratic society.

The conference produced a statement that had, in many respects, a different voice than that of the Cape Town Statement, because of South Africa's new political situation. The Vanderbijlpark Statement's focus was entirely on the Church in

---

25 Reconstruction and Development Program (RDP), Truth and Reconciliation Commission (TRC).
26 Pityana, Barney N., & Villa-Vicencio, 1995, pp. *ix*, 164; Nolan, Albert, 1995, p. 152. Some examples: Khoza Mgojo stated: "[...] If, on the other hand, the government fails to implement its Reconstruction and Development Programme (RDP), then it will lose the confidence of the people. This could be the beginning of a discontent playing into the hands of anti-democratic and counter-liberation forces". Mgojo, Khoza, 1995, p. 5; John W. de Gruchy stated: "One of the major problems facing the ecumenical church in South Africa is how to help build a new nation without being party to an uncritical and destructive nationalism, or silent in the face of any form of discrimination, corruption, or tyranny". De Gruchy, John W., 1995, p. 18; Saki Macazoma stated: "[...] The church must help build and be a critic of the state". Macazoma, Saki, 1995, p. 56; Charles Villa-Vicencio stated: "The call for prophetic ministry requires the church to be both a social and a critica partner of the building of the nation. [...]". Villa-Vicencio, Charles, 1995, p. 61.

a democratic South Africa, and it did not mention, for example, the churches' internal life and structures. This shift could be seen as the churches' response to being an important player in civil society's contribution to nation-building and the development of the society. The participants stated that African theology was intentionally inclusive, and the church was called to be ecumenical and not to withdraw into denominationalism. They also explained that the Church was part of God's inclusive plan, and dualisms such as men/women, black/white, and church/world were foreign to the gospel and to an African view of life. They acknowledged that the churches had fought apartheid, but there were now other challenges and enemies to face in the global context.[27]

The participants discerned four issues that had to receive special attention in the programme of action. They gave support to the government's plans to establish a Truth and Reconciliation Commission (TRC), which had been passed by Parliament, in order to bring about national reconciliation. They acknowledged that the process would need pastoral support, and training was needed for clergy and church workers. Education campaigns had to be established in order to educate people about the commission's purpose and to encourage people's participation.[28]

Johannesburg Consultation

A follow-up consultation was held in Johannesburg in October 1996, one-and-a-half years after the Vanderbijlpark Consultation. Unlike previous consultations, this meeting was arranged by the SACC alone. The Johannesburg Consultation produced neither a statement nor a programme of action. Nevertheless, it was important because it provided a platform for further discussion, and brought to light significant and relevant issues.[29]

One reason for the consultation was also an attempt to produce theology within the ecumenical body in South Africa that faced the questions of the new millennium. Four themes were in focus in the conference: African Culture, Land, Morality and Values, and Reconciliation and *Koinonia*. The papers delivered at the conferences were an important indicator of subjects that were on the agenda at the time of democratisation and before the TRC. Some of the issues, such as

---

27 Statement on Reconstructing and Renewing the Church in South Africa. Programme of Action, 1995, pp. 163–173.
28 Statement on Reconstructing and Renewing the Church in South Africa, 1995, pp. 163–173.
29 Pityana, Barney N., & Villa-Vicencio, Charles, eds., 1995, pp. iii–xi; Guma, Mongezi & Milton, A. Leslie, eds., 1997, Contents.

ethnicity, race and gender, were still important; but the representation of women was still low.[30]

2.3 The TRC's Faith Communities Hearing

The work of the Truth and Reconciliation Commission could be characterised as emphasising the importance of revealing the truth of what had happened during apartheid, and facilitating reconciliation and unity in the country. Church leaders had, since the Vanderbijlpark Consultation in 1995, supported the establishment of the TRC, even before it was known that many church leaders would lead the commission's work. The TRC was a creation of the democratic South African state for reconciliation in the society; but civil society organisations and the churches had visions of a reconstructed society. The TRC was not created by the churches; but theologians and church officials became heavily involved.[31]

The churches helped the TRC, for example, with premises, staff and counselling, in addition to their participation in the Faith Communities Hearing. The whole democratisation and reconciliation process in South Africa was in many ways an answer to the WCC's previous critique of the apartheid state and society and of the churches' inability to make sufficient changes.

Desmond Tutu, Archbishop-Emeritus of Cape Town, was appointed chairperson of the TRC, and the ideological foundation of the commission was similar to the churches' notion of catholicity. In the final report of the TRC, Tutu stressed the 'communion' character of the new South Africa as a society that could be compared with a family, as a common sister- and brotherhood. The source of this communion was understood to be God's family and the human family. The new society that Tutu imagined saw no differences between people, and did not divide human beings into different groups. Being human was not dependent on

---

30 Pityana, Barney N., & Villa-Vicencio, Charles, eds., 1995, pp. iii–xi; Guma, Mongezi & Milton, A. Leslie, eds., 1997, Contents.
31 The commissioners were made public on 15 December 1995. The Archbishop-Emeritus of the Church of the Province of Southern Africa, Desmond Tutu, was appointed Chairperson, and a former president of the Methodist Church of Southern Africa, Alex Boraine, was appointed Vice-Chairperson. Besides Tutu, two other ordained ministers were appointed as commissioners: the Revd Dr Khoza Mgojo came from the Methodist Church of Southern Africa, and the Revd Bongani Finca came from the Presbyterian Church in South Africa. Several others commissioners had church affiliations, including Piet Meiring. Boraine, Alex, 2000, p. 172; Truth and Reconciliation Commission of South Africa Report, Vol. 4, 1998, pp. 2, 148–150.

biological irrelevancies or other extraneous attributes that, according to the former apartheid society, were linked to ethnicity and skin colour.[32]

Tutu stressed a new united society that was not deeply divided, and he emphasised a sharing of opportunities for all South Africans. His report characterised a society that could embody a catholic vision of society in accordance with many ecumenical documents from the WCC. There was the image of a *koinonia* of people, and a very strong eschatological hope. It is not surprising that Desmond Tutu formulated an opinion similar to that of the ecumenical movement: he had previously been the general secretary of the SACC, and had many international engagements. Tutu's close relationship with the Community of the Resurrection, an Anglican monastic order, should also not be underestimated, as it also had influenced his theological background.[33]

Institutional Hearings

The TRC identified a number of institutions that were influential in the society – for example, business, the media, the faith community, and the health sector; and the TRC decided to investigate their responsibilities in connection with apartheid – whether the organisations and institutions had resisted or facilitated human rights abuses under apartheid. The churches and all the faith communities were invited to an institutional hearing, and they were asked to make submissions and statements in East London from 17 to 19 November 1997. Most of the churches responded and made submissions. All of the mainline churches investigated in this study, except for ELCSA and ELCSA-Cape, delivered submissions to the faith hearing. The bishop of ELCSA N-T wrote a letter to the commission stating that no submission would be provided to the hearing; but one was in fact sent six months later, and was included in the final report.[34]

---

32 Truth and Reconciliation Commission of South Africa Report, Vol. 1, 1998, p. 22.
33 Truth and Reconciliation Commission of South Africa Report, Vol. 1, 1998, p. 22.
34 Boraine, Alex, 2000, p. 172; Truth and Reconciliation Commission of South Africa Report, Vol. 4, 1998, pp. 2, 56–63, 148–150; Cochrane, James R. & De Gruchy, John W. & Martin, Stephen, 1999, pp. 192, 217.
Submissions to and materials about the TRC's Faith Communities Hearing in East London are from the South African History Archive (SAHA), William Cullen Library, University of the Witwatersrand. Audiovisual material about the Faith Communities Hearing has been obtained from the Department of Government Communication and Information System in Pretoria.

Roman Catholic Church

In 1996 the Roman Catholic Church delivered its submission to the TRC in the form of a book entitled *The Catholic Church and Apartheid*,[35] which was received by the research department of the TRC. The book dealt with the Roman Catholic Church in the apartheid state from 1948 to 1996. The Roman Catholic Church also delivered a submission to the Faith Communities Hearing, explaining that the church had members from different political backgrounds. Some had supported apartheid, while others had fought against the previous regime. Their members came from different 'races', languages, and classes. The church acknowledged that some of the victims were members of the Roman Catholic Church, and even the headquarters of the Southern African Catholic Bishops' Conference had been attacked. The church had not been vocal against apartheid in the early years of the Nationalist Party because of its own difficulties, and because it was seen as one of the enemies of the *volk*. The church had condemned apartheid in 1948 through a statement made by one of its bishops. There had been cautious writings in 1952 against apartheid, when the bishops called upon the government to use Christian principles to solve problems in the society. They opposed the Bantu Education Act in 1953 by keeping many Roman Catholic schools under their own governance, and they had opened Catholic schools to all pupils in 1976. They had continued to run their schools with private funds after they had lost state aid.[36]

The bishops were inspired by the Second Vatican Council, and became more vocal against state violence. They had drawn attention to the evil of apartheid in a pastoral letter in 1973. The statement had polarised the church both externally and internally. They also admitted that much more could have been done against human rights violations, although the church had emphasised that they had contributed to a culture of human rights, resistance and protest. They admitted that the church had neglected to resist apartheid, and had sometimes been more concerned with its own institutions and had remained silent. They had not entirely supported international sanctions, fearing increased poverty and unemployment. The church admitted that there were a Black church and a White

---

35 Abraham, Garth, 1989.
36 Submission to FCH, Roman Catholic Church, 15 August 1997. The earliest statement against apartheid was made by Bishop Henneman of Cape Town in 1948 when he condemned apartheid as against the law of God. The first time the bishops as a collective body issued a statement on race relations was in 1952. Race Relations and the Catholic Church in South Africa, 2005. The term *volk* means 'people', but was during apartheid often referring to the Afrikaners.

church because of the homelands system. The leaders of the church had had a tendency to address criticism to the state instead of addressing their members who elected the government.[37]

The church had started to provide group communication and counselling for victims, and the church would continue to promote human rights awareness in the country in a programme headed by the Justice and Peace Department of the SACBC.[38] Father Buti Thlagale added during the hearing that the church was committed to promoting rituals of reconciliation. He also stated: "There is a need to bring people from diverse cultural backgrounds together if we are going to achieve this goal of nation building".[39] He ended the message by saying that reconciliation could only be attained through the construction of a just economic system in the country.[40]

The Roman Catholic Church can be compared with the Anglican and Methodist churches' situations: all of them had a single church structure that was not divided by apartheid. In contrast to the other churches, the Roman Catholic Church refused to obey the Bantu Education Act, and continued to offer the same curriculum in all their schools. They refused to segregate their pupils, and continued with their schools. The Roman Catholic Church was seen by the National Party government as foreign, and was regarded as a national risk.

Church of the Province of Southern Africa (Anglican Church of Southern Africa)

The Anglican Church delivered a short submission to the TRC, while the message from Bishop Michael Nuttall during the hearing was much longer. The submission noted that they had a broad membership, some of whom had even been perpetrators and had violated human rights. The church had suffered during apartheid because of damage to its infrastructure, institutions, and schools, land expropriation, etc. The church stated that a complete picture of violations could only be given as individual members told their stories. The church acknowledged that there were occasions when it had been quiet and had also acted in submission to apartheid laws. They confessed that the church had made many statements that

---

37 Submission to FCH, Roman Catholic Church, 15 August 1997.
38 Submission to FCH, Roman Catholic Church, 15 August 1997.
39 TRC Special Hearing: Religion Tape 3, East London, DVD, (TRC0357 – 19971117), 1997.
40 TRC Special Hearing: Religion Tape 3, East London, DVD, (TRC0357 – 19971117), 1997.

were not reflected in the church's actions, which they saw as unfaithfulness to God. The church was committed to act as an agent for reconciliation and healing, address the injustices of the past, and eradicate poverty in order to maintain human rights.[41]

The message from Bishop Michael Nuttall emphasised that over many years the church had developed its own pattern of racial inequality and discrimination. English pride and prejudice, together with an attitude of moral superiority, had been directed towards the Afrikaner community. The 'White' Anglican minority had been beneficiaries of apartheid at the expense of the Black population, which included parishes, church facilities, and parsonages. There had also been a time when clergy stipends were paid according to race. They had allowed the appointment of Anglican priests as military chaplains, and they were slow to support economic sanctions, even though many in the church had advocated for their endorsement.[42]

The Methodist Church of Southern Africa

The submission of the Methodist Church to the Hearing was a limited document, but it was supplemented by an extensive statement by the presiding bishop, Mvume Dandala, during the Hearing. The Methodist Church stated that it had members from every section of South African society. They had people among their members who had suffered greatly under apartheid, and others who had committed serious human rights violations. The Methodist Church had rejected and opposed apartheid as unjust ever since apartheid had been introduced in 1948. They admitted, like other churches, that they had not always succeeded as a corporate body to be prophetic because of fear. A great number of their members had remained silent and uninvolved. They had fought against apartheid together with other churches through the SACC, and had contributed to the work of the Rustenburg Declaration. They were prepared, furthermore, to continue making the same efforts in the new democratic society. The Methodist Church committed itself to continuing its task of healing and reconciliation.[43]

Mvume Dandala's message at the Hearing added that the Methodists could not boast about their past efforts, and that they had failed to fulfil their mission as a church. They had also failed, together with other churches, to give justice and reconciliation a high priority. Dandala acknowledged, for example, that they had

---

41 Submission to FCH, Church of the Province of Southern Africa, 30 June 1997.
42 TRC Special Hearing: Religion Tape 3, East London, DVD, (TRC0357 – 19971117), 1997.
43 Submission to FCH, Methodist Church of Southern Africa, August 1997.

prevented an open discussion of economic sanctions, and the church had been divided over the issue of becoming a 'peace church'. They had paid unequal stipends to their ministers, and had stationed them on a racial basis, thus ensuring that both Black and White congregations were locked into their own separate cultural worlds instead of allowing them to be informed by the other side. The ministers were also not equipped by the church for the struggle against apartheid.[44]

Dandala said that their opposition to apartheid had been compromised by fear of the possible consequences of radical action. He named a situation where the church had been banned as an 'undesirable organisation' in one of the former homelands, Transkei – an area where the Methodist Church had the most members. Their properties had been confiscated, and they were not allowed to minister to their members. Dandala declared: "We will continue to build racially mixed congregations where individuals are honoured, and their heritage welcomed for the growth of all together".[45] He also stated that the church was committed, together with the other Christian communities, to fight hunger and poverty as a consequence of an unjust history. The Methodists were prepared to be in dialogue with people who would have claims on some of their properties, and they had opened their facilities for healing and counselling.[46]

Apostolic Faith Mission of South Africa

This church had once been divided along apartheid lines, but had recently been reunited. Their submission stated that they were founded as a single church, but had been seduced by the political and racial ideology, and had ended up being four churches – for Indian, Black, White and Coloured members. In the latter part of the freedom struggle they had explored the possibility of uniting, which was accomplished at Easter 1996. The AFM became the first church to unite after democratisation. They declared that their unification was more than structural unity: their identity as a church had been changed, and they were committed to attaining total unity. They acknowledged that not all of their members had agreed to church unity, and some had even withdrawn their membership. The church

---

44 TRC Special Hearing: Religion Tape 3, East London, DVD, (TRC0357 – 19971117), 1997.
45 TRC Special Hearing: Religion Tape 3, East London, DVD, (TRC0357 – 19971117), 1997.
46 TRC Special Hearing: Religion Tape 3, East London, DVD, (TRC0357 – 19971117), 1997.

believed that they had to pay the price for their convictions, but they perceived that it was in line with the word of God.[47]

They confessed that they had members who had committed transgressions. For example, many of their members had been employed by the state, had helped the system to work, and thus had extended apartheid's injuries. The submission even stressed that the AFM had not been able to monitor the subtle boundary between church and state, and many had believed that politics was not for Christians. Some had suffered because they thought that they were doing the right things, and others were suffering because of the guilt they were feeling for their deeds. They recognised that they had victims and perpetrators on both sides, and that they should have resisted, challenged and been more critical, but they had all failed.[48]

They had apologised collectively and individually to each other in the church, and they were facing the task of reconciliation, healing, and bridge-building. They declared that they had started to re-evaluate their training programmes, and they wanted to serve their community through social projects, and to create a spirit of sharing.[49]

When the president of the AFM, Isak Burger, made the church's presentation to the Faith Communities Hearing, he commented that their submission was unique. He said: "[…] It is to the best of our knowledge the only church submission to you in which members of all colours of the rainbow nation accept collective responsibility for the past".[50] He admitted that not long ago they had regarded unification as impossible. The delegation from the AFM had prepared a video to show the commissioners and participants in the Hearing about the re-unification of the church. It showed a public event where the divided church united. Burger, who had been the leader of one section of the church, made a public confession, and the previous leader of the other section, Frank Chikane, gave him absolution. They also made a promise that they would never again become divided. After the film, Isak Burger added that they had sinned for many years against the body of Jesus Christ by practising separation.[51]

---

47 Submission to FCH, Apostolic Faith Mission, 4 August 1997.
48 Submission to FCH, Apostolic Faith Mission, 4 August 1997.
49 Submission to FCH, Apostolic Faith Mission, 4 August 1997.
50 TRC Special Hearing: Religion Tape 11, East London, DVD, (TRC0366 – 19971119), 1997.
51 TRC Special Hearing: Religion Tape 11, East London, DVD, (TRC0366 – 19971119), 1997.

ELCSA, ELCSA N-T and ELCSA-Cape

The divided Lutheran church community in South Africa made a weak contribution to the TRC and the Faith Communities Hearing in East London. All the churches were invited, but ELCSA N-T was the only Lutheran church that submitted a submission. It was only received by the Commission the night before the closing date for contributions to the faith communities section of the final report.[52] ELCSA N-T was neither scheduled to be heard at the Hearing nor was it given time to make a presentation.[53] Piet Meiring said in an interview that they had expected ELCSA to have been part of the Hearing. The General Secretary of ELCSA, Manas Buthelezi, who was a former president of the SACC, was a very well-respected church leader. He had worked together with Beyers Naudé, and the TRC believed that ELCSA would come with a submission.[54]

ELCSA N-T acknowledged in their submission that, as a church and as individuals, they were deeply implicated in the injustice of apartheid. As members of the White society, they had enjoyed the privileges of apartheid, and were part of the section of the society that had governed the country. Their members, by and large, had identified with the interests of the White population, and their loyalty to the previous government had hardly been questioned. Most of the church's members were reluctant to criticise government policy, and some of the church's members had even been involved in developing and executing government policy. Their ministers, in general, avoided criticising the government, fearing conflict in their congregations and public ostracism.[55]

The church explained in their submission that they had failed to live in accordance with their understanding of the gospel. They had failed to speak out sufficiently against the exploitation and suffering of the majority of the Black community. They said: "[…] we have betrayed and denied God's unconditional love of all people irrespective of race, class, culture, education, achievement, gender or creed".[56] They had also failed to speak critically about public injustices and abuses of power. They regretted that they had not listened to the voices of their

---

52 Cochrane, James R. & de Gruchy, John W. – Martin, Stephen, 1999, p. 217.
53 The programme for the three days of hearing (with the names of the panelists), 1997. Materials from the Truth and Reconciliation Commission's Faith Communities Hearing.
54 Meiring, Piet, Interview Protocol 2011-03-05.
55 Submission to FCH, Lutheran Church of Southern Africa Natal – Transvaal, 19 March 1989.
56 Submission to FCH, Lutheran Church of Southern Africa Natal – Transvaal, 19 March 1989.

Black brothers and sisters, who had stated that apartheid should have been abolished. They declared furthermore that the church's council had not sufficiently encouraged the clergy to speak against apartheid.[57]

ELCSA N-T referred to the documents *A word of hope in the present situation in South Africa*, produced by ELCSA N-T in 1987, and *Christ is our Hope*, produced by UELCSA in 1986, which had been addressed to their congregations and to government. These documents had declared the church's position on theology, politics and economy in the country. The submission also referred to the church's position as a minority German-Lutheran church within the White population. They had safeguarded their cultural heritage and traditions, which isolated them from Black Lutherans and other Christians in general. This situation had kept them from being exposed to the Black social reality that included both Black and White members. They revealed their fears about the future, and noted that some of their ministers had attended a course on 'healing of memories' to learn a methodology that could be used among their members. They had, moreover, called their members to be involved in programmes and projects to develop and rebuild the country.[58]

The TRC's Final Report

Desmond Tutu wrote in one of his conclusions to the TRC that the Faith Communities Hearing in East London 17–19 November 1997 was more forthcoming than other institutional hearings. The religious communities had confessed their shortcomings, and they had acknowledged that they had acted in collusion with the apartheid government. They had confessed that they had been very vocal in criticising apartheid, while at the same time practising apartheid in their own institutions, and some had even been racially divided. He also wrote that, during the TRC, the faith communities had realised their special responsibility in healing a wounded people and in encouraging reconciliation and reparation among their members.[59]

The commission had the perception that the churches in South Africa had promoted and even supported apartheid in different ways, which included biblical and theological teaching. The commission highlighted the faith communities' failure to provide satisfactory ethical teaching as a counter against apartheid, in direct

---

57 Submission to FCH, Lutheran Church of Southern Africa Natal – Transvaal, 19 March 1989.
58 Submission to FCH, Lutheran Church of Southern Africa Natal – Transvaal, 19 March 1989.
59 Tutu, Desmond, 1999. p. 177.

contradiction of their own religious teaching. The churches followed state ideology and made it for possible apartheid ideology to survive, instead of keeping their own identity. The commission said that the church's position even contributed to and prolonged an undemocratic society, and perpetuated the apartheid myth that it was a Christian policy.

One important statement of the commission was the fact that the churches were seen to practise ecclesiastical apartheid by appointing ministers to parishes or congregations according to race – a practice that had economic consequences for the individual's salary or stipend. Churches could have appointed ministers from different backgrounds to parishes and congregations, independent of the state's apartheid segregation; instead they supported it and followed state ideology. The commission stressed that even the religious leaders mirrored apartheid, and thereby gave the lie to their profession of a loyalty that went beyond social divisions.[60]

The churches had approved and provided the apartheid state with ministers, priests, and pastors to serve, for example, as chaplains in the military and the police services. The commission was of the opinion that the churches were part of an illegal activity by entering into agreements with the state. According to the TRC, the chaplaincy was a window into understanding church-state relations, where churches even endorsed and supported the apartheid state structures. The commission believed that "[…] the military chaplaincy gave moral legitimacy to a culture characterised by the perpetration of gross human rights abuses".[61] The church-state situation also included numerous churches' members who were employed in the previous government's structures, with some even holding top positions in the former government. The churches' collaboration with the apartheid state also made them accountable for not objecting to state politics, and also for providing religious sanction and theological legitimacy for many actions of the armed forces.[62]

The previous apartheid ideology had created a divided society at every level, including residential, educational, workplace, transport, and social segregation. Total segregation was not achieved in the religious sector, but churches followed the apartheid pattern by structuring their organisations, parishes, and congregations according to the state's apartheid ideology. The commission stated in Report Number 4: "Despite their claim to loyalties that transcended the state, South

---

60   Truth and Reconciliation Commission of South Africa Report, Vol. 4, 1998, p. 65.
61   Truth and Reconciliation Commission of South Africa Report, Vol. 4, 1998, p. 70.
62   Truth and Reconciliation Commission of South Africa Report, Vol. 4, 1998, pp. 67–68; Truth and Reconciliation Commission of South Africa Report, Vol. 5, 1998, pp. 251–252.

African churches, whether implicitly or as a matter of policy, allowed them to be structured along racial lines – reinforcing the separate symbolic universes in which South Africans lived".[63] The commission noticed that in practice there had been a Black and a White church, even though some of the churches had not been divided organisationally. The Commission's statements made it very clear that the churches adapted to the conditions of the apartheid society without many objections. The commission believed that Black clergy were insufficiently empowered as leaders, giving them fewer possibilities for education and little supervision and guidance in leadership and ecclesiastical work.[64]

The TRC's Recommendations to the Faith Communities

Faith communities were mainly addressed because they were seen as having a privileged position in South African society. They were respected and had far-reaching moral influence. Besides the desire for the faith communities to embrace the position of providing a moral foundation for society, they were seen to have a key role in healing and reconciliation initiatives. The commission recommended that faith communities, among other things, should promote a culture of tolerance and peaceful co-existence, develop forms of worship that transcended language and cultural differences, and expose members from predominantly White and Black communities to one another. They further encouraged the churches to develop theologies designed to promote reconciliation and a true sense of community in the nation. Gender and class were mentioned in the final recommendation, but they were not specifically addressed to civil society or the faith communities.[65]

---

63 Truth and Reconciliation Commission of South Africa Report, Vol. 4, 1998, p. 68.
64 Truth and Reconciliation Commission of South Africa Report, Vol. 4, 1998, p. 69.
65 Truth and Reconciliation Commission of South Africa Report, Vol. 5, 1998, pp. 316–318. The Beyers Naudé Centre for Public Theology at Stellenbosch University, in collaboration with the Desmond & Leah Tutu Legacy Foundation, organised a "Re-enactment of the Truth and Reconciliation Commission's (TRC) Faith Hearing" 8–9 October 2014. There was a special focus on reconciliation in a post-TRC South Africa, and a revisiting of the commitments and recommendations that were made by the faith communities during the special hearing in East London in 1997. The outcome was not as positive as the faith leaders had hoped in 1997. Van der Riet, Louis, 2014, Truth and Reconciliation – A Matter of Faith?, Website.

2.4 Conclusion

The international ecumenical movement rejected any form of discrimination based on 'race' in the Christian community as early as the first World Assembly of the WCC at Amsterdam in 1948. Several statements and messages were made by the South African ecumenical movement in order to question segregation in church and society. The WCC organised meetings and consultations to negotiate with member churches that supported apartheid to change their theology.

The Rustenburg Conference, organised in 1990 in collaboration with the South African government and the SACC, took the first steps towards the society's and churches' transformation. The participants rejected apartheid and declared it a sin. The conference resulted in a declaration about forgiveness for the churches' contribution towards apartheid, and actions for restitution. The WCC and the SACC invited churches to consultations in Cape Town in 1991, before democratisation, and in Vanderbijlpark in 1995 after democratisation. The consultations acknowledged the churches' position under apartheid, but also emphasised important issues in the democratic South Africa that needed special attention. A follow-up consultation, organised by the SACC in Johannesburg in 1996, highlighted the churches' new position in a democratic environment.

The TRC made it possible for faith communities to contribute concerning their position in relation to the apartheid state during a special institutional hearing in East London in November 1997. The churches' submissions and responses showed very clearly that they had failed by becoming a divided community – but also that they had been victims of apartheid. The churches had also, to a certain extent, maintained inequality and sanctioned apartheid by collaborating with the apartheid government.

There was a discrepancy between the churches' many radical statements and resolutions and their actual practice. Several pastoral letters and documents had been produced and adopted that were not implemented. Some theologians had even questioned the usefulness of these documents and statements because they had not been implemented, and had argued that the churches could lose their credibility. The TRC was able to capture the churches' position during apartheid, but the significance of the commission's results is still debated.[66]

---

66 De Gruchy, John & de Gruchy, Steve, 2005, pp. 36, 258; Naudé, Beyers, 1991, p. 4; Van der Merwe, Hugo, & Chapman, Audrey R., 2008, pp. 241–245, 248–262.

The next chapter can be regarded as a response to the South African situation, and will describe the catholicity of the Church in a diverse ethnic society. This theory of the Church's catholicity comes from documents of the international ecumenical movement, which was engaged against racism, discrimination, apartheid and divisions within the Christian communion.

Chapter Three: Catholicity of the Church

In the previous chapter I illustrated how the South African ecumenical movement rejected apartheid. They gathered for conferences and consultations and produced documents, declarations and statements in order to work towards a democratic country. The churches stated during democratisation that differences between people were not a reason for dividing them, as had happened under apartheid. Segregation was perceived as foreign to the gospel and to an African worldview. In this chapter, I shall provide an overview of the notion of the 'catholicity' of the church that has been developed within the international ecumenical movement.

The South African churches selected for this study are members of the Faith & Order Commission (F&O) of the World Council of Churches (WCC) and of the SACC, and have either directly or indirectly contributed to the development of the ecumenical documents.[1] It is important to notice that the WCC is a fellowship of churches, and cannot legislate or act for its member churches. Every member church has the right to put into practice or reject the statements or actions of the WCC. Membership does not imply acceptance of a particular doctrine of the nature of Church. Nevertheless, the ecumenical documents about catholicity are in general consistent with the South African churches' doctrinal standpoints. It is helpful to use the key ecumenical documents to provide a normative view of catholicity in this thesis, even though the member churches do not consider the F&O and WCC documents to have the same status or authority as their own doctrines.[2]

---

1 ACSA, ELCSA, and MCSA are members of the WCC, and the RCC is represented in the F&O commission. ACSA, ELCSA, ELCSA N-T, MCSA, AFM and SACBC are members of the SACC, but ELCSA-Cape is not. The SACC is a member of the WCC, and thus its member churches are indirectly connected with the WCC. This is necessary in order for them to have a similar ecclesiological foundation for the concept of catholicity. WCC Membership Churches and Organisations in South Africa, 2013, Website; SACC Member Churches, 2013, Website.
2 At the third World Assembly at New Delhi in 1961, the WCC stated: "The World Council of Churches is a fellowship of churches which confess the Lord Jesus Christ as God and Savior according to the scriptures, and therefore seek to fulfil together their common calling to the glory of the one God: Father, Son and Holy Spirit". The New Delhi Report, 1962, p. 152. The WCC is not a super-church or the world church or the *Una Sancta* stated in the creeds. Membership of the WCC means that "each

I shall first give a general description of 'catholicity' as interpreted by the F&O and by WCC general assemblies, and from key documents of the ecumenical movement. In order to describe a general ecclesiology of the Church's catholicity, concepts such as 'body of Christ', 'Trinity', 'Christology', 'pneumatology', and the Christian communion as '*koinonia*' are inevitable. These concepts are used in the ecumenical discussions, and are ecclesiologically interlinked and intertwined. The terms will be used repeatedly and described from different angles when one of the other terms is examined. It is, for example, impossible to write about baptism and eucharist without referring to *koinonia* and Christology, and *koinonia* and eucharist must be referred to when writing about pneumatology and Christology. Figure I on page 73 describes how the diverse concepts are connected and intertwined in the catholicity of the Church within the body of Christ

Secondly, I shall present specific issues related to ethnicity that I have chosen as especially interesting in the South African context. These issues can be productively applied to the empirical material, particularly in the South African context, which is an ethnically-divided society. The issues are based on the Church's catholicity as set out in the ecumenical documents. These issues will become my analytical tool when I examine the congregations and churches that serve as case studies.

3.1 Catholicity in Faith & Order and the WCC

'Catholicity' emphasises the sharing (or *koinonia*) of the one universal community founded in the one baptism. This implies that people become members of the body of Christ, which is understood as a primary identity. Catholicity acknowledges that there are diverse expressions of the faith, recognised as the contributions that come from different global contexts.

The word 'catholic' is an ancient Greek term from the adjective καθολικός (*katholikos*) that was adopted by theologians. Used at first to distinguish between the whole church and the congregation, it later came to signify the *true* Church. Ignatius of Antioch is the first Christian author to use the term 'Catholic Church'. By it he means that the bishop is to the local congregation as Christ is to the Church.[3] In his catechesis, Cyril of Jerusalem wrote an interpretation of 'Catholic Church' that included, for example, universalism, unity, divine fellowship, and

---

    church retains the constitutional right to ratify or to reject utterances or actions of the Council". The Toronto Statement on "The Church, the Churches, and the World Council of Churches", 1950.
3   Schoedel, William R., 1985, p. 243.

inclusiveness.⁴ His description gave rise to one of the first theological discussions to develop the term in Christian antiquity. The teaching that the Church was a single universal community was also confirmed after the Council of Constantinople (381), when the Nicene Creed, which affirms belief in "[...] one holy, catholic, and apostolic Church [...]", was adopted.⁵ The word 'catholic' would best be understood in modern language as referring to an inclusive community, or as welcoming everyone into the community.⁶

The ecumenical documents of Faith and Order rarely used the word 'catholic' at the beginning of the modern ecumenical movement; but even if it was not mentioned explicitly, the subject could be traced in many early writings.⁷ The term was initially debated and considered to be controversial because of the contrast between catholic and evangelical at the time. The conflict was then resolved through a change of methodology in the ecumenical discussions.⁸ The Fourth World Assembly of WCC at Uppsala was more comfortable in using the word 'catholic' as a mark of the Church, and one of the assembly's sections dealt exclusively with the catholicity of the Church.⁹ The ecumenical theology of catholicity was developed later, and became a frequent explanation of the identity of the church within the ecumenical movement.¹⁰

---

4   Cyril of Jerusalem & Nemesius of Emesa, 1955, pp. 185–189.
5   Dulles, Avery, 1985. pp. 13–14.
6   Groome, Thomas H., 1998, p. 397.
7   The First World Conference on Faith and Order at Lausanne in 1927 did not use the term 'catholicity'. The documents use other terms – for example, God's family, the body of Christ, and the Temple of God. Reports of the World Conference on Faith and Order, 1927, pp. 5, 7. The Second World Conference on Faith and Order at Edinburgh in 1937 referred to a Holy Catholic Church and a common faith. They described the Church as the people of the new covenant, the household of God, the body of Christ, the kingdom of God. The catholicity of the church was not further described in the conference. Report of the Second World Conference on Faith and Order, 1937, pp. 230–232.
8   Vischer, Lukas, 1963, p. 24; Documentary History of Faith and Order, 1963–1993, 1993, p. 7; Fuerth, Patrick W., 1973, pp. 38–39, 53.
9   The Uppsala Report 1968, 1968, pp. 7–19.
10 Many books, articles and dissertations have studied the emergence of catholicity in the Faith and Order movement and the WCC. Dissertations cover topics such as: The concept of catholicity in the documents of the World Council of Churches, 1948–1968: A historical study with systematic-theological reflections, by Fuerth, Patrick W., 1973; The Concept of Catholicity in the Faith and Order Movement, 1910–1968, by Metzler, David G., 1973. Books include The Catholicity of the Church, by Dulles, Avery, 1985; and there are articles such as "Catholicity, Faith and Order, and the Unity of the Church" in The Ecumenical Review, by Gibaut, St-Helier, John, 2011, pp. 177–185.

The catholicity of the Church is described in ecumenical texts as "the fullness, integrity and totality of its life in Christ through the Holy Spirit in all times and places".[11] This means that the foundation of the Church is its life in Christ, who is also the model and character of a Christian community. The Church is the place where life and salvation is given to all humanity, irrespective of cultural background, sex, class, ethnicity, etc.[12]

The Church can change and adjust to changed times without becoming something different and losing its catholicity. The continuity of catholicity is found in the identity of the Church. It is important to notice that the catholicity of the Church discussed in the ecumenical documents is neither the number of many local churches that are joined together, nor the number of local churches that are connected to a certain 'catholic' church. Catholicity is expressed in every local church because every church is part of Christ. Nevertheless, a local church cannot be catholic in isolation: it has to be in communion with other Christian communities. The 'catholic church' already existed when there was only one Christian community in Jerusalem, because the Church was seen as the bearer of God's salvation for humanity. Later, other Christian communities were founded in Corinth, Thessalonica and Galatia, and these became catholic despite the differences between them. When new local churches are added, catholicity is not increased: the Church is extended. The Church as local and universal fulfils catholicity through its communion with other churches.[13]

Lorelei F. Fuchs has thoroughly described the concept of *koinonia*, relating the exegetical meaning to the ecumenical understanding of *koinonia*. She has also examined the concept of *koinonia* in the dialogues between churches, and challenges the churches to move beyond dialogue. Fuchs, Lorelei F., 2008.

11 God, in your Grace …, 2007, p. 257.
12 The Nature and Purpose of the Church, 1998, p. 10; Dulles, Avery, 1985, pp. 30–33.
13 Ecclesiology and Ethics, 1997, pp. 10–11, 37, 38, 42.

Figure I: The catholicity of the Church can be described as a community of members. God as three Persons and at the same time provides the pattern for the community, where diversity does not destroy unity, and unity does not choke diversity for the sake of uniformity. It is the same with Christ and the Church: the Church as the body of Christ cannot be separated from Christ, but there is at the same time a distinction between Christ and the Church. The communion is not sealed off by any boundaries, but the members are called from the world and sent into the world. Baptism is related to the eucharist; apostolicity and sharing as the other aspects of catholicity are interrelated and interlinked with each other. Catholicity is already present, but it is also an eschatological promise.

Church as Catholic, described as the Body of Christ

There are several images of 'Church' in the Bible, and some of them are frequently used in ecumenical texts that have particular significance for the Christian community. The analogy of 'the body of Christ' has been repeatedly used in several statements and declarations by F&O and the WCC, and has made fruitful contributions to ecumenical dialogue. As early as at the First and the Second World

Conferences on F&O at Lausanne and Edinburgh, 'the body of Christ' analogy claimed that any kind of division among Christians prevents the realisation of unity within the body of Christ.[14] The Fourth World Assembly of WCC at Uppsala even insisted that the greatest obstacle to unity was the inability to understand that the Church was the body of Christ.[15]

A significant factor in the ecumenical documents is that the body of Christ is more than an image or a metaphor: it is an analogy. The term 'body of Christ' establishes an identity between Christ and the Church, and also describes the Church as a living organism. The Church as the body of Christ cannot be separated from Christ; but there is at the same time a distinction between Christ and Church. The double nature of the Church was stressed in the Third World Conference on Faith and Order at Lund. Church and Christ were understood as belonging inseparably together, and there was an identity between Church and Christ. Members of the body of Christ are united with Christ and his death and resurrection. Union with Christ, with each other, and with the Church exists in every time and place.[16] Christ is the head of the body, and through the Spirit he is the giver of life. The image is described in the first letter to the Corinthians and in the letter to the Romans. All members of the body of Christ are given gifts conferred by the Holy Spirit for the building up of the body (cf. Rom 12:4–8; 1 Cor 12:4–30), reflecting their unity (cf. 1 Cor 12:12). The diversity and specific nature of these gifts enriches the Church's life.[17]

The body of Christ analogy can be expressed in sacramental terms that require – besides a Christological dimension – trinitarian and pneumatological dimensions as well. The Trinity is the image and example of unity within the body of Christ, where the focus is on communion. God as three Persons while being at the same time One sets a pattern in which diversity does not destroy unity, and unity does not choke diversity for the sake of uniformity. This kind of unity provides the foundation for the Church and for how unity is preserved. If one person in the Godhead excludes the other persons, there is no unity in God.

---

14 Reports of the World Conference on Faith and Order, 1927, p. 7; Report of the Second World Conference on Faith and Order, 1937, p. 235; Baptism, Eucharist and Ministry, 1982, p. 14.
15 The Uppsala Report 1968, 1968, pp. 17–18.
16 Confessing the One Faith, 1991, p. 83.
17 The Nature and Purpose of the Church, 1998, pp. 12–14; Together on the Way, 1999, pp. 134, 139, 144; The Nature and Mission of the Church, 2005, p. 8; God, in your Grace …, 2007, pp. 256–257.

The baptised person, as part of the body of Christ, participates in the trinitarian life of communion and love. This makes the Church a *koinonia*.[18]

The Christological dimension is expressed when baptised members of the communion are recreated in the image of Christ. The communion of members is the body, while Christ is the abiding head of his body who, by the gift of the Sprit, gives life to the body. Church as the body of Christ cannot be separated from Christ.[19] The Holy Spirit incorporates human beings into the body of Christ through faith and baptism, and enlivens and strengthened the baptised in the eucharist. The Spirit brings unity to the Church and gives diverse gifts for building up the body. The diversity and nature of the gifts enriches the life of the Church, and enables it to respond to its vocation of serving the world.[20]

There is, according to the ecumenical documents, a double character in the body of Christ: it is "being called from the world and sent into the world".[21] This expression stresses that Christians are called together to participate in forming a collective body that becomes the body of Christ, and to serve the world. The body that is Christ is not introverted, but is sent to be in cooperation with the world.[22] The dual character of the body of Christ is repeated several times in the ecumenical documents, emphasising that through baptism and eucharist people participate in God's creation.[23] The Church is, in this understanding, Christ's living Body, which exists in local congregations and as a worldwide communion that makes the Church catholic.[24]

The image of the body of Christ denies any form of segregation or division in the Church. People within the body of Christ are members of a new humanity in which barriers or divisions – for example, gender, ethnicity, or social status – are transcended. It is even understood that when segregation, exclusion or division

---

18 The Fourth World Conference on Faith and Order, 1964, pp. 82–83; Gathered for Life, 1983, pp. 62–63; Church and World, 1990, p. 23; Confessing the One Faith, 1991, p. 22; The Nature and Mission of the Church, 2005, pp. 4–5.
19 The Nature and Purpose of the Church, 1998, pp. 12–14; The Nature and Mission of the Church, 2005, p. 7.
20 The Nature and Purpose of the Church, 1998, p. 14; The Nature and Mission of the Church, 2005, pp. 4–5, 8.
21 The Third World Conference on Faith and Order, 1953, p. 18.
22 The Third World Conference on Faith and Order, 1953, pp. 17–21, 23; Baptism, Eucharist and Ministry, 1982, pp. 2–3; Confessing the One Faith, 1991, p. 83.
23 See for example: Gathered for Life, 1983, pp. 54–55.
24 Confessing the One Faith, 1991, p. 85; On the Way to Fuller Koinonia, 1994, p. 232; Towards Sharing the One Faith, 1996, p. 21.

occurs, it is a scandal that opposes being part of the body of Christ, and fundamentally destroys the body. Exclusion result in rejection: people are no longer part of the community. Divisions because of gender, ethnicity, or social status are irrelevant in the communion of the Church, and have no meaning or significance for baptised members who are united in the body of Christ. The new humanity created by Christ reconciles divisions, and the Church becomes part of the eschatological hope.[25] Breaking the bread during eucharist is a sign of the scarred and wounded body of Christ, and shows that the Church is itself broken.[26]

Despite the existence of diverse cultural, local, or separate expressions of churches or denominations, Christians are united in the community of the body of Christ. The same corporate communion is an expression of the catholicity of the Church. Diversity is an expression of the identity of being catholic, and should be visible in every part of the community. Diversity is not a reason for division, and the Christian community is encouraged to welcome cross-cultural experiences.[27]

Catholicity in Christology and Pneumatology

The body of Christ analogy requires, as mentioned, Christological and pneumatological dimensions. The ecumenical documents stress that the body of Christ analogy becomes a fundamental explanation of the Church's catholicity, because the analogy describes how the presence of Jesus Christ creates a catholic Church. Christ is the one who unites the Church in love for all humans, a love that transcends all existing barriers. Catholicity, moreover, includes the saints of all ages as well as all Christians of every place. This makes the local worshiping community central, and it also establishes the relationship of the local church with the universal Church in the present and in the past. The Christological perspective identifies Christ in the Church, and connects local worshiping communities together, transcending place and time. Catholicity is not primarily linked to a structure or organisation, but rather to life in Christ.[28]

---

25 First Assembly of the World Council of Churches, 1949, p. 56; The New Delhi Report, 1962, p. 127, 182–184; Baptism, Eucharist and Ministry, 1982, pp. 2–3; Gathered for Life, 1983, pp. 54–55; Church and World, 1990, pp. 20–23; Signs of the Spirit, 1991, pp. 248–250.
26 Christian Perspectives on Theological Anthropology, 2005, pp. 7–9.
27 Breaking Barriers, 1976, pp. 78–79, 92–94.
28 The Third World Conference on Faith and Order, 1953, pp. 23–24; The Fourth World Conference on Faith and Order, 1964, pp. 45–46, 57–59; On the Way to Fuller Koinonia, 1994, p. 232.

The Christological dimension considers Christ as the head of the body and – through the Holy Spirit – also as giver of life, as earlier described. The Holy Spirit creates the possibility for believers to enter into communion (*koinonia*) with God and with each other, which is incorporation into the body of Christ through faith and baptism. The Spirit is seen as the giver of life to the body through, for example, the preached Gospel, sacramental communion, and ministries of service. Every member of the body reveals gifts from the Holy Spirit for the common good of the body of Christ, and for service in the world in diverse forms.

The Holy Spirit nourishes and enlivens the body of Christ through the living voice of the preached Gospel, through sacramental communion, especially in the Eucharist, and through ministries of service. This is a Pentecostal act, since a new relationship is created with other believers that make it possible to learn to communicate across various divisions of issue and culture.[29] The Holy Spirit is the one who is the giver of the diverse gifts, but at the same time the one who brings unity to the Church.[30]

The catholicity of the church is a gift from the Holy Spirit to the Church. Catholicity even builds up the Church in each place and brings and maintains unity.[31] The gifts of unity from the Holy Spirit are demonstrated through the celebration of the eucharist, but are also visible in, for example, common prayers, having a corporate life, sharing resources, and manifesting unity with the whole Christian fellowship in all places. The Holy Spirit binds all humans together with all created life, and the catholicity given by the Spirit becomes visible when the Church becomes a unifying gift to the whole of society and all of humanity.[32]

Baptism as incorporation in the Body of Christ

Baptism in the ecumenical documents is a sacrament that expresses new life in Christ, and is inherently an incorporation into the body of Christ, which

---

29 The Third World Conference on Faith and Order, 1953, pp. 17–21, 23; The New Delhi Report, 1962, pp. 116–117; Towards Sharing the One Faith, 1996, p. 21; Church and World, 1990, pp. 26–27, 32; Signs of the Spirit, 1991, pp. 96–97; The Nature and Purpose of the Church, 1998, p. 14, The Church – Towards a Common Vision, 2012, p. 9.
30 The Nature and Purpose of the Church, 1998, p. 14; A Treasure in Earthen Vessels, 1998, pp. 29–30.
31 The Fourth World Conference on Faith and Order, 1964, pp. 51–53; The Uppsala Report 1968, 1968, pp. 13–18; Church and World, 1990, pp. 26–27; The Nature and Purpose of the Church, 1998, pp. 9–10, 12–14.
32 The New Delhi Report, 1962, pp. 116–117; Breaking Barriers, 1976, pp. 46–48; Signs of the Spirit, 1991, p. 97.

is understood as the Church. The incorporation is perceived as the work of the Holy Spirit through faith and baptism, as believers enter into communion with the Triune God. A new humanity is created through the water of baptism because everybody is identified exclusively with the crucified and risen Christ. Baptism grants unity with Christ and others in the Christian community, irrespective of time and place. The Church, through its baptised members, has no place for division, and is not intended to be part of a segregated society. Divisions of, for example, gender, ethnicity, language, or social status are transcended: there is a profound equality within the Christian community. According to this explanation, baptism is incorporation to the holy, catholic and apostolic Church, part of the eschatological hope that tears down walls of separation.[33]

Local churches are a fellowship bound together by baptism, eucharist, and confession of the one Gospel of Christ. Even if distance, culture, and time separate people, unity is preserved and revealed when baptised representatives of local churches came together for common meetings. Baptised members of a local church are united with the one Church of Christ, which transcends geographic, social, ethnic and temporal boundaries. Baptism creates a relationship with the whole body of Christ in every place and every time. The Church consists of baptised members both in local congregations and in a worldwide communion.[34] Because their membership transcends all boundaries in *koinonia* in the body of Christ, women and men, ethnic groups and nations are called to be incorporated into God's new people by baptism. Baptism is a new beginning in which all are made one with God and are inheritors of the *basileia* (dominion) of God.[35] The ecumenical documents also stress the importance of the eucharist to renew communion, alongside baptism.

---

33 The New Delhi Report, 1962, pp. 127, 182–184; Baptism, Eucharist and Ministry, 1982, pp. 2–3, 7; Church and World, 1990, pp. 20, 23; Confessing the One Faith, 1991, pp. 77, 92; On the Way to Fuller Koinonia, 1994, p. 248; The Nature and Purpose of the Church, 1998, pp. 9–10; Christian Perspectives on Theological Anthropology, 2005, p. 18; The Nature and Mission of the Church, 2005, pp. 4–5; Participating in God's Mission of Reconciliation, 2006, p. 24.
34 The Nature and Purpose of the Church, 1998, pp. 36–37; Confessing the One Faith, 1991, p. 85; The Nature and Mission of the Church, 2005, p. 17, One Baptism, 2011, p. 16.
35 The Nature and Mission of the Church, 2005, p. 20; Participating in God's Mission of Reconciliation, 2006, p. 24.

The Role of the Eucharist in Catholicity

Both baptism and eucharist lead Christians into communion with the triune God and into a communion within the body of Christ, which is the Church. Baptism and eucharist are clearly connected. The unity that is proclaimed and demonstrated through baptism is – as described earlier – an incorporation into *koinonia* with God and with the body of Christ. Unity is repeatedly expressed, nourished and reaffirmed in the eucharist. Every time the eucharist is celebrated and shared among the members of the body of Christ, *koinonia* is renewed in the body. This is visibly manifested in the eucharist through sharing the one bread and a common cup.[36]

The eucharist has to be practised in the Church in order to support and sustain the *koinonia*. Every time the eucharist is celebrated and shared among the members, unity with God and with other Christians is renewed. This includes unity with other Christians in other eucharistic communities, irrespective of time and place. Every local eucharistic celebration is connected with the whole Church, and the whole Church is involved in every local eucharistic celebration.[37] Local churches are bound together by baptism, by sharing the same eucharist, and by confessing the one Gospel of Christ. The eucharistic celebration becomes central when the local church expresses the catholicity of the Church. The eucharist urges every church to share the needs and hopes of others, and to overcome divisions that prevent a common celebration.[38]

Baptism and eucharist express the Christian community's new life in Christ – the creation of a new humanity. The ecumenical documents explain that Christians receive Christ by breaking the bread and sharing the cup in the eucharist. Participants simultaneously recognise themselves as Christ's body and become aware of the broken body. Participants in the eucharist in the *koinonia* are challenged by the inclusive practice of Jesus, who ate with the outcasts of society of his time. The

---

36 Baptism, Eucharist and Ministry, 1982, p. 14; Confessing the One Faith, 1991, p. 83; The Nature and Mission of the Church, 2005, pp. 9–10, 21, 34–35; One Baptism, 2011, p. 13.
37 Breaking Barriers: Nairobi 1975, 1976, pp. 46–48; Signs of the Spirit, 1991, p. 173; The Nature and Purpose of the Church, 1998, pp. 34–35; Baptism, Eucharist and Ministry, 1982, p. 14.
38 Breaking Barriers: Nairobi 1975, 1976, pp. 60–61; Baptism, Eucharist and Ministry, 1982, p. 14; A Treasure in Earthen Vessels, 1998, p. 31. The BEM document even stresses the importance of sharing in *one* bread and the *common* cup as demonstrating the oneness of the Christian community. Using individual communion cups can be questioned because the symbol of unity can be lost. Baptism, Eucharist and Ministry, 1982, p. 13.

Church becomes a sign of the scarred and wounded body of Christ, which means that the Church is united in brokenness.[39]

The eucharist requires reconciliation and sharing among Christians in communion, and participants are invited to reconcile before they worship together. It is the sacrament that builds up the community and challenges any form of segregation in worship that is based on injustice, ethnicity, racism or exclusion. Even social, economic and political life is challenged because the participants belong to the one body of Christ. The *koinonia* that was part of the eucharist in the early church involved ethical engagement – for example, when there was a need in Jerusalem and a collection to the poor was carried out (Rom 15:25). The ecumenical document *Costly Commitment*, for example, emphasises that the eucharistic *koinonia* always has an ethical dimension. The eucharistic celebration is the same as participating in the restoration of the world and of human dignity.[40]

Breaking bread and sharing wine in the eucharist is being part of a sharing *koinonia* with mutual prayers, offering services, giving material aid, working together for equality, justice and peace, etc. The eucharistic celebration expresses the catholicity of the Church, and challenges and questions all forms of division and disunity. The document *Baptism, Eucharist and Ministry* even stresses that the eucharist should be celebrated at least every Sunday, and that Christians should be encouraged to receive the eucharist frequently.[41]

Koinonia in Catholicity

Baptism is incorporation into the body of Christ, and the eucharist nourishes and reaffirms the community that is created in the body of Christ. The Christian community that is *koinonia* is described in the ecumenical documents in the same terms as the communion within the Trinity. There are three persons in God, and the persons are held together as one because of a relationship of *koinonia*. The Trinity's diversity does not destroy the unity, nor does the unity suppress the diversity. This *koinonia* in God is understood as a perfect communion of unity in love

---

39 Christian Perspectives on Theological Anthropology, 2005, pp. 7–9, 18–19.
40 The Uppsala Report 1968, 1968, p. 83; Breaking Barriers: Nairobi 1975, 1976, p. 49; Baptism, Eucharist and Ministry, 1982, p. 14; Ecclesiology and Ethics, 1997, pp. 22–33, 37, 39; The Nature and Purpose of the Church, 1998, pp. 21, 38–39.
41 The Nature and Purpose of the Church, 1998, pp. 9, 24–26; A Treasure in Earthen Vessels, 1998, p. 31; The Nature and Mission of the Church, 2005, p. 9; God, in your Grace …, 2007, p. 257; Baptism, Eucharist and Ministry, 1982, p. 13.

and, according to the ecumenical documents, has been revealed in the Christian faith throughout history.[42]

Humans are called to live in communion with each other, alongside the call to live in relationship with God. *Koinonia* in the Church echoes the relationships of the Trinity, and is interpreted as 'to have something in common', 'to share', 'to participate', 'to have part in', 'to act together' or 'to be in a contractual relationship involving obligations of mutual accountability', 'solidarity'. The word appears in the early church in the sharing of the eucharist, reconciliation, the collection for the poor, and the experiences and witness of the Church.[43]

The ecumenical documents explain that visible divisions reveal the brokenness of the Christian community, and also hamper the mission of the Church, even though *koinonia* is God's gift to the Church. *Koinonia* might not be fulfilled as perfect communion until a new heaven and a new earth are established; but there is an impulse in the foundation of the Church towards unity.[44] *Koinonia* has qualities that do not allow division and exclusion on the basis of ethnicity, age, language, sex, nationality, class or cultural background.[45] Divisions within the Christian community mean that *koinonia* cannot be passively assumed, but must be actively pursued. The aspiration to experience *koinonia* drives the members of the Church to seek visible unity with God and fellow beings.[46] Establishing *koinonia* involves a process of individual and collective forgiveness that leads to reconciliation and restitution, allowing the Church to overcome divisions and to bring about visible unity in the body of Christ.[47]

---

42 Confessing the One Faith, 1991, pp. 19, 22; On the Way to Fuller Koinonia, 1994, pp. 225–226.
43 Ecclesiology and Ethics, 1997, pp. 10–11; On the Way to Fuller Koinonia, 1994, p. 232; The Nature and Mission of the Church, 2005, pp. 8–9; The Church – Towards a Common Vision, 2012, p. 8.
44 On the Way to Fuller Koinonia, 1994, p. 233; Ecclesiology and Ethics, 1997, pp. 25–27; The Nature and Mission of the Church, 2005, pp. 8–9.
45 The First Assembly of the World Council of Churches, 1949, pp. 56, 67; The Third World Conference on Faith and Order, 1953, pp. 23–24, 239; The Evanston Report, 1955, p. 158; The New Delhi Report, 1962, p. 119; The Uppsala Report 1968, 1968, pp. 14–15; Breaking Barriers: Nairobi 1975, 1976, p. 74; Baptism, Eucharist and Ministry, 1982, pp. 2–3, 7; Church and World, 1990, p. 20; Signs of the Spirit, 1991, p. 172.
Confessing the One Faith, 1991, pp. 83, 87; On the Way to Fuller Koinonia, 1994, p. 232; The Nature and Purpose of the Church, 1998, pp. 9–10.
46 The Nature and Purpose of the Church, 1998, pp. 24–26; On the Way to Fuller Koinonia, 1994, pp. 225–226.
47 On the Way to Fuller Koinonia, 1994, p. 233; Ecclesiology and Ethics, 1997, pp. 25–27.

Each Christian community is related to other local Christian communities in *koinonia*, and they all belong to the same Church. One Christian community is not able to live in isolation from the rest: it has to be in relationship with the other communities. There is one Church, but there can be many local church communities at the same time. *Koinonia* is building bridges between different communities that also transcend all kinds of boundaries. Because of the unity that exists, and is supposed to come in the future, they can live the catholicity of the universal Church.[48]

There is one community within the Church; but there are also other churches that are called to seek unity. Furthermore, the community reaches out towards people of other faiths and convictions and even to all humanity. This means that many different communities and levels of communities exist simultaneously in the *koinonia* that proceeds from God.[49]

The Church as Local and Catholic

Koinonia is present in every local church where there are baptised members who practise the eucharist and reaffirm the one community. The meaning of 'local church' is discussed in the ecumenical documents – whether it is a local congregation of believers, a church with believers around an *episkopé* (church leader or bishop) or even several dioceses/areas. In the ecumenical documents the 'local church' is central as the foundation of the Christian community, and is defined as people living in one place. There could be many churches in one place, but they all belong to the same body because there is only one Church. This means that local congregations are related to each other, and they all belong to the same Church. There are no boundaries caused by church or denominational affiliation, ethnic, cultural or linguistic belonging, or even historical heritage. Unity within the body of Christ plays a crucial role and is given by *koinonia*, according to the ecumenical documents. *Koinonia* emphasises the interaction or sharing of believers within local Christian communities. When the term *koinonia* was used in the New Testament, it was to call for a collection for the church in Jerusalem to build bridges between different Christian communities. These communities transcended boundaries because they referred to a community that existed on the basis of people gathered around the gospel.[50]

---

48 The Fourth World Conference on Faith and Order, 1964, pp. 82–83; Ecclesiology and Ethics, 1997, pp. 10–11.
49 Breaking Barriers: Nairobi 1975, 1976, pp. 75, 78.
50 The Fourth World Conference on Faith and Order, 1964, pp. 82–83; On the Way to Fuller Koinonia, 1994, p. 232; Ecclesiology and Ethics, 1997, pp. 10–11.

All local churches in one place are related to one another, and one Christian community cannot be isolated from other Christian communities. If one church separates itself from other churches, that church is no longer part of the Christian community and has ceased being Church. According to this description, a local church in one place needs to be in relationship with other local churches. This relationship is not primarily based on organisational structures, but rather on a fellowship of local churches bound together by baptism, sharing the same eucharist, confessing the same Gospel, and serving one another – thus tying the community together.[51]

The gospel has been rooted and lived in every place, and has been proclaimed in language, symbols and images that are dependent on the particular time and context. The local becomes visible in rich diversity for cultural and historical reasons. The local reflects the global community because of this diversity. Even though there may be considerable differences, diversity is not the same as division. Unity within the communion of local churches is sustained by proclaiming and practising apostolicity and catholicity.[52]

Although local churches encounter diversity and face the problem of attaining unity, churches cannot be segregated in order to solve the problem of ethnicity. A local church must belong to the same communion, even if language is a barrier that necessitates separate local services. Local churches should reflect the ethnic variety found in the area where they serve. Local churches have to become a sign of hope to society by reflecting the global community.[53]

As described earlier, local churches are always related to the universal Church, and at the same time the universal Church is the foundation of the local churches. The worldwide Church is based on local churches, and local and worldwide communion is inseparable. People who are baptised into the trinitarian faith in a local church are at the same time united with the universal Church, which is the body of Christ that transcends geographic, social, ethnic and temporal boundaries.[54]

Catholicity Makes the Church a Sharing Community

Within the Triune God, there is *koinonia* with mutual sharing and, at the same time, unity in diversity. The sharing community is both local and universal. The

---

51 Breaking Barriers: Nairobi 1975, 1976, pp. 60–61; The Nature and Purpose of the Church, 1998, pp. 32–33; The Nature and Mission of the Church, 2005, p. 17.
52 The Nature and Mission of the Church, 2005, p. 17.
53 The New Delhi Report, 1962, pp. 103–104; Breaking Barriers: Nairobi 1975, 1976, p. 92.
54 Confessing the One Faith, 1991, p. 85.

sharing is visible to the Church through the understanding that God has become a partner with humanity shares creation with humanity. Christ shared his life, death and resurrection as a gift for salvation, and was an example to people on earth, without exception, of how life is to be shared. The ultimate sharing that is manifested in the Church is when Christ shares himself in the eucharist.[55]

The same divine sharing that is interpreted as proceeding from God is supposed to be visible in the Church, according to the ecumenical documents. God has called the Church to be an instrument and symbol of God's sharing with humanity. Resources, talents and gifts within the Christian community are believed to be exchanged. The fellowship of people have a vocation to share their lives, and they are invited and challenged to break down every division based on ethnicity, colour, caste, tribe, gender, class, or nationality. Instead, diversity is a gift to be shared within the body of Christ, which means that material resources and even different languages, symbols, traditions, cultures, and ethnic dimensions are to be shared with others. All the gifts are common goods for service within the community and to the world. Everyone has something to contribute through their diverse gifts to the *koinonia*.[56]

Sharing begins at local and individual level, just as the eucharist is shared within the local community. Sharing between and within different communities builds bridges between people and other communities. Mutual resources are shared as a sign of unity, and transcend any form of boundaries. Sharing is practised by coming together for common worship, celebrating eucharist, offering prayers, giving material aid, working together for humanity, witnessing together, etc.[57]

Prominent in the ecumenical documents is that every church is catholic, and that it fulfils its catholicity when it is in communion with other Christian communities. Each church is called to mutual giving and receiving of gifts. Denying or avoiding sharing is the same as denying the fullness of the catholicity of the Church.[58]

---

55 Empty Hands, 1980, p. 6; Confessing the One Faith, 1991, pp. 19, 22; On the Way to Fuller Koinonia, 1994, pp. 225–226.
56 The New Delhi Report, 1962, p. 119; Empty Hands, 1980, p. 6; Gathered for Life, 1983, pp. 62–63; Signs of the Spirit, 1991, pp. 97, 102; The Nature and Purpose of the Church, 1998, pp. 28–29.
57 Ecclesiology and Ethics, 1997, pp. 10–11; The Nature and Purpose of the Church, 1998, pp. 24–26; Together on the Way, 1999, pp. 135–134; The Nature and Mission of the Church, 2005, pp. 8–9; God, in your Grace …, 2007, p. 257.
58 On the Way to Fuller Koinonia, 1994, pp. 225–226; God, in your Grace …, 2007, p. 257.

The Catholicity of the Church: An *in via* Perspective

The ecumenical documents describe how the Church as the body of Christ is part of a new creation, but is still a subject to the conditions of the world with all its divisions. There are divisions that limit sharing in the Christian community. Political, historical, cultural and social factors, among others, damage the internal life of the Church. Discriminatory practices based on class, economic capacity, politics and ethnicity cause division. Discrimination occurs when individuals or groups are denied participation, based on such categories, without regard to their merit.[59]

Even if the Church is influenced because it is part of the surrounding society, the Church – despite its failures – is called to live in perfection. Although the Church has not yet reached this state, it is on the way towards a more perfect communion. It is like a pilgrimage. There is a relationship between the Church in history, the Church today, and the Church of the future. The Church is not only part of the past and the present: it is also the coming future. The documents describe how the Holy Spirit is the new age of the future but is already present, and how the Church belongs to the new age and to the fulfilment of the new creation. This can be described in the same way in which individual believers describe their Christian lives as being both justified and sinner (*simul justus et piccator*). The Church lives between two realities, between the historical Jesus and his second advent. This identity can be described as an *in via* perspective. The Church looks forward to the eschatological promise, and looks back to the apostolic community that was assembled at Pentecost.[60]

The Church has a direction, and the Holy Spirit is seen as leading humanity into a united community that is both a present and an eschatological reality. The task for the Church is to bring people together into an organic and living unity, even if this is not yet realised. Unity is something that is gradually achieved, and will finally reach its completion.[61]

---

59 The Third World Conference on Faith and Order, 1953, pp. 18, 45; The Nature and Mission of the Church, 2005, pp. 12-13; The Evanston Report, 1955, pp. 82-85; The Nature and Purpose of the Church, 1998, p. 18.
60 The Third World Conference on Faith and Order, 1953, pp. 17-21, 23; The Evanston Report, 1955, pp. 82-85; Confessing the One Faith, 1991, p. 87; The Nature and Purpose of the Church, 1998, pp. 12-14; A Treasure in Earthen Vessels, 1998, pp. 7, 30-31.
61 The Third World Conference on Faith and Order, 1953, p. 45; The Evanston Report, 1955, pp. 82-85; The Uppsala Report 1968, 1968, pp. 13-14; Church and World, 1990, p. 20; Signs of the Spirit, 1991, p. 97.

Unity in the Church is described as both a gift and a task given by the Holy Spirit to the imperfect Church. The ecumenical documents state that catholicity is supposed to be achieved in our own time – which means that the Church has an obligation to seek unity and to achieve catholicity. The Church is called to grow in God's gift of catholicity as part of an eschatological promise that tears down walls that separate people. Baptism has already united people in a *koinonia* with the triune God and with others; and the eucharist is a foretaste of Christ's eschatological meal with his people.[62]

Catholicity in Apostolicity

Since the time of the apostles, the Church has had a body of teaching that has been handed down, despite the Church's limitations due to the condition of being part of the world. The ecumenical documents define the Church as "one, holy, catholic and apostolic", as stated in the Nicene Creed.[63] These aspects of the Church are interdependent and reflect different aspects of the Church. The Church is not catholic if it is not also one, holy, and apostolic. The significance of apostolicity is that the Church continues the apostolic succession of teaching, which expresses the identity of Christians from the early Church throughout the ages. The Church is called at all times and in all places to continue the teaching inherited from the apostles, through Christ's sending them out. Apostolicity is also the continued transmission of the Gospel to humanity through witness, worship and service in the world. Apostolicity, together with baptism and eucharist, is part of life in the body of Christ, and together they support and sustain the *koinonia*.[64]

The diversity that occurs is an authentic expression of the apostolic vocation of the Church. One unchanged apostolic heritage has found different forms of expression in the world. Diverse ways of proclaiming the Gospel, presenting doctrines, and celebrating liturgy are visible signs of apostolicity. The ecumenical documents often refer to diversity as based on being called out of the world and at the same time being sent into the world. Diversity has to be respected as part of the Church's apostolicity, according to the ecumenical documents. When

---

62 The Uppsala Report 1968, 1968, pp. 14–15; Church and World, 1990, pp. 20, 23; The Nature and Mission of the Church, 2005, pp. 12–13; One Baptism, 2011, pp. 6–7.
63 The Third World Conference on Faith and Order, 1953, pp. 24, 28; Reports of the World Conference on Faith and Order, 1927, p. 7; God, in your Grace …, 2007, pp. 256–257.
64 The Uppsala Report 1968, 1968, pp. 12, 16; Confessing the One Faith, 1991, p. 83, On the Way to Fuller Koinonia, 1994, p. 239; Towards Sharing the One Faith, 1996, p. 21; The Nature and Purpose of the Church, 1998, pp. 34–35.

divisions occur as a result of ethnic, social class, or gender differences, there is no apostolicity, and catholicity is broken.[65]

The *ministry* as part of the Church's leadership has occasionally been studied in the ecumenical movement; but it was specifically emphasised when the document *Baptism, Eucharist and Ministry* (BEM) was produced. It stressed that there was a need in the Church to have some form of ministry that guaranteed unity. Historically, the ordained ministry, and primarily the ministry of the bishop, expressed and protected unity in the body of Christ. In areas with several eucharistic communities, the *episkopos* (church leader or bishop) provides and safeguards unity in the body of Christ, which includes both unity among local communities and the relationship with the universal Church. The ordained ministry also has a special mission to preserve and actualise the apostolic faith, as well as support and guarantee the apostolic teaching of the Church.[66]

Catholicity as Inclusion and Exclusion

As early as the First World Assembly of the WCC at Amsterdam in 1948, the WCC stated that exclusion because of race, colour, culture or class was no basis for division. The assembly even stated that the Church had, at times, privileged certain special groups – a situation that was intolerable because no-one should be excluded from any Christian place of worship on the grounds of race or colour. Exclusion occurs when individuals or groups are rejected and denied membership of a community; inclusion is the opposite: it is when somebody is incorporated into a community and embraced by others.[67]

Statements like that of the Amsterdam Assembly were repeated in later assemblies, and segregation and racism were frequently addressed as late as the Eighth World Assembly of the WCC in Harare in 1998. F&O and the WCC have particularly addressed unjust power structures. The documents state that churches have in general reflected the dominant patterns of society, and that most church members have been apathetic towards racism inside and outside the Church. Dualistic thinking about human nature has even received theological support, even though churches have at the same time repudiated the use of structures of domination and exploitation.[68]

---

65 The Uppsala Report 1968, 1968, p. 15; On the Way to Fuller Koinonia, 1994, p. 239.
66 Baptism, Eucharist and Ministry, 1982, pp. 22, 24–29; A Treasure in Earthen Vessels, 1998, p. 36; The Nature and Purpose of the Church, 1998, pp. 25, 45.
67 The First Assembly of the World Council of Churches, 1949, pp. 67, 76, 81, 93–94.
68 The New Delhi Report, 1962, pp. 103–104; Signs of the Spirit, 1991, pp. 57, 79.

The documents declare that the ecumenical movement rejects any form of racial prejudice and discrimination. Division because of race, wealth, social class, gender, etc. denies the dignity of humanity and undermines unity in Christ. Ecclesiastical division is even a contradiction of the meaning of worship, and a failure in the Church's ministry of reconciliation. The ecumenical documents assert that Christian worship should always be inclusive, and that every Christian community ought to work to avoid having homogeneous congregations. The Church denounces sin and re-establishes humanity by becoming inclusive.[69]

Baptism is the foundation of an inclusive Church in which all participate as equals and where there is respect for differences. All the baptised are welcome in such communities, and should be accommodated. Inclusiveness is full participation irrespective of age, gender, ethnicity, etc. and every worshiping community should also be a model of inclusive community.[70] The documents even stress that the Church should not create a multi-ethnic community where one dominant culture takes the lead, but rather a trans-ethnic community where the different ethnic identities are respected. According to the Third World Assembly of the WCC at New Delhi in 1961, minority groups are often hesitant to participate in churches that are dominated by other ethnic groups. The mission of the Church is to create a climate of acceptance and to make space for minority groups. These groups may have different ways of worshiping and contributing to the churches' life; but they will enrich the whole Church.[71]

Christians are to unite in the community of the body of Christ despite their differences. Culture holds communities together through, for example, language, lifestyle, attitudes, and symbols, and constitutes a collective memory. Even if cultural diversity is supposed to be accommodated, Jesus both affirms and judges culture. Cultural richness can become a problem when a culture denies life and oppresses people. When apostolicity is questioned and diversity divides the body of Christ, leading to exclusion, unity is destroyed and catholicity is violated.[72]

---

69 The Fourth World Conference on Faith and Order, 1964, pp. 70, 85–86; The Uppsala Report 1968, 1968, pp. 14–15, 18; Racism in Theology – Theology Against Racism, 1975, pp. 148–152.
70 Signs of the Spirit, 1991, pp. 118–119; On the Way to Fuller Koinonia, 1994, p. 248.
71 Participating in God's Mission of Reconciliation, 2006, pp. 17, 22; The New Delhi Report, 1962, p. 104.
72 Breaking Barriers: Nairobi 1975, 1976, pp. 78–79; Gathered for Life, 1983, p. 32; Signs of the Spirit, 1991, pp. 248–250; Towards Sharing the One Faith, 1996, pp. 7–8.

3.2 Catholicity as an Analytical Tool for Studying Ethnicity

Faith & Order and the WCC have produced several statements and documents about the catholicity of the Church. Some of the statements have emphasised subjects related to the church service as the ultimate form of catholicity, when a common eucharistic community shares the same fellowship. Other aspects of catholicity are also important and need special attention – for example, justice, distribution of wealth, and reconciliation. Becoming an inclusive Christian community regardless of ethnic background is a central aspect of the Church's catholicity, according to the ecumenical movement.[73] One of the first statements about catholicity made at the Third World Assembly of WCC in New Delhi acknowledged social relations as part of catholicity. The New Delhi Assembly said:

> We believe that the unity which is both God's will and his gift to his Church is being made visible as all in each place who are baptized into Jesus Christ and confess him as Lord and Saviour are brought by the Holy Spirit into one fully committed fellowship, holding the one apostolic faith, preaching the one Gospel, breaking the one bread, joining in common prayer, and having a corporate life reaching out in witness and service to all and who at the same time are united with the whole Christian fellowship in all places and all ages in such wise that ministry and members are accepted by all, and that all can act and speak together as occasion requires for the tasks to which God calls his people.[74]

The vision expressed in New Delhi stressed that part of being a catholic Church is "[…] having a corporate life … united with the whole Christian fellowship … and members are accepted by all […]". This vision indicates that those who are

---

73 See, for example, statements about catholicity made by WCC assemblies in New Delhi 1961: The New Delhi Report, 1962, p. 116; Nairobi 1975: Breaking Barriers: Nairobi 1975, 1976, p. 60; Canberra 1991: Signs of the Spirit, 1991, p. 173; Porto Alegre 2006: God, in your Grace …, 2007, p. 257. An example of a study of the catholicity of the church is that done by Jakob Tronêt. He has written a thesis about Max Thurian's understanding of ways towards the unity of the Church. Baptism, eucharist, and ministry are examples of practices that are investigated in order to understand the unity of the Church. Social issues are not considered; the goal of Church unity in Max Thurian's ecclesiology is attached instead to a sacramental unity of the Church. Tronêt, Jakob, 2014. In her thesis *Die eucharistische Vision* (The Eucharistic Vision), Margot Käßmann takes another approach to the Church as catholic. She argues that there is a connection between ecclesiology and ethics. Particularistic views are challenged in the eucharist as a sacrament, and there has to be resistance to any division between rich and poor. The social side of the eucharist has to be implemented; otherwise the sacrament will lose its meaning. Käßmann, Margot 1992.
74 The New Delhi Report, 1962, p. 116.

separated should be united in a common fellowship. The Christian fellowship is described as a communion in which Christians are united with Christ. This means that the Christian community should not be divided along stratified lines of differentiation, nor according to economic status, language, gender, etc.

In order to interpret catholicity as understood in the international ecumenical movement, I shall construct an analytical tool based on the texts of F&O and the WCC. I shall, in the next part, deal with specific issues about catholicity that I have chosen because they are especially interesting and visible in the case study material in the South African context. These issues are also useful as an analytical tool with which to study congregations and churches.

I am not concerned whether people of different churches or denominations are united in a single church organisation, but rather how ethnic diversity could cause either unity or division within a specific church or denomination.[75] The areas I want to explore in the next section are entitled: *The Christian Communion Transcends the Local Congregation, Ethnicity Transcends Division, Reconciliation of Ethnic Division is part of the Church's Ministry, Languages Contribute to the Church's Diversity,* and *Poverty Eradication Eliminates Ethnic Boundaries.* This analysis will indicate to what extent congregations' and churches' practices are consistent with the ecumenical documents, and how congregations and churches can be challenged by the catholicity of the Church.

The Christian Communion Transcends the Local Congregation

The foundation of a common Christian communion is baptism. The document *One Baptism* says:

> As a person is baptized into this trinitarian faith in a local assembly, that person is at the same time united with the one church of Christ that transcends geographical,

---

75 Another study could have been on how catholicity challenges denominationalism. The plurality of denominations and churches could also be questioned; but that would be another kind of study. It is important to state, however, that the existence of denominations is a contradiction of the concept of catholicity. Since the beginnings of the international ecumenical movement there has been a search for a shared structural belonging that is stronger than the present situation. There have been several attempts using various concepts, such as *Communio sanctorum*, which was introduced at Lund. The Third World Conference on Faith and Order, 1953, pp. 17–21, 23. *Koinonia* understood as 'fellowship' was stressed at New Delhi. The New Delhi Report, 1962, p. 119. *Koinonia* as 'the body of Christ' was the focus at Vancouver. Gathered for Life, 1983, pp. 62–63. *Conciliar Fellowship* at Nairobi. Breaking Barriers: Nairobi 1975, 1976, p. 60.

social, ethnic and temporal boundaries. That person is brought into relationship with the whole body of Christ in all places and in all times.[76]

Baptism transcends geographic, social, and ethnic borders, and unites people of diverse backgrounds in the Church. The Church is both local and universal; but F&O and the WCC identify several definitions of 'local'. The document *The Nature and Mission of the Church* has clarified the different definitions as follows:

> The term 'local church' is used differently by different traditions. For some traditions the 'local' church is the congregation of believers gathered in one place to hear the Word and celebrate the Sacraments. For others, 'local' or 'particular' church refers to the bishop with the people around the bishop, gathered to hear the Word and celebrate the Sacrament. In some churches the term 'local church' is used of both the diocese and of the parish. At another level, 'local church' can refer to several dioceses or to regional churches gathered together in a synodal structure under a presidency.[77]

Territorial definitions refer to local congregations of believers, a community gathered around a bishop or equivalent person, or a common organisational structure. The WCC and F&O often discuss Church unity beyond church or denomination.

My determination of the definition of 'local' is not dependent on those of the various churches or denominations. When I analyse the local church, I study a congregation where members gather. Furthermore, the congregation is connected with other congregations in a regional organisational structure such as a circuit or deanery or even diocese or district. In this thesis I have chosen to define 'local' as both a specific Christian community where members congregate, and also as members of the same church or denomination in one place. This means that Christian communities of the same church or denomination belong to the same church in one place. Anglican congregations in Johannesburg, Methodist congregations in Cape Town, or Lutheran congregations in Durban are local churches in one place. Local congregations belonging to the same local church in a city belong to the same *koinonia*.

---

76 One Baptism, 2011, p. 13.
77 The Nature and Mission of the Church, 2005, p. 18. A very similar explanation is given in the document: The Nature and Purpose of the Church, 1998, p. 33. The document Ecclesiology and Ethics has also described the different meanings of 'local' by stating: "The word 'local' means different things in different circumstances. It may mean a neighbourhood, or a nation, or a region of the world". Ecclesiology and Ethics, 1997, p. 14. A narrower definition was given at the beginning of the ecumenical movement: "[…] the fellowship of Christians gathered for the hearing of the word and celebration of the Lord's Supper according to Christ's ordinance". The Fourth World Conference on Faith and Order, 1964, p. 81.

According to this interpretation, a congregation in a suburb has to be in relationship with other congregations in the same city to ensure that diversity is attained. This implies that a congregation is not only supposed to be in a relationship with similar congregations, but also with congregations that are different. If one congregation is separated from other Christian communities, the congregation is not part of the *koinonia*. The document *The Nature and Purpose of the Church* has said: "The communion of the Church is expressed in the communion between local churches in each of which the fullness of the Church resides".[78] This means that the Church has its foundation in the diversity of local congregations where member congregate, and reaches its fullness in the Christian community.

The ministry has occasionally been studied in the ecumenical movement, but the theme was specifically emphasised when the document *Baptism, Eucharist and Ministry* (BEM) was produced. It stresses that the Church needs to have some form of ministry that acts as a focus for unity. Historically, the ordained ministry, and primarily the ministry of the bishop, expressed and protected unity in the body of Christ.[79] The document explains:

> The Church as the body of Christ and the eschatological people of God is constituted by the Holy Spirit through a diversity of gifts or ministries. Among these gifts a ministry of *episkopé* is necessary to express and safeguard the unity of the body. Every church needs this ministry of unity in some form in order to be the Church of God, the one body of Christ, a sign of the unity of all in the Kingdom.[80]

A bishop or an equivalent minister provides and safeguards unity in the body of Christ; and it involves unity among local communities as well as relationships with the universal Church. The ordained ministry also has a special mission to preserve and actualise the apostolic faith, as well as support and guarantee the apostolic teaching of the Church.[81]

It is important to my interpretation of the ecumenical documents that the local congregation is related to the universal Church, which transcends, for example, geographic, social, and ethnic boundaries. The document *On the Way to Fuller Koinonia* has said: "The koinonia of the Church is also universal. One community cannot be isolated from the rest. Again, the principle of authentic relationship is what binds particular communities within the universal. There is one Church

---

78 The Nature and Purpose of the Church, 1998, p. 32.
79 Baptism, Eucharist and Ministry, 1982, pp. 22, 24.
80 Baptism, Eucharist and Ministry, 1982, p. 25.
81 The Nature and Purpose of the Church, 1998, p. 45.

while there are many local churches at the same time".[82] In the catholicity of the Church, the relationship between local communities and the global community is central, and there has to be an exchange between these communities. Living conditions, spirituality, and environment in one place are the concern of other communities within local communities and of Christian communities in other places of the world.

Several documents have stressed the importance of sharing and receiving in the Christian community. The Sixth World Assembly of the WCC in Vancouver explained, for example, that healing and sharing life in community were an essential part of the life in the Church. The assembly agreed with the substance of the report from one issue group that said:

> Sharing is rooted in the very nature of the triune God as a "community of sharing" characterized by dynamic and creative mutuality. Christ is the concrete expression in time and space of God's *economia* of sharing. In Christ, God enters with us into an existential relationship of sharing and healing. The cross is the expression of Christ's complete sharing of himself. Hence, the Church as the living body of Christ, by its very nature and mission, is a *koinonia* of sharing and healing.[83]

Sharing and receiving is considered to be a central foundation of the Christian community, and it implies both spiritual and physical sharing. The sharing of resources within the community is even seen as a witness and sign of the local and universal Church of Christ.[84] My interpretation of the catholicity of the Church

---

82 On the Way to Fuller Koinonia, 1994, p. 232. Several other examples have expressed the same important relationship between the local and the universal. The Fourth World Conference on Faith and Order said: "Each congregation is a manifestation of the Church Universal". The Fourth World Conference on Faith and Order, 1964, p. 81. The document Confessing the One Faith declared: "The Church of Christ's living Body. It exists in local congregations and worldwide communion with each other". Confessing the One Faith, 1991, p. 85. The document A Treasure in Earthen Vessels stressed: "[…] catholicity binds all local communities together, thereby allowing them to contribute to one another's understanding and to broaden their horizons". A Treasure in Earthen Vessels, 1998, p. 31.
83 Gathered for Life, 1983, p. 62.
84 Other conferences and documents have affirmed similar statements. The Second World Conference on Faith and Order at Edinburgh stressed, for example, that the communion of saints implied "[…] the mutual sharing of both spiritual and temporal blessings on the part of all living Christians". Report of the Second World Conference on Faith and Order, 1937, p. 237. The WCC General Assembly in Uppsala stated: "Jesus Christ commanded us to be reconciled before we worship. As Christians we must refuse to participate in any form of racial or class segregation in worship, and our communion

implies that local communities should support one another and share their diverse gifts and resources; similarly, the universal Christian community should be part of the sharing and receiving.

The ecumenical documents stress, furthermore, that the community faces outwards towards people living in the same area who are not part of the same congregation. There is a human community with, for example, people doing the same work, or even with people of other faiths and convictions. The Fifth World Assembly of the WCC in Nairobi declared: "There is the community within a church or denomination and between the churches as pursued by the ecumenical movement. We then discussed a different dimension of community – that is, community with people of other faiths and convictions, and, in the widest sense, the community of all humanity".[85] The explanation implies that there are many different communities and levels of communities that exist simultaneously in the *koinonia* that proceeds from God. My view of catholicity implies that the Christian community does not live in isolation: there is a kinship with the whole human community. The local church is supposed to reflect the ethnic variety that is present in the area the church serves, even though the Church is part of a global community.[86]

---

    with Christ must show that we share our bread with his hungry brothers in the world". The Uppsala Report 1968, 1968, p. 83. The document Ecclesiology and Ethics declared: "Paul uses koinonia to describe relations between churches in different cities. The collection he takes up for the church in Jerusalem is itself called a *koinonia*". Ecclesiology and Ethics, 1997, p. 10.

85 Breaking Barriers: Nairobi 1975, 1976, p. 75.

86 One of the sections at the WCC General Assembly in Evanston reported that churches often try to justify separation in order to remain in or even sustain inherited patterns. Churches were nevertheless asked to repent of disunity because it was also seen as a separation from God, and 'racial' and ethnic prejudices were sins against God. The Evanston Report, 1955, pp. 153–155. The WCC General Assembly in New Delhi claimed: "The Church must not be a segregated society. Multi-racial or multi-ethical communities, churches and local congregations, whose membership is limited to people of one racial or ethnic group, must deal with this problem. […]". The New Delhi Report, 1962, pp. 183–184. The document Participating in God's Mission of Reconciliation said: "[…] churches often include members from different ethnic communities, and therefore have the opportunity – and obligation – to 'model' unity and harmony among such communities". Participating in God's Mission of Reconciliation, 2006, p. 17. These statements are examples that show that churches had to seek integration, and that any form of segregation was contrary to being part of the body of Christ.

Ethnicity Transcends Division

Christian communities have often been divided according to ethnicity, language, habits, features, or other factors that have provided a rationale for division. This differentiation of groups was especially visible during apartheid in South Africa, and it still creates barriers between groups of people. F&O produced several theological documents about division that questioned apartheid, and the WCC issued a number of statements condemning the same ideology, urging the churches to exert pressure to abolish the system. Racism in countries like South Africa was condemned as early as the Second World Assembly of the WCC in Evanston. It declared that:

> [...] any form of segregation based on race, colour or ethnic origin is contrary to the gospel, and is incompatible with the Christian doctrine of man and with the nature of the Church of Christ. The Assembly urges the churches within its membership to renounce all forms of segregation or discrimination and to work for their abolition within their own life and within society.[87]

The resolution was raised again at the next World Assembly of the WCC, that held in New Delhi, as a reminder that this position was in line with the ecumenical movement. The assembly even declared, using statements like those of Cottesloe, that:

> [...] 'The Church as the Body of Christ is a unity and within this unity the natural diversity among men is not annulled but sanctified. No one who believes in Jesus Christ may be excluded from any church on the grounds of his colour or race. The spiritual unity among all men who are in Christ must find visible expressions in acts of common worship and witness [...].[88]

Similar statements condemning the South African apartheid system were repeated in successive world assemblies until South Africa became a democracy.[89] Apartheid was seen as a heresy that contradicted the nature and purpose of the Church. The document *Ecclesiology and Ethics* even stressed:

> Instead of being agents of just social transformation, churches too often uncritically conform to unjust social and economic patterns within their cultural and national contexts. The result is moral malformation of the membership of the churches, which inevitably has a similar influence on the wider society. This was notably the case of South Africa [...].[90]

---

87 The Evanston Report, 1955, p. 158.
88 The New Delhi Report, 1962, p. 323.
89 See for example: Breaking Barriers, 1976, pp. 118–119; Gathered for Life, 1983, pp. 85–86.
90 Ecclesiology and Ethics, 1997, p. 62.

Teaching and practising apartheid represented a loss of the apostolicity and catholicity of the church. The ecumenical documents declare that the image of the body of Christ excludes any form of segregation, exclusion or division in the Church based on ethnicity, gender, social status, age, etc.

My use of the term 'catholicity', following that of the F&O and WCC documents, assumes that differentiations are human constructions, but that diversity is valuable in the Christian communion. Diversity, however, is subordinate in the Church's communion among the baptised members who are united in the body of Christ. I assume that a new humanity is created by Christ where there is a profound equality. This makes the Church part of the eschatological hope that tears down barriers of separation. People of any ethnic background should be accommodated and welcomed into any Christian community, and the Christian community should work against becoming homogeneous.

The Third World Assembly of the WCC in New Delhi said: "The complacency of a secure and homogeneous community may have to be disturbed by a Christian initiative in inviting people of different races into it".[91] The assembly stated, furthermore, that the churches should create an inclusive climate: "There is therefore a further task – the creation of a climate of warm acceptance of minority groups which may have different ways of worship, and other gifts, that will enrich the whole Church".[92] According to this practice, Christian worship is seen always to be inclusive.

Besides baptism, the eucharist also challenges the Christian community. The document *Baptism, Eucharist and Ministry*, for example, states: "All kinds of injustice, racism, separation and lack of freedom are radically challenged when we share in the body and blood of Christ".[93] The Christian community has an

---

91 The New Delhi Report, 1962, p. 104. The F&O document Racism in Theology – Theology against Racism (1975) had a similar interpretation: "But truly united worship will always include those who do not fit in. They are an inseparable sign of how radical the communication of God is. We ought to work hard to prevent totally homogeneous congregations, to secure worship which is truly hospitable to the wide diversity of Christian identity". Racism in Theology – Theology Against Racism, 1975, p. 148.
92 The New Delhi Report, 1962, p. 104.
93 Baptism, Eucharist and Ministry, 1982, p. 14. The document The Nature and Purpose of the Church is another example of questioning division in the eucharistic community. The document declares: "[...] Because Holy Communion is the sacrament which builds up community, all kinds of injustice, racism, estrangement, and lack of freedom are radically challenged when we share in the body and blood of Christ". The Nature and Purpose of the Church, 1998, p. 39. The same eucharistic challenge is stressed in the document Ecclesiology and Ethics: "Partaking in the same body and blood of Christ

ethical obligation to work for the restoration of the world and human dignity.[94] According to my analytical tool, the eucharistic fellowship has a special purpose to sustain the *koinonia*. The eucharist has to be practised in diverse communities, but also taught in Church in order to support unity. Breaking bread and sharing wine expresses the catholicity of the Church, and challenges and questions all forms of division in the human community.

My definition of catholicity, as interpreted from the F&O and WCC documents, assumes that baptised members in the Church should not lose their ethnic background and heritage, but should instead bring their gifts of diversity into a common space. This is stressed, for example, in the document *Confessing the One Faith*: "The Triune God is the ground of unity as well as diversity in his creation. The Trinity can be seen as a model of diversity that does not destroy unity and of a unity that does not suffocate diversity for the sake of uniformity".[95] The Christian community is supposed to live in reconciliation but not to create uniformity, and there should be an atmosphere of respect for diversity.[96] *Koinonia* has qualities that do not allow division and exclusion based on diversity. The desire to experience *koinonia* drives the members to seek visible unity with God and their fellow beings.

Reconciliation of Ethnic Division is part of the Church's Ministry

Reconciliation is central to the Church's practices, and is part of its worship, liturgy and confession. Reconciliation aims to restore the relationship between God and humanity, and relationships between individuals and between groups of people. Division in the Church based on diversity was considered early in the

---

they are called to a love without limits. They are called to transcend all barriers, in their celebrating community and in the world". Ecclesiology and Ethics, 1997, p. 37.

94 The Fifth WCC World Assembly at Nairobi declared: "Worship, especially the Eucharist, is the instrument through which all these communities open themselves up to God and his creation; thus it breaks down walls of division and stimulates creative forms of solidarity". Breaking Barriers: Nairobi 1975, 1976, p. 49.

95 Confessing the One Faith, 1991, p. 22. The document On the way to Fuller Koinonia emphasised that Christian *koinonia* had to overcome divisions because unity comes from God as a gift. The document declared: "Only a Church that overcomes ethnic, racial, and national hatred in a common Christian and human identity can be a credible sign of freedom and reconciliation". On the Way to Fuller Koinonia, 1994, p. 226.

96 The document The Nature and Mission of the Church states, for example: "Each local church must be the place where two things are simultaneously guaranteed: the safeguarding of unity and the flourishing of a legitimate diversity". The Nature and Mission of the Church, 2005, p. 15.

life of the ecumenical movement. The Fourth World Conference on Faith and Order at Montreal stated, for example: "[…] Ecclesiastical divisions based upon class, race or nation contradict true worship, because they represent a failure fully to carry out the common ministry of reconciliation to which we are all called in Christ".[97] Similar statements were made at several other meetings and assemblies that emphasised that the Christian community could not be divided. There should be a reconciled community reflecting diversity in the Church.[98]

The Fifth World Conference on Faith and Order at Santiago de Compostela declared, for example: "[…] Only a Church that overcomes ethnic, racial, and national hatreds in a common Christian and human identity can be a credible sign of freedom and reconciliation".[99] Such statements from ecumenical meetings and assemblies provide the basis for seeing that unity in a reconciled diversity is significant to the catholicity of the Church. Diversity is an important contribution to the richness of the life in the Church as catholic, and does not imply uniformity, division, or simply co-existence.[100]

My interpretation of the term 'reconciliation' in the context of ethnicity holds that ethnicity is important in the Church to create diversity; but when division occurs, the Church has to work for individual and collective reconciliation. The process requires the Church to overcome division and to attain visible unity that transcends ethnic diversities. The document *Ecclesiology and Ethics* addressed the South African situation after democratisation in these terms:

> […] Now the struggle against apartheid as the governing ideology is at an end, South African Council of Churches and its member churches, who were deeply engaged in that struggle, are being forced to give urgent attention to the recovery of a concern for

---

97   The Fourth World Conference on Faith and Order, 1964, p. 70.
98   Another example is a statement made at the WCC General Assembly in Canberra: "The calling of the church is to proclaim reconciliation and provide healing, to overcome divisions based on race, gender, age, culture, colour, and to bring all people into communion with God. Because of sin and the misunderstanding of the diverse gifts of the Spirit, the churches are painfully divided within themselves and among each other". Signs of the Spirit, 1991, p. 172.
99   On the Way to Fuller Koinonia, 1994, pp. 225–226.
100 In an article, Harding Meyer has explained the development of reconciled diversity in the ecumenical movement. The concept was developed by the F&O commission in Salamanca (1973) and by representatives of the Christian world communions in Geneva (1974). The concept of reconciled diversity has always been articulated in the ecumenical movement, and must lead beyond a plain and peaceful co-existence. Meyer, Harding, 1991, pp. 845–846.

ecclesial unity and fellowship in the task of national reconstruction, the development of a moral society and a just democratic culture.[101]

The document declared that the South African churches had a responsibility to support reconciliation and to make sure that it was achieved and that ecclesial unity was recovered. The South African churches were addressed by the international ecumenical movement even before the Truth and Reconciliation Commission had delivered its final reports about the faith communities' responsibility for reconciliation in society.

The eucharist itself enhances reconciliation among members of the Christian communion, and participants are invited to reconcile before they worship together. The document *The Nature and Purpose of the Church* declares: "[…] Because Holy Communion is the sacrament which builds up community, all kinds of injustice, racism, estrangement, and lack of freedom are radically challenged when we share in the body and blood of Christ".[102] A reconciled Christian community is part of the eschatological hope, and division is a failure of the church's ministry of reconciliation.

It is important to my interpretation of the F&O and WCC documents that reconciliation is incomplete if there is no restitution. The document *Signs of the Spirit* says: "[…] Reconciliation works when there is honest recognition of the actual sin committed against neighbour and when practical restitution has been made for it. In other words those who have been guilty of oppression and injustice must show genuine and costly repentance (metanoia)".[103] The Church has to practise a reconciled diversity so that ethnicity does not divide, but instead enriches the Church. Reconciliation is also followed by restitution so that Christian communion can be recovered.

Languages Contribute to the Church's Diversity

The ecumenical documents identified that the Church was influenced by the place where the Christian communion was rooted. The Third World Conference on Faith and Order at Lund said, for example:

---

101 Ecclesiology and Ethics, 1997, p. 27.
102 The Nature and Purpose of the Church, 1998, p. 39. The document Ecclesiology and Ethics has a similar definition: "Partaking in the same body and blood or Christ they are called to a love without limits. They are called to transcend all barriers, in their celebrating community and in the world". Ecclesiology and Ethics, 1997, p. 37.
103 Signs of the Spirit, 1991, p. 97.

> We recognise that Christianity makes itself at home in various cultures and takes a colouring from them. We believe that every nation will bring its tribute to the common treasury of Christian faith and life. Christianity is never to be equated with any culture, however, for it has a spirit of its own which always transcends social, political, and cultural conditions. The Spirit creates unity, while one of the causes of division lies in treating as absolute cultural factors which are only relative.[104]

The statement acknowledged that the Church was formed by its context, which became a legitimate expression of the Christian faith. But it is significant that Christianity can never be associated with a specific culture: every context has something to contribute to the Christian faith. My interpretation of the documents holds that, because of context, diversity should be perceived as a gift and contribution to the Christian community.

The catholicity of the Church, in the ecumenical documents, means that all local churches are bound together, contributing to enriching other local congregations and the whole Church. The document *A Treasure in Earthen Vessels* explains:

> To speak of contextuality and catholicity together clarifies the relationship between the local community and the wider community of all local communities. Contextual interpretations can contribute to a fuller interpretation of the Gospel and can thereby speak to the Christian community as a whole. ... Accordingly, catholicity binds all local communities together, thereby allowing them to contribute to one another's understanding and to broaden their horizons.[105]

The documents stress that contextual insights contribute to the wider Christian community, revealing new perspectives on the Church's catholicity. There are gifts in the local Christian communities that should be shared and received. The document *A Treasure in Earthen Vessels* even stresses that catholicity in the Church enables communities to be liberated from being bound to a specific context, and instead to be open to diverse contexts.[106]

The document *Church and World* is one of the few ecumenical documents that emphasise the importance of diverse languages. Language is one of the principal means to communicate between people, and can either include individuals or groups or exclude them from the community. This problem is especially complex in a multilingual context where a language such as English, French, or Portuguese predominates. The document *Church and World* explains:

---

104   The Third World Conference on Faith and Order, 1953, p. 32.
105   A Treasure in Earthen Vessels, 1998, p. 31.
106   A Treasure in Earthen Vessels, 1998, p. 32.

> Careful attention must be paid to the distinctive possibilities and problems of expression in the specific language(s) being used. This is especially important in a multi-lingual context. Issues and problems particular to one dominant language, for example English, should not be projected into other linguistic contexts. ... Especially in international and ecumenical contexts greater care should be taken not to let the use of language become an instrument of domination.[107]

In contexts where several languages are used, it is easy for a specific language to become the principal language and to dominate. It is important, in my interpretation of catholicity, that people are able to communicate; but there has to be equality between the diverse languages. The different languages that are spoken in the Church are signs that the gospel can be rooted in different contexts and among various people.

Catholicity as understood in the ecumenical documents states that the use of one dominating language could result in a Church that no longer expresses its full catholicity. One main language in a multilingual society creates power inequalities, and reduces the possibility of gaining a more profound understanding of the Christian message. Different languages in a community are supposed to be understood as gifts that are shared and received and that could reveal new insights. Using several languages is not the same as division.

Although a variety of languages can make it difficult for people to communicate, and separate church services may well be necessary, the ecumenical documents are clear that all members have to belong to the same communion. Local congregations should try to reflect the ethnic composition of the neighbourhood where they are placed – including the languages that are spoken there. The mission of the Church is to create a climate of acceptance and to make space for much diversity. This could, for example, include learning other languages and symbols that are used in the community – or at least learning parts of the liturgy in other languages. Diverse expressions have to be shared with other members in the community so that common goods could be given and received.

Poverty Eradication Eliminates Ethnic Boundaries

Sharing resources within the Christian communion was emphasised early on in the life of the ecumenical movement, and is an integral part of *koinonia*. The document *Ecclesiology and Ethics* says:

> [...] There is, for instance, koinonia in God, in the Holy Spirit, in Christ, in the faith, in the body of Christ, in the blood of Christ. This alone suggests wider usage. Paul uses

---

107   Church and World, 1990, pp. 65–66.

koinonia to describe relations between churches in different cities. The collection he takes up for the church in Jerusalem is itself called a koinonia. [...].[108]

Sharing resources with Christians in other places is a consequence of all belonging to the same communion, irrespective of geographic distance. Sharing begins in the sharing of the same eucharist, and continues into other aspects of life. The Sixth WCC World Assembly in Vancouver stated:

> The Church's conscious sharing and healing begins in the eucharist. It is the sign and locus of the Church's ministry of sharing and healing. The eucharist is essentially the self-giving of God in Christ to the world. It is both a recurrence and imperative. As we share in Christ's broken body, so we become bread for the world to *be* broken and shared – what we are and what we possess.[109]

Sharing of resources is based on Christ's own sharing of his life for the world, which establishes a pattern for the Christian community. Sharing begins at the local and individual level as the eucharist is shared within the local community, but it is also connected with the universal Church. Sharing between and within different communities builds bridges, and is a sign of a common *koinonia*. The Church is called from the world, but is also sent into the world – which means that the Church as catholic is called to become a common body that is open to serving the world.

My definition of catholicity, derived from the ecumenical documents, questions unequal conditions within the Christian community. *Koinonia* in the Church is supposed to be an image of the trinitarian relationship in which there is a mutual sharing. Christ shared his life, death, and resurrection, bringing salvation to humanity. This sharing is manifested in the Church in the practice of Christ sharing himself through the eucharist. The Christian community is supposed to follow Christ's example by becoming a sharing community and a witness in the world. The early Church practised sharing in the prayers, eucharist, reconciliation, collection for the poor, experiences, witness, etc. These practices are part of the Church's mission, and become apparent when the Church works for equality, justice, peace, and restitution, and when it offers services, gives material aid, etc.

The documents from F&O and the WCC furthermore urge the churches, the nations, and the international community to eradicate poverty in different contexts.[110] Sharing is also a matter of changing unequal economic structures and

---

108 Ecclesiology and Ethics, 1997, p. 10.
109 Gathered for Life, 1983, p. 62.
110 See for example: Empty Hands, 1980, p. 10; Together on the Way, 1999, pp. 135–134; God in your Grace ..., 2007, p. 294.

working for justice in society and the world. My interpretation of catholicity means that the Church has to identify unequal conditions in society and in the world in order to change the conditions in which the underprivileged live. Advocacy for socio-economic change and poverty eradication, for peace and justice in Church and society is part of the Church's ministry.

The New Delhi Assembly said: "We believe that the unity which is both God's will and his gift to his Church ... and that all can act and speak together as occasion requires for the tasks to which God calls his people".[111] Acting and speaking for one another within the Christian communion are part of the task of the Church as catholic. When members in local churches encounter poverty, or when human rights are violated, the Christian community has a duty to act together to eradicate poverty and to be a voice for the voiceless.

Similar statements were made at the Fifth World Conference on Faith and Order. The report of Section One stated:

> The Church as koinonia is called to share not only in the suffering of its own community but in the suffering of all; by advocacy and care for the poor, needy, and marginalized; by joining in all efforts for justice and peace within human societies; by exercising and promoting responsible stewardship of creation and by keeping alive hope in the heart of humanity. Diakonia to the whole world and koinonia cannot be separated.[112]

Diakonia and *koinonia* are kept together, and the whole Christian community has the task to engage in advocacy and to care for the poor, needy, and marginalised. The Church is supposed to safeguard and to be a voice not only for church members, but also for the whole of humanity as part of God's creation.

3.3 Conclusions

In this chapter I have offered an ecumenical interpretation of catholicity, based on Faith & Order meetings and WCC World Assemblies, and on key documents produced by the international ecumenical movement. I argue that catholicity as understood in the international ecumenical movement has far-reaching implications for the churches' life regarding diversity within Christian and human communities. It is important to emphasise that several of the statements, declarations and conferences of the South African churches and of the SACC, as presented in

---

111 The New Delhi Report, 1962, p. 116.
112 On the Way to Fuller Koinonia, 1994, p. 233. See similar statements in the reports of Section Two. On the Way to Fuller Koinonia, 1994, pp. 238–239.

the previous chapter, are consistent with the notion of catholicity articulated by the international ecumenical movement.

A number of specific issues are productive and interesting in relation to the South African ecclesial context. I have chosen a number of areas of the Church's catholicity that are drawn from the ecumenical documents; and this will be my tool when I examine South African congregations and churches. (See Figure II.)

In the next chapter, I shall provide a method for examining congregations and churches in South Africa and testing their catholicity by using an operative ecclesiology. My interpretation of catholicity in the ecumenical documents will be put alongside and tested against a contextual ecclesiology found among South African congregations and churches.

Figure II: Documents and texts from F&O and the WCC have provided a foundation for interpreting the catholicity of the Church. Specific issues concerning catholicity have been chosen to form my analytical tool, enabling me to test the ecumenical notion of catholicity with the collected case material. The issues are relevant to the South African context, and are evident in the case study congregations.

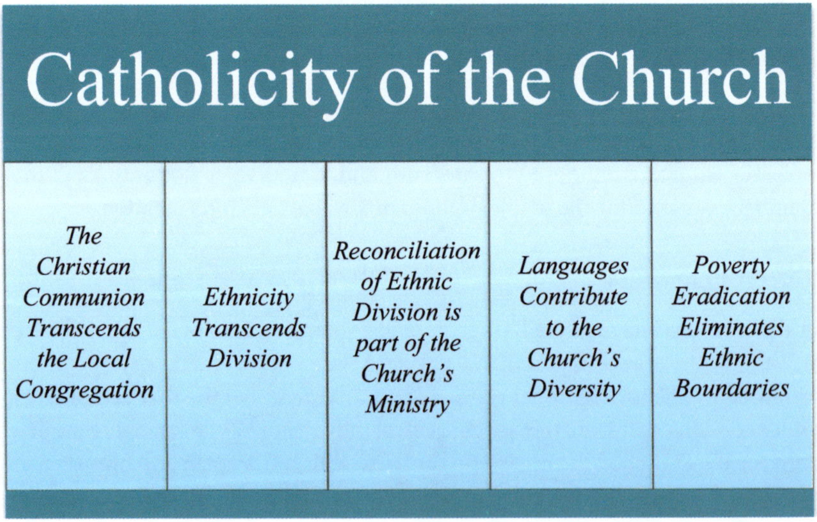

Catholicity of the Church

The Christian Communion Transcends the Local Congregation	Ethnicity Transcends Division	Reconciliation of Ethnic Division is part of the Church's Ministry	Languages Contribute to the Church's Diversity	Poverty Eradication Eliminates Ethnic Boundaries

Chapter Four: Ecclesiology in Practice

In the previous chapter, I described a catholicity that was based on Faith & Order and World Council of Churches documents, and that will be used as a normative theory of catholicity.

This chapter will present an explanation of an 'operative ecclesiology' derived primarily from the French theologian Yves Congar. An 'operative ecclesiology' illustrates how the Church can be studied through its documents, statements, resolutions, and creeds, but also through its various practices. I will describe the methodological foundation that was applied to the studied South African congregations and churches.

Firstly, I will discuss how the Church can be studied through different kinds of ecclesiologies. Secondly, I will describe the 'operative ecclesiology' and give a definition of 'practices'. Thirdly, I will explain how I conducted the case study through interviews, observation, and the study of documents.

4.1 'New Ecclesiology' and 'Modern Ecclesiology'

In several books and articles, the American theologian Nicholas Healy has emphasised the importance of the study of the Church's practices in ecclesiology. He argues for a 'new ecclesiology' that is focused on the practices of the Church, and he is critical of what he calls 'modern ecclesiology' which, according to Healy, has become overly systematic and theoretical. The 'new ecclesiology' recognises the actual Church and its identity, which is constructed by the actions and activities of the members. The shortcomings, failures, and fallibility of the members are acknowledged, and even the Church is part of a sinful world.[1]

Healy refers to Thomas Aquinas' understanding of Church through an *in via* ('on the way') perspective and an eschatological understanding of life. This kind of *in via* ecclesiology emphasises a clear distinction between *Ecclesia Militans* and *Ecclesia Triumphans* – terms that can be understood as equivalent to the earthly and heavenly Church. The earthly Church is not the same as the heavenly Church, and the earthly pilgrim Church is different from the heavenly Church. The earthly Church, according to Healy, does not need to become the heavenly Church, and it does not need to try to develop into some kind of ideal Church that is impossible to attain. Healy argues that there are various ways of describing the Church in the

---

1   Healy, Nicholas, 2000, pp. 5–9.

New Testament. He criticises what he calls 'blueprint ecclesiologies' such as those of J.-M. R. Tillard and John D. Zizioulas, both of whom emphasise communion ecclesiology. This kind of ecclesiology becomes very systematic, theoretical, and idealistic. The Church is portrayed in terms of perfection, and this ecclesiology turns into the only pattern for being Church.[2]

Gary Badcock, another American theologian, questions Healy's arguments about the importance of the 'new ecclesiology'. Badcock argues that Healy's practices deal with faith as it is lived, and that this has become more important than the doctrines of the Church. The *doing* in a particular time and place has replaced the teaching of the Church. Badcock gives effective examples, identifying gender equality in the Church, the churches' silence during the Second World War, or ecclesiastical tolerance of paedophilia as revealing a need for overarching ecclesiologies. Badcock insists that the so-called 'blueprint ecclesiologies', which are not contextually-driven, were a great help and resource for Christians during the Cold War years in Eastern Europe or the apartheid era in South Africa. The support for 'blueprint ecclesiologies', according to Badcock, arose because they were not *practical-prophetic*. He also questions whether the kind of ecclesiology that Healy advocates inspires significant change in the Church's life. Change requires motivation through vision, and practices do not have these qualities. Badcock nevertheless admits that there are ecclesiologies that are not relevant for the real Church and that might be questionable.[3]

The Swedish theologian Antje Jackelén has responded in a similar way to Healy's understanding of ecclesiology. She says that there are advantages to the so-called 'blueprint ecclesiologies': they provide visions that inspire people to reform and improve the Church, and they offer images of the Church as it is intended to be. These ecclesiologies are also a kind of anti-reductionism. The Church cannot be reduced to its successes or failures: it is more than its manifestation in reality.[4] Jackelén also says: "[…] where blueprint ecclesiology inspired the church to remain *ecclesia semper reformanda*, resulting in an ever-renewing church, contextual ecclesiology could reduce the church to an *ecclesia semper adaptanda*, becoming an ever-adapting church which runs the risk of losing its own identity".[5] The danger is that the Church could lose its uniqueness and thus its contribution to society through being by its very nature different. 'Blueprint ecclesiologies' can be a source

---

2 Healy, Nicholas, 2003, pp. 304–308; Healy, Nicholas, 2000, pp. 34–37.
3 Badcock, Gary D., 2009, pp. 2–7.
4 Jackelén, Antje, 1999, pp. 15–19.
5 Jackelén, Antje, 1999, p. 16.

of encouragement to the Church, and provide patterns that assist with constructive directions; but there is a need for both kinds of ecclesiologies.[6]

Healy nevertheless acknowledges and discusses the problem of the Church's practices. He states that there is no established definition of 'practices', and no consensus about criteria, which implies that every user of the term has to define what they mean by 'practices'. The aims of a practice may also differ; and the intentions behind an act are personal and might not be the same for others who participate in a certain practice.[7] Despite Healy's criticism, he does not reject 'blueprint ecclesiologies' outright. He recognises that both kinds of ecclesiology are necessary and have much to offer the Church. He also states that a 'blueprint ecclesiology' can respond adequately to a specific context.[8] Theological discussions of 'blueprint ecclesiologies' and ecclesiologies based on practices indicate that both kinds of ecclesiology are important, and can make significant contributions to the study of the Church.

One example of a combination of the two kinds of ecclesiology in the South Africa context is that advocated by the South African theologian Larry Kaufmann. He declares that an ecclesiology for South Africa always has to be contextual, but with assistance from important ecclesiologies proposed by, for example, Avery Dulles or Michael Cassidy. He proposed, during the last years of apartheid, a sacramental model of Church based on the eucharistic liturgy as a pattern for an ecclesiology that incorporates a contextual ecclesiology. Kaufmann's attempt shows that a practical contextual ecclesiology can be combined with a sacramental ecclesiology without giving rise to contradictions, and that they can instead be complementary.[9] I agree with Kaufmann that ecclesiology has to be both contextual and at the same time supported by other ecclesiologies.

In my thesis I will use the catholicity of the Church, as described in the analytical tool in the previous chapter, and an ecclesiology from South African congregations and churches. The method I have used to discern an ecclesiology is an ethnographic method through an 'operative ecclesiology'.

4.2 Ecclesiology and Ethnography

Several theologians have used ethnographic methods to study the Church with great success. It is not a new approach; but it has received greater attention since

---

6   Jackelén, Antje, 1999, pp. 15–19.
7   Healy, Nicholas, 2003, pp. 289–293.
8   Heally, Nicholas, 2004, p. 288; Heally, Nicolas, 2000, p. 47.
9   Kaufmann, Larry, 1985, pp. 6–23.

the Ecclesiology and Ethnography Network began to gather scholars working with theological approaches to qualitative research into the Church. The network also publishes *Ecclesial Practices*, a journal of ecclesiology and ethnography. In my research discipline, ecclesiology, the Faculty of Theology at Uppsala University has several researchers using ethnographic methods. Sune Fahlgren, for example, has analysed sermons, finding diverse approaches to being congregations; Jonas Ideström has studied the implicit ecclesiology in a specific congregation; and Kerstin Almegård is researching parishioners' experiences of church music.[10]

The British theologian Paul S. Fiddes has argued that ecclesiology has primarily used deductive methods based on accepted beliefs about the Christian community, while ethnography uses inductive methods. Ethnography is rooted in the study of observing people and their beliefs and practices. Fiddes declares that it is important to bring empirical studies of the Christian community into interaction with ecclesiology. It is interesting, for example, to investigate how the Church is influenced by different trends in society. Ecclesiology and ethnography may seem very different, but both are occupied in the study of a community or a *koinonia*. This means that the two disciplines are similar, despite approaching the Church from different angles. It could be very instructive to study the Christian community both from a systematic ecclesiological perspective and from a contextual ecclesiological perspective that is based on ethnography.[11] There is a range of definitions about what ethnography entails, and the term can have many definitions with various meanings. I will use the term in the sense of applying the use of qualitative methods such as interviews, observation, and collected material, to study the Church.[12]

Several scholars, especially in the USA, have used ethnographic methods – but from a sociological rather than an ecclesiological perspective – when they have studied the Church in relation to 'race'. Michael Emmerson, together with a group of scholars, has published several books studying racial segregation in religious institutions. Other scholars doing similar research into multicultural or intercultural congregations include George Yancey and Korrie L. Edwards.[13]

---

10 See, for example, Fahlgren, Sune, 2006; Ideström, Jonas, 2009.
11 Fiddes, Paul S., pp. 13–15, 18.
12 See, for example, the book *Perspectives on Ecclesiology and Ethnography* by Ward, Peter, ed., 2012.
13 See, for example, Christerson, Brad, & Edwards, Korie L. & Emerson, Michael O., 2005; DeYoung, Curtiss, et. al., 2003; Emerson, Michael O., & Smith, Christian, 2000; Yancey, George, 2003; Edwards, Korie L., 2008.

4.3 Ecclesiologies Revealed

The French theologian Yves Congar has noted that there have been several leading ecclesiologies of the Church as a communion in relation to the eucharist. He states that the liturgy, based on the tradition of the Church, has always stressed the Church as a community. Other ecclesiologies have sometimes taught that the priest represents the people, and the Church has become focused more on power and on the institution than on *ecclesia*, communion, and holiness. These different ecclesiologies found in the Church could be called 'operative ecclesiologies'. According to Congar, it is possible to find both explicit and implicit ecclesiologies in the Church.[14]

---

14 Yves Congar has written in the article: *L'"Ecclesia" ou communauté chrétienne, sujet intégral de l'action liturgique* (Congar, Yves M.-J., 1966) about different ecclesiologies that regard Church as a community in relation to the eucharist. He argues that the ancient writings of the Church Fathers about the sacraments, such as those of Justin, Irenaeus, and Augustine, were based on a biblical foundation when they accentuated the community as the people of God and the body of Christ (Peuple de Dieu et Corps du Christ). The vision that inspired the Church Fathers was the relationship between *caput* and *corpus*, Christ as the head and the Church as Christ's body, which could not be separated. '[...] La grande perception qui inspire ce que les Anciens nous disent est celle du lien entre *caput* et *corpus*, le Christ comme tête et l'Église comme son corps L'un ne va pas sans l'autre, on ne peut les séparer. [...]', p. 254. The ancient Christian community was only familiar with the celebration of the eucharist within a community. '[...] tandis que l'Antiquité n'avait connu que des célébrations eucharistiques faites pour une communauté [...]' p. 251. The eucharistic practice began to change because, among other things, the eremitic and monastic tradition was developing. The meaning of 'the faithful' became spiritualised, and the priest could celebrate the eucharist alone without a community. The liturgical communitarian ecclesiology was, however, maintained in the expression of the plural form in the liturgy. The doctrinal ecclesiology of the Church as a community was modified and even removed. Congar writes that the Church went from an ecclesiology of the *ecclesia* to an ecclesiology of powers, from an ecclesiology of communion and holiness to an ecclesiology of the institution. '[...] qu'on est passé d'une ecclésiologie de l'*ecclesia* à une ecclésiologie des pouvoirs, d'une ecclésiologie de la communion et de la sainteté à une ecclésiologie de l'institution et des moyens de salut fondés par le Christ. [...]'. p. 261. The *caput* and *corpus* relationship was changed from Christ as head to the ministerial hierarchy as the head of the body. The ecclesiology of the Church as a community, according to Congar, was restored by Vatican II when the communitarian aspect of the eucharist was rediscovered. Congar argues that it was the ecclesiology in the liturgy based on the tradition that had remained all along, and was made the foundation of a restoration. He states that liturgy is the great teaching of

There could of course be several readings of Congar's description of ecclesiologies, but the Swedish theologian Sven-Erik Brodd has interpreted Congar's 'operative ecclesiology' in the following terms: "Congar has pointed to the fact that behind liturgical patterns there are different ecclesiologies operative. These may be conscious or not. The ordering of the worship discloses a latent or open ecclesiology. This could be applied in all areas of ecclesial life".[15] Brodd explains that practices are hidden in, for example, liturgy, and create ecclesiological patterns that also influence the ecclesial identity as well as the way of being the Church. Different practices in the Church could be studied, such as preaching, liturgy, communitarian life, organisation, church music, and so on. In order to be able to study the practices, ecclesiological studies are supported by anthropology, sociology, linguistics, statistics, history, etc. Interviews, observation, historical documents, questionnaires, statements, and so on become an important tool in the study of the Church's practices.[16]

By this definition, ecclesiology becomes comprehensive, including all forms of Church activity other than the institutional Church, as well as every aspect of communitarian life in the Church, and different manifestations in life. Brodd states: "Dogma and empiricism are kept together, and the spiritual is not conceived as a parallel to the material but held together in an incarnational perspective when

---

the Church, and is the primary monument and witness of the *tradition*. Congar, Yves M.-J., 1966, pp. 242–246, 251–254, 261–262, 268.

15 Brodd, Sven-Erik, 2008, pp. xviii–xix.

16 Brodd, Sven-Erik, 2008, pp. xviii–xix. Brodd's interpretation of Congar's article could be discussed. Liturgy, according to Brodd, is an implicit ecclesiology; but liturgy could also be regarded as an explicit ecclesiology.
Several other theologians have used the concept of 'operational ecclesiology' with various meanings, and there is no clear consensus. Gesa E. Thiessen, for example, has explained operative ecclesiology in a way similar to Brodd, with reference to Karl Rahner. She uses intercommunion as an example, where there is one official ecclesiology and another 'operational ecclesiology' among people in the church. She stresses that the operational ecclesiology could contradict the official ecclesiology of the church. Thiessen, Gesa E., 2009, pp. 43–44. Kenan B. Osborne is another theologian who uses operational ecclesiology; but he stresses instead that this ecclesiology is the standard and dominant ecclesiology of the Roman Catholic Church. Osborne, Kenan B., 2007, p. 60; Osborne, Kenan B., 2009, pp. 28–30. Christopher Jamison describes an operational ecclesiology as an ecclesiology embracing new movements in church in contrast to a hierarchical ecclesiology. Jamison, Christopher, 2012, p. 83–84. A similar explanation to that of Jamison is offered by William A. Nordenbrock. Nordenbrock, William A., 2011, p. 127.

trying to understand what church is".[17] A distinction could be made between the Church as it is empirically observed and the Church as defined by the Church's teaching.[18]

In my study of the South African churches, I will use Sven-Erik Brodd's interpretation of 'operative ecclesiology'. The understanding of catholicity derived from F&O and the WCC is taken as normative, and will be an analytical tool to test ecclesiologies in the South African congregations and churches that are discovered through interviews, observation, statements, etc. My interest is to investigate whether there are great differences between an international ecumenical understanding of catholicity and an 'operative ecclesiology' among the congregations and churches in South Africa concerning ethnicity.[19]

Practices

The Scottish philosopher Alasdair MacIntyre has influenced several theologians who have used the concept of 'practices' in the Church.[20] MacIntyre argues that the world has lost a common moral society and has become morally incoherent as a result of the Enlightenment's individualism. This is caused by society's rejection of its narrative history and the lack of communal belonging. Society has instead become fragmentary and without aim, and people who are strangers to one another promote their own personal interests.[21] MacIntyre's claims could of course be questioned; but he suggests an Aristotelian tradition with practices and a clear common *telos* as an alternative to society's individualism.[22]

---

17 Brodd, Sven-Erik, 2008, p. xix.
18 Edgardh, Ninna, 2001, p. 183.
19 Documents about catholicity from F&O and the WCC are valid to use as a common international influential doctrine. Reformed churches have no common doctrine apart from statements made by the ecumenical organisations. The Roman Catholic Church has a *magisterium* (teaching office), but it is at the same time a member of the World Council of Churches' Commission on Faith and Order. For structuring factors in ecclesiology, see Brodd, Sven-Erik, 2006, pp. 124–125.
20 For example, scholars such as Dorothy C. Bass, Craig Dykstra, Reinhard Hütter, Nicholas Healy. See also, for example, books such as *Virtues & Practices in the Christian Tradition, Christian Ethics after MacIntyre*, by Dykstra, Craig, 1997 (1991); *Practicing Theology*, by Volf, Miroslav, & Bass, Dorothy C. eds., 2002.
21 MacIntyre, Alasdair, 1984, pp. 62–78, 251.
22 The term *telos* is Greek, and means 'end', 'purpose' or 'goal'.

MacIntyre has given a concise and oft-quoted description of 'practice':

> By a 'practice' I am going to mean any coherent and complex form of socially established cooperative human activity through which goods internal to that form of activity are realized in the course of trying to achieve those standards of excellence which are appropriate to, and partially definitive of, that form of activity, with the result that human powers to achieve excellence, and human conceptions of the ends and goods involved, are systematically extended. [...][23]

MacIntyre is referring here to the importance of all forms of cooperative human activities that are learned together and have a shared vision. The common acts are part of creating a communion of people, and the attachment to a community is the common aim of attaining a good life. He names, for example, playing football or chess, or farming as typical practices, while simply throwing a football, moving a chess piece, or planting seeds are not practices: they are activities within a practice. His image of farming as a practice is a good example that shows that experiences within a social community have been developed over time and have been shared with others. There is a common knowledge of how to cultivate, and there is the common purpose or aim (*telos*) of farming to produce food to sustain life. The *telos*, according to MacIntyre, is not something that is reached at a specific time, but a common way of orientating human life.[24] The image of farming does not end with a single harvest, but continues with the *telos* of being life-giving. A practice follows certain patterns, but changes over time. Farming is carried out differently around the world because of differences in landscape and climate, and it has changed over time through technical development; but it can still be recognised as the practice of farming. According to MacIntyre, this is a characteristic of a practice: it can be recognised, even if it is different or has changed, because the *telos* remains.[25]

A practice can, of course, be enacted individually, but it cannot exist in isolation, with no relationship to the rest of the community. An artist's painting would just become another drawing if it was not shared with a community, and it would have no purpose apart from the artist's own purposes. The practice is dependent on a community, because knowledge has to be taught within the community and transferred to other people. It is also in the community that the practice is

---

23 MacIntyre, Alasdair, 1984, p. 187. MacIntyre's definition of practices has been widely applied in various writings, and has been used constructively by, for example, McCann, Dennis P., & Brownsberger, M. L., 1995, p. 508; Bassham, Gregory, & Hamilton, Mark, 2007, p. 41; Fahlgren, Sune, 2006, p. 39; Ideström, Jonas, 2009, pp. 60–61.
24 MacIntyre, Alasdair, 1984, pp. 187–188.
25 MacIntyre, Alasdair, 1984, pp. 192–194, 202–203.

refined and corrected so that it can continue to exist and be relevant. The society's common *telos* is part of the practice, and also the driving force to maintain and develop the practice itself. Cooperative human activities will, in this way, reveal the *telos* and also the practice's own identity.

Ecclesial Practices

Two theologians from the USA, Dorothy Bass and Craig Dykstra, have developed MacIntyre's description of practices for the study of the Church. Ecclesial practices can be church services, sacraments, hospitality, forgiveness, prayers, and so on. Their definition is: "Christian practices are things Christian people do together over time to address fundamental needs and conditions of humanity and all creation in the light of and in response to God's active presence for the life of the world in Jesus Christ".[26] Practices, in the view of Bass and Dykstra, deal with essential needs in life. Their purpose is to make the Christian faith concrete and to support faith by making practices part of everyday life. They are performed in church, in public, and at home, and are shared activities even though they might be carried out by individuals. Nevertheless, individual actions have to be part of a common practice together in a community. Prayer can be named as an example: it can be performed in a group or by an individual. It is a Christian practice and is part of the Church, which means that it is a cooperative human activity.[27] Dykstra states: "Practice is participation in a cooperatively formed pattern of activity that emerges out of a complex tradition of interactions among many people sustained over a long period".[28] Practices, according to Dykstra, are not just carried out briefly in the Church: they have to be part of a larger context.

Bass and Dykstra explain that practices can take different forms, but are identifiable irrespective of culture, time, or place. Certain patterns can be recognised because the practices have the same constituent elements, whether the Church is in Europe, America, or Africa. Practices are not isolated activities: they have been performed for a long time and are part of the Christian tradition that is rooted in the Bible and in the ministry of Jesus. Practices have been taught over generations throughout the Church's history. This can be understood to mean that the Christian tradition is a search for a common *telos* for the Church. Practices are the Christian life skills and wisdom that have emerged from the community. They

---

26 Bass, Dorothy & Dykstra, Craig, 2010, p. 204.
27 Bass, Dorothy & Dykstra, Craig, 2010, pp. 6–7, 204–205; Dykstra, Craig, 1991, pp. 169–170.
28 Dykstra, Craig, 1991, p. 170.

may not always have been done well, and they remain open to critique and reform. Part of a practice in a community is the need for improvement and progress towards excellence. As MacIntyre explains it, practices are learned in a common framework, belong to a continuous process of actions, and are shaped over time.[29]

According to Bass and Dykstra, practices are interrelated and are difficult to separate and distinguish. There is a constant flow between the practices that keeps them interlinked and continuously connected, because they exist in a wider context and cannot be separated. People engage in many practices at the same time, and practices can be performed simultaneously. They become especially visible and central when the community is gathered in Christian worship.[30]

In studying the South African congregations and churches, I will make use of Bass and Dykstra's interpretation of practices. Several scholars in my research discipline of ecclesiology at Uppsala have used practices in their research with great success. Jonas Ideström, for example, has used Dykstra's definition in his thesis on the Church's practices, but has also related the practices to structures of identity. He argues that established collective activities can affect decisions made by the local church over time. These can be seen as aspects of an identity structure. A practice, according to Ideström, can be regarded as an element of an identity structure. He argues that it is possible to analyse a practice and to clarify the structure behind it.[31]

Sune Fahlgren has also used practices in church in his thesis, and has applied an image from the discipline of medicine concerning the human body. He compares practices with a cell's deoxyribonucleic acid (DNA), the chemical substance that carries genetic information. The body is the Church, the *koinonia*/communion of people that is understood as 'the body of Christ'. DNA contains the instructions needed to construct the cell components – how the cells should be formed. The DNA molecule is replicated by cell division, and a copy of the molecule is present in each daughter cell. The genetic information is passed on from one cell generation to the next.[32]

Fahlgren states that it is possible to trace the 'ecclesial genetic code' in the Church by examining how the 'Church body' appears in its practices. Just as DNA and its genetic code determines how a human body is developed and formed, common actions in the communitarian life of the Church reveal a specific 'ecclesial genetic code'. This analogy explains how ecclesial existence is incorporated

---

29 Bass, Dorothy & Dykstra, Craig, 2010, pp. 6–7, 204–205.
30 Bass, Dorothy & Dykstra, Craig, 2010, pp. 10, 205.
31 Ideström, Jonas, 2009, pp. 60–61.
32 Fahlgren, Sune, 2006, pp. 38–43.

into the ecclesial practices of the Church. It is possible, according to Fahlgren, to identify and describe an ecclesiology if the ecclesial practices are discovered and examined. Fahlgren's theory about practices is interesting and attractive, but has several weaknesses.[33]

Jacob Tronêt, in his thesis about Max Thurian's understanding of ways towards the unity of the Church, has used the analytical concept of 'catholic practices'. He states that catholicity is linked to the Church's actions, and indicates that catholicity is realised through the exercise of the practices. Tronêt stresses that the concept of 'catholic practice' can be compared with the marks of the Church (*notae ecclesiae*). The practices that he has used to study Thurian's texts are the eucharist, baptism, ministry, the bishop of Rome, and Mariology. Tronêt claims that a 'catholic practice' is a fundamental aspect of the life of the Church, and is a necessary condition for the Church's catholicity.[34]

South African Churches and their Operative Ecclesiology

The study of the South African congregations and churches is based on a case study in which I examined interviews, observation, statements, publications, and so on. I used implicit and explicit methods to discern an operative ecclesiology. So next I will describe the methodology I used when conducting the case studies.

4.4 Case Study Design

The case study was conducted from February to April 2011 – that is, twenty years after the South African parliament in Cape Town voted to repeal the framework of apartheid, and the country's transition to democracy began. Statistics South Africa, the South African government's national statistical service, conducted a

---

33 Fahlgren, Sune, 2006, pp. 38–43. Using the analogy of DNA has advantages but also weaknesses. It can be risky to mix the scientific image of DNA with the language of ecclesial practices. The consequence might be that practices become the 'true' ecclesiology. The image also does not take into account that there might be errors in the DNA, or in the 'ecclesial genetic code'. There might be failures or problems in the Church's genetic code – of which apartheid would be a good example. The body usually repairs the damage in a cell, but when the repair mechanism is not functioning, cells continue to divide unchecked and uncontrolled, and cancer cells develop into a tumour. The Church body can correct or reject practices; but if the mechanism is not functioning well, the practices are damaged and yet continue to be reproduced. MacIntyre's image of practices is preferable: he argues that practices are life skills and wisdom that have been developed in a community, and are refined.
34 Tronêt, Jakob, 2014, pp. 39–40, 258.

national census in 2011, thus providing the latest figures of the South African population. The twenty-year time span offered the society and the churches opportunities to act in response to democracy, and allowed the changes to become visible.[35]

Researcher's Background

I worked and lived in Kimberley, South Africa, from 1999 to 2003; and since that time I have spent shorter and longer periods in the country. During the years I was living in South Africa I worked, through the Church of Sweden and seconded to ELCSA, as a hospital chaplain in the Kimberley Hospital. My work there was in an ecumenical environment with chaplains from diverse churches and ethnicities. Besides the work in the hospital, I was also assigned as an assistant minister to St Sylvester congregation in Floors.

I realise that my position as a white male foreigner and minister in South Africa could have influenced situations during visits and interviews, but this has not significantly affected the outcome of my research. I acknowledge, for example, tensions when I was dealing with issues around ethnicity; but I adjusted the design of delicate issues after my first visits to the trial congregation and trial church leader.

Choice of Churches

I described earlier that I chose to study the Roman Catholic Church, the Anglican Church of Southern Africa, the Methodist Church of Southern Africa, the Apostolic Faith Mission of South Africa, and the Lutheran family of churches (the Evangelical Lutheran Church in Southern Africa, the Evangelical Lutheran Church in Southern Africa – Cape Church, and the Evangelical Lutheran Church in Southern Africa Natal-Transvaal).

When I selected the churches, I decided to choose mainline historical churches that had worked against apartheid before democratisation, that had more than one million members, and that had a significant place in South African society. The 2011 national census in South Africa did not include churches and religion as part of its study, and so I had to use statistics from Census 2001.[36] Although there were

---

35 South Africa's parliament voted in 1991 to repeal, for example, the Population Registration Act, the Group Areas Act, the Native Land Act, and the Native Trust and Land Act. Census 2011, Census in Brief, 2012, pp. 2–4.
36 Unfortunately questions related to religion and religious and church affiliation were not included in the Statistics South Africa questionnaire in Census 2011. The latest available data is from Census 2001.

major changes in church membership in those ten years, most mainline churches have maintained similar figures despite a gradual decline. The Pentecostal/Charismatic churches are not a single church or denomination, but together they have more than one million members. I have chosen the AMF as a representative of these churches, even though it has fewer than one million members. It is the largest and oldest Pentecostal church in South Africa, and it belongs to the SACC.[37] The Reformed churches together make up the largest mainline church family, and are very important in South African society. They are interesting to study, but their position in South African society was very different before democratisation. Much research has already been conducted into the Reformed churches, while the other mainline churches have been less well investigated. A possible future study would be to investigate the ecclesiologies of the family of Reformed churches, and their relationship with the international ecumenical movement.[38]

Choice of Congregations

I chose six congregations in three of the largest municipalities by inhabitants in South Africa: the City of Johannesburg Metropolitan Municipality, the City of Cape Town Metropolitan Municipality, and the eThekwini Metropolitan Municipality in Durban.[39] The reason for choosing cities is that they have a greater ethnic diversity in the population than do rural areas, and the largest municipalities were a natural choice. Selecting two congregations in each city also gave adequate variety and provided a manageable amount of material to examine. The congregations were selected from the five churches, but there are two Lutheran church

---

37   Church membership numbers in Statistics South Africa's Census 2001: Dutch Reformed Church 3 005 698, Zion Christian churches 4 971 932, Catholic churches 3 181 336, Methodist churches 3 305 404, Pentecostal/Charismatic churches 3 422 749, Apostolic Faith Mission of SA 246 190, Anglican churches 1 722 076, Lutheran churches 1 130 987. Census 2001: Primary tables South Africa Census '96 and 2001 compared Statistics South Africa, Report No. 03-02-04 (2001), 2004, p. 27.
38   There have been several dissertations and books about the Reformed churches in South Africa. See, for example, Van der Merwe, JM, 1990; Plaatjies-Van Huffel, Mary-Anne, 2008; De Beer, Jan Mathys, 2008; Kruger, Pieter, 2008; Van der Merwe, Barend Jacobus, 2010; Plaatjies, Mary-Anne, & Vosloo, Robert, 2013.
39   South Africa has eight metropolitan municipalities. The others are Buffalo City in East London, the City of Tshwane Metropolitan Municipality in Pretoria, Ekurhuleni Metropolitan Municipality in Germiston, Mangaung Metropolitan Municipality in Bloemfontein, and Nelson Mandela Bay Metropolitan Municipality in Port Elizabeth. In addition to the larger metros, there are district municipalities that in turn are divided into a number of local municipalities. The Local Government Handbook, 2014, p. 315.

congregations because the Lutherans are divided into three different church organisations.[40]

I have used a combination of convenience sampling and snowball sampling when I have selected the congregations. This method implies that the researcher makes contact with a small group of people who have knowledge of the project and who could establish contacts with others. This makes it possible to choose congregations strategically, with the research as the starting point. In my case I contacted people at diocesan, central, or equivalent level, and discussed various possible congregations; and they advised or assisted me to establish connections with particular congregations. In one case – the Anglican Church in Johannesburg – I contacted one congregation, but they had no openings for a visit. They suggested another congregation that was willing to participate. A similar situation happened with the AFM congregation in Durban when one congregation was prevented from participating, and another suggested congregation was contacted and was willing to be part of the project. It is important to emphasise that snowball sampling is not the same as random sampling, because it is impossible to get precisely representative congregations in the South African context. My aim was not to obtain a random sample, but instead to find a variety of South African congregations among the selected churches. The congregations' membership size is not comparable, but together they represent the range of South African congregations.[41]

Choice of Churches' Leaders and Resource Persons

In order to broaden the study beyond the six congregations, I included the central level of each of the churches through interviews with church leaders and key documents, materials, resolutions, etc. My aim was to increase the possibility of generalisation by adding central level material. I interviewed the churches' general secretary or the equivalent person who could be regarded as a church leader in the respective church. I also interviewed two former commissioners from the TRC to obtain insight into the churches' contributions to the reconciliation process in South Africa. One of them was in charge of the Faith Communities Hearing in East London, 17–19 November 1997; the other commissioner headed the Human

---

40 There would have been a significant domination of Lutheran congregations if I had chosen three Lutheran congregations. I decided to use only two of the Lutheran congregations because ELCSA-Cape and ELCSA N-T congregations are similar in many respects, and an ELCSA-Cape congregation would thus also represent an ELCSA N-T congregation.
41 Bryman, Allan, 2012, pp. 201–203.

Rights Committee. Two other persons were interviewed because they were working in congregations whose members came from other parts of Africa.[42]

Research Ethics

The case study was conducted in accordance with the ethical principles set by The Swedish Research Council and adopted by the Humanities and Social Science Research Council regarding principles of research ethics in the humanities and social sciences. The principles can be summarised as having four requirements: the requirement of information, the requirement of consent, the requirement of confidentiality, and the requirement of use.[43]

The requirement of information means that the researcher shall inform participants about the research and about the purpose of their part in the project. Participants should be informed that participation is voluntary and that they have the right to withdraw their participation. When I visited the congregations, I was first in contact with the local minister to inform them about the project and that I was going to be an observer. The church councils were informed about the research project before the interview started, and I also informed them about the research ethics that were guiding the case study. The same procedure was used before the interviews with church leaders and resource persons.[44]

The requirement of consent means that the researcher will obtain the participants' consent for their involvement in the research project. Participants have, for example, the right to be able to discontinue, and there should be no dependency

---

42 The two former commissioners are Prof. Piet Meiring and Ms Mary Burton. Mr Kiasso Ilunga-Mpomso was employed by the Evangelical Lutheran Church in Strand Street to minister to the French Lutheran community in Cape Town. Rev Jurie Goosen is a NGK minister in charge of an international fellowship in Stellenbosch. There were only two congregations from among the Lutheran churches, but three church leaders were interviewed. The Lutheran Church in Bellville belongs to ELCSA-Cape but is part of UELCSA. Both Bishop Horst Müller and Bishop Nils J. Rohwer from UELCSA were interviewed as spokespersons for this branch of the Lutheran church family. The reason for not having one more Lutheran congregation was to avoid an imbalance of churches or denominations.
43 Forskningsetiska principer inom humanistisk–samhällsvetenskaplig forskning, 2002.
44 Forskningsetiska principer inom humanistisk–samhällsvetenskaplig forskning, 2002, pp. 7–8.

between the researcher and the participants. All church councils, church leaders, and resource persons gave their consent to participate in the interviews.[45]

According to the *requirement of confidentiality*, the participants have the right to be guaranteed the utmost confidentiality.[46] None of the church councils had any objections to my use of the names of the congregations or of the church councils in the text of the thesis. I reflected on whether it was necessary to name the congregations in the thesis, but I concluded that it was essential for the reader to know where each of them was located. Detailed descriptions of the congregations are also important to discerning their ecclesial practices; and in any case, congregations would be revealed through their portrayals. It was also important for the congregations to examine the outcome of the visit to them. No individual names were listed during the church council interviews. Some ministers can be identified in the text, but no names are given. None of the church leaders or resource persons had objections to being named in the thesis.

The requirement of use means that collected information about individuals may only be used for research purposes, and is not to be used for commercial or other non-scientific purposes. The interviewees were informed that the interviews and collected materials were only to be used for my research project, not for other purposes.[47] The material in documents, resolutions, pamphlets, newsletters, minutes, and so on was either publically available or was given to me by church representatives. Visits to different archives in Johannesburg and Cape Town followed the South African principle of public access to official records for research purposes.

4.5 Case Study Approach

Several methods are available for the collection of material in ethnographic research. In what follows I provide information about the material and how the case study was conducted. Interviews were the primary source: church councils, churches leaders, and resource persons were approached about their congregations and churches. My own observation, diverse congregational publications, and websites have been supplementary materials to build pictures of the congregations. During and after the interviews, church leaders provided or referred to documents

---

45 Forskningsetiska principer inom humanistisk–samhällsvetenskaplig forskning, 2002, pp. 9–11.
46 Forskningsetiska principer inom humanistisk–samhällsvetenskaplig forskning, 2002, pp. 12–13.
47 Forskningsetiska principer inom humanistisk–samhällsvetenskaplig forskning, 2002, p. 14.

and materials that I have been able to access in the archives. These materials were used to provide a comprehensive understanding of the church leaders' references. All collected materials, such as recorded interviews, interview protocols, observation protocols, websites, and publications are digitally archived at DiVA.[48]

Interviews

I conducted semi-structured interviews, which means that the interviews had the character of conversations. I had a list of specific topics to be covered rather than specific questions, and the interviews followed a manual. The interviewer had considerable freedom to ask questions based on the situation, and issues that the interviewee mentioned also came into focus. The questions did not need to follow a particular order, and the situation was very flexible. The interviewees also had a part in directing the order of issues through their answers, and follow-up questions could be formulated dependent on previous answers. Semi-structured interviewing allows people to talk freely, and offers the interviewees' interpretations and focuses on the interviewees' perspectives.[49]

I conducted both individual interviews and group interviews. I am aware that these kinds of interviews are not comparable and generate different kinds of information. The group interviews were conducted in order to get information from elected representatives on the church councils. The individual interviews were conducted with the purpose of getting information from the churches' central levels.

All interviews were booked in advance or at the beginning of the case study process. The church leaders, former commissioners, and resource persons were contacted through a secretary or directly by phone. The interviews were conducted later in their offices or equivalent premises. The ministers of the different congregations were similarly contacted, and appointments were made to meet the church councils for interviews. These interviews were always conducted in the congregations' premises.

All the interviews were held in English, even though it was not the first language for most of the interviewees. Some interviewees had difficulties in expressing themselves in English, and this is evident in some of the quotations. All interviews were digitally audio-recorded, and nobody objected to being recorded. Recording interviews facilitated the ability to focus on the interview itself instead of having

---

48 DiVA is the Digital Academic Archive (Digitala Vetenskapliga Arkivet) at the University of Uppsala.
49 Bernard, H. Russell, 2002, p. 205; Bryman, Alan, 2012, pp. 469–472, 477–480, 493–497.

to take notes during the interview. The group and individual interviews were later transcribed into interview protocols according to themes. The advantage of recorded interviews is that they are a permanent record of primary information, and can become public for secondary analysis.[50]

St Mary on the Braak, an Anglican church in Stellenbosch, was chosen as a trial congregation representing the local level, and Shofar Christian Church in Stellenbosch was chosen as a trial church. I participated in one of the services at St Mary on the Braak, recorded an observation protocol, and met the executive of the church council to conduct an interview. I visited Shofar Christian Church in Stellenbosch and interviewed one of their leaders. The trials resulted in the modification of the issue relating to ethnic groups, and the number of questions was reduced to shorten the time required.[51]

The quotations in the texts have been carefully edited to eliminate repetition, hesitation, and stuttering. In some quotations the grammar has also been adjusted, while others have been left unchanged.

Individual Interviews

According to the anthropologist H. Russell Bernard, semi-structured interviews are suitable for interviewing leading members of a community. The issue-driven interview is time-efficient and allows the interviewer to follow new leads. The interview is a created situation because the time and place have been booked in advance, and it is an exclusive event between interviewer and interviewee.[52] The interviews were conducted in the interviewees' work places, and lasted on average between an hour and an hour-and-a-half. The individual semi-structured interviews were conducted with the churches' general secretaries or equivalent person, two former TRC commissioners, one person who was named several times during other interviews, and a minister who was part of a multicultural network of church communities in South Africa.

---

50 The anthropologist H. Russell Bernard stresses the importance of using digital audio tape because it is a permanent record of primary information and can be archived. Bernard, H. Russell, 2002, p. 220. The recorded interview with Horst Müller on 2011-03-04 was damaged. I was able, however, to reproduce the interview through reference to an interview report.
51 The observation at St Mary on the Braak was made on 2011-02-06, and the interview with the executive of the church council at St Mary on the Braak was conducted on 2011-02-08. The interview with Andries van der Merwe, one of the church's leaders in Shofar Christian Church, was conducted on 2011-02-21.
52 Bernard, H. Russell, 2002, p. 205.

Group Interviews

The group interviews were held with the church councils in the congregations' premises. Congregations variously call their highest local governing body 'church council', 'parish council', 'congregation council', or 'assembly council', but I will use 'church council' as the generic term.[53] The distinction between group interviews and focus group is not entirely clear, and sometimes the terms are used synonymously. A group interview often covered several issues, while a focus group emphasised a particular theme and had a greater focus on the interaction in the group. Group interviews typically involved six to 12 members and a moderator, and were constructive because they made it possible to have several topics discussed from the interviewees' points of view.[54]

The church councils were a natural choice for group interviews in the congregations. Other choices were also possible, but the councils had been democratically chosen by the whole congregation, and were given responsibility to govern the congregation together with the minister/s. They were key informants because they held a special position in the congregation. Other key informants, such as the women's league or the men's league, could also have been identified. Choosing the church council as a group does, nevertheless, have disadvantages; for example, it often does not include representatives from youth and children's groups or from different kinds of church organisations.[55] The size of the council was between six and 10, which was found to be suitable for group interviews. The representation of women and men was equal in all the church councils.[56]

---

53 St Michael's congregation is part of ELCSA, and belongs to a huge parish named Durban Central Parish. Athlone Methodist Church was not represented by their actual church council: they had selected a specific group for the purpose of the interview, several of whom were or had been part of the church council.
54 Bryman, Alan, 2012, pp. 213, 501–503; Bernard, H. Russell, 2002, p. 228.
55 Bernard, H. Russell, 2002, pp. 188–190.
56 St Peter Claver in Pimville in Soweto had six church council members – three women and three men. There were three who had isiZulu as their first language, two with Sesotho, and one with both Sesotho and isiZulu as first languages. The average age was 43 years. Church Council Interview Protocol 2011-02-27. St Thomas' in Linden had six church council members with four women and two men. Four had English as their first language, one with isiZulu, and one with Sepedi. The median age was 40–45 years. Church Council Interview Protocol 2011-03-06. Athlone Methodist Church had six church council members – three women and three men. All council members had English as their first language. The median age was around 80 years. Church Council Interview Protocol 2011-03-20. The Lutheran Church in Bellville had seven church council members – four women and three men. Six had German as their first language,

Group interviews are different from individual interviews. There are group dynamics that are influence the situation – for example, silent participants or persons who do not allow others to speak. Research also shows that groups can develop uncritical opinions or can be inclined to express expected or acceptable opinions. These group dynamics cannot be ignored. Church councils are groups that are used to discussing and debating various issues. These groups set the conditions for attaining the proper representation of diverse voices.[57]

The church council members were asked to disclose their gender, first language, and age, but not their names. They were asked about their gender in order to reveal whether there was an equal representation of men and women; their first language to observe whether the council and the congregation used the same or a variety of languages; and their age to get an idea of the age range in the congregations' decision-making bodies. They were not asked for their names because they represented the council rather than themselves as individuals, and they were also encouraged to talk without worrying about being identified. Names were irrelevant to and without significance for the research; and not asking for them also helped to ensure confidentiality.

It was often the case that not every member of the church council was present for the interview. This did not change the outcome, because the majority participated in the interviews. The interviews were always conducted at the congregations' premises, and all the interviews but one were conducted after a Sunday service. The interviews lasted for between three-quarters of an hour and one-and-a-half hours. The minister was part of the group interview in four congregations. The minister was often included in the council, but it was up to each church council and minister to decide whether the minister should be part of the interview. One church council added an employee as a participant in the interview.[58]

---

and one with Afrikaans. The average age was 56 years. Church Council Interview Protocol 2011-03-15. City Harvest Ministries in Ntuzuma had eight church council members – four women and four men. Seven had isiZulu as their first language, and one with isiXhosa. The average age was 36 years. Church Council Interview Protocol 2011-03-27. St Michael's in Durban had 10 church council members – four women and six men. Six had isiZulu as their first language, two with German, one with English, and one with Tshivenda. The average age was 55 years. Church Council Interview Protocol 2011-04-03.

57 Bryman, Alan, 2012, pp. 516–518.
58 The interview with the church council at the Lutheran Church in Bellville was conducted on Tuesday 15 March 2011 at 07.30 a.m., before an ordinary council meeting. The ministers were present at St Thomas' in Linden, the Lutheran Church in Bellville,

Observations

My position as an ordained minister who has previously lived and worked in a South African ecumenical environment facilitated my ability to conduct interviews and make observations. I have had previous experience in visiting churches, and have participated in church services in similar congregations to those that were chosen from the various churches or denominations.[59]

Church services were my principal source for observation. Services are regular events, and express and reveal the highest nature of the Church. They were not created for my research, but were part of an ongoing participatory religious gathering, and were suitable for observation.[60]

Observation can suffer from the problem that observers affect the situation that they study. For example, I was introduced to the members of the congregation in the services, but my presence was not strange, and it did not affect the situation because a church service is a public event with many participants. I made scratch notes and took photos before, during, and after the church services. I typed up the observations immediately after the services from the scratch notes and photos.[61]

Collected Printed Material, Websites, DVD

Printed material from churches' central levels primarily consists of constitutions, canons, service books, conference documents, synod reports, yearbooks, consultation reports, etc. These documents were provided by the central offices of the visited churches and from archives, with the assistance of helpful secretaries, archivists, and administrative staff. Printed material from congregations in the form of newsletters, information leaflets, pamphlets, liturgy, and so on were either publically available or were given to me by church representatives. The published websites of churches or congregations were printed and used like any other official document. Audiovisual material from the TRC's Faith Communities Hearing was purchased from the Department of Government Communication and Information System in Pretoria.

It was very evident that the congregations' ability to provide material depended much on their access to economic resources. Some congregations could provide

---

City Harvest Ministries in Ntuzuma, and St Michael's in Durban. The parish's director of music was also present at St Thomas' in Linden, probably to represent the staff.
59 Bernard, H. Russell, 2002, pp. 328–330; Bryman, Alan, 2012, pp. 445, 494.
60 "[…] la liturgie exprimant et manifestant au plus haut point la nature authentique de la véritable Èglise […]". Congar, Yves M.-J., 1966, p. 268.
61 Bryman, Alan, 2012, pp. 495–497; Sanjek, Roger, 1990, pp. 97, 324.

lots of material and documentation, while others had only a few papers. Congregations with limited resources did not have the staff to produce such materials. Also, both old and new congregations took part in the research, with different forms of documentation. This varying ability to deliver material influenced the possibility of building up a portrait of a congregation; but it did not significantly affect the outcome.

4.6 Conclusions

In the previous chapter, I outlined an ecumenical interpretation of catholicity arising from key documents and texts from Faith & Order and the World Council of Churches. Specific issues in relation to ethnicity that became evident in the case study were chosen, and will receive special attention in the thesis. Ecumenical catholicity is used as a normative international theory, and will serve as an analytical tool to test the ecclesiology of South African congregation and churches. (See the first square in Figure III.)

In this chapter, I have provided the methodological foundation that I used in the study of South African congregations and churches in order to reveal an ecclesiology. An operative ecclesiology based on that of Yves Congar was applied in the case study. This meant that the Church was studied through its implicit ecclesiology through different ecclesial practices, but also through the explicit ecclesiology found in its teaching in documents, statements, resolutions, creeds, etc. (See the second square in Figure III.)

Ecclesial practices are cooperative human activities related to the Christian community and performed in the Church. They are shared common activities rooted in the Christian tradition, and can be identified irrespective of culture, time, or place. Examples of ecclesial practices are church services, sacraments, hospitality, forgiveness, prayers, etc. The teaching of the Church becomes visible in vision and mission statements, conference papers, annual reports, etc. Both practices and the teaching of the Church are most visible in interviews, but also through observation and the study of relevant documents.

The next chapter describes the chosen congregations' and churches' history and background in the South African context. The chapters that then follow deal separately with various themes that are relevant and productive to examine in the South African context. The congregations' and churches' ecclesiology will be tested against the theology of catholicity arising from the ecumenical documents. (See Figure III.) In these chapters I investigate whether there are great differences between the congregations and churches and the catholicity of the

Church. I am also concerned to explore the main obstacles facing congregations and churches as a result of ethnicity.

Figure III: I use an 'operative ecclesiology' to examine South African congregations and churches. The catholicity of the Church that arises from F&O and WCC documents is used to test an ecclesiology that is revealed by examining the implicit and explicit ecclesiologies of South African congregations and churches.

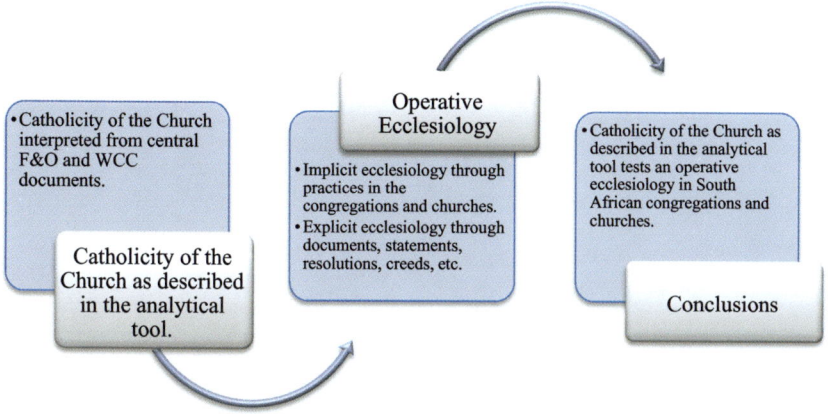

Part II

Chapter Five: Congregations and Churches on South African Soil

This chapter will briefly explore the history of the selected churches in South Africa, and in particular the case study congregations' histories and contexts. The purpose of the chapter is to set the scene for the congregations and churches that I am studying, and to provide information for the analysis that will be carried out in Chapters Six to Eleven. In this chapter, only descriptions will be offered, leaving the analyses to later chapters. However, in other chapters I will refer to information provided in this chapter that is important for analysis.

Firstly, I will give a brief introduction to the denominations, and describe how they dealt with apartheid before democratisation. Secondly, I will introduce the case congregations two decades after democratisation. I will describe where they are situated, their historical background, and the character of each of the congregations.

5.1 The Churches in South Africa

The churches in South Africa have very diverse histories. Some of them arrived early in its colonial history, while others were not allowed to minister to their members and to start mission work before the colonial power changed its policy. The churches also had different approaches to relating to the apartheid government. I will briefly describe how the selected churches were established in South Africa, and their various attitudes towards apartheid.

Roman Catholic Church

There were small number of Roman Catholics living in the Cape Colony when the Dutch East Indian Company was in charge of it. They had to conceal their faith because the Dutch Reformed Church was the only church that was recognised and allowed to operate in the Cape Colony. The situation changed at the beginning of the nineteenth century, when clergy were allowed to minister to Roman Catholic soldiers. The first Roman Catholic bishop was sent to the colony in the late 1830s, and several religious orders arrived soon after that. The church's object was to minister to Roman Catholics living in the cities, towns, and countryside,

131

and to establish parishes, churches, and schools for the children. The number of Roman Catholics grew through immigration from Europe and intermarriage.[1]

Mission work among indigenous people started around the 1860s, when mission stations were opened with schools, hospitals, orphanages, and churches. Mission work grew rapidly, and the church's position in South Africa had changed completely by the end of the nineteenth century. By then the church had many more members, priests, and members of religious orders, with excellent church institutions. The real growth of the church started in the twentieth century as a consequence of active Roman Catholic mission. The large number of missionaries, together with the church's independence from the apartheid state, helped the church to grow among the indigenous people. Today it is one of the largest mainline churches in the country.[2]

The church was for a long time seen as a foreign element in South African society because of the clear domination of the Protestant churches, and because the government primarily favoured the Dutch Reformed and Anglican churches. The Roman Catholic Church was heavily affected by the apartheid policy. The church's schools and hospitals were especially problematic for the government, because the church did not follow the government's education and health policies, and did not implement apartheid legislation. The church was not at the forefront of opposing apartheid in the early years, but it became very active in later years, during the struggle.[3]

Anglican Church

The London Missionary Society had already sent missionaries to the Cape Colony from 1799 onwards, and had established mission stations there. Despite that early mission work, the Anglican Church of Southern Africa's origins stem from the time when the British occupied the Cape Colony for the second time in 1806. The Anglican Church became the church for the English settlers and was the religion of the government, which gave the church a privileged position. A bishop was consecrated in the middle of the nineteenth century, and an Anglican province with several dioceses was formally established in 1870 as the English-speaking

---

1   Brain, Joy, 1997, pp. 195–196; De Gruchy, John & de Gruchy, Steve, 2005, p. 95.
2   Brain, Joy, 1997, pp. 198–200, 209.
3   Brain, Joy, 1997, pp. 195–197, 209. About 7.1 per cent of the South African population belonged to the Roman Catholic Church according to Census 2001. The church had approximately 79.4 per cent 'Black African', 11.1 per cent 'Coloured', 0.6 per cent "Indian or Asian", and 8.9 per cent 'White' members. Census 2001, 2004, pp. 27–28.

population grew. Great tensions arose at times between its mission work among the indigenous population and its close alliance with the colonial administration. For example, missionaries often took the side of the indigenous people in their struggle for justice and human rights.[4]

The Anglican Church had a privileged position when the Union of South Africa was created in 1910. The church, however, had an ambivalent stance towards racial discrimination, because it did not interfere in the government's policies. The church's position changed dramatically when the National Party came to power in 1948, and the Anglican Church started to oppose racial discrimination. The Episcopal Synod adopted the same resolution as the 1948 Lambeth Conference concerning the equality of all people regardless of 'race' or colour, despite external pressure to decide otherwise. The church made several compromises that reduced its credibility, although it simultaneously criticised the apartheid government. Together with many other churches, it increased its opposition to apartheid in the second half of the twentieth century, and many prominent Anglican leaders became important in the struggle for democratisation.[5]

Methodist Church

The Methodist Church of Southern Africa has a similar history to that of the Anglican Church, except that it was not connected with the government in the same way that the Anglican Church was. Members of the church arrived during the British occupation, and the Wesleyan Missionary Society in England sent the first missionary to the Cape Colony in 1815.[6]

The church was established not only to serve 'White' immigrants but also as a mission to 'Black' people. The Wesleyan Missionary Society's policy of ministering to both immigrants and indigenous people was not without tensions. The Methodist mission increased, and several mission stations were built. From the start the church had the largest number of 'Black' members among the mainline churches.

---

4   De Gruchy, John & de Gruchy, Steve, 2005, pp. 11–12, 36; Worsnip, Michael, 1991, pp. 1, 3, 5, 55.
5   De Gruchy, John & de Gruchy, Steve, 2005, pp. 53, 87. John de Gruchy states, for example, that the church was not critical of all racially discriminatory legislation, and was also conservative. De Gruchy, John & de Gruchy, Steve, 2005, p. 36. About 3.8 per cent of the South African population belonged to the Anglican Church of Southern Africa according to Census 2001. The church had approximately 64.3 per cent 'Black African', 20.9 per cent 'Coloured', 0.3 per cent 'Indian or Asian', and 14.5 per cent 'White' members. Census 2001, 2004, pp. 27–28.
6   Davenport, Rodney, 1997, p. 54; Hodgson, Janet, 1997, p. 75.

The church was committed to remaining united after the introduction of apartheid, even though its members worshipped in different buildings and belonged to different circuits based on colour. In 1948 the annual Methodist Conference adopted a resolution that no people, regardless of 'race', should be deprived of their constitutional rights. In 1958 the conference declared that the church should remain one, and that multi-racial co-operation was the will of God.[7]

Lutheran Churches

Unlike the Anglican and the Methodist churches, the Lutheran church did not come to South Africa as a single united church that served immigrants and carried out mission work among indigenous people.

The Evangelical Lutheran Church in Southern Africa (ELCSA) is by far the largest Lutheran church in South Africa, and has its background in mission work among indigenous people. Nine Lutheran mission societies from Germany and Scandinavia arrived in South Africa in the nineteenth century. They established congregations along 'Black' ethnic boundaries with a European church pattern. The mission societies started hospitals and schools, and a considerable number of missionary school pupils attended a Lutheran school.[8] The fragmented parts of Lutheranism began to consolidate in the mid-twentieth century: former regional churches merged and created dioceses within a united church, resulting in the establishment of ELCSA in 1975. The other Lutheran churches in Sothern Africa were invited to be part of the unification process, but they rejected the invitation.[9]

The Evangelical Lutheran Church in Southern Africa Cape Church (ELCSA-Cape) was founded by German immigrants early in South Africa's history – when the Cape Colony belonged to the Dutch East India Company. German settlers came to the colony in the middle of the seventeenth century, and formed a large proportion of its 'White' population. The first German Lutheran congregation was

---

7   Davenport, Rodney, 1997, p. 54; Hodgson, Janet, 1997, p. 75; De Gruchy, John & de Gruchy, Steve, 2005, pp. 13–14, 52; Minutes of the Seventy-Fifth Annual Conference of the Methodist Church of South Africa, 1958, p. 65. About 7.4 per cent of the South African population belonged to the Methodist Church of Southern Africa, according to Census 2001. The church had approximately 84.6 per cent 'Black African', 4.9 per cent 'Coloured', 0.1 per cent "Indian or Asian", and 10.4 per cent 'White' members. Census 2001, 2004, pp. 27–28.
8   Scriba, George & Lislerud, Gunnar, 1997, pp. 173, 177–179. In 1925, 18 per cent of all missionary school pupils attended a Lutheran school, but only one of twelve missionary hospitals was Lutheran. Scriba, George & Lislerud, Gunnar, 1997, p. 190.
9   Scriba, George & Lislerud, Gunnar, 1997, pp. 175–179, 181, 193.

founded in 1780 in Cape Town, and other congregations were soon established. Ministers came from Germany to serve in the congregations, and various mission societies also assisted with ministers. The congregations in the Cape formed a German Evangelical synod in 1895, and became a church in 1961. ELCSA-Cape's membership of the Lutheran World Federation was suspended at the LWF's Budapest assembly in 1984 because it had not publicly rejected apartheid. This suspension was lifted in 1992 in the light of ongoing unity discussions with the other Lutheran churches. ELCSA-Cape has been part of unity talks, but is still not united with the other Lutheran churches in Southern Africa.[10]

The Evangelical Lutheran Church in Southern Africa Natal-Transvaal (ELCSA N-T) was founded by a merger of ELCSA/Hermannsburg and ELCSA/Transvaal in 1981. The two former churches were started by two German mission societies. The Berlin Mission came to South Africa and opened their first mission centre in 1847, and the Hermannsburg Mission started mission work in Natal in 1857. A majority of the members of ELCSA N-T are descendents of German settlers and missionaries, as well as people of Scandinavian and American background. ELCSA N-T was not a member of the LWF when ELCSA-Cape was suspended in

---

10 Lutheran Churches in the World, 1989, p. 111; Scriba, George & Lislerud, Gunnar, 1997, pp. 174, 186, 193; "In Christ-Hope for the World", LWF Report No. 19/20, 1985, pp. 179–180. LWF declared at the general assembly in Dar es Salaam: "We especially appeal to our White member churches in southern Africa to recognize that the situation in southern Africa constitutes a status confessionis. This means that, on the basis of faith and in order to manifest the unity of the church, churches would publicly and unequivocally reject the existing apartheid system". In Christ - a new community, 1977, p. 180. The Report of the executive committee to the sixth assembly stated that the Evangelical Lutheran Churches of European background in Southern Africa had been hesitant to affirm some of the statements against apartheid, and neither had they been ready to declare clearly their opposition to the system of apartheid. The executive committee even wrote that the 'Black' churches were disappointed at the lack of support on the part of the 'White' churches, and that these churches stood in opposition to statements they had made. The Appeal to the Churches issued at the Swakopmund FELCSA meeting in 1975 was recognised as a call to all Lutheran churches in southern Africa. The appeal was probably the first statement about apartheid made by the Lutheran churches, and it played a significant role in the churches' emerging policies. The efforts towards the integration of ELCSA and ELCSA-Cape were not regarded as sufficient, in spite of statements such as the Declaration of Intention Concerning Church Unity by the Convocation of Pastors of ELCSA, Cape Church, and the Swakopmund - Appeal at the FELCSA meeting in 1975. Their rejection of apartheid was regarded as weak. Thus the LWF general assembly in Budapest in 1984 suspended the church's membership. Scriba, George & Lislerud, Gunnar, 1997, pp. 192–193.

1984, but it was accepted as a member when the suspension of ELCSA-Cape was lifted by the executive of the LWF in 1992. The church has been part of Lutheran unification discussions, but is still not united with the other Lutheran churches.[11]

ELCSA, ELCSA-Cape and ELCSA N-T belong to LUCSA, the Lutheran Community in Southern Africa, to which most of the main Lutheran churches in Southern Africa belong. The organisation is a common platform for cooperation across national and ethnic boundaries, and it works in close relationship with the LWF. ELCSA-Cape, ELCSA N-T, and ELCIN-GELC in Namibia are also members of UELCSA, an organisation for common matters among Lutheran churches with a German background. The divided Lutheran churches that are members of the LWF are based on two former 'White' churches and a major Lutheran church with a mostly 'Black' membership, but also with members of 'Coloured' and 'Indian or Asian' background. The division is a challenge, and several unification discussions have been initiated. Unification has been on the LWF agenda, but also indirectly through the TRC and the SACC. It is significant that the Lutheran churches together have the highest percentage of 'Black' members and the lowest proportion of 'White' members among the mainline churches in South Africa, according to Census 2001.[12]

---

11 Lutheran Churches in the World, 1989, p. 112; Scriba, George & Lislerud, Gunnar, 1997, pp. 175–178, 193. ELCSA/Hermannsburg was a member of the LWF from 1963, and ELCSA/Transvaal had so-called permanent connections with the LWF. The merger of the two churches as ELCSA N-T meant that it had to apply for new membership when it was formed. They applied for membership just before ELCSA-Cape and ELCIN-GELC were suspended at the general assembly in Budapest 1984, but withdrew their application and applied again when the suspension of ELCSA-Cape and ELCIN-GELC was lifted by the executive of the LWF in 1992. ELCSA N-T was accepted into LWF membership in 1992. Lutheran Churches in the World: A handbook, 1989, pp. 91–92. Confirmed by phone call to former bishop Dieter Lilje 2014-12-12.

12 Scriba, George & Lislerud, Gunnar, 1997, pp. 181, 184–185, 191; Farisani, Elelwani Bethuel, 2008, pp. 40–44; "[…] Lutheran Church, too, was racially divided; its white members consistently refused to join the unity movement that was to become the Evangelical Lutheran Church. […]". Truth and Reconciliation Commission of South Africa Report, Vol. 4, 1998, pp. 68–69. The SACC stated at the Cape Town Consultation that special attention was give to the Dutch Reformed family to challenge the 'White' Dutch Reformed church to unite with the other churches and become one church. This statement was also indirectly aimed at other churches that were divided. Cape Town Consultation Proposal for Action, 1991, p. 105. About 2.5 per cent of the South African population belonged to the Lutheran churches according to Census 2001. The churches had 87.1 per cent 'Black African', 10.5 per cent 'Coloured', 0.1 per cent 'Indian or Asian', and 2.3 per cent 'White' members. Census 2001, 2004, pp. 27–28.

Apostolic Faith Mission of South Africa

Many Pentecostal and charismatic churches in South Africa have their background in a movement started around the Dutch Reformed missionary Petrus le Roux in the town Wakkerstroom. He was a student of the NGK leader Andrew Murray, who was known for his powerful preaching. Murray's teaching, together with influences from John Alexander Dowie in Zion City, Illinois and his magazine *Leaves of Healing* had an impact on le Roux. The evangelist Daniel Bryant from the church in Illinois arrived in South Africa in 1904. Bryant baptised le Roux and many other converts in Wakkerstroom, which marked the beginning of the Pentecostal and Zionist movement in South Africa.[13]

As a consequence of the new movement and his baptism, Petrus le Roux had to resign from the NGK. He had adopted another confession, but most of his Zulu congregations agreed with his teaching, and they established the first Zulu Zionist Church. The Zion movement of Wakkerstroom grew rapidly and spread through the country. Le Roux later became hesitant about a development that he regarded as syncretism in the Zionist Church, and he left the movement and moved to the Witwatersrand. There he came into contact with the Pentecostal missionary John G. Lack who had arrived from the USA, and together they established the Apostolic Faith Mission of South Africa (AFM) in 1908. The first General Conference was held in 1911, when its constitution was adopted. The Rules and Regulations of AFM were adopted a year later. The church grew especially among 'Black' people and Afrikaans-speaking 'White' people.[14]

The AFM had a close relationship with the Dutch Reformed Church and the government. The 'White' members of the AFM were loyal to the National Party's apartheid policy. 'Black', 'Coloured', and 'Indian' sections of the church were gradually created, controlled and monitored by the 'White' section of the church. After an intense internal process in the church, apartheid was rejected in 1985 by the General Missionary Council. A committee was established to unify the different sections, and the church celebrated becoming a united church irrespective of ethnic background in April 1996. AFM is the largest Pentecostal church in South Africa, and one of the oldest in that tradition.[15]

---

13 De Gruchy, John, 2009, p. 84; Anderson, Allan H., & Pillay, Gerald J., 1997, p. 229; Burger, Isak, & Nel, Marius, 2008, pp. 24–29, 34–37, 80–81.
14 De Gruchy, John, 2009, pp. 84–85; Anderson, Allan H., & Pillay, Gerald J., 1997, pp. 229–234; Burger, Isak, & Nel, Marius, 2008, pp. 24–29, 34–37, 80–81.
15 Anderson, Allan H., & Pillay, Gerald J., 1997, pp. 229–234; Burger, Isak, & Nel, Marius, 2008, pp. 144, 220, 276, 301, 415, 431. Japie LaPorta, in the book *The Globalization of*

5.2 Congregations on the Ground

In the section that follows, the six case study congregations – situated in Johannesburg, Cape Town, and Durban – will be described. St Peter Claver in Pimville belongs to the Roman Catholic Church, and is in Soweto, Johannesburg. St Thomas' in Linden belongs to the Anglican Church of Southern Africa, and is in the northern suburbs of Johannesburg. Athlone Methodist Church belongs to the Methodist Church of Southern Africa, and is in Athlone on the Cape Flats, Cape Town. The Lutheran Church in Bellville belongs to ELCSA-Cape, and is in Bellville in the Tygerberg area of greater Cape Town. City Harvest Ministries belongs to the Apostolic Faith Mission of South Africa, and is in Ntuzuma township in Durban. St Michael's congregation is part of the Durban Central parish of ELCSA, and is in the Durban city centre.

Johannesburg – the Place of Gold

Johannesburg was founded on farm land that was unwanted because of its poor condition. However, gold was found on surrounding farms, and later on the Witwatersrand farm itself, in 1886. The discovery prompted a gold rush, and the population of Johannesburg grew by over a hundred thousand during the last years of the nineteenth century. People arrived from other parts of the country, from Europe, and from other African countries. The city was named after the two commissioners, Christian Johannes Joubert and Johannes Rissick, who had confirmed the discovery of gold in the area. For many years to come gold mines were the most important industry in Johannesburg; but later various other industries were developed, and the city became the economic centre of South Africa.[16]

The city of Johannesburg is today the provincial capital of Gauteng. It is South Africa's industrial, financial, and commercial centre, and many companies have their headquarters there. The city is also the home of the Johannesburg Stock

---

Pentecostalism, has described the unification of AFM. He states that the unification was only the first step, and that the AFM has to move towards a broader expression of unity, including ecumenical unity. LaPorta, Japie, 1999, pp. 151–167. In 2001 about 0.5 per cent of the South African population belonged to the Apostolic Faith Mission of South Africa, but 8.2 per cent of the South African population belonged to a Pentecostal or Charismatic church. The AFM had 60.5 per cent 'Black African', 11.3 per cent 'Coloured', 0.5 per cent 'Indian or Asian', and 27.7 per cent 'White' members. Census 2001, 2004, pp. 27–28.

16 Standard Encyclopaedia of Southern Africa, Vol. 6, 1972, p. 212; Encyclopedia of South Africa, 2011, p. 157.

Exchange. Industries consist primarily of gold mining, but the city is also an engineering and manufacturing centre. O.R. Tambo International Airport is South Africa's principal airport, and together with major developed road and rail networks, it makes the city a transport hub for southern Africa. Johannesburg has several major hospitals, museums, universities, and business schools. A number of media groups that own newspapers, magazines, TV stations, and radio channels are also based in the city.[17]

Johannesburg reflects almost a century of racially-based socially engineering; but it also reflects the changes brought by democratisation. The city of Johannesburg was never free of residential segregation according to 'race'. 'Black' people were not allowed to own or reside on land declared as a 'mining area', according to the Gold Law of 1885. The first population removal took place in 1904, when 'Black' people were relocated from other areas in the city to Klipspruit. Mine workers lived in the vicinity of the mines, and public service workers and domestic workers were accommodated in compounds dotted around the town and in servants' quarters in 'White' residential areas. Several forced removals took place, but the most radical change happened after the Group Areas Act was implemented from 1950 onwards.[18]

The city is marked by enormous contrasts, with skyscrapers and informal settlements, centres of education and a lack of good schools, luxury shopping centres and areas lacking clean water and sanitation. Democratisation made it possible for those who were previously not allowed to stay in the city to move to urban centres for work. Crime has increased, and companies, businesses, and the stock exchange have moved from the city centre to the northern suburbs. People with economic potential have also moved to the suburbs, and 'gated communities' have been formed, resulting in economic segregation.[19]

The City of Johannesburg Metropolitan Municipality had 4 434 827 inhabitants, according to Census 2011. This makes the city the largest in South Africa. There were 76.4 per cent who identified themselves as 'Black African', 12.3 per cent as 'White', 5.6 per cent as 'Coloured', and 4.9 per cent as 'Indian or Asian'. There were slightly fewer 'Black African' and 'Coloured', but more 'White' and 'Indian or Asian' people in Johannesburg, compared with the rest of the country. According to Census 2011, in Johannesburg 23.1 per cent had isiZulu as their first language,

---

17 The New Encyclopædia Britannica, Vol. 6, 1986, pp. 565–566; Standard Encyclopaedia of Southern Africa, Vol. 6, 1972, pp. 211–212, 224.
18 Parnell, S. M. & Pirie, G. H., 1991, pp. 129–131, 134–137.
19 Encyclopedia of South Africa, 2011, p. 157.

19.8 per cent English, 9.5 per cent Sesotho, 7.6 per cent Setswana, 7.2 per cent Sepedi, and 7.2 per cent Afrikaans.[20]

St Peter Claver, Pimville – Roman Catholic Church

St Peter Claver congregation is situated in Soweto, which is an abbreviated form of 'South Western Townships'. The area name Pimville, where the congregation is situated, was one of the first townships to be founded, and is named after James Howard Pim, a councillor in Johannesburg in the early twentieth century. The township grew together with other townships into the greater township that became known as 'South Western Townships' or 'Soweto' – the result of the increasing number of 'Black' mine workers who moved to Johannesburg and needed a place to live.[21]

The 'Black' population grew rapidly because of the economic opportunities offered by the mines, and rural people started to move into the city. Soweto became an area reserved for the 'Black' population as a result of apartheid's Group Areas Act. 'Black' people were forcibly removed to Soweto, or directed to live there. During apartheid the township was unplanned and overcrowded, with inadequate housing and poor infrastructure. It was a separate municipality, but after democratisation it became part of the City of Johannesburg Metropolitan Municipality. Soweto is an area full of contrasts. There are still areas where people live in poor conditions, with high crime and high unemployment; while other areas have large luxury houses where an elite group of South Africans live. Pimville can be regarded as typical of the older kind of South African township. There are several so-called 'council single family houses' that have since been improved. Some houses have been extended using corrugated iron sheets, and there are also informal settlements. Changed economic conditions are evident in the form of bigger modern houses with larger plots, and new shopping centres.[22]

---

20 Census 2011, City of Johannesburg Metropolitan Municipality, Statistics South Africa, 2013. Census 2011 identified that there were 79.2 per cent 'Black African', 8.9 per cent 'Coloured', 2.5 per cent 'Indian or Asian', 8.9 per cent 'White', and 0.5 per cent 'Other' in South Africa. Census 2011, Census in Brief, 2012, p. 21. The spelling of the official languages of the Republic of South Africa follows that used in the constitution. The Constitution of the Republic of South Africa, 1996, chapter 1, section 6.

21 Standard Encyclopaedia of Southern Africa, Vol. 10, 1974, p. 206; Encyclopedia of South Africa, 2011, p. 274.

22 St Peter Claver, Catholic Church, Pimville, 1928–2008, 80th Anniversary, 2008, p. 6, Church Publication; Standard Encyclopaedia of Southern Africa, Vol. 10, 1974, p. 206; Encyclopedia of South Africa, 2011, p. 274.

St Peter Claver is part of the Catholic Archdiocese of Johannesburg, which in turn is a member of the Southern African Catholic Bishops' Conference (SACBC), which is a formal geographic body of 24 dioceses and bishops created to support and coordinate common matters. The bishops in the SACBC maintain unity with each other and with the Bishop of Rome. St Peter Claver has over two thousand families as members.[23] It belongs to the Soweto district within the diocese, together with other congregations in the area. One of the biggest and most famous congregations is Regina Mundi in Rockville, where people gathered for meetings and debates during the time of apartheid. The Regina Mundi church was attacked by the previous regime's police during the Soweto uprising in 1976. Several Roman Catholic schools in Soweto are run and owned by the diocese.[24]

St Peter Claver was founded as a mission by the Missionary Oblates of Mary Immaculate (OMI) in 1928, and it is still served by priests from that religious order. The mission was also served by various women's religious orders primarily to assist the people with health services, education, and catechism. A Catholic school was established in 1809 by Dominican sisters. St Peter Claver Catholic primary school is still operating, and admits pupils from the area and is part of the congregation's church complex. A women's religious order, the Franciscans of Mary, has a small convent in Kliptown, which is within the congregation's boundaries.[25]

The congregation's name is derived from a saint who was a Spanish Jesuit priest who became a missionary in Latin America. According to the legend, St Peter Claver ministered to slaves from Africa, and he later became the patron saint of slaves. He was remembered for baptising many hundred thousand people. In their anniversary booklet the congregation compared him with people like Steven Bantu Biko and Martin Luther King Jr.[26] The name of the congregation is a legacy of European mission with its hope for the expansion of the Christian faith – but it

---

23 St Peter Claver, Catholic Church, Pimville, 1928–2008, 80th Anniversary, 2008, p. 30, Church Publication; St Peter Claver Parish, Pimville, Soweto, 2011, Website. The SACBC covers dioceses in Botswana, South Africa and Swaziland.
24 The Roman Catholic schools in Soweto are: St Matthew's Private Secondary School, founded in 1863, St Angela's Primary School, founded in 1863, St Matthew's Primary School, founded in 1818, Immaculata Secondary School, founded in 1864, St John Berchman's Primary School, founded in 1804, St Martin de Porres, founded in 1804, and St Peter Claver Primary School, founded in 1809.
25 St Peter Claver, Catholic Church, Pimville, 1928–2008, 80th Anniversary, 2008, pp. 12, 15–18, Church Publication.
26 St Peter Claver, Catholic Church, Pimville, 1928–2008, 80th Anniversary, 2008, pp. 12, 15–18, Church Publication.

also stands for political resistance. The legacy of mission is visible, furthermore, in the artwork of statues and paintings in European images.[27] However, the European mission congregation's heritage was not only visible in the name, fixtures, and various documents. The congregation's website declares:

> The Church, as St Paul stated in one of his letters, is "a Church which is self-supporting, self-administrating and self-propagating". St Peter Claver parish had to start embracing the fact that the Missionary time is over – no more Irish, German, Belgian priests, no more foreign monies to run the parishes. Yes, the local Church is faced with the challenge to be self sustaining – "to get off your crutches, and to walk".
>
> The Missionaries were very helpful – great men and women. Most of our Black children, some of whom are now important members of the community, were taught and educated by them. We thank them for putting up theses buildings and for providing the means of development for our children and parishioners. Those men and women are our unsung heroes. The challenge for us, children of the soil, is to improve their work, even making it better for ourselves – so that our children in the next generation may say, "indeed our ancestors left us a heritage and legacy we can be proud of, and with which we can empathise and identify.[28]

The text on the website stresses that a new time had arrived for the congregation. This was a new phase when people in the congregation had to take responsibility. Priests and missionaries were no longer coming from abroad, and less economic assistance for church activities and buildings could be expected from outside. The text continued to describe how the congregation had raised up a young man for the priesthood, and many lay groups and individuals were engaged in the congregation's life and future. They also announced further plans for the congregation that needed support, but also the development of church services and spiritual growth that was taking place. The explanation revealed that the congregation had a relatively long history with a heritage from the time when missionary religious orders came to South Africa. The congregation was growing in numbers, and the people in the congregation were ready for future challenges.[29]

The congregation, according to their anniversary booklet and their website, had over two thousand families as members.[30] Church services included a lot of children, youth, young adults, men and women, and middle-aged and elderly

---

27 Observation Protocol 2011-02-27.
28 St Peter Claver Parish, Pimville, Soweto, 2011, Website.
29 St Peter Claver Parish, Pimville, Soweto, 2011, Website.
30 St Peter Claver, Catholic Church, Pimville, 1928–2008, 80th Anniversary, 2008, p. 30, Church Publication; St Peter Claver Parish, Pimville, Soweto, 2011, Website.

people.[31] They had people from all age groups, but they were 'predominantly female'[32] according to the church council's own description. Those who attended church services and were members of the congregation were about 70 per cent women and 30 per cent men. On average, more than a thousand people attended church every Sunday – but, as the church council put it, 'It varies depending on the Sunday'.[33] One of the tasks for the church council was to extend and renovate the church building in order to accommodate more people.[34]

The church council said that most of the people who came to St Peter Claver lived in the area. The congregation was primarily for people who lived in Pimville and who belonged to that community. The congregation was also, according to the council, for all who were born in Pimville, and for any others who wanted to join it, even if they lived far away.[35]

St Peter Claver had several members who lived in other parts of Johannesburg but who travelled there for church services and church activities. The church council said that some people liked their vibrant way of worship with, for example, drums, music, choirs, and dances in a very African style of worship.[36] One of the council members explained the character of the services in these terms: "In fact, this is the vibrant church that I have been talking about, listen to the way we worship...the type of worship that Africans like. Others who are supposed to go to White parishes come to worship here".[37] The church council did not think that it was a problem that people travelled to a particular congregation, and said that it was a matter of choice. Some people liked the way St Peter Claver conducted their church services, and others preferred a different style of church life and worship. Another of the members of the church council said: "If you prefer people who don't sing you would go to church there and if you like music like us you come here".[38] The church council claimed that there was a difference between church services in the south and in the north of Johannesburg.

The diverse forms of worship made the church council able to accept people coming to their congregation. The council's description of people travelling from Soweto or from other parts of Johannesburg was evident outside the

---

31 Observation Protocol 2011-02-27.
32 Church Council Interview Protocol 2011-02-27.
33 Church Council Interview Protocol 2011-02-27.
34 Church Council Interview Protocol 2011-02-27.
35 Church Council Interview Protocol 2011-02-27.
36 Church Council Interview Protocol 2011-02-27.
37 Church Council Interview Protocol 2011-02-27.
38 Church Council Interview Protocol 2011-02-27.

church building: the huge car park, a green lawn, revealed that many people drove to church. Several of the cars were new and large, suggesting that members came from diverse economic backgrounds.[39] St Peter Claver experiences the same developments as many other congregations in the townships: people who have experienced greater prosperity move to areas with better conditions, but they are not able to find services in their own language or with attractive styles of worship. As result they have to travel to the congregation for Sunday services and other activities.

St Thomas' Anglican Church, Linden – Anglican Church of Southern Africa

The parish of St Thomas' in Linden belongs to the Anglican Diocese of Johannesburg. Thirteen congregations, including St Thomas', make up an archdeaconry, one of six in Johannesburg.

The Anglican Church of Southern Africa has 28 dioceses in seven countries in the southern part of Africa. The dioceses form a Province whose Provincial office and Archbishop are based in Cape Town. The Province is independent of other Anglican Provinces, but with them is in communion with the Archbishop of Canterbury, and thus is part of the Anglican Communion.[40]

Linden is a residential suburb in the north of Johannesburg, which is part of a greater area called Randburg. The name of the suburb originates from Gert van der Linden, who had many mining interests in Johannesburg. Before democratisation, Randburg was a separate municipality; today it is part of the City of Johannesburg Metropolitan Municipality.[41] Linden is mainly a residential suburb of houses, but there are also some flats and townhouses. The suburb has a number of nurseries, schools, retirement villages and old ages homes, bringing the congregation a broad

---

39   Observation Protocol 2011-02-27. Special fundraising projects for the congregation were organised by members and had to be approved by the church council. One of these projects was a trip to Cape Town that included travel, hotel and all fares to the cost of ZAR 6 500 each. St Peter Claver Parish, Pimville, Soweto, 2011, Website. The congregation also had a soup kitchen run by one of the groups in the congregation and by members of the voluntary organisation, the Society of St Vincent de Paul, reaching out to the poor. Church Council Interview Protocol 2011-02-27; St Peter Claver, Catholic Church, Pimville, 1928–2008, 80th Anniversary, 2008, p. 31, Church Publication.
40   Constitution and Canons of the Anglican Church of Southern Africa, 2012, p. 17–20b; Anglican Church of Southern Africa, Diocese of Johannesburg, Archdeaconries, 2014, Website.
41   Standard Encyclopaedia of Southern Africa, Vol. 9, 1973. p. 646.

spectrum of people of different ages.[42] Linden can be characterised as a typical residential or suburban area in a South African town or city that, before democratisation, was reserved for the 'White' population. However, the democratic South Africa is evident in the greater ethnic diversity among the residents of the area.

St Thomas' congregation was formed in 1952, but there was no church building to start with. The congregation had only a rectory, and church services were performed outdoors under a couple of marquees. The church building was completed in 1961; several extensions to and renovations of the church followed, as well as the construction of additional buildings. The church's architecture and fittings are very similar to the English Anglican tradition; the exception is a carved triptych in the narthex, made by a Zimbabwean artist to bridge the cultural gap between the African and English artistic styles. Music became a special feature of the congregation early on, and this is still very evident in church services, concerts, and music activities.[43]

In 2011 the congregation had several staff members who were either employed or self-supporting – a very rare situation in South African congregations. The number of staff suggests that the congregation was quite rich in both economic resources and volunteers. They had a rector, two self-supporting ministers, one retired assistant minister, a full-time music director, a secretary, a bookkeeper, a gardener, laundry and ironing staff, and an assistant cleaner. They had licensed lay ministers and a group of Anglicare counsellors, besides different guilds and various support groups.[44]

The congregation can be characterised as Anglo-Catholic in ethos, a fact that was emphasised by several members who noted that the eucharist was central and was frequently celebrated.[45] The Anglo-Catholic tradition of the congregation was stressed in various congregational documents, was regarded as an important

---

42 St Thomas' Anglican Church Linden, Parish Profile, 2011, p. 7, Church Publication.
43 St Thomas' Anglican Church Linden, Parish Profile, 2011, p. 4, Church Publication; Music at St Thomas', Leaflet about music at St Thomas' Anglican Church Linden, Church Publication; The St Thomas's Magazine April 2010, 2010. p. 7, Church Publication.
44 St Thomas' Anglican Church Linden, Parish Profile, 2011, p. 6, 12, Church Publication. The Anglicare counsellors are eleven people who are trained in counselling and are accredited by the church. At St Thomas' they volunteer in assisting the congregation and the community in various aspects such as victim support, relationship problems, and trauma.
45 Church Council Interview Protocol 2011-03-06.

part of the congregation's life, and was seen as something to be continued in the future.[46]

Most of the people who came to worship and were part of the congregation's many activities were members of the congregation and lived in Linden. There were, however, also some who lived beyond the congregation's boundaries and came to St Thomas' for services, for activities, and as volunteers.[47] There were 1 700 individual members on the parish roll, and the average weekly attendance was more than 500 people.[48] When the church council was asked why people came from other areas to participate at St Thomas', one of the members replied: "It is a very active church, it's very busy and I think it is because they could contribute and I think the spirit is good".[49] The many church activities, the various forms of worship, and the involvement of lay people in church life were also emphasised in several church documents and by the church council as factors that seemed to draw many people to the congregation.

The majority of the members were 'White' and were of English (or at least British) descent, but there were several members from other South African backgrounds. That the majority of the 'White' people were English-speaking was due to the fact that Johannesburg had historically been an area where many British immigrants settled, and most of the northern suburbs had been classified as 'White' under the previous government.[50]

The various church services on Sundays seemed to attract different kinds of people and age groups. The eight o'clock service, using the South African Prayer Book, mostly attracted senior citizens of a predominantly British background, with women predominating. The later family service, mainly following the Anglican Prayer Book, was more ethnically diverse and attracted families, children and youth. The Sunday school and St Thomas' youth church ran at the same time as the family service. There was also an afternoon service in an indigenous language, mostly for domestic workers in the area; and there was an evening service.[51]

St Thomas' congregational profile stated that they were a congregation of diverse people. The congregation had, according to their own perception in their congregation profile, a growing participation of people from all 'races'. This observation

---

46 St Thomas' Anglican Church Linden, Parish Profile, 2011, p. 2, Church Publication.
47 Church Council Interview Protocol 2011-03-06.
48 St Thomas' Anglican Church Linden, Parish Profile, 2011, p. 7, Church Publication.
49 Church Council Interview Protocol 2011-03-06.
50 Observation Protocol 2011-03-06.
51 Observation Protocol 2011-03-06; Linden St Thomas, Normal Schedule of Services, 2011, Website.

could be a sign that an increasing number of people from different ethnic groups had either moved into the area or were commuting to services at the church. The congregational profile said that they enjoyed social gatherings and wanted to create a sense of belonging in their fellowship.[52]

St Thomas' Church follows a pattern that is typical of English-speaking congregations in cities or suburbs that have become more ethnically diverse since democratisation. People who have benefited from economic opportunities are moving into the area and becoming involved in the nearest congregation that uses an accessible language. Suburban churches that use Afrikaans do not reflect the same development, because the majority of people do not have sufficient knowledge of Afrikaans.[53]

Cape Town, the Mother City

Cape Town is the oldest urban area in South Africa, and early in its history became one of the first ethnically-diverse places in the world. The settlement was originally used only as a stop-over and provisioning post for merchant fleets before Europeans began to visit the southern tip of Africa. The fleets stopped at the Cape to load fresh water and to exchange goods for cattle with the Khoikhoi people. The Dutch East India Company occupied the area in 1652, and Jan van Riebeeck became the leader who built a fort and supply station to serve the trading company on its route between Europe and Asia. A small colony was soon established in the Cape with emigrants from Europe. The story is told that Van Riebeeck planted a hedge to separate the settlers and the Khoikhoi people – the beginning of ethnic separation.[54]

In the early eighteenth century the company began to import slaves from Mozambique and Madagascar, and from as far as Indonesia, India and Ceylon. The Cape slaves had very diverse backgrounds in language, religion and social context. The colony grew, and new areas were incorporated and developed. Marriages between people of diverse backgrounds were not uncommon in the Cape. Great Britain took control of the Dutch colonies, capturing the Cape in 1795. The colony

---

52 St Thomas' Anglican Church Linden, Parish Profile, 2011, pp. 3, 8, Church Publication.
53 Jon Orman has explained the strong connection between the Afrikaans language and the Afrikaner community. The language is not widely spoken, especially since democratisation, and the language serves the Afrikaner myth of a homogeneous group. Orman, Jon, 2009, pp. 112–116, 120–124, 130–133.
54 Thompson, Leonard, 2001, pp. 32, 35–38; Cook, G. P., 1991, p. 26.

was returned to the Netherlands by a treaty in 1803, but Great Britain returned in 1806 and again occupied the Cape.[55]

When the British came to the Cape they immediately announced that there had to be absolute separation between the people in the colony and the Xhosa. The British immigrants in the Cape were the first not to assimilate with people of different backgrounds. They had no interest in the Cape beyond the peninsula, but the colony expanded as (mainly Dutch) farmers moved further inland, and especially as diamonds and gold were discovered in Kimberley and on the Witwatersrand to the north. After a succession of wars between the two Boer Republics and the British colonies of Natal and Cape, the Union of South Africa was created in 1910. From the beginning the Union required that 'Black Africans' should carry passes and seek exemption to live outside specific locations. There were areas with mixed populations, but when the National Party came to power in 1948 and the policy of apartheid was introduced, a huge part of the population was allocated to new areas.[56]

The city of Cape Town has been formed by many years of social engineering that has structured it along the lines of separate ethnic groups, reinforcing economic injustices. The extent of change to the city following democratisation has depended on economic conditions and socio-economic developments. The city attracts many 'Black African' migrants who find residence in one of the townships; and a large part of the population continues to live in poor conditions.[57]

Census 2011 estimated that the City of Cape Town Metropolitan Municipality had a total population of 3 740 025 people, making it the second largest city in South Africa. There were 42.4 per cent who identified themselves as 'Coloured', 38.6 per cent as 'Black African', 15.7 per cent as 'White', 1.4 per cent as 'Indian or Asian', and 1.9 per cent as 'Other'. The statistics show that a greater proportion of 'Coloureds' live in this municipality, compared with numbers in the rest of the country. The Western Cape Province has the highest population of 'Coloureds', who make up almost half the population of the province. There are also proportionally more 'White' and fewer 'Black African' and 'Indian or Asian' people, compared with the rest of South Africa. According to the Census 2011, of first-language speakers in Cape Town, 34.9 per cent are Afrikaans, 29.2 per cent isiXhosa, and 27.8 per cent English.[58] IsiZulu is one of the most widely-spoken

---

55 Thompson, Leonard, 2001, pp. 51–52; Cook, G. P., 1991, p. 26.
56 Thompson, Leonard, 2001, pp. 53, 56, 115–121; Cook, G. P., 1991, pp. 27–29.
57 Cook, G. P., 1991, pp. 39–42.
58 Census 2011, City of Cape Town Metropolitan Municipality, Statistics South Africa, 2012; Census 2011, Census in Brief, 2012, p. 21.

languages in South Africa, but it is virtually absent in the municipality; by contrast, isiXhosa as a first language is well represented. People with either Afrikaans or English as their first language are also well represented in the municipality. This is because most 'Coloureds' have Afrikaans as their first language, while some are English-speaking.

Athlone Methodist Church – Methodist Church of Southern Africa

The Methodist Church in Athlone has a history closely connected with the area where the church is placed. Athlone is part of the Cape Flats, a sandy flat area on the periphery of the metropolitan area. It was not highly populated when the city first began to develop, and the houses were mostly wood and iron shanties. A school for the blind was opened in 1927, which the Earl of Athlone, who was the Governor-General of the Union of South Africa, was invited to open. The area that had been known as 'Milner' was renamed Athlone in honour of his visit and to avoid confusion with the area named Milnerton. The establishment of a metrorail in Cape Town, with a railway station in Athlone, contributed to economic growth and to an increase in the number of shops and business centres.[59]

Methodists who lived in the Athlone area worshipped in Mowbray together with many other people from nearby areas. Methodist church leaders of the Cape district decided to divide the Mowbray circuit in 1860. The Rondebosch circuit was created to serve the 'White' population, and the new Mowbray circuit served the immediate surrounding areas. The latter was also responsible for missionary work in the Cape Flats, including Athlone. In 1904 a simple wood and iron building, known as 'Blik kerk' ('zinc church'), was built on Church Street in Athlone to serve the growing number of people moving into the area. The population increased rapidly, and a new brick church was built in 1943 to accommodate the members.[60]

The Cape Flats changed dramatically from 1950 onwards as the Group Areas Act was implemented. Large numbers of people were forced to move from other areas to the Cape Flats. Athlone was declared an area for people classified 'Coloured'. The church building became too small as the population grew, and in 1958 a new church was built next to the older church, which then became the church

---

59 Athlone School for the Blind, History, 2014, Website.
60 Jacobs, G. A., 1992, Church Publication; Athlone Methodist Church, Church History, ca. 2010, Church Publication; Athlone Methodist Church, Athlone Society Profile, c.a. 2008, p. 1, Church Publication.

hall. The church has since been extended several times by building additional premises.[61]

The history of Athlone Methodist Church shows that many people in the congregation have gone through difficulties because of the previous government's policies. Members are mainly English-speaking, and Athlone Methodist Church is also known as the 'Coloured' cathedral in the Western Cape.[62] Today Athlone is mostly a residential area, but there are also a football stadium, a theatre, and a commercial area with shops and petrol stations. Several bus and taxi routes pass through Athlone, particularly along Klipfontein Road, the main route between the city centre and the N2 highway.[63]

Athlone Methodist Church belongs to the Methodist Church of Southern Africa (MCSA), which, besides South Africa, includes Lesotho, Mozambique, Swaziland and Namibia. The MCSA has twelve districts with bishops, and is part of the World Methodist Council. Athlone Methodist Church is part of the Cape of Good Hope District. There are nineteen circuits and societies in this District, and Athlone Methodist Church belongs to the Dumisani Circuit together with congregations in Langa, Pinelands, Rosebank and Thornton.[64]

Most of the people who belong to Athlone Methodist Church live in the area. One church council member explained: "I think most of them are from Belgravia. There are families that travel because they grow up in the church and are sentimental, you know, and still come to service".[65] Belgravia is an area in Athlone bordered by Klipfontein Road, Belgravia Road, Duine Street, and Johnston Road. Belgravia is opposite Athlone Stadium and across Klipfontein Road from the church. This explains partly why the church has a huge parking area. Klipfontein Road is very busy, and it is not an easy place for most people to walk. Crime is also high in the area, even though a police station is situated close to the Athlone shopping district.

The congregation has members who travel some distance to the church. A council member explained: "They come from the whole peninsula, eventually,

---

61 Jacobs, G. A., 1992, Church Publication; Athlone Methodist Church, Church History, ca. 2010, Church Publication; Athlone Methodist Church, Athlone Society Profile, c.a. 2008, p. 1, Church Publication.
62 Athlone Methodist Church, Athlone Society Profile, c.a. 2008, p. 1, Church Publication.
63 Scott, Peter, 1955, pp. 157, 161; Bickford-Smith, Vivian, & van Heyningen, Elizabeth, & Worden, Nigel, 2000, pp. 186–187.
64 The Methodist Church of Southern Africa, Circuits and Societies in the Cape of Good Hope District, 2014, Website.
65 Church Council Interview Protocol 2011-03-20.

Steenberg, Grassy Park, you name it, we even have people in Kayleden".[66] The areas mentioned by the councillor are on the opposite side of the Cape Flats. People have travelled to the church because they grew up in the congregation and wanted to remain members, even though there are several other Methodist churches closer to their homes.

The congregation had about 480 members at the time of this study, according to the congregation's statistics. The average Sunday attendance was 181 congregants. A church council member declared: "I think a large group, aged between forty and sixty".[67] The church council's estimation agreed with the congregation's own statistic that showed that half of the members came from the age group between 41 and 100 years old.[68] The church council was able to say that more people came to church at specific times. One member explained: "There are those who especially come for Christmas and Easter".[69] Attendance figures during special festival seasons showed that the congregation had a community that consisted of people who were regular participants and others who occasionally came to church. Common to all was that they predominantly came from the so-called 'Coloured' community, according to the congregation's own description.[70] A large number of congregations with 'Coloured' people are found in the Western Cape and Northern Cape Provinces. These congregations have not changed much ethnically since democratisation.[71]

Lutheran Church Bellville – Evangelical Lutheran Church in Southern Africa Cape Church

Bellville can be said to have been founded because the South African Railway Company began to build a railway line between Cape Town and Stellenbosch in 1859. The area was mainly farmland, but a village was developed because of the new transport system. The railway was opened in May 1862, with one of the stations at Durban Road. The government named the new village Bellville in

---

66 Church Council Interview Protocol 2011-03-20.
67 Church Council Interview Protocol 2011-03-20.
68 Athlone Methodist Church, Athlone Society Profile, c.a. 2008, p. 2, Church Publication.
69 Church Council Interview Protocol 2011-03-20.
70 Jacobs, G. A., 1992, Church Publication; Athlone Methodist Church, Church History, ca. 2010, Church Publication; Athlone Methodist Church, Athlone Society Profile, c.a. 2008, p. 1, Church Publication.
71 There are, according to Census 2011, about 48.8 per cent 'Coloured'in the Western Cape and 40.3 per cent 'Coloured' in the Northern Cape provinces. These provinces have the largest number of 'Coloureds' in South Africa. Census 2011, Census in Brief, 2012, p. 21.

honour of the governor, Charles Davidson Bell. For a long time there were only two hotels close to the station, and a small chapel called the Mission Hall that was erected by the German Lutheran congregation. Soon shops and a school were also built in the Bellville village.[72]

The area had fewer than a thousand inhabitants in the first decades of the twentieth century, a majority of whom were 'White' people; but there were also some 'Coloured' people who had settled in the area. The population began to increase rapidly, and Bellville develop into a town. About half of the people spoke Afrikaans, but English was mostly used as the main language. By the middle of the twentieth century, the three small towns of Parow, Bellville and Durbanville had grown into one urban area. There had been segregation according to 'race', but from 1950 the Group Areas Act reinforced segregation through the removal of 'non-White' people within the Tygerberg area. When apartheid was abolished after democratisation, people could live where they wished, according to preference and affordability, and the area's ethnic composition was totally changed.[73]

Bellville is now a suburban area in greater Cape Town, and is part of the City of Cape Town Metropolitan Municipality. Bellville has several shopping centres, hotels, schools, businesses, residential and industrial areas, etc. The University of the Western Cape, The Cape Peninsula University of Technology, and the Stikland Hospital for mental health care are also situated in Bellville. The N1 highway to Worcester and the north-west of the country goes through Bellville, as does Voortrekker Road to Somerset West.

The Lutheran Church in Bellville was founded in 1890 as a daughter congregation of St Martini in Long Street. A property was bought the same year, but services were held in different homes. A wooden chapel was built in 1898, and was extended in 1910. The congregation had to look for a new place to establish a church building because of the Group Areas Act. The chapel was handed over to the Lutherans of the 'Coloured' community. A new plot was bought in Middle Street, and a new church centre, the *Kreuzkirche* (Church of the Cross) was inaugurated in 1963; extensions and new buildings were added later. The architecture and fittings of the church are modern, and represent the style of the time when the church was built.[74]

---

72 Wesson, Alf, 1998, pp. 56–59, 60; Myburgh, D.W., 1998, pp. 67, 69–70, 79.
73 Wesson, Alf, 1998, pp. 56–59, 60; Myburgh, D.W., 1998, pp. 67, 69–70, 79; Census 2011, Bellville, Statistics South Africa, 2013.
74 Ottermann, Reino, 1995, pp. 90–91; Wesson, Alf, 1998, p. 57; Lutheran Church Bellville, Who Are We?, 2011, Website. The original chapel that was handed over to the 'Coloured' congregation because of forced removal was later demolished when the area was taken

The congregation belongs to ELCSA-Cape, which was started by German immigrants in the former Cape Province and Orange Free State. (The provincial boundaries were changed after democratisation, and they are known today as the Western Cape, Eastern Cape, Northern Cape, and Free State Provinces.) Almost all the congregations in ELCSA-Cape offer services in German, but also in English and Afrikaans. The church's head office and bishop are located in the Cape Town area; the church and diocese coincide. ELCSA-Cape Church belongs to UELCSA – as described earlier, an organisation of other Lutheran churches in Southern Africa with German descendants. ELCSA-Cape Church is also part of LUCSA and the LWF.[75]

The Lutheran church centre in Middle Street, known by the German name *Kreutzkirche* (Church of the Cross), is situated in a residential area of mainly private homes. The church council said that they had about 460 members, and that the congregation was multilingual, with German-, Afrikaans-, and English-speaking members. They were almost exclusively 'White', and came from middle class and upper middle class backgrounds, according to the church council. One member of the council said: "It's a bit of an age gap among those aged around forty-five. So there are young people and elderly people".[76] The council's description is not unusual, and many other churches struggle with the same issue of lacking certain age groups. The congregation had a full-time minister, a retired minister who assisted when needed, and a part-time administrator. In the past the congregation had a co-worker for the youth, and they were hoping to appoint a new youth worker. Several lay people volunteered as churchwardens, vergers,

---

over by industry and road construction. The Lutheran Church in the Cape, n.d., p. 9, Church Publication; Observation Protocol 2011-02-20.

75 Ottermann, Reino, 1995, pp. 11–16, 82–85. ELCSA-Cape has only fourteen congregations, and is organised like a German *Landeskirche*. Ottermann, Reino, 1995, p. 90–124. UELCSA is the abbreviation for United Evangelical Lutheran Churches in Southern Africa. It is a union of ELCSA-Cape, ELCSA N-T and ELCIN, which are churches with German descendants, and are organised like the German *Landeskirchen*. LUCSA is a communion of Lutheran churches in Southern Africa related to the LWF. ELCSA-Cape is a member of the SACC but not of the WCC. ELCSA N-T is another Lutheran church started by German immigrants in the former Natal and Transvaal provinces, which, after democratisation, became the North West, Limpopo, Gauteng, Mpumalanga, and KwaZulu-Natal Provinces. ELCSA N-T is also a member of UELCSA, LUCSA and the LWF. It is member of the SACC but not of the WCC. The bishop and the ELCSA N-T head office are located at the Lutheran Centre in Bonaero Park, Kempton Park, Johannesburg.

76 Church Council Interview Protocol 2011-03-15.

organists, music leaders, children and confirmation teachers, as well as many others for practical duties.[77]

The church council characterised their congregation as "The oldest church in Bellville in the middle of Bellville".[78] The Lutheran Church was the first to start services in the area because many people of German background had settled in the former village. One of the church council members said: "People from the outside normally describe us as the German Church".[79] That statement indicated that the church had gained the reputation of being a somewhat ethnic church for people of German background. This description might be an advantage for people of German background who wanted to find a church with a German heritage. However, the reputation could also be a disadvantage if people assumed that the church was only for those of German descent, and not an option for other people.

Their German heritage has influenced the congregations of ELCSA-Cape in various ways. They have been able to remain a community with German roots that has kept the German language alive. But this has led the church community not to become totally integrated into South African society. One member of the council commented:

> In the past the Lutheran church felt like a guest in South Africa also with the political issues in that background, but I think in recent years the Lutheran voice with the message of the cross has come more to the forefront, and I think Lutherans are more bold to voice their opinion as well in a family of churches in South Africa […].

The description given by the church council reinforces the notion that the German heritage had been understood as something foreign. They kept their language, and did not assimilate with the English or Afrikaans groups, as many other European settlers had done. However, according to the church council the church did change, and dared to become part of the public debate. Another member of the council stated:

> The Lutheran church in the Cape is a very quiet district church and that is because of its history. In the eighteenth century all the Germans or Lutherans that came to the Cape were forced to become Dutch Reformed. In other words, in order to stay Lutherans they had to be quiet. For example, the Cape church never really has had an act of outreach. For example, Table View is an area that is mushrooming. We are very careful about getting in there immediately […].[80]

---

77 Hahne, Albrecht, 2011, pp. 2–3, Church Publication.
78 Church Council Interview Protocol 2011-03-15.
79 Church Council Interview Protocol 2011-03-15.
80 Church Council Interview Protocol 2011-03-15.

The Lutheran church was established early in the Cape Colony, but it had to follow the rules of the Dutch Reformed Church. ELCSA-Cape congregations have their origins in the late seventeenth century, when German immigrants settled in the Cape, but when only Reformed denominations had the right to hold church services. In the late eighteenth century Lutherans were able to have their own minister, but the church had to use an order of the service that was very similar to that of the Reformed Church. The historical background of ELCSA-Cape has led the church to adopt an unobtrusive profile. Also, most of the congregations are situated in the Eastern and Western Cape Provinces, which is only one part of the country. The congregations are scattered, and many members live far from their congregations. The strong German heritage, together with the small number of congregations, affects the church's position in society, making it a rather isolated entity.[81]

The situations of the other Lutheran churches in South Africa are very diverse. ELCSA N-T was started by German missionary societies for people who were mainly related to mission work, and ELCSA was founded by missionary work from Lutheran churches in Germany, Scandinavia and the USA, and is a church of South Africans. Both ELCSA-Cape and ELCSA N-T were founded by German-speaking settlers. ELCSA is much more part of South African society because it has always been a church for South Africans.

Some of the people in the Lutheran Church's Bellville congregation lived in the vicinity of the church building, but most of the people travelled to church. One council member explained: "In that sense we are different to other churches that have a congregation with a short distance to the building. We are very widely spread".[82] That statement shows that members lived in various places in the city, not in any one area. Another council member added that they even had members who lived very far from the church: "They are from St Helena which is a hundred and eighty kilometres, then there is Gansbaai which is probably ninety kilometres away and those people don't come so regularly. Quite a few come from Tygerberg".[83] The statements confirmed that a group of members lived in areas near the church, but they also had members from other towns in the Western

---

81 Ottermann, Reino, 1995, pp. 11–12.
82 Church Council Interview Protocol 2011-03-15.
83 Church Council Interview Protocol 2011-03-15. Both St Helena Bay and Gansbaai are popular tourist destinations and fishing centres. St Helena Bay is a town about 150 km north of Cape Town, and Gansbaai is located approximately 100 km southeast of Cape Town. Tygerberg is the area around the northern suburbs of Cape Town, and includes Bellville, Durbanville, Parow and Goodwood.

Cape.⁸⁴ A congregation with members living in various places confirmed that ELCSA-Cape churches were different from many other churches in South Africa, and ministered principally to people of German background. Members who lived in other areas indicated that other churches in their own areas were not an option for them, and that the German heritage was important to them.

The church council estimated that about 12 to 15 per cent of their members out of a total of 460 regularly attended church services. A church council member explained: "I was just thinking about that; I think we've got a percentage of round about twelve to fifteen percent regular presence. Last Sunday, if we take that, I think we had a quarter in the church services. Once a month we have over a hundred of our local membership. [...]".⁸⁵ Similar figures were acknowledged in the minister's annual report that was delivered at the general meeting in 2011. The minister stated:

> In general attendance at worship services has increased by 14 per cent last year against the figures of 2009. A development for which we can be grateful. On the third Sunday of the month about 100 people attend our various services. The service in the St Johannis Heim is especially attended.⁸⁶

Church attendance was relatively fair, and the numbers had even increased. Once a month the church had three separate services in the different languages. St Johannis Heim – the German retirement village that is supported by the congregation – enjoyed well-attended Sunday services. The statement from the church council and the minister's report stated that they had stable participation in their services.

The congregation had many people who appreciated it through either passive membership or being friends of the congregation in addition to the regular members. One church council member said:

> [...] I want to say we've got a lot of friends of the congregation, and whenever there is something on they flock here. I mean, they would not like to miss the bazaars of the Easter market or so. ... We have the kindergarten that also is very good. The people feel it is a *wie ein festung oder wie kann man sagen?* [like a fortress or how can you say?]. It's a place which will stay, which will be there. They might not even be members of the church at all, but when they've got a problem or death in the family they will contact the pastor.⁸⁷

---

84   Church Council Interview Protocol 2011-03-15.
85   Church Council Interview Protocol 2011-03-15.
86   Hahne, Albrecht, 2011, p. 2, Church Publication.
87   Church Council Interview Protocol 2011-03-15.

People who did not attend the church at other times of the year would come for special events. The council acknowledged that there was a wider community that extended the membership of the congregation. They had many friends of the congregation, and according to the church council, the church was seen as a constant and firm place in people's lives. If something happened to these friends of the congregation, they knew that the church was available for them. One of the church council members described the community around the congregation: "Active membership. Inactive membership and then circuits outside and around, but then one of the arms that reaches out is our kindergarten which actually, at the moment, we've got no members of the church, so it is a service of the community starting from three months to preschool".[88] The kindergarten or preschool was regarded as part of the congregation's community, even though none of the parents or children were members of the congregation, and it was run by a school organisation. The language at the kindergarten was German, but it was open to anybody in Cape Town. The basis for contact within the congregation was some kind of German or Lutheran connection, although the congregation was open to anybody in the area. The Lutheran Church in Bellville reflects the ethnic situation in a typical ELCSA-Cape congregation, but not that of an ELCSA N-T congregation. Several congregations in ELCSA N-T have become very diverse, and some have predominantly 'Black' members. The reasons for the differences relate to language use: most ELCSA N-T congregation use English almost exclusively every Sunday.[89]

Durban or eThekwini

Vasco da Gama sailed past the shores of the east coast of southern Africa in 1497, and gave the territory the name *Terra do Natal*. Colonists started to settle in Port Natal, and a trading post was established. The settlement grew when people arrived, mainly from the Cape. A town named after the governor of the Cape, Sir Benjamin D'Urban, was founded in 1835. Several groups of Boers moved to the Natal area, and Pietermaritzburg was founded and became the capital of the

---

88 Church Council Interview Protocol 2011-03-15.
89 Several ELCSA N-T congregations have members from diverse ethnic groups. They use German and English. See, for example: Friedenskirche, Johannesburg, Overview, 2011, p. 1, Church Publication; St Johannes Lutheran Church, Kelvin, Overview, 2011, p. 1, Church Publication; St Peter's Congregation, Pretoria, Overview, 2011, pp. 1–2, Church Publication; St Peter's by the Lake Lutheran Church, Overview, 2011, pp. 1, 3, Church Publication; Evangelical Lutheran Church in the Vaal Triangle, Vanderbijlpark, Overview, 2011, p. 1, Church Publication.

Republic of Natalia. Port Natal was later incorporated into the Boer republic, but the British government decided to occupy Natal in 1845 and it came under British rule. The Natal constitution of 1858 determined that 'Black' people were excluded from permission to trade, and 'White' people were assured political power. From about 1846 there were specific 'native reserves' for the 'Black' population.[90]

Large numbers of people from India were invited to Natal to meet the need for agricultural labour from 1860 onwards. The Indian workers were initially not a threat to the colonial power, but they increased in number and became urbanised. Some started to trade, and others began to work in the city. Durban experienced rapid economic expansion between 1870 and 1890 because of the development of a harbour with attached industries. The harbour became even more important when a railway line from Johannesburg was completed in 1895. Raw materials, fruit and vegetables, sugar, textiles etc. were exported from the harbour, and with mining in Johannesburg the trade increased.[91]

The people who came from India as guest- or contract-workers developed economically and became the largest single group in Durban, and thus were seen as a threat to the people of European descent. The Indians' trading rights were suppressed, and the Asiatic Land Tenure Act in 1946 became the first official segregation that was imposed upon people of Indian descent. The Group Areas Act was implemented in Durban in 1958, creating clearly-defined areas for the specific 'race groups'. 'Black' people were restricted to locations on the periphery far to the north of the city. The Durban city council played a central role in the development of segregation legislation, and the city was organised in accordance with the apartheid laws. Segregation was completed in 1970.[92]

Democratisation has rearranged the map, but the legacy of the Group Areas Act remains in the form of huge townships on the city's periphery. Durban follows the same pattern as many other South African cities: companies and businesses are leaving the inner city. Shopping malls are developed, and better housing is available according to affordability. Economic rather than ethnic differentiation is creating new boundaries. Flats in the city, together with middle- and lower-income suburban areas, are most affected by economic mobility. Problems related to illegal immigrants from other African countries have resulted in xenophobia;

---

90 Standard Encyclopaedia of Southern Africa, Vol. 4, 1971, pp. 112, 114; Encyclopedia of South Africa, 2011, p. 92; Davies, R.J., 1991, p. 72.
91 Standard Encyclopaedia of Southern Africa, Vol. 4, 1971, p. 112, 117; Encyclopedia of South Africa, 2011, p. 92; Davies, R. J., 1991, p. 73.
92 Encyclopedia of South Africa, 2011, p. 92; Davies, R. J., 1991, pp. 73, 76, 79–80.

and eThekwini Municipality – the third largest city in the country – experiences many challenges.[93]

The eThekwini Metropolitan Municipality in Durban had a total population of 3 442 361 people, according to Census 2011. Of these, 73.8 per cent identified themselves as 'Black African', 16.7 per cent as 'Indian or Asian', 6.6 per cent as 'White', 2.5 per cent as 'Coloured', and 0.4 per cent as 'Other'. This suggests that there are many more people who are 'Indian or Asian', and slightly more 'Black African', but fewer 'Coloured' and 'White' people in the municipality, compared with the rest of the country. According to Census 2011, 62.2 per cent had isiZulu, 26.5 per cent English, 3.9 per cent isiXhosa, and 1.7 per cent Afrikaans as their first language.[94] It is noteworthy that the municipality has a much larger 'Indian or Asian' population than is found in other parts of the country. There are also fewer 'White' and 'Coloured' people in Durban than in the rest of the country. It is natural that isiZulu should clearly be the dominant language, but many also have English as their first language. It is significant that very few people in Durban have Afrikaans as their first language. Limpopo is the only other province to have very few Afrikaans-speaking people.[95]

City Harvest Ministries, Ntuzuma – Apostolic Faith Mission of South Africa

City Harvest Ministries is an assembly/congregation in the Ntuzuma township, about 20 km from the centre of Durban. It is thus part of the eThekwini Municipality. The congregation, part of the AFM, has around a hundred members. Local AFM assemblies are organised into 43 geographic regions or non-geographic networks in South Africa, which are led by regional committees and regional leaders. City Harvest Ministries is part of the Durban Region network. The AFM head office is in Centurion, Gauteng, staffed by its President, General Secretary, and other office bearers.[96]

Ntuzuma is joined with the nearby areas of Inanda and KwaMashu in a node of townships known as the 'INK' townships. At the beginning of the millennium these three townships, together with some other areas in South Africa, were identified as the most severely impoverished areas in South Africa, and so needed

---

93 Encyclopedia of South Africa, 2011, p. 94; Davies, R. J., 1991, p. 88.
94 Census 2011, eThekwini Metropolitan Municipality, Statistics South Africa, 2013.
95 The Limpopo province has 2.6 per cent Afrikaans first language speakers. Census 2011, Census in Brief, 2012, p. 25.
96 Constitution of the Apostolic Faith Mission in South Africa, 2010, Chapter 3, 4.

special attention. The INK townships had one of the largest concentrations of low-income households in South Africa. Inanda is the oldest township, having been established in the mid-1800s as a special area for 'Black African' people. KwaMashu was built between 1957 and 1968 to accommodate people displaced through forced removals. Ntuzuma is the most recent of the three townships, having been established in 1970. Because of the poverty and huge inequalities that marked South African society, the township became a centre of political violence during the final years of apartheid.[97]

The INK townships were part of the apartheid planning that directed sections of the population to the periphery of the city. The townships became isolated and fragmented: a river valley and hilly terrain were natural barriers between them and other townships. People's work and social services were located in the Durban city centre; yet the public transport system was inadequate, fragmented, and uncoordinated. The situation of the INK townships is not much changed in post-apartheid South Africa. Most of the people who have employment work outside the INK area, with most of them working in the Durban city centre. The majority of the residents commute to their work in the city by rail and minibus taxi. The vast majority of the people in the INK area are unemployed.[98]

The INK townships have a mix of formal and informal settlements. Water, sewerage, and electricity are not available for every household in the area.

South Africa has a high proportion of HIV-infected people. KwaZulu-Natal Province has the highest rate in the country, and INK is one of the areas with the greatest number of infected people in the province. The townships have a high level of crime because of the underprivileged conditions. Many residents who experience improved economic conditions leave the area and move to Durban, where they can gain better access to housing, employment, and education, and experience a lower crime rate. Ntuzuma is very similar to many other townships in South Africa, with poor living conditions and few possibilities for people to improve their situation.[99]

---

97 Nodal Economic Development Profile (INK) Inanda, Ntuzuma and KwaMashu KwaZulu Natal, 2007. p. 14, Provincial and Local Government Print; Township Renewal: INK Case Study, 2009, p. 5, Provincial and Local Government Print.
98 Nodal Economic Development Profile (INK) Inanda, Ntuzuma and KwaMashu KwaZulu Natal, 2007, pp. 2, 8–9, Provincial and Local Government Print; Township Renewal: INK Case Study, 2009, p. 2, Provincial and Local Government Print.
99 Nodal Economic Development Profile (INK) Inanda, Ntuzuma and KwaMashu KwaZulu Natal, 2007, pp. 10, 15, Provincial and Local Government Print; Township Renewal: INK Case Study, 2009, pp. 3, 6, Provincial and Local Government Print.

The congregation's history is similar to that of many other Pentecostal and charismatic congregations that have started with a group of people and a leader who have decided to come together to form an assembly/congregation. City Harvest Ministries started in Ntuzuma township in 2009; but the congregation had already been established in the centre of Durban in 2005, as a satellite church of the Maranatha Ministries in the township of KwaMashu. The congregation first rented a hall in one of the hotels in the central business area of Durban, but in 2008 it moved to a location in an industrial and office area just outside the city centre. The congregation was recognised by the AFM the same year, as they began to rent a permanent place for worship and became an independent assembly. The congregation grew in membership; many students joined them for worship, so that the congregation had a high turnover of members who came and left.[100]

In June 2009 City Harvest Ministry begun a project in the Ntuzuma township. One of the new members of the congregation offered it the use of part of her yard in Ntuzuma for a church, instead of transporting people to town. The congregation left central Durban a year later, and a tent became the congregation's new worship space. One of the church council members described their history in these terms:

> The church started three years ago in town, but unfortunately we did not have a premise so we were renting in town. First we were renting at a hotel and then we moved to another area ... one of the difficulties that we experienced of being in town, we used to have mostly students coming to worship with us, but unfortunately as soon as they finished their studies they would leave and go back home. So we got new people all the time. So for about a year ago, the pastor saw that this was an area where we could come [...].[101]

The church council described the short history of the congregation and its troubles with renting places in Durban, as well as having many students as members. The group of people who had established the congregation had a vision for finding a better place where they could minister to people. Ntuzuma did not have many churches, and so they decided to move the whole congregation. It is notable that they chose an underprivileged area and began to worship in a tent.[102]

The area next to the tent church had poor-quality houses, which is typical for a township. One of the church council's members characterised the houses close to the tent church as 'informal settlements'.[103] Another member added:

---

100 City Harvest Ministries, The life of City Harvest Ministries, 2013, Website; Observation Protocol 2011-03-27; Church Council Interview Protocol 2011-03-27.
101 Church Council Interview Protocol 2011-03-27.
102 Observation Protocol 2011-03-27.
103 Church Council Interview Protocol 2011-03-27.

Mostly they are governmental sponsored with subsidies, but mostly it is people who are unemployed, low income, what else. They are mostly, the family structures, you will find that it is one single parent that is heading the house. Maybe she is working or not working, hey, it's a lot of poverty. It's got more and more poverty than any other areas.[104]

The church council member's description of the area was very similar to other reports about the INK townships. There was significant unemployment, poor housing, single parent households, informal settlements that did not provide basic necessities. The average age of the people in Ntuzuma was relatively low. One church council member stated: "It's a mixture of sixteen up to forty-five, fifty".[105] The estimate of a young population in Ntuzuma is similar to the total population of the province of KwaZulu-Natal, where more than half of the population are younger than twenty-five years old.[106]

Most of the people who came to City Harvest Ministries were living in Ntuzuma, which was also why the congregation had moved to that specific area. One of the church council members described the people who came to worship: "It is mostly the people from around this area but also the rest of us that came from town that started the work of the Lord".[107] It is notable that, although the church had been in Ntuzuma less than two years, the majority of the worshippers came from that area. A core group of people still travelled to the church, and had been part of the congregation from its origins in the city.

The congregation's members were entirely 'Black African', and almost everybody had IsiZulu as their primary language – like the population of Ntuzuma.[108] The congregation had no members from other African countries. A church council member explained: "No, we don't have them here but we had some in town. A guy from Zimbabwe and one from Nigeria".[109] Presumably most people from other African countries do not settle in an area like Ntuzuma. People from other African countries have been victims of xenophobia, and live in other areas. Durban city centre has many immigrants, as described earlier. Both international students and people from other African countries found it easier to attend City Harvest Ministries when the congregation was in the city, owing to better transport options.

---

104   Church Council Interview Protocol 2011-03-27.
105   Church Council Interview Protocol 2011-03-27.
106   Census 2011, Census in Brief, 2012, p. 28.
107   Church Council Interview Protocol 2011-03-27.
108   Church Council Interview Protocol 2011-03-27.
109   Church Council Interview Protocol 2011-03-27.

The church council estimated that they had around hundred members in the congregation.[110] One council member stated: "I give a measurement. We say that we have about hundred in church, so we are mostly hundred people including children".[111] A congregation of a hundred members, children included, could be characterised as a small congregation among the mainline churches in South Africa. However, the congregation had increased rapidly in membership in the short time of its existence.

City Harvest Ministries' members seemed to have the same age demographic as in the province. A council member acknowledged the age of the congregation's members by saying: "They are mostly young".[112] A congregation with young members and many children can also achieve a high profile in the local community on Sundays.[113] Pentecostal and charismatic churches in South Africa have also been growing in number in recent years.[114]

Membership was granted to people who were identified as 'born again' and had received believer's baptism, according to the constitution of City Harvest Ministries. Members had to accept the doctrinal, ethical, and liturgical pronouncements approved by the management of the church. Members could also transfer their membership to the congregation from another assembly, but all new members had to be accepted by the congregation's management committee. This committee also had the right to terminate membership. The members were encouraged to maintain a good relationship with the Lord Jesus and with the community at large.[115]

St Michael's Evangelical Lutheran Church – Evangelical Lutheran Church in Southern Africa

Durban Central Parish consists of six congregations. One of them, St Michael's congregation in the Durban city centre, can be regarded as the main church of the parish. Like the other case congregations in the study, St Michael's will be described as an entity in its own right.

The parish covers a vast area, and the whole parish had about a thousand members in 2011. The parish estimated that St Michael's congregation had 276 members, but many people came to worship without being members. Durban

---

110 Church Council Interview Protocol 2011-03-27.
111 Church Council Interview Protocol 2011-03-27.
112 Church Council Interview Protocol 2011-03-27.
113 Observation Protocol 2011-03-27.
114 Yong, Amos, & Attanasi, Katy, 2012, pp. 67–72.
115 City Harvest Ministries Constitution, 2011, pp. 2–3, 4–5, Church Publication.

Central Parish and St Michael's congregation are part of ELCSA, and the parish belongs to the Durban circuit and the South Eastern Diocese. The bishop's office and diocesan administration are located in Umpumulo, KwaZulu-Natal, and the head office of ELCSA is located at the Lutheran Centre in Bonaero Park, Kempton Park, Johannesburg. ELCSA is also a member of LUCSA and LWF.[116]

St Michael's Lutheran Church is situated between the International Convention Centre (ICC) and the beach front. The church building and its furnishings are plain, but its hammer beam roof with open timber trusses was inspired by English Gothic architecture, giving the impression of a sacred space. No South African works of art are visible in the church, even though ELCSA and the diocese have an art and craft centre.[117]

The congregation has its origins in the Norwegian Mission Society, when the Revd Ole Stavem began work in the harbour town of Port Natal in 1890. Many Lutherans had moved into the city from rural areas to find employment. The mission society was able to obtain a plot in Milne Street, where a building was erected and a congregation was started. A new and bigger church was built in 1906, replacing the former building in order to accommodate all the Lutheran members in the city. Another Norwegian missionary, the Revd Sven Eriksen, took over the work in Milne Street when the new church was built.[118] One church council member described the beginning of the Milne Street church like this:

> I think in the beginning, if we go back to the history, it was mostly men, I think, working here, coming from the mission churches working here in Durban, and they had services here by missionaries and also evening classes. They tried to educate, to further the education, and it was Norwegian missionaries here.[119]

The Lutheran mission had concentrated on the rural areas, but there was a need to start congregations in the cities too, because Lutheran members had begun to move to the urban areas. A new phase began when the Revd Petrus Lamula, the first 'Black' South African Lutheran minister, took charge of the Lutheran church in Milne Street in 1915. Lamula became very involved in the situation of the many men working and living in severe conditions in the hostels in the harbour

---

116 Lüdemann, Joe, 2012, pp. 1–5, Church Publication.
117 Observation Protocol 2011-04-03. ELCSA runs Rorke's Drift Art and Craft Centre, which has a worldwide reputation.
118 Durban Central Parish, Short history of the congregations, 2014, Website; The St Olav Lutheran Church 1880–1980, 1980, p. 81. Port Natal was later renamed Durban.
119 Church Council Interview Protocol 2011-04-03.

area. He gathered the workers for Sunday services, but also for educational and social meetings.[120] Another member of the council explained the situation:

> I think what I heard, it was at that time when it was mainly migrant labourers here and many men also living in the hostels in insanitary conditions. That's the time of pastor Lamula who was very active and who also acted in the whole area of the trade unions. It attracted big masses among the workers as well. It seemed to have been a conflict between the Norwegian mission headquarters and these new tendencies, and then Lamula left the church. He had to leave the church and I think with him a large group of workers. [...].[121]

Petrus Lamula was much engaged as a minister and teacher, and was concerned about social issues that also had political consequences. Lamula's ministry occurred at the beginning of the labour union movement in the Durban area, and what he did was apparently not in accordance with what the Norwegian Mission Society expected. He had to resign from the work at the Milne Street church, and was replaced by the Revd B. A. Mpanza in 1924. Lamula's resignation shows how the missionary societies once related to politics and the indigenous people. Urbanisation increased in Durban as many labourers moved into the city. The Milne Street church had to start a daughter congregation in Moore Road in 1926 to cater mostly for domestic employees.[122]

A congregation of missionaries and traders with Norwegian and other Scandinavian ancestry began at the same time as the mission work of the Norwegian Mission Society in Durban. The Norwegian and Scandinavian congregation had ministers from the mission societies, among them Ole Stavem and Sven Eriksen, who also served the Milne Street congregation. The Norwegian and Scandinavian congregation, named St Olav's, was established in 1880, and a church was built on Winder Street in 1892. The congregation grew, and in 1962 St Olav's built a new church centre on St Thomas' Road, Berea. The church was also used by the Norwegian Seamen's Mission, but as its work increased it needed larger premises. So the Norwegian Seamen's Mission built a church on Mansfield Road, Berea, which was inaugurated in 1967.[123]

The Church of Norway had intended that St Olav's would be part of ELCSA when the former Lutheran mission churches in Southern Africa founded ELCSA in 1975. However, St Olav's insisted on not joining ELCSA, despite attempts in 1985 to persuade the congregation to become a member. The situation caused a

---

120 Durban Central Parish, Short history of the congregations, 2014, Website.
121 Church Council Interview Protocol 2011-04-03.
122 Durban Central Parish, Short history of the congregations, 2014, Website.
123 The St Olav Lutheran Church 1880–1980, 1980, pp. 72–73, 81.

split, and a group of about 40 members left St Olav's and began to worship in the chapel of the Norwegian Seamen's Mission on Mansfield Road. They began to call their congregation 'St Michael's'. St Olav's congregation became independent of the Church of Norway, and the congregation was served by ministers from other denominations.[124]

At this time, the Lutheran congregation in Moore Road had burned down under suspicious circumstances, and they too found a place to worship in the Norwegian Seamen's Mission. The Norwegian Seamen's Church Board in Norway decided, however, to close the church in 1987 because of fewer seamen were visiting Durban. There was a plan that St Michael's with its 'White' members and the congregation from Moore Road with its 'Black' members would together take over the premises. The Norwegian Seamen's Mission board in Norway decided, however, to sell the church building to the Deaf Association Natal despite protests. Some people accused the Norwegian Seamen's Mission board of succumbing to pressure from people in South Africa not to transfer the property to the St Michael's and Moore Road congregations. Once the property had been sold, the two groups had no place to worship.[125]

This situation resulted in a merger of the St Michael, Moore Road, and Milne Street congregations as one congregation, and they shared the church building in Milne Street. The new congregation was named 'St Michael's', and it held services in both English and isiZulu. The history of St Michael's shows how the Lutheran mission societies and mission churches created parallel church organisations by simultaneously planting separate churches for 'Black' South Africans and for people of European descent. The situation in which a Norwegian or Scandinavian church refused to unite with ELCSA is not unique: the German Lutheran churches in South Africa, ELCSA N-T and ELCSA-Cape, did not unite with ELCSA during the unity talks either, and they remain separate churches. In central Durban, for example, there were St Paul's Lutheran Church and Lutherkirche, which belonged to ELCSA N-T and had been ministering to English-speaking and German-speaking

---

124 Hagen Agøy, Berit, 2000, pp. 267–268; "The Turning Point", 2002, pp. 2, 5–7, Church Publication; Observation Protocol 2011-04-03. St Olav's congregation decided on 1 June 1997 to become a member of the Church of England in South Africa, and the formal agreement was signed on 4 October 2001. The congregation left the Lutheran confession, but kept the congregational name as a sign of its Norwegian heritage. E-mail from Monica Geyer, Secretary in St Olav's church. Geyer, Monica, 2014, Email 2014-02-12.
125 Lindekleiv, Heidi Marie, 2008a, p. 12–13; Lindekleiv, Heidi Marie, 2008b, p. 12.

people of American and German descent. ELCSA N-T and ELCSA-Cape have several congregations in South Africa, and Scandinavians and Americans have had similar congregations in, for example, Johannesburg. Comparable patterns can be found in other Protestant churches in South Africa, such as the NGK and URCSA, each of which has parallel church organisations.[126]

The history of St Michael's Lutheran church in Milne Street indicates that people in the congregation come from very diverse backgrounds, with a diversity of ethnic groups and languages. Members had moved from rural to urban areas, mergers of various congregations had created new forms of community, and the democratic South Africa had changed living conditions for large groups of people, all of which affected St Michael's. The congregation described itself as a multicultural and multilingual congregation that was striving to celebrate its diversity. St Michael's is unique because there are not many 'White' members in other ELCSA congregations, apart from a few co-workers from other countries.[127]

Durban Central Parish includes many different kinds of residential areas. St Michael's is situated in an area where many people live in flats and hostels, and several people in St Michael's travel to attend services.[128] The situation changed significantly following democratisation, when people could decide for themselves where to live and spend their social life. One of the council members who had been in St Michael's for a long time explained:

> I think there was a great change when the change of government took place in ninety-four. Maybe a few years before that but especially since then. Families moved in here. Before when we came here it was predominantly ladies who were working in households and maybe five percent men working in businesses, and that has changed dramatically.[129]

---

126 Overview of the Durban Congregation, n.d., ELCSA N-T, ELCSA N-T, Church Publication. Johannesburg also has a church that was started by the Church of Sweden Mission and ministered to Scandinavians. The church was later named St Johannes Lutheran church and became a full member of ELCSA N-T in 1995. St Johannes Lutheran Church, Kelvin, Overview, 2011, Church Publication. Another congregation in Johannesburg that is part of ELCSA N-T and was first ministered to by the American Lutheran Church is St Peter's by the Lake Lutheran Church. The congregation became a full member of ELCSA N-T in 1984. St Peter's by the Lake Lutheran Church, Overview, 2011, Church Publication. For Reformed churches with parallel church organisations, see: Van der Linde, Hugo Hendrik, 2002.
127 Durban Central Parish, Who are we?, Congregations, St Michael's, 2011, Website.
128 Lüdemann, Joe, 2012, p. 2, Church Publication.
129 Church Council Interview Protocol 2011-04-03.

This explanation illustrates that the church had been a typical inner city church with few residential members other than the official ethnic groups. Democratisation changed the situation, and St Michael's received new groups of people who had moved into the Durban city centre. Female domestic workers had been in the majority before, and women were still in the majority at St Michael's. In discussion a church council member said: "I think it is about 10 per cent men", and another person replied: "Not nearly 10, the church has 20 men".[130] The discussion indicated that between 10 per cent and 20 per cent of the members were men, and 80–90 per cent were women.

St Michael's received new groups of people because they could choose where to live according to their preference and ability to afford it. They also received people from other areas because of the current transportation system. One council member explained: "Most people live in central town, and then you get people from other parishes that choose to come here for worship who are not members. So, I'd say 60 per cent are living in central Durban".[131] This showed that more than half of the people who came to church lived in central Durban; but they also had a huge group of people who travelled to church. The minibus taxi industry is an important part of the South African transport sector, and is an inexpensive alternative for people to travel. One member of the council stressed:

> Yes, we have interesting categories. You have those coming from the urban area environment because of the transports changes. It is more convenient ... You maybe want to travel to St Michael. You take one taxi. It is easier than attending a local church in the rural area when you take maybe two or three transports to reach church. It becomes cheaper. And because of this the numbers are going up.[132]

Durban city centre is a hub for most of the minibus taxis, which made it easier and cheaper for people to come to St Michael's instead of trying to get to the Lutheran church closest to where they lived. The transport situation in Durban enabled St Michael's to receive many participants because of its convenience. People came from other parts of the city without becoming members of the congregation.

There were also many young people who attended church regularly or during their stay in Durban for studies or work. The church council estimated that about 60 per cent of those who came to church were young adults.[133] One council

---

130   Church Council Interview Protocol 2011-04-03.
131   Church Council Interview Protocol 2011-04-03.
132   Church Council Interview Protocol 2011-04-03.
133   Church Council Interview Protocol 2011-04-03.

member said: "We have a number of young people who come here for education, higher education... and also workers. There is also a migration from rural to urban areas because of job options".[134] Durban is a city with many education institutions, such as the Durban University of Technology, Berea Technical College, business schools, and several campuses that are part of the University of KwaZulu-Natal. The urban area has many more job opportunities for younger people than do the rural areas.

Having many young people in St Michael's made the congregation fluid both in attendance and in membership. One church council member clarified the situation of having many young people in the church in these terms: "For temporary students and also workers, whose homes are in the rural areas, which are here most of the time, and those are the ones who are going home at least once a month".[135] The young people in St Michael's came to worship in the church but had still contacts with their homes in the rural areas. Some of the people occasionally went home to their families in the villages and were members of the local congregation there. They attended St Michael's during their time in the city. A council member explained:

> [...] Some of them will remain officially members of their rural congregations and then they come here for three or four years during their duration of their studies, but they would still remain members at home. Because they are thinking of, well, if I'm baptising my children or if I'm getting married or die. That's where all of these important things are going to happen.[136]

People's heritage was very important when it came to the main celebrations in their lives. Students especially regarded their home congregation as their principal community.

Their membership affected the economic situations of both the rural and the urban congregations. The rural congregations kept their members and received economic advantages, while St Michael's had high attendance – but fewer members who contributed through pledges. St Michael's had many young congregants, but also quite a few congregation members who moved to rural areas when they retired. One council member said: "But aren't there also some people like the older people who when they're retiring actually leave this congregation? They are no longer working, so they are going back to the rural areas. We do lose

---

134   Church Council Interview Protocol 2011-04-03.
135   Church Council Interview Protocol 2011-04-03.
136   Church Council Interview Protocol 2011-04-03.

them!".[137] The church council acknowledged that people had strong roots in the rural areas and moved back when they retired. The situation was different for people who were brought up in the city or who had adjusted to life in the city, and also had children and perhaps grandchildren in Durban.

The congregation had younger and older members, rural and urban people, English, isiZulu or other first languages, and various other forms of diversity. St Michael's people described themselves as a congregation with cultural diversity. One church council member portrayed the congregation in these terms:

> I would say we have all nations. We have two services. The first service is in English for English-speaking people from all over the world, from around Africa and from Europe. Sometimes some of them come as students or workers. We have the eleven o'clock service which is predominantly for people who are from the South Eastern diocese and other parts of South Africa.[138]

The comment about "all nations" indicates that St Michael's had people who came from various ethnic groups, and that they catered for people with English and isiZulu. The services in English also accommodated people from other parts of Africa and other parts of the world who knew English.

5.3 Conclusions

The former colonial power, and later the governments of the Union of South Africa and the Republic of South Africa, supported the stratified division of the population according to 'race'. The division influenced the churches' congregations by their being divided according to ethnic group, and some even according to a specific ethnic church or denomination.

The Anglican and Methodist churches were established to serve immigrants and the mission to indigenous people, but remained single church organisations. Their churches were established when the British conquered the country. The Roman Catholic Church arrived later in South Africa, owing to resistance from the colonial power. Catholic churches were not divided into different ethnic churches, and rejected any form of division. Their congregations were, however, divided according to ethnic groups as a consequence of members' residence; but the churches remained part of a single church organisation at the central and regional levels.

---

137 Church Council Interview Protocol 2011-04-03.
138 Church Council Interview Protocol 2011-04-03.

The AFM was a single church when it was first organised, but it divided into different sections along ethnic lines during the apartheid years. The church managed to unite during democratisation, and today it is not divided on 'racial' lines.

The Lutheran Church was divided into various churches from its beginnings. Churches for people of German descent were established, as were churches for indigenous people reached through mission work. The divisions still exist despite unification talks, but the strict ethnic divisions of the past have begun to break down, mainly because of people's ability to choose more freely where to live.

The churches did not in general oppose division along ethnic lines before the National Party came to power. The Anglican and Methodist churches began to resist when the apartheid laws were enforced, and ELCSA and the Roman Catholic Church followed suit later, during the struggle. The Lutheran churches of German descent, ELCSA-Cape and ELCSA N-T, were questioned by the international Lutheran community because they did not publicly denounce the government's apartheid policy. The AFM was loyal for a long time to the government's apartheid policy, but started to question the divisions in later years.

The six case study congregations from the five church families, in Johannesburg, Cape Town and Durban, were still struggling with the legacy caused by the former Group Areas Act. They showed that there was still ethnic stratification in the congregations two decades after democratisation; but the differentiation tended to relate more to economic factors. Some people moved into other areas after the Group Areas Act was abolished. Most people, however, lived and attended church according to the same pattern as before democracy.

The congregations mostly had members who lived in the area of the church, but they also had some people who travelled to the congregations for church services and other activities. The reason for travelling to a congregation was a preference for a specific style of church service, its spirituality, convenient transportation, or language. The congregations had in general a high proportion of women, who were in the majority as participants in services and in diverse church activities.

The congregations and churches are challenged in various ways, according to my analytical tool of the Church's catholicity. There is a need to work towards reconciliation, to become inclusive communities, to increase the diversity of their expressions, to enhance diverse language use, to strengthen contacts between the congregations, and to support social transformation. The chapters that follow will examine diverse themes of the Church's catholicity that can be productively studied in the South African context. In the next chapter I will explore how the congregations and churches have been dealing with reconciliation as part of the Church's catholicity.

Chapter Six: Reconciliation as Part of the Church's Ministry

The WCC and the SACC supported the establishment of the Truth and Reconciliation Commission as a contribution to the reconciliation of the human community after several decades of ethnic division in South Africa. Reconciliation was a way to deal with the past and to help lead the country away from a divided past to a future built on reconciliation and national unity. The previous chapter showed, however, that congregations were still struggling with the legacy of apartheid two decades after democratisation.

This chapter will explore the ministry of reconciliation as part of church's practices. Firstly, I will examine how the congregations were influenced by the TRC and how they perceived reconciliation in their communities. I will focus on the legacy of the TRC, and then on reconciliation from a general perspective. Secondly, I will analyse whether reconciliation was reflected in the congregations' vision and mission statements. These statements capture the congregations' primary objectives and purposes, and reveal whether reconciliation is central to their practices.

6.1 Congregations as Communities for Reconciliation

During democratisation, congregations and churches were encouraged to work for reconciliation to unite the divided churches and society. The SACC developed special reconciliation liturgies that were supposed to be used in the congregations. Sermons, symbolic events, counselling, storytelling, dialogue and community-building were other examples that were expected to be organised. The SACC also organised special meetings, conferences, and consultations to promote reconciliation and restitution in the country.[1]

It is important to note that the TRC's hearings were broadcast nationally on radio and television in 1996 and 1997; they were difficult to avoid, and had an impact on South African citizens. The majority of South African citizens have, nevertheless, not seen the final recommendations of the TRC. The Faith Communities Hearing in East London in 1997 was held at the same time as many

---

1 Van der Merwe, Hugo, 2003, pp. 277–279; See, for example, Liturgy of Reconciliation, Unity and Equality, 2008; Rite of Reconciliation, 1996. The consultations in Vanderbijlpark in 1995 and in Johannesburg in 1996 were two important national SACC events; but there were also several others at regional and local level.

other hearings, and when this research was undertaken, a long time had passed since the TRC had completed its work.

St Peter Claver in Pimville – Roman Catholic Church

The congregation is located in Soweto, as described in the previous chapter. The Roman Catholic Church has several congregations in Soweto. The township can be seen as a separate part of the municipality, and in other parts of South Africa it would be regarded as a town or a city. The congregation belongs to the Soweto district within the Diocese of Johannesburg.

The church council at St Peter Claver was asked whether the TRC and the reconciliation process had had any impact on the life as a congregation. The council replied that they did not think that the TRC had had any effect on the congregation or the congregation's life. Neither did they believe that the Faith Communities Hearing, which was part of the TRC, had had any implications for their congregation. They stated, although, that they believed their bishop had been invited and had participated in the TRC.[2] Their response was not a sign that reconciliation was unnecessary, but that the congregation had not been involved in the TRC as a community and that they had not performed any reconciliation services. The congregation was also far from the city centre and from the northern suburbs, where diverse ethnicities could meet and take part in reconciliation discussions and services.

They agreed that reconciliation was part of the church, and that they practised reconciliation in the liturgy in their services. Reconciliation with God and each other was part of the Sunday service, and they saw their own congregation as a model of reconciliation. They did not, however, mention any acts of reconciliation with other congregations of other ethnicities.[3] The response shows that the church council believed that reconciliation was already practised within their community, but not together with other congregations of other major ethnicities in Johannesburg. Because the congregation is located in Soweto, the council did not expect that congregations of other major ethnicities would come to Pimville for reconciliation services. Large groups of other ethnicities seldom visit Soweto. They were already in communion with congregations in the same diocese and with the congregations closest to them in Soweto.

It is understandable that the church council considered that the TRC and the reconciliation process had not had any impact on the life in the congregation

---

2 Church Council Interview Protocol 2011-02-27.
3 Church Council Interview Protocol 2011-02-27.

because of their being situated in Soweto. Almost everybody belongs to the same ethnic group, and few other groups would come to worship there, apart from a few individuals. It is a problem, according to the analytical tool concerning the catholicity of the Church, that the congregation was not practising reconciliation across ethnic borders. Practising the liturgy of the eucharist, including reconciliation, together with other congregations with other ethnicities shows that the Christian communion transcends ethnic diversities. Nevertheless, the diocese sometimes arranged functions where people in the diocese could meet across congregational boundaries.[4]

The outcome of the TRC was to some degree present in the congregation's mission statement, even though the work of the TRC was not seen as central to the congregation's life. Their vision and mission statements were placed on a signboard in one of the church's aisles. The statements were also published in other documents and papers that were accessible to its members. According to the church council, the vision and mission statements were created by the congregation.[5] They read:

> Vision: St Peter Claver will become an Evangelised and evangelizing community of Believers who give witness to the universal scope of God's saving plan in Jesus Christ.
> Mission: Our mission is to transform our community and the world by following Jesus' Truth and sharing Jesus' life according to divine principles of the Gospel.[6]

The vision emphasised a church that witnessed to God's salvation. This message had universal legitimacy, which should indicate the catholicity of the Church, because it emphasised that the community transcended national and ethnic borders. The mission statement revealed a link with the country's reconciliation process by mentioning transformation, which was central to the democratisation process. 'Transformation' is a key term in the democratisation process of the country, and is commonly used to make a clear connection with that process.[7] The statements needed to be explained and interpreted, but very little was described in any documents. When the church council was asked about the vision and mission statement,

---

4   Church Council Interview Protocol 2011-02-27.
5   Church Council Interview Protocol 2011-02-27.
6   St Peter Claver, Catholic Church, Pimville, 1928–2008, 80th Anniversary, 2008. p. 43. Church Publication.
7   About the transformation of the education system, see for example: Rembe, Symphorosa Wilibald, 2005; about political transformation see: Harshe, Rajen, 1993, pp. 1980–1983; about the transformation of the police see: Gastrow, Peter & Shaw, Mark, 2001, pp. 259–275.

one of the members replied: "We would like to see that the Roman Catholic Church is growing".[8] The response explained that the mission was to grow the church numerically, but also to extend the ministry that the Roman Catholic Church could offer to society, to all people in the country, overcoming any divisions.

St Thomas' in Linden – Anglican Church of Southern Africa

The congregation is situated in one of the northern suburbs, and since democratisation has become more ethnically diverse. The members of the church council in St Thomas' were very aware of the truth and reconciliation process in the country, and saw that democratisation had changed the country and their community. One council member commented on the TRC:

> You know that the Truth and Reconciliation Commission was so much a part of who we were and what was happening in our lives at that stage. It became like the air that we breathe and we changed because of it. I don't think that I know when I changed which way or why. That was things that happened long before that was important. People who understood what was happening in this country and it was not easy for any of them. I mean you just have to read Beyers Naudé's book, and you know that there were people on every side that were really struggling. I think the Truth and Reconciliation ended up well in the very end, but I don't think that it changed anything immediately because of that.[9]

The response of the council is interesting, because the TRC was not the only process that had an impact and changed peoples' attitudes to the new South Africa. The TRC was regarded as a national symbol for truth and reconciliation, together with many other changes in the society. The church council was not convinced that the TRC as such had changed their congregation; rather, the whole democratisation process in the country had changed people gradually.

They had not organised or held special reconciliation services. One member stated: "We did not have our own services of reconciliation".[10] The SACC and other organisations had developed rites and liturgies for congregations and faith communities to bear witness to reconciliation, unity, and equality. Some of these rites were even intended to be inter-faith services.[11] Another member responded: "I went to one Truth and Reconciliation, a massive one where we all went".[12] The

---

8   Church Council Interview Protocol 2011-02-27.
9   Church Council Interview Protocol 2011-03-06.
10 Church Council Interview Protocol 2011-03-06.
11 See for example: Rite of Reconciliation, 1996; Liturgy of Reconciliation, Unity and Equality, 2008.
12 Church Council Interview Protocol 2011-03-06.

SACC had held several reconciliation services in one of the main churches in Johannesburg in the past. It is notable that members had participated in such a service even though they had not organised their own reconciliation service in their congregation. Linden is not far from many of the main churches in Johannesburg, which meant that these services were more accessible to its members than to, say, people who lived in Soweto.

Other similar services had been held more recently. A council member said: "Well, we went to St John once, quite recently, and there has been a service".[13] The service was probably at St John the Evangelist in Sandton, which indicates that some Anglican congregations still held reconciliation services two decades after democratisation. It is interesting that these services are still held, not just in the earlier years of democratisation. Another member of the council responded: "It is more of a once-off experience".[14] The council member's response showed that the reconciliation services could not be repeated too often, and participation in one service was not an experience that was easily reproduced. Reconciliation, however, is central to the Christian liturgy, and is constantly repeated at the prayer of penitence and absolution.

It is noteworthy that St Thomas' had not held their own reconciliation service. Its ethnic diversity had increased since democratisation as more people from diverse ethnic backgrounds were able to move into Linden, and so joined the congregation. There were some who found it difficult to join the congregation, and they had struggled to become part of the community.[15]

The minister in charge of the congregation had, nevertheless, encountered a delicate situation in his previous congregation of St Gabriel's in Florida, West Rand, Johannesburg, before he came to work at St Thomas.[16] The minister described his experience thus:

> I was in Florida previously, and that was a parish that went through a very rapid demographic shift from being a very conservative and traditional West Rand parish and then just in a space of a couple of years to becoming 90 per cent a Coloured parish as the community moved out ... That caused lots of tensions in the parish because there was a well-established core of old White people who had been running the parish forever and

---

13 Church Council Interview Protocol 2011-03-06.
14 Church Council Interview Protocol 2011-03-06.
15 See, for example, the testimony offered by one of the church council members and a church warden, recorded in the next chapter. The St Thomas' Magazine March 2011, 2011, pp. 12–13, Church Publication.
16 Florida was declared an area for 'White' people during apartheid. Many people from neighbouring 'Coloured' townships moved into Florida after democratisation.

could remember the early days. And then a whole new group of people who said well, this is our parish too now. How are we going to be part of it? Are you going to accommodate us? We have our own traditions and a different view of things, and that needs to be expressed when we are now worshiping. So, there was a lot of tension and we actually deliberately, there, grew on some of the, let's call it, techniques of TRC to get people together and sit down and just try and find a common story in a scene, and to get people to unpack a little bit where some distrust was coming from, where some of the suspicion was coming from. And be able just to hold that and say this is your hurt, this is our hurt and this is where we are coming from, but we somehow want to go together, and to draw people along that process was an incredible healing in that community where I was. But there it was very obvious issues that needed to be addressed.[17]

That experience came out of a situation after democratisation, when people could choose to live according to affordability, and no longer according to apartheid laws. The tensions that occurred among Anglican people from different ethnic groups were solved by a methodology that was inspired by the TRC. The practice could be categorised as an intercultural experience applied in the congregation. The minister had experienced a reconciliation methodology that originated from the TRC, but a similar practice had not been followed at St Thomas'. That congregation had not experienced rapid demographic change as St Gabriel's in Florida had; but St Thomas' could also have experienced the constructive effects of practising a similar reconciliation ministry.

Because of the social changes after democratisation, St Thomas' became a congregation of diverse ethnicities. Reconciliation practices in other Johannesburg congregations with a different ethnicity were less evident. Some members had contact with other congregations in the city, but not with the practice of reconciliation and restitution.

St Thomas' had not produced their own vision and mission statements, although the congregation had adopted the mission statement of the Anglican Diocese of Johannesburg. This mission statement was reproduced in several of the congregation's documents and leaflets in either summary or complete form. The mission statement was not interpreted in the congregation's documents.[18] It declared:

---

17 Church Council Interview Protocol 2011-03-06.
18 St Thomas' Anglican Church, Linden, Parish Profile, 2011, p. 1, Church Publication; Linden St Thomas, Welcome to St Thomas' Linden, 2011, Website; Information sheet for the Sunday, 6th March 2011, 2011, Church Publication; Welcome to St Thomas' Anglican Church, Linden, 2011, p. 1, Church Publication.

The Ministry of All Believers – God in each of us transforming church and world.
Spiritual Formation – A lifelong process of growth and learning in Christ.
Visionary Servant Leaders – Leaders whose example empowers others.
Vibrant Christian Community – The growth of our Christian community.
Focused Outreach – Commitment to social justice issues and action, Christian unity, evangelism and new church planting.[19]

The statement emphasised that all people in the church were part of the church's ministry, contributing to the life of the church and to the broader community. All believers were part of transforming the church and the world, and the church had the task of equipping members in their ministry. The term 'transformation' is used in agreement with the TRC and the democratisation of South African society. Part of 'outreach' included social justice issues and action. The mission statement can be seen as consistent with the analytical tool for catholicity in respect of reconciliation, because of its stress on transformation and on working towards social justice. However, the reconciliation of ethnic divisions in congregation and church is not evident.

The Diocese of Johannesburg had set out the mission statement in a particular document. 'Spiritual formation' was defined as a personal devotion to prayer, worship, witness and Bible study, but also as a dedication to justice, reconciliation, concern for the environment, and voluntary and financial contributions to the church.[20] It is notable that spiritual formation was attached not only to the church, but also to a ministry of peace, justice and socio-economic action, and to transformation in the South African society and the world. It is also remarkable, however, that unity in the diverse South African society was not mentioned.

Athlone Methodist Church – Methodist Church of Southern Africa

The congregation is situated in Athlone, not far from the Cape Town city centre. The area was designated for the 'Coloured' population before democratisation. The area still had a large 'Coloured' population, and there had not been major changes to its ethnic make-up since democratisation. Before democratisation the congregation was allocated to a circuit with congregations of the

---

19 St Thomas' Anglican Church, Linden, Parish Profile, 2011, p. 1, Church Publication.
20 Anglican Church of Southern Africa, Diocese of Johannesburg, Diocesan Vision, 2002, Church Publication.

same ethnic group. After democratisation the demarcations of circuits were changed to be ethnically diverse.[21]

The church council members in Athlone Methodist Church did not believe that the TRC had affected their congregation's life. They responded: "No, No", "Not, really".[22] There was a long silence, and then another member said: "Not very much, I don't think it had any effect".[23] The answers might be a consequence of the fact that Cape Town, and especially Athlone, was not one of the major areas to experience unrest during apartheid. A member in the council added: "I think more people who were politically, at that time and involved ... They felt they needed that kind of help. But we followed that in the newspaper. Our church was never really part".[24] The statements revealed that the TRC had not been a focus for individuals or for the congregation. They had noticed that the reconciliation process had been carried out in their society, but this reconciliation was intended for people who had been involved in the struggle. Their answer should not be interpreted to mean that the members were unconcerned; but people in Athlone had not been involved to the same extent as those living in other areas. Their statement does not represent the Methodist Church as a whole, which was deeply involved in the TRC through its staff and church leaders.

The church council statement about reconciliation also has to be understood from the people's point of view concerning racial classification. As described in the introduction, the 'Coloured' ethnic group was a construction of the apartheid government. 'Coloureds' become reconstructed in social relationships and in the public space. The people in the 'Coloured' group shared the same identity through their forced removal by the apartheid government into an area such as Athlone. They did not choose to be differentiated as a specific group. So the question that had to be asked was: To whom should they be reconciled in society and in the church?

The church council members did not refer to any reconciliation services that had been celebrated in their congregation or in other congregations in Cape Town. Nor did they mention that they had been invited to any reconciliation services, 'healing of memory' talks, or other reconciliation events. Nor had the

---

21 87 per cent identified themselves as 'Coloured', which is the vast majority of the population in the area. Census 2011, Athlone, Statistics South Africa, 2013. The congregation belonged to a circuit together with congregations in Langa, Pinelands, Rosebank and Thornton. Church Council Interview Protocol 2011-03-20.
22 Church Council Interview Protocol 2011-03-20.
23 Church Council Interview Protocol 2011-03-20.
24 Church Council Interview Protocol 2011-03-20.

congregation had frequent interactions with other congregations in the circuit and district. There were still wounds from the past that had not been discussed and that were not yet reconciled. The statement made by the church council – that they had not been involved – could indicate that the reconciliation process in the church had not yet started two decades after democratisation. The initiative had to come from those who represented the perpetrators. The congregation and its members were not frequently in contact with congregations of other ethnicities, but they had tried in the past. Nor did they celebrate the eucharist across ethnic boundaries as a sign of the Church's catholicity and reconciliation.[25]

The Methodist Church had been involved in the TRC, even though the church council responded that their local congregation had not been so engaged. Alex Boraine, for example, was a Methodist minister and former president of the Methodist Church who served as deputy chairperson of the TRC.

The congregation had no vision statement, but it had a mission statement. The mission statement was displayed on one of the tapestries in the church's chancel, and on its official letterheads and other documents. The statement read:

> Empowered to touch the world for Christ.[26]

The congregation explained that ministry and social engagement in Athlone Methodist Church was rooted in the mission statement. Activities such as the women's and men's organisations, school feeding scheme, soup kitchen, etc. were a consequence of their mission statement.[27]

The mission statement emphasised that they were a congregation who sought to be an active church, serving the community in various ways through their ministry. The statement was very brief, and did not reflect the reconciliation or transformation that were part of the country's democratisation.

Lutheran Church in Bellville – Evangelical Lutheran Church in Southern Africa Cape Church

The Lutheran Church in Bellville is situated in one of the suburbs of Cape Town. The congregation had a German background, and most of the members were of German descent. They emphasised their German heritage, and supported the German community in Cape Town.

---

25 Church Council Interview Protocol 2011-03-20.
26 Athlone Methodist Church, Athlone Society Profile, c.a. 2008, p. 1, Church Publication.
27 Athlone Methodist Church, Athlone Society Profile, c.a. 2008, p. 1, Church Publication.

The church council was not very familiar with the TRC's work. They were asked whether the TRC had affected the congregation, and the council answered with a unanimous "No".[28] One of the members added: "Not at all".[29] Issues around the TRC were not important to the church council. They were also asked whether they had considered following any recommendations made in the TRC's final report, and in response the council was silent. Their reaction was not unusual: few church councils had any knowledge of the TRC's final reports. They did not mention that they had participated in any reconciliation services.

The responses about reconciliation and the TRC have to be understood against the church's background and history. ELCSA-Cape had to follow the rules of the colonial power when the church was established in the Cape Colony, and they had catered for the German community in South Africa. They were a church in South Africa; but at the same time they ministered to people of German background. The situation set the church apart from the rest of South African society.[30]

The church council did not mention that they had participated in any reconciliation services, but in the past, before democratisation, they had had services and eucharists together with ELCSA congregations across ethnic boundaries. These services were no longer held.[31] The situation could be characterised in these terms: that, together with other congregations, the congregation had started a process of reconciliation as part of the Church's catholicity, but this practice had been discontinued.

The congregation did not have a vision and mission statement displayed in the church, or in its magazines or liturgical documents. The congregation instead had a motto or slogan that could be regarded as a mission statement:

> A church for you — a church for you in the heart of Bellville.[32]

The motto was explained in the minister's reports to the annual general meeting: "[…] This motto spells out the mission into which we and our church have been called. To create a space, where people can find a home – a place where we bear each other's burdens and joys, a place where you may rest with your joys and

---

28 Church Council Interview Protocol 2011-03-15.
29 Church Council Interview Protocol 2011-03-15.
30 One of the council members stated, for example: "In the past the Lutheran church felt like a guest in South Africa […]". Church Council Interview Protocol 2011-03-15.
31 Church Council Interview Protocol 2011-03-15.
32 Hahne, Albrecht, 2010, p. 1, Church Publication; Hahne, Albrecht, 2011, p. 1, Church Publication.

your frustrations and still be accepted without having to fulfil any preconditions. [...]".[33] The church was described not as an organisation but as a relationship. This relationship was expressed as communion with God and among the people. Everybody had a place in this communion, the church. The congregation also had a mission to reach out to the world, and the congregation was located in Bellville, where they had a task to accomplish.[34]

The motto focused on the local church community, and nothing reflected the history of South Africa or the need for reconciliation. There was, however, the image of an inclusive community. The church was for everybody, and the minister's interpretation described a community of people where everybody had a place to go. The inclusive message could be seen as a goal to achieve, but it required sensitivity to people's needs in Bellville.

City Harvest Ministries in Ntuzuma – Apostolic Faith Mission of South Africa

People who lived in Ntuzuma, outside Durban, had not experienced significant social change in the area since democratisation. Unemployment, poor communication, inferior education, poverty, inadequate housing, etc. had not undergone main changes in their township. The work of the TRC, with the concomitant expectations of restitution, had not been realised. The TRC's effect on the church was unclear, but was mostly understood as social. A church council member said about the TRC's effects on the church: "I don't think so. In a way, it does".[35] The answered was developed by another person, who stated:

> It's a social issue. You can't say that it is not affecting you. ... there was a guy who was working as a mechanic and he did not get a pension. Yes, he did not get a pension and lost his job as a mechanic, and you cannot say that it did not affect you as a person. When you know somebody who has been affected by the issues of apartheid, and what is reconciliation. It did not come up. Nobody came up and said 'I did this'. So those are the issues that still are not resolved. And people had to go to counselling, to counselling, to counselling, and others had hope but reconciliation did not come.[36]

Reconciliation had not become visible, and there were still unresolved issues from the TRC process. The church council's description was not about the changes their church might have experienced, but rather their disappointment about the

---

33 Hahne, Albrecht, 2010, p. 1, Church Publication.
34 Hahne, Albrecht, 2011, p. 1, Church Publication.
35 Church Council Interview Protocol 2011-03-27.
36 Church Council Interview Protocol 2011-03-27.

outcome of the TRC process. City Harvest Ministries was established in the democratic South Africa and after the TRC had taken place; and so it had not been part of the democratisation process. They did not hold reconciliation services, 'healing of memory' talks, or other acts of reconciliation with other AFM congregations of other ethnic groups. A congregation in a township has very limited contact with congregations of other major ethnicities in Durban, because those other groups seldom visit the townships. City Harvest Ministries was, however, ministering in an area where there were many people who would be considered marginalised and needing social change.

They had established the congregation in Ntuzuma on purpose, because it was an underprivileged area. They wanted to minister in a deprived area in what could be seen as an act of reconciliation. The members of the congregation were from the same ethnic group, and they did not have much contact with congregations of other ethnic groups. Signs of a reconciled church that transcends ethnic boundaries and celebrates the eucharist to enhance Christian communion were not mentioned by the church council.[37]

One member mentioned that affirmative action was something that had changed the situation from the past, although the TRC had not changed the lives of people in Ntuzuma. A church council member acknowledged that the policy had been good both for the underprivileged and for women:

> Yes, because it has redressed some issues that were there when we had apartheid as you were talking about women now. So, even in the workplace you would say that there are mostly men, and there have been a majority of other races, and we haven't been seeing the black people. So, I think for now, it's good. It will come to a point when we say we will redress and go back to normal.[38]

Affirmative action was something temporary in order to change the situation for 'Black' people and for women. It is interesting that, even though the congregation emphasises the spiritual conditions in life, the council member highlighted the need for certain social changes in society. Affirmative action, RDP, BEE, ABET, GEAR programmes, etc. were important, even if the people did not see that the TRC had managed to make the necessary changes in society.[39] External

---

37 Church Council Interview Protocol 2011-03-27.
38 Church Council Interview Protocol 2011-03-27.
39 RDP (Reconstruction and Development Programme), BEE (Black Economic Empowerment), ABET (Adult Basic Education and Training), GEAR (Growth, Employment and Redistribution).

factors such as affirmative action might, in the future, even influence the social situation, and people's ethnic diversity would become less important.

City Harvest Ministries had created vision and mission statements that were part of their constitution. The statements did not address any social change or reconciliation. Their vision statement exclusively emphasised the congregation's need for numerical growth. The vision was "To be a God-centred and effectively harvesting family; that extends the Kingdom of God".[40]

The phrase, "extends the Kingdom of God", could have many interpretations, and could include reconciliation for unity with other people. Another interpretation is that the church should grow numerically. The mission statement was quite clear that the congregation's intention was to increase its membership. The mission statement declared:

> Inviting individuals to become members of the family of Christ; (John 1:39)
> Equipping them to effective spiritual growth; (Ephesians 4:11–13)
> Sending them to fulfil the Great Commission (Matthew 28:18–20).[41]

The congregation's mission statement called their attention to conversion, spiritual development, and making new disciples according to the so-called 'Great Commission'. It is noteworthy that the vision and mission statements did not consider the social situation in Ntuzuma, and exclusively emphasised the spiritual extension of the Kingdom of God – although 'the Kingdom of God' could possibly include the interpretation that a just society was sought. Reconciliation or transformation were not mentioned.

The congregation stated in their constitution that their main objectives were to minister to the needs of the total person. The congregation's first objective was to proclaim God and to preach the gospel of Jesus Christ, but the second was to provide community service and to develop projects in collaboration with other organisations. Their second object could be characterised as a response in order to change unequal conditions in society.[42]

City Harvest Ministries in Ntuzuma interpreted 'reconciliation' as changes that reduced inequality in society. The process required restitution, which had not been visible. Reconciliation within the AFM was not mentioned by the church council, and the privileged congregations had not yet begun to act. City Harvest Ministries could possibly work for reconciliation and begin the process

---

40 City Harvest Ministries Constitution, 2011 p. 1, Church Publication.
41 City Harvest Ministries Constitution, 2011 p. 1, Church Publication.
42 City Harvest Ministries Constitution, 2011 p. 1, Church Publication.

of recognising community beyond ethnicity; but congregations of other ethnicities had to be prepared to participate.

St Michael's Evangelical Lutheran Church – Evangelical Lutheran Church in Southern Africa

St Michael's is situated in the city centre of Durban. The congregation belongs to ELCSA, and is one of few congregations in that church that have members from diverse ethnicities. Their diversity is the result of a merger of three separate congregations to form St Michael's.

The church council was asked whether the TRC had affected the congregation. Their answer came after a long silence: "Not directly".[43] They knew that Desmond Tutu, the former Anglican archbishop, had an important role in the TRC, and that several church leaders had been involved in its work. The church council believed that the TRC had been focused on individuals, and they did not see that they as a church were affected by the commission's work.[44]

The answer should not be understood as a lack of interest, but rather as reflecting the complexity of relating the commission's work to a local congregation's situation. The church council had not seen the report of the TRC, and their church had not emphasised any of the recommendations directed at the faith communities.

Nobody in the council mentioned whether they had participated in healing and reconciliation services. Members could have participated in these services in the past because they were held in central Durban churches. ELCSA is part of the SACC; and the church council stated that they were members of and participated in the Diakonia Council of Churches in Durban. Several ecumenical organisations had been promoting reconciliation services during and after democratisation.[45]

They had, however, been engaged in workshops run by the Institute for the Healing of Memories, even though the church council did not at first sight believe

---

43 Church Council Interview Protocol 2011-04-03.
44 Church Council Interview Protocol 2011-04-03.
45 Church Council Interview Protocol 2011-04-03. The Diakonia Council of Churches is an ecumenical organisation in Durban working with churches and church-related organisations to improve life for poor people and to change unjust structures in society. Diakonia was founded in 1976, during apartheid, to mobilise churches to work for a just society. After democratisation Diakonia merged with the Durban & District Council of Churches. The Diakonia Council of Churches today facilitates, enables and equips churches in Durban and the coastal region of KwaZulu-Natal to deal with challenges in South African society.

that their congregation was affected by the TRC.⁴⁶ These workshops had been run in the circuit together with ELCSA N-T, and there were plans to extend these workshops. The institute can be described as a continuation of the TRC process. One of the ministers who was part of the church council explained:

> Yes. The area which we are working at started actually with pastors in NT and from ELCSA and from the whole circuit, not so much from this parish. We took part in a 'healing of memories' from the Healing of Memories Institute. It was quite moving for all of us and we then decided to scale up to parish and congregational level. Subsequently there has been one 'healing of memories' workshop which has been attended by congregation members from St Michael's and from Lutherkirche, that's St Paul's, and our aim is to let more and more people of our congregations take part in these workshops. They play an important role bringing together and sharing. That's one entry between NT and ELCSA [...].⁴⁷

As noted by the minister, the workshop had been arranged in cooperation with the Institute for the Healing of Memories, and had participants from an ELCSA congregation, which had predominantly 'Black' members, and ELCSA N-T with its predominantly 'White' members of German descent. The members came from various parishes in the circuit and from St Michael's. The plan was to continue with the workshops and extend the participation so that more people from parishes and congregations could be part of the workshops.

The members in the church council might not have seen the connection between the TRC and the Institute for the Healing of Memories. The Institute flowed out the commission's work and philosophy. The workshops can be characterised as the practice of a reconciliation process in which members of the divided Lutheran churches, who were also diverse ethnic groups, could tell their

---

46 The Institute for the Healing of Memories was started by Fr Michael Lapsley, an Anglican priest who was a member of the ANC. He received a letter bomb when he was living in exile in Zimbabwe. He lost both hands and the sight of one eye through injuries caused by the bomb. He participated in the TRC, and told his story as a victim of the previous government; but nobody confessed to having sent the bomb to him. In 1998, after his experience of the reconciliation process in South Africa, he established the Institute for the Healing of Memories (IHOM). The institute facilitates workshops that make it possible for people from different background to reach a better understanding of themselves and of other people's contexts and history. The institute seeks to contribute to the healing journey of individuals, communities, and nations. Through listening and sharing, human relationships can be transformed and restored. The institute is based in Cape Town, but works throughout South Africa and internationally.

47 Church Council Interview Protocol 2011-04-03. NT is an abbreviation for ELCSA N-T.

stories. They could gain new insights into the current situation, and together strive for a different kind of community.

The workshops can also be characterised as the start of reconciliation towards a united Lutheran community in South Africa. St Michael's already had members of diverse ethnicities, and they worshipped together and celebrated the eucharist. This can be seen as a congregation practising reconciled community in accordance with the understanding of the Church's catholicity put forward in this thesis. However, the journey of reconciliation towards a united Lutheran community in South Africa had just begun, and it would not be completed before the churches achieved unity.

The congregation had a vision statement that was based on three terms; *Rejoice*, *Renew*, and *Reach out*. The statement stressed the present situation of diversity and challenges in the country, with their background in the country's reconciliation process. The vision statement declared:

> Rejoice in the Lord always! We as Lutheran Christians in Durban rejoice in the fact that we are God's children, created and loved by him in our diversity. Rejoicing in song and dance, with food and laughter. God is with us!
>
> Renew – Create in me, O Lord, a pure heart! We live out of God's mercy and forgiveness – a refreshing new start, whenever we turn to Him. As a nation with a past full of hurt and a present with many challenges and temptations, renewal through God's presence is vital and vitalizing.
>
> Reach Out your hand and put it into my side – stop doubting and believe! Jesus' call to Thomas encourages us to reach out and share with others the blessings of God's presence. We share the doubts and fears of those whose everyday life is a struggle. We are open to God calling us to bring love and hope in word and deed. We are part of God's mission to the world and as such see all our work as mission work.[48]

It is notable that the vision statement emphasised diversity as something positive, a cause for rejoicing. Diversity can be seen as a burden; but the vision statement emphasised that diversity was a gift, a contribution to the congregation's life and even to the country. In the analytical tool's understanding of the Church's catholicity, diversity is seen as very important.

The vision statement also stressed that the history of the country had caused hurt, and that at the present time there were many challenges and temptations. The hurt was caused by apartheid, and the challenges were how the people of South Africa could create a democratic country and a more equal society. The temptations could be interpreted as the advantages and benefits that some would

---

48 Lüdeman, Joe, 2012, pp. 2–3, Church Publication.

get at the expense of others. There was, however, hope that the people would be helped to renew and revitalise the society. The members were encouraged to share the gospel, even though they were doubtful about the possibility of transforming the congregation and community. They were encouraged to believe and acknowledge that they were part of God's mission.

The vision statement reflected an already diverse congregation where there were members from diverse ethnic groups, languages, and economic conditions. It is very interesting that the congregation's vision reflected the past, and that the members of the congregation could make changes. They recognised contemporary problems and stated that they could make a contribution. They acknowledged a wider community, and tried to work together with other churches globally towards unity, justice, peace, and reconciliation. The statement clearly reflected the truth that the congregation was not an isolated entity, and that the work of the reconciliation process would continue. It is also important that the congregation was not only describing the past, but also looking at challenges, both present and future. The vision statement was in accordance with the catholicity of the Church, acknowledging a wider community where diverse gifts were exchanged. It is significant, for example, that the parish's annual report named support for those infected and affected by HIV/AIDS in interpreting their vision.[49]

The mission statement referred back to the vision, and declared:

> Rejoice, renew, reach out! This statement envisions a church that rejoices, its members being renewed, and thereby the church itself constantly renewing its outlook, objectives and operations, on the basis of the gospel. This leads the church to reach out, not only to its own members, but to those beyond the church walls. All initiatives of Durban Central Parish are to be seen as mission work.

> The church's mission is therefore to provide the resources – spiritual, intellectual and administrative – to enable members to take up their tasks (priesthood of all believers) with confidence, joy, forgiveness and the support they need.[50]

Their view of mission was to manifest their own vision statement. The mission was described as a holistic approach, in which everything that was done in the congregation was part of the church's mission. Everybody in the congregation had the responsibility to contribute to it according to their own specific gift; and this included the abilities of every member, without exception. It is interesting that they motivated the congregation's contribution in the Church's mission through

---

49 Lüdeman, Joe, 2012, p. 3, Church Publication.
50 Lüdeman, Joe, 2012, p. 3, Church Publication.

the notion of 'the priesthood of all believers', which has been central in Lutheran teaching in South Africa.

6.2 Church Leaders' views of Reconciliation

The aim of this thesis is to investigate how ethnicity is practised and perceived two decades after democratisation, and how the catholicity of the Church, in terms of the analytical tool, challenges South African congregations and churches about ethnicity. Reconciliation can be understood as a ministry to unite an ethnically-divided church, even though the TRC was primarily a mechanism to attain reconciliation between victims and perpetrators.

The church leaders who were general secretaries, or who held equivalent positions, in the selected churches and denominations were also approached about their church's or denomination's responses to the country's reconciliation process. The views of the church leaders are especially interesting because they possess insights into the approach of the churches or denominations during democratisation and into initiatives that followed in later years. They also have an overview of the diverse incentives to stimulate reconciliation. The Faith Communities Hearing that took place in 1997, and its effects on the churches' situation, is of particular interest.

The general secretary of the Southern African Catholic Bishops' Conference, Vincent Brennan, was asked whether the TRC had influenced the Roman Catholic Church. Brennan responded: "It was so much an individual thing".[51] He thought that it had not affected the church directly, and it was more of an individual conversation. He reflected that it had often been said that the TRC may have succeeded in letting the truth be spoken, and had given people a platform where they could tell their story, but had failed to bring about reconciliation. He referred to Desmond Tutu who had, according to Brennan, said: "That is the role of the church, to work on the reconciliation".[52] The Roman Catholic Church responded to the recommendations of the TRC, according to Brennan, by contributing to nation-building, but less to internal reconciliation within the church. His statement might indicate that reconciliation across ethnic divisions had not been completely attained.[53]

Brennan also declared that the churches should have become more involved in the reconciliation process of the TRC. Churches had been more engaged during

---

51 Brennan, Vincent, Interview Protocol 2011-03-01.
52 Brennan, Vincent, Interview Protocol 2011-03-01.
53 Brennan, Vincent, Interview Protocol 2011-03-01.

the struggle because there was an enemy who gave a sense of unity and purpose. This kind of unity had disappeared when the churches had gone back to focusing on their own affairs.[54] Most churches could be described in similar terms as the Roman Catholic Church: they had fought against apartheid as a common enemy, and other problems in the churches had been put aside to be dealt with at a later time. Churches had to deal with internal matters when democratisation arrived, and the impetus to continue the reconciliation process was lost. The common enemy that united the churches was also no longer present.

When Brennan was asked about one of the recommendations of the TRC to faith communities about organising their own TRC, he responded: "Not the church nationally, not the whole church, individual dioceses did have programmes of looking at the residue of racism within the church. ... They looked at their own structures, their own management, and their own government".[55] The issue of an internal TRC was never on the bishops' conference agenda, and it was not considered at central level. Brennan acknowledged that the issue had been discussed by the Southern African Council of Priests, an organisation for diocesan priests in Southern Africa. They had dealt with truth, reconciliation and healing within their own structures after the country's democratisation. However, the SACBC had a land desk that was dealing with land re-distribution.[56] Brennan's answer revealed that the church could have made much greater efforts to work on internal reconciliation. Few attempts had been made to address the church's own segregation as a response to the TRC.

One effort to deal with 'race' relations in the Roman Catholic Church was the report named *Race Relations and the Catholic Church in South Africa a decade after apartheid*, produced by the SACBC in 2005 and mentioned by Vincent Brennan.[57] The report had been much debated, and was part of a process of dialogue, reflection, and consultation that had been taken place throughout the Roman Catholic Church in South Africa in 2003 and 2004, through eight regional seminars in different dioceses. The report highlighted the legacy of apartheid that still affected people's lives in their congregations, parishes, dioceses, and social

---

54 Brennan, Vincent, Interview Protocol 2011-03-01.
55 Brennan, Vincent, Interview Protocol 2011-03-01.
56 Brennan, Vincent, Interview Protocol 2011-03-01. One example of dealing with truth and reconciliation within the Southern African Council of Priests took place during the 1995 annual general meeting, when RDP, TRC, reconciliation, and healing were studied and debated. Entre Nous, 1995.
57 Race Relations and the Catholic Church in South Africa, 2005.

interactions.⁵⁸ These regional seminars can be seen as a continuation of the TRC process, but the seminars did not continue.

Another project that Brennan named, and that could be related to the TRC, was an inter-diocesan consultation that discussed the unity of the church. This consultation process took place over several years, and looked at the meaning of being a Catholic church in South Africa. The consultation was a way of identifying the challenges facing the church at the time, including the challenge to contextualise itself. It was not about reconciliation alone, but about facing the reality two decades after democratisation. The consultation had three phases, according to Brennan: the first examined the present in the light of the past, and was completed in 2010. The second phase dealt with theological reflection on the nature of the Church; and the third stage was intended to chart a way forward through the adoption of new goals for the church in Southern Africa.⁵⁹

Brennan said also that the SACBC had founded the Denis Hurley Peace Institute after the TRC. The institute arose in response to a request from other parts of Africa for a South African contribution to similar situations where there had been violence. The institute was established by the SACBC in order to help other parts of Africa. It worked outside South Africa, while the Justice and Peace Department of the SACBC worked with justice issues within South Africa. The Justice and Peace Department dealt with, for example, liberation, violence, wages, and employment issues. They tried, according to Brennan, to bring the theological voice of the church's social teaching to society.⁶⁰

Brennan also maintained that the relationship between the different churches in South Africa had improved. The relationship between the Roman Catholic Church and the Dutch Reformed Church, for example, had been hostile in the past. Brennan said that they were currently good friends, and were working very well together. He considered that the relationship was dramatically different from the past, and there were new ways of relating to each other.⁶¹ Brennan's statement has to be understood from an historical point of view. The Roman Catholic Church had not been welcome to be established in South Africa. Under the previous government, the Dutch Reformed Church was favoured, and could have been considered as virtually a state-church. After democratisation the situation changed, and all faith communities were accorded the same status. The present

---

58 Race Relations and the Catholic Church in South Africa, 2005. Preface.
59 Brennan, Vincent, Interview Protocol 2011-03-01. Inter-Diocesan Consultation 2012, 2011.
60 Brennan, Vincent, Interview Protocol 2011-03-01.
61 Brennan, Vincent, Interview Protocol 2011-03-01.

close relationships between the faith communities can be characterised as a response to the recommendations of the TRC.

The Roman Catholic Church had achieved many improvements in accordance with the TRC, although Brennan said that the church could have made many more efforts to promote reconciliation. There were external programmes in the form of the redistribution of land; some dioceses had participated in dialogue programmes; and an inter-diocesan consultation was dealing with important contemporary issues in the church. Furthermore, they had a Justice and Peace Department that was engaged in human rights issues within the country. Dealing with the past was still important, because many of the church's congregations still reflected apartheid's patterns. External actions to bring about restitution and social change were possibly perceived as essential if unequal economic conditions in the country were to be changed.

The Roman Catholic Church has many characteristics that could be identified as reflecting the Church's catholicity. It was not divided on ethnic lines, and the central church organisation shared in national reconstruction for a just society with restitution. Reconciled diversity is less evident, however, because the congregations continue to reflect apartheid's patterns.

The Provincial Executive Officer of the Anglican Church of Southern Africa, Allan Kannemeyer, could not comment on his church's response to the recommendations of the TRC, as they – and the process of democratisations itself – had been made before he became Provincial Executive Officer. He commented that the church did not have its own TRC, and that there had not been any formal process to reflect on their own church's practices during the apartheid years. Kannemeyer explained that the Anglican Church had never had to stand up and say: "We are sorry for what we have done".[62] The church never saw itself as a perpetrator of apartheid, according to Kannemeyer.[63] The Anglican Church is not unique in this. Several churches did admit their collaboration with the previous government during the Faith Communities Hearing; but most churches or denominations have not dealt with the past. It is important to note that a church that has not confessed previous guilt will find it difficult to practise restitution as part of living out the Church's catholicity.

Kannemeyer stated that, unlike some of the Afrikaner churches, the Anglican Church did not see the need to reconcile with the past. The church did not think it had done much wrong, and Kannemeyer thought that TRC had not gone far

---

62 Kannemeyer, Allan J., Interview Protocol 2011-03-16.
63 Kannemeyer, Allan J., Interview Protocol 2011-03-16.

enough in their church. He could not recall any Anglican bishop, priest, or congregation making a confession, even though this was a vision of former Archbishop Desmond Tutu. Kannemeyer believed that the Anglican Church was affected by the TRC, although he could question the church's performance after the TRC.[64] Kannemeyer's recognition is representative of the Anglican Church in Southern Africa. The church was very engaged in the struggle against apartheid, but at the same time it adopted the system as part of the society in which it was located; and the church had not acknowledged the need for internal reconciliation.

Kannemeyer mentioned one example where the church had not yet addressed the need for reconciliation. Archbishop Thabo Makgoba had delivered a speech during the Provincial Synod of the Anglican Church of Southern Africa in September 2010.[65] Makgoba mentioned the damage that was experienced by 'White' people through their conscription into the national defence force during apartheid, and said that this was a challenge to the church. Young 'White' men who just had left school were forced to participate in the defence force, and some had even killed other people. This had never been addressed before, and some of the men had become ministers in the Anglican Church. The archbishop's message, according to Kannemeyer, resulted in a massive outpouring of emotion at the synod. Kannemeyer stated: "White clergy came to the podium, started to talk about this, and collapsed, crying".[66] Kannemeyer said that it was too emotional to deal with, and the archbishop held a follow-up discussion to see how deep these issues went in the church. He stressed that there was an ongoing conversation in the church at the time about how to deal with the wounds of apartheid. He was asking himself how the church could heal these memories.[67] The TRC had mentioned in their report the churches' support for the previous government especially by supporting the military chaplaincy, which had given moral legitimacy to the culture of gross human rights abuses.[68] Kannemeyer's example indicated that internal reconciliation had not yet been accomplished, even though many in the church believed that it had not contributed to apartheid. Other churches had similar unfinished issues that needed to be addressed if they were to achieve reconciliation.

Nevertheless, Kannemeyer mentioned the Institute for the Healing of Memories, run by an Anglican priest, as an example of a response to the TRC. The

---

64 Kannemeyer, Allan J., Interview Protocol 2011-03-16.
65 The Provincial Synod is the highest decision-making body of ACSA, and meets every third year.
66 Kannemeyer, Allan J., Interview Protocol 2011-03-16.
67 Kannemeyer, Allan J., Interview Protocol 2011-03-16.
68 Truth and Reconciliation Commission of South Africa Report, Vol. 4, 1998, p. 70.

institute did not address the Anglican Church only: it was not confined to the Anglican Church, but addressed the whole nation. It was not surprising, said Kannemeyer, that the Institute for the Healing of Memories was an initiative arising from the Anglican Church, because of its spirituality.[69] The Institute was started by an Anglican minister who was a victim of apartheid, and it ran reconciliation workshops. The unique Anglican spirituality that Kannemeyer mentioned is, among other things, devoted to social engagement in the society, and has had a long tradition in South Africa.[70]

Kannemeyer was also asked about the significance of having had a former Anglican archbishop as chair of the TRC. Kannemeyer replied that Desmond Tutu had not signed the Kairos Document in 1985, when he was Archbishop of Cape Town. He explained: "Tutu was very careful not to be aligned to any particular grouping. He was protective of his prophetic voice, and prophets speak as lone voices".[71] Kannemeyer clarified that prophets did not speak on behalf of an assembly, but addressed the assembly. Kannemeyer added that, even when Tutu called for sanctions, he was careful not to speak on behalf of the church. This was his way of maintaining his independence.[72]

Kannemeyer explained that, when Tutu was appointed to be the chair of the TRC, he was both tied to his church and independent of his church. The church was proud of him, and they thought that they owned him; but the TRC was not a church process. It was a government process, and the church did not even second him. Kannemeyer explained that there was sufficient distance between the church, Archbishop Tutu, and the government. This made Tutu's independence possible, because the TRC was also going to say some uncomfortable things about the church. Kannemeyer's response makes it clear that the Anglican Church had been proud of having Desmond Tutu as the chair of the TRC, but that Tutu was not captive to the church, and represented the people of South Africa in a way that went beyond church, denominational, and faith borders.[73]

---

69 Kannemeyer, Allan J., Interview Protocol 2011-03-16.
70 One example of a socially-engaged spirituality is that of the Community of the Resurrection, an Anglo-Catholic religious community originating from England. The community trained Desmond Tutu and many other South African Anglican clergy at St Peter's College in Rosettenville, Johannesburg. One of the community's members was Trevor Huddleston, a well known anti-apartheid activist and a mentor to Tutu.
71 Kannemeyer, Allan J., Interview Protocol 2011-03-16.
72 Kannemeyer, Allan J., Interview Protocol 2011-03-16.
73 Kannemeyer, Allan J., Interview Protocol 2011-03-16.

The general secretary of the Methodist Church of Southern Africa, Vuyani Nyobole, had participated in the work of the TRC. He believed that its advantages were to open doors, but that a lot of unfinished business remained. The TRC was about truth and reconciliation, but very little reconciliation took place during the process. He stated that the legal framework of the TRC had favoured the perpetrators rather than the victims, which he obviously believed was not right. Nyobole was also asked about the Methodist Church's participation in the country's truth and reconciliation process. He replied that the Methodist Church was not challenged by the TRC. For example, they did not pass any resolutions about moving the church forward, and neither did they have their own TRC, as had been suggested by the commission.[74]

Neither the Anglican Church nor the Methodist Church had been divided on ethnic lines at the regional and central level. Their unity could be considered as being true to the Church's catholicity. They were, however, divided in practice at the local level because of where people lived, and a major restitution process had not been established after democratisation.

Nyobole's remarks were similar to those of Allan Kannemeyer about the Anglican Church. The Methodist Church was active in the TRC process, and one of their former ministers and presidents had served as the deputy chairperson of the TRC. Despite the involvement of many prominent Methodists in the TRC, Nyobole nevertheless believed that the church had not been challenged by the commission's work.[75] His statement indicates that after the TRC there was no movement to seek reconciliation. The church had to take care of internal matters after democratisation, and the national ecumenical movement did not take the kind of lead it had taken during the struggle.

The general secretary of the Apostolic Faith Mission, George Mahlobo, did not explicitly identify the TRC as important, but said that the whole democratisation process of the country had inspired their church. He recognised that the unification of their church was made possible because of the positive attitude of the former 'White' section towards bringing the two churches together. Frank Chikane, who had been the leader of the former 'Black' section of the AFM, and had also been general secretary of the SACC, had a good relationship with Isak Burger from the former 'White' section, and this had facilitated the unification. The environment created in the country during the democratisation process was

---

74 Nyobole, Vuyani Gladstone, Interview Protocol 2011-02-28.
75 Alex Boraine was a minister in the Methodist Church and had been a president of the MCSA. He served as deputy chairperson of the TRC.

specifically important, according to Mahlobo. Changes in the church, and the making of agreements, were particularly favourable during that time. He also affirmed that personal relationships were essential for the sake of reconciliation in the church.[76] The church's unification process, in which ethnic division is opposed, is a clear pointer towards being a catholic church. The Church is a communion of diversity, and ethnic diversity is no reason for division.

Mahlobo believed that the TRC had affected the AFM, but not to the extent that he had hoped. He thought that the church should have embraced the issue of reconciliation and restitution; but this did not happen at a corporate level. The TRC had affected the church in a number of other ways, but the emphasis on truth and reconciliation had taken place more at a personal level. Mahlobo described, for example, the situation when Frank Chikane met Adriaan Vlok in 2006, and Vlok had washed Chikane's feet.[77] Ceremonies and even liturgies were supported by the ecumenical movement as part of reconciliation; and such examples could have been applied on other levels in the church.

Mahlobo declared: "Out of that, as a leadership of the church, we were encouraging people not to sit with their guilt, those who had done wrong. We were encouraging our people, the victims, those who had been affected by what happened in the past, to be willing to forgive".[78] Mahlobo's examples confirmed the opinion about the TRC as a process that had affected the church on an individual level, but not collectively. His observation was similar to the other church leaders' remarks. All these conclusions are noteworthy. The catholicity of the Church, according to the analytical tool, emphasises that the church is a body where reconciliation takes place in the community. The TRC was perceived, rather, as an individual process of reconciliation.

George Mahlobo declared, like the other church leaders, that the AFM had not had their own TRC, but that the church had, at particular meetings at a national

---

76 Mahlobo, Mphikeleki George, Interview Protocol 2011-03-01.
77 Adriaan Vlok was Minister of Law and Order in the last apartheid government. He had discussed the situation of Khotso House (the building housing the SACC and a number of other anti-apartheid organisations) with the head of the security police. President Botha was informed about the situation and gave orders to take necessary steps to make the building unusable. Khotso House was bombed in 1988; Adriaan Vlok was responsible for ordering the secret police to do so. He received amnesty from the TRC. Amnesty Decision, 1999. Vlok contacted Frank Chikane in August 2006, and washed the feet of the former head of the SACC as a sign of reconciliation. Day, Katie, 2009, Website.
78 Mahlobo, Mphikeleki George, Interview Protocol 2011-03-01.

level, asked people to address the issue of reconciliation. The meetings created an environment that allowed people to tell their stories and to describe how the past had affected their lives and how they saw the future. Mahlobo stated that they had expected that the regional structures would roll out a similar process that would have been passed on to the congregations. He declared that they had not had a continuation of reconciliation, and the process remained personal.[79] His acknowledgement that the church had met at times to practise storytelling was similar to the method that had been developed out of the TRC.

Bishop Horst Müller from ELCSA N-T believed that neither the TRC nor the Faith Communities Hearing had had any consequences for the church as a whole. There had been those on the political right who were in favour of apartheid, and those who struggled against apartheid; and both types belonged to ELCSA N-T. The bishop's response made it clear that the church had members on both sides during apartheid. Some members had participated in the TRC as individuals, but the church did not participate as a whole community.

Müller confirmed, furthermore, that ELCSA N-T had not had their own TRC.[80] He said that the most important statement of the church had been a paper from 1986, which was more significant than the submission that ELCSA N-T had delivered to the TRC. Müller was probably referring to the document *Christ is Our Hope*, issued by UELCSA to their congregations, in which they declared that the church could no longer support the government's policies at that time.[81] The bishop's statement that there were different opinions about the past had still not been addressed. A fairly small church like ELCSA N-T, with members holding conflicting views, could easily initiate some kind of process to discuss the past of the church. A church with more members would require more funds to start a similar process.

The bishop of ELCSA-Cape, Nils Rohwer, declared that their church had not participated in the Faith Communities Hearing. When he was asked why the church had not done so, he answered: "Simply because of time … we are such a small group of people".[82] They did not even discuss the possibility of participating

---

79 Mahlobo, Mphikeleki George, Interview Protocol 2011-03-01.
80 Müller, Horst, Interview Protocol 2011-03-04.
81 UELCSA confessed in the statement that many people in the churches had supported government policies. They stated that they could no longer support such policies, especially in a political situation with much violence. Message of the Church Council to the congregations on the instruction of the General Synod, "Christ is our Hope", 1986, Church Publication.
82 Müller, Horst, Interview Protocol 2011-03-04.

in the hearings, and it was for practical rather than ideological reasons, according to Rohwer.[83] His response revealed that ELCSA-Cape did not see that they were fully part of the South African society, despite being one of the first churches to be established in the country.[84] Both ELCSA N-T and ELCSA-Cape had begun to receive members from different ethnic groups, but reconciliation with ELCSA had not yet begun. The Lutheran churches were still divided, which could be regarded as denying the Church's catholicity. The churches were still following the patterns from the time before democratisation, although some congregations had begun to be ethnically diverse.

The general Secretary of ELCSA, Bheki Mathe, was approached about ELCSA's absence from the Faith Communities Hearing. Mathe did not have a direct answer about why ELCSA contributed its submission to the TRC very late. He explained that the presiding bishop was not a full-time position, and the bishop at that time did not find it possible to give an answer in time.[85]

Mathe believed that the TRC was a good process, and a continuation of what the churches had been doing during the struggle against apartheid. He stated, though, that the TRC process had not been carried out properly. The wounds of the past were not clearly healed, because people still felt that there were those who had managed to escape. He believed that the TRC had happened too early for the 'Black' community, which had been excluded in many ways, to face their previous oppressors. Many of those who expressed themselves through the TRC were not yet accustomed to speaking publicly. They were still in the mentality that 'Blacks' were inferior to others. Mathe said: "They asked for forgiveness; what else could we do?"[86] Mathe's conclusions about the TRC are important. Living in a democratic South Africa with freedom of speech was not something that

---

83 Rohwer, Nils J., Interview Protocol 2011-02-09.
84 Rohwer, Nils J., Interview Protocol 2011-02-09.
85 The Berliner Mission is a German mission society that started the Lutheran mission in South Africa. It was one of the societies that were part of establishing ELCSA; and it was inspired by the TRC. The Berliner Mission produced a statement, published in 2000, that recognised and confessed attitudes, practices and a lack of sensitivity towards African history, culture and customs. They confessed that they did not resist apartheid legislation, and profited from the privileges of the 'Whites' and the colonial government. The statement was produced long after the TRC, and was received with reluctance among some within ELCSA. Statement on the History of the Berliner Mission in South Africa, 2000.
86 Mathe, P. Bheki, Interview Protocol 2011-03-07.

everyone experienced. Making demands of and challenging the perpetrator was not possible during that time either.

Mathe questioned whether it was possible to get amnesty without doing justice, or without being involved one hundred percent with the victims. He said: "When we come together about our bad past, there should be some programme of action and interaction at different levels to try to clear up the past".[87] Mathe was doubtful about the results of the TRC. It was not a critique of the commission's work, but rather of the results that later became visible when reconciliation had not been achieved in the society. He also acknowledged an inequality: some people in the society had not contributed to reconciliation, and there was a lack of restitution. There was, furthermore, an inequality when people who were victims were not ready, at that time, to give a full testimony. His questioning of the TRC's results, of not achieving restitution, is consistent with what the understanding of catholicity in the analytical tool demands.

The late contribution – or the lack of contribution – to the TRC's Faith Communities Hearing in East London in 1997 reveals the Lutheran churches' weak participation in the TRC's reconciliation process. They could have helped to accelerate the churches' unification process if all three Lutheran churches had participated in the hearing and contributed submissions. The churches, despite limited participation in the TRC, were challenged by the commission for having been racially divided, and for the fact that the 'Whites' had resisted unification.[88] Two decades after democratisation, the churches were still not united, despite several attempts and pressure from the LWF. A divided Lutheran church – even though there are no doctrinal differences, when they co-exist in the same society, and when the divisions are based on former divisions – is clearly an ecclesiological issue, and it denies the catholicity of the Church according to the analytical tool.

---

87 Mathe, P. Bheki, Interview Protocol 2011-03-07.
88 The TRC wrote in its final report: "Besides the Afrikaans churches and the Apostolic Faith Mission, the Lutheran Church, too, was racially divided; its White members consistently refused to join the unity movement that was to become the Evangelical Lutheran Church". Truth and Reconciliation Commission of South Africa Report, Vol. 4, 1998, pp. 68–69. It is striking that ELCSA N-T did not mention the divided Lutheran community in their submission. In the document from 1987, *A word of hope in the present situation in South Africa*, the church stated that they wanted to take practical steps towards church unity at all levels with their predominantly 'Black' sister church. Lutheran Church of Southern Africa Natal-Transvaal, Submission, 19 March 1998; A Word of Hope in the Present Situation in South Africa by the council of the Evangelical Lutheran Church in Southern Africa (Natal-Transvaal), 1987.

6.3 Commissioners of the TRC's views of Reconciliation

Piet Meiring and Mary Burton were two commissioners of the TRC who were interviewed about the churches' involvement in the TRC. Piet Meiring had been a professor in theology at the University of Pretoria and a member of the Dutch Reformed Church. Mary Burton was a former president of the Black Sash, and a member of the Anglican Church.[89]

Piet Meiring was the commissioner in charge of the Faith Communities Hearing in East London in 1997. He explained that most newspapers had been present at the hearing, and there were huge hopes surrounding the churches' contribution to the truth and reconciliation process. He stressed that there were many expectations and challenges about how the churches could promote reconciliation. They had hoped that a large number of small TRCs would develop in communities, towns, and cities. He also explained that they had hoped that there would have been groups of people who were brought together to tell their stories. During the TRC, the commissioners had understood the power of stories as an important contribution to reconciliation. Meiring explained that storytelling was part of African culture. Mary Burton expressed a similar view, that the TRC had created a mechanism for opportunities for people to listen to one another.[90]

Piet Meiring explained that the Faith Community Hearing was a very good experience, but that the result was disappointing. He said that many people had later expressed the view that the churches had missed an opportunity to contribute to reconciliation, and that this was seen as an embarrassment. The churches' participation had not accomplished or realised what had been expected. One reason, Meiring said, was that the SACC had a new role after democratisation. It had been the guiding institution for the churches, but the organisation had lost its sense of purpose, and could not complete its tasks.[91] Meiring was referring to the SACC's leading position in the country's protests against apartheid. When apartheid was abolished, one of the SACC's most important issues disappeared.

The SACC found it difficult to adjust to the new situation, and lost its direction. Meiring also commented that many talented people had left the organisation and

---

89 The Black Sash started in 1955 as a non-violent 'White' women's anti-apartheid movement. The organisation initially protested against separate representation in the Cape Province legislature. The women continued to protest against the pass laws, and later advocated against apartheid.
90 Meiring, Piet, Interview Protocol 2011-03-05; Burton, Mary, Interview Protocol 2011-03-23.
91 Meiring, Piet, Interview Protocol 2011-03-05.

gone to work for the government. The SACC was drained, and became diminished.[92] Meiring's explanation of the SACC's shortcomings is relevant; and there was also a lack of support from the churches. In addition, the SACC found it difficult to re-orientate after the political changes. The organisation had been against the previous undemocratic government, and was positive towards the new democratic government. It was difficult to continue to have a critical voice vis a vis the new government. Churches had, for example, to deal with particular social issues that had been largely ignored before democratisation. Meiring confirmed the notion that many church leaders had mentioned, that the churches found it difficult to continue the reconciliation process.[93]

Mary Burton also believed that, for various reasons, South Africa had not done well with reconciliation. She believed, for example, that the TRC's recommendations had not been followed, and few people had even read the TRC's reports and recommendations. She expressed the view that there had been too many recommendations, and that this had reduced the possibilities of achieving the goals. The recommendations would have been received differently – and would have been given more attention – if there had been fewer of them, she said.[94]

When Burton was asked about the TRC's recommendation to the churches, she agreed that South Africa was a religious country, but that the churches had found it difficult to change. She said that it was unusual for people of different backgrounds to come together in the churches. There were places like cathedrals, however, where people of different backgrounds could meet. There were small groups of people that wanted to bring about reconciliation, but the process was not led by the churches.[95] She said: "It is uphill work. We are still very, very divided. We

---

92 Meiring, Piet, Interview Protocol 2011-03-05.
93 Several messages delivered at the SACC's Vanderbijlpark consultation in 1995 and the Johannesburg consultation in 1996 mentioned the churches' difficult position in the new democratic South Africa. Both consultations also named several social issues that churches needed to address, such as poverty and HIV. Being the Church in South Africa Today, 1995; An African Challenge to the Church in the 21st Century, 1997.
94 Burton, Mary, Interview Protocol 2011-03-23.
95 Mary Burton said that she belonged to a congregation in Rondebosch that had a link with a congregation in Gugulethu. When she went to church in Gugulethu she was warmly welcomed, but she got special attention. She was longing for the day when people could go to different churches without much notice being taken of the fact. St George's Cathedral in Cape Town was a church where people of different backgrounds could meet without much fuss, but it was not easy to achieve. The cathedral had a committee for justice and reconciliation, and it had taken a number of initiatives. She explained that there were small groups of people who wanted to

are divided by language, by appearance, by economic issues, and just because they don't know each other".[96] Burton's experience of a divided society where, two decades after democratisation, the churches have not been able to change, is notable. According to the understanding of catholicity developed in the analytical tool, the churches are supposed to practise reconciliation, overcome divisions, and achieve a visible unity; but this was obviously not the case.

Burton declared that, despite problems, contradictions, and criticisms, the TRC had accomplished its tasks as well as it possibly could, given the situation and the specific circumstances. In her view, the TRC did a reasonable job of confronting the South African public with the truth of what had happened during apartheid. She added: "You don't find anybody now that can deny the atrocities that happened. There is still more to be discovered of course, but the denial that was customary is no longer possible".[97] Burton was referring to the past, when people avoided recognising the abuses of the undemocratic government. The commission had been able to reveal and expose the human rights violations, and nobody could deny the truth any longer.

Both commissioners agreed that reconciliation was difficult to attain, particularly in a country that had been damaged by apartheid. Meiring explained that South Africa was a very racially-structured society. He said: "Racism is an ugly dragon, and is always there. It is always there. Even in churches with a long ecumenical tradition, it is difficult to kill the dragon".[98] He added that it was one thing to erase the word 'apartheid' from people's speech and writings, but erasing the word from their hearts and minds was difficult. Meiring gave examples from the political discussions, which had seen many accusations by the different ethnic groups. Politicians, for example, polarised the nation by talking about the country as a 'Black' and a 'White' nation.

Burton also referred to the political racial debates in the news. She said that race was a product of the country's history, and South Africa was a racist society. Everyone had been socialised into racism, and it was a political and economic reality.[99] The former commissioners' explanations made it clear that reconciliation between groups in the society was not an easy task, and it would take a long time

---

work for justice and reconciliation, but they were not led by the Church. Burton, Mary, Interview Protocol 2011-03-23.
96 Burton, Mary, Interview Protocol 2011-03-23.
97 Burton, Mary, Interview Protocol 2011-03-23.
98 Meiring, Piet, Interview Protocol 2011-03-05.
99 Meiring, Piet, Interview Protocol 2011-03-05; Burton, Mary, Interview Protocol 2011-03-23.

to recover from the apartheid legacy. The construction of 'race' had penetrated deep into peoples' perception of humanity, and was difficult to eliminate. Reconciliation had not yet been achieved, and the churches still had a task to fulfil as part of their catholicity.

Burton acknowledged one complexity about reconciliation. She said that she could understand it when 'Black' people did not want to meet 'White' people with great enthusiasm. She declared:

> We try to impose our own White desire to come closer, and many Black people say, 'Why should we do that? Why should we make White people feel good? It doesn't make us feel good. It is not for us to salve their conscience. If they want to do something, that is fine, but why should we? … In the past, it was we who suffered under apartheid' […].[100]

She could understand 'Black' peoples' opinion, and emphasised that reconciliation was not a one-way track, and that reconciliation needed restitution. A lack of enthusiasm could possibly also be the expression of a strategy of resistance. The Church's catholicity, according to the analytical tool, means that restitution is part of reconciliation, and it would build bridges between people and eliminate resistance.

Burton also mentioned issues around language as part of the inequalities in the society. She noted that 'White' people did not make any effort to speak isiXhosa, for example, while 'Black' people had to learn English. Burton used the example of her congregation's twin congregation in Gugulethu. The members of that congregation could speak two or three languages, while her congregation used only one language. If her congregation used a different language every Sunday, they would soon learn some of the words in the prayers.[101] Burton stressed that reconciliation was not only a matter of coming together from diverse ethnic groups. Reconciliation was also a matter of power, and that the privileged literally had to restore the past. Issues of power cannot be underestimated because of inequalities in the society. The catholicity of the Church in the analytical tool emphasises a mutual sharing through which unequal conditions have to be eradicated. Language was another example of the issue of power and inequality. 'White' people did not make any effort to learn one of the indigenous languages, while many 'Black' people had to manage several languages, including English. Her views made it clear that reconciliation was not only a spiritual matter: it was closely linked to restitution.

---

100   Burton, Mary, Interview Protocol 2011-03-23.
101   Gugulethu is a previous 'Black' township in Cape Town. Burton, Mary, Interview Protocol 2011-03-23.

6.4 Conclusions

The TRC was an independent commission initiated by the government. Several prominent church leaders were commissioners, and the whole process was supported by the churches and the national ecumenical movement through the SACC. The process was not established by the churches, but the commission's mission was in accordance with the churches' view of reconciliation as being part of the Church's doctrine of catholicity. The responses from church councils, church leaders, and former commissioners made it clear that reconciliation was not easy to accomplish.

Almost all the church councils in the case study congregations stated that they had not been influenced by the TRC. Some of the council members indicated, however, that the whole democratisation process had influenced their congregations. It was the whole process, and not specifically the work of the commission, that had gradually changed people. The years during democratisation were even seen as creating a unique atmosphere in which unity within the churches could be realised. The TRC and its work did not bring about any significant change and transformation in the congregations, but together with other elements of democratisation and reconciliation, congregations were transformed. Despite the fact that the church councils claimed not to have been influenced by the TRC, some of the council members referred to practices of storytelling and methods of reconciliation that originated with the TRC. Council members were unaware of the TRC's impact on the reconciliation process in the country.

It is important to stress that the TRC was not primarily a mechanism to attain reconciliation between diverse ethnic groups in South Africa. It was an instrument to disclose gross violations of human rights and human dignity. Its mandate, furthermore, was to bring about reconciliation between perpetrators and victims so that they could continue to live together in the same society. The church councils' lack of knowledge about the TRC is due to the fact that they were neither victims nor accused of being perpetrators. That also helps to explain why the councils had limited knowledge of the TRC.

According to their responses, the church councils did not demonstrate that the congregations had been major agents of reconciliation and change, as the TRC had hoped. It is important to state that practising reconciliation was not absent from the congregations' life, and reconciliation was seen as something that was part of their ordinary services, especially at the liturgical confession. Reconciliation was practised within the congregations, but not in relation to congregations of other ethnic groups. The catholicity of the Church, as used in the analytical tool, stresses that reconciliation has not been attained if congregations remain divided along ethnic lines. Worshipping and celebrating the eucharist, and thus transcending ethnic boundaries, took place in some of the congregations, but it was rarely seen occurring across congregational boundaries.

The statements regarding reconciliation reveal an unequal power relation. Reconciliation cannot be implemented among congregations if relationships with congregations of predominantly different ethnicities are not established. Congregations in the suburbs were able to become ethnically diverse, while congregations in the townships remained as before. The privileged congregations have a particular responsibility to work for reconciliation and to draw closer to underprivileged congregations. To accomplish reconciliation, it is necessary to tell stories that challenge conditions in the society and that are followed by restitution, according to my analytical tool for the Church's catholicity.

None of the congregations mentioned that they had held any reconciliation services with liturgies inspired by the SACC. Some church council members had participated in such services, and they could also affirm that such services were still practised. These liturgies were seen, however, as a one-time event. But the catholicity of the church challenges the churches to see that reconciliation is part of the Church's ongoing ministry, and is a continuing process. Even though the TRC came to an end, churches still have a responsibility to establish truth and reconciliation processes that lead to social transformation. The church councils, church leaders, and former commissioners stated that many issues still needed to be addressed, and there were still opportunities for the churches to continue working for reconciliation in the society.

The country's history as an ethnically-divided society, and thus the need for reconciliation, were largely absent from the congregations' vision and mission statements. The main expressions in the statements were spiritually-oriented, although transformation and social engagement were also present. One congregation had very clear statements referring to the country's previous division on ethnic lines. Diversity in this congregation was seen as something to be appreciated, as a cause for rejoicing. Their statement was based on their already being a diverse congregation that included various ethnic groups and languages.

The church councils declared that the TRC was seen as something affecting only individuals. Individual testimonies and confessions were a major part of the TRC's public hearings, unlike most other institutional hearings. Individual hearings were also the main focus of the media.

The statements of the church councils about the weak continuation of the TRC were confirmed by the responses of the church leaders and former commissioners. Several of the church leaders stressed that the TRC was an individual process. They stated that the churches had not continued the reconciliation process, and had not been challenged by the TRC. The former commissioners also acknowledged that the TRC had not managed well with reconciliation, and that reconciliation was difficult to realise.

It is noteworthy that church councils, church leaders, and former commissioners emphasised that the reconciliation process had been generally viewed as an individual process. This perception indicates that the meaning of reconciliation has shifted towards being more individualistic. The catholicity of the church in the analytical tool emphasises, rather, a collective image of the church as a body or a communion. The individualistic approach was visible in the church councils' explanations for not participating in the reconciliation process. The responses emphasised the necessity of dealing with the differences between collective and individual reconciliation.

The society had had great expectations of the churches, but the churches did not continue with the process as the commission had hoped. One reason might have been that there were too many recommendations that were not possible to manage. Churches, for example, did not have their own TRC's, despite being encouraged by the commission to do so. Churches' internal engagements, and the SACC's new position, were mentioned as reasons for not continuing the reconciliation process. The SACC had experienced shortcomings that made it difficult for the organisation to continue to work as before.[102] Some church leaders stated that they had included storytelling in national conferences, had organised workshops, or had mentioned issues in meetings, but that these had not been part of a movement within their churches.

This chapter has explored how congregations and churches have dealt with reconciliation between ethnic groups since democratisation. The next chapter will investigate how ethnicity in general is reflected and perceived in the congregations and churches two decades after democratisation.

---

102 See, for example, Piet Meiring's analysis of the SACC's shortcomings after democratisation. Meiring, Piet, Interview Protocol 2011-03-05.

Chapter Seven: Ethnicity and the Christian Communion

The apartheid ideology implied a divided society at all levels, including residential, educational, work-place, transport, and social segregation. Segregation was not fully achieved in the religious sector, but churches followed the apartheid pattern by structuring their organisations and their congregations in line with the state ideology, as described in Chapter Five.

The international ecumenical movement rejected any form of segregation based on racist ideology. The WCC urged the South African churches to give attention to ecclesial unity, national reconstruction, and the development of a moral society and a just democratic culture when the country became democratic. Faith communities were specifically addressed by the TRC because they were seen as occupying a privileged position in South African society. They were respected and had far-reaching moral influence, as described in Chapter Two. The churches were seen to have a key role in healing and reconciliation initiatives, apart from the hope that the faith communities would embrace the responsibility to lay a moral foundation for the new society. Church members came from diverse groups in the society, and were encouraged to develop communities that transcended ethnic diversity. However, as described in the previous chapter, reconciliation was not easy to realise.

This chapter will examine ethnicity in the congregations and churches two decades after democratisation. It is primarily based on interviews with church councils and church leaders about how they perceived ethnic diversity in their congregations and churches. Firstly, I will examine the ethnic make-up of the case congregations and churches. Secondly, I will explore what influences ethnic diversity in the congregations, and whether it is possible for denominations to promote ethnic diversity in their communities.

7.1 Congregations Affected by Division

The previous government's apartheid policy forced the whole country, whether urban or rural, to be divided into different areas according to 'race'. There were specific areas for 'White', 'Coloured', 'Indian or Asian' and 'Black' people. 'Black' people could live in the cities because of their labour was needed, but they had to be citizens of one of the so-called 'Bantustans'. The Group Areas Act of 1950 laid the foundations of the apartheid policy, which became a reality in virtually every sphere of society. The law was repealed in 1991 as the democratisation process began, and people were allowed to choose where to live according to preference and affordability. Residential areas, and thus the churches' congregations, are still marked by the former government's dividing up of the society, but minor population movements are in progress.[1] The following description will show how congregations saw ethnicity in their communities.

St Peter Claver in Pimville – Roman Catholic Church

St Peter Claver congregation is situated in Soweto (an abbreviation of 'South Western Townships'). According to Census 2011, Soweto had a population of 1 271 628 inhabitants in 355 331 households, of whom 98.5 per cent described themselves as 'Black African'.[2] This indicates that South Africa's former 'Black' townships remained almost unchanged after democratisation. St Peter Claver congregation covered Pimville Zones 1–8, Klipspruit, and Kliptown, which had 85 873 inhabitants in 22 691 households. Around 98 to 99 per cent of the population identified themselves as 'Black African' in Zones 1–8 and Klipspruit. The only significant exception in the congregation's area was Kliptown, which had 68.2 per cent 'Black African' and 30.55 per cent 'Coloured' inhabitants.[3]

People who came to St Peter Claver were almost exclusively 'Black', either because they lived in Soweto or because they travelled to worship in that church. Those who travelled to services attended them specifically to be able to worship in isiZulu or Sesotho, or occasionally in Setswana. Some also travelled because they liked the style of the church services.[4] Travelling to the congregation was a consequence of vertical and lateral mobility for people who wanted to remain part of the congregation's community. Travelling across Johannesburg to attend a specific congregation becomes an ecclesiological structuring factor.

The congregation also had people from other African countries who attended their congregation and services. In addition, the congregation had occasional visitors from other continents, including Europe. People from other parts of Soweto and from rural areas moved into the congregation's area, as happened in many other townships. However, ethnic mobility in receiving new groups after democratisation was not significant, according to Census 2011. Diversity

---

1 Lemon, Anthony, 1991, pp. 17–22.
2 Census 2011, Soweto, Statistics South Africa, 2012.
3 Census 2011, Pimville Zones 1–8, Klipspruit and Kliptown, Statistics South Africa, 2013.
4 Observation Protocol 2011-02-27.

did not increase, which negatively affected the Church's catholicity in terms of the analytical tool.[5]

St Peter Claver had had a number of ministers and missionaries from Europe in the past, but more recently the ministers were South African. The church council was asked whether the ethnicity of the minister was an important issue in the congregation. They responded that for them it was not an issue whether their minister was 'White', 'Indian', or 'Coloured'. They said: "It is a big challenge to get people to become Christians… It is no way of fussing around the background of the priest as long as he is a true Christian … It does not matter as long as he is Christian".[6] Their response was an indication that ethnicity was unimportant as long as the minister was a devoted Christian. The congregation was used to having many ministers from diverse backgrounds, and they had no objection to receiving ministers from other ethnic backgrounds. The situation of having ministers from diverse backgrounds would happen less in the future because fewer missionaries – especially those from Europe – were coming to South Africa.[7] The church council's response could be seen as consistent with a catholicity that did not regard the ethnic background of the minister as significant.

Because of the apartheid policy, Johannesburg was still an ethnically-divided city, with certain areas inhabited predominantly by specific ethnic groups. Thus congregations remained separated along ethnic lines. The church council stated, however, that they had contact with other congregations in the diocese. They also took part in special meetings to which the bishop invited many people from around the diocese. And there were different kinds of exchange between congregations that were important signs of belonging together. The church council said, for example, that they had had two choirs visiting the congregation, and that this had reminded them of the unity of the church. The council said that the bishop was very important for the unity of the church, as a sign that they all belong to each other, irrespective of background.[8]

The congregation's contacts with other congregations within the diocese were regarded as an important basis for people of diverse ethnicities to meet. They were united by the diocese and their bishop, even though they were separated geographically. The ecclesiological perception of church unity that originates from the ministerial hierarchy is a distinctively Roman Catholic theology. The

---

5   Church Council Interview Protocol 2011-02-27; St Peter Claver Parish, Pimville, Soweto, 2011, Website.
6   Church Council Interview Protocol 2011-02-27.
7   Church Council Interview Protocol 2011-02-27.
8   Church Council Interview Protocol 2011-02-27.

ecumenical documents – and especially the BEM document – also stress that church leaders have a special responsibility for safeguarding and protecting the unity of the Christian community; and the church council confirmed this in their statement. Their image of the church leader as one who gathered people irrespective of ethnicity is a clear sign of the Church's catholicity according to the analytical tool. The church council also revealed aspects of catholicity when they said that they were in contact with other congregations through exchanges such as choirs visiting them. The church council's statement suggests that the most important task for the diocese and the church's ministry was to sustain a catholicity that transcended ethnic divisions.

The church council did not see it as a problem that there were congregations in Sandton City, for example, that mainly had 'White' members. Neither was it a problem that there was not a greater mix of different ethnic groups in the congregations. People attended church where they lived, and it was better for people to go to a church close to where they were staying instead of attending other congregations.[9] The council's statement indicated that they were at ease with geographically-based ethnic divisions. However, this did not mean that ethnicity was not seen as problematic, nor that divisions were accepted and internalised. Visions for another kind of church or society were not mentioned by the council.

The council acknowledged that they had people who travelled to their congregation because they liked its way of worship. Travelling to a specific congregation was accepted and not seen as strange. They confirmed that there were different types of Roman Catholic congregations, and that they worshiped in different styles. People could choose a church that they liked. Much, though, depended on the minister and on how the congregation worshiped, its choice of language, etc.[10] One of the council members said: "There are times when I prefer to go to other churches especially during Easter […]".[11] The statement was a sign that the council member appreciated different styles of worship, and that there were times when the member preferred to attend another church in order to experience another kind of church service. The experience also showed that 'local' could be fluid and could mean that baptised people in one place were part of a greater communion.

The church council explained that a person who did not like singing could choose to attend another church. If people liked music and dancing, they would, for example, attend a service at St Peter Claver in Pimville. One council member

---

9   Church Council Interview Protocol 2011-02-27.
10 Church Council Interview Protocol 2011-02-27.
11 Church Council Interview Protocol 2011-02-27.

explained: "Some people feel that it's better to worship where you come from. We in Soweto say it is nearer for us to come to church here... if we went to church in Sandton it would not be a problem".[12] This explanation showed that most people who attended St Peter Claver went to the church where they lived, but they would not have a problem with attending other churches' services within the Roman Catholic Church. The church council's responses showed clearly that there was an affinity between members of the church and the diocese, regardless of congregational membership. There was a generous attitude towards people attending other congregations according to personal preferences; and there was mutual recognition between the congregations in the diocese. Their perception of belonging to the same Roman Catholic Church, irrespective of where a congregation was located in Johannesburg or anywhere else, was in accordance with the Church's catholicity as understood in the analytical tool.

Catholicity as reflected in the ecumenical documents stresses that a local church should reflect the ethnic diversity that is found in the area the church serves. Local communities in the same area should also be in contact with each other. St Peter Claver in Pimville serves an area where most of the people are 'Black', which implies that they reflect the local composition of the people.

St Thomas' in Linden – Anglican Church of Southern Africa

According to Census 2011, Randburg, where Linden is situated, had 337 053 inhabitants in 123 767 households. There were 45.7 per cent that described themselves as 'White', 36.8 per cent as 'Black African', 8.6 per cent as 'Coloured', and 7.5 per cent as 'Indian or Asian'.[13] The suburb of Linden, part of greater Randburg, had a population of 8 629 inhabitants in 3 360 households. There were 66.7 per cent of people who described themselves as 'White', which was higher than in the rest of the area. There were 21.8 per cent 'Black African', which was lower than in the rest of Randburg. There was almost the same number of 'Indian or Asian' people at 7.9 per cent, but fewer 'Coloured' with only 2.5 per cent in Linden. The statistics confirm that there is an increased mix of different ethnic groups in this former 'White' suburb.[14]

St Thomas' congregation reflected the same ethnic diversity as the suburb of Linden. It was very obvious that the congregation had changed since democratisation. Church wardens, altar servers, musicians, choir members, Sunday school

---

12 Church Council Interview Protocol 2011-02-27.
13 Census 2011, Randburg, Statistics South Africa, 2013.
14 Census 2011, Linden, Statistics South Africa, 2013.

members and church attendants came from various ethnic groups, although the majority of the people were 'White' with English as their first language.[15] The variety of ethnic groups was also visible in the congregation's information leaflets and in the parish magazine. For example, people from different ethnic groups were shown in the profile page and in congregational and diocesan news in the parish magazine.[16] The change of ethnicities in the area and in the congregation is due to upward social mobility, combined with lateral geographic mobility. The increased ethnic diversity arising from new economic possibilities helped the congregation to transcend divisions as part of the Church's catholicity.

The church council was approached about why their congregation had become more diverse. One of the members replied: "Those who can afford it move to the areas they can afford, and the new apartheid of this country is going to be economic classes. I think that race will disappear quite quickly".[17] Linden is an upmarket residential area. The area has, for example, many excellent schools and easy access to highways, and is close to Rosebank's shopping centres and exceptionally good transportation options. Ethnic groups that previously had not lived in Linden were now residents, and several of them had leading positions in St Thomas'.[18] The congregation reflected in many respects the local composition of diverse ethnicities that lived in the area, which is an important aspect of the catholicity of the Church in the analytical tool. The change was not created by the congregation, but arose as a consequence of changed economic conditions. Ethnic transformation will continue in the future because of new economic possibilities. The congregation had a majority of 'White' members, but the municipality was differently composed – a fact that could give rise to additional interactions with congregations of other ethnicities.

The congregation had a rector, two self-supporting assistant ministers, and one retired assistant minister on its staff. All the ministers were English-speaking 'White' people, but there were two 'White' and one 'Black' lay ministers in the

---

15 Observation Protocol 2011-03-06.
16 See for example: St Thomas' Treble Choir, n.d., Church Publication; The St Thomas' Magazine January & February 2011, 2011, pp. 11, 16, Church Publication; The St Thomas' Magazine March 2011, 2011, pp. 12, 14, 16, Church Publication; The St Thomas' Magazine April 2011, 2011, p. 7, Church Publication; The St Thomas' Magazine May 2011, 2011, pp. 6, 12, 16, Church Publication; The St Thomas' Magazine August 2010, 2010, pp. 6–7, 16, Church Publication.
17 Church Council Interview Protocol 2011-03-06.
18 See for example: The St Thomas' Magazine March 2011, 2011, pp. 12–13, Church Publication.

congregation.[19] The church council were asked whether they would have any problems about receiving a minister coming from an ethnic group that was different from that of the majority. They answered: "We have people in training, we are a training parish".[20] Their response emphasised that the congregation regularly had students, curates, and other people from diverse ethnic groups coming to it for training for shorter or longer periods. The council did not regard different ethnic groups as strange or problematic.

The congregation had five assisting staff who were 'White' and three who were 'Black'. Among the twelve members of the church council, three were 'Black' and nine 'White', and they had one 'Black' and two 'White' people as church wardens.[21] The ethnic background of the congregation's leaders was seen as subordinate, in accordance with the catholicity of the Church. It is remarkable, however, that there were no larger ethnic representations among the ministers. The congregation had members of various ethnicities, but there were only 'White' ministers who had no knowledge of other languages besides English. The clergy did not reflect the ethnic composition as the congregation, even though they received people of diverse ethnicities for training.[22]

The church council said that all 'racial' groups were represented in the congregation, except at the two o'clock service on Sundays. One council member declared: "Only the two o'clock service is not very representative, and never has been".[23] The service used one of the South African indigenous languages, and gathered only 'Black' people – most of them domestic workers. The division of people according to ethnic groups at the afternoon service was explained by the church council as a result of language. Some people were not comfortable with English, and could not come to worship at other times of the day.[24] One of the council members said:

---

19 Welcome to St Thomas' Anglican Church, Linden, 2011, pp. 3, 4, Church Publication.
20 Church Council Interview Protocol 2011-03-06.
21 Welcome to St Thomas' Anglican Church, Linden, 2011, pp. 3–8, Church Publication. One example of a 'Black' minister who had worked at St Thomas' was Mo Tshule, who had been a youth minister. The St Thomas' Magazine March 2011, 2011, pp. 14–15, Church Publication. The congregation also had an organist named Mduduzi Ndlovu, who had begun to play at St Thomas'. The St Thomas' Magazine August 2010, 2010, p. 11, Church Publication.
22 St Thomas' got a new rector in January 2014 when Fr Moses Thabethe was instituted by the Rt Revd Steve Moreo, Bishop of Johannesburg. He was the first 'Black' rector of the parish. The St Thomas' Magazine January 2014, 2014, pp. 1–5, Church Publication.
23 Church Council Interview Protocol 2011-03-06.
24 Church Council Interview Protocol 2011-03-06.

"It is kind of the price for that kind of service".[25] The excuse of a divided worship community according to ethnic group was made in order to offer a Sunday service for everybody. They wanted to make provision for those who had been working during the morning services, and wanted to have a service in other languages besides English.[26] It is remarkable that the afternoon service had participants who were exclusively 'Black', but that the membership and the people in the area had a different ethnic composition. The service could not be regarded as reflecting the catholicity of the Church in the analytical tool, and it was mostly a consequence of the women's working hours and their knowledge of a specific language.[27]

One of the members in the church council, who did not have English as a first language, stated: "[…] We are sort of making some games. It's not that we are going backwards. From the time I joined there has been lot of retrievals and also issues around diversity that are being addressed in a way, yes".[28] The council member's statement made clear that the congregation had made progress with diverse ethnic groups, but that there had been some struggles. Another member who was 'Black' and had been elected church warden was interviewed in the parish magazine. She told her story about coming to St Thomas'. She had begun to worship in the congregation because her father had moved into the area. She explained:

> It wasn't easy at first – I would sit down in a pew and people would pick up their handbag and shift as far as they could down the pew! … I'd like to see more synergy at St Thomas', more meeting of minds. There are lot of different things going on at St Thomas' but everybody seems to be doing their own things – there's no real St Thomas' family.[29]

This observation revealed that the council member had not been able to interact with other members as she had expected in the beginning. She had remained in the congregation and continued to attend the church services. Then there was a change of sorts, and the person was elected to the church council and then elected church warden.

---

25   Church Council Interview Protocol 2011-03-06.
26   Church Council Interview Protocol 2011-03-06.
27   An intersectional connection was revealed among the 'Black' women who were domestic workers using another language. An inequality in the society and the church was revealed. Fish, Jennifer N., 2006, pp. 112–114.
28   Church Council Interview Protocol 2011-03-06.
29   The St Thomas' Magazine March 2011, 2011, pp. 12–13, Church Publication. The new elected church warden was Ntombi Langa-Royds. The parish council and wardens were elected on 14 November 2010 to lead St Thomas' during 2011. The St Thomas' Magazine November & December 2010, 2010, p. 1, Church Publication.

Even if some people in the congregation saw it as making space for diversity, others stated that St Thomas' could be seen as being scattered and having lost a sense of familiarity. The 'Black' council members could affirm that there had been progress in the congregation; but there had also been times of struggle. The fact that they were church officials – members of the council and church wardens – suggested that they had brought something new into the congregation. There were changes taking place at St Thomas', as both women and men and people of diverse ethnic groups were able to find space. Even the congregation's decision-making body had been enriched with diverse ethnicities. Such diversity in the church council is consistent with the catholicity of the Church.

Athlone Methodist Church – Methodist Church of Southern Africa

The Methodist church in Athlone is deeply attached to the area where it is placed. Athlone is part of the Cape Flats, a sandy flat area some distance from the city centre. Athlone had 237 414 inhabitants and 51 891 households in Census 2011. Of these, 87 per cent identified themselves as 'Coloured' – the great majority of the population in the area. This high number is a consequence of the previous government's policy of separating ethnic groups into specific areas through forced removals. Only 5.9 per cent were 'Black African' and 4.5 per cent 'Indian or Asian' in Athlone. The statistics confirm that Athlone and other previously 'Coloured' areas in the Western Cape Province remained intact in the democratic South Africa. Other wards in metropolitan municipalities had experienced vertical mobility, where former 'Coloured' and 'Indian Asian' areas had received people from other ethnic groups, but not many from the 'White' population.[30]

---

30 Census 2011, Athlone, Statistics South Africa, 2013. Rylands in Cape Town during apartheid was classified as an 'Indian or Asian' area, according to Census 2011, and was 76.88 per cent 'Indian or Asian', 13.3 'Coloured', 7.59 per cent 'Black African', 2.2 per cent Other, and 0.05 per cent 'White'. Census 2011, Rylands, Statistics South Africa, 2013. Lenasia in Johannesburg during apartheid had been classified as an 'Indian or Asian' area. The area, according to Census 2011, had about 55.9 per cent that identified themselves as 'Indian or Asian', 40.38 per cent 'Black African', 2.55 per cent 'Coloured', 0.95 per cent Other and 0.21 per cent 'White'. Census 2011, Lenasia, Statistics South Africa, 2013. Bosmont in Johannesburg during apartheid was classified as a 'Coloured' area. The area, according to Census 2011, had about 70.81 per cent that identified themselves as 'Coloured', 18.46 per cent 'Black African', 5.52 per cent 'Indian or Asian', 4.49 per cent Other and 0.7 per cent 'White'. Census 2011, Bosmont, Statistics South Africa, 2013. Chatsworth in Durban during apartheid was classified as an 'Indian or Asian' area. The area, according to Census 2011, had about 60 per cent that identified

'Population group' or 'race' was regarded by the church council as an issue that belonged to the past, and it was not part of the new democratic South Africa. The church council showed great aversion to any form of classification. When the council was approached about diverse groups in the congregation, one member responded: "It is mixed now".[31] This statement showed that there was no need to create any boundaries between people. Another member added: "We have moved away from race now".[32] This response indicated that 'race' was part of the previous society; as a third member explained simply: "We are South Africans".[33] The only thing that mattered in the new democratic South Africa was that they were all the same people and belonged to the same country. Tensions about divisions into groups among 'Coloured' people demonstrated that they wanted to leave behind any talk of classification; it was irrelevant after liberation. The 'Coloured' group was, as earlier described, a purely South African construction of the previous government, and not self-chosen. The church council's response was also a reaction against ethnic divisions and in favour of a vision of another kind of society.

'Coloureds' had been underprivileged under the previous government, and were still underprivileged in the democratic South Africa.[34] A woman in the

---

themselves as 'Indian Asian', 38.2 per cent 'Black African', 1.18 'Coloured', 0.5 per cent Other, and 0.15 per cent 'White'. Census 2011, Chatsworth, Statistics South Africa, 2013. Wentworth in Durban during apartheid was classified as a 'Coloured' area. The area, according to Census 2011, had about 60.5 per cent that identified themselves as 'White', 18.7 per cent 'Black African', 10.8 per cent 'Indian or Asian' and 10 per cent 'Coloured'. The large proportion of 'White' people is due to the fact that the ward was merged with a beach front area. Census 2011, Wentworth, Statistics South Africa, 2013. Another former 'Coloured' area is Newland East. The area, according to Census 2011, had about 69.3 per cent that identified themselves as 'Black African', 24.2 per cent 'Coloured', 5.75 per cent 'Indian or Asian', 0.52 per cent Other, and 0.23 per cent 'White'. Census 2011, Newland East, Statistics South Africa, 2013.

31 Church Council Interview Protocol 2011-03-20.
32 Church Council Interview Protocol 2011-03-20.
33 Church Council Interview Protocol 2011-03-20.
34 The practice of 'affirmative action', for example, does not favour 'Coloured' people, and individual politicians have at times severely criticised it. Government spokesperson Jimmy Manyi said in 2011 that the Western Cape had an over-concentration of 'Coloureds' and that they should be denied jobs; they should be spread around the rest of the country. See, for example, Mtyala, Quinton, & Serrao, Angelique, & Davis, Gaye, & Williams, Murray, 2011, p. 1. Statistics South Africa still used 'Coloured' as a population group in the latest census (2011) questionnaire. Census 2011, Census in Brief, 2012, pp. 21–27, 41–46, 53–54; Household Questionnaire A, Demographics, Statistics South Africa, 2011, p. 2.

council explained: "But in former years we were known as the Coloureds".³⁵ The response acknowledged how they had previously been socially constructed as a specific ethnic group. Classification was part of the past, but the present government was still using differentiating terms. The church council members' attitude was consistent with the theme of catholicity in the ecumenical documents, where there is no demarcation, and ethnicity is fluid. The church council's position was an explicit rejection of the previous and present governments' policies regarding fixed ethnic groups and how the term 'Coloured' was used in society.

The congregation had a predominance of so-called 'Coloured' members. There had been no vertical or lateral mobility in the area, and so people from other ethnic groups had not joined their congregation. The high number of 'Coloureds' in the City of Cape Town Metropolitan Municipality makes mobility less common. In cities with fewer 'Coloureds', other ethnic groups have moved into those areas.³⁶

The church council declared that some of the congregations in the Methodist Church had become more ethnically mixed. Rosebank and the Metropolitan Methodist Church, for example, were changing and had become more diverse. The same was not happening in other areas – including their own congregation. A council member explained: "People move out of the area and instead go to the church where they belong".³⁷ Social mobility is mostly the result of socio-economic changes, as people move to better areas.

A council member added: "[...] they go to the church where they want".³⁸ There were others who had chosen to belong to congregations near their new homes, although the congregation had some members who continued to come to their church. The responses indicated that the council acknowledged that people should belong and be part of a congregation in the area where they lived, or through choice.

The council was asked whether exchanges with other ethnic groups had increased in their circuit since democratisation. Their response indicated that interactions happened in some circuits, but that they had not had many meetings in their own circuit. One council member stated: "We only had that one time when

---

35 Church Council Interview Protocol 2011-03-20.
36 There were 42.4 per cent who identified themselves as 'Coloured', 38.6 per cent in the City of Cape Town Metropolitan Municipality according to Census 2011. Census 2011, City of Cape Town Metropolitan Municipality, Statistics South Africa, 2012; Census 2011, Census in Brief, 2012, p. 21.
37 Church Council Interview Protocol 2011-03-20.
38 Church Council Interview Protocol 2011-03-20.

three churches met".[39] The demarcations for geographic circuits in the Methodist church had changed after democratisation. This adjustment was decided by the church synod in order to change the boundaries of the past. A council member explained: "It has increased now since this new dispensation. Now we have nine churches in the circuit".[40] The Dumisani circuit, to which Athlone belonged, included congregations in Langa, Pinelands, Rosebank and Thornton. The congregations had people from diverse ethnic groups, which after the demarcation were united in one circuit. The Methodist Church wanted to move away from an organisation that had been structured according to the previous government's policy. Reorganising the circuits in order to become ethnically diverse can be regarded as being in accordance with the analytical tool of catholicity, which affirms diversity. The church council's response showed, though, that new demarcations were not enough. The practices of the past continued despite the new circuits.

A council member declared: "In the beginning when Rosebank circuit came in we used to have a combined evening service, once a month in Athlone and once a month in Rosebank. But then, you know how people are, Rosebank did not come to Athlone. We came to Rosebank but they never came to us […]".[41] The statement revealed disappointed hopes of greater interaction with congregations of other ethnic groups within the same circuit. Athlone congregation was willing to meet the people in Rosebank, but Athlone was not met with the same willingness, according to the council. The experience shows that the people in the Athlone Methodist Church had tried to have more interaction with the congregation in Rosebank. This situation demonstrates an inequality that is attached to ethnic background. Practising greater ethnic diversity, as part of the Church's catholicity in the analytical tool, has to be accomplished by meeting with other congregations.

There were no signs that Athlone Methodist Church had made any attempt to have more contacts and exchanges with, for example, a congregation in Langa that had predominantly 'Black' members. Thus the members of the Athlone Methodist Church were acting in the same way as the congregation in Rosebank. The church council showed that it was resigned about accomplishing greater interactions across ethnic borders as part of the task to create greater diversity. There were still difficulties in having exchanges with congregations of predominantly

---

39 Church Council Interview Protocol 2011-03-20.
40 Church Council Interview Protocol 2011-03-20. The synod in 2003 started a programme of restructuring the geographic circuits with the goal of creating 'non-racial' circuits in the MCSA. 2003 Yearbook of the Methodist Church of Southern Africa, 2003, p. 124.
41 Church Council Interview Protocol 2011-03-20.

another ethnicity, even though the national church had changed the demarcations for the circuits, which would be consistent with the analytical tool of the Church's catholicity.

There were about eight ministers in the Dumisani circuit who met frequently, despite limited interactions between the congregations' members. The staff in the circuit met monthly for fellowship and planning. All ministers were expected to exchange pulpits with their colleagues every fifth Sunday of the month.[42] However, the planned exchange had not happened lately. One church council member stated: "They are supposed to … we haven't had it happening very often lately. … They have a planned roll and they are supposed to. Each one is supposed to go and preach somewhere else".[43] The plan was not followed, and the congregation had its own lay preachers to cover their needs. A council member added: "Then of course we have a lot of preachers too".[44] Several members were used to leading and preaching at the services when necessary. The lack of greater exchange of ministers did not facilitate contacts between the congregations and diverse ethnic groups within the circuit.[45] Even if the church had tried to offer incentives for greater exchange between various groups, exchange between congregations was not often done. The responses indicated moreover that there was not much enthusiasm among the circuit's ministers to visit other congregations.

A sign of increased ethnic diversity was the fact that the Athlone Methodist Church had a minister who came from another ethnic group than that of the majority of the congregation's members. One council member said: "Our minister comes from a different population group".[46] According to the Methodist Church, the local congregation has the choice to invite according to a call system. The Connexional Executive reviews all the appointments annually and assigns the ministers. It is rare that the Executive places ministers in specific congregations.[47] A member of the council stated about their minister: "He is Xhosa … he is from the Eastern Cape".[48] Because the congregation used English, it had a minister who, even though he was from another ethnic group, could speak English. The minister's ethnicity was of minor importance; but using the same language as the

---

42 Athlone Methodist Church, Athlone Society Profile, c.a. 2008, p. 31, Church Publication.
43 Church Council Interview Protocol 2011-03-20.
44 Church Council Interview Protocol 2011-03-20.
45 Church Council Interview Protocol 2011-03-20.
46 Church Council Interview Protocol 2011-03-20.
47 The Laws and Discipline of the Methodist Church of Southern Africa, 2007, pp. 38–38; Nyobole, Vuyani Gladstone, Interview Protocol 2011-02-28.
48 Church Council Interview Protocol 2011-03-20.

members of the congregation was central. The minister's different background could be considered as an expression of the Church's catholicity in the analytical tool, because ethnic background was perceived to be subordinate in the congregation's communion. Diversity was also enhanced when a leader in the local congregation was appointed to work in a congregation of a predominantly different ethnicity.

One left-over from the past in the Methodist Church that still divided people along ethnic lines was the establishment of the different leagues, associations, or groups with diverse organisations. One woman explained: "The older women, we belong to the Women's Association which is a recognised organisation of the Methodist Church. [...]"[49] The Methodist Church has, for example, the Women's Association, Women's Auxiliary, Women's Manyano, Methodist Men's League, and Young Men's Guild. The organisations are socially segregated, even though their constitutions do not separate people according to ethnic groups, and they are open to everyone.[50] The different organisations could be regarded as a relic of the past, and do not reflect the catholicity of the Church according to the analytical tool. Diversity is supposed to be appreciated, and ethnicity has a subordinate importance. The practice of having diverse organisations may be necessary for the members, but it does not facilitate interactions between ethnicities, and it does not increase diversity as part of the catholicity of the Church. Diverse organisations become an ecclesiological structuring factor because ethnicity becomes a reason for division. Diverse organisations in the church that still divide church people according to their different ethnicities does not facilitate the sharing and receiving of diverse gifts that is emphasised in the analytical tool of the Church's catholicity.

---

49 Church Council Interview Protocol 2011-03-20.
50 The Laws and Discipline of the Methodist Church of Southern Africa, 2007, pp. 183, 188,189, 196, 202, 216. The division of the organisations along ethnic lines was confirmed by a phone call to District Bishop of Cape of Good Hope Michael Hansrod 2013-10-18. Twenty years after democratisation, the MCSA stated at its annual conference: "We are still trapped in the apartheid ghetto which will in time reverse gains made in the past 20 years of moving towards a 'one and undivided' Church. We must, as a matter of urgency, create platforms for life-giving, *wet cement conversations* – thoughts that are open to reshaping, rethinking and reconsidering at all levels of our structure (Society, Circuit, District and Connexion)". 2014 Yearbook, The Methodist Church of Southern Africa, 2014, p. 15.

Lutheran Church in Bellville – Evangelical Lutheran Church in Southern Africa Cape Church

Bellville could be considered a suburban area in greater Cape Town, and is part of the City of Cape Town Metropolitan Municipality. Bellville had 112 507 inhabitants and 34 796 households, according to Census 2011. There were 50.3 per cent in the area who identified themselves as 'White', 33 per cent as 'Coloured', 15.7 per cent as 'Black African', 3.1 per cent as 'Other', and 1.5 as 'Indian or Asian'. There were 11 788 who lived in the area closest to the congregation, in 3 585 households. About 56 per cent identified themselves as 'White', 15.2 per cent as 'Coloured', 19.3 per cent as 'Black African', 8.5 per cent as 'Other', and 1 per cent as 'Indian or Asian'. There were, however, 39 per cent who identified themselves as 'Black African', 35 per cent as 'White', 23 per cent as 'Coloured' and 3 per cent as 'Other' in Kempenville, which is the ward where the church building is situated.[51]

Approximately half of the population considered themselves to be 'White', and the rest were mostly 'Coloured', 'Black African' and 'Other'. This makes the area fairly ethnically diverse. This diverse population confirmed that there was an increasing change among the various ethnic groups in an area previously reserved for 'White' people, where the church building is situated. Greater Bellville was mixed even before democratisation, with diverse ethnicities; but people lived in specific areas. Census 2011 indicates that diversity has increased in all the wards since democratisation. There has been a lateral mobility combined with vertical social mobility.

Most of the members of the Lutheran Church in Bellville had some kind of connection with a German background, by family or by intermarriage; and the members were almost exclusively 'White'. ELCSA N-T congregations in other provinces where ELCSA-Cape was not established had begun to get Lutheran members from other ethnic groups, especially from ELCSA.[52] ELCSA-Cape had not experienced the same pattern. The minister of the congregation emphasised:

> That is a move that you find in Johannesburg and in Pretoria and so forth, not in the Cape, and Strand Street has got an element of that … the Moravian Church which is also part of the federation of Lutheran churches here, they are a very strong and stable church with good qualifications also for their pastors. The ELCSA is not that well and

---

51 Census 2011, Bellville, Avondstil, Bellville Central, Chrismar, Eversdale Ext 21, Harry De Villiers, Hillrise, Kempenville, Kingston, Oakdale, Sunkist, Statistics South Africa, 2013.
52 Müller, Horst, Interview Protocol 2011-03-04; Rohwer, Nils J., Interview Protocol 2011-02-09.

I don't think there is a lot of growth there, but the people don't come over here to us from ELCSA. Not yet. I get the first enquiries, people wanting to come over, but it's not yet that rush that you find in Johannesburg and so forth.[53]

The ELCSA-Cape congregations had not found that people from ELCSA had started to attend services in their congregations, as had happened in ELCSA N-T congregations. It was only the Lutheran Church in Strand Street in Cape Town, part of ELCSA-Cape, that exclusively used English. The Strand Street congregation also had members from various ethnic groups. One reason for congregations not having the same development as ELCSA N-T congregations could be that ELCSA-Cape congregations did not adopt English as their principal language, but continued with German and Afrikaans.[54]

It is noticeable that the Lutheran Church in Bellville had very strong connections with its German heritage, which it supported and maintained. German descent became an ecclesiological structuring factor: the heritage was more important than other aspects of church life. ELCSA-Cape congregations had the advantage of relating to EKD in Germany, which facilitated exchanges with German congregations. The connection with EKD at least helps congregations to relate to a global community – which is one kind of visible unity, but not in relation to the local context. It is important to notice that the relationship with EKD can release the congregation and the church from building stronger relationships with ELCSA congregations and church.

The congregation did not entirely reflect the conditions of its local area, because not many 'Coloured' and 'Black African' inhabitants were found in the congregation. The church council declared that they occasionally had visitors from diverse ethnic groups. One member stated: "We quite often get visitors of colour, but it seems as if they are not totally at home here. Somehow I think it's more a cultural thing, and we try our best to make them feel at home, but they

---

53 Church Council Interview Protocol 2011-03-15.
54 Several ELCSA N-T congregations have many members from diverse ethnical groups, and some congregations have a majority of 'Black' members. Examples of such congregations in ELCSA N-T are Friedenskirche and St Peter's by the Lake Lutheran Church in Johannesburg, St Johannes Lutheran Church in Kelvin, Evangelical Lutheran Church in the Vaal Triangle in Vanderbijlpark, St Peter's Church in Pretoria.
Friedenskirche, Johannesburg, Overview, 2011, p. 1, Church Publication; St Johannes Lutheran Church, Kelvin, Overview, 2011, p. 1, Church Publication; St Peter's Congregation, Pretoria, Overview, 2011, pp. 1–2, Church Publication; St Peter's by the Lake Lutheran Church, Overview, 2011, pp. 1, 3, Church Publication; Evangelical Lutheran Church in the Vaal Triangle, Vanderbijlpark, Overview, 2011, p. 1, Church Publication.

don't and they leave. [...]".⁵⁵ The council emphasised that people did not feel comfortable as part of the congregation for various reasons, and so they did not continue to come for worship.

Visitors did indicate that they had some interest, and that the congregation might have been considered as an alternative place of worship. Another member of the council explained: "After church we've got coffee and tea, and we invite everybody to come to participate and socialise, and some people come and others just go out".⁵⁶ This statement showed that the congregation had an environment where people could meet after church services, but that some visitors did not have time to stay, while others did not feel that they were included in the community. The catholicity of the Church according to the analytical tool invites the Christian communion to create a climate of warm acceptance where diverse groups can meet.

The council was asked whether they would consider having a minister who came from a different ethnic group than that of the majority of the congregation's members. There were different opinions in the council about this. One council member stated: "It would be a language problem. If he knows all the languages I wouldn't have a problem. For me it's the language, it is important".⁵⁷ Another member of the council declared: "If he is a Lutheran pastor I wouldn't have any problem".⁵⁸ A third person added: "But it might be that in the whole congregation that there are those who are against that".⁵⁹ A fourth person emphasised the cultural and language aspects by declaring: "It is one thing that has to be considered and mentioned, and that is the cultural aspect. The language is always imbedded in a culture and these cultures differ. It would be easier to get preachers in on a more irregular basis, but a local pastor I think the people would react [against]".⁶⁰ The responses revealed that some had hesitations related to language. The minister had to be able to speak German, Afrikaans, and English, but also had to be able to fit into their particular environment.

The discussion at the council revealed that there would still be people who would have difficulties with a minister from another ethnic background, even if the minister met all the stipulated criteria. German identity was more important than diversity as part of the Church's catholicity in the analytical tool.

---

55 Church Council Interview Protocol 2011-03-15.
56 Church Council Interview Protocol 2011-03-15.
57 Church Council Interview Protocol 2011-03-15.
58 Church Council Interview Protocol 2011-03-15.
59 Church Council Interview Protocol 2011-03-15.
60 Church Council Interview Protocol 2011-03-15.

City Harvest Ministries in Ntuzuma – Apostolic Faith Mission of South Africa

City Harvest Ministries is situated in Ntuzuma, a township about 20 km from the city centre of Durban, and part of the eThekwini Municipality. Ntuzuma had a population of 125 394 and 29 988 households according to Census 2011. It is primarily a residential area characterised by hilly terrain and dense housing. A total of 99.7 per cent of the population identified themselves as 'Black African', 0.2 per cent as 'Indian or Asian', 0.2 per cent as 'Coloured', 0.1 per cent as 'Other', and 0.1 per cent as 'White'. The figures show that many former so-called 'Black' townships remain intact in the democratic South Africa. A vast majority of the people in Ntuzuma are 'Black African', as was also evident among the members of City Harvest Ministries.[61]

City Harvest Ministries had only 'Black' members, which could be explained by its location in a township where almost no other ethnic groups were present.[62] Similar situations are found among other congregations and churches in townships and rural areas in the countryside where there is no greater ethnic diversity. The situation in Ntuzuma confirmed that townships with predominantly 'Black' people had not changed since democratisation. City Harvest Ministries reflected the ethnicity of their area, and they had few contacts with congregations of other ethnicities. The ethnic homogeneity of the congregation could be described as an ecclesiological structuring factor.

Diverse ethnic groups did not appear to be an issue in the church council. There were no other major ethnic groups living in the area, but the council was in favour of the democratic South Africa.[63]

The church council was asked whether they would have any objections to having a minister from a different ethnic background. Their answer was clear and unanimous: "No".[64] Their response showed that for them ethnic background was subordinate. The church council named other aspects apart from ethnicity that divided people. City Harvest Ministries had, for example, developed their own way of worship and of being a congregation. A church council member explained:

> You know, I think it is more of the culture of how we worship. It is still with us. I give an example. The others, the White, Indian and Coloured, they only have one service

---

61 Census 2011, Ntuzuma, Statistics South Africa, 2013.
62 Church Council Interview Protocol 2011-03-27; Observation Protocol 2011-03-27; Census 2011, Ntuzuma, Statistics South Africa, 2013.
63 Church Council Interview Protocol 2011-03-27.
64 Church Council Interview Protocol 2011-03-27.

during Easter and we have the whole weekend. We have services from Friday, Saturday, and Sunday. So what they usually do, they would come maybe once, if they come. Usually we have our whole Easter weekend from Friday to Sunday. Maybe they will attend one service.[65]

The differences practices of those from other ethnic groups were evident in their diverse forms of worship and the amount of time that was spent in church. People of other ethnic groups only want to be in church for a limited time, while the City Harvest Ministries members preferred to spend a lot of time in church. The difference was explained as the result of historical factors, and would, as a matter of course, disappear with greater interaction with other ethnicities. It is also a matter of age: younger generations have other priorities. The style of worship and time spent in church could be seen as part of being a church where there is space for diversity as long as the diversity does not create divisions. Variety does not need to be seen as a problem; on the contrary, it could be seen as part of the Church's catholicity in the analytical tool, as long as local congregations have mutual relationships.

The council was asked whether there was a need for greater integration of ethnic groups. One member answered: "It is a need, but the way I look at it, it goes past the issue of race. It is the style of worship that now comes in between us".[66] The explanation was developed further by another member:

> Because we want to dance, clap and sing the whole weekend, as the pastors are saying, but they would like, the other cultures, they want something that got a start and finish time and to go home and do other things. We are more comfortable spending the whole day with singing and spending time in front of the Lord. It's not really a race issue how we do things. It is cultural differences.[67]

The style of worship was the greatest difference between congregations of different ethnicities, and it became the cause of division. Diverse styles of worship became a dividing factor, which is the opposite of the inclusive nature of the Church's catholicity.

Worship was, nevertheless, not the only factor that kept people apart. The way that the church and the AFM were organised, together with the congregations' interests in each other's activities, were also understood as a source of division. A church council member said:

> Another issue that I think is mostly in the AFM. All the local assemblies, they have their own programmes and they have the right to be their own and all reports go directly to

---

65 Church Council Interview Protocol 2011-03-27.
66 Church Council Interview Protocol 2011-03-27.
67 Church Council Interview Protocol 2011-03-27.

the national office which makes it very difficult to say 'Let's meet' to come together. It is very difficult because of that.[68]

The independence of the assemblies or congregations, which is part of the AFM's ecclesiology, allowed the congregations to be very independent. There is a weak church hierarchy, with no deaneries or circuits that gather the local assemblies and require them to cooperate, as happens in other main-line churches.

One council member said: "If you have your own programme you have to respect that, but we would send an invitation […]".[69] Local church services and activities had to be respected, according to the council's reply. The lowest level of interaction with other congregations was apparently to issue an invitation. The church council wanted to have increased interactions with people of other ethnicities, but every congregation had their own programmes.[70] City Harvest Ministries is situated in Ntuzuma, an underprivileged area. People from other areas do not often visit townships. The independence of assemblies or congregations does not facilitate sharing and receiving as part of the Church's catholicity, according to the analytical tool.

The AFM had chosen to be organised as a church with largely independent assemblies and with the advantages of substantially autonomy. But that advantage could also become a disadvantage, because there was no external agency that helped to create greater interactions between people. Congregations in a church like the AFM have to make more effort to increase their ethnic diversity, as part of the Church's catholicity, than do more hierarchical churches like the Roman Catholic and Anglican churches. The unification process of the AFM during democratisation helped to create greater unity among people of diverse ethnicities on the central level, but at the local level it could be greater.

City Harvest Ministries nevertheless had great interaction with other AFM congregations of the same ethnic group. It was linked to Maranatha Ministries in KwaMashu. They regularly held conferences with other congregations in the area, and speakers came from other parts of South Africa and even from other African countries.[71] Their contacts with other congregations and even with churches aboard are visible signs of the Church's catholicity according to the analytical tool. Diversity was appreciated and practised, but not across the ethnic lines created by the former divisions in South Africa.

---

68 Church Council Interview Protocol 2011-03-27.
69 Church Council Interview Protocol 2011-03-27.
70 Church Council Interview Protocol 2011-03-27.
71 City Harvest Ministries, The life of City Harvest Ministries, 2013, Website.

St Michael's Evangelical Lutheran Church – Evangelical Lutheran Church in Southern Africa

St Michael's Church is situated between the International Convention Centre (ICC) and the Durban beach front. The city centre includes Durban Central, North Beach, and South Beach, where St Michael's is located. It had about 55 666 inhabitants and 19 556 households according to Census 2011. There were 72 per cent in the area who identified themselves as 'Black African', 16.5 per cent as 'Indian or Asian', 3.5 per cent as 'Coloured', 6 per cent as 'White', and 2 per cent as 'Other'. The figures indicate that there has been a big shift of ethnic groups in the city centre, which was mostly reserved for the 'White' population before democratisation. It is significant that there has been lateral mobility. The ethnic figures in the area where St Michael's was located were almost the same as in the whole municipality, according to Census 2011. The only differences from the figures of the municipality were that there were more 'Coloureds' and fewer 'Indian or Asians'.[72]

St Michael's was a diverse congregation with several ethnic groups. There was even a small group of 'White' members in this ELCSA congregation. The 'White' people's presence was, as explained earlier, due to the unusual history of the merger between St Michael's and the Milne Street and Moore Road congregations. The 'White' group of people came to the congregation because of a split at St Olav's when ELCSA was established. St Michael's is one of the few congregations in ELCSA with a group of 'White' South African members.

A majority of the members of the congregation were 'Black' and Zulu, but St Michael's also had members from other parts of South Africa. There were, for example, people who were Phedi, and there was no conflict between the diverse groups. St Michael's had separate worshiping communities because of ministering in both isiZulu and English. The two worshiping groups met occasionally for services and other activities. The church council stated that they want to accommodate everybody in the congregation.[73] The composition of the

---

72 Census 2011, North Beach, Statistics South Africa, 2013; Census 2011, South Beach, Statistics South Africa, 2013; Census 2011, Durban Central, Statistics South Africa, 2013. The eThekwini Metropolitan Municipality had 73.8 per cent who identified themselves as 'Black African', 16.7 per cent as 'Indian or Asian', 6.6 per cent as 'White', 2.5 per cent as 'Coloured', and 0.4 per cent as 'Other'. Census 2011, eThekwini Metropolitan Municipality, Statistics South Africa, 2012.
73 Lüdemann, Joe, 2012, p. 2, Church Publication; Church Council Interview Protocol 2011-04-03.

St Michael's membership reflected the ethnic variety that was found in the area around the church. Such ethnic diversity is a sign of the Church's catholicity, with people coming from various groups in South African society.

The church council was unanimous that 'race' was not an issue in their congregation.[74] One of the members of the council declared:

> I hope that a lot of people look at it that the most important is the spiritual aspect. Whether I can't have that as White, I can't have that because I am German-speaking, I can't have whatever. But the most important is that I can relate to anybody that has the same desire of growing spiritually. That's more important than the visible differences.[75]

This statement showed that people's ethnic or language differences were subordinate, and the response revealed a wider context where a community of Christians were growing together as a community in the church. The response could be considered as being in accordance with the ecumenical texts, where the Christian community transcended any divisions based on ethnic background. The statement could also be interpreted as confirming that they could imagine another kind of society where ethnicity was of minor importance. The council said, however, that they were grappling with the many languages, and that they had not yet found an easy way to deal with the linguistic diversity.[76]

Ministers from different ethnic groups were not a problem, according to the council. The minister-in-charge came from Germany, and the previous minister – who was still assisting in the congregation – was also of German background. They had another full-time minister, a volunteer minister, and several lay preachers who together represented the diversity of the South African population.[77] The ministers' background showed that diversity was also appreciated.

---

74 Church Council Interview Protocol 2011-04-03.
75 Church Council Interview Protocol 2011-04-03.
76 Church Council Interview Protocol 2011-04-03.
77 Church Council Interview Protocol 2011-04-03. The ministers in the congregation were Revd Dr Joe Lüdemann (Parish Pastor), Revd Sybil Chetty (Parish Pastor), Revd Sabelo G. Mkhathini (Pastor, Tent Making Ministry) and Revd Fred von Fintel (Retired). Revd Dr Joe Lüdemann came from Germany and was employed by the Evangelical-Lutheran Mission in Lower Saxony (ELM) to work in ELCSA. ELM is a German Protestant mission organisation. Durban Central Parish, Leadership team, 2014, Website.

7.2 Ethnic Diversity or Division

The denominations' church leaders were also asked about ethnic diversity in their churches. A view from the central level broadens the context and explains the circumstances of the congregations' approach to ethnicity. The church leaders' perception of ethnicity will be examined in order to reveal changes, obstacles, and challenges.

Roman Catholic Church

The general secretary of the Southern African Catholic Bishops' Conference, Vincent Brennan, explained that the congregations were, in many cases, physically separated because of the legacy of the past. This was less obvious after democratisation because 'Black' people were moving into previously 'White' areas. Most congregations in the inner cities were ethnically more integrated, but the physical division that was part of apartheid had, according to Brennan, an effect on the actual integration. He believed that ethnic integration of the church would come because of changes in society as people moved into new areas. More 'Black' ministers would also lead these congregations in the future. He emphasised that people did not move in the opposite direction – from previously 'White' areas to previously 'Black' areas.[78] Brennan confirmed the conclusion that was evident in many of the case congregations: there was an upward vertical social mobility combined with lateral mobility that affected certain areas. The opposite 'downward' mobility, combined with a lateral mobility, was less evident.

Brennan stressed that he had never heard that ethnic integration had been a problem in the Roman Catholic Church in South Africa. Many of the traditionally 'White' congregations already had 'Black' priests. He said, though, that there had always been complaints about divisions in the church.[79]

Brennan recognised that people's knowledge of different languages, or the lack of it, was an issue that separated them. He stressed, for example, that most people from the 'White' community would not participate in diocesan functions or open air services. They would, according to Brennan, always explain that the function lasted too long. He questioned whether time was the real reason, when people did not come late or left early. He stated that it became an issue of culture when 'White' people had no problem spending half a day watching a cricket match,

---

78 Brennan, Vincent, Interview Protocol 2011-03-01.
79 Brennan, Vincent, Interview Protocol 2011-03-01.

but did not participate in a church function or an open air service.⁸⁰ Brennan's statement revealed diverse approaches to becoming a united community beyond ethnic divisions. Unequal power relations might also be an issue, because some groups are willing to contribute through their diversity, while others are resistant.

Brennan stressed that there were conversations in the church to overcome racism among clergy and especially in the congregations. He was of the opinion that there was a rather open discussion about these issues and about how the church could overcome the problem of racism. The general secretary's response was not to deny that there were still problems in relation to ethnicity within the church. Language, time, and various other differences, as well as racism, had been debated within the church, and they had even produced conference reports and printed material about these matters.⁸¹

Brennan declared that the Roman Catholic Church had made statements about the church and the new democracy during the first free national elections. There had also been statements and policy documents about integration in the church. Brennan referred to a 2003 document entitled *Pastoral Letter of the Southern African Catholic Bishops' Conference on Race Relations*. It stated that the bishops were sad to see that people in the church failed to come together – for example, when people of other ethnic groups stayed away from celebrations, blaming problems of language or the length of the services.⁸²

In the document, the bishops urged members to look for ways to bring people of different ethnic traditions into greater contact with each other. They emphasised that the people of South Africa should grow into one community. The church was encouraged, in congregations and dioceses, to build relationships between groups that previously had been separated from each other. The bishops ask the church's members to participate in church and civic activities where there were different expressions.⁸³

---

80 Brennan, Vincent, Interview Protocol 2011-03-01.
81 Brennan, Vincent, Interview Protocol 2011-03-01.
82 Brennan, Vincent, Interview Protocol 2011-03-01; Race Relations and the Catholic Church in South Africa, 2005. pp. 3–5.
83 Brennan, Vincent, Interview Protocol 2011-03-01; Race Relations and the Catholic Church in South Africa, 2005. pp. 3–5. Several statements of the SACBC have addressed the government – such as: Southern African Catholic Bishops' Conference Statement on Race Relations, June 1952; Southern African Catholic Bishops' Conference Pastoral Letter, February 1960; SACBC Statement on Unscriptural Racial Policies (8/6/82), 1982; The Church and Racism: Towards a more Fraternal Society, February 1989. Archbishop Denis Hurley in Durban was one of the most outspoken religious

The pastoral letter that Brennan referred to stressed a catholicity of the church that emphasised that people belonged to the same community regardless of ethnicity, and that diversity was supposed to be shared within the church. The document had similar tasks for the church as those that can be found in an ecumenical view of the Church's catholicity, as well as in the final report of the TRC. The bishops' letter could be characterised as reflecting a catholicity that emphasised a united Christian community without ethnic borders, in accordance with the ecumenical documents.

Brennan explained, moreover, that the church had produced a pastoral plan in 1989 entitled *Community Serving Humanity*. The plan dealt, among other things, with church as a community, and removing discrimination because of racial barriers erected by government policy.[84] One outcome of the document was a planned new inter-diocesan consultation initiated by the SACBC, starting in 2012.[85]

The SACBC had also produced a document in 2005 entitled *Race Relations and the Catholic Church in South Africa, A Decade after Apartheid*. The document challenged church people to transcend cultural comfort zones, and to stop explaining divisions as justified by irreconcilable cultural differences and language. The document also emphasised an intersectional approach by highlighting that ethnicity could not be treated in isolation, because issues of gender, poverty, the

---

opponents of the apartheid regime. Kearney, Paddy, 2009. One example of addressing ethnic integration within the Roman Catholic Church is the document, Declaration of Commitment on Social Justice and Race Relations within the Church: SACBC Plenary Session, February 1977, 1997. The SACBC, for example, addresses the inappropriate use of language, the availability of church premises for everyone, bringing various 'races' together, and re-assessing the distribution and functions of church personnel. All the statements are also archived in DiVA as Church Publication. The Roman Catholic Church was among the first to appoint 'Black' priests to 'White' congregations, and opened 'White' parochial schools to all 'races'. Black Priest due in White African Congregations, 1977.

84 Community Serving Humanity, 1989, pp. 18, 24–25. The document stated, for example: "In Southern Africa we have inherited a legacy of barriers. There are the racial barriers erected by a political policy that has fed on people's racial prejudices… There can be no meaningful search for community that does not strive to remove those barriers… Discrimination, whether based on race or on sex, is found not only in society but also in our Church communities. In pursuing the theme of Community Serving Humanity we must therefore give special attention to demolishing these barriers, removing discrimination, and fostering a genuine experience of equality before the Lord". Community Serving Humanity, 1989, pp. 24–25.

85 Inter-Diocesan Consultation 2012, 2011; Brennan, Vincent, Interview Protocol 2011-03-01.

economy, etc. were related to racism. The document called for discussions and dialogue in the church's different levels.[86]

All the documents and papers produced by the SACBC could be regarded as a way of opposing ethnic divisions in the church and the society. The documents stressed that 'race' was a social construction, and that ethnic diversities were subordinate in the Christian community. People were encouraged to relate to people of other backgrounds; and this could be described as a sign of Church's catholicity according to the analytical tool.

Brennan said that there was no policy in the church of having 'White' ministers in traditionally 'White' congregations, but they had a custom of placing 'Black' ministers in traditionally 'White' congregations. Brennan said: "In a lot of the traditionally White parishes there are Black priests. It is not just a matter of having to, it is a matter of policy that they are put there".[87] He had not found that the appointment of ministers to particular areas on ethnic grounds had caused any problems. Brennan pointed to examples from the diocese of Pretoria, where the cathedral congregation and the congregation of Sunnyside had 'Black' ministers. He mentioned these specific examples because these congregations were situated in the city centre of Pretoria, which during apartheid had been reserved for the 'White' population. There was a visible change in the church's placement of ministers that became evident even in the city congregations.[88] The placement of ministers could be regarded as opposing ethnic divisions.

Brennan admitted, nevertheless, that there were still a lot of 'White' ministers in the traditionally 'White' congregations in Johannesburg, for example. The reason he gave was that these ministers had been working in the same congregations for a long time, and the situation had not changed for those communities. These ministers did not speak any of the indigenous languages, which made it difficult to place them in other areas. 'White' ministers in former 'White' congregations were, according to Brennan, only an issue in cities. He explained that some congregations belonged traditionally to a particular religious order – for example, the Franciscans – and that this also influenced the situation. They nominated a minister,

---

86 Race Relations and the Catholic Church in South Africa, 2005, pp. 3–5, 27–28, 29–32.
87 Brennan, Vincent, Interview Protocol 2011-03-01.
88 Brennan, Vincent, Interview Protocol 2011-03-01. The Roman Catholic congregation of St Martin de Porres is situated in Sunnyside. The suburb is a residential area with many flats, close to the city centre and to the University of Pretoria.

and the bishop appointed the minister.[89] The situation that Brennan illustrated was going to change because in the future ministers would be predominantly 'Black'.

Vocations to the ministry influence the appointment of ministers. Brennan explained: "At the moment the White vocations are very, very few, minimum, local White vocations in South Africa. Our seminaries are almost completely Black. So within the next ten years there will be very few White priests left, unless it changes around".[90] There were not many young 'White' men offering themselves for ministry, and neither were they receiving any more Roman Catholic clergy from abroad. In the past ministers had come from Europe, but the Roman Catholic Church in Europe also had very few vocations.[91]

The picture of the ethnic situation of ministers in the church showed that the dioceses could appoint ministers according to a planned strategy. The church had the advantage of appointing ministers independent of ethnicity; but it would, according to Brennan's estimates, have almost only 'Black' ministers in the future. Fewer 'White' vocations and ministers could be regarded as failing to reflect the ethnic diversity in South Africa and in the Roman Catholic Church in South Africa. The situation could be perceived as problematic; but ethnicity could also be regarded as subordinate, with the background of the minister having no significance.

Anglican Church

The Provincial Executive Officer of the Anglican Church of Southern Africa, Allan Kannemeyer, stated that the Anglican Church was forced to be part of apartheid in the past, even though they did not agree with the previous government's policy. They had to live and be a church under apartheid's conditions. The consequence was a church with congregations for each ethnic group. He stated that local congregations were racially defined under apartheid. All congregations were nevertheless managed by the same 'chapter', independently of the priests and members. Neither the church as a Province nor its constituent dioceses were divided by apartheid's rules.[92] Kannemeyer said that the congregations in the urban centres may have been more mixed for various reasons – for example, the presence of domestic and

---

89 Brennan, Vincent, Interview Protocol 2011-03-01. Some congregations are served by a specific religious congregation, such as the OMI in St Peter Claver, Pimville and the Jesuits in Holy Trinity, Johannesburg.
90 Brennan, Vincent, Interview Protocol 2011-03-01.
91 Brennan, Vincent, Interview Protocol 2011-03-01.
92 The province is an autonomous unit within the Anglican Communion.

other workers in the cities.⁹³ Similar situations with mixed congregations would also be found in Roman Catholic and Methodist congregations in the cities. It is noteworthy that some denominations were able to remain united as a single church organisation despite pressure from the apartheid government to put racial divisions in place. Kannemeyer said, though, that the church was divided into diverse worshiping communities despite trying to remain united. His statement echoed the conclusions of the TRC, as described in Chapter Two.⁹⁴ Racial divisions were an ecclesiological structuring factor in the past, but democracy had changed the situation in some places.

According to Kannemeyer, the present situation with ethnically-segregated congregations was a legacy of apartheid. The suburbs, and particularly the former 'White' residential areas, had started to become diverse through the redistribution of wealth. People of other ethnic groups were able to buy property in well-developed areas when they gained access to better jobs. They thus started to attend churches in the areas where they lived. The congregations in the townships remained very much as they were in the past. The townships had less ethnic diversity than the suburbs. He explained that this was due to economic conditions and language issues.⁹⁵ Kannemeyer's reflection was similar to the case congregations' situations and to other church leaders' statements. Congregations in former 'White' privileged suburbs became more ethnically diverse, while former 'Black' townships did not change much after democratisation. The reason for greater ethnic diversity without any transformation was mainly increased economic possibilities. There was an 'upward' vertical social mobility that combined with a lateral mobility from townships to suburbs. Money and wealth became the new ecclesiological structuring factor.

Kannemeyer noted that the 'race' issue was always on the agenda of all national church meetings, and that resolutions arose out of these meetings.⁹⁶ The

---

93 Kannemeyer, Allan J., Interview Protocol 2011-03-16. Kannemeyer's reference to the 'chapter' meant that the Anglican Church in Southern Africa was united by having the same corporate ecclesial body independent of diverse ethnical groups.
94 "Despite their claim to loyalties that transcended the state, South African churches, whether implicitly or as a matter of policy, allowed them to be structured along racial lines – reinforcing the separate symbolic universes in which South Africans lived." Truth and Reconciliation Commission of South Africa Report, Vol. 4, 1998, p. 68.
95 Kannemeyer, Allan J., Interview Protocol 2011-03-16.
96 The CPSA made several statements against apartheid after 1948. The book: *The Churches and Race Relations in South Africa* has a collection of statements and resolutions. The synod of Bishops, for example, issued a statement in 1949: "The Synod calls upon

issue would also be brought to the attention of various synods and other meetings within the Anglican Church of Southern Africa, and resolutions were passed at diocesan level, especially in metropolitan areas such as Cape Town and Gauteng.[97] Kannemeyer did not mention any practical documents helping congregations to bring about increased integration between different ethnic groups, although he stressed that the Anglican Church had made many statements and passed many resolutions since democratisation. Kannemeyer did not name any conferences, exchange programmes or twin congregation initiatives within the church. Such projects were run by the dioceses, and were not an issue for the provincial structures of the church.

Kannemeyer did comment that there was a good mix of bishops from diverse ethnic groups in the Anglican Church of Southern Africa. He declared that there used to be 'White' bishops with a sprinkling of 'Blacks', but the situation was the opposite today. He explained that the changed situation was due to social transformation, but was also a result of greater access to education. There were now opportunities, and people could prepare themselves for leadership and responsibility.[98] Changed ethnic patterns in the leadership in the church were a significant change that had increased diversity. The appointment of bishops of diverse

---

all Church people to recognize the truth that all men and women, of whatever race, are made brethren in Christ by baptism, and to face fearlessly the implications of this truth in the life of congregation and diocese". Cawood, Lesley, 1964, p. 62. The same synod issued a statement in 1950: "Every churchman should be assured of a cordial welcome in any church of our Communion, and no one should be ineligible for any position in the Church by reason of his race or colour … the Church has not in practice been always faithful to her own principles and has allowed herself to be infected by the racial prejudices prevalent in the world about her. It therefore calls upon all members of the church to re-examine their racial attitudes in the light of the Christian Gospel, that in every congregation witness may be borne to the equal standing of all churchmen before God and to their brotherhood one with another in Christ". Cawood, Lesley, 1964, p. 61. The CPSA has had many leaders known for opposing apartheid, such as Trevor Huddleston and Desmond Tutu. John de Gruchy, however, believes that while there was no lack of official protests against apartheid by the CPSA, there was a gap between syndical resolutions and the congregations' resolve and action. De Gruchy, John & de Gruchy, Steve, 2005, pp. 86, 91.

97 Kannemeyer, Allan J., Interview Protocol 2011-03-16. Gauteng is the name of one of the South African provinces; it mainly includes Johannesburg and Pretoria and the areas immediately around them.
98 Kannemeyer, Allan J., Interview Protocol 2011-03-16.

ethnic backgrounds reflects South African society and reinforces the catholicity of the Church.

The Anglican Church did not have any statements or policies about ministers' appointment related to ethnic background. Kannemeyer explained: "It used to be an area of sensitivity. Not so much anymore. Congregations now look beyond colour. You find prejudice here and there but it does not influence the deployment of the particular priest".[99] He explained that it was the bishop together with the chapter that decided where ministers were placed.[100] Kannemeyer believed that the church had defined some kind of policy during the apartheid years, but even under apartheid 'Black' ministers were appointed to so-called 'White' areas. They had, at that time, to have special dispensations from the police to work in a congregation and live in a rectory in a 'White' area.[101]

Ethnicity and the appointment of ministers, according to Kannemeyer, was no longer an issue within the Anglican Church. The development had occurred naturally because of changes in the country.[102] Kannemeyer's response demonstrated the advantages of a strong central church organisation that had the responsibility of appointing ministers. The church could control the appointments of ministers, and make ethnicity less important. Diversity in the church could be supported as part of the Church's catholicity, according to the analytical tool. However, the congregations' lack of influence and a powerful church hierarchy also has the disadvantage that the congregations cannot decide for themselves who should be their minister.

Kannemeyer believed that one obstacle to becoming a more ethnically-integrated church was structural and institutional forms of racism. Future generations would not have lived under apartheid, and children who were not taught racist attitudes by their parents would not have the same mindset as the present generation. The coming generations, according to Kannemeyer, would hopefully grow up in a situation that would be free from prejudice.[103] He stressed that ethnicity was a social construction, and he acknowledged that the next generation could still be socialised into earlier patterns. Time would transform the society, and he hoped for a more ethnically-integrated church in the future.

---

99   Kannemeyer, Allan J., Interview Protocol 2011-03-16.
100 The chapter is the bishop's advisory body.
101 Kannemeyer, Allan J., Interview Protocol 2011-03-16.
102 Kannemeyer, Allan J., Interview Protocol 2011-03-16.
103 Kannemeyer, Allan J., Interview Protocol 2011-03-16.

Methodist Church

The Methodist Church of Southern Africa, like the Roman Catholic and Anglican churches, never divided its organisation on 'racial' lines under apartheid. The general secretary of the Methodist Church of Southern Africa, Vuyani Nyobole, stated that at a certain stage some groups in the church wanted to divide the church in line with the previous government's policy. The Methodist Church resisted these demands, and remained a united church, as confirmed in a statement in 1958. The church's annual conference that made the statement declared that the church should be one and undivided, and that an increase in multi-racial co-operation was the will of God. Nyobole claimed that the church was proud of that statement, which had been repeated in all the yearbooks because they thought it was an important resolution.[104]

The decision was in accordance with the ecumenical documents from F&O and the WCC. It is interesting that the church took the decision during the implementation of the Group Areas Act of 1950 – and more than two years before the Cottesloe Consultation in December 1960. The statement reflects an ecclesiology that perceives ethnic diversity as subordinate in the church's communion, and shows that inclusivity is a sign of Church's catholicity as described in the analytical tool.

The church was still influenced by apartheid despite opposition to the government. Nyobole explained that ministers were still classified according to 'race' within the church, and that ministers' stipends were also determined by 'race' until 1976, when the racial categories were abolished.[105] Differentiating stipends and classification according to 'race' was not unique to the Methodist Church. The Anglican, Lutheran, and Apostolic Faith Mission churches paid different stipends to their ministers according to 'race'. It was only the Roman Catholic

---

104 Nyobole, Vuyani Gladstone, Interview Protocol 2011-02-28. The conference stated: "The Conference declares its conviction that it is the will of God for the Methodist Church that it should be one and undivided, trusting to the leading of God to bring this ideal to ultimate fruition, and that this be the general basis of our missionary policy. ... Conference affirms that members of all races have their place, as God calls them, in all parts of His Vineyard, and points out that there is abundant room for more workers, and that saturation point is never likely to be reached. Moreover, Conference believes that an increase, not a decrease, in multi-racial co-operation is God's Will. The Spirit of God is already revealing new avenues of service and opening doors of opportunities." Minutes of the Seventy-Fifth Annual Conference of the Methodist Church of South Africa, 1958. p. 65.
105 Nyobole, Vuyani Gladstone, Interview Protocol 2011-02-28.

Church that paid the same stipends to all their ministers.[106] The TRC also identified the differentiated stipends as a previous inequality, as mentioned in Chapter Two.[107] Nyobole's statement recognised that even churches that had tried to remain united and had questioned division had implemented aspects of apartheid.

Nyobole also recognised that the church was divided according to 'racial' groups during apartheid because people lived in different areas. He stated, nevertheless, that no one would have been expelled if a person of another 'racial' group had gone to a congregation where there were people of a different 'colour'.[108] He declared that there had been social division within the church because of apartheid, but it had always been possible to attend church services anywhere, irrespective of congregation.

Several ethnic divisions were still visible in the church's associations, leagues, and units, although it had remained a united church organisation during the apartheid years. There were, for example, different women's, men's, and youth organisations that followed the former social structures. The church's constitution states that all of its organisations are open to all 'races'; but there remains the social practice of being ethnically divided.[109] These divided church organisations show how deeply segregationist policies had penetrated into the Christian community.

---

106 Nyobole, Vuyani Gladstone, Interview Protocol 2011-02-28; Cawood, Lesley, 1964, pp. 54, 69–70, 81, 105. The AMF had separate churches for the different 'race' groups, and the Lutheran churches were divided into different churches. Missionaries from the missionary churches and societies also received different stipends from those of South African ministers, even though they were employed by the same church.

107 "Stipends were drastically different for black and white clergy, reinforcing racial stereotypes of lifestyle differences." Truth and Reconciliation Commission of South Africa Report, Vol. 4, 1998, p. 69.

108 Nyobole, Vuyani Gladstone, Interview Protocol 2011-02-28.

109 The Laws and Discipline of the Methodist Church of Southern Africa, 2007, pp. 190–161, 188, 202. The division of the organisations by ethnicity was confirmed by a phone call to the District Bishop of the Cape of Good Hope, Michael Hansrod, 2013-10-18. Women's organisations in the Methodist and Anglican churches see themselves as ethnically inclusive. The Methodist Church set up racially-divided women's groups. These organisations remain ethnically divided, even after democratisation. Gaitskell, Deborah, 2002, pp. 386–387. The Anglican Church had the Mothers' Union, which is an international organisation. 'White' and 'Coloured' women started the Anglican Women's Fellowship in 1960, which became a more 'liberal' alternative to the Mothers' Union in its openness to divorced women and unmarried mothers. Some women belong to both organisations, which have strong links and cooperate with each other. Gaitskell, Deborah, 2004, pp. 271–273, 281.

Church organisations had been allowed to develop into separate units, and this was not easy to transform.

After democratisation the church made several statements about the church as a communion for everybody. Nyobole emphasised the importance of resolutions and statements made at annual conferences about racism and increased ethnic integration. The annual conference in 2002, for example, declared that the church was undivided and denounced racism in church and society. The statement was repeated a year later, in the 2003 conference, when delegates challenged the church to make real the 1958 statement. Several annual Methodist Church conferences had also dealt with issues of domination and racism.[110] The church had, for example, facilitated increased linguistic competence and the sharing of experiences to advance ethnic integration, and had stated that circuits could no longer be divided along racial lines.[111]

It is noteworthy that the church did not have the same focus on ethnic integration in later conferences, ten years after democratisation. Other issues – such

---

110 Nyobole, Vuyani Gladstone, Interview Protocol 2011-02-28. Examples of statements from the 2002 conference: "We are a one and undivided Church believing that Southern Africa needs the church to offer models of reconciliation and unity that will point the way for all within the many divided societies". 2002 Yearbook of the Methodist Church of Southern Africa, 2002, p. 55, "Conference, in denouncing racism, calls on all Methodists to continue striving against all forms of racism in Church and Society and commits the MCSA to co-operate with all agencies working towards similar objectives". 2002 Yearbook of the Methodist Church of Southern Africa, 2002 p. 56; 2003 Yearbook of the Methodist Church of Southern Africa, 2003, pp. 13, 124–125. It was decided to integrate circuits in 1997. 1997 Year Book of the Methodist Church of Southern Africa, 1997, p. 73. The annual meetings in 1998, 2000/2001 dealt with domination and racism. 1998 Year Book of the Methodist Church of Southern Africa, 1998, p. 5; 2000/2001 Yearbook of the Methodist Church of Southern Africa, 2001, p. 3.

111 "All Circuits have continued struggling with issues relating to integration, particularly in regard to distribution of resources, power and authority, and growing understanding of cultural differences. Furthermore, investigation into language courses has been conducted and several options have been made available to ministers wishing to increase competence in this regard. Those engaged in cross-cultural ministry have met regularly to discuss the strain of adjustments needing to be made, and have designed the outline of a course for those who are to be initiated into this work". 2000/2001 Yearbook of the Methodist Church of Southern Africa, 2001, p. 44. Similar statements were made in 2002 and 2003, for example, when the conferences also stated that no existing geographic circuit should be divided along 'uniracial' lines. 2002 Yearbook of the Methodist Church of Southern Africa, 2002, p. 56.

as crime, human sexuality, corruption, and xenophobia – received more attention in later conferences. The changed focus indicates that the environment for ethnic integration had declined.[112] Nyobole believed that it was inevitable for the church to become ethnically integrated. This happened in residential areas and schools. Integration, according to Nyobole, would start when people moved into and lived in new areas. The change would come for economic reasons, as people could afford to live in other areas. He assumed that economic reasons would cause the country and the church to become more ethnically integrated. His description was exclusively about integration in previously 'White' areas; he did not apply the term to the situation in former 'Black' areas.[113]

Nyobole indicated that there was an upwards social vertical mobility that combined with a lateral mobility from townships to suburbs. Economic opportunities would become an ecclesiological structuring factor. Downwards vertical mobility in former 'Black' townships was not mentioned.

Nyobole explained that a few ministers were placed across the racial lines during the apartheid years, and that this still happened, but only very rarely. He explained that the reluctance to appoint ministers across ethnic lines was due to the church's invitation system: local congregations could choose which ministers to call; only rarely did the church's conference place ministers. There were, however, areas in South Africa that were progressive, and Nyobole named the Central District as one example.[114] He stated: "The central district, I think, is the most progressive in terms of that most Black ministers in particular are in White circuits. There are very few White ministers who are in Black local churches at the moment".[115] The situation that Nyobole described was not unusual in some of the other denominations. 'Black' ministers were appointed to serve in former 'White' areas, but it was unusual that a 'White' minister served in a former 'Black' area. The 'call system' of appointing ministers would reduce the possibilities of placing ministers regardless of ethnicity. Diversity, as part of the Church's catholicity that transcends divisions, was difficult to attain.

The stipends of Methodist Church ministers were assessed in the different circuits, but paid to the minister from the central church office, according to

---

112 See for example: 2006 Yearbook of the Methodist Church of Southern Africa, 2006; and: 2009 Yearbook of the Methodist Church of Southern Africa, 2009; and: 2011 Yearbook of the Methodist Church of Southern Africa, 2011.
113 Nyobole, Vuyani Gladstone, Interview Protocol 2011-02-28.
114 The Central District includes three provinces: Gauteng, the North West from Lichtenburg to Vryburg, and one town in the Northern Cape, Christiana.
115 Nyobole, Vuyani Gladstone, Interview Protocol 2011-02-28.

Nyobole. This system made a fairer allocation of resources within the church possible. Congregations that could not afford to pay stipends were assisted. Ministers received a basic stipend, but local congregations and circuits could offer more than the stipend that was centrally paid. Because of this arrangement, salaries for individual ministers could differ according to circuits' and local congregations' ability to afford them.[116] As mentioned in Chapter Two, the TRC also stated that unequal stipends reinforced the stereotypes about different lifestyles being linked with ethnic background.[117]

The system of church stipends was an obstacle to the attainment of a greater ethnic mix of ministers in congregations. Nyobole believed that the issue of different church stipends was a reason why 'White' ministers were not found in predominantly 'Black' congregations. He stated also that unequal stipends were a sign that the church had not yet emerged from the apartheid mentality. He explained this by saying: "White people think that a White minister would be much more understanding in terms of their needs, in terms of their worship style, in terms of everything".[118] His statement was in fact true of any church where there were hesitations about diversity in the church. His example showed that there was still a perception that people of diverse backgrounds did not have anything to contribute in a different environment. Congregations that did not embrace the challenge could instead risk preserving old patterns.

Apostolic Faith Mission

During apartheid the AFM was divided into different sections, as described earlier, but united as one church during democratisation. The general secretary of the Apostolic Faith Mission, George Mahlobo, stated that the unification process had already started before the democratisation of the country. The new democratic president, Nelson Mandela, created a very favourable situation with reconciliation as the primary focus, which helped people to develop hope. The unification talks of the racially-divided church resulted in the creation of an ethnically-integrated church between 1997 and 1998.[119] Mahlobo identified this time as specially significant and advantageous for unification. Mandela's view of democratisation and reconciliation promoted a collective image of the South African people regardless

---

116 Nyobole, Vuyani Gladstone, Interview Protocol 2011-02-28.
117 Truth and Reconciliation Commission of South Africa Report, Vol. 4, 1998, p. 69.
118 Nyobole, Vuyani Gladstone, Interview Protocol 2011-02-28.
119 Mahlobo, Mphikeleki George, Interview Protocol 2011-03-01.

of ethnic background, thus facilitating transformation.[120] Others also identified a similar environment during democratisation when people in the country began to change.[121]

Mahlobo stated the importance of the 'White' church leader Isak Burger and the 'Black' church leader Frank Chikane in facilitating the unification process. Both churches were positive about church unity, and the church leaders had met and got to know each other personally. The unification was made known during the TRC's Faith Community Hearing in 1997. Mahlobo believed that it would have been more difficult to unite later because of greater polarisation between the ethnic groups. He identified increased levels of crime, for example, as a complex factor at the time that caused polarisation.[122] Mahlobo's response showed the importance of personal relationships that bridged ethnic differences in order to build unity in the church. Church unity would have been more difficult to achieve after Mandela's presidency. There are certain moments in history when change is more likely to occur.[123]

Some congregations were still situated in the apartheid-classified residential areas, and continued to minister as in the past. Mahlobo stressed that there was a small shift in the urban congregations. Some of them could even be classified as 'multi-racial'. Mahlobo said that the challenges were at the local level, and there was not much the national level could do to change the local situation.[124] The inability of the church's central level to affect the situation was due to the church's organisation: congregations had considerable independence, with the advantage of substantially autonomy. But this autonomy could also be a disadvantage, because the regional or central levels could not 'interfere' by encouraging greater ethnic integration.

---

120 See for example Xolela Mangcu's description of the reconciliation environment that Nelson Mandela created. Mangcu, Xolela, 2003, pp. 105–107.
121 See for example the parish council at St Thomas', mentioned in the previous chapter. Church Council Interview Protocol 2011-03-06.
122 Mahlobo, Mphikeleki George, Interview Protocol 2011-03-01. Chikane and Burger showed a film about the unification during the Faith Communities Hearing. TRC Special Hearing: Religion Tape 11, East London, DVD, (TRC0366 – 19971119), 1997.
123 There are certain times when political policies have had special advantages. Some political scientists have tried to explain this process with a theory named 'policy window'. John W. Kingdon has described this theory as special moments when ideas are more likely to succeed. There are several actors, and because of diverse developments a certain policy can become prioritised. Kingdon, John W., 1995. pp. 21–22, 67–72, 165–178, 179–182.
124 Mahlobo, Mphikeleki George, Interview Protocol 2011-03-01.

Some people moved from previously 'Black' areas into previously 'White' areas. However, there were barriers in the congregations – language and culture, for example – that made ethnic integration difficult. Mahlobo also noted that 'White' people moved to other areas when crime increased in the cities. He believed that there were social factors that led to the mobility of certain groups. He added that the inner cities had become predominantly 'Black' and cosmopolitan – which represented a different kind of diversity. Congregations in the inner cities accommodated, apart from South African citizens, people from other countries.[125]

Mahlobo's statement about social mobility in the South African context was similar to other church leaders' impressions of the situation. He noted that 'Black' people had moved into previously 'White' areas since democratisation, but that the opposite had not occurred. There was an upwards vertical social mobility combined with lateral mobility. Previously 'White' congregations had the opportunity to become ethnically diverse as a sign of the Church's catholicity, while previously 'Black' areas remained as before. Inequality became visible when privileged congregations enjoyed greater diversity, while underprivileged areas lacked those advantages.

Social mobility towards the cities did not necessarily create a greater ethnic mix, because some of the 'White' people moved to new areas. Nevertheless, the mix of people from various African countries occurred in those congregations that enjoyed diversity as a sign of the Church's catholicity in the analytical tool.[126] The pattern that Mahlobo described, of social mobility in the church, becomes an ecclesiological structuring factor.

George Mahlobo mentioned other examples of ethnicity-related issues that could cause division in the AFM. The church was managed in geographic regions; but they also had five so-called 'non-geographic' regions. People in the church had 'City visions', and wanted to establish inner city churches in Durban, Johannesburg, Cape Town, and even London. The 'City visions' were the reason for developing non-geographic regions. Mahlobo explained that these non-geographic regions happened to be mostly 'White' people. He acknowledged that the establishment of the non-geographic regions could give the impression

---

125 Mahlobo, Mphikeleki George, Interview Protocol 2011-03-01.
126 There is, for example, the trend of people with economic potential moving into secure and gated communities. For example, Midrand and Centurion (between Johannesburg and Pretoria) have several exclusive areas for people with the resources. The division between people is primarily an economic stratification, not ethnic.

that they were reverting to past patterns, that the non-geographic regions were a challenge, and that they were trying to manage the situation.[127]

Mahlobo also noted that there were specific ministries in the church that were mostly attended by 'Black' members – for example, children, youth, and women. They had previously had 'mission departments' consisting of predominantly 'White' participants, and now the situation was reversed. These kinds of issues were, according to Mahlobo, challenges for the church.[128] It is noteworthy that a divided Pentecostal church such as the AFM was able to unite, but that they still struggled with issues of ethnicity. New internal problem arose, for example, with 'White'-dominated non-geographic regions and with the absence of 'White' participants from particular ministries. Church unity creates new diversities that become difficult for a church to manage.

George Mahlobo said that the AFM had in the past adopted a presbyterian system of appointing ministers to congregations. They had then changed to a hybrid version of the presbyterian and congregational systems. This ensured that the local congregation had a certain power that included decisions about ministers. According to the deployment policies, the local congregation had to ask the regional leader to chair a meeting where they considered the requests for a minister. The congregation would select a suitable candidate, determine the stipend, and then call the minister to the position. They would turn to the general secretary's office when the partners had agreed, and the church would appoint the minister. After confirmation from the central office, the local congregation could enter into a contract between itself and the minister. Mahlobo believed that they had to deal with this system of appointing ministers in the future, because there were inequalities between rural and urban areas. Congregations in the cities, for example, could afford to have ministers, while congregations in rural areas did not have the same economic conditions. There were also many ministers who had to be allowed to work part-time.[129] Mahlobo's description was of a method of appointing ministers that did not facilitate the appointment of ministers across ethnic boundaries. The system hampered the possibility of social transformation where ethnic diversity was needed as part of Church's catholicity according to the analytical tool.

The AFM and the Methodist Church shared many similarities in their systems of calling or inviting ministers. The choice of ministers was made, in practice, by the local congregations, even though the central level had to approve the

---

127 Mahlobo, Mphikeleki George, Interview Protocol 2011-03-01.
128 Mahlobo, Mphikeleki George, Interview Protocol 2011-03-01.
129 Mahlobo, Mphikeleki George, Interview Protocol 2011-03-01.

appointments. Differentiated stipends or additional benefits also made congregations with better economic conditions more attractive. The Methodist Church at least had an equalisation system that guaranteed all ministers a basic stipend, while the AFM had some ministers who could not survive on their stipend and had to work part-time. The calling or invitation system, together with unequal stipends, could obstruct the possibility of appointing ministers from one ethnic group to serve a congregation of predominantly another ethnic group. The Roman Catholic and Anglican churches also had different stipends from diocese to diocese, and diverse allowances that depended on the ability of individual local congregations to provide them. Their situation, however, was different, because the central level of their churches chose candidates and appointed the ministers. The Roman Catholic and Anglican churches made it possible for churches to increase in diversity, but this also reduced the local church's ability to influence the choice of ministers.

Lutheran Churches

The Lutheran community in South Africa is, as described earlier, divided into three churches owing to different historical developments. First the people of German Lutheran Church background came to the Cape Colony to participate in the work of the Dutch East India Company. They obtained permission to worship in the Lutheran tradition, even though the Reformed Church was the only church that was allowed to worship in the area. Later, German, Scandinavian, and American mission societies began mission work, followed by settlers and other immigrants of European background. The Lutherans organised different churches and became segregated along the lines of the apartheid policy. It is important to acknowledge that the ethnically-divided churches, together with the apartheid state, became formative in South African society. It is not possible to escape the importance of the ecclesiastical traditions' participation as an identity-shaping factor in the society. The Lutherans remain divided because of their heritage, and repeated attempts to unite have failed. The churches' division, originating in a segregated society, becomes an ecclesiological structuring factor.[130]

---

130 Scriba, George & Lislerud, Gunnar, 1997, pp. 174–178, 191–194. On church unity, see also for example: Winkler, Harald, E., 1989; Florin, Hans, W., 1967; Fosseus, Helge, 1974. There is also the Moravian Church in South Africa, established in 1737. The Moravians began mission among the Khoi and established a mission station in Genadendal. The church has about 50 000 members and is part of LWF but not of ELCSA. Du Preez, Hannetjie, 2009, p. 13; Scriba, George & Lislerud, Gunnar, 1997,

Bishop Nils Rohwer from ELCSA-Cape was of the view that unity between the divided Lutheran churches was especially experienced under apartheid. They had joint services with eucharist, demonstrating that they belonged to one another and to the Lutheran confession. The ministers used to meet three or four times a year; congregations came together; and choirs used to meet regularly. Unity between the Lutheran churches was no longer practised as it had been because of a lack of engagement. Rohwer stressed that having fewer interactions was dangerous because they tended to drift apart, showing that unity was no longer regarded as necessary as it had been in the past.[131] This statement indicated that it was easier to have interactions when the society was divided by apartheid and when boundary-crossing relationships were prevented by government policy. The government could no longer be blamed when the country became democratic. The intention of the church to seek unity was tested when the country became democratic and external factors no longer prevented unification.

A similar development was recognised by bishop Horst Müller from ELCSA N-T, who said that the negotiations between ELCSA, ELCSA N-T, and ELCSA-Cape began in the 1980s and came to an end in 1994. There were many reasons for the discontinued negotiations, but discussions between the churches had resumed. Müller thought that there would be no problems for ELCSA N-T and ELCSA-Cape to unite, but that this would have created a greater distance and polarised the situation if the two former 'White' churches had united. Such church unity, according to Müller, would have emphasised that there were separate 'Black' and 'White' churches, which was not desirable.[132]

It is interesting that church unity discussions came to an end during democratisation. Several other church leaders and church councils had pointed to the special environment that made unity talks particularly favourable during the period of democratisation. Since its founding in 1975, ELCSA had had the aim of becoming a united church for all Lutherans in Southern Africa. ELCSA was the result of a merger of several regional churches established by the former missionary societies; but the other Lutheran churches in South Africa had decided not to become part of ELCSA. Several unity talks had been held, and even the LWF had pressured the churches to unite.[133] The divisions in the Lutheran community are not consistent with the catholicity of the Church in the analytical tool. Divisions

---

pp. 174–178. The Dutch Reformed churches are also ethnically divided into several churches with roots in the former segregation policy.
131 Rohwer, Nils J., Interview Protocol 2011-02-09.
132 Müller, Horst, Interview Protocol 2011-03-04.
133 Scriba, George & Lislerud, Gunnar, 1997, pp. 173, 185–186, 191–194.

that are consistent with government policy before democratisation are in conflict with unity in the Christian community.

The general secretary of ELCSA, Bheki P. Mathe, confirmed that the divided Lutheran churches continued to hold unity talks, but that the discussions were still a struggle. He believed that the churches would overcome their divisions, but also that there were many misunderstandings.[134] Mathe's optimism about future church unity was shared by the two other church leaders; but all of them identified several obstacles. Horst Müller noted that there were different views about and patterns of church hierarchy: the lifelong episcopate of ELCSA, for example, would not work for ELCSA N-T or ELCSA-Cape.[135] Bishop Rohwer had the same opinion, and added that bishops in ELCSA-Cape and ELCSA N-T were not consecrated like the bishops in ELCSA, but instead were simply inducted. ELCSA had a top-down structure that ELCSA-Cape would not accept, according to Rhower. ELCSA's general secretary identified similar differences over the position of bishops in the church.[136]

The opinion of the church leaders and bishops revealed diverse traditions about the episcopacy within the Lutheran communion of churches. ELCSA N-T and ELCSA-Cape elected and re-elected bishops, while the bishops in ELCSA were elected once and remained in their positions until retirement. The differences might appear to be vast; but in fact the bishops of ELCSA N-T and ELCSA-Cape spent a similar amount time in office as did the bishops in ELCSA.

Bheki Mathe said that ELCSA was a sending church and that ELCSA N-T and ELCSA-Cape were calling churches. Sending ministers to congregations was important for ELCSA. For example, the church had no power to give a minister a position if the minister was not called anywhere. Mathe said, however, that the 2006 ELCSA general assembly was willing to use both a sending and a calling system; so there might be some space for compromise in the talks between the churches.[137]

Another difference between the churches related to ministers' salaries. Mathe said that in ELCSA the dioceses were responsible for ministers' salaries, while in the other two Lutheran churches the congregations were responsible for them. He noted that ELCSA had much lower salaries for their ministers than ELCSA

---

134 Mathe, P. Bheki, Interview Protocol 2011-03-07; Fosseus, Helge, 1974, p. 36–40.
135 Müller, Horst, Interview Protocol 2011-03-04.
136 Bishop Rohwer identified the Swedish tradition, because the Church of Sweden has a life-long episcopacy; and Swedish theologians took part in the discussions leading to the formation of ELCSA. Rohwer, Nils J., Interview Protocol 2011-02-09; Mathe, P. Bheki, Interview Protocol 2011-03-07.
137 Mathe, P. Bheki, Interview Protocol 2011-03-07.

N-T and ELCSA-Cape. ELCSA, however, had started a programme to eliminate the salary gap between the churches, and they were close to removing the differences. He also recognised that the minister's salaries in ELCSA were dependent on the individual dioceses' ability to afford them, which varied.[138] The ownership of church property was also mentioned by the ELCSA N-T and ELCSA-Cape bishops as a source of difference between the churches. Bishop Müller said that every local congregation in ELCSA N-T and ELCSA-Cape owned its property, whereas property in ELCSA was owned by the central church.[139] Bheki Mathe explained that issues around property were a cause of misunderstanding between the churches. He explained, for example, that ELCSA congregations could fundraise and expand their buildings and buy additional property. The properties that the congregations occupied would, however, be owned by the whole church and not by a single congregation.[140] Issues regarding church organisation were another difficult area to resolve. However, the differences between the churches were less difficult to solve than those of the rest of society, which had undergone a major transformation.

It was important, however, that the three Lutheran churches had accepted one other's ordination; but a minister from ELCSA who wanted to serve in ELCSA N-T or ELCSA-Cape was required to have a recognised academic degree in order to be employed. Most of the ministers in ELCSA had only three or four years' training.[141] The bishops' view on the education of people for ministry emphasised a more functional understanding of the ministry. The church leaders' responses revealed divergent understandings of the ministry among the churches. ELCSA N-T and ELCSA-Cape are more influenced by the German Lutheran tradition, while ELCSA, with its more diverse background, is also influenced by Lutheran churches in Scandinavia and the USA.[142]

---

138 Mathe, P. Bheki, Interview Protocol 2011-03-07.
139 Müller, Horst, Interview Protocol 2011-03-04.
140 Mathe, P. Bheki, Interview Protocol 2011-03-07.
141 Müller, Horst, Interview Protocol 2011-03-04; Rohwer, Nils J., Interview Protocol 2011-02-09.
142 The Lutheran churches in the Nordic countries and the Evangelical Lutheran Church in America (ELCA) emphasise the apostolic succession much more than the Lutheran churches in Germany. The differences are visible in far-reaching unity between the Church of England and the Nordic Lutheran churches and between the Episcopal Church in the USA and ELCA. The German Lutheran churches do not have these kinds of agreements with Anglican churches.

All three Lutheran church leaders declared that no doctrinal issues separated their churches in South Africa. They recognised one other's ministries; they were united in pulpit and altar fellowship; and all three churches were members of and shared the same communion in the LWF.[143] They also belonged to LUCSA, a sub-region of Lutheran churches in Southern Africa attached to the LWF. All three church leaders said that the Lutheran churches intended to create a united church in South Africa. They already had a bishops' conference that meets regularly, and some congregations from the different churches meet occasionally at a local level for services, projects, and celebrations of the common Lutheran confessional heritage.[144] It is important to note that a divided Lutheran community is an ecclesiological structuring factor. The division reveals an ecclesiology of a broken *koinonia,* where ethnic and economic factors are more important in constituting the churches.

Many of the ELCSA N-T and ELCSA-Cape congregations had become more ethnically diverse. Lutherans from ELCSA had moved into areas where there was already a Lutheran church, and had become involved in, for example, an ELCSA N-T congregation. The ELCSA N-T congregations also used English, which opened them to people of different backgrounds. There were even congregations in ELCSA N-T with a majority of 'Black' members.[145] Müller said that ELCSA N-T was almost entirely German-speaking until the 1980s, but today it was multicultural and multilingual. Demographic changes and the economy had caused the church to become more multi-ethnic.[146]

Rohwer said that the Lutheran Church in Strand Street in Cape Town, an ELCSA-Cape congregation, had more 'Black' than 'White' worshipers on a Sunday, and many 'Black' people had become members. However, diverse ethnicities were not evident in every ELCSA-Cape congregation. Rohwer had rarely seen

---

143 The arguments for having pulpit and eucharist as the only signs of church unity were criticised by the LWF's ecclesiological study programme on *status confessionis* (1973-76), and were brought to the attention of the LWF's general assembly in Dar es Salaam in 1977. In Christ – a new community, 1977, pp. 91–32; Lodberg, Peter, 1988, pp. 76–77.
144 Rohwer, Nils J., Interview Protocol 2011-02-09; Müller, Horst, Interview Protocol 2011-03-04; Mathe, P. Bheki, Interview Protocol 2011-03-07.
145 Rohwer, Nils J., Interview Protocol 2011-02-09; Müller, Horst, Interview Protocol 2011-03-04. See for example: Friedenskirche, Johannesburg, Overview, 2011, p. 1, Church Publication; St Peter's Congregation, Pretoria, Overview, 2011, pp. 1–2, Church Publication; St Johannes Lutheran Church, Kelvin, Overview, 2011, p. 1, Church Publication.
146 Müller, Horst, Interview Protocol 2011-03-04.

people from different ethnic groups at the Lutheran Church in Stellenbosch, for example.[147]

Mathe also confirmed that ELCSA people became members of ELCSA N-T or ELCSA-Cape congregations; and that, he believed, helped these churches to understand the rainbow nation. He recognised that the opposite – members from ELCSA N-T or ELCSA-Cape becoming members of ELCSA – was not happening. He also said that ELCSA N-T and ELCSA-Cape were at an advantage because they had fewer members, and receiving 'Black' members improved their image. The 'Black' members who moved into the cities and became members of an ELCSA N-T or ELCSA-Cape church were generally better off, and this meant that ELCSA was the economic loser.[148]

Mathe's observation confirmed the development that leaders from other denominations had identified: there was a move from former 'Black' to former 'White' areas, while the opposite was not true. A social upwards vertical mobility, together with lateral mobility from townships to suburbs, was evident.

The other denominations kept their members in the same church tradition or denomination, but there was movement between congregations. ELCSA members were transferring to ELCSA N-T or ELCSA-Cape congregations. These moves made ELCSA N-T and ELCSA-Cape more diverse, simply because of increased economic opportunity. Lateral mobility caused ELCSA not just to lose members, but specifically to lose its most economically-advantaged members.

The whole South African society has been adjusted after democratisation, as was obvious in, for example, public administration, school institutions, and laws; but ELCSA, ELCSA-Cape, and ELCSA N-T have found it difficult to become a united church organisation despite pressure from the LWF. It is also notable that the other mainline churches studied were united as a single church organisation, while the Lutheran church family was divided from the start – much in line with South Africa's divisions before democratisation.

7.3 Conclusions

Most of the congregations in the study reflected the ethnic composition of the area where they were situated, which is consistent with the catholicity of the

---

147 Rohwer, Nils J., Interview Protocol 2011-02-09.
148 Mathe, P. Bheki, Interview Protocol 2011-03-07; Desmond Tutu was the first to coin the expression 'rainbow people of God', in a sermon in Tromsø, Norway on 5 December 1991. The expression has continued to be used to describe the people of South Africa as diverse but belonging to the same community. Tayob, Abdulkader, 1999, p. 85.

Church in the analytical tool. Congregations in former 'White' areas had become more ethnically diverse, while congregations in other areas had not experienced the same development. Congregations in former 'Black' areas had not become more diverse than they had been before democratisation.

Increased ethnic diversity was not primarily a consequence of congregations and churches changing their policies, but of socio-economic shifts that enabled people to choose their residential areas. A visible social upwards vertical mobility combined with a lateral mobility from townships to suburbs. The opposite lateral mobility – from city centres and suburbs to townships – was not evident in the congregations, nor was it mentioned by the church leaders. This new form of division in the society is inconsistent with the catholicity of the Church in the analytical tool. Segregation – whether because of apartheid or changed socio-economic conditions – is inconsistent with an understanding of Christian communion.

Congregations in former 'White' areas – and to some extent in 'Coloured' and 'Indian or Asian' areas as well – had been advantaged by becoming ethnically-diverse congregations in line with the catholicity of the Church according to the analytical tool. Congregations in former 'Black' areas could not reflect the same ethnic diversity; and this became a problem because the same diversity found in other areas did not appear in their communities. It is significant that these congregations were unable to achieve greater diversity, even had they wished to do so. Increased ethnic diversity in congregations located exclusively in wealthier areas is not consistent with the analytical tool of the Church's catholicity. Accomplishing diversity is a task for the whole Christian community, and diversity is supposed to be shared and received. The catholicity of the Church requires a mechanism that supports ethnic exchange between congregations across ethnic borders.

Some of the church councils and church leaders were able to indicate that there was another kind of movement among the urban population. People who had economic opportunities moved from the city centres into suburbs or new housing estates to escape crime, urban decay, and ethnic change. The move into 'gated communities' is related to socio-economic conditions, and not primarily to ethnicity. However, after democratisation ethnicity combined with socio-economic conditions become an ecclesiological structuring factor. It is very clear that socio-economic stratification is more important than ecclesiological reasons for ethnic integration. Non-theological reasons became more important when the ethnic pattern was changed after democratisation.

Becoming a member of a congregation of a different ethnic group was not always easy; and this brought to the fore a catholicity that challenged congregations to create an accepting and hospitable environment for minority groups. Some congregations changed gradually in their approach when new ethnic groups were embraced, and ethnic diversity was even reflected in some of the congregations' decision-making bodies. Safeguarding representation in decision-making bodies also creates opportunities for diversity in the churches.

The catholicity of the Church as used in the analytical tool challenges the congregations and the churches, furthermore, to increase connections between people of various ethnicities in order to permit diversity within the churches. Of course, the way the churches have chosen to be organised affects their ability to become ethnically diverse and thus to represent variety in the South African Christian communion. Strong central and regional church organisations and hierarchies, such as the Roman Catholic and Anglican churches, could make diversity possible by rearranging circuits and districts and by appointing ministers regardless of ethnicity. These two churches were organised such that the dioceses appointed ministers; but this reduced the congregations' independence. The ministers in the Methodist and AFM churches were appointed entirely by the congregations, but approved by the church's central structures. The congregations had far-reaching autonomy in appointing their ministers; but this reduced the likelihood that they would choose ministers from a different ethnicity from that of the majority in the congregation. The churches' leadership, however, had become more ethnically diverse in most churches. Education and social change were contributing factors that could change the churches' leadership in the future.

The Roman Catholic, Anglican, and Methodist churches have never been ethnically divided as organisations, but in practice they were divided at the local level before democratisation. The AFM had been divided along ethnic lines, but became a united church during democratisation. The Lutheran churches are still divided despite holding the same doctrines; and disagreement on practical matters does not make church unity any easier. The catholicity of the Church according to the analytical tool stresses that ethnicity is not a reason for division within the Christian community.

Congregations and churches could still be ethnically divided even after there were no longer laws and systems of governments that imposed ethnic divisions. Various organisations, such as women's and men's leagues, still separate members according to their ethnicity, and this creates division in the churches. Greater ethnic interaction as part of Church's catholicity does not occur automatically. A lack of teaching about catholicity, and the failure to achieve a thorough reconstruction of the denominations, are the reasons for continued ethnic divisions. Denominations that are divided in practice ensure that ethnicity becomes an ecclesiological structuring factor.

Few of the church councils or church leaders revealed their vision for how they would like to see the church, or the wider society, in respect of ethnicity in the future. They were not asked, and some gave implicit information. Some of them stated that ethnicity should be seen as of minor importance in the church. Nobody, however, referred to the visions that were promoted before and during democratisation by bodies such as the SACC and the TRC. It is interesting, too, that few church councils referred to important persons from the past who had advocated against apartheid, while they were named by several of the church leaders. The failure to name people and church organisations that were important in bringing about change suggests that the anti-apartheid legacy was not particularly present after democratisation.

This chapter has examined ethnic diversity in congregations and churches two decades after democratisation. The next chapter will investigate how ethnicity becomes visible in church services, as an important ecclesial practice, in the different congregations and churches.

Chapter Eight: Church Services Gathering Christian Communion or Ethnic Groups

The previous chapter examined ethnicity in the congregations and churches studied. It was clear that there had been vertical and lateral mobility after democratisation, and that some areas had become more ethnically diverse. This chapter will explore how ethnicity becomes visible in the congregations' and churches' services.

Church services are the main ecclesial practices in congregations where Christians gather as a community. Services could be viewed either as a single main practice, or as a collection of several practices. According to Alasdair MacIntyre, a service could be described as a recurring event in a community that has developed through the long tradition of the Church. It is a practice that is learned through the generations, following certain patterns; and it can be recognised, irrespective of time and place, and even if worshiping communities are separated.[1]

The previous chapter was almost entirely based on interviews with church councils and church leaders about how they perceived ethnic diversity in their congregations and churches. This chapter will also use observations made during Sunday services. I will analyse the services as an ecclesial practice using observation, hymn books, worship materials, congregation profiles, missals, and descriptions that were given in the interviews.

I will examine how the services are performed in the South African context, and how ethnicity becomes visible in the studied congregations. Firstly, I will focus on how these congregations conduct their services in relation to ethnicity, and then explore some important practices that became visible and are worth examining. Secondly, I will examine how the congregations and churches confess their catholicity according to the creeds in the church services. The terms used in confessing catholicity could have implications for the realisation of an ethnically-diverse Church.

---

1   One example of emphasising the church service as an important practice of the church is given by Yves Congar. He states that the liturgy in the Church is an expression of the nature of the Church. "[…] la liturgie exprimant et manifestant au plus haut point la nature authentique de la véritable Église […]" Congar, Yves M.-J. 1966, p. 268. See MacIntyre's description of practices: MacIntyre, Alasdair, 1984, p. 192–194, 202–203.

8.1 Similarities and Differences

The case congregations showed many similarities, but their life as worshiping communities also took diverse forms. They belong to different denominations, and they are situated in different parts of the country – factors that influenced the ethnic makeup of the congregations and how they conducted their church services.

St Peter Claver in Pimville – Roman Catholic Church

This congregation, situated in Pimville, Soweto, had two church services every Sunday, at seven o'clock and nine o'clock in the morning respectively. There was no need for additional services on Sundays because the church building could accommodate more than a thousand people at a time. Nor was there any need to have separate services in different languages. The people who worshiped at St Peter Claver could understand isiZulu and Sesotho, both of which were widely used in the congregation and in the area.[2]

They also had a eucharist service on Tuesday, Thursday, and Friday mornings at eight o'clock. On Wednesday mornings they had adoration and benediction together with a eucharist service in one of the zones in the area. Twice a month they had a eucharist service at an outstation named Kliptown, which could be characterised as a squatter camp. People in the congregation were encouraged to go to confession, for which a special time on Saturday afternoons at half past four was assigned.[3]

The strong emphasis on the eucharist is consistent with the Roman Catholic tradition, but is also in line with the catholicity of the Church according to the analytical tool. The eucharist supports and sustains the Christian community, and also requires reconciliation and a sharing of common gifts. Celebrating the eucharist frequently is important in the ecumenical documents, but they do not stipulate the frequency of the eucharistic celebrations other than every Sunday. Unity with the bishop was emphasised by the church council members as a unifying factor that connected all the members to one another in the diocese,

---

2   St Peter Claver Parish, Pimville, Soweto, 2011, Website; Observation Protocol 2011-02-27; Church Council Interview Protocol 2011-03-06. In Soweto, 98.5 per cent of the people described themselves as 'Black African' according to Census 2011. Census 2011, Soweto, Statistics South Africa, 2012.
3   St Peter Claver Parish, Pimville, Soweto, 2011, Website; Church Council Interview Protocol 2011-03-06.

regardless of ethnicity. The BEM document also stresses that church leaders have a particular task to safeguard the unity of the church.[4]

The church services with the eucharist, known in the Roman Catholic Church as 'Mass', follow the Roman Missal. With few exceptions, all Roman Catholic services around the world follow this text; but the services are held in local languages, and often use contextualised music, hymns, symbols, etc.[5] Using a common liturgical order was regarded as important. A council member stated that it was possible to visit other Roman Catholic congregations and recognise virtually the same liturgy.[6] Identification with, and knowledge of, the same liturgy gave a sense of unity with other members of the Roman Catholic Church. Using a particular common liturgy is not central to the ecumenical documents, but should not be underestimated as helping to express the Church's catholicity according to the analytical tool.

The church council at St Peters Claver explained that their services were "[…] vibrant, lot is happening".[7] Many members participated in the services as choir-singers, musicians, servers, and other ministries. The congregation also characterised their worship as "Spirit-filled Worship and Dynamic Music, Powerful Preaching. Youth on the move for Christ, Social outreach, Evangelisation, Religious Education for Children and Adults, Faith Formation, Bereavement and Sick ministry" on the congregation's website.[8]

Music and singing also played a central role, especially during Sunday services. The congregation had several people in the choirs; many people were part of processions; and at times more than 20 people served at the altar. The members had strong voices, and there was a lot of movement in the services. People danced, waved hands, used instruments such as muffled hand drums or hand bells, and ululated. The hymns were sung in the traditional South African style, with many tunes and rhythms unaccompanied by an organ or other similar instruments.

---

4   St Peter Claver Parish, Pimville, Soweto, 2011, Website; Church Council Interview Protocol 2011-03-06; Baptism, Eucharist and Ministry, 1982, pp. 24–29.
5   Missale Romanum, 1969. All Roman Catholic dioceses had to use the Roman Missal after the Council of Trent, unless they had used a specific liturgy for more than two hundred years. Examples today include Milan in Italy, which uses the Ambrosian Rite, and Toledo and Salamanca in Spain, which use the Mozarabic Rite. There are also autonomous Catholic Churches in full communion with the Holy See that follow their own liturgical tradition. Senn, Frank C., 1997, p. 489.
6   Church Council Interview Protocol 2011-02-27.
7   Church Council Interview Protocol 2011-02-27.
8   St Peter Claver Parish, Pimville, Soweto, 2011, Website; St Peter Claver, Catholic Church, Pimville, 1928–2008, 80th Anniversary, 2008, p. 43, Church Publication.

Incense and bells at the consecration, together with a rich liturgical development, were part of the services. The sermons could be described as spiritual, with space for both laughter and seriousness. The congregation said in one of their documents that they wanted to celebrate the liturgy in accordance with the Vatican II Council's norms.[9] Vatican II declared, for example, that congregations should use music, songs, and languages from their contexts, and involve many people in the church services.[10]

An indication of the catholicity of the Church according to the analytical tool became evident during the prayers and the special 'Prayers of the Faithful' that were part of the liturgy. The church council stressed that they prayed for the church, their families, the sick, prisoners, the community, the departed, themselves, etc. The focuses of the prayers came from the community, and they prayed for everything that was necessary – even prayers for ancestors, according to the church council.[11] The practice of praying for others helped the community to include people of diverse backgrounds and ethnicities in the community, the country, and even abroad. Prayers for ancestors are especially important in the African context, and are implicitly mentioned in the ecumenical documents: the notion of communion beyond time is stressed in several documents that deal with Holy Communion.[12]

The congregation confessed that they believed in a church *eliKhatholika* during the creed. This means that they believed in a 'catholic' church – the term that would be used in an English-language service. The word 'catholic' would also be used in all creeds in other languages used by the Roman Catholic Church.[13] The

---

9 Observation Protocol 2011-02-27; St Peter Claver, Catholic Church, Pimville, 1928–2008, 80th Anniversary, 2008, p. 31, Church Publication.
10 Sacrosanctum Concilium, 1963, Ch. 1:14–20, 37–40.
11 Church Council Interview Protocol 2011-02-27; Observation Protocol 2011-02-27.
12 The communion of saints is repeatedly stressed in several ecumenical documents. See for example: "[…] Him who has knit together the whole family in heaven and in earth in the communion of saints, united in the fellowship of service, or prayer, and of praise". Reports of the World Conference on Faith and Order, 1927, p. 5. The BEM document says about the eucharist: "United to our Lord and in communion with all the saints and martyrs, we are renewed in the covenant sealed by the blood of Christ". Baptism, Eucharist and Ministry, 1982, p. 12.
13 The word 'catholic' is used in English, *katolieke* in Afrikaans, and *eliKhatholika* in Nguni languages. The translation *katolieke* in Afrikaans could be perceived as foreign to Afrikaans because of the language's strong connection with reformed (and therefore anti-Catholic) theology. The Sacramentary, 1998, p. 435; Die Sakramentarium, 1989, p. 370; Incwadi Yamamisa Ngamasonto, 1983, pp. 436–437.

use of 'catholic' in the creeds emphasised the ecclesiological meaning of being church in South Africa and in the world.

St Thomas' in Linden – Anglican Church of Southern Africa

The congregation, which belongs to the Anglican diocese of Johannesburg, is situated in Linden, a residential suburb on the northern side of Johannesburg. The congregation had various services in English and one in an indigenous language. In Linden 66.7 per cent of the population described themselves as 'White', and 21.8 per cent described themselves as 'Black African', according to Census 2011. Similar numbers of people attended the various services. The congregation had four services every Sunday in order to accommodate all the people in the church building, but also to provide a range of services and one indigenous language service.[14]

The church council members said that St Thomas' had its roots in the Anglo-Catholic tradition, which was regarded as very strong.[15] One of the council members explained:

> It is very clear that the eucharist is very central. Take the eight o'clock service. I think as a parish, in terms of what we teach, and how we treat this across the borders, we have what is called a high regard for the eucharist, that it's important and some kind of focus, presence of Christ amongst us [...].[16]

Most of the different services during the week were eucharistic, emphasising the importance of the eucharist to the congregation. The rich liturgical life in the services was evident, for example, in the presence of several altar servers and choirs dressed in liturgical vestments. They had processions with the cross, candles, and gospel, and used incense, consecration bells, and benediction in front of the Blessed Sacrament.[17] They emphasised the importance of the eucharist to the congregation in the same way as the Roman Catholic congregation in Pimville did. This was also stressed in several ecumenical documents, including BEM. Breaking bread together and sharing wine challenges and questions all forms of

---

14 In Linden 66.7 per cent of the population described themselves as 'White', 21.8 per cent as 'Black African', 7.9 per cent as 'Indian or Asian', and 2.5 per cent as 'Coloured'. Census 2011, Linden, Statistics South Africa, 2013.
15 The Anglo-Catholic tradition was emphasised in the parish profile. St Thomas' Anglican Church Linden, Parish Profile, 2011, p. 2.
16 Church Council Interview Protocol 2011-03-06.
17 Observation Protocol 2011-03-06; St Thomas' Anglican Church Linden, Parish Profile, 2011, p. 7, Church Publication.

division in the human community, and also reaffirms the unity of the body of Christ.[18]

The ministry of all believers and the growth of the Christian community were evident in the church services, and were stressed in the church's Vision and Mission statements, as mentioned in Chapter Six. Several people of all ages were church servers, and many lay ministers participated in the worship. The congregation's five Sunday services were at six thirty, eight o'clock, quarter to ten in the morning, at two o'clock in the afternoon, and at six thirty in the evening. They also had several weekday services, and all of them included the eucharist, in accordance with the congregation's profile. The sermons would typically be short, lasting for ten to fifteen minutes. The services would have a set ending time because another service would start soon after the previous one. Each of the various Sunday services had its own character; they used a variety of prayer books, including An Anglican Prayer Book, the South African Prayer Book, or a special liturgy for a particular service.[19] Using the various liturgies stressed the importance of diversity and of members' preferences for different traditions. Unity as part of the Church's catholicity in the analytical tool does not suppress diversity for the sake of uniformity.

The church council stated that Sundays began with a said Mass from An Anglican Prayer Book at six thirty in the morning. The service had no music, hymns, or sung liturgy, and was said by the minister, altar servers, and congregants. The eight o'clock service was a sung High Mass with traditional Anglican hymns led by organ and piano music and choir. This service followed the South African Prayer Book, and had many participants, most of whom were women and men in their late middle age and senior citizens who were 'White' and of British descent; only a few 'Black' members attended. The hymns were traditional Anglican hymns of mainly English origin. Several parts of the liturgy – for example, the Gospel, the Lord's Prayer, Kyrie, Gloria, Agnus Dei – were sung.[20]

---

18 See for example: Baptism, Eucharist and Ministry, 1982, p. 14–16. See especially D:19-21 and E:31.
19 Observation Protocol 2011-03-06; St Thomas' Anglican Church Linden, Parish Profile, 2011, p. 1, Church Publication.
20 St Thomas' Anglican Church Linden, Parish Profile, 2011, p. 7, Church Publication; Church Council Interview Protocol 2011-03-06. The hymn book used in the service was The English Hymnal, London 1906, Forty-third impression, 1979. Observation Protocol 2011-03-06. The South African Prayer Book was published in 1928, and has similarities with the Church of England's Book of Common Prayer. An Anglican Prayer Book is the ACSA's revised liturgy, published in 1989.

The quarter to ten service was a Mass with music – a 'family Mass' – using An Anglican Prayer Book. It met the needs of families, and took place simultaneously with Sunday School and the St Thomas' Youth Church. The service was often accompanied by a marimba liturgy from the *Lumko Marimba Mass*, with elements in Xhosa, Zulu, and Sotho.[21]

The service at two o'clock in the afternoon was a so-called 'vernacular Mass' in one of the South African indigenous languages, following the South African Prayer Book. The service did not have the same high profile as the morning services in respect of music or the number of people attending. The church bells were not used, and hymns were chosen by a group of participants just before the service started. No organ, piano, or other instruments were used in the service: the hymns were sung in the traditional South African way, with unaccompanied voices in four parts. The minister used either an indigenous language or English translated into an indigenous language. The services had few participants, and most were women domestic workers, some of them wearing the Mothers' Union uniform.[22]

When the church council was approached about the afternoon service, one member said: "I've never been to that service".[23] Several other members also admitted that they had not attended the two o'clock service, and that they had limited knowledge of it.[24] The response from the church council indicated that the Sunday afternoon service was not a high priority for the congregation. As it was mainly for women domestic workers in the area, an intersectional inequality in the society and the church related to gender, class, and ethnicity may have been evident.[25] The service was an opportunity for women who had been working during the mornings to be able to attend a service on a Sunday. A church council member explained:

---

21 Observation Protocol 2011-03-06; Marimba Mass, St Thomas' Anglican Church, 09h45 Family Mass, n.d., pp. 4, 10–12, 13, Church Publication. The Lumko Marimba Mass was developed within the Roman Catholic Church in South Africa in conjunction with the former music department at the Lumko Institute. Lumko is a conference centre, and pastoral formation and training institute run by the SACBC at Germiston in Gauteng. Confirmed by phone call to Miriam Dyantui at Lumko Institute 2013-11-27.
22 Observation Protocol 2011-03-06; Church Council Interview Protocol 2011-03-06.
23 Church Council Interview Protocol 2011-03-06.
24 Church Council Interview Protocol 2011-03-06.
25 The notion of 'Black' women as domestic workers continues to reinforce the social construction of the household as an underpaid, feminised, and radicalised space. Fish, Jennifer N., 2006, pp. 112–114.

That two o'clock service has a demographic of its own. The other services are mostly for people who live in the area. The two o'clock service tends to be more for domestic workers who work for people who live in the area, and they're working in the morning so that's why they can't come [earlier].[26]

This response showed that the two o'clock service was different from the other Sunday services. In addition to using a language other than English, it was for 'Black' women who were domestics working in the area, but who did not live there. The custom of having afternoon Sunday services in areas where people have domestic workers is not new, and was also offered by other churches in the area and in other cities.[27] One council member explained:

> It has always been as long as I know… In all the churches … They would meet on a Sunday afternoon because most of them are working, they are domestics, and they have no other chance. They also meet on Thursday afternoon with the Mothers' Union. The Mothers' Union still meets on a Thursday afternoon because that's their afternoon off. So they get together and worship, and they also catch up and socialising and working on various programmes […].[28]

The South African system of domestic workers could be characterised as a legacy of apartheid that was also evident in St Thomas' church services. The two o'clock service was maintained because the women's labour market had not undergone significant change. Domestic work is still the largest sector of employment for 'Black' South African women, and it continues to reinforce social constructions of women's positions in the society.[29] The domestic workers' free time is Sunday and Thursday afternoons, when the women are free to attend church services, to be engaged in the church's women's leagues, and to volunteer for various projects.

It could be argued that St Thomas' was unable to change the domestic workers' working hours, but it could at least have offered the women the option of access to a particular church service that they could attend. It is noteworthy, however, that the service was regarded as different from the other services, and had a lower profile than the morning services. Several of the women who attended the afternoon service might well have been working that morning in the home of church members, and so not been able to participate in the morning services. It is noteworthy

---

26   Church Council Interview Protocol 2011-03-06.
27   See, for example, St Charles Borromeo Roman Catholic Congregation, Victory Park, Linden, which had a similar approach to St Thomas', with Sunday services in English at 06.30, 08.00, 10.00, and 17.30, and one in Sesotho/ isiZulu at 15.00. St Charles Borromeo Roman Catholic Congregation, Holy Masses, 2013, Website.
28   Church Council Interview Protocol 2011-03-06.
29   Fish, Jennifer N., 2006, pp. 107, 109, 112–115.

that the two o'clock service became an ecclesiological structuring factor in the congregation because it served a specific group of people. A service that causes an intersectional inequality cannot be regarded as being consistent with the Church's catholicity according to the analytical tool. The two o'clock service had limited contact with the other worshiping groups in the congregation, and exposed a division based on ethnicity, gender, and class.

The congregation had tried to have a number of combined services during the year in order to learn from each other, to bring different traditions together, to let people get to know each other, and to break down barriers. These combined services were not explicitly intended to include the two o'clock service, but rather to let people of the different morning services meet each other.[30] One council member stated:

> I think that's the one thing about our parish, it is very diverse but it is fragmented ... we tried four times a year to have one service, to ask everybody to come together in one service, and we would have traditions from each. Some liturgy, some family words, and just come together so we would learn from each other and greet each other.[31]

The combined services could exemplify a search for unity to sustain catholicity. Diversity that develops into different worshiping communities with limited contact risks breaking catholicity.

The last service on Sundays was at six thirty in the evening. It was a 'said' service using An Anglican Prayer Book's *lectio divina,* or (on the last Sunday of the month) a service of evensong and benediction. This was a quiet service with meditation, according to the church council. The service had only a few participants – either people who had attended a service previously, or those who had been working earlier on Sunday.[32] One council member described the evening service: "[…] It's practically those who have come in the morning, but are looking to end the day. It's a very quiet service. … There is no sermon, but we do a meditation on the scripture that we all reflect on in silence […]".[33] The variety of Sunday services was a way of accommodating people's preferences, and making it possible to attend a service on a Sunday. One council member explained that

---

30 Church Council Interview Protocol 2011-03-06.
31 Church Council Interview Protocol 2011-03-06.
32 St Thomas' Anglican Church Linden, Parish Profile, 2011, p. 7, Church Publication; Church Council Interview Protocol 2011-03-06.
33 Church Council Interview Protocol 2011-03-06.

Johannesburg was a busy city, and that a lot of people worked on Sundays and needed different worship times.[34]

The variety of Sunday services to accommodate people's preferences was described by one council member:

> I see it very open to different kinds of people. It is quite a conservative group at the eight o'clock service, it's a much more relaxed group at the nine thirty service, and then in the evening, the six-thirty in the evening, it's a much more plain church group ... People could slot into where they are.[35]

The council stressed the variety of people and services, and that there was a place for everyone. It is obvious that the council members could not have a complete picture of all the different services in the congregation. The many forms of worship services, reflecting a huge diversity, could be described as emphasising diversity in order to avoid uniformity – which is part of the Church's catholicity. Diversity can be encouraged as long as the diversity does not destroy the unity.

The very diverse forms of services could, however, cause division and could easily develop into different communities. It is obvious that the various services at St Thomas' had fragmented the congregation, as one of the council member stated. This was particularly evident for the two o'clock service, which some of the church council members had not even attended.

The congregation also had several church services during the week. They had a Healing Mass every Tuesday afternoon at five forty-five, and a said Mass every Wednesday, Friday, and Saturday morning. They had a weekly service at the Darrenwood Village every Friday and monthly services at Elm Park retirement village, both of which were enclosed retirement villages. Monthly services were also held at various retirement homes, nursing institutions, and schools. These services were mostly performed by one of the associate, assistant, or self-supporting ministers, and occasionally by a lay minister or the rector. The additional staff made it possible for the congregation to minister to a variety of different institutions and also to have many services during the week.[36]

Making attendance possible for people who would otherwise find it difficult to attend ordinary services could be seen as including them in the ordinary community. These services nevertheless run the risk – as the Sunday afternoon service shows – to develop into their own separate communities. Symbols of unity,

---

34 Church Council Interview Protocol 2011-03-06.
35 Church Council Interview Protocol 2011-03-06. Note that, although the respondent said the service was at nine thirty, it was in fact at a quarter to ten.
36 St Thomas' Anglican Church Linden, Parish Profile, 2011, p. 7, Church Publication.

or even the presence of other members of the congregation, would help to sustain catholicity in the congregation.

One important part of the Sunday church services – and a symbol of a united community – was the distribution of 'family crosses' at the end of the services. Wooden crosses, each holding a candle like a small private votive altar, were distributed to individuals or families for anniversaries and birthdays, and to those in need of special prayers. The distribution was made publicly, and it was explained why a particular person or family was being given the cross.[37] The delivery of the crosses was followed by a special 'family cross' prayer by the minister, and the recipient was given a printed copy of the prayer. Those who had received a cross were named in the information leaflet each Sunday, and congregants could participate in the prayers for those who received them.[38]

The liturgy around the 'family cross' was a way of communicating that every member of the congregation belonged to the one community, and that there was communal prayer and care. Special anniversaries, illnesses, incidents, etc. were not merely a private matter, but were part of the wider community through prayers that were linked with the congregation's services. The 'family crosses' were a sign of a fellowship, of a *koinonia* that constituted the congregation.

Intercessions and prayer in church were a way of making the issues of the wider community visible. New perspectives were brought to the church's attention, and members could make their own responses to the needs of individuals, the congregation, the society, and the world. A council member explained:

> I think prayer is a sign of our unity, and there is a cycle of prayer that is published by the diocese. People in the pews are not even aware of where it comes from, but we always include elements from that cycle in the weekly prayers. That brings us together as a diocese, so in the diocese we pray for the whole Anglican community through the world.[39]

The intercessions that were produced by the diocese and used in every congregation were seen as a way of bringing the diocese together, and of uniting them with the Anglican Communion and the whole international Christian community. The practice of praying for other people in the community, in South Africa, and around the world, facilitated by the diocese, could be a sign of the catholicity of the Church

---

37 St Thomas' Anglican Church Linden, Parish Profile, 2011, p. 12, Church Publication; Observation Protocol 2011-03-06.
38 St Thomas' Anglican Church Linden, Parish Profile, 2011, p. 12, Church Publication; Church Council Interview Protocol 2011-03-06; Information sheet for the Sunday, 6th March 2011, 2011, Church Publication; Observation Protocol 2011-03-06.
39 Church Council Interview Protocol 2011-03-06.

according to the analytical tool. The local and the global were kept together, and the prayers transcended geographic and ethnic boundaries. People of diverse ethnicities, social backgrounds, and economic conditions offered the same prayers, and were even connected with communities in other contexts and countries, thus making the Christian communion visible. The character of the prayers showed that a centrally-produced prayer could facilitate the emphasis on Christian community.

The congregation used the word 'catholic' in the English services and *eliKhatholika* in the indigenous afternoon service, when the congregation confessed their credal faith on Sundays. The term 'catholic' was also used in other translations of the liturgy in the languages used in the Anglican Church.[40] Using the term 'catholic' emphasised the theological foundation of the church's ecclesiology.

Athlone Methodist Church – Methodist Church of Southern Africa

Athlone Methodist Church is situated in one of the former 'Coloured' areas in Cape Town. The congregation had one main church service every Sunday, apart from a special eucharist service once a month, conducted exclusively in English. The church building is big, and accommodated all the people who came to Sunday services. The great majority of the population of Athlone identified themselves as 'Coloured', as described in Chapter Five; and this was consistent with those who worshiped in the church. The congregation did not need separate services on the basis of language or available space; and this meant that the congregation did not need to be divided. Unity was retained – although ethnic diversity was less visible.[41]

Apart from the single worship service on most Sundays, other services were held during the week. They had a youth service on Friday evenings, and devotions when, for example, the women met, as they did regularly. The Sunday service started at nine o'clock, and lasted for about one and a half hours. The average Sunday service attendance was about 180 members. They had significantly more participants at special festivals such as Christmas and Easter, according to the church

---

40 The word 'catholic' is used in English, *katolieke* in Afrikaans and *eliKhatholika* in indigenous languages. An Anglican Prayer Book, 1989, p. 109; 'n Anglikaanse Gebedeboek, 1989, p. 109; Incwadi Yokukhuleka yaseTshetshi, 1989, p. 109.

41 There were 87 per cent who identified themselves as 'Coloured', the great majority of the population of Athlone. There were only 5.9 per cent 'Black African' and 4.5 per cent 'Indian or Asian' in Athlone. Census 2011, Athlone, Statistics South Africa, 2013; Observation Protocol 2011-03-20.

council. At the same time as the church service, a Sunday school ran in a nearby building, with a weekly attendance of about 60 children.[42]

The congregation had several lay people involved in the Sunday services. For example, they played the organ, led prayers, read the scriptures, and were in charge of making announcements. One person was in charge of the computer and projector that displayed messages and pictures. A specific family was in charge of practical matters every Sunday: greeting members at the entrance, taking the collection, lighting candles, etc. The families were like church wardens, and their responsibilities followed a roster. The involvement of many people in the services showed that volunteering was significant in the congregation.[43]

The congregation did not celebrate eucharist every Sunday: they had eucharist at 07.30 and 09.30 every first Sunday of the month, according to the congregation's profile. That pattern of celebrating eucharist is common among Methodist congregations; and most follow a set order of service that has been translated into various languages. There were congregations, however, that used various contemporary liturgies, which varied according to congregation.[44]

The services in the Athlone Methodist Church could be regarded as using a very free liturgy. The church council stressed that the ministers decided how the service would be conducted. A member of the council stated: "They decide".[45] The services were nevertheless planned in cooperation with the church musicians. Another member added: "They would liaise with the church organist".[46] The services were highly dependent on the minister, even though they followed a set order. The space for congregations to use freely-developed liturgies ensured diversity; but too much freedom could endanger the unity within the same denomination.

Newcomers and visitors were presented at the beginning of the service as a sign of welcome. People who were celebrating birthdays, anniversaries or other important life events were identified by public announcement. Members were also invited to receive a personal prayer with laying on of hands by the minister.[47] Identifying members in these ways was a sign that acknowledged the Christian community and sustained the congregation's *koinonia*.

---

42 Athlone Methodist Church, Athlone Society Profile, c.a. 2008, p. 2, Church Publication; Observation Protocol 2011-03-20.
43 Observation Protocol 2011-03-20.
44 Methodist Church, Athlone Society Profile, c.a. 2008, p. 2, Church Publication.
45 Church Council Interview Protocol 2011-03-20.
46 Church Council Interview Protocol 2011-03-20.
47 Observation Protocol 2011-03-20.

Part of the initial liturgy was to light a so-called 'AIDS candle'. A church council member explained: "We do that every service".[48] In 2011 South Africa had more people living with HIV than any other country in the world. Many received antiretroviral therapy, but there were still many new HIV infections. Lighting the candle reminded the congregation of the pandemic, and acknowledged that infected and affected people were in the church and the society. When they lit the candle they also offered a prayer for those who were infected.[49] The lighting of the candle and the prayer stressed that the pandemic was a concern for the Christian community, and people infected or affected became part of the congregation's effort for an equal and just society.

The congregation occasionally prayed for other issues in the society. A council member said: "Sometimes we do. If there are some problems in Klipfontein we bring it to prayer".[50] Klipfontein Road is the very busy main road that goes through Athlone. The council member's statement referred to disturbances or troubles that sometimes occurred. The practice of praying together in the services could be seen as strengthening the community and extending their own boundaries. The community was bigger than their own congregation, and a wider human community was included in the congregation's concern. The prayers could be interpreted as emphasising a wider community as part of the Church's catholicity according to the analytical tool.

The congregation used traditional Methodists hymns along with modern choruses. The computer and projector enabled the congregation to use a great variety of songs and hymns. The congregation also had a worship team in some services that played guitars, drums, etc., and both music and liturgy became more contemporary.[51] The participation of choirs was another important contribution to the services. A woman in the council explained: "We have two services a month where the choirs are singing. One Sunday a men's choir and one Sunday a ladies' choir [...]".[52] The men's and women's choirs also sang together sometimes. The choirs' participation, together with the worship team's leadership, enabled the

---

48 Church Council Interview Protocol 2011-03-20.
49 Observation Protocol 2011-03-20; How to get zero, 2011, pp. 7, 20, 30.
50 Church Council Interview Protocol 2011-03-20.
51 Athlone Methodist Church, Athlone Society Profile, c.a. 2008, p. 1, Church Publication; Nyobole, Vuyani Gladstone, Interview Protocol 2011-02-28. There are several different Methodist hymnbooks in various languages. One interesting hymnbook that was developed during democratisation was 'Sing Together', a multi-lingual hymnbook that was published just before the first election. Sing Together, 1992.
52 Church Council Interview Protocol 2011-03-20.

congregation to have several different forms of music in the services.[53] The computer and projector facilitated the incorporation of songs, hymns, and choruses from diverse Christian traditions without the limitation of using a single hymn book.

The congregation used the word 'catholic' when they confessed their faith during the liturgy. The Methodist Church used different terms in various languages. In an Afrikaans service they would use *algemene*, meaning church 'in general' or 'in common'. In indigenous languages such as isiZulu, they used the term *lomhlaba wonke*, which could be translated 'the whole world' or 'universal', and is used in Genesis 11:9 as a description of when God scattered people over the face of the earth after the incident of the tower of Babel.[54] The diverse terms used for 'catholic' is a sign of inculturation.

Lutheran Church in Bellville – Evangelical Lutheran Church in Southern Africa Cape Church

The congregation is situated in Bellville, a suburban area in greater Cape Town. There is a large variety of ethnicities in Bellville because it is a large area encompassing great differences. The area around the church building also had a wide variety of ethnicities. The congregation principally catered for people of German descent, and thus its catchment area was significantly greater. The congregation had services in German and Afrikaans, and on some Sundays in English. The holding of many services in the church was simply a consequence of its members' diverse first languages, and not for any other reason, such as liturgical preferences.[55]

The congregation had one, two, or three services on a Sunday, depending on a special five-week roster, according to their worship service description. They had an Afrikaans service at ten o'clock on the first Sunday, and on the second Sunday they had a German service at nine o'clock and an Afrikaans service at ten fifteen. On the third Sunday they had an English service at nine o'clock, a German service at nine fifteen, in different venues, and an Afrikaans service at ten fifteen.

---

53 Athlone Methodist Church, Athlone Society Profile, c.a. 2008, p. 1, Church Publication.
54 Methodist Worship, 1999, p. 135; Die Metodiste-gesangboek, 1987, p. 375; Incwadi yenkonzo, kunye neminye imithandazo, nezingoma, emiselwe libandla Lamamethodisi aseningizimu Neafrika: Ibalwe ngesizulu, 1938, p. 16.
55 About 56 per cent identified themselves as 'White', 15.2 per cent as 'Coloured', 19.3 per cent as 'Black African', 8.5 per cent as 'Other', and 1 per cent as 'Indian or Asian' in the area closest to the congregation. Census 2011, Avondstil, Bellville Central, Chrismar, Eversdale Ext 21, Harry De Villiers, Hillrise, Kempenville, Kingston, Oakdale, Sunkist, Statistics South Africa, 2013.

The fifth Sunday had a trilingual or combined service at ten o'clock, at which all three languages were used. The purpose of the trilingual service was to bring the various language groups together.[56]

Most of the people who lived close to the church building had Afrikaans and English as their first languages, but not German. The use of German was a consequence of the church's history, as described in Chapter Five. The holding of different language services could be seen as an acknowledgement of the diversity that was found in the area, and as taking minority groups into consideration. This diversity recognises language differences as part of the Church's catholicity in the analytical tool; but it does not accommodate diverse ethnicities.[57]

The congregation had German evening services periodically at Table View and devotions at the German retirement village of St Johannis Heim. Almost every service, except for those at St Johannis Heim, had Children's Church, which was a kind of Sunday School service. The services at the retirement village could be seen as a way of including members in the congregation's ordinary community services. The services at Table View could be considered as an extension for future development of the congregation.[58]

The use of three languages showed the importance of members' first language in the church services, but also how language could become an obstacle in a single congregation. The congregation developed several worshiping communities in one congregation. They aimed to ensure unity with a combined service every fifth Sunday.

The German services used a hymn book from Germany named *Evangelisches Gesangbuch*; the Afrikaans services used hymns from *Laudate*, a South African Lutheran hymn book; and the English services used the Lutheran Australian hymn book named *Lutheran Hymnal with Supplement*. All services used the liturgy of

---

56 Lutheran Church Bellville, Worship Services, 2011, Website; Hahne, Albrecht, 2010, p. 3, Church Publication.
57 About 50.6 per cent had Afrikaans as their first language in the area close to the church building, and 16.4 per cent had English, 9.8 per cent Other, and 4.3 per cent isiXhosa. Census 2011, Avondstil, Bellville Central, Chrismar, Eversdale Ext 21, Harry De Villiers, Hillrise, Kempenville, Kingston, Oakdale, Sunkist, Statistics South Africa, 2013.
58 Lutheran Church Bellville, Worship Services, 2011, Website; Lutheran Church Bellville, Kalender, Februar 2011–Maart 2011, 2011, Church Publication; Hahne, Albrecht, 2010, p. 3, Church Publication. Table View is a west coast suburb named for its panoramic view of Table Mountain. It is a suburb that has grown rapidly in recent decades.

UELCSA, but the liturgy and hymn books were only suggestions, and each congregation in ELCSA-Cape could decide how to design their own services.[59]

The congregation had, for example, recently revised the Afrikaans liturgy. One change was to how God and the congregation were addressed, using the second person singular and plural instead of the third person. New techniques with projectors made it possible to use the congregation's own hymns, choruses, and songs. Occasionally the congregation also had free forms of services such as youth and family services.[60] The diverse hymn books, mostly from the church in other countries, revealed a delicate situation when the congregation had to use diverse languages. Nor did the many hymn books reflect the South African context; but new technologies could ensure that new traditions were accommodated in the congregation.

Church services on a Sunday were attended by about 100 people when they had services in the different languages, according to the congregation's reports. The Children's Church or Sunday School was not very well attended, and the congregation had experienced a decline in attendance. Parents did not bring their children to church, and so the congregation tried to attract more children as participants. They also had plans to establish a mothers' room where parents could be together with their small children during services. They were planning to have more youth services, and they had also had services for their youth together with other Lutheran churches in Cape Town.[61]

The congregation battled with problems similar to those of many churches in Europe that are trying to attract a new generation. Trying to maintain their German heritage in South Africa presents an additional difficulty. It could be an advantage when gathering people of German background for services; but at the same time the language could keep other South Africans from becoming part of the worshiping community.

---

59 Lutheran Church Bellville, Worship Services, 2011, Website; Lutheran Church Bellville, Kalender, Februar 2011–Maart 2011, 2011, Church Publication; Observation Protocol 2011-02-20; Hahne, Albrecht, 2010, p. 3, Church Publication; Müller, Horst, Interview Protocol 2011-03-04; Rohwer, Nils J., Interview Protocol 2011-02-09. The hymnbooks that the congregation used were: Lutheran Hymnal with Supplement, 1989; Evangelisches Gesangbuch (Niedersachsen, Bremen), 1994; Laudate: Gesangboek van die Verenigde Evangelies-Lutherse Kerk in Suider-Afrika, 1982.
60 Lutheran Church Bellville, Worship Services, 2011, Website; Observation Protocol 2011-02-20; Rohwer, Nils J., Interview Protocol 2011-02-09.
61 Hahne, Albrecht, 2010, p. 3, Church Publication; Hahne, Albrecht, 2011, p. 2, Church Publication; Rubow, Hürgen, 2011, pp. 1–2, Church Publication.

Preserving and promoting language and cultural identity is in accordance with the South African constitution, but it can result in isolation, which conflicts with the catholicity of the Church according to the analytical tool. Preservation of a specific identity in a constantly transforming society where there are social changes endangers a congregation's survival. Reaching out to new groups of people in accordance with the church's ministry could threaten ecclesiological patterns.[62]

The Lutheran Church in Bellville had several lay people involved as churchwardens, organists, scripture readers, Children's Church leaders, computer and technical assistants, and so on. The organ was the principal instrument in the services, but other musicians played during special services and events in the church. The services followed a set liturgy with hymns from the hymn books, scripture readings, and prayers.[63]

The sermon had a prominent place in the services. The prayers of the church named people in public life, those with problems, and members celebrating birthdays, etc. The prayers included personal, community, and wider matters, emphasising both local and global concerns. The prayers can be characterised as a sign of care for the local community, but also for their task of serving the world.[64]

The eucharistic liturgy was brief, and individual communion cups were used to distribute the wine to congregants. The use of individual communion cups could, however, reduce the symbolism of sharing the blood of Christ. After the services tea and coffee were served in a room next to the kitchen, enabling members to interact and helping newcomers to feel included. This practice was vital in a congregation that otherwise was divided by times of services and language.[65]

The congregations in ELCSA-Cape, and all the other UELCSA congregations, used the term 'Christian' as a free translation of 'catholic' in the creed in the English services. In German services they used the word *christliche*, and in the Afrikaans services they used *algemene*. The use of 'Christian' in the English service is influenced by the German Protestant translation of the creeds, and *algemene* is influenced by the Dutch Reformed Church's practice.[66] Using such different terms for 'catholic' could endanger the ecclesiological foundation of the Church.

---

62 Ospino, Hosffman, 2008, p. 65.
63 Observation Protocol 2011-02-20.
64 Observation Protocol 2011-02-20.
65 Observation Protocol 2011-02-20.
66 Lutheran Hymnal with Supplement, 1989. p. 28; Evangelisches Gesangbuch (Niedersachsen, Bremen), 1994. No. 06.1; Laudate: Gesangboek van die Verenigde Evangelies-Lutherse Kerk in Suider-Afrika, 1982, p. 6.

City Harvest Ministries in Ntuzuma – Apostolic Faith Mission of South Africa

The congregation is situated in the Ntuzuma township, about 20 km from the city centre of Durban, as described in Chapter Five. The great majority of the people in the township were 'Black African' and had isiZulu as their first language; and this was evident among the members of City Harvest Ministries.[67]

The congregation had around a hundred members, and was part of one of the oldest Pentecostal churches in South Africa. This congregation, however, was newly-established, and used a tent in which to worship and hold its other activities. The plot on which the tent was pitched belonged to one of the congregation's members, and they hoped to be able to build a church in the future.[68]

Proclaiming God through preaching was an important part of Sunday services in City Harvest Ministries. They had one main church service every Sunday at nine o'clock that lasted for about two hours. The congregation also had other kinds of services throughout the week – for example, intercession services, prayer meetings, and youth services, according to their notice board. They had several church conferences and special fellowships and outreaches, with additional services during holidays and on special weekends.[69]

The church council described City Harvest Ministries as a charismatic church, stating: "It is more charismatic than anything else".[70] The emphasis on being charismatic was seen as quite important to being part of the AFM and having contacts with many other charismatic and Pentecostal congregations. The church services followed the same pattern as many other AFM congregations. Every congregation in the AFM had the freedom to create their own services, but a consistent order

---

It is interesting that the LWF uses the term *catholic* in all of the federation's official languages. Constitution of the Lutheran World Federation, as adopted by the LWF Eighth Assembly, Curitiba, Brazil, 1990, including amendments adopted by the LWF Ninth Assembly, Hong Kong, 1997 and by the LWF Eleventh Assembly, Stuttgart, 2010. 2010, Paragraph III.

67 There were 99.7 per cent of the population that identified themselves as 'Black African', 0.2 per cent as 'Indian or Asian', 0.2 per cent as 'Coloured', 0.1 per cent as 'Other', and 0.1 per cent as 'White'. In Ntuzuma 91.58 per cent had isiZulu as their first language. Census 2011, Ntuzuma, Statistics South Africa, 2013.
68 Church Council Interview Protocol 2011-03-27; City Harvest Ministries, The life of City Harvest Ministries, 2013, Website.
69 City Harvest Ministries, The Notice Board of C.H.M., 2013, Website; City Harvest Ministries, Year Plan for the year 2012, 2013, Website.
70 Church Council Interview Protocol 2011-03-27.

had developed among the congregations – a common tradition about how a service was performed.[71]

A Sunday service at City Harvest Ministries had singing with several songs of praise, a sermon, prayers, and testimonies. A keyboard, an essential part of the worship, was played throughout the service except during the sermon, when no music was played. A service could start with songs of praise, prayers, prayer in tongues, a peace greeting, and songs that continued with the word of welcome.[72] The peace greeting and the presentation of newcomers to the congregation was a natural practice in a congregation that was relatively new in the area. The greeting could be a sign of a practice to recognise and confirm the local Christian community.

The services included several testimonies from congregants about God's action in their lives. Offering money to the church was a natural part of the service: people walked to the front where there was a stand into which funds were placed. The practice of walking together as a group sharing their resources stresses the collective task of the congregation, that they are a sharing community.[73]

The sermon was preceded by songs of praise and prayers. The sermon was delivered extempore, without a script. The sermon had a particular focus in the service, and considerable time was dedicated to the sermon as a sign that preaching was important. People could receive special individual prayers at the end of the service, and a common blessing was proclaimed at the end. Several congregants were engaged in the service, both men and women, and people of different ages. Young people were especially encouraged to speak in church, and the congregants responded with "Amen", "Hallelujah" or "Thank you Jesus" as signs of appreciation.[74]

The songs and choruses were sung in English, not using traditional Zulu harmonies but rather a style inspired by an international charismatic way of singing. The prayers were mostly offered in isiZulu, but with elements of English. The sermon was mostly in isiZulu, but the language could change depending on the preacher; and the sermon could also be in English and interpreted into isiZulu.[75] The use of many languages made diversity visible. The songs and choruses in English and the style of music connected the congregation to the international

---

71 Observation Protocol 2011-03-27; Mahlobo, Mphikeleki George, Interview Protocol 2011-03-01.
72 Observation Protocol 2011-03-27.
73 Observation Protocol 2011-03-27.
74 Observation Protocol 2011-03-27.
75 Observation Protocol 2011-03-27.

charismatic movement, but also reduced diversity and emphasised the hegemony of English and of the western style of worship.

The congregation's order of service was an example of how a denomination could develop similar services but still have services that were locally influenced. The order of service was recognisable to other members of the AFM and even to members of other charismatic and Pentecostal churches. City Harvest Ministries gathered around 50 people; the majority of them were young women, and many of them were teenagers or young adults.[76]

The eucharist was not part of every Sunday service, but it was regularly celebrated. When the church council was asked how many times they had eucharist, one church council member answered: "Once a month".[77] Celebrating eucharist was, the church council explained, something personal; and it was part of confessing Christ and his second coming, as one council member said.[78] Their interpretation and practice were not consistent with the catholicity of the Church in the analytical tool. The Church's catholicity emphasises that the eucharist is supposed to be celebrated every Sunday and frequently to support and sustain the community.

The services provided many opportunities for corporate and individual prayers that were offered freely, not from books or sheets of paper. The prayers had a central place in the service, and were spontaneous. The church council explained that they were praying for various issues: "Needs, … any needs… we pray for the families… for others, for the government, for this country, everybody".[79] Another council member emphasised life in the congregation and the spiritual needs by saying: "Community, spiritual growth".[80] Others were also hoping and praying that they would be able to have a church building, and named it "Church House".[81] Social needs in an area with many problems were described by another council member who identified a special area of attention: "To reach the other people from crime".[82] Healing was also a subject that was mentioned; one member stated: "We pray for the sick".[83] The list of matters for prayer presented by the church council was narrowly focused on issues affecting the members and where they were ministering.

---

76 Observation Protocol 2011-03-27; City Harvest Ministries, The life of City Harvest Ministries, 2013, Website.
77 Church Council Interview Protocol 2011-03-27.
78 Church Council Interview Protocol 2011-03-27.
79 Church Council Interview Protocol 2011-03-27.
80 Church Council Interview Protocol 2011-03-27.
81 Church Council Interview Protocol 2011-03-27.
82 Church Council Interview Protocol 2011-03-27.
83 Church Council Interview Protocol 2011-03-27.

The prayers emphasised the local community, and were not aware of a community of Christians that extended to people in other countries.[84] The issues in the prayers showed that the congregation was very locally-based. The AFM congregations have considerable independence, giving them the advantage of substantial autonomy and an emphasis on the local situation. Their autonomy in respect of the regional and central levels of the church could also be a disadvantage, as it meant that the greater community became less important.

The congregation did not use any creeds in their services, which is consistent with the practice of Pentecostal or charismatic churches. Songs, choruses, personal witness, and sermons, together with responses from the congregation, played the role of a creed for the members. The AMF has not included the Nicene or Apostolic Creeds in their doctrines, but they do have the *Confession of Faith* in their constitution, which could be characterised as having been inspired by the ancient creeds. The Faith & Order Commission has recognised that churches without the ancient creeds continue to function within the same context.[85] The 'catholic' Church is not mentioned in the *Confession of Faith*; instead the Church is defined as consisting of born-again believers, and as a community and fellowship that builds up one another.[86] The absence of the term 'catholic' could influence the church's ecclesiology; but that does not need to make the church any less catholic.[87]

---

84 Church Council Interview Protocol 2011-03-27.
85 Confessing the One Faith, 1991, p. 3.
86 AMF's *Confession of Faith* declared: "We believe that Jesus Christ is the Head of the Church which is constituted by the Holy Spirit and consists of born again believers. The Church is responsible for the proclamation and demonstration of the gospel and God's will to all people. As a charismatic community they fellowship with and edify one another". Constitution of the Apostolic Faith Mission of South Africa, 2010, P. 3.8. The South African theologian Daniël Nicolaas Andrew has written a thesis in which he discusses the AFM and the catholicity of the Church. Andrew, Daniël Nicolaas, 2005, pp. 169–200.
87 Daniël Nicolaas Andrew says about the AFM: "In the past, Pentecostals had a tendency to treat the local church as the visible Body of Christ, but were reluctant to speak of any visible embodiments of the universal church. It reflected a historic Protestant mistrust of church institutions and also a concern not to make exclusive claims for their own denominations. Pentecostals understand today that they are part of a catholic and universal church". Andrew, Daniël Nicolaas, 2005, p. 223.

St Michael's Evangelical Lutheran Church – Evangelical Lutheran Church in Southern Africa

St Michael's is situated in the city centre of Durban, between the International Convention Centre (ICC) and the beach front. A majority of the people who lived in the areas around St Michael's identified themselves as 'Black African'. The most commonly-spoken languages in the area were English and isiZulu.[88] ELCSA's membership comes from every South African ethnic group except 'White' people. As noted earlier, St Michael's was an exception to this rule: with a split in the Norwegian or Scandinavian congregation of St Olav's in Durban, a group of 'White' members wanted to become members of ELCSA; and a merger of three congregations formed St Michael's with people of diverse ethnicities. St Michael's catchment area was considerably larger than the area around the church building, and there were even people who worshiped in the church because travel to the city centre was convenient.[89]

Diversity as a principal cause for rejoicing was emphasised in the congregation's vision statement. The diversity was also visible in the congregation's Sunday services, which included people from different ethnic groups in Durban, but also from other parts of South Africa and from other countries. People spoke a range of languages, and there were different forms of liturgies, hymns, and styles of worship.[90]

St Michael's had two church services every Sunday. The first service at nine o'clock was in English, and the second at eleven o'clock in isiZulu. St Michael's had to have two services on Sundays in order to accommodate all the members. Peoples' first language was, however, the primary cause for the different services. Durban Central Parish also had other congregations, but St Michael's could be regarded as the main congregation – and it was the only congregation using both

---

88 There were 72 per cent in the area that identified themselves as 'Black African', 16.5 per cent as 'Indian or Asian', 3.5 per cent as 'Coloured', 6 per cent as 'White', and 2 per cent as 'Other'. There were 32.8 per cent who had English and 31 per cent who had isiZulu as their first language in the area. Census 2011, North Beach, Statistics South Africa, 2013; Census 2011, South Beach, Statistics South Africa, 2013; Census 2011, Durban Central, Statistics South Africa, 2013.
89 Church Council Interview Protocol 2011-04-03.
90 Durban Central Parish, Who are we?, Congregations, St Michael's, 2011, Website.

isiZulu and English.[91] Their choice of languages showed that St Michael's reflected local conditions as part of the Church's catholicity in the analytical tool.[92]

Two diverse worshiping groups were separated because of language, and could easily have grown apart. The division would have arisen primarily not because of ethnicity, but because of language. The Church's catholicity, however, emphasises that language is not a reason for division. The church council were aware of the problem of diverse worshiping groups, and tried to find ways to overcome divisions. The church council said that St Michael's had occasionally held combined services for the English- and isiZulu-speaking service groups. Combined services were not regularly scheduled, but they were held, for example, during Lent and Easter.[93]

The English-language nine o'clock service had 'White', 'Coloured', and 'Black' members. A small group of people still came to the English service from the original St Michael's, which had begun in the Norwegian Seamen's Mission church. The service clearly had fewer participants than the eleven o'clock service in isiZulu; around fifty members attended the average nine o'clock Sunday service. A preaching plan involved different people, including lay preachers. People of different ethnic groups led the services, read the scriptures, or made the announcements. The liturgy was very plain: there were no processions, vestments, or other forms of liturgical expression. The sermon was also considerably shorter than at the eleven o'clock service in isiZulu.[94]

The services followed the ELCSA liturgy, but the hymns came from the English Hymn Book, special edition, prepared by the Evangelical Lutheran Church in Malaysia and Singapore in 1980.[95] One church council member explained:

> The liturgy itself is actually the same as ELCSA, but why all of these hymn books? They were looking for a hymn book which had all the old English hymns but also had some newer English worship songs, but I'm not talking about new, meaning thirty years old. Because these books are obviously from 1980. They have a little bit more classical English hymns, so that's when some pastors in the 1970s looked at other English-speaking communities and provinces and some got books from Australia or Malaysia, and I think that

---

91 Durban Central Parish, Who are we?, Congregations, St Michael's, 2011, Website.
92 Census 2011, North Beach, Statistics South Africa, 2013; Census 2011, South Beach, Statistics South Africa, 2013; Census 2011, Durban Central, Statistics South Africa, 2013.
93 Church Council Interview Protocol 2011-04-03.
94 Observation Protocol 2011-04-03.
95 Observation Protocol 2011-04-03; ELCSA-SED-Durban Central Parish–Preaching Plan-April to August 2011, 2011, Church Publication.

was the reason behind it, why these books. You will find in Malaysia that there are hymns that you don't find in other English hymn books.[96]

The church council explained that ELCSA had produced no English hymn books, and neither were there any other South African English hymn books that reflected the Lutheran heritage. There had been an option to use a Lutheran hymn book from Australia, but the books from Malaysia and Singapore were cheaper and better suited for use in South Africa.[97]

The use of a Lutheran hymn book from Malaysia and Singapore connected the congregation with the worldwide Lutheran community, and especially with Lutheran churches in Asia. The catholicity of a wider community was strengthened, going beyond national, ethnic, and cultural borders. South African hymns were, nevertheless, not part of the hymn book; and it is interesting to note that ELCSA-Cape and ELCSA N-T used the Australian Lutheran hymn book instead.

Coffee and tea was served after the English service, when members could stay for talk, discussion, and planning. The time of coffee and tea was important among the English-speaking group because they were in the minority in St Michael's, and were also the most diverse group. The coffee and tea helped that group to interact and welcome newcomers.[98]

The eleven o'clock service in isiZulu had considerably more participants than the earlier English service, and they even had to extend the seating with movable chairs. An ordinary service could have more than two hundred participants. These services were much richer liturgically than the English services. There were, for example, different harmonies in the hymn singing and hand-clapping; and the service began with a procession with a cross-bearer, candle-bearers, church servers, and the minister. A procession down the aisle with cross- and candle-bearers also took place before the gospel reading in the centre of the congregation. The church servers – both girls and boys – wore liturgical vestments.[99]

The previous minister-in-charge of the parish had introduced church servers or acolytes as well as the use of processions, incense, bells, and vestments, according to a document about liturgical practice in the congregation. His successor was more guarded about using incense, for example, whose use had been questioned

---

96 Church Council Interview Protocol 2011-04-03.
97 Church Council Interview Protocol 2011-04-03.
98 Observation Protocol 2011-04-03; Church Council Interview Protocol 2011-04-03; Liturgical Practices in our Congregation, 2010, pp. 5–8, Church Publication.
99 Church Council Interview Protocol 2011-04-03; Liturgical Practices in our Congregation, 2010, pp. 5–8, Church Publication.

by some members. It was reserved for special occasions, and the custom was explained as having been influenced by other mainline churches in South Africa.[100]

This so-called 'high church spirituality' was also partly connected to the heritage of Swedish missionaries, acording to the parish minister-in-charge. The English-speaking services did not use incense, for example; and different practices were supposed to be respected during joint services at parish and circuit level.[101] The liturgical differences between the two worshiping groups revealed diverse and conflicting traditions, but they were allowed to coexist in the same community. Diversity was preserved, and uniformity was not enforced at the expense of the catholicity of the Church.

The majority of the participants in the eleven o'clock service were women, and several were involved in a range of roles in the services – for example, reading the scriptures, leading the prayers, and singing. The dominance of women could also be seen in the presence of a large group of women belonging to the Women's League, in their black and white uniforms. The congregation had also many students and young people who had moved to Durban for work, according to the church council, and this was evident in the presence of many young adults in the services. Children and teenagers attended the Sunday school during the first part of the service. The sermon would last for about half an hour, which was longer than in the English services. The hymns were from the ELCSA hymn book in isiZulu, most of them written and composed by European men two or three centuries ago. The hymns were sung with South African harmonies and rhythms even though they originated in Europe.[102]

The hymns of European heritage are not a particular ELCSA issue: all mainline churches, apart from the Pentecostal churches, used hymns with similar backgrounds. Immigrants and missionaries brought their hymn traditions to South Africa, which in many ways became contextualised and reinterpreted through indigenous styles of singing and harmonies. European hymns can be seen as a symbol of catholicity that transcends geographic borders; but they can also been seen to lack catholicity through not reflecting the local context. Supporting and introducing locally-developed hymns in both services, combined with typical denominational hymns, could connect diverse traditions.

---

100   Liturgical Practices in our Congregation, 2010, pp. 5–8, Church Publication; Lüdeman, Joe, 2012, p. 8, Church Publication.
101   Liturgical Practices in our Congregation, 2010, pp. 5–8, Church Publication; Lüdeman, Joe, 2012, p. 8, Church Publication. Incense, acolytes, or altar bells are influences from the Anglican and Roman Catholic churches.
102   Observation Protocol 2011-04-03; Church Council Interview Protocol 2011-04-03.

The offertory collection took the form of a procession: the congregants sang as they walked towards the altar. People could put money in collection boxes or leave their contribution in envelopes on the altar. The emphasis on the collection reinforced the communitarian aspect, as sharing gifts and resources became a visible part of the Church's catholicity.[103]

The service ended with announcements and singing, and new visitors were welcomed and introduced. Those who had become widows or widowers were recognised, and the newly-married were congratulated.[104] The announcements about the people in the congregation indicated that members were important to the whole community.

The church council also recognised that there was a need to find new ways and different styles of church services, particularly because many young people came to worship. They had, for example, installed a new loudspeaker system and projector. A church council member explained:

> There are practical sides that tell us that everybody in the back could listen, and that was important that they could do that. The loudspeakers also enabled us to use different music instruments in a professional way and also with the screen to use PowerPoint, pictures maybe and to see that we are a little bit more multimedia-driven approach, which I think is important for an inner city church.[105]

The loudspeaker system and projector allowed St Michael's to use different musical instruments, solo singers, and various forms of multimedia. The projector also helped with hymn texts when people came to church without hymn books. The church council had discussed the renewal of the services, but also acknowledged the importance of the tradition.[106] One council member explained:

> I would say ... the question of new ventures in music or service. Looking at the group of people that we are having here, they are very young, and there is a fertile ground for trying out different service styles, and this has to be balanced against the need for continuity and the strong sense of tradition, and a sense of belonging, which also young people have when they come here. They do enjoy finding a service which they basically know from home in villages and rural areas. So that is always something that has to be balanced.[107]

The council gave voice to the dilemma involved in trying to maintain the traditional way of celebrating the Sunday service, while also responding to the demand

---

103 Observation Protocol 2011-04-03.
104 Observation Protocol 2011-04-03.
105 Church Council Interview Protocol 2011-04-03.
106 Church Council Interview Protocol 2011-04-03.
107 Church Council Interview Protocol 2011-04-03.

for a new style of worship. The discussion in the church council acknowledged the importance of meeting the challenges of an inner city congregation. The discussion revealed an ongoing reflection about how services could be contextualised. Local conditions are part of the Church's catholicity according to the analytical tool; but church services must also acknowledge an order that has been developed over a long period in the church's life.

The eucharist was regarded as important by the congregation, but there was no agreement about how often it should be celebrated. When the church council was asked about the frequency of the eucharist, one member replied: "It depends on the pastor".[108] They had nevertheless found that there more people came to Sunday services when there was eucharist. A council member confirmed this by saying: "[…] I have noticed that when people know that there is a certain date, the attendance is higher when we have Holy Communion […]".[109] It is interesting that the eucharist was not celebrated more frequently at Sunday services, even though the leaders had noticed that more people came to church on these Sundays. The BEM document argues that Christians should be encouraged to receive the eucharist frequently, and that it is appropriate that it is celebrated at least every Sunday.[110]

Eucharist was essential for the personal life as well as for the whole community. One council member explained the eucharist in these terms: "[…] When we have it, I think it revives us. It is what it does for me".[111] Another member stressed: "I think it is an identification. I think so. When we drink from the same cup and eat from the same bread it is a symbolic act".[112] Both statements acknowledged that the eucharist was significant for the individual Christian's life, but also that it united the people in the church. The eucharist influenced the life of the congregation, but they celebrated it in different ways, according to the various services on a Sunday. One member of the church council said:

> Just as a comment. We have two different ways of having Holy Communion. Because of the small numbers at the nine o'clock services, people do kneel on this altar rail. That has a strong influence on how the community is orientating their experience. The eleven o'clock service, people just come by, come through, because it otherwise would take a long time. This community aspect is a little bit difficult to really experience then. If you stand around the altar as one group, immediately there is a group feeling. It's a little bit

---

108 Church Council Interview Protocol 2011-04-03.
109 Church Council Interview Protocol 2011-04-03.
110 Baptism, Eucharist and Ministry, 1982, p. 16.
111 Church Council Interview Protocol 2011-04-03.
112 Church Council Interview Protocol 2011-04-03.

more meditation and silence. While here you stay in the queue, you take your wafers, you take your wine, and go back.[113]

The statement explained that St Michael's had different traditions of receiving the eucharist at the nine o'clock and eleven o'clock services. The differences were due to the number of participants in the services. The congregants at the nine o'clock service could kneel at the altar rail, thus reinforcing one aspect of community. The eleven o'clock service did not use the altar rail, and people received the elements standing in front of the altar. They became part of a queue that instead emphasised another communitarian aspect. Both practices could accentuate community aspects of the congregation.

The congregation at the English services used the term 'catholic' in the creeds, in accordance with the official translation and liturgies of ELCSA. Some ELCSA congregations would, however, also use the term 'Christian' instead of 'catholic' in the creeds. St Michael's used the term *lomhlaba wonke* in the isiZulu service, like the Methodist Church. The same term was also used in other indigenous languages, and ELCSA congregations would use *algemene* in the Afrikaans services.[114] Using diverse terms for 'catholic' could broaden the understanding of its theological implications, but could also make the term vague and not applicable to the communion.

8.2 Diversity as an Obstacle for Communities

The many different church services in the case study congregations showed great diversity in the ways that they acknowledged language, liturgies, time, space, and duration. This diversity showed that different factors could divide congregation communities and create barriers to increased integration. Congregations with several church services could easily develop into separate worshiping communities with limited contact between members. These congregations ran the risk of the community becoming fragmented and of damaging the catholicity of the Church according to the analytical tool. The separate communities became evident in, for example, morning and afternoon services, various language services, family or

---

113 Church Council Interview Protocol 2011-04-03.
114 Altar Book Evangelical Lutheran Church in Southern Africa, 1995. pp. 9–10; Altaarboek Evangelies-Lutherse Kerk in Suidelike Afrika, 1995. pp. 4–5; Incwadi Yase Altare Ye-Evangelical Lutheran Church in Southern Africa, 1995. pp. 9–10. One example of an ELCSA congregation using 'Christian' instead of 'catholic' is the Eastwood Lutheran Church in Pietermaritzburg. Eastwood Lutheran Church, The Liturgy. p. 11, Church Publication.

traditional liturgical services, or services on different premises where different categories of people attended church. Members met briefly or had no contacts with the other worshiping communities. The catholicity of the Church emphasises that the Christian community transcends all kinds of boundaries, and does not allow division or exclusion.

It is interesting that the ecumenical documents do not mention any solutions to maintaining the catholicity of the Church when there are several worshiping communities within one congregation because of ethnicity, language, or other differences. Unity in the local church is supposed to be achieved in the present; but the documents do not offer any suggestions about how to deal with diversity, even though a range of issues can divide a congregation. The documents challenge the church to counteract fragmentation and to build bridges between people and groups. The churches are challenged to reject ethnic fragmentation and at the same time to maintain diversity, even though natural diversity is part of the social reality.

The case congregations had many diverse practices in their church services. Ethnic diversity brings advantages, but it can also threaten the catholicity of the Church.

Next I will explore some important practices related to ethnicity that became evident in the congregations' church services.

Diverse Church Services

All the congregations in the study had one or more church services on Sundays and devotions or services on weekdays. The reason that some congregations had more than one church service on Sundays was primarily to do with language and, to a certain extent, ethnicity.

Some congregations used several languages, such as English, isiZulu, Sesotho, Afrikaans or German. Members had a range of first languages that required a range of services to be held in formerly 'White' congregations. Examples included the congregations in Linden, Durban city centre, and Bellville. The other congregations used one language exclusively, even though members could use or understand several languages. The knowledge and use of language was a cause of division in many congregations, and was related to power inequality; and this was not consistent with the Church's catholicity in the analytical tool. The issue of language needs to be more thoroughly explored, which I shall do in the next chapter.

A number of congregations with several Sunday services used different forms of liturgies. One, for example, could be formal, another family-orientated, a third quieter and more meditative, and others vibrantly African. There were also different preferences for when during the day the worship took place, and for how long it lasted. Some people preferred attending an early morning service; others were working and had to attend an evening service. A number of congregations had such high attendance on Sundays that a single service would not accommodate everyone. In general, these factors cannot be considered as related to ethnicity; but they were still ecclesiological structuring factors, as they influenced the congregations and how members attended services.[115]

Some congregations, such as St Thomas' in Linden, St Michael's in Durban, and the Lutheran Church in Bellville tried to accommodate diverse worshiping communities because of language and ethnicity by having combined Sunday services a couple of times every year. The practice implied, for example, using several languages, or English alone, or using interpreters so that everybody could understand. In St Thomas' the diverse worshiping groups contributed something unique from their traditions, while the Lutheran Church in Bellville had a set liturgy for the combined services. In a number of congregations, such as St Peter Claver in Pimville, members had a good knowledge of a range of languages; in others, like St Thomas' in Linden, the knowledge of other languages was limited. Combined services were necessary so that members from diverse groups would meet, but these services were not seen as a solution to be used every Sunday.[116]

The practice of having combined services was one way to sustain a united Christian community, but other shared congregational gatherings and activities could also support the one community as part of the Church's catholicity. Some worshiping groups in congregations were assured of being represented on the

---

115 St Thomas' Anglican Church in Linden had several services in English and one in an indigenous language; the Lutheran Church in Bellville had services in German, Afrikaans, and English; St Michael's in Durban had one service in English and one in IsiZulu. St Thomas' Anglican Church in Linden used different liturgies for the Sunday services. They had also services on Sunday mornings and evenings. Athlone Methodist Church and City Harvest Ministries in Ntuzuma are examples of congregations that had only one service each Sunday. The Lutheran Church in Bellville had services in other premises, such as Table View St Johannis Heim; and both Athlone Methodist Church and City Harvest Ministries were examples of congregations having devotions as part of their outreach programmes.
116 St Thomas' Anglican Church in Linden, the Lutheran Church in Bellville, and St Michael's in Durban had combined Sunday services a couple of times every year. Every worshiping group at St Thomas' Anglican Church contributed something from their tradition during the combined Sunday services. People in St Peter Claver in Pimville and City Harvest Ministries in Ntuzuma, for example, had good knowledge of several South African languages, while most people in St Thomas' and Athlone Methodist Church probably knew English and Afrikaans.

church councils, as at St Michael's in Durban; while other congregations had worshiping communities with limited contact with the decision-making body, such as St Thomas' in Linden. This, of course, limited greater participation in positions of leadership. There were also other congregational activities that gathered people of diverse ethnic backgrounds and gave them to opportunity to meet. Combined services with other worshiping communities of the same denomination, but located in other areas of a city and representing other ethnicities, were limited, thus hampering inter-ethnic relationships.[117]

The congregations had weekday devotions and services both in their church buildings and in other venues such as community centres, homes, retirement villages, nursing homes, convents, and places of outreach. St Peter Claver Roman Catholic parish in Pimville and St Thomas' Anglican Church in Linden had weekday services with eucharist in their church buildings, but also in other places where they had members. Theses congregations also had tabernacles with the reserved sacrament, from which the eucharistic gifts were taken to sick and absent members. This practice emphasised the sharing of the same worshiping community.

Other congregations had services or devotions in members' homes, in areas for so-called church planting, or at outreach projects. Athlone Methodist Church and City Harvest Ministries in Ntuzuma, for example, often had specific youth services on Sunday evenings or on a weekday evening. All the congregations in the study had Sunday School or similar activities for children during at least one of the services on a Sunday. The practice of having several services or of bringing the eucharist to members confirmed that the congregational community was extended to others beyond those who congregated for Sunday services. Youth services, Sunday Schools, or services at nursing homes, for example, showed that people of diverse ages or situations in life were included in the congregational communities and were not left isolated.

The practice of including a wider worshiping community indicated that the congregational communities extended beyond the Sunday services, and included people of all ages and those who lived in diverse areas.

---

117 The indigenous language afternoon service in St Thomas' Anglican Church in Linden, for example, had very limited contact with the decision-making body of the congregation, while at St Michael's in Durban central, both worshiping communities were assured representation on the church council.

Liturgy and Hymns

The orders of service or liturgy in the studied congregations and churches were mostly determined by the particular denomination, but also to a certain extent by ethnicity. St Peter Claver Roman Catholic Church in Pimville, St Thomas' Anglican Church in Linden, and St Michael's (ELCSA) followed their denominations' particular liturgies, in accordance with their churches' regulations.

The Roman Catholic congregation used the Roman Missal, but the music and hymns could differ from congregation to congregation. Each language group had their own hymn book of translated traditional hymns, and congregations often used locally-composed hymns.[118] The Anglican Church had similar liturgies for its congregations, with official hymn books translated into diverse languages, but it also had locally used songs, choruses or hymns.[119] St Thomas' Anglican Church in Linden, for example, used The *English Hymnal* or locally-chosen hymns and choruses alongside the *South African Prayer Book* or *An Anglican Prayer Book*. ELCSA used the same liturgy and hymn books translated into diverse languages, while congregations with English-language services used hymn books from other English-speaking Lutheran churches.[120] St Michael's in Durban, for example, used the official ELCSA liturgy, the ELCSA hymn book in isiZulu, and the *English Hymn Book* produced by the Evangelical Lutheran Church in Malaysia and Singapore.[121]

The Athlone Methodist Church, City Harvest Ministries in Ntuzuma (AFM), and the Lutheran Church in Bellville (UELCSA) followed recommended orders of service because their denominations did not prescribe exactly how the services should be conducted. The Methodist Church had a liturgy and hymn book translated into various languages for use in the diverse congregations. Congregations with predominantly 'White' members mostly used a range of contemporary

---

118 The general secretary of the SACBC, Vincent Brennan, stated that music and hymns could vary in Roman Catholic churches depending on the congregation, because they did not need to follow the same hymnbook. Each language group had their own hymnbook of translated traditional hymns, and congregations often used locally-composed hymns. Brennan, Vincent, Interview Protocol 2011-03-01.
119 See for the Anglican Church: An Anglican Prayer Book, 1989, 'n Anglikaanse Gebedeboek, 1989, Incwadi Yokukhuleka yaseTshetshi, 1989. There are also translations into various indigenous languages and into Portuguese.
120 ELCSA used different translations such as the Altaarboek Evangelies-Lutherse Kerk in Suidelike Afrika, 1995; Altar Book Evangelical Lutheran Church in Southern Africa, 1995; Incwadi Yase Altare Ye-Evangelical Lutheran Church in Southern Africa, 1995; Observation Protocol 2011-04-03.
121 Incwadi Yokuhlabelela yeBandla lamaLuthere, 2008; English Hymn Book, 1980.

liturgies, but the eucharistic liturgy in the Methodist Church was the same for the whole church. The Methodist Church had also developed a multi-lingual hymn book named *Sing Together*, which could be regarded as a model in which several languages and ethnicities were acknowledged. This hymn book could be used in combined services, but also as a tool so that the richness of diversity could be shared with the whole church.[122]

The AFM congregations followed an order of service that was characteristic of charismatic and Pentecostal churches. The church had for a long time developed a common tradition of organising the services with singing, testimonies, preaching, collection, prayers, etc. Every congregation was nevertheless free to organise and develop their own liturgy with hymns, songs and choruses, but there was a consistency of practice throughout the AFM about how to conduct a service. City Harvest Ministries, for example, had a fixed order of worship consisting of songs of praise, sermon, prayers, and testimonies.[123]

ELCSA N-T and ELCSA-Cape had developed a joint liturgy within UELCSA, with recommended hymn books for congregations to use. The liturgy and hymns were only suggestions, and every congregation decided how it wanted to design its services. The Lutheran church in Bellville, for example, used the *Evangelisches Gesangbuch* in German, *Lutheran Hymnal with Supplement* in English, and *Laudate* in Afrikaans.[124]

---

122 See for example: Incwadi yenkonzo, kunye neminye imithandazo, nezingoma, emiselwe libandla Lamamethodisi aseningizimu Neafrika: Ibalwe ngesizulu, 1938; Die Metodiste-gesangboek, 1987; Methodist Worship, 1999; Sing Together, 1992. For example, the general secretary of the Methodist Church, Vuyani Nyobole, said that most 'Black' congregations used the same liturgy translated into different languages. The 'White' congregations instead used various contemporary liturgies that could differ from congregation to congregation. When Methodist churches had ethnically-mixed congregations, the dominant culture often determined the style of worship. This dynamic was not unique to the Methodist Church, and could be seen in most churches. The eucharist liturgy in the Methodist Church was, nevertheless, the same for the whole church. Nyobole, Vuyani Gladstone, Interview Protocol 2011-02-28.

123 The AFM general secretary, George Mahlobo, explained that every congregation was free to choose their own liturgy, hymn books, etc. but there was a consistent practice among all the congregations in the church. Over a long period the church had developed a common tradition of organising its services, with singing, testimonies, preaching, collection, prayers, etc. Mahlobo, Mphikeleki George, Interview Protocol 2011-03-01.

124 Müller, Horst, Interview Protocol 2011-03-04; Rohwer, Nils J., Interview Protocol 2011-02-09. ELCSA N-T and ELCSA-Cape, for example, used the Evangelisches

It is notable that congregations in denominations with recommended order of services had different practices according to ethnicity. Congregations that were predominantly 'Black' were more inclined to use a fixed order of service, following their church's regulations; while predominantly 'White' congregations tended to prefer a more locally-designed or contemporary liturgy and service. These differences became visible at least in the Methodist and Lutheran churches, where ethnicity was a significant factor in the choice of liturgy and hymn books. A different, locally-designed liturgy or order of service does not need to be a dividing factor, and could be seen as a sign of the Church's diversity. The congregations belonged to the same denominations, and chose a liturgy or order of service in accordance with their churches' regulations. Recognising diversity is consistent with the catholicity of the Church in the analytical tool, as long as unity is not undermined and inclusivity is preserved.

It is interesting that recognition of a similar liturgy or order of service was seen as important by some church council members. Members could visit other congregations, regardless of their ethnicity, and be familiar with the way they worship. They could even recognise the liturgy and become part of another community without knowing, for example, the language or local customs. Such experiences emphasise that the local congregation is part of a greater communion of churches; and this reveals the catholicity of the Church. Church services are communitarian practices that develop over time in the Christian tradition, with certain recognisable patterns, irrespective of people's ethnic background or location.[125]

All of the congregations in this study mostly used hymn books of European, or at least Western, origin. The hymns and songs might be inspired by the specific

---

     Gesangbuch (Niedersachsen, Bremen), 1994, Lutheran Hymnal with Supplement, 1989, Laudate: Gesangboek van die Verenigde Evangelies-Lutherse Kerk in Suider-Afrika, 1982.

125 One example is when a council member in St Peter Claver in Pimville said that members could recognise the same form of liturgy when they visited other congregations, which gave them a sense of unity with other Roman Catholics. Similar experiences were recounted by members of the church council in the Athlone Methodist Church when they visited other congregations. The BEM document, for example, outlines important historical elements in the eucharistic liturgy that should be followed. BEM adds: "The liturgical reform movement has brought the churches closer together in the manner of celebrating the Lord's Supper. However, a certain liturgical diversity compatible with our common eucharistic faith is recognized as a healthy and enriching fact. The affirmation of a common eucharistic faith does not imply uniformity in either liturgy or practice". Baptism, Eucharist and Ministry, 1982, pp. 13-14.

denomination, but the ethnic composition of South Africa was rarely visible in these hymn books.

Hymns and songs were, however, 'recreated' in services with predominantly 'Black' members. They sang the hymns and songs in an indigenous language, and used harmonies and rhythms arising from the South African context. It is important to notice that the hymns were not seen as 'foreign', and were accepted as part of the members' spiritual heritage. These services also used several spontaneous South African indigenous songs or choruses. It is notable that congregations that did not have predominantly 'Black' members had not yet integrated South African indigenous choruses into their services.[126]

Previously foreign elements such as hymns could be examples of a global Christian community exchanging liturgical gifts; but they could also be interpreted as symbols of cultural dominance. Using the same hymns across several churches could be a symbol of an ecumenical community, but South African choruses were sung almost exclusively in congregations that used indigenous languages.

The liturgies and forms of music used in the various congregations could be called into question for not fully reflecting the range of South African contexts. Diverse expressions make the catholicity of the Church visible. However, some congregations had incorporated various elements into some services that signified an ethnically-diverse community; and the Methodist Church had even produced a multilingual hymn book.[127] The catholicity of the Church as interpreted

---

126 The only exception was the quarter to ten service in St Thomas' Anglican Church in Linden, which used parts of the *Lumko Marimba Mass* with elements in isiXhosa, isiZulu, and Sesotho.

127 The main-line churches' congregations followed similar patterns to those introduced by European missions. The Roman Catholic congregation in Pimville followed the Roman Missal, the Anglican congregation in Linden followed several Anglican prayer books that had similarities with the Book of Common Prayer, and used Anglican hymn books. Athlone Methodist Church was very free in its liturgy, but was inspired by the Methodist tradition. They used traditional Methodists hymns as well as modern choruses. The Lutheran Church in Bellville was also liturgically free, but used a liturgy inspired by the Lutheran churches. They used Lutheran hymn books from German and Australian churches, and a South African Afrikaans Lutheran hymn book. City Harvest Ministries in Ntuzuma followed the same pattern of service as many other AFM congregations, and sang charismatic choruses. St Michael's in Durban followed the ELCSA liturgy and used an English Lutheran hymn book from Malaysia and Singapore and an ELCSA hymn book in isiZulu. South African choruses were only sung in congregations holding services in indigenous languages.

in the analytical tool challenges congregations and churches to be open to cross-cultural experiences with a diversity of hymns, songs, and music.

Congregations using computers and data projectors were able to be independent of specific printed hymn books, as they were able to display hymns, texts, information, new styles of liturgies, and pictures, and allow their services to be driven by multimedia. This technology also enabled them to use several languages and a variety of songs or choruses in their services in order to incorporate diversity across ethnicities.[128]

The Residence of Worshipers and their Attendance at Services

Most of the people who attended the church services in the various case congregations lived in the area where the congregation was located, as described in Chapter Five. The residential area of worshipers influenced, of course, the churches' ethnic composition. All of the congregations, nevertheless, had smaller or larger groups of people who commuted to the churches from other areas. The reason that people commuted was mainly that they lived far from the church building, liked a specific way of worshiping, shared the same first language as the other worshipers, preferred that specific community, found communication easy, or had historical or family connections with those congregations.

Ethnicity as a reason to travel to a particular congregation was an obvious factor. Some travelled a short distance – for example, within Soweto, or from the north of Johannesburg to the south. A smaller group of people travelled greater distances to attend worship with a particular language and community group. The German-speaking services are an example of a community whose members travelled very far. Nevertheless, the church council did not see this as a problem, and they regarded the practice as a natural consequence of social diversity.[129]

St Thomas' Anglican Church in Linden was an exception: they used both traditional hymns and contemporary worship songs during their family services.

128   Athlone Methodist Church, the Lutheran Church in Bellville, and St Michael's in Durban had installed computer and data projectors in their buildings, and used these facilities in their services.

129   St Peter Claver in Pimville had a large parking place, but most of its members lived in Pimville because the congregation covered a large area. The church council confirmed that the congregation was for all who were born in Pimville and for those who wanted to come to the congregation even though they lived further afield. Observation Protocol 2011-02-27; Church Council Interview Protocol 2011-02-27. St Thomas's in Linden did not have a large parking area, and most of its members lived in Linden; but many members lived beyond the congregation's boundaries.

The previous chapter described a vertical upward social mobility combined with a lateral mobility. A geographic movement from townships to suburbs was evident in former 'White' areas because of socio-economic changes after democratisation. An opposite lateral mobility was not very obvious in the studied case congregations. Some 'Black' people travelled to a specific congregation because they had had the opportunity to move into other areas after democratisation. Other people started to worship in congregations close to where they had moved, increasing the ethnic diversity in these congregations. There were also people who travelled or commuted to a church because of good communication or preference.[130] Commuting can strengthen the relationships in a local community; but if it reduces the ethnic diversity of a congregation, the catholicity of the Church is also reduced. Travelling becomes an ecclesiological structuring factor for congregations and churches.

The congregations' openness to people living in other areas confirmed that the congregations realised that being in a particular area was not reason enough to create barriers to membership in the community. People who lived in other areas – even those far beyond the congregation's boundaries – could belong to the community. The congregations welcomed everybody who wanted to participate in services in their church. Travelling distances to attend church services is frequently practised in large cities around the world, mostly due to communication and preferences. The ecumenical documents stress that the Christian community

---

Observation Protocol 2011-03-06; Church Council Interview Protocol 2011-03-06. Athlone Methodist Church also had a large parking area, but most of its members lived in the area, and some commuted for historical reasons. Observation Protocol 2011-03-20; Church Council Interview Protocol 2011-03-20. The Lutheran Church in Bellville had members who lived in that part of Cape Town, but also some who travelled far to have access to a German-speaking congregation. Church Council Interview Protocol 2011-03-15. City Harvest Ministries in Ntuzuma had a number of members who came from Durban, where the congregation had previously been located, as well as new members from Ntuzuma. Church Council Interview Protocol 2011-03-27. St Michael's in Durban had members who lived in areas close to the congregation, but several people commuted because transport to the city centre was convenient. Church Council Interview Protocol 2011-04-03.

130 St Peter Claver in Pimville had several people who travelled within Johannesburg to attend a church service. St Thomas' had received members who had moved from a township to Linden. St Michael's in Durban had many people coming because of convenient transportation. Church Council Interview Protocol 2011-02-27; Church Council Interview Protocol 2011-03-06; Church Council Interview Protocol 2011-04-03.

is present in every local church. The word 'local' in these documents can mean people living in a specific neighbourhood around a church, in a village or town, in a city, or those who gather around a church leader or bishop; or it can even mean a diocese. It is important to notice that the ecumenical documents are very vague about the meaning of 'local church' apart from defining it as 'people living in one place'. 'Local' in catholicity is challenged in a situation where modern transport systems allow people to travel easily; and a more refined definition is needed. 'Local' in the congregations examined in this study is first and foremost seen as the people coming together in a place of worship.

All congregations had members that regularly attended church services, but several church councils commented that they enjoyed higher attendance during major festival seasons such as Christmas and Easter. This increased participation at specific times of the year could indicate that the congregations saw the worshiping community as larger than just those who came regularly.

However, the AFM congregation was an exception to this: they required that all members should be active participants. They nevertheless had many visitors – people living in the area who were recognised as part of their community, but who were not actual members. It is significant that the Christian community making up the congregation was understood as an extended community, and that it did not only consist of regular members. The community was wider than the regular members who came to Sunday services. The catholicity of the Church in the analytical tool does not set the boundaries of a community, but emphasises the importance of a community with regular participants. The extended community based on baptism is a visible sign that the Christian communion transcends ethnicity.

Eucharistic Celebration

The frequency of celebrating eucharist was exclusively a factor of denominational tradition and not a matter of ethnicity. Ethnic diversity when the eucharist was practised was exclusively related to the congregation's location. The catholicity of the Church stresses that the eucharist is necessary to sustain and support the communion. The eucharist demands reconciliation and sharing among Christians in the communion, and challenges any form of segregation. According to the Church's catholicity, the eucharist should remind the congregations that the Church is broken but that it is also united in the body of Christ. The unity that is supposed to be demonstrated in the eucharist challenges the divisions that occur within congregations and churches. Practising the eucharist is therefore necessary – a primary collective action to maintain and build communion. The eucharist is also a practice that expresses unity with other Christians in other eucharistic communities, irrespective of time and place, that transcends ethnic diversity.

The Roman Catholic and Anglican congregations celebrate eucharist at every service on Sundays and also several times during the week. The ELCSA and ELCSA-Cape congregations celebrated eucharist at least once a month, sometimes every second Sunday, or depending on the minister. The Methodist and the AFM congregations celebrated eucharist once a month.[131]

Most of the ecumenical documents do not prescribe how often the eucharist should be celebrated. The BEM document, however, stresses that Christians should be encouraged to receive the eucharist frequently, and that the eucharist should be celebrated at least every Sunday.[132]

The eucharist as celebrated in the local congregations and the Christian community reflected the ethnic composition of the congregations. The ethnic diversity was greater in former 'White' areas than in other areas, as described in the previous chapter. Congregations with a greater ethnic diversity could better show that the eucharist transcended and challenged ethnic boundaries. Few congregations demonstrated that they had contacts with congregations of predominantly another ethnicity, as will be described in Chapter Eleven.

There was, however, evidence of eucharistic practices that transcended ethnic boundaries. The minister and church council at St Peter Claver Roman Catholic Church in Pimville, for example, described (as set out in the previous chapter) that they held events and open air services together with other congregations within the diocese. The church council at St Thomas' noted that they had twinned with a congregation in an area of a predominantly different ethnicity, where they joined them for services. One church leader even stated, as described in the previous chapter, that common services with congregations across ethnic boundaries had ended after democratisation.[133] The ecumenical documents

---

131 The Roman Catholic congregation of St Peter Claver in Pimville and St Thomas' Anglican Church in Linden celebrated eucharist every Sunday and several times during the week. The Lutheran Church in Bellville celebrated the eucharist at one of its services about every second Sunday. Athlone Methodist Church, City Harvest Ministries in Ntuzuma (AFM) and St Michael's Lutheran Church in Durban celebrated the eucharist once a month.
132 Baptism, Eucharist and Ministry, 1982, p. 16.
133 Church Council Interview Protocol 2011-02-27; Brennan, Vincent, Interview Protocol 2011-03-01. Mary Burton described how she used to visit a twinned congregation in Gugulethu, and St Thomas' had a twin congregation in Soweto. Burton, Mary, Interview Protocol 2011-03-23; Church Council Interview Protocol 2011-03-06. Bishop

stress that the ministers, and especially the bishops or equivalent leaders, have a particular task to safeguard the unity between diverse worshiping communities.

Furthermore, congregations had different practices when distributing and receiving the eucharist. These were related to denominational tradition, not to ethnicity. Some congregations distributed the eucharist at one or more stations where congregants queued to receive the gifts. Some churches had altar rails where congregants knelt to receive the bread and the wine. A third practice was the use of individual communion cups that were distributed to the congregants either in the pews or at the altar.[134]

Different ways of receiving the eucharist could result in diverse emphases on being one communion. The ecumenical documents do not describe precisely how the eucharist should be distributed, but the BEM document stresses the importance of sharing the *same* bread and the *same* cup; and this symbolism could be lost in some of the practices.[135]

Diversity in Duration of Services

A difference in the length of church services was observed, related to denomination and also to ethnicity. This difference was also stressed by some church councils and church leaders. Congregations with a predominance of 'Black' members usually had longer services than congregations that were predominantly 'White'. The church council at St Michael's emphasised the different expectations that members had of their services. Those attending the English-language services were used to one-hour services, while the services in isiZulu could last for two or even three hours. The church council at City Harvest Ministries in Ntuzuma also emphasised that ethnic diversity influenced the amount of time spent in church.

For example, the general secretary of the AFM, George Mahlobo, declared: "In most Black townships, you find that services take a little bit long and in suburbs services are short".[136] Both Vincent Brennan from the SACBC and Nils Rohwer

---

Nils Rohwer described how common services between ELCSA and ELCSA-Cape had ended after democratisation. Rohwer, Nils J., Interview Protocol 2011-02-09.

134 The members at St Peter Claver in Pimville, for example, received the eucharist after standing and queuing. The congregants at St Michael's received the eucharist kneeling at the altar rails at the first service and standing at the second service. The congregants in the Lutheran Church in Bellville could receive the eucharist in individual communion cups. Observation Protocol 2011-02-27; Observation Protocol 2011-04-03; Observation Protocol 2011-02-20.

135 Baptism, Eucharist and Ministry, 1982, p. 16.

136 Mahlobo, Mphikeleki George, Interview Protocol 2011-03-01.

from ELCSA-Cape also spoke about the length of worship as related to ethnic background. Brennan questioned whether the length of services was the real reason for the excuse of 'White' members for not participating in such services, or whether it was actually a matter of priorities. Rohwer mentioned the length of the sermons as a difference that was also related to ethnic background.[137]

Differences in the length of worship could be interpreted as church-dividing and as an obstacle to achieving a united community. The differences in duration between services have arisen because communities have been isolated, and their practices have developed in different directions. The length of a service is a constructed difference that can be reduced when worshiping communities get closer to one another and develop new patterns of church services. The catholicity of the Church according to the analytical tool does not prescribe the length of sermons or services. And generational differences over the 'right' duration of worship should not be underestimated.

Cultural Diversity

Ethnic differences were also obvious when church councils mentioned culture as a reason for holding separate services. 'Culture' was not defined by any of those who were interviewed, but it was identified as a dividing factor between the various ethnic groups in congregations. Culture was not seen as a 'race' issue, but it was attached to ethnicity. One church council, for example, said that their services were 'vibrant African', and another stated that they wanted to dance, clap hands, and sing, which was seen as part of a cultural difference. Two other congregations said that they followed an English or German tradition. Culture was understood to be a dividing factor rather than something that could contribute to the communities by including new elements and bringing new insights.[138]

---

137   Brennan, Vincent, Interview Protocol 2011-03-01; Rohwer, Nils J., Interview Protocol 2011-02-09.

138   The church council at City Harvest Ministries in Ntuzuma, for example, stressed that time that was spent in church was not an issue of 'race' but of cultural difference. The church council at St Michael's in Durban also emphasised that time spent in worship was more than a 'racial' question, and arose rather out of the church's history. The difference expectations about time are ethnically constructed, and will change with ethnic integration. The church council at St Peter Claver in Pimville noted that they had vibrant African services, and City Harvest Ministries in Ntuzuma said that they liked to dance, clap, and sing during services. St Thomas' in Linden stressed that theirs was an Anglican church in South Africa with an English-speaking heritage. The Lutheran Church in Bellville emphasised their German tradition.

The catholicity of the Church according to the analytical tool stresses that cultural and ethnic diversity are something to be appreciated. The Christian community is not supposed to demand uniformity, and there should be an atmosphere of respect for diversity. Different expressions communicate the richness of the Christian faith, which is part of the catholicity of the Church. This does not mean that congregations have to change their own traditions, but rather should be open to new insights that could contribute to the Churches' catholicity. It is significant that the ecumenical documents do not help churches to manage cultural diversity in their congregations.

Prayers and Intercessions in Church Services

Prayers and intercessions were central in the various congregations' services. All of them had special places in the liturgy or the order of service where the congregations prayed for the community and the society. A range of prayers, varying in both style and content, were used in the case congregations, and included common and individual prayers, silent and spoken prayers.

Some congregations used set prayers from liturgical books, offered by a member or provided by the diocese; other congregations used extempore prayers offered by the minister and members. Congregations mostly prayed for the community, families, people who were absent, society, government, and activities in the congregation. Intercessions and prayers were a way of making issues visible to members as well as bringing them before God. One example was a congregation that began the service by lighting a candle and offering a special prayer for people living with HIV. Another congregation distributed a leaflet on Sundays in which there was a summary of the intercessions and issues for particular attention during the week. By using the leaflet members could continue to address the issues in their personal prayers. Another example was the congregation that distributed the 'Family Cross' so that members could hold other members in their prayers.[139]

---

[139] All the congregations had space for common and individual prayers during their services. Some congregations, such as St Thomas' in Linden, even had a special rack for votive candles. Athlone Methodist Church and City Harvest Ministries in Ntuzuma mostly used extemporaneous prayers and addressed local issues. St Peter Claver in Pimville, St Thomas' in Linden, the Lutheran Church in Bellville, and St Michael's in Durban had predominantly set prayers, which came from liturgical books or from the diocesan office, as was the case at St Thomas' in Linden. Set prayers from the diocese had the advantage of including perspectives of a wider community, but left out the local. A church council member at St Thomas' thought that the intercessions and prayers in church were a way of making the issues of the wider community visible.

It is notable that congregations that used set prayers during the so-called 'Prayers of the Faithful' had very comprehensive prayers. They addressed the wider society, extending the prayers to include the global Church community, as well as other church leaders, churches and countries. These prayers extended the community and crossed even ethnic boundaries. Congregations using only free prayers tended to limit them to their own community and needs. The set prayers were well elaborated, while the free prayers captured the moment. The style of praying was not related to ethnicity but rather to denominational background and tradition. Congregations that addressed a wider communion, or even the wider society, included people beyond ethnicity – and that is consistent with the catholicity of the Church according to the analytical tool.

Congregations that belong to a denomination with stronger hierarchical structures that prescribe set prayers could facilitate the inclusion of a wider community that transcends ethnicity, and of the global church, in their intercessions. By contrast, congregations from denominations with decentralised structures were able to include the local situation in their intercessions.

The catholicity of the Church as described in the analytical tool challenges the congregations and churches to include both local and global perspectives in their prayers and intercessions. The local perspective is important in order to acknowledge the situation in the local community and in other local congregations. The local congregation is related, furthermore, to the universal Church. The global perspective is central to the local congregation because it is part of one Christian community. Congregations in other places around the world are a concern for every local congregation.

Confessing Catholicity

In the creeds they recited, the congregations and churches used different words for the Greek word καθολικόν (catholic). The Roman Catholic and Anglican churches used the word 'catholic' and its cognates in all their creeds, irrespective of language – for example, *katolieke* in Afrikaans and *eliKhatholika* in the Nguni languages. The Methodist and the ELCSA churches used 'catholic' in their English liturgies. Some ELCSA congregations, and all the congregations in UELCSA, instead used 'Christian', which was also used in German with the term *christliche*.

St Thomas' distributed a leaflet at Sunday services with a summary of intercessions. Another example was Athlone Methodist Church, which began the service with a special prayer for people living with HIV and AIDS.

The congregations in the Methodist and Lutheran churches used *algemene* in Afrikaans, meaning a church 'in general' or 'in common'; and in the Nguni languages, *lomhlaba wonke*, which could be translated 'the whole world' or 'universal'. The AFM did not use the ancient creeds, but instead had a 'Confession of Faith' as part of their constitution. The word 'catholic' or a related term was not mentioned in their confession. The AFM could be viewed as a non-credal church because it did not affirm the ancient creeds. However, 'non-credal' churches can function within the context of the ecumenical creeds.[140]

Using other terms for 'catholic' is a legacy of European church history that was transferred to South African churches. Using other words in the indigenous languages could be seen as a sign of inculturation. The use or non-use of the term 'catholic' in the creeds is, however, of lesser importance, as long as the churches practise and teach the catholicity of the Church, and emphasise a communion that transcends ethnic borders.

There are no terms in South Africa's official languages that correspond completely with the meaning of the Greek word καθολικόν (catholic). The term *lomhlaba wonke* emphasises the geographic dimension of the Church, while *algemene* and 'Christian' or *christliche* are very general and superficial. One possible solution would be not to translate the term, but instead to use the original Greek word in order to preserve its original meaning.[141]

The common confession and interpretation of catholicity in congregations and churches is important for their self-understanding. Divergent interpretations of catholicity, and the use of other words, could have ecclesiological implications, with the precise meaning of a church as 'catholic' possibly being lost.[142] To act and speak together, in addition to confessing the faith, are important signs of the Church's catholicity according to the analytical tool. This definition indicates that unity requires that the local church should act and speak together. Confessing the

---

140 Confessing the One Faith, 1991, p. 3.
141 Ekenberg, Anders, 1996, pp. 49–50.
142 John de Gruchy gave, as an example of the lack of a church's teaching, what happened when the Anglican Church issued official statements against apartheid. He explained that there was a gap between synodical resolutions and congregational resolve and action. There were, he said, a lack of grass-roots teaching and a lack of action. Similar examples could be found when churches did not teach catholicity, and thus it did not inform every level of the Church. De Gruchy, John, de Gruchy, Steve, 2005, p. 91.

Church's catholicity also involves a wider communion beyond the local congregation that can act and speak on behalf of every local Christian community.[143]

8.3 Conclusions

There were several reasons why the case congregations had diverse forms of church services. The use of various languages, which is related to ethnicity, was an important element that divided the congregations into separate worshiping communities. There were also other issues, such as liturgies or orders of service, time, and location that led congregations to have different services. Congregations ran the risk of becoming fragmented through being divided into different worshiping communities; and this risked damaging the catholicity of the Church.

Liturgical differences along ethnic lines were visible between congregations situated in different areas. Congregations' styles of worship – evident in the music, songs, choruses, harmonies, and to a certain extent how the church services were conducted – were different. The liturgies or orders of service in the Methodist, Lutheran, and AFM congregations were more local and contemporary in design among congregations that were predominantly 'White', and more traditional in those that were predominantly 'Black'. However, Roman Catholic and Anglican congregations followed the same liturgies, independent of ethnicity or where the congregations were situated.

Recognising the same liturgy or order of service among congregations of the same denomination, irrespective of ethnicity, was seen by some church council members to be important. The liturgy or order of service became a sign of unity that transcended ethnic boundaries. Because of the common liturgy, people from diverse ethnicities could have a sense of belonging to one Christian community. The catholicity of the Church challenges congregations and churches to appreciate diversity, but not to become divided into different worshiping communities. The length of services was also an element that could vary because of

---

143 The New Delhi Assembly said: "We believe that the unity which is both God's will and his gift to his Church is being made visible ... with the whole Christian fellowship in all places and all ages in such wise that ministry and members are accepted by all, and that all can act and speak together as occasion requires for the tasks to which God calls his people". The New Delhi Report, 1962, p. 116. Keith Clements, in the book *Learning to Speak,* has given several examples of when the Church has spoken on special occasions in modern history. He particularly describes two cases: the Barmen declaration in Germany and the Kairos Document in South Africa. Clements argues that the churches are expected to speak on major public issues. The Church is also always speaking on behalf of a community. Clements, Keith, 1995, pp. 2, 24–50, 44.

ethnicity; but it is related to church tradition and generational differences, and is constructed.

The hymn books used in the congregations did not reflect the South African ethnic context, but reflected a European tradition because of the denominations' heritage. In some of the congregations the hymns were often re-created and adapted to the context by using indigenous harmonies. By contrast, songs and choruses were contextual, but were not used in all the congregations, irrespective of their ethnic composition. The South African song tradition with choruses was not shared in or received by all the congregations. The technologies of computers and data projectors could, however, allow new forms of hymns, songs, and worship that were more contextual. Congregations are challenged by the catholicity of the Church, as described in the analytical tool, to reflect the South African context and to receive diverse traditions as shared gifts.

Prayers and intercessions were often focused on the congregation, its members, and its projects. Some congregations included other congregations – and even a national and a global perspective – in their prayers and intercessions, thus broadening the sense of community. It was evident that congregations in a denomination with stronger hierarchical structures included a wider community that transcended ethnicity in their intercessions. By contrast, other congregations – those in denominations with decentralised structures – could include the local situation in their intercessions. The catholicity of the Church challenges congregations and churches to include both local and global perspectives in their prayers and intercessions.

Confessing catholicity as expressed in the ancient creeds was apparent in the liturgies and services of the studied congregations. Other terms or expressions were used in several of them to express the sense of the word 'catholic' – the effect of European church mission and inculturation. The use of such diverse terms is related to denominational tradition, but also in some churches to language. Using other terms for 'catholic' could be advantageous, as long as the concept is taught and practised; but it could also threaten the ecclesiological foundation of the Church's perception of catholicity in relation to ethnicity. To act and speak together as a Church are visible signs of a Church as catholic.

A majority of the people who took part in a church service were worshiping in the congregation in the area where they lived. The residential area of members attending church services affects, of course, the ethnic make-up of the gathered people. Some nevertheless commute from more distant areas in order to attend a specific church service in a particular community. Such commuting can be excused on the basis of preference, language, communication, or family connections;

but if it endangers diversity in congregations, the catholicity of the Church is also threatened, because diversity is lost.

People travelling from one area to another also challenge the definition of 'local'. The ecumenical documents use a range of definitions of 'local'; but in an era of better communication, this needs further research. The definition of 'local' in the congregations studied here is mostly understood as the people who come together in a place of worship.

The meaning of 'local' as people belonging to a specific denomination in a city is not particularly evident among the studied congregations. Services and eucharistic celebrations with worshiping communities of predominantly different ethnicities were limited. Catholicity as 'local' – defined as people belonging to the same denomination in one place – stresses that people should be in relationship and should meet across geographic and ethnic boundaries. This sense of catholicity requires, at the very least, that there be signs that such catholicity extends the boundaries of the congregation.

The frequency of celebrating the eucharist related entirely to denominational patterns. Some congregations celebrated the eucharist every Sunday and several times during the week. Other congregations celebrated the eucharist a couple of times a month, or once a month. Celebrating the eucharist, however, is important to sustaining and supporting a community that transcends ethnicity. The catholicity of the Church, as described in the analytical tool, states that eucharist should be celebrated frequently, and at least every Sunday.

This chapter has focused on several issues that emerged through observation of the congregations' services. Diversity of language is one of the most significant causes of division in the Christian community; and this will receive special attention in the next chapter, where I will explore how languages influence the situation of congregations and churches in the South African context, and how language either unites or divides the Christian community.

Chapter Nine: Tower of Babel or Day of Pentecost?

Language is one of the principal means of communication. This is the case in the Church, too, when sermons are delivered, when liturgy is conducted, or when members build community and gather for social events.

The previous chapters have shown that linguistic diversity was particularly difficult for the congregations and churches to manage: it was both an advantage and a disadvantage when congregations and churches were building community and gathering for church services across ethnicities. This chapter is based on interviews with church councils and church leaders about linguistic diversity, and on congregational publications and statistics.

In this chapter I will examine how the congregations and churches deal with the situation of having several official languages in the democratic South Africa. I will focus on language practices that are found in the diverse congregations and churches. It is important to examine what influences the choice of language. Firstly, I will investigate how the language practices are related to the Church's catholicity as defined in my analytical tool. Secondly, I will explore situations where one language dominates, and how these situations might be seen in relation to the catholicity of the Church.

9.1 Congregations' Accommodation of Languages

The different congregations in the case study solved linguistic diversity in various ways, depending on their background, location, and members' first language. Most congregations have chosen to use the language of the place where they are situated. A number of congregations use several languages in the same service; others use a range of different services for different language groups, with common services a couple of times every year; and some congregations exclusively use one dominant language. English has gained a prominent position through becoming the lingua franca of the society. A situation where one language is dominant, however, creates unequal relationships between the different languages in the church communities.

St Peter Claver in Pimville – Roman Catholic Church

This congregation, situated in one of the oldest parts of Soweto, had a strong emphasis on indigenous languages. 37.1 per cent of the church members used isiZulu as their first language, 15.5 per cent used Sesotho, and 12.9 per cent used

Setswana as their first language, according to Census 2011.¹ The St Peter Claver congregation covered zones 1-8 in Pimville and the Klipspruit and Kliptown areas of Soweto – with 85 873 inhabitants and 22 691 households. A variety of languages was spoken within the congregation's area, although the dominant languages were isiZulu and Sesotho. Other languages had a prominent position in specific areas. For example, 32.8 per cent had isiXhosa as their first language in Zone 8, and 32.4 per cent in Kliptown had Afrikaans as their first language. Zone 4 had 28.1 per cent speaking Xitsonga as their first language, and 16.2 per cent used Setswana as their first language in Zone 3. The high number of Afrikaans-speaking people in Kliptown was due to the fact that they had a large number of 'Coloured' people living in that area.²

Of those living in the area close to the church building, 37.1 per cent spoke isiZulu as their first language, 15.5 per cent Sesotho, and 12.9 per cent Setswana.³ Of the people in the congregation who worshipped at St Peter Claver in Pimville, most came from Soweto, and isiZulu and Sesotho were the main languages.⁴

St Peter Claver was bilingual without being divided by that, and it accommodated at least two of the national languages in the congregation. The church council members used isiZulu or Sesotho as their first language, but they also spoke other languages, including English.⁵ The liturgy and the hymns were in isiZulu, Sesotho, or another chosen language, and even small parts of the liturgy were in Latin.⁶

When the church council was asked about language, one person replied: "[…] like today the sermon was in both Zulu and Sotho; some other days it could be in Tswana or English".⁷ The use of language was also dependent on the minister's knowledge of languages. The congregation, furthermore, had people from other African countries attending services and activities, but they had to learn one of the languages used in the congregation.⁸ A person would need to learn either isiZulu or Sesotho – or both – in order to participate in the life of St Peter Claver. The many languages spoken in the congregation showed that people had no problems mastering several languages. Their knowledge of languages helped

---

1   Census 2011, Soweto, Statistics South Africa, 2013.
2   Census 2011, Pimville Zone 1-8, Klipspruit and Kliptown, Statistics South Africa, 2013.
3   Census 2011, Soweto, Statistics South Africa, 2013.
4   Church Council Interview Protocol 2011-02-27.
5   Church Council Interview Protocol 2011-02-27.
6   Observation Protocol 2011-02-27.
7   Church Council Interview Protocol 2011-02-27.
8   Church Council Interview Protocol 2011-02-27.

the congregation to remain a united worshipping community. The use of diverse languages was also consistent with the catholicity of the Church as described in the analytical tool. Diversity was visible, and the languages spoken in the area were used.

English was used in the congregation's website, information leaflets, and other publications, although isiZulu and Sesotho were the main languages in the area and in the congregation.[9] Most of the congregation's members and those in the area could speak English. The use of English for information and announcements indicates that there is an unequal power relationship, in which English is regarded as the language of communication in the society, and becomes the norm. Having one dominant language does not reflect the Church's catholicity, described in the analytical tool.

St Thomas' in Linden – Anglican Church of Southern Africa

This congregation is situated in Randburg, and the main languages spoken by the people were English 52.0 per cent, Afrikaans 17.6 per cent, and isiZulu 6.6 per cent.[10] The population's first language in Linden as a suburb and as part of greater Randburg was English 49.8 per cent, with the others being Afrikaans 30.3 per cent, Other 4.1 per cent, isiZulu 3.7 per cent, Setswana 3.6 per cent, and Sesotho 2.1 per cent.[11] The high number of people with English as first language is characteristic of those who live in the northern suburbs of Johannesburg. The figure for Afrikaans-speaking people indicated that there were both 'White' and 'Coloured' people in the area who had Afrikaans as their first language. There are 'White', 'Indian or Asian', and some 'Black African' people who would consider English to be their first language. It was striking that indigenous languages were of minor importance, although several domestic workers were not included in the Census 2011 because their home was elsewhere.

St Thomas' was an English-speaking congregation, but also had members from various ethnic groups who had other first languages. Using English in the congregation was not strange because almost half of the population in Linden used English as their first language. Using the language that was spoken in the area is

---

9   St Peter Claver Parish, Pimville, Soweto, 2011, Website; St Peter Claver, Catholic Church, Pimville, 1928–2008, 80th Anniversary, 2008, Church Publication.
10 Census 2011, Randburg, Statistics South Africa, 2013.
11 Census 2011, Linden, Statistics South Africa, 2013.

consistent with the Church's catholicity, but minority groups also have to be accommodated.[12]

The church council emphasised very strongly that they were English-speaking, and that their heritage as an Anglican church in South Africa was English. One of the church council members stated: "We are going to be an English parish, and somebody who cannot cope with English is not going to feel at home here".[13] The statement made it very clear that the main language in the congregation's services, social life, and activities would continue to be English. The statement was not intended to create barriers so that people would not feel welcome in the congregation; it simply emphasised that it would be difficult for people to become part of the community if they did not know English. A council member added:

> It's tricky, I think the idea of a lingua franca is that it's part of Anglicanism. It is why it still exists when it drew away from the Latin, it's in English. And I guess the tricky thing is that do you have a service in a language that anyone can follow, or do you try to have a service in a language that everybody hears with parts in their mother tongue, but not necessarily follow those parts in other mother tongues? I think everybody understands English. I can't see that this parish rapidly changes from English services.[14]

The English roots were very strong, underlining the fact that many members were of British descent. The congregation was part of the Anglican Church of Southern Africa, which in turn is part of the Anglican Communion, for which English is the common language, connecting the congregation to other congregations and dioceses around the world. It is important to state that the dominant position of English in the Anglican Church does not imply that every Anglican congregation in South Africa uses English. In fact, most Anglican congregations use one of the indigenous languages; but English is the common language.[15]

The statement stressed that there would have to be radical demographic changes in the congregation for it to change to another language. The dominance of English in the Anglican Church, however, indicates the colonial history attached to the language. The statement also said that there were difficulties in accommodating several languages in a congregation where most people had little knowledge of languages other than English.

The congregation used to gather all members of the different Sunday services in one combined Sunday services four times a year. One of the council members

---

12 Church Council Interview Protocol 2011-03-06.
13 Church Council Interview Protocol 2011-03-06.
14 Church Council Interview Protocol 2011-03-06.
15 De Gruchy, John & de Gruchy, Steve, 2005, p. 85.

said: "In our [combined] services we have mixed ..., I think we have had those four times a year".[16] The practice, introduced by the previous rector, was confirmed by other council members. The combined services were held in order to unite the people in the congregation. It was a way of bringing different worshipping traditions together.[17]

According to the council, however, a combined service with a mix of different languages was not seen as the way to accommodate people from different language groups. One member said: "If you are mixing the languages you are also missing the message... all of us can't speak all the languages".[18] The statement showed that everybody in the congregation could understand English, but that few had knowledge of other languages. The central position occupied by English showed that it had a higher status than other languages.

The dominance of English became very obvious when there was a reluctance to learn other languages. A church council member stressed:

> My own feeling is that we as English-speaking people are lazy, and that is an international thing, right to America, and we don't take anyone's language easily. And traditionally we're in the education in this country, it was English and Afrikaans, and only about twenty years [ago] did we start having other languages. But I have tried to do another language but gave up.[19]

The council member's statement reveals an inequality between languages. Most 'Black' people spoke several indigenous languages and English, while 'White' people of English background would know some Afrikaans – but very few would know any indigenous South African languages. Learning other languages was seen as difficult, while 'Black' people were more or less forced to learn English. A change in the education system will gradually transform the situation.

The council member was supported by another member:

> I agree with you that it is hard to learn another language, but sometimes you have to be careful that we are not assuming that this is what they want. For example, at the eight o'clock service, which is an English service. If you look at the people who enjoy that service and come to that service, it is a completely mixed congregation. If I speak to, sort of, Toby's mother, she would say no, no, no, she has to go to the English church. And this is why she apparently loves it, and they want the good old traditional English hymns. They

---

16 Church Council Interview Protocol 2011-03-06.
17 Church Council Interview Protocol 2011-03-06.
18 Church Council Interview Protocol 2011-03-06.
19 Church Council Interview Protocol 2011-03-06.

want the organ. So it is tricky to assume that they want services in their own languages, and that is not always that way. For some, it is, but not for all.[20]

The council member emphasised that people's tradition of worship was also an important consideration, and language could be attached to vestments, rituals, and beliefs. People who were brought up in the English tradition of hymns, liturgy, and sermons appreciated that particular style of worship. A situation with a learned religious language had to be acknowledged, while at the same time there were people who would prefer a service in one of the indigenous languages.

The congregation tried to accommodate diverse languages, even though English was the congregation's primary language; and the council members had different views about language. The two first Sunday services were exclusively in English, while the next two services had elements of an indigenous language, or parts of the liturgy in another language. The family service, which often used marimbas, followed the liturgy in English according to *An Anglican Prayer Book*. But they also used elements of isiXhosa, isiZulu, and Sesotho in the songs and in parts of the liturgy. The Marimba Mass that was frequently used came from the *Lumko Marimba Mass*, which was sung in English, together with the original version in indigenous languages. The service also used the Lord's Prayer from a Caribbean liturgy, emphasising that the church had connections with Christians in other parts of the world.[21] The use of other languages in addition to English made diversity visible. The South African context became apparent, and can be recognised as a trace of the Church's catholicity according to the analytical tool.

The afternoon Sunday service at two o'clock was called 'Vernacular Mass', 'African Language Mass' or 'Sesotho-Nguni service' in various information leaflets, parish magazines, church documents, and on the website.[22] It is notable that the service was called 'vernacular' in some of the congregation's documents – as if

---

20 Church Council Interview Protocol 2011-03-06.
21 The service at St Thomas' had five liturgical parts or songs that were sung in an indigenous language, sometimes alternating with English. Marimba Mass, St Thomas' Anglican Church, 09h45 Family Mass, n.d., pp. 4, 10–12, 13, Church Publication. The *Lumko Marimba Mass* was developed within the Roman Catholic Church in South Africa in collaboration with the former music department at the Lumko Institute. Lumko is a conference and pastoral formation and training institute run by the SACBC at Germiston, Gauteng. Confirmed by phone call to Miriam Dyantui at Lumko Institute, 2013-11-27.
22 St Thomas' Anglican Church, Linden, Parish Profile, 2011, p. 7, Church Publication; Welcome to St Thomas' Anglican Church, Linden, 2011, p. 2, Church Publication; Linden St Thomas, Normal Schedule of Services, 2011, Website.

some languages were vernacular and others were not. The naming of the service indicates that languages were valued differently: English was the norm, and other languages were compared with the dominant language.

The two o'clock service was the only one that was almost entirely in a language other than English. It used several languages, including isiXhosa, Setswana, and Sesotho, depending on the participants, the minister, or the interpreter. The service was either completely in an indigenous language, or was led by a lay minister with some parts – such as the sermon – interpreted from English. The possibility of using only an indigenous language was dependent on the ministers who served in the congregation and on their knowledge of languages.[23]

One of the church council members declared: "[…] The two o'clock service, we don't currently have clergy who preach or celebrate in one of the vernacular languages, but we have a translator at the services".[24] This statement confirmed that the ministers did not know another language – or at least, that they had not tried to learn to lead the liturgy in an indigenous language, suggesting that indigenous languages were not given high priority, and that this arose from an unequal power relationship. English was superior, and there was no need to learn other languages. The dominance of English in the congregation becomes an ecclesiological structuring factor.

The two o'clock service could signify that the congregation tried to accommodate minority groups, consistent with the Church's catholicity; but the indigenous afternoon service was not given priority in this respect. The church bells were not rung, hymns were chosen by the congregants just before the service started, and no instruments were used in the service, as indicated in the previous chapter.

Athlone Methodist Church – Methodist Church of Southern Africa

Athlone is on the Cape Flats, on the periphery of metropolitan Cape Town. The area is a product of the apartheid policy of forced removals, and many so-called 'Coloured' people live there. About 52 per cent of people in Athlone used Afrikaans as their first language, while 43.6 per cent used English, according to Census 2011. Only 1.9 per cent had isiXhosa as their first language. The high number of Afrikaans- and English-speaking people shows that many so-called 'Coloured' people used either English or Afrikaans as their first language. This was also evident in the congregation.[25]

---

23   Observation Protocol 2011-03-06.
24   Church Council Interview Protocol 2011-03-06.
25   Census 2011, Athlone, Statistics South Africa, 2013.

The people in Athlone Methodist Church primarily spoke English and Afrikaans, and Athlone Methodist Church was an English-speaking congregation. There are Afrikaans-speaking congregations in the Methodist Church, but Athlone Methodist Church had an historically English background. The dominance of English in the Methodist Church is also due to its British heritage.[26] The use of English in the Athlone Methodist Church was not strange, because a significant group of people in the area spoke English as their first language. Thus the language used in the congregation reflected one of the main languages used in its context.

All the people in the church council spoke English as their first language, and they estimated that the majority of the members spoke English as their first language. One member stated: "I would say it is 60 per cent English and 40 per cent Afrikaans, most of the services are in English".[27] Afrikaans was also spoken, but only occasionally. A council member explained: "Most of it. Occasionally they would switch in the service. The minister would say something in Afrikaans and then in English. But everybody understands both languages".[28] Most of the people in the congregation were bilingual, knowing both English and Afrikaans. It is strange, however, that the congregation did not have services in Afrikaans, despite there being quite a number of members who spoke Afrikaans as their first language, and everybody knowing both languages. The English language has a strong position in the so-called 'English-speaking churches', although the majority of Methodist Church members in South Africa speak other languages as their first language.

The strong emphasis on English in the congregation is an ecclesiological structuring factor. The majority of the people in Athlone, including the church members, had either English or Afrikaans as their first language. English was the only language used in the congregation and Afrikaans was almost invisible. Using English exclusively could indicate a stratification of languages, where English was considered superior to Afrikaans.

The church council members confirmed that English was dominant in the society, and in many ways was displacing Afrikaans. For example, they had grandchildren who spoke only English, not Afrikaans.[29] The council members' responses indicated that the English language had increased in favour, and that other languages such as Afrikaans had faded away, even in the private sector. The language situation shows that Afrikaans lost importance among some groups in society and in private life after democratisation.

---

26 Athlone Methodist Church, Athlone Society Profile, c.a. 2008, p. 1, Church Publication.
27 Church Council Interview Protocol 2011-03-20.
28 Church Council Interview Protocol 2011-03-20.
29 Church Council Interview Protocol 2011-03-20.

Their present minister knew English and isiXhosa; but the congregation had not considered introducing isiXhosa, even though it is one of the most widely-spoken languages in the Cape Town metropolitan municipality, alongside Afrikaans and English. One church council member stressed: "Then it would be a language problem".[30] The need to use additional languages in the congregation had not arisen, and there was no real interest in learning more languages.[31] The minister's knowledge of languages could have been seen as an advantage, but accommodating other languages was not considered. Introducing prayers or choruses in isiXhosa could have been a sign of catholicity, as it was one of the major languages in Cape Town.[32] The minister's knowledge of isiXhosa could also have been important in the congregation's connections with isiXhosa-speaking Methodist congregations.

Lutheran Church in Bellville – Evangelical Lutheran Church in Southern Africa Cape Church

The suburban area of Bellville in Cape Town already had diverse languages and diverse groups living in the area before democracy. Approximately 64.9 per cent of its inhabitants used Afrikaans as their first language, 25.2 per cent spoke English, 4.8 per cent Other languages, and 2.5 per cent isiXhosa. Other South African languages were also spoken in Bellville, but by less than one per cent of the population. In the area close to the church building, 50.6 per cent used Afrikaans as their first language, 16.4 per cent English, 9.8 per cent Other, and 4.3 per cent isiXhosa. In the ward of Kempenville, where the church building was situated, 42 per cent spoke Afrikaans as their first language, 21 per cent Other languages, 21 per cent English, and 12 per cent isiXhosa.[33]

The majority of South Africans with Afrikaans as their first language are 'White' Afrikaners and the so-called 'Coloured' people. People who have English as their first language are 'White' and mainly of European background, with some 'Black African' and 'Coloured' people. The group who spoke 'Other' languages could be people from other African countries, and – in the case of Bellville – people with

---

30 Church Council Interview Protocol 2011-03-20.
31 Church Council Interview Protocol 2011-03-20.
32 In Cape Town 34.9 per cent had Afrikaans as their first language, 29.2 per cent isiXhosa, and 27.8 per cent English. Census 2011, City of Cape Town Metropolitan Municipality, Statistics South Africa, 2012; Census 2011, Census in Brief, 2012, p. 21.
33 Census 2011, Bellville, Avondstil, Bellville Central, Chrismar, Eversdale Ext 21, Harry De Villiers, Hillrise, Kempenville, Kingston, Oakdale, Sunkist, Statistics South Africa, 2013.

a German background. The congregation's catchment area was, however, bigger than the area close to the church building.

The congregation did not reflect the demographics of the surrounding area, as the Church's catholicity in the analytical tool would suggest. The congregation, however, used the languages that were spoken among those who gathered for worship and were members of the Lutheran Church in Bellville. There was a contradiction between the geographic location of the congregation and the languages spoken by those who gathered there for worship. The issue relates to the definition of 'local'. It has diverse meanings in the ecumenical documents, but most of the studied congregations would regard 'local' to mean the people who come together for worship, as stated in the previous chapter.

Language was regarded as a very important element in the congregation's identity. It was connected with their German heritage, and to preserving the German community in South Africa. The German language helped the congregation and the church to have a strong connection with Germany and EKD, and was an advantage because it also connected them with the greater Christian community in Germany, as part of the Church's catholicity. The local congregation could be in relationship with a community that transcended geographic boundaries, although it ran the risk of becoming isolated from the surrounding society.

When the congregation was established in 1890, as described in Chapter Five, it used German exclusively. According to a former minister in the congregation, however, there had almost always been some families in the congregation in which one person spoke Afrikaans as his or her first language. Later there was a need to introduce Sunday services in Afrikaans when the congregation incorporated more Afrikaans-speaking members. These services began in the mid-1960s.[34]

The congregation experienced conflict when Afrikaans was introduced, according to the church's documented history. Some members felt that they were losing their German church. The congregation initially held one Afrikaans service a month, which meant that there was one fewer service in German. The congregation, however, had the custom of using German and Afrikaans hymn books in parallel in the different language services. The congregation also allowed individuals to say the Lord's Prayer and the Creed in their preferred language. After some years it became apparent that there was a need to have more services in Afrikaans. The congregation began with an Afrikaans service at nine o'clock and a German service at 10.15 on one Sunday every month. The conflict over the introduction of

---

34 E-mail from Pluddemann, Gerhard, 2014-07-09; Ottermann, Reino, 1995, p. 91.

Afrikaans was settled in the 1980s, with no further disagreement. Both German and Afrikaans became accepted languages in the congregation.[35]

Marriages with English-speaking people led to nearly one quarter of the members having English as their first language, making it important to introduce a third language. English began to be used to accommodate English-speaking members and to facilitate their remaining members of the Lutheran church. Worship services in English began to be held once a month in 2002.[36] A council member explained: "The other languages came in because of mixed marriages. Children marrying Afrikaans and English and we don't want to lose the English-speaking people going over to somewhere else. That's why we use the English. [...]".[37] Introducing Afrikaans and English arose from intermarriage, and the fact that German was no longer the first language in some families, as it had been in the past.

Accommodating Afrikaans and English in the congregation could be explained as an act of survival. All three languages were used on signs and in pamphlets and other documents. Some knowledge of all three languages was more or less necessary in order to be part of the congregation's life and activities. One example of the importance of knowing several languages was access to articles in the congregation's magazine. Several articles were in two languages, but some were in only one of the three languages.[38] There were still problems about multilingualism in the congregation, although the members were reconciled to the situation. A council member said: "One cannot say it's not an issue any more. It is an issue. ... It's quite a battle to get everybody happy".[39] The statement indicated that managing three languages in the congregation still created problems.

The council described the congregation as 'multilingual'. One member of the council said: "[...] Although we are trilingual, the centre is around German descendants".[40] The German language still played an important role in the congregation's services and activities, even though it was no longer as prominent. The situation was very like that of other migrant churches where there had initially been a dominant foreign language, but where later generations began to

---

35 E-mail from Pluddemann, Gerhard, 2014-07-09; Ottermann, Reino, 1995, p. 91.
36 Hahne, Albrecht, 2002, p. 14, Church Publication.
37 Church Council Interview Protocol 2011-03-15.
38 Observation Protocol 2011-02-20. See, for example, Kreuzkirchengemeidebrief, Evangelical Lutheran Church Bellville, Kruiskerk Nuusbrief, 04/05 2009, 2009, Church Publication; Kreuzkirchengemeidebrief, Evangelical Lutheran Church Bellville, Kruiskerk Nuusbrief, 02/03 2011, 2011, Church Publication.
39 Church Council Interview Protocol 2011-03-15.
40 Church Council Interview Protocol 2011-03-15.

adopt the dominant languages of the society.[41] Retaining a strong emphasis on German and Afrikaans could be problematic, because both languages in many ways represent social divisions.

The vast majority of the church council members still spoke German as their first language, and there were several other indicators that German had a special position in the congregation. The kindergarten used German, and employees had to be able to speak the language. The German identity survived even after several generations because the German community in South Africa – with German schools, congregations, and social clubs – had a stronger position than many other migrant communities in South Africa.[42] The high priority of the German language, as well as the use of Afrikaans, becomes an ecclesiological structuring factor. German is the principal language, and other languages are accommodated primarily because of intermarriage.

The church council was asked whether English had also grown in importance in their congregation because of its strong position in society. A member stated: "It is the same".[43] Another member said: "It is the most stable group in the congregation".[44] A third council member added: "What I have found, what I have observed is that it draws, say, also Black people. They can't associate with German or Afrikaans. English they can understand, so now we are also having Black people coming in".[45] English had not previously grown in importance in their congregation, and the congregation had had the same attendance figures.[46]

The congregation had a five-week plan for different services. Afrikaans services took place on four Sundays, German services on three Sundays, and an English service on one Sunday. The fifth Sunday had only one service, which was

---

41 For example, Anya Woods has studied migrant churches in Australia. Migrant people's first language has been important for the first generation, but later generations have begun to use English. Woods, Anya, 2004, pp. 26–40, 175–178.
42 Church Council Interview Protocol 2011-03-15; See for example: Kreuzkirchengemeidebrief, Evangelical Lutheran Church Bellville, Kruiskerk Nuusbrief, 02/03 2011, 2011, Church Publication. There are, for example, the Deutsche Internationale Schule Kapstadt (DSK) in Cape Town, Die Deutsche Internationale Schule Johannesburg (DSJ) in Johannesburg, and Deutsche Schule in Durban. There is also the Deutsche Schule Hermannsburg (DSH) in Kwazulu-Natal with boarding facilities. Larger cities have a German Club, and there are several German retirement villages in South Africa.
43 Church Council Interview Protocol 2011-03-15.
44 Church Council Interview Protocol 2011-03-15.
45 Church Council Interview Protocol 2011-03-15.
46 Hahne, Albrecht, 2011, p. 2. Church Publication.

a trilingual or combined service.⁴⁷ It was obvious that English-language services were not the most frequently-held services in the congregation, but they had a constant number of attendees. Having fewer English services might hamper drawing in other ethnic groups to attend the congregation's services, while continuing with Afrikaans might attract, for example, 'White' Afrikaner and 'Coloured' Afrikaans-speaking people. The congregation might experience the same growth in 'Black African' attendants as ELCSA N-T has done if English services were to become more frequent and the emphasis on its German heritage reduced.

Accommodating the German-speaking minority is consistent with the catholicity of the Church, as described in the analytical tool. The Church needs to create a climate of acceptance and to make space for minority groups: they contribute to the diversity of the Church, and should be seen as enriching the whole church. However, catholicity presupposes that the congregation does not live in isolation, but is in relationship with other congregations of other languages and ethnicities.

The council was asked whether they would consider adding another South African language in order to accommodate new members. A council member said: "We battle with three".⁴⁸ Already using three languages, the congregation felt that they could not cope with yet another one. The people in Bellville were mostly Afrikaans- and English-speaking; but 12 per cent of the residents of the ward where the church building was situated spoke isiXhosa. Another council member added: "Language is based on the composition of what the congregants can speak, so we've got a German section and an Afrikaans and a small English section".⁴⁹ This answer reflected the languages spoken in the congregation at the time. Another church council member added: "I wouldn't have an objection if the situation is right. I would say we could accommodate them".⁵⁰ These responses indicated that there were many opinions in the church council about language use in the congregation. One of the responses also showed a very pragmatic attitude toward change in society, and indicated that the congregation could adjust to a new situation.

---

47 Lutheran Church Bellville, Worship Services, 2011, Website.
48 Church Council Interview Protocol 2011-03-15. The Lutheran Church on Strand Street was established in 1780 as the first Lutheran Church for German settlers in the Cape Colony. For a long time the congregation used Dutch services with German hymn-singing, until a new hymnbook was introduced early in the twentieth century. English was only introduced in 1889, and today the congregation only uses English. The congregation became a member of UELCSA in 1965, but did not join ELCSA-Cape until 1993. Ottermann, Reino, 1995, pp. 94–95.
49 Church Council Interview Protocol 2011-03-15.
50 Church Council Interview Protocol 2011-03-15.

In the church council, the minister used the example of a new group of people attached to the church:

> But, for example, there comes a question along now amongst the French-speaking. We are able to support them, support them with bibles and so forth because that is what they need. There is this mission from Strand Street congregation amongst the French-speaking people, and that is something that might come along. But I would like to stress very clearly that we are more multi-lingual than many other churches. From our physical constraint, we can't do more. We would have to employ somebody.[51]

The Lutheran Church in Strand Street, Cape Town had begun to support a group of French-speaking people, and had begun a mission project in Maitland, in an abandoned Dutch Reformed Church building.[52] Several congregations in ELCSA-Cape supported the project in various ways. It is interesting that none of the congregations within ELCSA-Cape had offered the French-speaking group the use of any of their premises. Instead, another building was rented to accommodate the French-speaking group. The minister in Bellville, however, was open to supporting new developments, but stressed at the same time that their congregation was already catering for more languages than most others. They had limited resources, and if they were to accommodate another language in the congregation, they would need to provide language competence. Some church council members were also hesitant about accommodating people of other language groups. A church council member declared: "And the need is not there. If we would have ten in our service every Sunday then it would probably be a chance, but as I say there is not at the moment, they are not feeling at home here".[53] This statement made it clear that they did not have people of other language groups in the services, and that therefore there was no need to incorporate another language. Another council member said: "They are not in the vicinity here, so they go to churches, Lutheran churches, which are closer to them where they are comfortable. They are good in relating to people and so forth going there".[54] This statement suggested that Lutheran members speaking other languages would rather go to congregations where they felt more comfortable.

It is admirable, of course, that the congregation and the ELCSA-Cape congregations supported people from Francophone countries in Africa. Support for minority groups is important, and is part of the Church's catholicity. Not accommodating

---

51 Church Council Interview Protocol 2011-03-15.
52 Ilunga-Mpombo, Kiasso, Interview Protocol 2011-03-18.
53 Church Council Interview Protocol 2011-03-15.
54 Church Council Interview Protocol 2011-03-15.

the group in any of the congregations' premises, however, does not facilitate integration as part of the Church's catholicity in the analytical tool.

City Harvest Ministries in Ntuzuma – Apostolic Faith Mission of South Africa

All the church council members in City Harvest Ministries were first-language isiZulu speakers, apart from one who spoke isiXhosa.[55] IsiZulu is the main language in KwaZulu-Natal, and particularly in the Ntuzuma township outside Durban: 91.58 per cent spoke isiZulu, 2.3 per cent English, 1.6 per cent isiNdebele, and 1.6 per cent isiXhosa, according to Census 2011.[56] The vast majority of the people in Ntuzuma had isiZulu as their first language, and this was also evident among the members of City Harvest Ministries.

The congregation sometimes had visitors who used other languages. One church council member said:

> It depends on what kind of visitors we have … Sometimes we have visitors that speak different languages, then we accommodate them to give them the interpretation according to their language. We use all the languages, and I think for us, I think in fact it is three with Xhosa.[57]

IsiZulu and isiXhosa are Nguni languages and are closely related. They have many similarities in syntax, vocabulary, and pronunciation, and a person speaking one of these languages can easily acquire knowledge of the other.[58] When the church council was asked which language was most commonly used in the congregation, they answered unanimously: "Zulu".[59] The language of services was mainly isiZulu, but elements in English were also used in prayers, songs, and choruses. Members of the congregation could easily interpret into another language if necessary.[60] Most South Africans are multilingual: most 'Black' people know one or more indigenous languages as well as English; but 'White' English- and Afrikaans-speaking people have a limited knowledge of indigenous languages, although they are fairly fluent in each other's languages.[61]

---

55 Church Council Interview Protocol 2011-03-27.
56 Census 2011, Ntuzuma, Statistics South Africa, 2012.
57 Church Council Interview Protocol 2011-03-27.
58 Chen, Yiya, & Downing, Laura J., 2011, p. 251.
59 Church Council Interview Protocol 2011-03-27.
60 Observation Protocol 2011-03-27.
61 Orman, Jon, 2009, pp. 85–88, 90–92.

The congregation used isiZulu as their primary language, which is consistent with the Church's catholicity according to the analytical tool. The congregation's language was determined by its context; but they still included elements of other languages to reveal new perspectives of the Christian faith. City Harvest Ministries could easily accommodate visitors because most of the members could speak English as well as indigenous languages. Part of the service could be interpreted if necessary, but isiZulu would be the primary language in the congregation, and there was little need to introduce additional languages in an area such as Ntuzuma.

It is interesting that English was used in the congregation's website, official documents, and other publications, even though City Harvest Ministries was almost entirely IsiZulu-speaking.[62] English was the official language at a central level, which explains why they used it in official documents. The use of English indicated the dominance of English in the society's communication and in the church. IsiZulu does not have the same status as English in official documents and communication.

St Michael's Evangelical Lutheran Church – Evangelical Lutheran Church in Southern Africa

In the centre of Durban, where St Michael's is situated, 32.8 per cent of the residents spoke English as their first language, while about 31 per cent spoke isiZulu, 14.6 per cent Other languages, 8.5 per cent isiXhosa, 2 per cent Afrikaans, 1.3 per cent isiNdebele, and 1.2 per cent Sesotho, according to Census 2011. English and isiZulu were the two major languages in the areas close to St Michael's. In central Durban, almost the same proportion as in the entire eThekwini Municipality were first language English-speakers; while half as many had isiZulu as their first language. It is interesting that many people in central Durban spoke other languages, a fact that is not reflected in the municipality as a whole.[63]

St Michael's used English and isiZulu, and the majority of the members spoke isiZulu as their first language. English and isiZulu were also the two major languages in the area around the church building. The linguistic character of the congregation could be seen as having been formed by its context, which reflects the Church's catholicity.

---

62 See for example: City Harvest Ministries, The life of City Harvest Ministries, 2013, Website; City Harvest Ministries Constitution, 2011, Church Publication.

63 Census 2011, North Beach, Statistics South Africa, 2012; Census 2011, South Beach, Statistics South Africa, 2012; Census 2011, Durban Central, Statistics South Africa, 2012.

The different ethnic groups with their many languages were a difficulty for the congregation, and they had not found ways of dealing with the diversity. St Michael's had two services in different languages every Sunday. There was one service in English at nine o'clock, and one in isiZulu at eleven o'clock. The parish's ministers mastered several languages between them: two knew isiZulu, English, German, and Afrikaans; while the other two spoke English and either Afrikaans or isiZulu. This language fluency helped the parish's leadership to master the services in different languages.[64]

The church council stated that the members were very accepting of ministers who did not know a language perfectly. More important was the message, and not how the minister pronounced certain words, or if the minister has a strange accent. Their attitude towards people's language skills was very generous, and suggested a wide acceptance of people's attempts to learn isiZulu, for example.[65]

One of the council members originally came from ELCSA Central Diocese, where they had a mixture of people from different parts of South Africa. The member explained that congregations in the Central Diocese had liturgy in English, and the hymns, choruses, and songs were in some of the other South African languages. They could alter the language of the hymns, but use the same melody, allowing them to sing the hymns in different languages.[66] He stated:

> I come from the Central Diocese where you have Coloureds, you've got Zulu-speaking and Pedi-speaking in one church. How we overcome that was just to have the liturgy? That would be normally in English and always songs that you would have in especially Zulu and the Pedi. The songs that you do are similar. They would mix them or sing one in Zulu and one Sotho and one in English.[67]

English could be viewed as a language that everybody understood; but others in the church council at St Michael's questioned whether having a single language was the answer. When the council was asked whether English would be the language to take St Michael's into the future, one member replied: "I think English is the language, but the problem is that you have elderly people that don't understand English. A problem as a church, how far do you go where we are? The pastor would have to try too, in preaching possibly in English and translate in some way".[68] Even if English were used as some kind of lingua franca, and St Michael's tried to merge

---

64 Durban Central Parish, Leadership team, 2014, Website.
65 Church Council Interview Protocol 2011-04-03.
66 Church Council Interview Protocol 2011-04-03.
67 Church Council Interview Protocol 2011-04-03.
68 Church Council Interview Protocol 2011-04-03.

the two services in English and isiZulu, there would still be some people who would not entirely understand and feel at ease with English.

If they had just one service, they would need to translate the sermons. They occasionally had common services, but interpretation made the services very long. The use of English would unify the church at the expense of people's first language, and the diversity and catholicity of the Church according to the analytical tool would be lost.

There was also an issue of time, arising from the language used in services, which divided the different worshipping groups at St Michael's. One of the church council members said:

> I think that there probably is more than a racial question. It is, the main challenges are the questions of languages and different history regarding length of services, for instance, where people could feel at home and say when they finished the service, 'This was a service', and it wasn't only a devotion. I think that it is very interesting because we are battling with these issues in this parish. It is not only an issue here in St Michael's because of the two different services, nine and eleven. It is also an issue in the parish itself. You got an English-speaking congregation in Wentworth, where coloured people are members, and it is also a challenge for us at parish level, to see that we accommodate different people with different songs and different kinds of services and traditions as well. And I think there are no easy answers. For instance, at one point when we come together for a parish rally when all congregations are together and you would see that members from the English service's groups will take part in a short space usually, because they are used to a service being one hour, and in Zulu-speaking services usually people, let's say, two or three hours is fine and it also relates to other parts of the service. I would say that this is something we are grappling with and trying to find compromise and try to accommodate everybody which you can't, and we are trying out seeing which works, and I'm quite happy that people do voice their opinion and so on, and they are vocal [...].[69]

The church council acknowledged that there were diverse practices relating to the duration of services, and diverse traditions in the two language services. The church council tried to find ways of dealing with the language issues and made compromises, but they had not found any common solutions.

The council's statements showed how language, traditions, and practices were interrelated; but the connections should be seen as constructions. They said that they sometimes had consecutive interpretations of the sermons, but that this would significantly prolong the service. The extra time added to a service when an interpreter was used discouraged the congregation from having bilingual services very often. The council mentioned as an example the time that the bishop visited

---

69 Church Council Interview Protocol 2011-04-03.

the congregation, and the sermon with an interpreter easily lasted one and a half hours.[70]

The language groups in the congregation, furthermore, coincided with how activities were structured in the congregation. The English-speaking group, for example, had no organisations or leagues, but had groups that were not part of ELCSA's official church organisations. Such differences become noticeable in the organisation of the whole church, where the various leagues and organisations had official status, even in the constitution. According to the council, the congregation tried to accommodate the English-speaking groups by recognising that they were an equally valid expression of the Lutheran faith in ELCSA. They strove to make the English-speaking group feel part of the wider church, and not to become isolated. The English-speaking people, at the same time, had to be challenged to be open to some of the practices in the isiZulu-speaking part of the congregation.[71]

It is interesting that language could become a dividing factor, based on its status in the church and even in the activities that the congregation organised. It is also notable that the church council was aware of the need for the English-speaking service to introduce elements in isiZulu, which would be in line with Church's catholicity according to the analytical tool. Language diversity is supposed to be shared and received.

9.2 Language Change in the Churches

The general secretary of the Southern African Catholic Bishops' Conference, Vincent Brennan, stated that Roman Catholic congregations in the cities, which formerly were predominantly English-speaking, had opened up to the use of other languages in hymns and songs. The sermons and prayers in city congregations were still in English alone, as this language had become the lingua franca due to the cosmopolitan character of the congregations. Some congregations in the cities also held different services in various languages, and some even used French for members who came from the Great Lakes region of East and Central Africa and from the Congo.[72]

Language diversity increased in the city centres after democracy as people were able to move into the cities, as described in Chapter Seven. Elements in other languages had been introduced into the services, although English was still the dominant language. The introduction of hymns and songs in other languages could be

---

70 Church Council Interview Protocol 2011-04-03.
71 Lüdemann, Joe, 2012, p. 10, Church Publication.
72 Brennan, Vincent, Interview Protocol 2011-03-01.

323

seen as signs of the Church's catholicity. Different languages revealed new perspectives of the church, and related the local congregation to the greater communion.

Brennan acknowledged that some of the older ministers knew only English, and did not know any indigenous languages. He also recognised that congregations in the cities mainly used English, whereas churches in townships and in rural areas used other South African languages.[73] Brennan's thoughts about language were very similar to the case congregations' experiences. English held a strong position in the cities, but there was a need to use several other languages. The new generation of ministers would be able to speak several languages to accommodate people who spoke a range of first languages.

The Provincial Executive Officer of the Anglican Church of Southern Africa, Allan Kannemeyer, had the same perspective as Vincent Brennan about English as the main language in many city congregations. He also noted that English was increasing in public life. It had become a uniting factor that brought people together. He mentioned, for example, that English was spoken in workplaces and in institutions of higher learning, apart from a few universities that used both Afrikaans and English. Furthermore, the use of English had become part of the process of changing social class.[74]

Kannemeyer's statement revealed an unequal power relation between the languages defined as official, and the English used in higher educational institutions and the workplace. The dominance of English as the main language in many sectors in society, together with the aim of promoting an upward social mobility, affected language status in the society: English became superior to the other South African languages. It is important to notice that there was a connection between language, upwards vertical mobility, and lateral mobility. Upwards vertical mobility, together with lateral mobility, influences language use. The strong position of English becomes an ecclesiological structuring factor. One dominating language can endanger the catholicity of the Church when inequalities are created.

The general secretary of the Methodist Church of Southern Africa, Vuyani Nyobole, also recognised that English had grown in importance, but stated that it was not good that English had developed into the dominant language. He noted that language would always be an issue in their church. He said that the operating language in the Methodist Church was English, but English was not always accessible to everybody. Not everything was translated into indigenous languages because

---

73 Brennan, Vincent, Interview Protocol 2011-03-01.
74 Kannemeyer, Allan J., Interview Protocol 2011-03-16.

of the high cost of doing so. Most 'Black' people could speak English, but the use of different languages was an obstacle to integration, especially for 'White' people.[75]

It is noteworthy that Nyobole, coming from a so-called 'English-speaking church', acknowledged the unequal relationship in his church between English and other languages. Not all had access to English, and thus an unequal power relationship was created between those who had English as their first language and those who had to learn English. His response about 'White' people's inability to learn indigenous languages is interesting. Their attitude – that it was not necessary to learn other languages – reveals an unequal power relationship, but could, at the same time, endanger their own integration.

English was used at all levels of the church, but church services were held in several languages. The church had encouraged ministers to study one African language in order to increase the language competencies in the church.[76] This initiative was interesting, because the Methodist church's language use was inherited – but at least they tried to facilitate the introduction of indigenous languages by encouraging ministers to undertake further studies. The decision could be seen as consistent with the Church's catholicity because the diversity of the Church was enhanced.

The Anglican and Methodist churches are often referred to as 'English-speaking churches', even though the majority of their members do not have English as their first language. The situation for these churches of British heritage is complicated. They have a common language that is inherited for the purposes of communication, but most of their members speak other first languages. Promoting other languages is important, but it requires large and expensive resources.[77]

The AMF had many members who spoke Afrikaans or indigenous languages, adding another layer of complexity to the use of English as the common language. The general secretary of the Apostolic Faith Mission, George Mahlobo, said that their congregations were still located in areas with specific language affiliations. Afrikaans had been important in urban areas, but English had recently become increasingly indispensable in that context. When people moved from previously 'Black' areas into previously 'White' areas, language and cultural differences became an obstacle to ethnic integration.[78]

---

75 Nyobole, Vuyani Gladstone, Interview Protocol 2011-02-28.
76 Nyobole, Vuyani Gladstone, Interview Protocol 2011-02-28; See also: The Laws and Discipline of the Methodist Church of Southern Africa, 2007, p. 64.
77 De Gruchy, John & de Gruchy, Steve, 2005, p. 85.
78 Mahlobo, Mphikeleki George, Interview Protocol 2011-03-01.

Mahlobo said: "The barrier now becomes the language and the way of doing things, because in most suburbs the dominant AFM churches would be the Afrikaans-speaking churches. These people, Black guys, coming in, most of them would be English-speaking".[79] Mahlobo identified another difficulty that arose when few church members spoke English as their first language, but English was used as the only common language for everybody in the AFM. The issue was not the same as in the 'English-speaking' churches, where people had the advantage of English as their first language. There was not necessarily an unequal power relation, but English was the only common language.

The AFM supported church planting and the establishment of urban churches that were multilingual, according to Mahlobo. Language knowledge, intercultural competencies, and a desire to work in an environment with people from diverse backgrounds were necessary in the bigger cities. Mahlobo revealed another obstacle. There could be ministers with the desired skills, and congregations that had become intercultural; but some groups in the society moved to other areas. People with options and who were predominantly 'White' left the inner cities and moved to other, more congenial areas.[80] Mahlobo's statement stressed that there was a social mobility that was not related to language but to economic capacity, and that this destroyed the possibility of establishing multilingual and intercultural congregations. The mobility was not vertical but lateral, in the form of a move from the city centres to suburbs or even enclosed communities. Such mobility made it increasingly difficult to become a sharing and receiving community of diversity, in accordance with the Church's catholicity.

The Lutheran church family in South Africa, which is divided into three churches, cannot be regarded as a so-called 'English-speaking church' because of its origins in Germany, Scandinavia, and America.[81] ELCSA-Cape and ELCSA N-T had a strong German heritage, but they also used English and Afrikaans. ELCSA used various indigenous languages as well as English and Afrikaans.

ELCSA was, as described earlier, established as different synods or regional churches, mainly along ethnic lines, by the mission societies. The regional churches were united in 1975 and formed ELCSA, made up of several dioceses. The Cape Orange diocese was mainly Afrikaans-speaking, South Eastern diocese was predominantly isiZulu-speaking, the Northern diocese used Sepedi and Tshivenda, and the Western diocese used Setswana. The Central diocese had

---

79 Mahlobo, Mphikeleki George, Interview Protocol 2011-03-01.
80 Mahlobo, Mphikeleki George, Interview Protocol 2011-03-01.
81 De Gruchy, John & de Gruchy, Steve, 2005, p. 86.

adopted a multilingual approach to accommodate language diversity among its members. The 'Indian' Lutheran congregations used English, as did some city congregations. All of ELCSA's official documents were drawn up in English – the church's common language.[82]

The Lutheran churches did not reveal a large power inequality between languages. Most of the members did not speak English as their first language, but English had to be used as the lingua franca at least at the central level.

ELCSA-Cape and ELCSA N-T had undergone a change concerning language. English and Afrikaans had been introduced because the German settlers and their descendants had been assimilated into English and Afrikaans groups, and trilingualism was adopted in many of the congregations.[83] Bishop Horst Müller of ELCSA N-T explained that the congregations had become more open to people of different backgrounds as a result of the introduction of English. ELCSA N-T was almost entirely German-speaking until the 1980s, when the church became multilingual. After democratisation the church also received Lutherans from ELCSA as they moved into areas where there was an ELCSA N-T congregation. There were even some congregations where the majority of their members were "Black", and some ELCSA N-T congregations had services in one of the indigenous languages because they had received members from other ethnic groups. Müller stated that there were only two congregations in ELCSA N-T that used German exclusively.[84]

The bishop of ELCSA-Cape, Nils Rohwer, said that most people who belonged to the church were of German descent, but their congregations used German, Afrikaans and English. ELCSA-Cape had also begun to move in the same direction as ELCSA N-T by receiving members from ELCSA once some congregations had begun to use English. The congregations in ELCSA-Cape used English exclusively, or alternated languages, or had different services, each of them using all three languages every Sunday. Only St Martini in Cape Town, which belonged to ELCSA-Cape, was almost exclusively German-speaking.[85]

The changes in language use in ELCSA N-T and ELCSA-Cape indicated how communities were affected by the surrounding society. The churches were

---

82 Scriba, George & Lislerud, Gunnar, 1997, pp. 180–181, 184–185; Florin, Hans Wilhelm, 1999, p. 155.
83 Scriba, George & Lislerud, Gunnar, 1997, pp. 182–183.
84 Müller, Horst, Interview Protocol 2011-03-04. One example is West Rand Lutheran Community Church, which used Setswana every Sunday in addition to German and English. West Rand Lutheran Community Church, Overview, 2011, Church Publication.
85 Rohwer, Nils J., Interview Protocol 2011-02-09.

exclusively German-speaking for many years, and the use of English and Afrikaans began relatively late. Language could help to preserve a community by continuing to use its mother tongue – in this case, German. The introduction of English, and to a certain extent Afrikaans as well, could accommodate new members from other ethnicities. The language practices in ELCSA-Cape and ELCSA N-T congregations show that language can both exclude and include.

The leaders of both ELCSA-Cape and ELCSA N-T believed that it was an advantage to use English because it was the common language for all in South Africa. Because the ELCSA-Cape and ELCSA N-T congregations in the cities were using English, they had drawn members from ELCSA.[86] English was the lingua franca, and was the most dominant of the official languages – which could indicate unequal power relations. However, ELCSA-Cape and ELCSA N-T showed that the introduction of English could help to build ethnic integration.

9.3 Conclusions

Language is a complex matter in South African congregations and churches because several languages are used in South African society. The catholicity of the Church is also challenged because the reality is rather different from the ideal state of having either a single language or minor differences of language.

The first mainline churches to be established in South Africa were attached to the colonial powers, and used English or Afrikaans or, in some small groups, German. The missionaries coming to South Africa emphasised the importance of local languages so that everyone could have access to the churches' message in their own language. The missionaries even developed the South African indigenous languages into written languages so that the Bible could be translated and used in various languages. Moreover, since democratisation the South African constitution has recognised eleven official languages and acknowledged several minority languages. There are, however, other tendencies in language use in South Africa that might change the linguistic scene in the future. Indigenous languages will increase in importance through, for example, changes to educational requirements. Such changes threaten some groups in the society, and question current power relations.[87] The increased use of a variety of languages in churches

---

86 Müller, Horst, Interview Protocol 2011-03-04; Rohwer, Nils J., Interview Protocol 2011-02-09.
87 The Senate of the University of KwaZulu-Natal approved a rule in 2013 that students registering for undergraduate degrees were required to pass or obtain a credit in isiZulu before they could graduate. The policy is part of a plan to promote and facilitate the

is consistent with the catholicity of the Church as described in the analytical tool, because diversity reveals insights into the Christian message that need to be shared and received within the Christian community.

Two decades after democratisation, all of the studied congregations were using the same languages as before. All but two of the congregations were using the main languages spoken in their area. The two exceptions used other languages because of their background and heritage.[88] Some of the church leaders explained that a number of congregations in city centres had introduced indigenous languages or elements of other languages into their services since democratisation, as new groups of people had moved into the areas. The catholicity of the Church emphasises that local congregations should reflect the ethnic composition of their localities. This implies that congregations do not need to use languages that are not spoken in the area, but that they are encouraged to incorporate elements of other languages to increase diversity. Catholicity emphasises that, when different languages are spoken in an area where a congregation is situated, it should reflect that diversity and become a multilingual community. And when there are language changes in an area, the congregations should also introduce these new languages into its life.

Church councils' and leaders' responses illustrated the complexity of the relationship between language and Church in a multilingual society, and there were diverse practices. Language use was dependent on where the congregation was situated and on the congregation's denominational affiliation. It was particularly noticeable that the Anglican and Methodist churches, and one Lutheran congregation, used the languages inherited from their denominations' history. Anglican and Methodist congregations used English because of their British heritage, and one of the Lutheran congregations used German because of its German origins.

---

use of isiZulu as an academic language alongside English. The change could be seen by some to be a threat because, even if only a small amount of teaching were done in isiZulu, the need for everyone to be bilingual would be unavoidable. UKZN Pioneers the Introduction of isiZulu in Undergraduate Degrees, Media Release UKZN, 2013.

88   In Athlone, about 52 per cent spoke Afrikaans as their first language, and 43.6 per cent spoke English as their first language, according to Census 2011. Athlone Methodist Church had a British background, and those in the congregation who were Afrikaans-speaking used English as their religious language. Bellville Lutheran Church used German and Afrikaans, and on some Sundays English as well. In Bellville 64.9 per cent were Afrikaans-speaking and 25.2 per cent were English-speaking. However, 12 per cent spoke isiXhosa as their first language in the ward where the church building was situated. Bellville Lutheran Church was, however, ministering principally to people of German descendent.

Congregations in cities were more English-speaking than were rural ones, which used indigenous languages. English primarily – but also Afrikaans and German in Lutheran churches – was used in the suburbs, while indigenous languages were used more in the townships because they reflected the ethnicity of their contexts. Indigenous languages were also used in special services in suburbs and some city centres congregations, where domestic workers worshiped, or where people had moved into these areas and had brought with them their indigenous mother tongue.[89]

The many languages in the studied congregations resulted in diverse practices. One congregation was able to accommodate several languages in a united worshiping community because the members could master several languages. A number of congregations used only one language because most of the members shared it as their first language. Congregations using only one language, however, ran the risk of failing to accommodate people who spoke other languages. Several congregations had different services for diverse language groups. Holding diverse services for various language groups could easily produce a fragmented congregation with separate worshiping communities.

Combined services were held in the congregations that had separate services for different language groups. These were held a couple of times a year to bring the different language groups and worship traditions together. Combined services, however, were not seen as a solution by the church councils because they could create discomfort. Some people did not know the other languages; they felt uneasy, and the message could be lost. The use of consecutive interpreting resulted in very long services. Some congregations used elements of other languages for hymns and songs during at least one of the services, thus accommodating variety and acknowledging ethnic diversity.

The ecumenical documents are very clear that a diversity of languages is no reason for division within the Christian community. The baptised members belong to one Church that transcends language boundaries, and there is a profound equality within the Christian community. Congregations that have a single language have to take care that they are not excluding people by failing to make space for

---

89 The case congregations showed that, for example, St Peter Claver in Pimville and City Harvest Ministries in Ntuzuma used indigenous languages but could also occasionally use English. Athlone Methodist Church used English alone. St Thomas' in Linden had English as its primary language, but used elements of an indigenous language in one service, and an indigenous language in a service intended mainly for domestic workers. The Lutheran Church in Bellville mainly used Afrikaans and German, but used also English. St Michael's in Durban city centre used both an indigenous language and English.

diversity. And congregations that are multilingual have to take care not to create boundaries between language groups and thus create unequal opportunities. It is important to notice that the catholicity of the eucharistic *koinonia* expects there to be diverse expressions within the community, and common gifts should be shared. Congregations that do not use languages that accommodate people of diverse ethnicities are reducing the possibilities of achieving wider views of the catholicity of the Church, according to the analytical tool.

It is noteworthy that congregations' choice of a specific main language or of several languages can be inclusive – but at the same time it can preserve groups in the society. A congregation that continues to use a language that has always been used in an area is not opening itself up to new expressions, and does not make it possible to accommodate minority groups in ways that are consistent with the Church's catholicity as described in the analytical tool. Even the TRC, in its final recommendations, encouraged faith communities to develop forms of worship that transcend language and cultural differences.

There is a contradiction concerning catholicity in at least the Anglican, Methodist and German Lutheran churches. The Anglican and Methodist congregations using English, and the Lutheran congregations using German, are strengthening their relationships with churches in England and Germany respectively as a way to express the Church's catholicity. There is an advantage to using a specific language that can unite and that transcends national borders. But at the same time the use of English or German damages or inhibits catholicity in the local context.

Ministers' knowledge of languages was crucial for congregations and for the possibility for churches to create an environment that accommodates several languages. Most of the ministers in the various congregations studied here could speak at least two of the official South African languages, and some could speak several. Only in two congregations did the ministers not know an indigenous language.[90]

Nevertheless, learning other languages was regarded as a difficult task among the congregations with predominantly 'White' and so-called 'Coloured' church council members. 'Black' people were more or less required to learn English.

---

90 The ministers at St Thomas' used English only, and had to have an interpreter for the service in an indigenous language. The Lutheran Church in Bellville was multilingual in the sense of using German, Afrikaans and English, which the minister spoke, but it was not multilingual in the sense of accommodating an indigenous language. Athlone Methodist Church was an exclusively English-speaking congregation, but was situated in an area where people spoke English or Afrikaans as their first language. The minister spoke English and isiXhosa, but the congregation itself did not use an indigenous language.

The need to learn other languages exposed an unequal hierarchy among the languages, and their status in the congregations and churches was becoming an ecclesiological structuring factor.

Societies that use several languages often develop so that a particular language becomes the lingua franca. Afrikaans and English were previously the official languages, but Afrikaans has lost most of its privileged status and is no longer compulsory in schools. English has become the only lingua franca in the democratic South Africa, with both advantages and disadvantages. A lingua franca often becomes an official language, and that results in unequal power relations, cultural dominance, and exclusion.[91]

Most of South Africa's official languages are visible in the media – mainly on TV, on news and radio channels, and in state institutions such as Parliament; but several languages are not used in other sectors of public life. Socio-political changes have led to indigenous languages being displaced by English – in public life, at least. Although English has a colonial history, it is also attached to economic power, with the accompanying prestige and status. Especially among 'Black' urban communities there is a language shift in order to achieve upwards social mobility – which, of course, includes religious language. Church leaders indicated that changing to English was a strategic move for some people. Transformation is class-related, and also affects communication between generations. Similar patterns have been evident in other communities when language has been related to, for example, status, attitudes, socio-economic values, and education. Historical examples of language shifts can be found in the Indian and Khoisan communities in South Africa, who abandoned their languages in favour of a dominant language. It is notable that the language shift has not come about suddenly, but has gradually been established by bilingualism.[92] It is important to notice that, even if English has become a uniting factor, it is still attached to ethnicity and class. Pronunciation, vocabulary, and grammar differ according to ethnic background, even if education is sometimes able to erase boundaries.[93]

It was clear that English was increasing in importance in the studied congregations and churches. They used English almost exclusively as their primary language at national level, and all the congregations used English in their official documents such as information leaflets, policies, and websites. It is crucial that that information should be available to as many people as possible, and there is

---

91 Meierkord, Christiane, 2007, pp. 212–214.
92 Kamwangamalu, Nkonko M., 2006, pp. 86–96, 93; Kamwangamalu, Nkonko M., 2003, pp. 226–227.
93 Meierkord, Christiane, 2012, pp. 120–127; Steyn, Melissa, 2001, pp. ix–x.

a need for a common language. Translating key documents into all the official languages would be very expensive. The use of English indicates that there is an unequal power relationship when English is seen as the language for communication in the society and becomes normative.

However, there is a paradox about having English as the dominant language. English has become superior, which is not consistent with the Church's catholicity; but at the same time it has also facilitated communication between people of diverse ethnicities. Churches need a common language; but at the same time the notion of catholicity stresses that no language should dominate. The equation is impossible to resolve, and it reveals unequal power relations between languages. If English continues to be promoted at the expense of other languages, the Churches' catholicity will be damaged, and the churches will lose parts of their diverse expressions.

An ecumenical catholicity challenges congregations and churches – and society as a whole – over several different aspects of language use. Churches and congregations are encouraged to develop pedagogies, techniques, and so on to monitor the use of different languages in congregations and churches.

This chapter has exposed the complexity of having diverse languages in the society and churches of South Africa. The next chapter will explore the congregations' relationships and contacts with other local congregations across language and geographic boundaries.

Chapter Ten: Congregations' Relationships with Other Congregations and Churches

The previous chapters have investigated how local Christian communities that congregate in one place are ethnically composed, how they conduct their services, and what languages they use. Geographic and linguistic diversity in particular have created boundaries between congregations. This chapter will investigate whether there are paths of catholicity that unite congregations that are predominantly of one ethnicity with others beyond their own denomination. The chapter will be based on interviews with church councils and on various congregational publications.

There are several definitions of the term 'local church' in the ecumenical documents. As explained in Chapter Three, 'local' can refer to a congregation of believers gathered in one place, a community gathered around a bishop or equivalent person, a geographic area, or a regional church structure. Chapter Eight revealed that the congregations being studied emphasised that 'local' related first and foremost to those who congregated in one place. Furthermore, it is important to investigate whether 'local' could also imply that the Christian community transcends the boundaries between congregations of different dominating ethnicities.

Firstly, I will investigate whether the case study congregations use the term 'local' as referring to a community beyond the congregated people in one place. Secondly, I will focus on whether the congregations have any contacts or relationships with congregations that belong predominantly to another ethnic group.

St Peter Claver in Pimville – Roman Catholic Church

St Peter Claver belongs to the Soweto district in the Roman Catholic Archdiocese of Johannesburg. The church council said that they had many connections with Roman Catholic congregations in Soweto and throughout the whole diocese through various forms of exchange and meetings. Unity with the bishop was central; and being acquainted with the ways in which the liturgy was done in other congregations, as described earlier, built a sense of unity with other members of the Roman Catholic Church.[1]

---

1   Church Council Interview Protocol 2011-02-27.

Unity with the bishop was seen as very important. Their understanding of the bishop's position can be compared with the catholicity of the Church, which states that the function of the bishop or equivalent person is to safeguard the unity of the body of Christ. The bishop's functions involve unity among local communities, as well as relations with the universal Church. The emphasis on the bishop's position in the church reveals that 'local' refers to both the diocese and the congregation. Their emphasis on the bishop means that St Peter Claver in Pimville is connected with other congregations in the Archdiocese of Johannesburg through the bishop. The unity with the church hierarchy granted unity among the members, irrespective of the ethnic or social background or geographic location of other local congregational communities.[2]

St Peter Claver occasionally invited members of other denominations, and they also visited other denominations' churches, especially when they had functions or events. These kinds of meetings happened frequently, according to the church council.[3] The mutual relationship was stressed, for example, when a visiting member of another denomination came to participate in the inauguration of new members of a guild or a league. The church council said that all Christians were united, and all were citizens of the Kingdom of God, even though they did not belong to the same denominations.[4]

The communion of Christians in a geographic area such as Pimville was emphasised. There were several congregations in the same area; together they were the local Christian community, even though they belonged to diverse denominations. There were, however, visible boundaries within the Christian community. Visitors from other denominations, for example, could not receive the eucharist in their communion. The church council explained that only Roman Catholics were allowed to receive the eucharist in their church. They explained that the body of Christ was a sign of oneness associated with the eucharist for the people in the congregation. People could become members of their community if they went through a course, and after a special service they could be admitted into the Roman Catholic Church.[5]

However, one of the council's members stressed: "In the spirit everybody is one".[6] This response was a sign that, even if a person was not part of the Roman Catholic Church, they were still joined in some kind of mutual unity. The church

---

2   Observation Protocol 2011-02-27.
3   Church Council Interview Protocol 2011-02-27; Observation Protocol 2011-02-27.
4   Church Council Interview Protocol 2011-02-27.
5   Observation Protocol 2011-02-27.
6   Church Council Interview Protocol 2011-02-27.

council revealed some ambiguity about this: on the one hand they emphasised that people became members of the Church through baptism, and that they would welcome another Christian from another denomination to participate in their community; but on the other hand, they simultaneously stressed that other Christians were not part of their eucharistic communion.[7] Their responses indicated that there was a geographic Christian community among the congregations in the same area, but that they belonged to diverse denominations between which there were boundaries.

Most contacts and relationships with other congregations and Christian communities were within Pimville and Soweto. The congregation occasionally had individual visitors from other Christian communities of other ethnicities. Furthermore, they had various forms of exchange and meetings within the diocese where people of diverse backgrounds could meet.[8] The diocese became an important platform where people from the same denomination, irrespective of ethnic background, could meet for common functions, services, or activities.

St Thomas' in Linden – Anglican Church of Southern Africa

The congregation is situated in one of the northern suburbs of Johannesburg, It is part of the Anglican Diocese of Johannesburg, and belongs to one of the archdeaconries. Its members came from diverse ethnicities.

The church council declared that they had several contacts with other Anglican congregations. In the St Thomas' parish profile, they stated that they wanted to be actively involved in the diocese, archdeaconry, and community.[9] Furthermore, individual members or groups in the congregation were engaged in committees, projects, and meetings in the diocese, as well as in the Anglican Province, and had contact with Anglicans in other countries.[10] One example of interactions with other Anglican congregations was through music and worship. One council member said:

> We have concerts with some churches together, so on the music side like Sophiatown we had concerts together. Our closest Anglican church which is Christ the King in

---

7 Church Council Interview Protocol 2011-02-27.
8 Church Council Interview Protocol 2011-02-27.
9 St Thomas' Anglican Church Linden, Parish Profile, 2011, p. 2, Church Publication.
10 Church Council Interview Protocol 2011-03-06.

Sophiatown, I think it is the closest, so we had a concert with them and then we came here and they came here [...]¹¹

Sophiatown is south of Linden, and is one of the 'Black' Anglican churches closest to the affluent northern suburbs of Johannesburg. The collaboration between the two congregations, as explained by the council, was especially interesting, because they belonged to different archdeaconries, and the socio-economic contexts of Sophiatown and Linden were very different, not least because the residents in these two areas are very different ethnically.

Another church council member described an experience of being exposed to interactions with other Anglican congregations in Johannesburg in these terms:

> I think that we are having different experiences of that. Once again that goes back to the prayer group that I am involved in, and one of the people in that prayer group is permanently now involved in a congregation in Soweto, so I go to that parish quite often, and that has opened different doors for me. I think a number of people in this parish have been to Holy Cross, and that has opened doors and given us different words for community in Anglicanism. And I think that would be nice if we would do that a little bit more often, but that doesn't happen.¹²

The council member's explanation specified that interaction with people in another area of Johannesburg was not an obvious practice. There were no natural connections just from living in the same city. Involvement in a congregation, and being part of a congregation in the diocese, presented opportunities for interaction between people of diverse ethnic backgrounds. The council member's example showed that the church created opportunities for people of different ethnicities living in other parts of Johannesburg to meet.

Both experiences, as exemplified by the music exchange and the visits to a twin congregation, show the importance of the church organisation. St Thomas' had links with other congregations that were predominantly another ethnicity.

---

11 Church Council Interview Protocol 2011-03-06. Sophiatown is an area where many 'Black', 'Coloured' and 'Indian or Asian' people lived before and during apartheid. They were forcibly removed in 1955, the area's name was changed to Triomf ('Triumph' or 'Victory'), and it became a suburb for poor 'White' Afrikaners. Triomf was renamed Sophiatown after democratisation. The well-known Anglican priest and anti-apartheid activist, Trevor Huddleston, worked at Christ the King, Sophiatown, and was part of the resistance to the forced removal of people from Sophiatown.

12 Church Council Interview Protocol 2011-03-06. Holy Cross Anglican congregation is situated at 7354 Sisulu Street, Orlando West, Soweto. The Community of the Resurrection started the congregation, and one of its first ministers was Trevor Huddleston. Smit, Johannes A., 1999, p. 385.

The church council did not explicitly name the bishop as a uniting factor for the congregations, but the diocese clearly saw that its task was to unite the people living in the same city. The Anglican Communion, furthermore, made contacts with churches in other countries possible. 'Local' meant not only the congregation, but also a community gathered in a diocese where the bishop was the leader.

The diocese helped to prevent individual communities becoming isolated or avoiding people of other backgrounds; this was also stressed by the minister of the congregation. He stated:

> [...] Obviously the local church needs to support and meet people's needs, be a place of rest in the local community. I am also involved in work at the diocesan level. There's a bigger picture of 'church' that I have been involved in, and certainly as a diocese what we are trying to do is to grapple with 'church' in a broad sense as a model for what the wider society should look like. So at that level we are trying to be quite intentional about doing reconciliation. Just because of our history we traditionally tend to have black parishes, coloured parishes and white parishes and so on. It is because of geography, people were divided, but we realised that we are the Anglican Church in a broader sense, representing the entire spectrum of people in the country from Oppenheimer mining magnates down to informal shack, township members and we need to find ways of bringing across that spectrum of people together. So we have been looking at ways of linking parishes, to reshuffle deaconries into larger groups and trying to make bridges between different types of communities.[13]

The diocese became important, especially as a mediator of linked communities to each other, and making connections between groups of people from different backgrounds. The church could assist with greater interaction between ethnically diverse communities, even when people did not live close to each other. The church's organisation facilitated increased interaction.

The minister stressed, however, that congregations sometimes found it difficult to catch a broader view of the church than simply being a congregation. He explained:

> I suspect that clergy are aware of the diocesan bishop in terms of embodying history because we are all part of structure. My suspicion is, most Anglicans have a very congregational mind-set. If the archbishop says something, that's important, of course, we want to get behind him when he speaks for us. But in the office, I don't think that people think in those terms of a body in Anglicanism. That is my suspicion.[14]

That comment stressed that the connection with the diocese and a wider Anglican fellowship was not always obvious for congregation members. There was, however,

---

13 Church Council Interview Protocol 2011-03-06.
14 Church Council Interview Protocol 2011-03-06.

a feeling of belonging regarding the episcopacy, although people's sense of belonging to an Anglican communion in Southern Africa could be questioned.

The church council's image of the bishop was much influenced by the role that former Archbishop Desmond Tutu had played during his time in office. One church council member said:

> [...] If you think about the Anglican Church during apartheid years ... you know, the Anglican Church was together trying to find one thing as a body and the archbishop was the spokesperson, he saw what everybody was feeling, so for me that was a sign of unity and the one person that could express what we all felt. I think that is vital. And for the Methodists that was the head of the Methodist Church who was Peter Storey at that time, and he could express what we could not express ... Now, I think it would be the same. I don't think they are as vocal, and I think they could be more vocal, but I certainly as much regard our present archbishop who we have now. I think the archbishop of South Africa is wonderful.[15]

The archbishop, along with other church leaders, became representatives and a voice for the churches in South Africa. They had a prominent role to play, and the image of a church leader's position was shaped by the time of the struggle. The church leaders' role of speaking for the members was also something that they wanted to see happen today, and more often. The bishop became a symbol of the united Anglican members' common voice. The diocese and the bishop's voice were not absent from St Thomas'. The congregation was involved in several projects together with the diocese, and there was information about the diocese in, for example, the parish magazine. Examples included announcements from and activities in the diocese, and the bishop's letters were published in the magazine for the special information of members.[16]

Athlone Methodist Church – Methodist Church of Southern Africa

The congregation is situated in one of the former so-called 'Coloured' areas, and belongs to the Dumisani circuit within the Methodist Church. The congregation did not have much to do with other congregations in the circuit or in the district. They met occasionally, not frequently. The church council stated that they would go to other congregations in the circuit if there were special events, and

---

15 Church Council Interview Protocol 2011-03-06.
16 Church Council Interview Protocol 2011-03-06. For diocesan information see, for example: The St Thomas' Magazine January & February 2011, 2011, p. 9, Church Publication. For a bishop's letter, see for example: The St Thomas' Magazine January/February 2010, 2010, p. 11, Church Publication.

they would also invite others to come to their church. A church council member said: "We sometimes have a service in a church and we are invited to that other congregation".[17] These kinds of gathering did not happen frequently. A member stated: "Not so often",[18] and another member added: "Occasional".[19] The ministers in the circuit, in contrast, had regular twice-monthly ministerial staff meetings for fellowship and joint planning.[20]

The Methodist Church in Southern Africa has districts with a bishop, and each district is divided into several circuits. The congregation did not have much contact with the other congregations in the districts or circuit, but they met for special occasions, activities, or services. The geographic demarcation of circuits in the Methodist church was changed after democratisation, as described in Chapter Seven. The new demarcations required the Athlone Methodist Church to meet with congregations of other ethnicities.

The district of the Cape of Good Hope had a bishop, and the council was asked whether they had contact with him. One member of the council replied: "For certain services he would come".[21] They did not have much contact besides special occasions, but the ministers had more contact with the bishop. One member stated: "The ministers have more contact with him. Only during special services we would meet".[22] He would come if they invited him; and it was important to have a bishop as leader. If there were complaints about a minister they would go to the bishop, and he would come and sort out the problems.[23]

The district and the bishop's function was not emphasised much by the church council, but the denominational organisation made the congregation have at least some kind of relationship with other congregations. The ministers also had a natural forum in which they met to deal with common matters across ethnic diversities. The connection with the bishop and the district was not as clear as in the Roman Catholic and Anglican churches, but the organisational structure uniting the church and its members was visible. The members might not have much of a relationship with the bishop, but the ministry of safeguarding the unity of the church as part of catholicity was obvious.

---

17 Church Council Interview Protocol 2011-03-20.
18 Church Council Interview Protocol 2011-03-20.
19 Church Council Interview Protocol 2011-03-20.
20 Church Council Interview Protocol 2011-03-20; Athlone Methodist Church, Athlone Society Profile, c.a. 2008, p. 1, Church Publication.
21 Church Council Interview Protocol 2011-03-20.
22 Church Council Interview Protocol 2011-03-20.
23 Church Council Interview Protocol 2011-03-20.

Some of the youth, women, and men in the congregation were part of one of the Methodist church's official organisations that had meetings with other members of the Methodist Church. One woman in the council said: "The women. There is an organisation that meets on a regular basis, once a year".[24] The youth's, women's, and men's organisations gathered in the district, and they also sent representatives to national meetings.[25] The district, and even the national organisation of the church, became an important platform where people in the church would meet, irrespective of ethnic background.

The congregation sometimes had visitors, occasionally from other countries. One council member explained: "Members bring them, and today we had a Jewish lady and another lady".[26] Visitors came mainly through a member's invitation when they brought them to church, but the council confirmed that they had contact with other churches in the area.[27] One member explained: "Especially during Easter time we have churches meeting together".[28] Members of diverse congregations from various denominations in the area would come together for a common service during the Easter celebration. Furthermore, the women met once a year for the Women's World Day of Prayer; and there was a ministers' forum where church leaders in Athlone met.[29]

Athlone Methodist Church's interactions with congregations in the area showed that there was a community of Christians in the same geographic area that transcended denominational borders. They met during special services and also for prayer meetings, when they manifested the local Christian community in one place as part of the catholicity of the Church, as described in the analytical tool.

Lutheran Church in Bellville – Evangelical Lutheran Church in Southern Africa – Cape Church

The congregation is part of ELCSA-Cape, to which most of the congregations in the Western Cape Province belong. Their bishop and the church's office are located in the Cape Town area. The Lutheran Church in Bellville is situated in

---

24 Church Council Interview Protocol 2011-03-20.
25 The Laws and Discipline of the Methodist Church of Southern Africa, 2007, p. 145.
26 Church Council Interview Protocol 2011-03-20.
27 Church Council Interview Protocol 2011-03-20. There are several different churches in Athlone: The Baptist on Pliny Street, the Anglican on Bamford Avenue, the Lutheran on 8th Avenue, the Roman Catholic on Lawrence Road, and the Seventh-day Adventist on Buckley Road.
28 Church Council Interview Protocol 2011-03-20.
29 Church Council Interview Protocol 2011-03-20.

a suburb that has become more diverse since democratisation, as described in Chapter Seven.

The congregation had contact with other congregations in ELCSA-Cape, but they did not meet regularly apart from official church meetings. The members of the church council in Bellville had different opinions about their relationship with the bishop and the church's central structure. One council member explained their relationship with the bishop by saying: "To me he is very far away".[30] Another member stated: "He is the leader of our church".[31] Most of the council members did not have much contact with the bishop, and he was simply seen as the leader of the church.[32] The minister in the council stated, however:

> He is an extra minister to us. He is the pastor of the pastors, and this office he really maintains. He's got his own congregation, his own congregation of the pastors which here we are very far apart, you know, Western Cape, Eastern Cape and he definitely, he knows exactly what is going on in the congregations, what is happening amongst the pastors [...].[33]

The minister in the congregation recognised that the bishop ministered to the ministers in the church and that he was leading the church – despite the fact that the congregations were scattered around the province and were also in other, more distant, provinces. The bishop at least had contact with the ministers and knew what was happening in the congregations. Not all church council members had the same opinion about the bishop, but they recognised that the bishop had occasional gatherings and that he sometimes came to preach when they had special services.[34] The minister in the council recognised that the bishop had been important when their congregation had had a crisis. He said: "For example, we had a mega-crisis in this congregation. He was hands-on. He was here from the first day until the problem was solved [...]".[35] The bishop was a leader of the church and could assist in the event of difficulty.

The function of the bishop was mostly centred on being a leader. The church also had a limited organisation because of the small size of the church, and there were not many meetings for members besides the annual synod of the church. The bishop, together with the synod, was important for the church, even though

---

30 Church Council Interview Protocol 2011-03-15.
31 Church Council Interview Protocol 2011-03-15.
32 Church Council Interview Protocol 2011-03-15.
33 Church Council Interview Protocol 2011-03-15.
34 Church Council Interview Protocol 2011-03-15.
35 Church Council Interview Protocol 2011-03-15.

there was a tendency to have a more congregational approach to the church. The bishop was important for safeguarding the unity of the church, and would even personally assist when there were disagreements.[36]

The congregation did not have much of a relationship with congregations from other denominations in Bellville.[37] The church council was asked whether they had any ecumenical contacts with other churches in the area. One member of the council responded: "Very little. They have soup day once a year ... I think it is the Anglican Church and they invite the people who come on a Thursday, and then the women's prayer day we come together, but it is very little".[38] Ecumenical activity among the congregations from the various denominations was weak, apart from the above-mentioned soup day and the Women's World Day of Prayer. They had a pastors' fraternal, but the minister in the council stressed:

> The pastors' fraternal worked quite well until about three years ago and also fell apart. We still have contact by e-mail if something happens. ... What happened here is that the Dutch Reformed Church is very strong here, and they actually meet on a regular basis. So there are Dutch Reformed meetings.[39]

The Dutch Reformed Church's congregations were dominant in the area, which made ecumenical relationships less important. The local Christian congregations from the diverse denominations in Bellville did not have many contacts because of this dominant congregation in the area.

The divided Lutheran community in South Africa, with their different major ethnic groups, did not have many interactions after democratisation. The church council was approached about whether they had any contact with ELCSA congregations. A council member replied: "We had in the past, but unfortunately since '94 it's sort of flattened out".[40] The answer stressed that they had more contacts with ELCSA before democratisation than since. Another member answered similarly, saying: "Ironically it was more during the apartheid years when their

---

36   Church Council Interview Protocol 2011-03-15.
37   There are several different churches in the area, for example: Uitsig Gemeente, NGK, on Mountainview Road; Bellville Baptist Church on Fifth Avenue; The Full Gospel Church of God, Bellville on Mable Street; Bellville Methodist Church on Krige Street, Boston; Church of the Transfiguration, Anglican, on the corner of Durban & Sydney Streets; and Our Lady of Fatima, Roman Catholic Church, on the corner of Rhos and Welgemeend Streets.
38   Church Council Interview Protocol 2011-03-15.
39   Church Council Interview Protocol 2011-03-15.
40   Church Council Interview Protocol 2011-03-15.

ministers came and gave a sermon here and so on".[41] This statement is interesting in stating that contacts with ELCSA were more frequent before democratisation. More contact would have been expected when the country had achieved democracy and the society had abolished apartheid laws. The minister in the church council explained:

> This is the most amazing that we can think. The [year] 1994 actually divided the churches again because it was no longer politically, anything to look to the other churches. Virtually the racial divide was after '94. So far so that we actually four years ago we had an annual combined service. ... The ELCSA-Cape church as long as it had the chairmanship we called for these meetings. Since the ELCSA has got the chairmanship nothing happens in spite of us protesting. [...].[42]

The statement questioned the commitment that the members in the divided Lutheran community had to increased interaction across the ethnic divides. The above statement identified one reason for the reduced contact; but the divided church organisation did not facilitate interaction among peoples of diverse ethnicities as part of the Church's catholicity as understood in the analytical tool.

City Harvest Ministries in Ntuzuma – Apostolic Faith Mission of South Africa

City Harvest Ministries is located in Ntuzuma, which was dominated by one ethnicity. The congregation is part of the Durban Region Network of AFM, which is the regional level of the church. Links with the church's regional structure were very loose. The minister in the congregation explained the regional church organisational structure in Durban in these terms: "It is the pastors that meet from now and then, and then in the regional committee usually ... but I think they are there as a structure to collect the tithes from the local assemblies through to the national office".[43] Engagement with the church's regional organisation appeared not to be seen as very important. The regional organisation could be seen as a network, but it did not assist the congregations with greater interactions between them or across ethnic borders.

The central and local levels are the most important ones in the church. The limited contacts at regional level are due to the AFM's organisation, which allows the assemblies or congregations considerable independence. The local level is the most important; the central level provides for the needs for the whole church.

---

41 Church Council Interview Protocol 2011-03-15.
42 Church Council Interview Protocol 2011-03-15.
43 Church Council Interview Protocol 2011-03-27.

The regional structure is, for that reason, not as developed as those of many other main line churches. The church has no bishops, but it has a National Leadership Forum that can be regarded as the leadership level of the church where everybody, irrespective of ethnicity, is united. The Leadership Forum can be viewed as safeguarding the unity of the church, as described in the analytical tool for the Church's catholicity.

However, City Harvest Ministries had several contacts with other congregations, despite the weak regional organisation of the AFM. As described earlier, the congregation started as a satellite church of the Maranatha Ministries in the township of KwaMashu. The minister at City Harvest Ministries, furthermore, had a mentor at the El Shaddai Assembly in Durban. The congregation held several conferences and outreach activities together with other congregations, and there was also a pulpit exchange when visitors came to preach at City Harvest Ministries in Ntuzuma. They were part of an interdenominational network, and they had speakers from, for example, New Glory Dominion Centre International Church, Life Abundant Church, and Life Renewal Centre in Durban. Conferences that were organised together with other congregations even had speakers invited from other African countries. Such networks strengthened the diverse congregations belonging to the same Christian community.[44]

The congregation's relationship with many other congregations showed that a strong regional structure was not necessary in order to foster such contacts and relationships. Congregations could be connected locally, and even internationally, with many other congregations through other forms of networks. A strong hierarchical organisation is not needed to develop relationships with a variety of congregations. The congregation's far-reaching interaction with other congregations could also be recognised as an example of the Church's catholicity, as described in the analytical tool. The networks were chosen, however, and did not necessarily imply that the congregation had relationships with congregations of predominantly another ethnicity. Networks can be interrogated by the analytical tool. Networks are incidental meetings that might result in pulpit exchanges, joint conferences, and so on. The relationships are fluid, and a congregation or a church can easily leave a network when there is conflict or when one partner no longer benefits from it. By contrast, the ecumenical documents emphasise that the body of Christ is much more than just a network.

---

44 City Harvest Ministries, The life of City Harvest Ministries, 2013, Website; Apostolic Faith Mission of SA City Harvest Family, 2008, p. 1, Church Publication.

There were other congregations in Ntuzuma with which City Harvest Ministries had limited contact. One of the church council members explained: "We only know them by their pastors. There is one, I think it is a charismatic one, Ethiopian Church, what else ... the Shembe. Shembe is one of the African Traditional Churches".[45] Another council member added:

> Shembe are not mostly Christian. ... They belong to African Traditional so they are a mixture of whatever. We don't have Muslims ... we don't have much of them but we have another social group which is called the Rastafarians. I'm serious, I have noticed them. It is a social group [...].[46]

The church council mentioned the Nazareth Baptist church, the Ethiopian church, and the Rastafarians. They did not have much contact with them because they were not regarded as having the same religious creed as their church.[47] There were also other mainline churches in Ntuzuma that were not mentioned by the church council. They were not situated close to the church tent of the City Harvest Ministries.[48]

A local Christian community of diverse congregations in one place was less evident. The council recognised, though, that there was a Christian community where Christians were united. One church council member explained the image of the body of Christ:

> We are the body of Christ, which means we support each other, we are part of one another. That is how we understand. If we are the Christians, you are my brother, you are my sister. Every difficult is my difficulties. Every joy that you have is my joy. Combine every, our happiness, our difficulties together. There's one body. ... Only the Christians belong to the, those who accept the Lord and are saying that they believe in the Lord and in the Spirit and the Son, those who are Christians [...].[49]

This statement declared that there was a community among those who believed in the triune God. The membership of their church was, however, a different

---

45 Church Council Interview Protocol 2011-03-27.
46 Church Council Interview Protocol 2011-03-27.
47 'Shembe' is the name given to followers of Isaiah Mloyiswa Mdliwamafa Shembe. The official name of the church is Nazareth Baptist Church or *iBandla amaNazaretha*, and it is regarded as an AIC in South Africa. The Ethiopian church is a church movement originating from the Anglican and Methodist churches, constituted by a group of people who rejected 'White' control and supremacy in the churches. The name 'Ethiopian' is used in a wider sense to include a church originating in Africa.
48 For example: St Saviours Anglican Church, Ntuzuma, Society Methodist Church, and KwaKristo Umsindisi Catholic Congregation.
49 Church Council Interview Protocol 2011-03-27.

community. Members were required to be born again and to have received believer's baptism, according to the church's constitution.⁵⁰

St Michael's Evangelical Lutheran Church – Evangelical Lutheran Church in Southern Africa

The congregation is situated in the city centre of Durban. It had convenient transportation and attracted many young adults and students. Diverse ethnicities were represented in the congregation because of a previous merger of three diverse worshipping groups. St Michael's and Durban Central Parish are part of the South Eastern Diocese of ELCSA, and the parish had frequent contacts with other parishes within the same circuit and diocese. Furthermore, many people came to worship who belonged to other ELCSA congregations. The congregation tried to get people to become members, but anyone was welcome and could be part of their congregation and community.⁵¹

The dean was the leader of the circuit, and the bishop was the leader of the diocese, according to the church council. People in St Michael's regularly met other Lutheran members in the circuit for Sunday school, youth, partnership committee meetings, league meetings, rallies, retreats, ministers' conventions, etc. There were also many contacts within the diocese, such as ministers' meetings, various committees, and meetings of leagues and organisations. Much of the bishop's work within the parishes was to visit them and to attend circuit ministers' meetings. The church's local and regional organisational structures seemed to be essential for greater interactions between parishes, congregations, and individuals. Both the dean and the bishop, with the diocese and the circuit, were named in this regard, and were seen as important for providing a platform where people could meet.⁵²

The role of the bishop, the church council explained, was as the leader of the diocese, but also as a kind of 'father figure' in the church. Several church council members said that the bishop was the spiritual leader of the church; and one council member took this further, saying: "He is a spiritual leader, father figure for the congregation. In fact, that he will be coming, the reaction to that is that he is the leader, spiritual leader for the congregation for spiritual growth".⁵³ The bishop, as leader of the diocese, could be regarded as a uniting factor for the congregations

---

50 City Harvest Ministries Constitution, 2011, p. 3, Church Publication.
51 Church Council Interview Protocol 2011-04-03.
52 ELCSA–SED 2010 Year Plan, 2010, Church Publication; ELCSA–SED Durban Circuit 2011 Year Plan, 2011, Church Publication.
53 Church Council Interview Protocol 2011-04-03.

in the diocese – again reflecting an aspect of the Church's catholicity, in terms of the analytical tool.

Nevertheless, contacts between the bishop and the congregation were not very strong. One council member said: "We hardly ever get to see him, except in diocesan meetings, because he is leading the diocese, not the parishes. [...]".[54] The bishop was far away from the congregation. He was understood to be a leader for the diocese, not for the parishes or congregations. They were not in direct contact with the bishop, but it was a big event when he came to visit.

Congregations, parishes, circuits, and the diocese were linked together, and there were several functions when the people of the diocese met. The different leagues and organisations had links to the diocese, and they met several times a year. The relationship between the English-speaking group in the congregation and the diocese was weaker because they organised their activities without being part of leagues.[55]

Contacts with congregations belonging to other denominations in the local area in Durban were made through the Diakonia Council of Churches, to which the congregation belonged. One church council member explained: "Diakonia Council of Churches where we also are participants in what they offer, workshops, seminars, meetings, especially related to social issues and like what we did in the past, also preparing for elections because most of the majority had never voted, and voter education".[56] The congregation cooperated with congregations from other denominations in the Diakonia Council of Churches, especially over societal issues. This cooperation was enhanced every second year when they focused on an issue during a special 'social justice season'. A council member explained:

> I think that one has to distinguish between congregation members, for whom it is quite new, and pastors or certain members. I think that in the congregation itself, one point is the social justice season for instance, which cause we have been involved in, which happens every two years in Durban, where bible studies are developed; are having many churches in Durban from the whole ecumenical spectrum. I think a second point is the ecumenical council which on Good Friday, early morning, are having ecumenical services in which we [are] partners ... I'm member of the inner city ministry network where we meet as pastors from different churches to exchange ideas. [...][57]

The interactions with other Christian communities differed, depending whether meetings were among church workers or congregation members. The ministers

---

54 Church Council Interview Protocol 2011-04-03.
55 Church Council Interview Protocol 2011-04-03.
56 Church Council Interview Protocol 2011-04-03.
57 Church Council Interview Protocol 2011-04-03.

in the various churches in Durban met frequently on matters of common concern, while congregational members did not have the same contact with other churches' members. Ministers met during workshops, seminars, and courses, and congregational members particularly met for special services. There was, for example, a tradition that all churches in Durban had an ecumenical early morning service on Good Friday.

Other meetings with other Christians in one place included funerals. One church council member explained:

> Yes, I would say one part, really, where we do see that is with funerals. There you would not really see boundaries between denominations. Because everybody who wants to show their respect or console, they will be there. Seeing for instance the Women's League for the different churches. All of them are together, and one very unifying factor is the hymns, especially the chorus which everybody knows, irrespectively which church you belong, and for me that is always a strong sign.[58]

Thus a local Christian community transcending denominational borders became visible, for example, at funerals. People were united as a Christian communion, but these gatherings were not necessarily ethnically mixed. Knowing the same hymns and choruses also made the people of different denominational backgrounds part of the same practice. The hymns and chorus that everybody knew, independent of denomination, became a unifying factor for those who knew the same language. Church practices went beyond denominational borders – but not necessarily beyond ethnic borders.

The parish's minister-in-charge came from Germany, which broadened the contact with other Christian communities in the world. A person coming from a partner church in another country to work among them became a sign that the Christian community extended beyond national and even ethnic borders. The minister from Germany also helped the congregation to develop partnerships with other churches globally. This was explained by a council member: "Also on a practical level, yes, we have a partnership with a congregation near Cologne, and one of the ministers, a lady, she was here for a week, last week".[59] The congregation had a partnership with a congregation in Melle, Germany, named Evangelisch Lutherische St Martini-Kirchengemeinde Buer. They met occasionally by visiting each other, and the congregations gave each other support in various ways. A council member explained:

---

58 Church Council Interview Protocol 2011-04-03.
59 Church Council Interview Protocol 2011-04-03.

We are also having a trip of six members of our parish. Three of them are from St Michael's who are going to Germany in the end of May for a trip. It is the first time that they finance their own trip, and the partners in Germany are taking care of the time when they are there [...].[60]

The visitation was another way to strengthen the partnership, and it was important that the people in South Africa were financing their own flights to Germany. The partnership became more equal when there was no need for financial assistance from the churches in Europe. The people in the congregation in Melle took care of the visitors from South Africa, and when the people from Germany came as visitors to South Africa, they were hosted by their partner congregation in South Africa.

Another sign of international Christian community was in the person of three volunteers who came to work with the organisation, Lutherans United in Action (LUA). Their presence indicated that social justice issues in South Africa were important to the wider international community. It is noteworthy that the same opportunity for South Africans to be part of social justice issues abroad was not established.[61]

The congregation had limited contact with ELCSA N-T congregations in Durban, but they did engage in common social outreach programmes with some of them. Furthermore, another form of cooperation had been established through LUA. They had, for example, services with ELCSA N-T congregations twice a year, and combined Lenten services. One church council member explained: "We also combine for the weekly Lenten services, it is combined, and then there are also other collaborations on the social level, I think LUA, Lutherans United in Action [...]".[62] Services were held together with ELCSA N-T congregations every midweek evening during Lent, and they also had other kinds of services, devotions, and workshops during the year. The goal was to work towards church unity between ELCSA and ELCSA N-T, which, according to the church council, was supported at grassroots level.[63]

The division between the Lutheran churches in South Africa was described by the church council as problematic, but they said that there had recently been remarkable changes. A minister on the council described the changes through the example of one of the ELCSA N-T congregations:

---

60 Church Council Interview Protocol 2011-04-03.
61 Lüdemann, Joe, 2012, p. 6, Church Publication.
62 Church Council Interview Protocol 2011-04-03.
63 Lüdemann, Joe, 2012, p. 4, Church Publication.

[…] about the change in ELCSA itself maybe it couldn't more dramatically be seen in New Germany Lutheran church, a NT congregation, which has probably 70 per cent members with Zulu as mother tongue, and it used to be a central white congregation, and that has happened in the past 10–15 years or so. So I think the doorsteps are getting lower, and it is getting easier to start to try some successful ways of meeting. As pastors we are also really trying to drive this process forward, but at the moment we are not seeing much happening on highest administrative level of the two churches. So we say, we as pastors should on grassroots level drive this process forward […].[64]

New Germany is a suburb in an area situated inland from Durban, and is part of eThekwini municipality. It was an area reserved for the 'White' population during apartheid, but it became a mixed area after democratisation. New Germany was established by German immigrants who came to Natal in 1847, and a congregation was started with the support of German missionaries. It is the oldest among the congregations in ELCSA N-T, and has gone through major transitions. The congregation was originally only German-speaking, but it changed to become both German and English because of inter-marriage. According to the latest census, almost half of the population in New Germany was 'Black African', and about 33 per cent was 'White'. The congregation had experienced a decline in attendance at German-language services and an increase at English-language services. The latest census estimated that about half of the population had English as their first language, while about 30 per cent had IsiZulu as their first language. A similar trend was visible in the two ELCSA N-T congregations in central Durban – Lutherkirche and St Paul's – which had also received members from various backgrounds and had become multi-lingual. The shift in many ELCSA N-T congregations to having many 'Black African' members raised hopes for unification between ELCSA and ELCSA N-T. The barrier was lowering because of the greater ethnic mix, and it was going to be easier to try some successful ways of meeting.[65]

A more diverse ethnic situation, together with shared workshops and collaboration on social issues, had increased interactions between the two Lutheran churches. They did not have the same bishop or organisational structures, but there were other networks that brought them together. The networks were, nevertheless, chosen on the basis of personal relationships, and could easily end if one of the congregations withdrew its participation.

---

64 Church Council Interview Protocol 2011-04-03.
65 Census 2011, New Germany, Statistic South Africa; New German Lutheran Church, 2011, Church Publication; Overview of the Durban Parish, n.d., Church Publication.

Conclusions

All the congregations indicated that 'local' referred to a congregation of believers gathered in one place. They also showed by their practices that the 'local' Christian community was the Christian community in one geographic area, but was also a regional church structure.

All the congregations showed that a regional structure around a bishop or equivalent person within their own denomination was important for relationships with other local congregations. The links with the churches' regional structure were more or less visible, and the relationship with the bishop or equivalent person differed, depending on denomination. Ethnic boundaries could be transcended through the regional churches' organisational structures within, for example, a diocese, district, circuit, or deanery. The catholicity of the Church, in terms of the analytical tool, did not explicitly identify the churches' organisational structure as important, but it was the function of the bishop, an equivalent person, or the church leaders to safeguard unity in the body of Christ. Unity involved unity among local communities as well as relationships with the universal Church.

St Peter Claver in Pimville met other people and groups for diocesan meetings and services that transcended ethnic boundaries. St Thomas' in Linden had music and choir exchanges, as well as a twin congregation within the diocese that was predominantly of another ethnicity. Athlone Methodist Church did not have many contacts with other congregations apart from a couple of services during the year. The ministers in the circuit, nevertheless, met frequently during the year, and representatives from diverse organisations came together for special meetings at the regional and central level. These gatherings were with people from diverse ethnic backgrounds.

City Harvest Ministries did not have a strongly hierarchical organisational structure, but they were involved in several networks that kept the congregations together. The networks did not necessarily need to transcend ethnic boundaries, and were a loose form of relationship that could more easily be terminated than in other forms of church organisation.

AFM ministers met, nevertheless, at regional level, and representatives from diverse organisations met annually at a central level across ethnic boundaries.

The Lutheran Church in Bellville, part of ELCSA-Cape, did not have many relationships with other congregations, but the bishop was regarded as a leader of the church. They had a common church organisation where people from various congregations met at least during synod meetings. St Michael's, which belongs to ELCSA, regarded the bishop as central, and members met across congregational boundaries at circuit and diocesan level. The Lutheran churches that were historically divided did not facilitate relationships with congregations of a predominantly different ethnicity. St Michael's was, however, part of a local network of ELCSA and ELCSA-NT congregations that facilitated contacts with other congregations across ethnic borders. A simple network was not sufficient, however, to create sustainable ties within the local Lutheran community. The catholicity of the Church, according to the analytical tool, challenges churches of the same confession, but belonging to different organisations, to unite.

Furthermore, the churches' organisations made it possible for local congregations to relate to local congregations in the universal Church. Most of the congregations had occasional visitors from other countries. All of the churches were part of a greater communion of churches, such as the Anglican Communion for Anglican congregations, LUCIA for Lutherans, or international networks for AFM congregations. These organisations or networks made it possible for the local congregation to have contact with other local Christian communities across national and ethnic boundaries. Some congregations even had personal exchange programmes or staff from other countries, thus enhancing the catholicity of the Church. Personal relationships and exchange programmes between congregations in the universal Church should not be underestimated for their role in affirming the Church's catholicity.

All the congregations, more or less, had relationships, common activities, and services with other congregations of another denomination in the area where they were located. These contacts were not necessarily with congregations of another ethnicity. There were, for example, personal or group invitations for special services, ministers' meetings, common annual services, or social projects.

This chapter has explored the meaning of 'local' church. The case study congregations' practices showed that 'local' also meant a community beyond the people congregated in one place. 'Local' also referred to several congregations in one place, such as a city. The churches' organisational structures became important for connecting the congregations. Several congregations had relationships with other congregations of a predominantly different ethnic group. The churches' organisational structures or other networks did not guarantee greater inter-ethnic interaction, but they could facilitate relationships. Churches' organisational structures or other networks could, furthermore, facilitate relationships with the universal church, which is important for the catholicity of the Church. Various kinds of network can facilitate voluntary relationships, but their sustainability is open to question.

The next chapter will investigate congregations' and churches' engagement with, and activities for, people in their communities, in their society, and in their work for poverty eradication. These activities are important in order to eradicate boundaries between ethnic groups, because of the geographic differences created before democratisation.

Chapter Eleven: Congregations' and Churches' Ministries and Work towards Poverty Eradication

Some of the congregations studied for this research had become more ethnically diverse, while other congregations had not changed significantly since democratisation. Changed socio-economic conditions were the main cause for increased ethnic diversity in the congregations. The previous chapter showed that the churches' organisational structures or networks were important to a certain extent in increasing ethnic diversity in parishes of a predominantly different ethnicity.

This chapter will investigate the contribution of congregations and churches to social change. Various forms of sharing can be identified as a way of reducing ethnic barriers in churches and in the wider society. There is one Christian communion, and its members are called to eradicate boundaries so that ethnic diversity can be shared and received in every part of the Church. New economic possibilities in previously underprivileged areas can facilitate increased ethnic diversity. This chapter is based mainly on interviews with church councils and church leaders, and on diverse congregational publications.

Firstly, I will explore activities and ministries that the congregations undertake in their communities and in the wider society. Secondly, I will investigate whether the congregations and churches are engaged in poverty eradication as part of reducing ethnic barriers between people in the Christian community.

11.1 Local Engagement Serving Community and Society

The case congregations celebrated Sunday services every week, but also had several activities, engagements, and ministries in the communities where they were located. The congregations responded to the call to build local community, but also to be sent to serve the wider society – as became apparent in their ministry.

St Peter Claver in Pimville – Roman Catholic Church

St Peter Claver, located in one part of Soweto, was a large congregation with many members. The church services played a prominent role, especially on Sundays, when people came together for two services. The congregation also had several other activities, groups, guilds, and unions on weekdays. There were, for example, the Sacred Heart men and women, and the Catholic Women's and Men's Leagues, each with a large membership. These groups gathered people for services, Bible study and prayer, visitations, and social projects. The congregation had several choirs, drama groups, youth groups, social outreach programmes, a soup kitchen for the needy, home visitations, support groups, etc. Confirmation classes, catechism education, parents' preparation classes for infant baptism, and programmes for marriage were other examples of the main activities that the congregation ran.[1]

Several activities of the congregation could be regarded as training in community development. Participating in societies and diverse groups was training in democracy, and several groups supported individuals in outreach programmes, home visitations, and the soup kitchen. The ministry could be viewed as a sharing of knowledge and of personal needs in the community.

Raising funds was a significant concern, according to the church council. There were plans to extend and renovate the church and to build a house for the priest. They also had plans to start a catechetical centre and to provide better facilities for the soup kitchen. The congregation had a close relationship with the St Peter Claver Primary School, although it was an independent entity administered by the Catholic Schools Office of the Archdioceses of Pretoria and Johannesburg. It was one of seven Roman Catholic schools in Soweto. St Peter Claver Primary admitted children who lived in the area.[2] Roman Catholic schools have a long tradition in South Africa, continuing to operate even after the apartheid government had taken over many schools run by other churches. Education can be regarded as a form of community development, through which pupils are equipped with skills to change society.

St Peter Claver had many relationships with other groups in the society, alongside those with other Roman Catholic congregations and members of other denominations. A church council member said that their ministry was for everybody in the community, and not only for Roman Catholics. Anybody could get assistance and help, because they were all part of the human community. Faith was subordinated, and there were no expectations of drawing new members into the church through their social projects.[3] Their approach to the wider community can be regarded as consistent with the Church's catholicity according to the

---

1   St Peter Claver Parish, Pimville, Soweto, 2011, Website; Observation Protocol 2011-02-27; St Peter Claver, Catholic Church, Pimville, 1928–2008, 80th Anniversary, 2008, pp. 32–34, 40–42, Church Publication.
2   Church Council Interview Protocol 2011-02-27; St Peter Claver, Catholic Church, Pimville, 1928–2008, 80th Anniversary, 2008, p. 31, Church Publication.
3   Church Council Interview Protocol 2011-02-27.

analytical tool. There is a human community; and the church serves the world. The church council's statement that their ministry was for everybody, regardless of faith, indicated that they recognised a community that transcended faiths and convictions.

An indication of the congregation's commitment to the wider society was the different subjects that were highlighted during the prayers, especially in the 'prayers of the faithful' that were part of the liturgy. The church council stressed that they prayed for the church, families, people who were in jail, the community, those who had departed, the sick, etc. The focuses of the prayers came from the community, and they prayed for everything that was important – even for ancestors.[4]

The list of activities identified by the church council could be seen as a demonstration that the congregation had a mission to serve the people who lived in the area around it. They supported education, social groups, home visitation, food for the needy, and various other social projects. The ministry was mainly focused on individuals rather than on broad changes in the society. The projects and activities were not intended to eradicate poverty as part of transforming the community.

St Thomas' in Linden – Anglican Church of Southern Africa

The congregation had many people involved in church services and in different groups and activities. Several lay people supported the congregation by voluntary work – for example, maintenance, administration, finance, various ministries, counselling, communication, and worship services.[5]

A number of groups in the congregation were attached to the church services. The congregation had altar servers, sacristans, sidepersons as a welcoming team, and a team of licenced lay ministers who assisted in the running of the services. They had so-called 'flower ladies' – a group of people who arranged flowers weekly for church services and for special occasions. There was also a special group called 'InVestment' that cared for and developed new vestments.[6]

The congregation also had a team of people who were in charge of the congregation's intercessions. They took special responsibility for praying for those in need of long-term prayer. There was also a prayer chain of people, in addition to the prayer team, who were responsible for praying for people in time of crisis. People who were in need of prayer, or who had asked for special prayers, could also have their names published in the information leaflet each Sunday. A grief

---

4   Church Council Interview Protocol 2011-02-27; Observation Protocol 2011-02-27.
5   St Thomas' Anglican Church Linden, Parish Profile, 2011, pp. 10–14, Church Publication.
6   St Thomas' Anglican Church Linden, Parish Profile, 2011, p. 10, Church Publication.

support group met regularly during the day, and anybody was welcome to join them to deal with personal loss. Pastoral care visits in homes or institutions were regularly carried out by ministers or lay ministers, and four house groups constituted smaller communities within the larger congregation.[7]

The groups and activities attached to the church services were primarily to support and sustain the local Christian community at St Thomas'. The ministry can be seen as a calling to build the local Christian community through equipping them with gifts to serve society.[8]

A notable activity at St Thomas' was the development and high profile of music. A full-time music director was in charge of the congregation's many choirs and music groups, a marimba group, a worship band, etc., which gave music a prominent place in the congregation's life. A full-time employed music director is most unusual in South African churches. The high profile of music reflects the congregation's economic status, but also the importance that music played in the life of St Thomas' church.[9]

The congregation also had Sunday school, St Thomas' Youth Church, GHETTO Jnr, and GHETTO Snr for children of pre-high school age and high school age, in addition to the many choirs and music groups for youth and children. On Mondays they had a coffee shop that was open for a few hours during the day, and a monthly senior citizens' tea with entertainment, provided free of charge. They also had a group that carried out pastoral care visits, several guilds that supported congregational life, and a Wednesday ladies' group that was open even to men, and that made items for sale or as donations.[10]

The various groups were social events that were established to serve the people in the area around the congregation. It was not for members only, but for the whole community. Some of those who attended the groups were not even

---

7   St Thomas' Anglican Church Linden, Parish Profile, 2011, pp. 11–12, Congregation Print; Information sheet for the Sunday, 6th March 2011, 2011, Church Publication.
8   The Third World Conference on Faith and Order declared that the Church was: "being called from the world and sent into the world". The Third World Conference on Faith and Order, 1953, p. 18.
9   St Thomas' Anglican Church Linden, Parish Profile, 2011, p. 4, Congregation Print; Music at St Thomas', Leaflet about music in St Thomas' Anglican Church Linden, Church Publication.
10 St Thomas' Anglican Church Linden, Parish Profile, 2011, pp. 11–12, Congregation Print; Church Council Interview Protocol 2011-03-06; Welcome to St Thomas' Anglican Church, Linden, 2011, p. 2, Congregation Print; Observation Protocol 2011-03-06. GHETTO consists of afternoon activities for children and youth.

members of the congregation.¹¹ The catholicity of the Church emphasises that there are several levels of community, and that there is a wider society beyond the membership of a specific denomination.

The congregation hoped to continue to be a teaching and educational centre. According to the church council, their profile for education and teaching was very important. St Thomas' had, for example, youth and adult confirmation classes, adult formation programmes such as Lenten courses as part of the church year, weekend retreats, marriage preparation courses and support courses for the newly-married, prayer groups, house groups, and a heritage group that regularly wrote articles for the parish magazine. There was also a four-week course of baptismal preparation for parents and godparents, and an admission to communion course preparing young people for the eucharist.¹² The high profile of education revealed the parish's interest in equipping, not just members of the congregation, but also people throughout the diocese with the capacity to develop and deepen knowledge in the Christian community. This ministry extended to serve the whole community in the diocese, but it was still focused on individual members.

A special counselling centre was developed at St Thomas' that ministered to congregation members, the diocese, and the wider community. Several trained and licensed Anglicare counsellors – all of them lay people – volunteered to work in the counselling centre.¹³ One church council member explained the work:

> [...] in terms of community services we have an important counselling centre for the diocese. We have a lot of people who are trained, certified counsellors who offer that service to the parish, but also to the local police station with, for example, rape, crime counselling. That's lay people trained to do that. [...].¹⁴

Through the counselling service, the parish profile explained, the trained counsellors served the congregation and the community in all aspects, including victim support and trauma debriefing.¹⁵ An Anglicare counsellor was always present at the Sunday morning services, and contact details were given in the information leaflet every Sunday.¹⁶

---

11 Church Council Interview Protocol 2011-03-06.
12 St Thomas' Anglican Church Linden, Parish Profile, 2011, p. 11, Church Publication.
13 St Thomas' Anglican Church Linden, Parish Profile, 2011, pp. 6, 12, Church Publication. The Anglicare counsellors were eleven people who had training in counselling and who were accredited by the church.
14 Church Council Interview Protocol 2011-03-06.
15 St Thomas' Anglican Church Linden, Parish Profile, 2011, p. 12, Church Publication.
16 Information sheets for Sunday 6ᵗʰ March 2011, 2011, Church Publication.

It is interesting that while the counselling centre was run by the congregation, its mandate was not limited to the congregation's boundaries. Counselling was part of the congregation's activities, but was made available to the diocese and even to the local police station. The counselling and the church services were held together, and were not seen as two different entities. The counselling was for individuals and was open to everybody, irrespective of their church or faith affiliation. The ministry could be seen as a service to the human community.

Special outreach and ministry was offered by the congregation and by individual members through financial support and visits to Bethany House in Bertrams, close to Hillbrow, Doornfontein, for abused women and children; and to St Joseph's Children's Home in Sophiatown. Individual members were also involved in courses for the unemployed, home-based care, a refugee ministry, a soup kitchen, etc.[17] The congregation also participated in the coalition that ran the Anglican children's home, which was part of the Diocese of Johannesburg. Special donations from members were encouraged in order to support the children's homes.[18]

All the different ministries were offered by the congregation, the diocese, or individual congregation members; but all were seen as ministries that were part of the congregation. It is notable that even initiatives and engagements by individual or small groups at St Thomas' were viewed as ministries that were based in the congregation's community. It is also interesting that the ministries had strong connections with the church's services through the collections and announcements made during services on Sundays.

The congregation's buildings, staff, services, and various activities required financial support. The collection of funds was seen as a major challenge, according to the church council. One of the members said:

> Money! Let's just look at our treasury. I think it is that we are just great as far as it is how finances are going. … What we'd love to do is to develop in different ways, but until we actually could work out how we could get money for that. … salaries and rates and taxes are non-negotiable […].[19]

The economic situation of the congregation was relatively stable, but the fixed charges increased at the same rate as other costs in the wider society. If the congregation wanted to expand its activities or its buildings, they needed more donations to meet the budget. They needed regular funding that had to increase, but special donations had to be found for special projects, even if the congregation had many

---

17 St Thomas' Anglican Church Linden, Parish Profile, 2011, p. 13, Church Publication.
18 Linden St Thomas, Our Outreach Project, 2011, Website.
19 Church Council Interview Protocol 2011-03-06.

people who offered their time, skills, and experiences voluntarily. The economic situation could not be ignored; and this too affected the congregation's outreach and ministry.

Prayers and intercessions in the church services were offered for activities in the congregation, for South African society and its leaders, for other communities and bishops within the Anglican Communion, and for people and nations around the world that faced unrest or needed support. They also prayed for institutions such as schools and universities, individuals who were ill or in special need, the whole Church of God, unity among people, all nations globally, and different kinds of leaders.[20] The prayers indicated that they were involved in the society at both local and global levels.

One church council member acknowledged that the prayers opened windows to the wider community: "For me the awareness that we're doing this and we're aware of the needs and the prayers of others […]".[21] Intercessions and prayers in church were a way of making the issues of the wider community visible. New perspectives were brought to their attention, and members could make their own responses to the needs of individuals, the congregation, the society, and the world.

Athlone Methodist Church – Methodist Church of Southern Africa

The Athlone Methodist congregation is situated in an area that was developed and grew because of the apartheid policy of forced removals. People lived in other areas, but had to move to Athlone because the previous government constructed an ethnic group called 'Coloured', who were located to live in areas like Athlone.

Apart from Sunday services, Athlone Methodist Church had a range of activities during the week. One church council member said: "There is a youth group, and they meet on Friday nights, young men take them, and then we have two women's groups. We have two choirs, a men's choir and a ladies' choir".[22] According to the church council, the women's and men's choirs, together with the worship team, were essential in enriching the Sunday services. The congregation had a youth group that met every Friday. The youth also had occasional camps and conferences.[23] One church council member added: "One thing that we didn't mention

---

20 Observation Protocol 2011-03-06. One example of intercessions is visible in the information sheet. Information sheet for the Sunday, 6th March 2011, 2011, Church Publication.
21 Church Council Interview Protocol 2011-03-06.
22 Church Council Interview Protocol 2011-03-20.
23 Athlone Methodist Church, Shukuma 20.02.2010, 2010, p. 2, Congregation Print; Athlone Methodist Church, Athlone Society Profile, c.a. 2008, pp. 1–2, Church Publication.

is that we have Sunday schools, we do have a Sunday school in every Methodist church. That is where we are trained and where we would go for confirmation".[24] Many children participated in the Sunday schools, and confirmation was a natural continuation of the children's Christian formation. The youth group's regular meetings made it possible to accommodate the youth in the congregation and to support them in their spiritual training.

Other activities related to the Sunday services included a coffee fellowship after the Sunday service that was organised by the members. A worship team assisted with issues relating to the services, and a group of people were in charge of the sound system and the projector. Others helped to transport people who had difficulties coming to church. The families in the congregation, as described earlier, had responsibilities for practical matters in the services, following a roster. A particular group of people also committed themselves to be part of a specific prayer ministry, and met every second Thursday of the month.[25]

The congregation had two different groups for women, as mentioned in a previous chapter: the Women's Association, and the Women's Fellowship. The Women's Association was one of the official organisations of the Methodist Church, while the Women's Fellowship was a local group of younger women. A council member said: "There is a men's group, they just started it".[26] Some of the men had just begun a group that gathered men in the congregation. The minister also gathered people for Bible studies every Wednesday morning.[27] Some of the members belonged to a so-called 'cell group', a form of small community within the congregation. These cell groups were also responsible for pastoral work in different geographic areas. Other groups in the congregation gathered widows and widowers, married couples, or those who dealt with finance and property.[28] The main activities in the

---

24 Church Council Interview Protocol 2011-03-20.
25 Athlone Methodist Church, Shukuma 20.02.2010, 2010, p. 1, Congregation Print; Athlone Methodist Church, Shukuma Task Group – 3rd November 2010, 2010, pp. 2–3, Congregation Print; Observation Protocol 2011-03-20.
26 Church Council Interview Protocol 2011-03-20. The MCSA has two official men's organisations: the Methodist Men's League and the Young Men's Guild. The Laws and Discipline of the Methodist Church of Southern Africa, 2007, p. 202, 216. The men's organisations, like the women's organisations, are socially divided: the Men's League is mostly for 'Coloured' and some 'White' people, while the Young Men's Guild is mostly for 'Black' people. Confirmed by a phone call to District Bishop of Cape of Good Hope, Michael Hansrod, 2013-10-18.
27 Athlone Methodist Church, Athlone Society Profile, c.a. 2008, p. 1, Church Publication.
28 Athlone Methodist Church, Shukuma 20.02.2010, 2010, p. 2, Congregation Print; Athlone Methodist Church, Shukuma Task Group – 3rd November 2010, 2010, p. 3.

congregation were focused on the church community itself. The ministry could be characterised as supporting the members in their spiritual formation and their ministries in society.

Finance and fundraising for the congregation's operations were always an important issue. One council member stressed: "I think the problem here is, the fact that our church, basically, there are many pensioners in this church, and that creates a bit of a problem. You don't need to worry as a pensioner in any case, but pensioners here in South Africa don't get much, so we have a problem. That is why finances are not so good".[29] About 30 per cent of the members were older than 60, and about 20 per cent were younger than 18, according to the congregation's own statistics. About half of the members were of working age, which made it difficult for the congregation to collect sufficient funds. It held special events to improve its finances by, for example, arranging fundraising brunches, and increasing transparency through regular financial reports, thus ensuring accountability.[30] The concern about the congregation's finances was valid, because only a minority of the congregation were able to support the work.

Apart from its internal programmes, the congregation ran several social projects either in its own right or in cooperation with other Methodist churches. They had special ministries of supporting people living with cancer and those affected by HIV. They were also involved in prison ministry.[31] In addition, they ran various kinds of outreach projects, and once a year they collected groceries. One of the members in the council explained: "We have a harvest festival. That is also one of our projects where people bring whatever they have, like fruits and stuff and things to old aged homes and to children's homes and so on".[32] Delivery of food supplies to specific homes was one of the congregation's social ministries, but they were also engaged in a soup kitchen and in feeding schemes.

A member of the council said: "There is also a feeding scheme at the church where people get fed. Once a week".[33] People in need in the area were invited to receive soup and bread at the premises of the Athlone Methodist Church. They also assisted schools with soup and bread, together with an organisation named 'H.E.L.P. Ministries'. A woman in the council explained: "There is an organisation

---

29 Church Council Interview Protocol 2011-03-20.
30 Athlone Methodist Church, Shukuma 20.02.2010, 2010, p. 3, Congregation Print; Athlone Methodist Church, Athlone Society Profile, c.a. 2008, p. 2, Church Publication.
31 Athlone Methodist Church, Shukuma Task Group – 3rd November 2010, 2010, p. 3, Congregation Print; Church Council Interview Protocol 2011-03-20.
32 Church Council Interview Protocol 2011-03-20.
33 Church Council Interview Protocol 2011-03-20.

serving soup during winter at schools, that's another part of our church".[34] H.E.L.P. Ministries was a project supported by the United Methodist Church in the USA.[35] The council member added: "We target certain schools in the area, and we divide [the people] into groups, and each gets a turn to go for lunch".[36] The soup was prepared in a central kitchen and then delivered to school children and unemployed adults.[37] The soup kitchen could be regarded as sharing with people in the community as part of the catholicity of the Church, according to the analytical tool.

The soup kitchen brought the congregation into greater contact with the surrounding community. The church council was asked why they undertook this kind of ministry. One member answered: "We care, the church cares, we're reaching out to them".[38] They had a vision to reach out to the wider society, and when they were asked whether they wanted to convert people to their faith, they answered unanimously that the soup kitchen was not that kind of ministry. One member in the council stated, however: "They do have a prayer before they eat. They know that they are welcome to come, and they have come to us for church service".[39] Everyone was welcome to come to the congregation, but there was a religious element – an opening prayer. The member in the council added: "We don't [put] pressure on them to come".[40] People could participate in their ministry, and there were no hidden motives, according to the council.

The church council's statement that anybody was welcome to use the soup kitchen could be seen to mean that their ministry was open to the wider community. The congregation's social outreach engagement could be regarded as a sign that the congregation was part of a broader community that involved all the people living in that area. The community could even include people of other faiths and convictions, who were part of the human community according to the Church's catholicity.

The congregation's ecumenical involvement had increased when Athlone Methodist Church started a pre-school. They became engaged as board members, staff and parents. The project involved not only people in their own congregation

---

34 Church Council Interview Protocol 2011-03-20. H.E.L.P. is an acronym for Healing, Evangelism and Leadership Programmes. H.E.L.P. The centre of the organisation is based in Cape Town. H.E.L.P. Ministries International Trust, 2014, Website.
35 H.E.L.P. Ministries International Trust, 2014, Website.
36 Church Council Interview Protocol 2011-03-20.
37 H.E.L.P. Ministries International Trust, 2014, Website.
38 Church Council Interview Protocol 2011-03-20.
39 Church Council Interview Protocol 2011-03-20.
40 Church Council Interview Protocol 2011-03-20.

but also people from other denominations. Through the pre-school, the project enabled the congregation to contribute to the local area, giving the congregation, as they put it, greater relevance in society.[41] This contribution to the wider society can be seen as a ministry that extended the congregation's boundaries, helping to create a more inclusive community.

Despite the many local initiatives, the church council wanted to affect the whole society. The council believed that the church needed to be more vocal in the wider society. A man in the church council stated:

> […] the church isn't standing firm towards the government. The church should show its principles, what it agrees and disagrees with. Recently I heard that they had a meeting in Pretoria, a conference, and the ministers were concerned about certain things that came from parliament and they discussed that … the churches need to stand firm.[42]

This statement expressed a disappointment about the churches' voice, or lack of it, in public debate with the government. There were obvious issues with which people in the council disagreed, and the church needed to have a voice in the society. The congregation's members wanted the leadership of the Church to contribute to the public debates, but the Athlone Methodist Church itself was not involved.

Youth and drugs were other issues that were brought to the fore, and that were a concern to the church council. A member stated:

> And a big problem also in churches is how we're going to deal with the drug problems with our young people. Because we don't know that there are, but the young people are focused on that, and I think those who are in charge of the young people they do keep their eyes opened, but you know, you sometimes hear that there's unhappiness because they suspect maybe there are of the young people that's going that way. I think it's in all churches, the problem comes up now.[43]

The council was concerned about the younger generation and drugs, and they did not know how to deal with these issues as a church – but they hoped that their youth leaders would help to protect the youth. Drugs were obviously perceived as a danger to the youth, and they wanted to protect them.

The ministry of Athlone Methodist Church was mainly intended to minister to individuals and to maintain support for minority groups. It was not intended to seek major change in society, but rather to support people in need.

---

41 Prins. D. ca. 1993, p. 4, Church Publication.
42 Church Council Interview Protocol 2011-03-20.
43 Church Council Interview Protocol 2011-03-20.

Lutheran Church in Bellville – Evangelical Lutheran Church in Southern Africa Cape Church

The Lutheran congregation in Bellville was centred on its German background, as was obvious in their activities, projects, and ministries. The congregation had several lay people – readers, organists, musicians, tea-makers, flower-arrangers, sound and computer engineers – involved in the Sunday services. The congregation also had Children's Church for children aged between 3 and 12 years, which was similar to Sunday School. This group had several leaders who met for planning during the week.[44]

Quite a number of people were engaged in church activities during the week. A mothers' group met once a month, and a seniors group met on the first Thursday of the month for outings or to listen to a guest speaker. Two Bible study groups met every Thursday: the German-speaking group in the morning, and the English study group in the evening. *Haus der offenen Tür* ('Open Door') was a social gathering on Thursday mornings after the German Bible study, when there was opportunity for tea and coffee. A brass band rehearsed on Tuesday evenings, and they also organised concerts. A special group was engaged in the sale of new and second-hand books, and another carried out maintenance and renovations to the church centre. Other activities in the congregation included a sewing group, bring-and-braai Saturdays, communication through a magazine for the congregation, emails and SMSes, a winter dance, dance classes, bazaars, and festivals.[45]

Some of the congregation's activities supported the local Christian community, and can be regarded as a ministry to build it up. Other activities had a more social character to support the local German community.

When the church council was asked about important issues in the church's life, one council member replied: "Youth work. Try to get that working again. We want to get a youth leader, for example, so that has been an issue that we have been grappling with the past months".[46] The purchase of a neighbouring house was a way to provide premises both to increase the youth work and to make an apartment available for new staff.[47] Another council member said: "Activating or reactivating the 30 to 40, 50 age group, which then also includes the children,

---

44 Hahne, Albrecht, 2011, p. 4, Church Publication.
45 Lutheran Church Bellville, Activities, 2011, Website; Rubow, Hürgen, 2011, p. 2, Congregation Print; Hahne, Albrecht, 2011. p. 4, Church Publication.
46 Church Council Interview Protocol 2011-03-15.
47 Rubow, Hürgen, 2011, p. 2, Church Publication.

because these children are not getting in and one of the reasons is affluence".[48] Youth, children, and families are important target groups for the survival of a small Lutheran church in South Africa. The congregation had to maintain its membership numbers into the future if it was going to survive as a congregation in Bellville.

Children's ministry had been central for many years, and the congregation had extended the church centre with a kindergarten in 1989. The kindergarten was a private school association that rented the premises, but at the same time the congregation regarded it as a ministry offered by the Lutheran Church in Bellville as part of their community. The congregation was represented on the board, and the minister visited the kindergarten once a month, and a layperson once a week, for teaching. Few of the parents and children were involved in the congregation's services or weekly activities, and closer cooperation between the congregation and the kindergarten was promoted by the council.[49]

The kindergarten taught in German, but was open to anyone. When the church council was asked whether the kindergarten was only for the German community, one member said: "Also for others but their tuition is in German. In other words, the children actually learn another language".[50] The kindergarten was an initiative of the congregation as part of the church centre in Bellville, and it was regarded as part of the congregation's activities to reach the wider community. It was open to all, but there were still requirements in the form of fees that most South Africans would not be able to afford.[51]

The congregation had previously investigated whether to establish another German kindergarten in Table View, in the northern part of Cape Town. The German School in Cape Town was prepared to support the kindergarten financially, but when the project was supposed to start there were not enough children. The congregation had wanted to start such a project and to establish a permanent presence of the Lutheran Church in that part of Cape Town.[52] It is notable that an English-speaking kindergarten – or even an Afrikaans-speaking one – had not been considered, showing that there was a strong link between the German community and this ELCSA-Cape congregation.

The congregation was engaged in several social projects. One member, for example, was in charge of organising home visitations for the sick and those in

---

48 Church Council Interview Protocol 2011-03-15.
49 Rubow, Hürgen, 2011, pp. 1–3, Congregation Print; Observation Protocol 2011-02-20.
50 Church Council Interview Protocol 2011-03-15.
51 Deutscher Kindergarten Bellville, Fees, 2014, Website.
52 Hahne, Albrecht, 2010, pp. 1-2, Church Publication.

need of care. They had also established a social and welfare fund to provide support when the need arose.[53]

When the church council spoke of the importance of being church, one member said: "The church services are basically the centre of our spiritual life. We've got quite a lot of church services, often two or three a Sunday, but we focus primarily on our own congregation. We don't have much outreach. Am I correct? We support iThemba Labantu [...]".[54] iThemba Labantu, a social project in Cape Town started by the German Lutheran mission society BMW, is a Lutheran community centre in Philippi, one of Cape Town's townships, where ELCSA-Cape previously had a congregation. The organisation had a diaconal project among the people of Philippi. The congregation also had a special collection each month for projects run by the German mission societies ELM and BMW.[55] Their statement showed that the congregation was primarily occupied with its own community, and that their support of projects was mainly connected to the German community. Their support for iThemba Labantu was nevertheless a project that transcended ethnic boundaries, as a sign that the Christian community went beyond the local context.

Other council members stated that they supported the German retirement village and old age home, St Johannis Heim, a non-profit organisation that ELCSA-Cape founded in 1981 as a diaconal work. ELCSA-Cape was one of the sponsors of St Johannis Heim, and was also a stakeholder in the German-speaking community together with the Roman Catholic Church in the Cape, the German Club, and the Johanniter Hilfswerk of the Cape branch.[56]

In addition, the congregation joined with other churches and organisations in Bellville in supporting the Tygerberg Association for Street People (TASP), a community-based organisation that provided food, clothing, shelter, rehabilitation, and other services to refugees and immigrants in Tygerberg. There was also a collection box in the church centre where people could donate food that was later distributed to people in need.[57] The support of TASP was one of the few projects

---

53 Lutheran Church Bellville, Activities, 2011, Website; Hahne, Albrecht, 2011. p. 3, Church Publication.
54 Church Council Interview Protocol 2011-03-15.
55 Church Council Interview Protocol 2011-03-15; Ottermann, Reino, 1995, pp. 97–99.
56 Church Council Interview Protocol 2011-03-15; St Johannisheim, The Sponsors, 2014, Website.
57 Church Council Interview Protocol 2011-03-15; Hahne, Albrecht, 2011, p. 3, Church Publication; Lutheran Church Bellville, Activities, 2011, Website.

that were directed to the wider community and that involved cooperation with other organisations in civil society.

The activities, projects, and ministry of the Lutheran Church in Bellville were focused primarily on their own congregation. Support for specific issues beyond the congregation was mainly centred on Lutheran members, on people of German descent, and on German mission societies that were active in South Africa. Their focus indicated that it was important to serve the German community and projects related to the Lutheran heritage.

City Harvest Ministries in Ntuzuma – Apostolic Faith Mission of South Africa

City Harvest Ministries is situated in the township of Ntuzuma, outside Durban. The congregation was established in 2005 in the Durban city centre, but moved to Ntuzuma in 2009. They had a tent church, and carried out several activities during the week apart from their Sunday services. Monday evenings were dedicated to intercessions, Thursday evenings to Bible classes, Wednesday or Saturday evenings to a prayer meeting, and Friday evenings to youth services. Saturday evenings were reserved for worship practice before the next day's service.[58]

The congregation had a children's ministry in the form of a Sunday school, which was part of the congregation's outreach programme in the area.[59] Outreach and evangelism, according to the congregation's description, were central to the life of City Harvest Ministries. They encouraged outreach programmes and invited individual members to make home visitations, and also to strengthen the ties of friendship between members and those who came to the church.[60] One church council member described the congregation's mission in these terms: "I think mostly, I put it according to the statement, the mission that we have, firstly invite people and secondly equipping for the spiritual and sending them to get others as well".[61] Drawing in others to increase membership and spiritual growth was essential for the life in the congregation. They had not yet started any social work in the community, but this was part of the plan for the future. Nevertheless, social

---

58 City Harvest Ministries, The Notice Board of C.H.M., 2013, Website; Observation Protocol 2011-03-27.
59 City Harvest Ministries, Good News to the young generation, 2013, Website.
60 Observation Protocol 2011-03-27. One example of outreach is on National Youth Days. City Harvest Ministries, The Notice Board of C.H.M., 2013, Website.
61 Church Council Interview Protocol 2011-03-27.

projects were not a focus in the church's constitution, and were not mentioned in the Vision and Mission statements.[62]

The congregation's activities, projects and ministry can be characterised as concentrating on the congregation and equipping members in their ministry to reach new people. The congregation had a vision for numerical growth and supporting those who were already members in their ministry in the area.

The congregation held several conferences and special services during the year, either on its own or together with other congregations within the AFM. They had a regional Easter weekend conference, a Regional Men's fellowship, a Christmas conference, a National Sisters conference, a Harvest Time conference, etc.[63] Dedication to church activity was part of being a member of the congregation: according to the City Harvest Ministries' constitution, members were obliged to be actively involved in the fellowship of the congregation. Membership also included financial support, prayer for the work, and personally witnessing to the Lord Jesus Christ and giving their testimony, as stated in their constitution. The members were expected to be present at all church meetings, home cells, and services.[64] The case congregations of the other denominations did not require such dedication to the church in the way that City Harvest Ministries did.

The congregation had a number of contacts with other groups and many other charismatic churches in the Durban area. The members of City Harvest Ministries said that God had told them to start a church in Ntuzuma, and that they had chosen to be located in the area and to establish an assembly. The church council confirmed that all who came to their community were welcome.[65] One church council member emphasised their presence in the area by explaining that the local people were also part of their community:

> [...]. Because if they have funerals, like we are just getting invited, and they say they need a pastor, so they saw that there is a church here, and if they need a pastor and we can go there, and at time they need instruments. So we are part of the community in a sense. When we are needed we are there.[66]

This explanation showed that there was a reciprocal confirmation of a common community. The congregation's decision to be located in an underprivileged area

---

62 Church Council Interview Protocol 2011-03-27; City Harvest Ministries Constitution, 2011 p. 1, Church Publication.
63 City Harvest Ministries, The Notice Board of C.H.M., 2013, Website.
64 City Harvest Ministries Constitution, 2011, pp. 3, 5, Church Publication.
65 Church Council Interview Protocol 2011-03-27.
66 Church Council Interview Protocol 2011-03-27.

and to share their resources as a community could be regarded as a sign of the Church's catholicity according to the analytical tool. There was also recognition of a greater community that went beyond their own membership, and that had been part of the congregation's founding. The congregation was willing to serve the community, and the people of Ntuzuma had invited the congregation to be among them. Another council member explained:

> I think those who are living here understand the importance of having us. Because you see, an area like this, a tent like this, they can take [i.e. steal] the whole site and do up their house and cover their house if they want to, but they don't do that. Because they actually understand that for us being here is going to help either directly or indirectly for the community. Like the pastor has said, sometimes we are invited to families, to go there, those people, some of them, they are not even our members, but we go there and assist, even they are not part of our church's members, even they are not members.[67]

The council member stressed that the people in the area protected the congregation, and so they were not targeted for theft, destruction, or harm. The people in the area appreciated their presence, and the congregation wanted to be good for the people in Ntuzuma. They were invited by families – even by those who were not members of City Harvest Ministries. The council's interpretation of their presence showed that they considered themselves part of the community in Ntuzuma. They had a mission to reach the people to become members of their congregation, and the people in the area appreciated them because they would benefit from the church's presence.

The church council described their role in the area through the words of a council member: "Meet the needs of the community around us, and of those who are in need among the people that come to church".[68] Another member clarified the needs: "At the moment, what we can say is that most of the people who come here are children, so obviously they want jobs, they want to go to school. Those are the needs that we should as a church look into or are trying to meet".[69] The economic situation of unemployment and the need to provide sufficient education were also identified as important issues among the people of Ntuzuma.

They had not made any progress in social activities in the area, but this was something that was part of the congregation's plans. A church council member stated: "We haven't started but we have plans, we will do social work in the

---

67 Church Council Interview Protocol 2011-03-27.
68 Church Council Interview Protocol 2011-03-27.
69 Church Council Interview Protocol 2011-03-27.

community".[70] City Harvest Ministries emphasised that they were a very charismatic church, and they had not yet begun their social activities; but this element was included in the job description of the minister. The minister was supposed to contextualise the congregation's work by being socially involved in the area. For example, the minister was supposed to be engage in feeding schemes, care for the elderly, and networking with existing structures in society such as prisons, schools, and the police forum. The minister was also supposed to support HIV-prevention projects – a very relevant issue in an area like Ntuzuma.[71] The church council's identification of the needs in the area – and its willingness to relocate the congregation to Ntuzuma, as earlier described – indicated that the congregation was dedicated to becoming an important player in doing mission but also in supporting social change.

The church council stressed the role of assisting the government rather than taking a critical stance. One member of the church council said:

> Is to be as neutral as possible … you know in relation to that you must always look at the government how to move us. We must reach a point when the church, where you could ask the government, "What can we do for you?" That would be the ultimate good. How can we help the government? Not only by praying but doing other projects as well for the government.[72]

The church council's outlook emphasised that they were part of the South African society, and that their role was to assist and to serve the government's programmes. It was notable that the church council did not mention the church's role as a prophetic and critical voice in relation to the government. On the contrary, they stressed the importance of a shared community and of how the society could be improved together with the government.

City Harvest Ministries were not engaged in any programmes supporting poverty eradication in Ntuzuma that could reduce ethnic barriers. Their presence in an underprivileged area, however, could be an indication that they wanted to bring about social change in Ntuzuma.

St Michael's Evangelical Lutheran Church – Evangelical Lutheran Church in Southern Africa

This congregation, situated in the Durban city centre, had people coming from various areas in the city because of convenient transportation systems. The con-

---

70 Church Council Interview Protocol 2011-03-27.
71 Apostolic Faith Mission of SA City Harvest Family, 2008, p. 2, Church Publication.
72 Church Council Interview Protocol 2011-03-27.

gregation had several visitors who were not members of the congregation but who belonged to ELCSA; they came to the city to study or to work. There were members from diverse ethnicities, as became apparent particularly in the English-speaking service. The presence of these diverse ethnicities was mainly a consequence of the merger of three different worshiping communities, as described earlier.

The congregation had several activities and services during the week in addition to church services on Sundays: for example, bible study groups, congregation festivals, various conferences and meetings for the different leagues and organisations, youth services, breakfasts for specific professions, special Christmas and Easter programmes, retreats, and rallies.[73]

Every congregation in ELCSA is responsible for organising Sunday Schools and confirmation classes for children and youth. St Michael's had a Sunday School that was attended by a large group of children who came to church on Sundays with their parents. They also had confirmation classes in order to fulfil their aim of having Christian formation that would encourage members to participate in the church's mission and in the life of the congregation. The Sunday School's organisers aimed to equip its teachers through training and workshops. They were supposed to meet regularly for lesson preparation, arranging functions, and encouraging parents' active participation. The congregation supported the Sunday School's activities through an annual Sunday School rally over a weekend with games, Bible stories, traditional dancing, etc.[74] The Sunday School was a particularly important part of the congregation because it gathered a large group of children at the church for religious formation.

The Women's League gathered women for prayer and offered spiritual and material support to its members, the congregation, and the whole community. They had weekly meetings, made home visits to people in need, and assisted in many important ministries in the congregation. They were also particularly active in the Sunday School and confirmation class teaching and with the 'help desk' activities. They had a special role in caring for people with addictions or those who were abused. The congregation also had a group of women named *iMbokodo* who met with a particular focus on fundraising for the congregation's

---

73 Durban Central Parish 2011 Activity Plan, 2011, Congregation Print; Lüdemann, Joe, 2012, p. 3, Church Publication.
74 Durban Central Parish, Leagues and Organisations, Abasizikazi, Amadoda, Abasha, iMbokodo, Youth Adult League, Sunday School, ELCSASO, ELCSAMO, 2001, Website; Objectives for Christian Education in ELCSA, 1984, pp. 1–2, Church Publication; Durban Central Parish 2011 Activity Plan, 2011, Congregation Print; Observation Protocol 2011-04-03.

activities. They especially provided catering when needed for church conferences and a range of other activities.[75]

The Men's League had similar activities and tasks to those of the Women's League. They met at least once a week for Bible study and prayer, and to support people who had been bereaved or were ill. They were especially encouraged to develop their talents to serve the church and the society.[76] Young people aged between 12 and about 35 could join the Youth League. They met on Saturday evenings for discussion, services, exploring future trends, music, and addressing topics that were important to the church. Central to the life of the Youth League were several youth conferences during the year. They began on a Saturday evening and continued through the night to the next morning. These youth conferences had a programme with services, Bible studies, testimonies, discussions, social gatherings, etc.[77]

The Young Adults League had members aged 25 years and upwards. It was founded in order to cater for younger adults – a group that had previously been neglected by the church. The Lutheran church had found, for example, that some younger adults changed denomination and joined another church. The Young Adults League had the task of using their members' professional skills to develop the church. They met at least once a month, and had an annual conference.[78]

Durban had several educational institutions, and the congregation had a large number of students who came to worship. The ELCSA Student Organisation was not directly part of the congregation, but was linked in many ways to Durban Central Parish. Branches of the ELCSA Student Organisation were founded in 2009 at the University of KwaZulu-Natal (Howard Campus) and at the Durban University of Technology (Steve Biko campus).[79] The organisation encouraged

---

[75] Durban Central Parish, Leagues and Organisations, Abasizikazi, Amadoda, Abasha, iMbokodo, Young Adults League, Sunday School, ELCSASO, ELCSAMO, 2011, Website; Constitution of the Prayer Women's League of the Evangelical Lutheran Church in Southern Africa, 1998, Chapter 3, Church Publication; Lüdemann, Joe, 2012, p. 6, Church Publication.

[76] Constitution of the Prayer Men's League of the Evangelical Lutheran Church in Southern Africa, Chapter 1, Church Publication.

[77] Durban Central Parish, Leagues and Organisations, Abasizikazi, Amadoda, Abasha, iMbokodo, Young Adults League, Sunday School, ELCSASO, ELCSAMO, 2011, Website; Constitution of the Youth League of the Evangelical Lutheran Church in Southern Africa, 2011, Part 3, Chapter 1, Church Publication.

[78] Constitution of the Young Adults League of the Evangelical Lutheran Church in Southern Africa, 2010, Chapter 1, 5, 7, 8, Church Publication.

[79] Durban Central Parish, Leagues and Organisations, Abasizikazi, Amadoda, Abasha, iMbokodo, Young Adults League, Sunday School, ELCSASO, ELCSAMO, 2011, Website;

its members to take part in the life of the congregation and to develop the leadership of the church. Every branch of the organisation was supposed to meet at least once a week, and to relate to its nearest congregation.

The ELCSA Music Organisation was present in the congregation, and had a local committee. Its aim was to promote music and singing in the church through workshops, seminars, music education, organising church choirs, music conferences, and choir competitions. The ELCSA Music Organisation committee at Durban Central Parish organised, for example, a music talent show called 'Music Explosion' where individuals, groups, and choirs could perform and offer their talents to the church.[80]

It was evident that several activities in the congregation were organised to gather specific groups in the congregation, in order to equip their members with spiritual formation, but also to support their members in their diverse needs. Some of the leagues were also engaged in a range of social projects for individuals.

Most of the activities in ELCSA congregations were organised by the different leagues – a fact that had both advantages and disadvantages. It was sometimes difficult to involve people, even though the congregation offered a range of activities. A council member said: "Another issue is to get our congregants to participate outside the Sunday services. That is always an issue of getting people into different structures. … They are there, but they just have to either be identified or be given small projects and to come up with something […]".[81] The council member's statement was about those members who did not belong to a particular group or league. The various organisations in ELCSA congregations played an important role in monitoring the various activities, and provided organisational structure to these activities. The different leagues and organisations also offered many activities that were not always coordinated. The local leading team, however, had the job of bringing together the different activities. People who were not part of a league or an organisation had to be approached to become involved; and this, obviously, was not always easy at St Michael's.

Maintenance of the buildings was another activity – and an ongoing issue in the church – that needed particular attention. One church council member explained:

Constitution of the Student Organisation of the Evangelical Lutheran Church in Southern Africa, 2005, Chapter 5, 11, 13, Church Publication.

80 Durban Central Parish, Leagues and Organisations, Abasizikazi, Amadoda, Abasha, iMbokodo, Young Adults League, Sunday School, ELCSASO, ELCSAMO, 2011, Website; Constitution of ELCSA Music Organization, n.b., Chapter 1 and 5, Church Publication.

81 Church Council Interview Protocol 2011-04-03.

"One of the burning issues is always renovations".[82] They had carried out a complete internal and external renovation of St Michael's church. The building had previously not been in good shape, and they needed suitable premises for church activities, to develop the services and to attract members.[83] The congregation had different fund-raising events to support its expenditure on its activities, social work, and buildings. The most common was the Sunday collection, when members were encouraged to use personalised envelopes so that their offering could be recorded. St Michael's was able to meet its annual budget through the regular offerings and other fundraising initiatives, but other congregations in the parish had difficulty covering their costs.[84]

The congregation's main focus in its social projects was on refugees, because of xenophobic attacks that had taken place in Durban. Their focus on this issue can be regarded as consistent with the analytical tool of the Church as catholic. The members of the church knew no national borders, and were part of the Christian communion. The congregation belonged to the Diakonia Council of Churches, and become involved in mediation work in one of Durban's informal settlements. They had formed a partnership with the Children's Care Centre, which had a crèche run by the Union of Refugee Women. Their support was not financial, but they offered advice and various supplies. The congregation had also offered St Michael's Church to a Congolese congregation so that they could hold services and prayer meetings.[85] The congregation's engagement in the refugee situation was particularly noteworthy because of the increased xenophobia in South Africa.

The congregation was engaged in many different social projects for people in Durban, and many of them were done together with the Diakonia Council of Churches, other congregations, churches, Christian communities, and organisations in the society. These projects were intended to serve everybody, irrespective of church membership, religion, or background. The church council stated that they were doing the work for humanity, and not to win new members or to make people become Christian. One council member said: "It is an act of [social] responsibility".[86] The congregation's cooperation with a range of organisations, both religious and non-religious, indicates that the congregation was willing to work together with various groupings in the society. Their social action can be

---

82 Church Council Interview Protocol 2011-04-03.
83 Church Council Interview Protocol 2011-04-03.
84 Lüdemann, Joe, 2012, p. 9, Congregation Print; Observation Protocol 2011-04-03.
85 Durban Central Parish, Projects, Inner–City Outreach, The P.U.S.H. Project, Lutherans Uniting in Action, 2011, Website; Church Council Interview Protocol 2011-04-03.
86 Church Council Interview Protocol 2011-04-03.

seen as ministry to a broader community that transcended particular faiths and convictions, as part of the Church's catholicity in the analytical tool.

Apart from humanitarian assistance, the congregation also undertook projects as ways to unite the Lutheran church family in Durban. A council member said: "The other reason for having these projects was uniting the three churches. Instead of always saying we need to be one, we run a project together. We have one project, yes, and we also have a help desk which also takes care of issues outside the church".[87] Instead of waiting for the Lutheran churches to unite, they were working together on social projects. Lutherans United in Action (LUA) begun as a result of a workshop with ELCSA N-T. Ministers from ELCSA and ELCSA N-T in the Durban area had met at this workshop, run by the Institute for the Healing of Memories. It resulted in a joint service with participants from St Michael's, Lutherkriche, and St Paul's. In addition, the church council members met after the workshop and decided that a joint committee for social outreach should be established. The committee devised strategies to raise awareness of social justice in the congregations, and jointly they became involved in different projects.[88] Although the churches had difficulties in uniting at a central level, the congregations found areas for cooperation at a local level. Social projects became a tool for church unity.

The congregations from ELCSA and ELCSA N-T in Durban had also registered a non-profit organisation called 'The PUSH Project', with a coordinator and a board that monitored its activities. The organisation was involved in home-based care for people living with HIV, and care for child-headed households and for orphans as a result of AIDS. The PUSH Project also trained care-givers for home-based care, orphans, and vulnerable children. They had received funds from PEPFAR to set up a small bakery in one of the townships in order to finance the project. However, the bakery found it difficult to remain sustainable without proper marketing of its bread and a good business plan. The congregation had found that the project did not have committed members from the congregations to help it to become successful as a social outreach work. The Help Desk had, nevertheless, begun to incorporate the PUSH Project into its work.[89]

---

87 Church Council Interview Protocol 2011-04-03.
88 Durban Central Parish, Projects, Inner-City Outreach, The P.U.S.H. Project, Lutherans Uniting in Action, 2011, Website; Lüdemann, Joe, 2012, pp. 6, 11, Church Publication. St Michael's belongs to ELCSA, and Lutherkriche and St Paul's belong to ELCSA N-T.
89 Durban Central Parish, Projects, Inner-City Outreach, The P.U.S.H. Project, Lutherans Uniting in Action, 2011, Website; Lüdemann, Joe, 2012, p. 11, Church Publication. The

Street Kid Outreach was carried out by the congregation together with other organisations. Members from the ELCSA Student Organisation, and a volunteer from the congregation's partner organisation ELM in Germany, were involved in 'I Care', a non-profit Christian organisation. I Care had drop-in centres for street children, and was trying to rehabilitate those who were living without families. I Care was also involved in reunification programmes with the children's families, offering housing, education, training, and awareness programmes.[90]

It is interesting that the congregation cooperated with many organisations instead of running its own projects independently. This indicated that there was a great willingness in the congregation to work together with other units in civil society for the sake of humanity. The boundaries were broadened to include the wider community, embracing church and society. The congregation's activities, projects, and ministries served its own members and the wider community. The ministry, however, was primarily focused on assisting individuals, and not on major social change. The congregation cannot be seen as being primarily engaged in poverty eradication in order to bring about social change and thus to reduce ethnic boundaries. Their engagement in social justice issues and in social transformation, however, can be characterised as an act of changing the society.

11.2 Difficulties in Making an Impact on Democratic Society

The various church leaders were approached about their churches' efforts towards poverty eradication through advocacy, statements, and social projects. The general secretary of the Southern African Catholic Bishops' Conference, Vincent Brennan, responded that the SACBC had spoken about the issues of unemployment, redistribution of wealth, and land distribution. He questioned whether the voice of the church had made any impact on the public debate. Brennan referred to Archbishop Denis Hurley, and said:

> What voices have we in the public debate? There's so much unemployment, there's so much inequality, there's so much poverty. Where is the voice of the church? And people will always point to the past of apartheid when church had a strong voice and people listened. Now with the new government and [the end of] apartheid it's a thing of the past. Are the people even willing to listen anymore? 'Cause you're criticising the democratic

---

President's Emergency Plan for AIDS Relief is also known as PEPFAR. It is a USA-based initiative to respond to the global HIV pandemic.

90 Durban Central Parish, Projects, Inner-City Outreach, The P.U.S.H. Project, Lutherans Uniting in Action, 2011, Website; Annual Review, October 2011, I Care – giving children a future, 2011, pp. 2–4, Church Publication.

government and you are pointing out issues that they maybe don't want to have pointed out.[91]

Brennan communicated a sense that the society was no longer interested in receiving the kind of criticism from the churches that it had before, despite many inequalities in the country. He said that political parties only wanted to meet with the church when they wanted to promote their own agenda. He also said that the media was not listening to the voice of the church any more.[92]

He explained that the SACBC had established a parliamentary office after democratisation, through which the church could participate actively in decision-making processes. The church discussed social issues and took stands, but the problem was to speak in such a way that the voice was heard. He asked himself where the prophetic voice of the church was today.[93]

The SACBC's Justice and Social Department was working with justice issues within South Africa. The department had, for example, produced a range of theological training materials about economic justice and democracy for local community development, participation, and advocacy. The materials were used in local communities to educate citizens in democracy and participation in communities.[94]

The Provincial Executive Officer of the Anglican Church of Southern Africa, Allan Kannemeyer, emphasised that the church was continuously taking stands to promote work for poverty eradication. As examples he mentioned how the archbishop had spoken about the issue and had participated in a seminar about poverty. He also stated that SACC was seen as the church's ecumenical ministry for social justice. Apart from the SACC, a number of local church organisations were working for poverty eradication. Kannemeyer said that interfaith movements were also addressing poverty, and the Anglican Church had played a prominent role in this. He added that the Anglican Church had a tradition

---

91 Brennan, Vincent, Interview Protocol 2011-03-01.
92 Brennan, Vincent, Interview Protocol 2011-03-01.
93 Brennan, Vincent, Interview Protocol 2011-03-01.
94 Brennan, Vincent, Interview Protocol 2011-03-01. The SACBC has produced a number of study materials for local advocacy. Examples are: *Masisukumeni, Let's Stand Up*, a booklet dealing with democratisation, local government, community participation and challenges. *Acting Against Poverty* deals with democracy, economic justice and HIV in relation to church action for change. *Theological Refection* is study material about ecumenical justice issues in a global context. Masisukumeni, Let's Stand Up, 2004; Theological Refection, 2005, Acting Against Poverty, 2005.

of addressing these issues, and many of the organisations had been started by Archbishop-Emeritus Desmond Tutu.[95]

Kannemeyer declared that the Anglican Church had various social and diaconal programmes, as well as development work in congregations, dioceses, and the province. A provincial body, 'HOPE Africa', promoted and implemented social development programmes for the Anglican Church in Southern Africa. The church's social and diaconal work was intended to serve all the people of South Africa, not just Anglicans; and this was part of God's mission.[96]

The general secretary of the Methodist Church of Southern Africa, Vuyani Nyobole, claimed that the country and the Church would become more ethnically integrated as a result of economic changes in the country. This would happen when people could afford to live in different areas and pupils could attend different schools. The church opposed economic inequality by making statements and meeting government officials, but also through the SACC and similar channels. The churches acted together through ecumenical organisations in order to have a stronger influence. The political stands of the church, and its advice to the government and society, were not always disseminated, because the media was not always seen as interested in the church's statements, according to Nyobole.[97]

Public statements about society were often made during the church's annual conferences. They had passed resolutions in recent years about the militarisation of society, legalisation of prostitution, xenophobia, and crime; and a decade earlier the issues addressed had included poverty, capacity-building, and the basic income grant. The presiding bishop had also particularly addressed poverty in his opening sermon at the 2009 Methodist conference.[98]

---

95 Kannemeyer, Allan J., Interview Protocol 2011-03-16.
96 Kannemeyer, Allan J., Interview Protocol 2011-03-16.
97 Nyobole, Vuyani Gladstone, Interview Protocol 2011-02-28.
98 On poverty, see: 2003 Yearbook, The Methodist Church of Southern Africa, p. 121, 2003. On human resources and capacity building see: 2005 Yearbook, The Methodist Church of Southern Africa, p. 119, 2005. On the basic income grant see: 2006 Yearbook, The Methodist Church of Southern Africa, pp. 74–75, 2006. On child trafficking and prostitution, public health issues, and crime see: 2008 Yearbook, The Methodist Church of Southern Africa, pp. 75–76, 78, 2008. On prostitution see: 2010 Yearbook, The Methodist Church of Southern Africa, p. 84, 2010. On military conscription see: 2011 Yearbook, The Methodist Church of Southern Africa, p. 103, 2011. Economic justice was an important area, for example, during the 2002 Conference, but it did not receive the same attention in later conferences. 2002 Yearbook of The Methodist Church of Southern Africa, 2002, pp. 104–108.

The Apostolic Faith Mission was running several social programmes about HIV and the adoption of children, among others, according to the AFM's general secretary, George Mahlobo. They encouraged the local churches to run social projects and skills development for their communities.

Mahlobo believed that it was a challenge for the church to act collectively on socio-political issues.[99] Members of the church did not always have a shared understanding of the situation, and the AFM did not always have a common voice because the social situation was interpreted differently by various groups. He identified, for example, the issue of affirmative action, which they had not yet addressed within the church. It was seen as a delicate issue, especially among 'White' men. Mahlobo stated that the church should say something about this issue, but that other disadvantaged groups would oppose it. They had tried to reach consensus over crime, but it had not been easy. Some wanted, for example, to reintroduce the death penalty, which others opposed. He said: "Social-political issues have changed tremendously from where it was when we became one, and there are more polarisations today, you know".[100] Mahlobo's statements acknowledged that it was difficult for the church to find a united voice about society and the government. The church's unification had resulted in greater diversity, making it harder to present a unified voice. It was easier during apartheid to find alliances against the previous government and to take strong stands in the public debate. A diverse church with many opinions complicated its ability to make joint declarations.[101]

The AFM had, nevertheless, addressed many statements to the government on a number of social and moral issues. They were part of the SACC, and when they approached the government about, for example, poverty, unemployment and crime, they did so through the ecumenical bodies together with other churches. Under the previous president, Thabo Mbeki, they had held a National Religious Leaders Forum that met with the president regularly and dealt with several issues. The AFM would, however, issue its own statements on moral issues, because not all the churches held the same opinions.[102]

---

99 Mahlobo, Mphikeleki George, Interview Protocol 2011-03-01.
100 Mahlobo, Mphikeleki George, Interview Protocol 2011-03-01.
101 Mahlobo, Mphikeleki George, Interview Protocol 2011-03-01. Anders Göranzon has written a thesis about the SACC as a prophetic voice. He states that it has addressed the democratic government and other actors in the South African society. He argues that the SACC has articulated a prophetic voice, but that there is an uncertainty whether the voice has been heard. It is mainly through the media that the prophetic voice can be heard. Göranzon, Anders, 2011, pp. 494–495.
102 Mahlobo, Mphikeleki George, Interview Protocol 2011-03-01.

Bishop Horst Müller from ELCSA N-T explained that they did not make any political statements as a single church. They were members of the SACC, and they were working together with ecumenical organisations that approached the government and society about the situation in South Africa.[103] The general Secretary of ELCSA, Bheki Mathe, said much the same thing, referring to the SACC. Statements about poverty eradication were made through the ecumenical bodies. ELCSA also directly approached the government departments that were responsible for a particular issue, instead of going public. Mathe explained:

> For example, there is the Department of Rural Development and Land Reform. We are highly involved through our diakonic arm, which is ELCSA Development Services. They are working towards a programme of action in helping the government and challenging the government or pushing the government towards taking care of the poverty-stricken members of our country.[104]

ELCSA also participated in stakeholders' meetings or consultations with, for example, the Department of Social Development. Mathe believed that it was easier for churches that had communication offices or policy departments dealing with public policies issues, because they had contacts through the media. Mathe stated: "[…] But we as ELCSA, if we write statements they don't appear, they will just summarise paragraphs in the newspaper, and sometimes they will change the statement, and that has de-motivated us in many ways".[105] His statements were much the same as those of the other church leaders who were interviewed. Churches found it difficult to get their message through the media 'noise', and they did not have the resources to bring a strong voice to the debate. This is a new era in which churches have to compete with other public actors. There were fewer public operators during the apartheid years, and the media no longer had the same influence as in previous years. Churches, however, often forget the tremendous opportunity they have to influence public opinion through the public's strong confidence in them. Their messages could be conveyed via the pulpits in Sunday services.

All the Lutheran churches were part of LUCSA, dealing with social development, justice, health, etc. They were also members of the LWF, which had global departments for humanitarian aid and development that also operated in southern Africa.[106] It was only ELCSA among the Lutheran churches that had a central

---

103 Müller, Horst, Interview Protocol 2011-03-04.
104 Mathe, P. Bheki, Interview Protocol 2011-03-07.
105 Mathe, P. Bheki, Interview Protocol 2011-03-07.
106 ELCSA Almanac 2011, 2011, p. III; Mathe, P. Bheki, Interview Protocol 2011-03-07. LUCSA is a communion of Lutheran churches in southern Africa that deals with

department for development service, running several projects. All the churches, nevertheless, had several local social projects. Horst Müller said that many in ELCSA N-T believed that the church was not very active in social and diaconal work. The head office had nevertheless invited the congregations to an exhibition, and they had been amazed at the amount of activity it revealed. Many congregations were deeply involved in various projects that went far beyond their own community in the form of soup kitchens, care for orphans, etc.[107] Congregations within ELCSA-Cape also showed a commitment to social and diaconal work, particularly in relation to a programme in one of Cape Town's townships.[108]

The church leaders' responses indicated that the churches had made several decisions and passed various resolutions about inequalities in the society, and had issued statements about poverty eradication. They had met with the government and the president, and had occasionally approached governmental officials.

The various church leaders regarded the SACC as an important organisation that gave the churches a strong common voice about, for example, unemployment, social justice, and poverty. Ecumenical organisation gave the churches a stronger voice so that they could influence the society and the government. Some of the churches had also their own departments or offices at the central level to advocate for social issues to both society and government – and also to their own members. The Roman Catholic Church, for example, had a parliamentary office and a Justice and Social Department; the Anglican Church had its provincial office; and the Lutheran churches had LUCSA. Establishing central departments for social issues was, however, regarded as an issue of having sufficient resources and funds.

Churches in a better economic condition could establish offices that engaged in advocacy and become a public voice. There were also issues about which the churches had different or contradictory opinions – for example, moral issues – and this complicated their ability to make joint proclamations. Churches also

---

    several common issues, such as different development projects. LWF has DWS (Department for World Service) and DMD (Department for Mission and Development), which between then deal with global humanitarian aid and development service, among other things.

107 Müller, Horst, Interview Protocol 2011-03-04.
108 Several ELCSA-Cape congregations, for example, supported iTemba Labantu, a Lutheran community centre in the township of Philippi. The ELCSA-Cape had representatives on its board, and congregations supported the project in various ways. See for example: Kreuzkirchengemeindbrief, Kruiskerk Nuusbrief, 12/2007, 01/2008, 2007. p. 8, Church Publication.

experienced internal disagreements, making it difficult for them to make official statements.

Most churches also had central departments or organisations that were engaged in social and diaconal projects. They promoted and implemented social development programmes, and several of these were done in cooperation with local congregations. The diaconal projects that were carried out by the churches can be regarded as a sign that *koinonia* and *diakonia* were held together, as described in the analytical tool about the catholicity of the Church.

The churches had strong credibility in the South African society; but several church leaders acknowledged that their voice was not as strong as in the past. Churches could make statements and pass resolutions, but the media were not interested – or they misunderstood their messages. The churches had realised that they now had a different position in the democratic society. They acknowledged that it was difficult to communicate their messages through the media 'noise'.[109]

11.3 Conclusions

The case congregations had several ministries that were attached to Sunday services and to local congregations. Members had duties such lay ministers, lectors or readers, altar servers, people in charge of intercessions, churchwardens, and various practical duties. The congregations ran courses and conferences, and offered education as part of spiritual formation. Education could be seen as the members' training in justice, democracy, and community development; but these local activities were almost entirely intended to build up the congregations and their members.

As part of worship's role of sending people out, together with prayers and intercessions, the congregations responded through several ministries such as home visitations, support groups, counselling, evangelisation, senior citizens activities, and social outreach programmes. Such programmes – soup kitchens, counselling, community projects, and so on – revealed that the congregations were engaged in issues in society that were not necessarily aimed at their own members, nor a way of getting new members. Church council members stressed that they supported everybody in the church, the society, and the human community.

---

109 The World Values Survey 2010-2014 indicated that more than half of the population considered themselves to be active members of a church or a religious organisationm while 77 per cent of the population had a great deal or quite a lot of confidence in the churches. World Values Survey (2010-2014) – South-Africa 2013, V 25 and V 108.

Some of the projects were carried out in cooperation with other congregations and churches, and even across ethnic and confessional boundaries. Cooperation in social projects could also become a shared platform for increased interaction between people of diverse ethnic backgrounds. A number of congregations also received support for their social projects from churches in other countries and on other continents, enhancing the global responsibility of the Christian community, and transcending ethnic and geographic borders in order to change inequalities in society.

Sharing, as part of the Church's catholicity, became apparent when congregations shared their resources within the community. Some congregations established special funds, volunteered their skills, or enabled donations. However, exchanges between privileged and underprivileged congregations were less visible in the case congregations.

Congregations' social programmes were mainly focused on alleviating local poverty and addressing local social injustices. Their ministries were primarily focused on individual assistance, and not on major social changes. Nevertheless, some congregations worked together in networks of local churches or civil society that tried to effect change in a specific area or a city.

Local congregations cannot, of course, eradicate poverty or promote sharing in a whole society; but their contexts reveal an inequality in the South African society that challenges the catholicity of the Church. Congregations have to be connected to a broader community such as a diocese or a district – and the ecumenical Church – in order to act and speak together in line with the analytical tool for catholicity. *Diakonia* and *koinonia* should be held together, and the whole Christian community is called to advocate and care for the poor, needy, and marginalised.

Advocacy about poverty eradication at the churches' central level was mainly done in collaboration with ecumenical bodies such as the SACC. Some churches issued statements and passed resolutions in their general assemblies, and some had even their own departments or organisations working on social justice, democracy, and the economy. The church leaders stated, however, that their voice did not have the same impact on society as in the past. Churches had had a clear voice under the apartheid government in opposing apartheid; but the situation since democratisation was different, given that there were more actors in the public space.

Congregations and churches showed, through their social and diaconal projects, that they imagined another kind of society with fewer differences between people. The primary aim of the ministries was not to reduce the gaps between ethnic groups but to alleviate poverty and to reduce social injustice. Advocacy for poverty eradication and social justice could, however, result in fewer barriers between the different ethnic groups.

Part III

Chapter Twelve: The Church in an Ethnically-diverse Society

This thesis is about the catholicity of the Church in relation to ethnicity in South African congregations and churches. Some scholars might argue that it is impossible to compare catholicity and ethnicity. I have found it productive, however, to use key documents from Faith & Order (F&O) and the World Council of Churches (WCC) to investigate how South African congregations and churches dealt with ethnic diversity two decades after democratisation.

The first part of the thesis gave the background to how South African churches have rejected apartheid, and their positions regarding the transition from apartheid before and after democratisation. I continued this part of the thesis by developing my analytical tool about the Church's catholicity, which has been derived from key documents from the international ecumenical movement. This part of the thesis also described how I studied a number of South African congregations and churches by using an operative ecclesiology. This method has been used to reveal their understandings of the Church by examining their implicit and explicit ecclesiologies.

In the second part of the thesis, I examined several themes in the South African congregations and churches that were productive to analyse in relation to ethnicity. By using an operative ecclesiology I could reveal an ecclesiology that I could test with my analytical tool about the Church's catholicity. In Chapter Five I described the parishes and churches that I studied. I selected five mainline churches: Roman Catholic, Anglican, Methodist, Lutheran, and Apostolic Faith Mission. From these churches, I selected six case congregations in the three largest metropolitan municipalities in South Africa: Johannesburg, Cape Town, and Durban. The congregations were St Peter Claver in Pimville, St Thomas' in Linden, Athlone Methodist Church, the Lutheran Church in Bellville, City Harvest Ministries in Ntuzuma, and St Michael's Lutheran Church in Durban.

Chapter Six investigated how the congregations and churches have dealt with reconciliation across ethnic boundaries since democratisation. The legacy of the TRC was explored, as well as how congregations and churches pursued reconciliation across ethnic boundaries. Special attention was given to the congregations' vision and mission statements in order to examine whether they reflected the Church's task of achieving reconciliation.

Chapter Seven specifically focused on ethnic diversity and on the ethnic composition of the congregations and churches two decades after democratisation.

Chapter Eight examined how ethnicity became visible in the church services and how diversity became apparent. The churches' confession of the ancient creeds as part of the liturgy was also investigated. Chapter Nine focused on the language issue as a specific concern that united or divided people in the churches.

In Chapter Ten I investigated the congregations' relationships with congregations of a predominantly different ethnicity. The churches had diverse organisational structures that influenced how they related to other communities. Chapter Eleven focused on the congregations' ministries and their work towards poverty eradication. A more equal and just society was part of the churches' vision before and after democratisation. Poverty eradication could become an important incentive to reduce divisions within the human community.

In this final chapter, Part III of the thesis, I will present the results of the research. Initially I discuss how the documents from the international ecumenical movement became important in discerning a sense of the catholicity of the Church, and how I developed my analytical tool. Then I turn to the operative ecclesiology that I have used to reveal an ecclesiology in South African congregations and churches. After this theoretical and methodological discussion, my conclusions are presented. These will determine the structure of this chapter, rather than following the structure that I have previously used in the thesis. Finally, I will discuss the theory and method, and how this kind of research could be applied in other areas of interest.

12.1 Theoretical Background, Analytical Tool, and Methodology

I have analysed documents from the world conferences of F&O from 1927, and documents of the WCC's world assemblies from 1948 until 2011, in so far as they dealt with ethnicity. Apart from these documents, I have analysed key ecumenical documents regarding ethnicity over the same period to develop my analytical tool about the Church's catholicity.

The F&O movement and the WCC are fellowships of churches and have no legal power to influence their member churches. Every church has its doctrines about the nature of the Church. However, the documents of the international ecumenical movement are generally consistent with their member churches' doctrines. These ecumenical documents are useful in providing a normative view of the Church's catholicity. From the documents, I have developed an analytical tool in which I have distinguished five areas of special concern related to ethnicity. The five areas are briefly discussed below.

1. The Christian Communion Transcends the Local Congregation
People are united through baptism into a shared communion with Christ that transcends geographic, social, ethnic, and temporal boundaries. The Christian communion is a specific community where members congregate, usually as members of the same church or denomination. A bishop or an equivalent person has the task of providing and safeguarding the unity of the Church – both the unity of local communities and unity with the universal Church.

2. Ethnicity Transcends Division
Any differentiation of the human community is a social construction, and diversity is valuable in the Christian communion. Diversity is, however, a secondary factor in the Church's communion of baptised members, because all are united in the body of Christ. Members are part of a new humanity in which there is a profound equality. The Church as a communion of believers becomes part of an eschatological reality that tears down barriers of separation. People of any ethnic background should be accommodated and welcomed into any Christian community, and every community is called to work against uniformity. Ethnic diversity should be seen as a gift that needs to be shared and received in the Christian community.

3. Reconciliation of Ethnic Division Is Part of the Church's Ministry
Reconciliation aims to restore the relationship between God and humanity and the relationships between individuals as well as groups of people. Ecclesial division contradicts the Christian message, and is regarded as a failure to carry out the ministry of reconciliation. Unity-in-reconciled-diversity is significant for the catholicity of the Church, and it does not imply uniformity, division, or mere coexistence. The eucharist has become a vital part of reconciliation because participants are invited to reconcile before worship. The eucharist, furthermore, sustains the Christian communion. The sharing of the same bread and wine also establishes a pattern of reconciliation followed by restitution so that Christian communion can be recovered.

4. Languages Contribute to the Church's Diversity
The Church is influenced by its context, which includes the languages that are spoken in the area where the congregations are situated, and that they use. These languages are legitimate expressions of the Christian faith. Language diversity is not the same as division, and the variety of languages enriches local congregations and even the universal Church. Diverse languages reveal new facets of the Church's catholicity. Languages are supposed to be shared and received. In contexts where

one language is dominant, other languages should also be accommodated and used to attain equality between the diverse languages.

5. *Poverty Eradication Eliminates Ethnic Boundaries*
The Church is called to act and speak in order to combat poverty and to safeguard human rights. Sharing resources with other Christians, irrespective of the geographic distance between them, is a consequence of all the baptised belonging to the same communion. *Koinonia* and *diakonia* should be held together. Sharing resources is based on Christ's own sharing of his life with the world. The practice begins with sharing the same eucharist, and extends to other aspects of life. Allocating resources between and within different communities builds bridges between them, and reflects an aspect of the Church's catholicity. The Church's work for equality, justice, peace, and restitution, as well as its advocacy for socio-economic change and poverty eradication, are also part of sharing in the Christian communion.

I have developed these five areas as my analytical tool, which I have named 'the catholicity of the Church', from the international ecumenical movement's documents. I treat this analytical tool as a normative theory in my thesis, and I have used it to test the findings in the case congregations and churches.

The method I have used to discern a South African ecclesiology originates with the French theologian Yves Congar and is called 'operative ecclesiology'. Congar argues that it is possible to find explicit and implicit ecclesiologies in the Church. There are different interpretations of the meaning of 'operative ecclesiology', and I have chosen to use one of these interpretations.

I argue that, according to Congar, it is possible to find both explicit and implicit ecclesiologies. An implicit ecclesiology is hidden in the Church's practices, which create ecclesiological patterns. The practices were studied in a range of churches in South Africa in 2011, two decades after apartheid had been dismantled. Group interviews were conducted with church councils and individually with the respective churches' leaders, general secretaries, or equivalent persons. The case congregations' church services were observed, and various materials were collected at local and central levels. An explicit ecclesiology can be discovered in the congregations and churches by examining their creeds, documents, and statements. Implicit and explicit studies of the Church made it possible to reveal an ecclesiology.

The practices were studied with the help of a method developed by the Scottish philosopher Alasdair MacIntyre. He argues that practices are cooperative human activities that are learned collectively over a long period. The common acts are part of making a communion of people. Two theologians from the USA, Dorothy Bass and Craig Dykstra, have developed MacIntyre's view of practices for an ecclesial context. They argue that ecclesial practices are something Christian people do together over time, and are cooperatively-formed patterns of activities. The practices address fundamental needs as a response to the Christian message. Typical ecclesial practices include church services, sacraments, hospitality, forgiveness, and prayers.

In my thesis, I have used the analytical tool as a normative theory of the Church's catholicity for the purpose of testing the established ecclesiology that I have discerned through an operative ecclesiology. Through my research into the South African congregations and churches, questions emerged that were worth investigating. In particular, it has been productive to investigate how South African congregations and churches have dealt with issues of ethnicity two decades after democratisation, and to discover what has determined ethnic integration. It was also interesting to examine whether there were differences between the congregations' and churches' practices concerning ethnicity on the one hand, and the Church's catholicity deduced from the ecumenical documents on the other hand. The congregations and churches belonged to different denominations, and it was useful to analyse different manifestations of a realised catholicity.

12.2 The Churches before Democratisation

The indigenous people at the southern tip of Africa were kept apart from the colonisers from the time that the Europeans settled in the area. An inherited myth relates how the leader of the first European settlers, Jan van Riebeeck, planted a hedge to separate the settlers from the indigenous people. When the colonisers captured the area and established their colonial administration, they enacted laws in their province to protect their interests. People who did not come from Europe could not own or live on certain land because of their background. There were also special laws that excluded people of certain backgrounds from holding specific positions in public life. Political power was also reserved for the 'White' colonial power.

The policy of segregation continued when the Union of South Africa was created in 1910, along with many discriminatory laws. For example, there had to be an absolute separation between people of diverse ethnic backgrounds. 'Black Africans' had to carry passes and had to apply for an exemption to live outside specific locations. The most severe policy was the Land Act of 1913, which enabled the 'White' minority to have exclusive access to valuable land and other natural resources in the country.

The National Party came to power in 1948, and the segregation policy continued and indeed was intensified. Apartheid was introduced through several laws that protected 'White' supremacy. One of the laws – the Group Areas Act of 1950 – was one of the most far-reaching in its effect of separating the population into particular areas. Different residential and working areas were created in the cities and in specific homelands for the 'Black' population. Forced removals were a consequence of the Act, as the implementation of apartheid was completed.

The churches had an ambivalent attitude towards the segregation of society. Churches did not interfere with the policies of the colonial administration or of the governments that followed it. Opposition to segregation was not substantially voiced before apartheid was introduced. The churches, however, passed resolutions, made statements, and instituted policies against discrimination, forced removals, and the introduction of the Group Areas Act when apartheid was introduced after 1948. However, little action was taken about discrimination in the churches' own practices, and the absence of protests by congregations at a local level was noticeable. For example, churches practised ecclesiastical apartheid by appointing ministers to congregations according to 'race', the leadership of the churches mirrored apartheid, and the churches did not question the intensifying social divisions.

Furthermore, the churches collaborated with the government in respect of military and police chaplaincies. They made agreements with the apartheid state that gave legitimacy to the apartheid policy. Ecclesial education did not provide ethical teaching to counteract apartheid. Moreover, a consequence of the Group Areas Act was that the churches became divided in practice, even though some of them were not divided organisationally. The AFM, however, became divided into different church sections under apartheid. The separation of the Lutheran churches coincided with the government's division of the people, and they are still not united.

Apartheid became an ecclesiological structuring factor in terms of which ethnicity became an important reason to divide worshiping communities. The international ecumenical movement condemned the policy and the laws that divided both society and Church on the basis of race, colour, or ethnicity. The notion of the Church's catholicity that emanated from the international ecumenical movement condemned apartheid policy. The discrimination revealed the brokenness of the *koinonia*, and hampered its prophetic mission and service in the world. South Africa's churches were seen as an example of a distortion of the Church's catholicity.

12.3 The Churches' Visions for a New Society

The South African ecumenical movement and churches met for several consultations and conferences when the country began to dismantle apartheid and to make the transition to democracy. Consultations continued after the advent of democracy, and the majority of the churches presented their perceptions of the past and their future hopes.

Church leaders came together at Rustenburg in 1990, where they agreed to reject apartheid, which had divided the population into separate groups. In a later consultation – in Cape Town in 1991 – the church leaders and delegates declared that people should not be divided on the basis of ethnicity or skin colour. During a special Faith Communities Hearing arranged by the TRC, several church leaders stated that the churches were prepared to participate in the work of reconciliation. They also stressed that they wanted to build a new society, one that was not damaged by separation. The church leaders stated further that reconciliation could not be accomplished without a just economic system. The society had to offer equal access to education, health, land, etc. There was also a need to create a culture of sharing in which all citizens had similar opportunities. The church leaders who were part of the TRC's special Faith Communities Hearing in East London in 1997 confessed that they wanted to work for a church in which diversity was welcomed and in which diverse heritages could flourish together. The TRC's final report stated that they encouraged the churches to develop communities that transcended language and cultural differences and where people from diverse backgrounds could encounter one another.

The churches' vision just before and after democratisation can be characterised as being consistent with the notion of the Church's catholicity according to my analytical tool. Ethnicity, language, habits, physical features, and similar forms of diversity were not reasons for division. According to the notion of catholicity discerned in the ecumenical documents, churches needed to practice reconciliation and to work towards a just society with equal access to education, employment, health care, living conditions, etc. Sharing as part of life in the Christian community was also consistent with catholicity as set out in my analytical tool.

12.4 Reconciliation as a Practice of Catholicity

South African society had been extremely divided because of the apartheid government's segregation policy, which created both perpetrators and victims. Part of the South African vision for the future was to become a reconciled community where people of diverse ethnic backgrounds could live together. The churches were challenged by the national and international ecumenical movement and the TRC to practise reconciliation – but also by the churches' own teaching about reconciliation.

Two decades after democratisation, my study of the case congregations and churches indicated that they had hardly been influenced by the TRC. Rather, they emphasised that they had been challenged and changed by the whole democratisation process in the country. None of the churches had continued the TRC's reconciliation process in their own structures after the Commission had ended its work. There were, however, other initiatives that had been inspired by the TRC that enabled people from diverse backgrounds to meet for reconciliation and healing.

It is important, however, to note that the TRC was not primarily a mechanism to attain reconciliation between diverse ethnic groups in the society. The commission's mandate was to reveal gross violations of human rights and human dignity that had been carried out during apartheid. Its mandate was also to bring about reconciliation between perpetrators and victims. The limited knowledge of the TRC's work on the part of the congregations and churches is due to the fact that they were not directly involved in the truth and reconciliation process.

Some of the people encountered in the case congregations had experienced reconciliation services. These services had been encouraged by the national ecumenical movement, the SACC, and were still sometimes practised in some congregations. Members of the church council at St Thomas' Anglican Church in Linden had participated in reconciliation services. St Michael's Lutheran Church in Durban had participated in workshops for the 'healing of memories', which can be regarded as an outflow from the TRC process. The services were seen as one-off events, not as a recurring practice. Reconciliation was part of ordinary Sunday services, but this kind of reconciliation would not necessarily occur with congregations of a predominantly different ethnic group. Few practices that transcended ethnic boundaries were evident in the case congregations. The Roman Catholic congregation, St Peter Claver in Pimville, had contact with other congregations in Soweto, but not with other congregations in Johannesburg other than through diocesan functions. Athlone Methodist Church had not held any reconciliation services, and – despite the rearranged local circuits – meetings with other congregations were seldom arranged. The AFM congregation, City Harvest Ministries in Ntuzuma, held services and outreach events with similar congregations, but interactions with congregations across ethnic boundaries were limited.

It is noteworthy that reconciliation was regarded by the church councils and church leaders as a process for individuals, not as a collective practice. However, the catholicity of the Church assumed in my analytical tool stresses that the reconciliation of the individual is integral to a communal practice where diversity is present. Reconciliation aims to overcome division based on ethnicity and to recover ecclesial unity and fellowship.

Reconciliation is also associated with restitution, according to the notion of catholicity used in my analytical tool. The case congregations at a local level did not support specific underprivileged congregations apart from engaging in social projects and the distribution of resources within their own church organisations such as a diocese or district. St Thomas' Anglican Church in Linden, for example, arranged a soup kitchen to distribute food for the needy and supported various institutions in Johannesburg. St. Michael's Lutheran Church in Durban ran a bakery in an underprivileged area and supported diverse social projects in the city centre. The Lutheran Church in Bellville contributed funds to a community project run by a German mission society in a township, undertook voluntary work in a retirement village, and supported an association for street people. They also collected resources for a local fund in the congregation. Nevertheless, some of the churches' central structures had programmes for the redistribution of wealth between congregations. The funds were collected from the congregations in a diocese or a district to support the ministers' stipends and particular projects in the congregations.

12.5 Ethnicity and Socio-economic Conditions Challenge Congregations and Churches

After two decades, the democratisation process in South Africa has resulted in a great deal of ethnic diversity in many congregations and churches. People of various ethnicities are, according to the country's constitution, able to live, work, and worship in any part of the country irrespective of their ethnic origin.

The Church is – and has always been – influenced by the surrounding society, and this has also been evident in the South African context. Congregations and churches are part of a society and do not exist independently of surrounding factors. The findings of this thesis indicate that both theological and socio-economic factors shaped the congregations and churches. Ethnic diversity grew in some areas, but segregation was enhanced and sustained in other areas.

The increased mobility of people in South Africa became evident after it became possible to choose where to live according to preference and affordability, but also through more convenient ways to communicate. This increased mobility has become a significant ecclesiological structuring factor. Before democracy, the society limited people's mobility: the Group Areas Act imposed restrictions on people's residence and movement. These restrictions also shaped the congregations and churches, and became an ecclesiological structuring factor. The catholicity of the Church could not be realised because of the state's restrictions.

Democratic South Africa now offers opportunities that could not be taken in the past. Nevertheless, most people live in the same areas as they did before democratisation, and this continues to influence the ethnic composition of most congregations. The study shows that socio-economic conditions were the main forces that changed the ethnic situation of some of the congregations. The mobility of people is another ecclesiological structuring factor for the congregation and churches. Socio-economic conditions have determined where people could live and have also sustained economic segregation; and this too shaped the congregations and churches.

Socio-economic conditions that give rise to a new form of segregation in society are inconsistent with the analytical tool. Likewise, any form of segregation within the Christian communion is inconsistent with the catholicity of the Church according to the analytical tool.

People moved into new areas mostly as a result of economic opportunities. A vertical and lateral mobility from former 'Black' areas to former 'Coloured', 'Indian Asian' and 'White' areas, and from former 'Coloured' and 'Indian Asian' areas to former 'White' areas, changed the ethnic make-up of the congregations. St Thomas' Anglican Church in Linden is situated in a former 'White' area, but it became more ethnically diverse after democratisation. It was, nevertheless, only a minority of the population that could take advantage of this vertical and lateral mobility. Lateral mobility in the opposite direction did not occur. St Peter Claver in Pimville and City Harvest Ministries in Ntuzuma, both in former 'Black' areas, and Athlone Methodist Church, in a former 'Coloured' area, had not become ethnically diverse. In this respect the congregations reflected the wider society.

Suburbs and city centres that were 'White' areas before democracy became more ethnically diverse. These areas always had a small amount of diversity even before democracy. Churches' main buildings are often located in city centres, while domestic workers have stayed in the 'servants' quarters' of suburban homes. Former 'Coloured' and 'Indian or Asian' areas had also become ethnically diverse because there was a greater mix of 'Coloured' and 'Indian or Asian' people in these areas, and 'Black Africans' had also moved into these areas according to Census 2011.

The case congregations in the suburbs and city centres had become ethnically diverse, but the ethnic diversity of congregations was also affected by language. Congregations that introduced English found it easier to accommodate people of diverse backgrounds, while congregations that emphasised the use of Afrikaans or German, for example, were less likely to become diverse. The Lutheran Church in Bellville was an example of a congregation that used Afrikaans and German in almost every Sunday service but used English only about once a month. The area where the church building was situated had become ethnically diverse, but the congregation did not reflect the changes that had taken place in that area. The ability to create a hospitable environment is part of my analytical tool for catholicity, and this is also a factor influencing the possibility of becoming a diverse community.

City centres had begun to become residential areas for predominately 'Black African' people, as was evident in the congregations located in the city centres. St Michael's Church in the Durban city centre was an example of a congregation that had received new members. Several of the church leaders indicated the same development. The Roman Catholic Church in Sunnyside, Pretoria, the Lutheran Friedenskirche or Church of Peace in Johannesburg, and the main AFM congregation in Pretoria had received huge numbers of 'Black African' people as new members.

There was nevertheless an indication of another lateral mobility: that of the 'White' population leaving the city centres mainly because of crime. People moved into enclosed or 'gated' communities where those with economic opportunities could enjoy residential security. This mobility into enclosed or gated communities is another form of vertical and lateral mobility that is not mainly to do with ethnicity, but with economic conditions. People living in enclosed or gated communities create another kind of ecclesiological structuring factor. Congregations situated in these communities are segregating themselves from the rest of society, and so cannot be regarded as living in accordance with the analytical tool that I have developed about the Church's catholicity.

The social mobility of people who had opportunities to move into other areas, but who were still worshiping members of a congregation in the area where they had previous lived, created another kind of ecclesiological structuring factor. St Peter Claver, for example, had members who had moved but who continued to worship in the parish because of language and liturgical preferences. Athlone Methodist Church had members who lived in other areas but who, because of their previous connections, continued to be members of the congregation. City Harvest Ministry in Ntuzuma had several members living in the city centre of Durban who continued to attend services in the township. Convenient forms of transport – cars or minibus taxis – made it possible for them to choose their congregation according to their language and liturgical preferences. The analytical tool for catholicity stresses that 'local church' refers to territorial definitions: a local congregations of believers, a community gathered around a bishop or equivalent person or common organisational structure. The mobility of members is not taken into account in the ecumenical documents and so this needs to be investigated further.

Ethnicity was an ecclesiological structuring factor during apartheid because of the separate residential areas and worshipping communities; but two decades after democratisation socio-economic conditions have also become an ecclesiological structuring factor alongside ethnicity. Ethnicity is still a marker that divides people, but economic conditions determine where people live, and these create new patterns of segregation. Socio-economic conditions as a structuring factor are not unique to South Africa. Most societies are socially structured, but the development is not consistent with the visions that were expressed by the churches and the ecumenical movement just before and after democratisation.

The congregations in former 'White' areas – and to a certain extent, congregations in former 'Coloured' and 'Indian Asian' areas as well – have become privileged because they have been able to become ethnically diverse, more clearly reflecting the Church's catholicity as I have defined the term in my analytical tool. Congregations in former 'Black' areas have not changed ethnically. People who live in these areas have not had the same economic opportunities nor the experience of vertical or lateral mobility, and they have remained in the same area.

Socio-economic conditions as a structuring factor created a situation of inequality. Some congregations could become ethnically diverse, in line with the Church's catholicity; other congregations were segregated, and had no possibility of becoming ethnically diverse. Segregation was forced on them because the majority of the people did not have the option of moving into an environment with a mainly different ethnicity. Socio-economic conditions determine the possibility of congregations and churches becoming ethnically diverse. The situation might even re-create the previous social divisions through the churches' practices, so that they reflect and perpetuate social patterns instead of becoming a force for change.

New theological questions emerge in a situation when ethnicity and socio-economic issues together become ecclesiological structuring factors. This thesis has revealed that there are three areas that particularly challenge congregations and churches to safeguard the catholicity of the Church as I have used the term in my analytical tool. 1) The churches' organisations or networks become vital to connecting people across ethnic and socio-economic boundaries. 2) Poverty eradication eliminates boundaries between people. 3) Using and learning different languages links people of diverse ethnicities, and offers fresh insights into the Christian message.

Church Organisations Serving Catholicity

The Church's catholicity, according to my analytical tool, emphasises that neither ethnicity nor other demarcations are grounds for segregation or division within the Christian communion. Diversity should be regarded as a gift to be shared and received in the communion of baptised believers. The findings of my thesis show that church organisations are important to safeguarding the unity of the Church and connecting people of diverse ethnicities. The churches' organisations were not simply administrative units for monitoring the congregations' common interests. Circuits, deaneries, dioceses, districts, networks, ecumenical bodies, and so on, were vital to transcending the divisions based on ethnicity or people's backgrounds.

The Roman Catholic congregation, St Peter Claver in Pimville, had an almost entirely 'Black African' membership, and they belonged to the Soweto district within their denomination. They were part of the Catholic Archdiocese of Johannesburg, which connected the congregation to other congregations in the city that consisted of other ethnicities. The diocese offered a common area where people of diverse backgrounds could meet and share their resources and needs. The congregation was also, through the diocese, part of the Southern African Catholic Bishops' Conference (SACBC) which in turn united them with the Bishop of Rome. The contacts and interactions between different communities might be limited, but the church's organisation offered a platform for uniting people of diverse ethnicities. When a member from one congregation visited another congregation, the same liturgy could be recognised, and they could share the same eucharist because they belonged to the same church. Clergy and religious orders also had networks at the same regional level and with a global community that transcended ethnic diversities.

St Thomas' Anglican Church in Linden mainly had 'White' members, but the congregation had become more diverse since democratisation as people of diverse ethnicities moved into the area. The congregation belongs to the Anglican Diocese of Johannesburg, which in turn is part of the Anglican Province of Southern Africa – an independent province with dioceses and congregations in the countries of Southern Africa. The province is in communion with other Anglican churches through the Anglican Communion. The congregation itself is part of one of the archdeaconries. These subdivisions within the diocese brought together congregations with a variety of diverse ethnicities. The diocese used St Thomas' as a teaching congregation that received students and curates from diverse backgrounds who stayed for longer or shorter periods. St Thomas' was twinned with a congregation in Soweto that some of the members often visited. The contacts with the Soweto congregation had broadened the sense of belonging to the same community. St Thomas' also had many choirs, providing opportunities for exchange programmes with other choirs in the diocese across ethnic boundaries. Their emphasis on music also made it possible to attend workshops elsewhere in the Anglican Communion. The diocese was responsible for developing intercessions for every Sunday service; and these identified issues in the Anglican Communion, the diocese, and the local congregation, thus connecting people in the congregations to others of diverse backgrounds and locations.

Athlone Methodist Church had members who were mostly 'Coloured'. They belong to the Cape of Good Hope District, part of the Methodist Church of Southern Africa. The Methodist Church is a member of the World Methodist Council, an organisation connecting Methodist churches around the world. The Methodist Church of Southern Africa has districts and congregations in the countries of Southern African. Athlone Methodist Church belonged to a circuit of other congregations with members from diverse ethnicities. The congregation did not have many contacts with the other congregations, but the ministers in the circuit met frequently. Delegates from the congregation participated in annual national meetings where people of diverse backgrounds met and discussed common matters. The congregation's membership of a specific denomination facilitated the appointment of a minister from a different ethnicity than that of the majority of the members of Athlone Methodist Church. The congregation and the district cooperated, moreover, with a global organisation within the Methodist Church, which was another form of network that transcended national and ethnic boundaries.

The Lutheran Church in Bellville, situated in one of the suburbs of Cape Town, belonged to ELCSA-Cape. The congregation – and ELCSA-Cape as a whole – was started by people of German background who had moved to South Africa. The church had predominately 'White' members of German descent. ELCSA-Cape was part of a network of other southern African Lutheran churches of German background; they shared similarities, but were located in other areas. Because of its German background, the church had strong relationships with EKD in Germany. However, this strong sense of community with the churches in Germany could become an excuse for not developing stronger relationships with ELCSA.

The church was also a member of the LWF and the sub-area LUCSA, to which people from other Lutheran churches of diverse ethnicities also belonged. Nevertheless, LWF and LUCSA did not constitute an organisation where people of diverse backgrounds could meet. Before democracy the Lutheran Church in Bellville had contacts with congregations of mainly other ethnicities, but the meetings later became infrequent. The common Lutheran confession and membership of LWF do, however, provide a platform for future unification.

It is strange that LWF is not actively involved in seeking visible church unity in Southern Africa. LWF did not even expect the churches to try to merge after democratisation. Lutheran ecclesiology is content as long as the word of God is proclaimed and the sacraments are rightly administered.

City Harvest Ministries in Ntuzuma is located in one of the townships of Durban and consists of 'Black African' members. It belongs to the AFM of South Africa, which is divided into regions or non-geographic regions. The regional and central levels of the church were not very strong and did not offer shared opportunities for meeting. The congregation was, however, part of several other networks for Pentecostal and charismatic churches that gathered people from diverse congregations in a city, nationally, or internationally. These networks provided opportunities for diverse ethnicities to come together for worship and meetings.

St Michael's is located in the Durban city centre. The majority of its members were 'Black African', but the congregation had members from diverse ethnicities because of its unique history. The congregation is a member of ELCSA, which emerged out of foreign mission work; most of ELCSA's members were of South African indigenous background. The congregation still had contacts with the churches in Europe and the USA that had established ELCSA. They had partnership programmes that enabled people from diverse continents to meet and support each other with intercessions, funds, and visits. Staff exchange was another form that transcended both national and ethnic boundaries. ELCSA is a member of LWF and LUCSA, but these organisations did not provide additional meeting opportunities for local members. Instead, the congregation, with an ELCSA N-T congregation, created a local network for people to meet across ethnicities. Their initiative can be seen as a pattern for church unity at regional and central levels for Lutheran churches.

Several congregations and churches were connected with other congregations and churches through various networks. It is important to stress that a network is different from a church's own organisations. Networks are fluid, and a congregation or a church can easily leave a network when it suits it; it is easy to leave a network when one partner no longer benefits from the relationship. Belonging to a network is a matter of choice, and it can facilitate interactions with people of diverse backgrounds. But it can also be an excuse for not seeking stronger links within a church in order to achieve catholicity. Acting and speaking against injustice and human rights violations is part of catholicity, but this is difficult to do through loose networks. The organisations of dioceses, districts, and churches are different: they are not left to choice, and they are integral to being Church.

Apart from the churches' own organisations, there were also ecumenical networks such as the SACC at national and regional levels that provided opportunities to meet such as workshops, joint services, and social projects. The ecumenical networks facilitated interactions between people from various backgrounds in South Africa.

My thesis has shown that church organisations should not be underestimated as a way to increase interaction between people of diverse ethnic backgrounds. The organisational structures make it possible to transcend ethnic boundaries and create common platforms where people can come together for meetings, services, and discussions. The churches have structured organisations that enable people to meet across boundaries – a feature that other organisations or associations in society lack. Interactions might still be limited, but the organisations can provide further engagement in the future. This study shows that church organisations are important for the Church's catholicity as understood in my analytical tool.

Sharing as an Instrument to Change Society and the Church

The previous government's policy divided the population into different groups, creating unequal conditions and opportunities in respect of wealth, health, education, land, and political power. South African society was extremely divided when the country became democratic. The legacy of the two decades since democratisation was still tied up with ethnicity, but economic conditions began to emerge as a new dividing factor.

The Church's catholicity, according to my analytical tool, stresses that sharing resources is part of belonging to the same Christian community that has its foundation in the one baptism. Sharing begins with the sharing of the eucharist, praying for others, and serving one another, and continues in giving aid and working for justice, peace, and equality. Sharing resources with other Christians in other places is a consequence of all belonging to the same communion, irrespective of geographic distance.

The case congregations' social programmes were primarily centred on alleviating local poverty and local social injustices. Congregations ran soup kitchens, supported social projects such as institutions for street children and homeless people, retirement homes, and schools. They also organised home visitations, support groups, counselling, home-based care, etc. However, the congregations were not involved to any large extent in wider social change such as advocating for local or regional governments to change their policies. Some congregations, such as St Michael's, nevertheless worked together with other congregation or networks like Diakonia in Durban, and tried to bring about change in a particular area in a city.

Of course, local congregations cannot eradicate poverty in South African society. Their actions, however, point to an inequality in the society that challenges the Church as catholic. Churches need to have a notion of catholicity that will make them act and speak together. A centralised – and even national and international – Christian community that is in full agreement about this issue is necessary in order to promote poverty eradication and sharing within the Christian community.

In contrast, the churches' central levels were engaged in advocacy for poverty eradication with the national government. This work was primarily done in collaboration with ecumenical bodies like the SACC. Some of the churches had departments or organisations running social programmes and advocacy for social justice, but their level of engagement was determined by the churches' available resources. The SACBC, for example, had a Justice and Peace department and an office attached to the national parliament. The Anglican Church had established an organisation named HOPE Africa that promoted and implemented social development programmes. AFM were running programmes concerning HIV, and the Lutheran churches together had a department for social development.

Churches made statements and passed resolutions at their general assemblies concerning social inequality that were addressed to the government. The Methodist Church, for example, had passed resolutions against the militarisation of the society and increased xenophobia. They had also supported the introduction of a basic income grant, and passed resolutions against prostitution and child trafficking. The Anglican Church regularly made statements to promote poverty eradication, and the AFM directed several statements to the government concerning moral and social issues.

The church leaders admitted that their churches' statements were seldom highlighted in the public media. The statements were valuable; but they also revealed a gap between resolutions and the churches' concrete actions. The churches' voice in advocacy was seen to be not as strong as in the time before democracy, and there was an opinion that there were fewer possibilities to penetrate the media noise. Church leaders, however, often underestimated the people's confidence in the churches and their potential to engage in advocacy through the churches' own channels. The World Values Survey 2010–2014 indicated that more than half of the population considered themselves to be active members of a church or a religious organisation; and more than three quarters of the population had a great deal or quite a lot of confidence in the churches, showing that the churches occupied an important position in shaping public opinion. Apart from the central level of the churches, the international Church as an ecumenical movement, according to the analytical tool, is challenged to act and speak together to eradicate poverty and become a sharing community.

Language as a Means to Communicate

There were two official languages in South Africa before democratisation, but several indigenous languages were also used in congregations and churches. The situation changed after democratisation, when eleven official languages were acknowledged. Other community languages were also supposed to be promoted and respected in terms of the Constitution. The South African situation of linguistic diversity can be seen as a major problem – but also as an advantage for experiencing greater diversity. It is a problem when people have many different first languages and almost nobody can understand and speak all the national languages. People have to learn other languages; and only a few people can communicate in their first language in the public space using, for example, isiXhosa, isiZulu, or Setswana. Recognising several different national languages can be an advantage for a society. People can express their opinions in various ways – and learning more languages can open up new perspectives.

The catholicity of the Church, according to my analytical tool, emphasises that the church should be formed by its context. This means that the church should use the languages that are spoken in the area where the church is located. Linguistic diversity should be regarded as a gift to be shared and received in the Christian community. Every language reveals new aspects of the Christian message that enrich congregations. There are, however, situations when one language dominates and inhibits diversity. The use of one dominant language reveals that there is an unequal power relation between the languages, and that not all languages are considered as important as the dominant language. Learning other languages – or at least using parts of the liturgy, hymns, or texts in other languages – is a way of acknowledging diversity as part of the Church's catholicity.

The same languages were used in the case congregations and churches as they had used before democratisation – that is, the peoples' first language. St Peter Clavier in Pimville used isiZulu and Sesotho, but they were also able to use Setswana or English. St Thomas' in Linden was English-speaking, but held a Sunday afternoon service in an indigenous language. Athlone Methodist Church used English entirely, but the members could also speak Afrikaans. The Lutheran Church in Bellville had German and Afrikaans as its main languages, but about once a month it held a service in English. City Harvest Ministry in Ntuzuma was entirely isiZulu-speaking, but also used English in the choruses that were sung there. St Michael's used isiZulu and English. St Thomas' in Linden was the only congregation that incorporated hymns and songs in various South African languages into one of their Sunday services.

Affiliation to a specific denomination determined the choice of language to a certain extent. The Anglican and Methodist churches are traditionally English-speaking, and the Lutheran Church in Bellville used German because of its German background. The situation after democratisation changed the scene because of the vertical and lateral social mobility that brought new groups of people into some of the areas. Bellville, for example, became more diverse. Many isiXhosa-speaking people moved into the area where the Lutheran Church was located, but this had no impact on the congregation.

The case congregations and churches showed that several indigenous languages were used in the townships where a majority of 'Black African' people lived. These congregations could manage with one service because the members could master several indigenous languages, including English. The congregations that used English, Afrikaans, or a community language such as German, and were located in a suburb or a city centre, exclusively used one language, or had to hold different services based on language. People who were English, Afrikaans or German first-language speakers might master one of the other languages, but not as their liturgical language. Congregations that had several different language services combined services a couple of times every year to bring the different worshiping groups together.

The languages that were used in the congregations and churches revealed unequal power relations between the languages. Learning and using an indigenous language was seen as too complicated by those who did not have an indigenous language as their first language. People with an indigenous language as their first language were more-or-less required to know English.

English became the lingua franca in South Africa after democratisation, and Afrikaans gradually declined in importance as the use of English grew. A common primary language was necessary for the churches' central levels and for common purposes when members of the same denomination met for services or functions. English became a unifying language that promoted communication between groups of people. The *lingua franca* is, however, often made the official language, which involves unequal power relations, cultural dominance, and exclusion. Having one dominant language would endanger the Church's catholicity, according to my analytical tool. Diversity and insights into the Christian message can be lost when one language dominates, and when it is not possible to attain sharing and receiving.

More research into language and churches in relation to catholicity is needed. Further study is especially necessary in a context like South Africa where there are several official languages. The Church's catholicity particularly challenges language domination and power stratification in the churches' language practices.

12.6 Denominational Belonging Influences a Realised Catholicity

I have investigated six congregations from five denominational communities, and their central denominational structures. It is relevant to question whether belonging to a particular denomination influences a realised catholicity. My definition of a realised catholicity implies that congregations and churches reflect the teaching of the Church about catholicity, as envisaged in my analytical tool, in their actions and practices.

The way a denomination chose to be organised considerably influenced its ability to realise the catholicity of the Church in relation to ethnicity. My interpretation of the Church's catholicity, based on the ecumenical documents, acknowledges that there are several ways to be organised as a church. The documents do not explicitly define how a church should be organised, and the structures are not mentioned explicitly. The function of a bishop, or the equivalent person, to safeguard unity in the body of Christ is central. This function involves the unity of local communities as well as relationships with the universal Church.

Congregations that were part of a denomination with a strong regional and central level – such as the Roman Catholic and Anglican churches – had several advantages in seeking to transcend ethnic boundaries. These churches had ready-made platforms for organising common meetings, gatherings, and services for everybody in a diocese regardless of ethnic background. There were also twinning projects that connected diverse worshiping communities. The churches' central levels could prescribe liturgies and prayers that everybody would use, regardless of ethnic community. They could, moreover, rearrange their deaneries as a sign of a common community. The central levels could also appoint their ministers regardless of ethnicity. A congregation with predominantly 'White' members could, for example, have a minister who was 'Black', or vice versa.

Congregations that were part of a denomination with a weaker regional and central level had much more local independence, as was the case with the AFM and ELCSA-Cape congregations. These congregations could, among other things, decide on their form of service or the appointment of ministers to the local congregation. These congregations did not have the same platform to gather in a common space regardless of ethnicity in the way that more centralised and hierarchical denominations could. They did not have any external influences from other levels of the church that could force a congregation to change or interact with other congregations. The congregations were independent and did not have frequent meetings at regional and central levels. Instead, these congregations had far-reaching independence when compared with congregations connected to a church with a strong regional and central organisation. Such independence reduces the possibilities of safeguarding the Church's catholicity, because a bishop or equivalent person did not have the same authority in these local communities.

Church families such as the Lutherans had a particular problem: they were not united into a common church organisation at the regional and central levels. Their church organisations coincided with the divisions in the country before democratisation. Some congregations in the former 'White' churches had begun to become ethnically diverse because of vertical and lateral social mobility. But none of these churches could achieve greater diversity because they had separate church organisations. There were no common platforms where people from ELCSA, ELCSA-Cape, and ELCSA N-T could mee; there were only occasional locally-formed meeting places. The divided Lutheran churches could not be considered as being consistent with the Church's catholicity according to my analytical tool, because ethnicity still separated the churches, and they were still not united as a single church.

Another issue attached to denominational belonging was the way the liturgy or order of service was enacted. Congregations that belonged to a denomination with a more fixed liturgy or order of service, such as the Roman Catholic, Anglican, and ELCSA churches, had an advantage because members could recognise each other's services regardless of ethnic factors or the location of a congregation. The liturgy or order of service could become a sign of unity that crossed boundaries. Congregations that belonged to denominations with only recommended liturgies or orders of service, such as the Methodist, ELCSA-Cape, and AFM churches, reflected the context in which the congregation was located, but they lost the mutual recognition of the services.

The eucharist is part of the liturgy or order of service, and denominations celebrated the eucharist with varying frequency. The catholicity of the Church, according to my analytical tool, stresses that the eucharist should be celebrated at least every Sunday and that Christians should be encouraged to receive the eucharist frequently. The Roman Catholic and Anglican congregations celebrated the eucharist every Sunday and also on weekdays. All the congregations that belonged to other denominations celebrated the eucharist once or twice a month. The celebration of the eucharist is, according to my analytical tool, a reaffirmation of the unity of the Christian community. When people celebrate the eucharist they are simultaneously affirming their unity with other Christians, which transcends ethnic boundaries. Celebrating the eucharist, even together with other worshiping communities, is vital for the unity of the church. There were also visibly different understandings of the eucharist between the congregations, related to denomination. Some congregations, such as the AFM congregation, emphasised a more individualistic approach, while others, like the Roman Catholic and ELCSA congregations, emphasised a more collective understanding of the eucharist. Individualistic or collective emphases affect the understanding of communion in relation to the eucharist.

Part of the liturgy or order of service was the common confession of the Christian faith. All churches in one or another way confessed that they were a catholic church in their practices, but they were confessing 'catholicity' differently. The Roman Catholic and Anglican churches used 'catholic' (and their equivalents in other languages, such as *eliKhatholika* or *katolieke*). The Methodist and ELCSA churches used 'catholic' in English, but in other languages terms like *lomhlaba wonke* ("the whole world" or "universal") or *algemene* ("the church in general" or "in common"). ELCSA N-T and ELCSA-Cape used terms like 'Christian' and, in other languages, *christliche* or *algemene*. AFM as a non-credal church did not use or translate the ancient terms; instead, it had a confession that could be considered as inspired by the ancient creeds.

Confessing 'catholicity' may seem irrelevant in relation to the practice of catholicity, but it influences a denomination's self-understanding. Denominations like the Roman Catholic Church, which emphasise the significance of a strong, hierarchical regional, central, and even global organisation, are inclined to stress the importance of the church as 'catholic'. A denomination like AFM, which emphasises a decentralised organisation, does not need to emphasise the church as 'catholic' because a united church organisation is not as important to them as it is to a church that emphasises the church as an organisation. Acting and speaking together, apart from confessing the faith, are important signs of the Church's catholicity according to the analytical tool. This definition suggests that unity involves local churches acting and speaking together.

Diverse interpretations of the term 'catholicity', and the use of other words, have ecclesiological implications; and the specific meaning of a church as 'catholic' might be lost. Members of the Christian community will only sustain and capture catholicity if they are part of a church that acts, speaks, lives and teaches catholicity. People learn by participating in catholicity in a church that is confessing, teaching, and practising catholicity. A parallel can be drawn with a society that wants to sustain and develop democracy. There is, however, a difference between democracy and catholicity. Democracy is a chosen form of governance, while catholicity is part of the Church's foundation, and the creeds are part of the Church's doctrines. Furthermore, confessing catholicity connects the local congregation to a wider communion that can act and speak on behalf of every local Christian community.

12.7 Final Comments

This thesis has been an attempt to capture the relationship between catholicity and ethnicity. The connection between the two concepts is not usually investigated. They could be regarded as not amenable to comparison because catholicity is an entirely theological term, while ethnicity comes from sociology and anthropology. I have, however, found the method constructive and productive in the study of contemporary ecclesiology.

I recognised that the ecclesiology of the South African case congregations and churches were in many ways consistent with the catholicity arising from the ecumenical documents. I have, however, chosen to investigate a topic that has been problematic in the South African context of diversity. South Africa is unique and thus has something to teach other churches in the world concerning catholicity in relation to ethnicity.

I have found it constructive to apply a methodology that uses an operative ecclesiology to discern an ecclesiology among South African congregations and churches. I could have chosen exclusively to use published documents from the congregations and churches, but practices are interesting because they can reveal another kind of ecclesiology. If further research were to be carried out, using the notion of 'operative ecclesiology', it could yield very interesting and constructive results, especially when an operative ecclesiology is tested against the catholicity of the Church.

I chose to use ecumenical key documents from F&O and the WCC to define a normative theory of catholicity. The documents were produced in an international environment, and do not specifically address South Africa; churches from other contexts are part of developing a consensus about the Church's teaching. Several scholars have used ecumenical documents in their research into the Church and have found that very productive. Few scholars, however, have tried to develop the notion of catholicity from the ecumenical documents, especially in relation to ethnicity. I find the use of the concept of 'catholicity' derived from the ecumenical documents productive; and it could be applied in the study of other subjects such as the environment, migration, xenophobia, ecumenism, or economics. It is strange, therefore, that 'catholicity' is not used more often by theologians as a tool to describe the Church's foundation. Using this kind of material is problematic, however: there is no collection or single document that explains catholicity as it is understood in the ecumenical movement. The notion of catholicity has to be culled from several documents in which the ecumenical movement has expressed a consensus. It would have been easier to examine, for example, the eucharist or baptism, because ethnicity is not always explicitly named in the documents. It was possible, however, to discern some connection between catholicity and ethnicity in the documents, showing that it might be possible to examine other issues concerning the Church. It would be valuable for other researchers if F&O and the WCC developed a single document, or initiated a special programme, about the catholicity of the Church to facilitate further studies related to various issues in the Church and in the world. The concept of 'catholicity' is rarely mentioned in later ecumenical documents, and it is seldom used as an instrument to analyse various issues in the Church. Further research could usefully examine how catholicity is taught and practised in congregations and churches.

I chose to examine five church families, and this had both advantages and disadvantages. It would have been easier to study just one church tradition, with congregations from the same denomination. This would have been an interesting study, but at the same time it would have been very limited. The selection of several churches has revealed where there are differences, which is important from an ecumenical point of view. Testing is also constructive in revealing diverse patterns of how churches can deal with ethnicity.

My research has particularly revealed that language diversity and socio-economic differences have to be investigated ecclesiologically in relation to the catholicity of the Church. These issues of catholicity are a challenge not only in the South African context, but in every society where barriers occur in the Christian community.

References

Unpublished Sources

Unpublished sources in the form of interview protocols, interviews, observation protocols, websites, e-mail correspondence, and church and congregation publications are archived as attachments to the thesis in DiVA (Digital Academic Archive) at the University of Uppsala. DiVA is a digital archive for long-term preservation. The material can be accessed through the Faculty of Theology at the University of Uppsala.

Submissions and transcriptions from the Truth and Reconciliation Commission's Faith Communities Hearing in East London in 1997, provincial and local government publications, Acts of Parliament, newspaper articles, and media releases are also archived in DiVA. Statistics from Census 2011 can be accessed from the Statistics South Africa database in Pretoria. Audiovisual productions from the Faith Communities Hearing in East London in 1997 can be accessed from the Department of Government Communication and Information Systems in Pretoria.

Church Council Interview Protocols

Church Council Interview Protocol 2011-02-27.
   St Peter Claver Roman Catholic Church, Pimville, Soweto, Johannesburg.
Church Council Interview Protocol 2011-03-06.
   St Thomas' Anglican Church, Linden, Johannesburg.
Church Council Interview Protocol 2011-03-15.
   Bellville Lutheran Church, ELCSA-Cape Church, Bellville, Cape Town.
Church Council Interview Protocol 2011-03-20.
   Athlone Methodist Church, Methodist Church, Athlone, Cape Town.
Church Council Interview Protocol 2011-03-27.
   City Harvest, AFM, Ntuzuma Area, Durban.
Church Council Interview Protocol 2011-04-03.
   St Michael's Lutheran Church, ELCSA, Durban.

Individual Interview Protocols

Brennan, Vincent, Interview Protocol 2011-03-01.
   General Secretary, SACBC, Paul Kruger St, Pretoria.

Burton, Mary, Interview Protocol 2011-03-23.
   Former Commissioner in TRC, UCT, Rondebosch, Cape Town.
Goosen, Juri, Interview Protocol 2011-04-09.
   Domini, NGK, Khaya Building, Van Ryneveld Street, Stellenbosch.
Ilunga-Mpomso, Kiasso, Interview Protocol 2011-03-18.
   St. Martin's Church, ELCSA-Cape, Long Street, Cape Town.
Kannemeyer, Allan J., Interview Protocol 2011-03-16.
   Provincial Executive Officer, ACSA, Bishopscourt Drive, Bishopscourt, Cape Town.
Mahlobo, Mphikeleki George, Interview Protocol 2011-03-01.
   General Secretary, AFM, Centurion, Gauteng.
Mathe, P. Bheki, Interview Protocol 2011-03-07.
   General Secretary, ELCSA, Bonaero Park, Kempton Park, Johannesburg.
Meiring, Piet, Interview Protocol 2011-03-05.
   Professor and former Commissioner in TRC, Camellia Avenue, Lynnwood, Pretoria.
Müller, Horst, Interview Protocol 2011-03-04.
   Bishop, ELCSA N-T, Bonaero Park, Kempton Park, Johannesburg.
Nyobole, Vuyani Gladstone, Interview Protocol 2011-02-28.
   General Secretary, MCSA, Morning Hill, Bedfordview, Johannesburg.
Rohwer, Nils J., Interview Protocol 2011-02-09.
   Bishop, ELCSA-Cape Church, De Beer Street, Stellenbosch.
Van der Merwe, Andries, Interview Protocol 2011-02-21.
   Pastor, Shofar Christian Church, Andringa Street, Stellenbosch.

Congregation Observation Protocols

Observation Protocol 2011-02-20.
   Bellville Lutheran Church, Kreuzkirche, ELCSA-Cape Church, Bellville, Cape Town.
Observation Protocol 2011-02-27.
   St Peter Claver Roman Catholic Church, Pimville, Soweto, Johannesburg.
Observation Protocol 2011-03-06.
   St Thomas' Anglican Church, Linden, Johannesburg.

Observation Protocol 2011-03-20.
Athlone Methodist Church, Methodist Church, Athlone, Cape Town.
Observation Protocol 2011-03-27.
City Harvest Ministry, AFM, Ntuzuma, Durban.
Observation Protocol 2011-04-03.
St Michael's Lutheran Church, ELCSA, Durban.

Email Correspondence

Geyer, Monica, monica.geyer@stolav.co.za, 2014. *St Olav Church, Durban.* [email] Message to Erik Berggren (erik.berggren@teol.uu.se). Sent Wednesday 12 February 2014: 06:00.

Pluddemann, Gerhard, igpluddemann@universe.co.za, 2014. *Pastor emeritus ELCSA-Cape.* [email] Message to Erik Berggren (erik.berggren@teol.uu.se). Sent Wednesday 9 July 2014: 21:07.

Church Publications

Anglican Church of Southern Africa, Diocese of Johannesburg, Diocesan Vision, 2002, Adopted at the Diocesan Synod Conference in March, 2002. Johannesburg: ACSA, Diocese of Johannesburg.

Annual Review, October 2011, I Care – giving children a future, 2011. Durban: I Care.

Apostolic Faith Mission of SA City Harvest Family, 2008. Durban: City Harvest Ministries.

Athlone Methodist Church, Athlone Society Profile, c.a. 2008. Cape Town: Athlone Methodist Church.

Athlone Methodist Church, Church History, ca. 2010. Cape Town: Athlone Methodist Church.

Athlone Methodist Church, Shukuma 20.02.2010, 2010. Cape Town: Athlone Methodist Church.

Athlone Methodist Church, Shukuma Task Group – 3rd November 2010, 2010. Cape Town: Athlone Methodist Church.

City Harvest Ministries Constitution, 2011. Durban: City Harvest Ministries.

Constitution of ELCSA Music Organization, n.d., Johannesburg: ELCSA.

Constitution of the Prayer Men's League of the Evangelical Lutheran Church in Southern Africa. Johannesburg: ELCSA.

Constitution of the Prayer Women's League of the Evangelical Lutheran Church in Southern Africa, 1998. Johannesburg: ELCSA.

Constitution of the Student Organisation of the Evangelical Lutheran Church in Southern Africa, 2005. Johannesburg: ELCSA.

Constitution of the Young Adults League of the Evangelical Lutheran Church in Southern Africa, 2010. Johannesburg: ELCSA.

Constitution of the Youth League of the Evangelical Lutheran Church in Southern Africa, 2011. Johannesburg: ELCSA.

Durban Central Parish 2011 Activities Plan, 2011. Durban: Durban Central Parish, ELCSA.

Eastwood Lutheran Church, The Liturgy, n.d. Pietermaritzburg: Eastwood Lutheran Church, Pietermaritzburg South Parish.

ELCSA-SED 2010 Year Plan, 2010. Umpumulo: ELCSA-SED.

ELCSA-SED – Durban Central Parish – Preaching Plan – April to August 2011, 2011. Durban: Durban Central Parish, ELCSA.

ELCSA-SED Durban Circuit 2011 Year Plan, 2011. Durban: ELCSA-SED Durban Circuit.

Evangelical Lutheran Church in the Vaal Triangle, Vanderbijlpark, Overview, 2011. Johannesburg: ELCSA N-T.

Friedenskirche, Johannesburg, Overview, 2011. Johannesburg: ELCSA N-T.

Hahne, Albrecht, 2002. English Worship Services in Bellville. In: Plüddemann, Ulrich, ed. 2002. *Cape Church Newsletter, April 2002, No. 1*. Cape Town: Communication Desk of ELCSA Cape Church. pp. 14–15.

Hahne, Albrecht, 2010. *Pastor's Report Tabled at the Annual General Meeting on 7th March 2011*. Cape Town: Bellville Lutheran Church.

Hahne, Albrecht, 2011. *Pastor's Report Delivered at the Annual General Meeting of the Cross Church, Bellville on 27th February 2011*. Cape Town: Bellville Lutheran Church.

Information sheet for the Sunday, 6th March 2011, The ninth Sunday of the Year, 2011. Johannesburg: St Thomas' Anglican Church Linden.

Jacobs, G. A., 1992. *The Athlone Circuit*. Cape Town: Athlone Methodist Church.

Kreuzkirchengemeidebrief, Evangelical Lutheran Church Bellville, Kruiskerk Nuusbrief, 04/05 2009, 2009. Cape Town: Evangelical Lutheran Church Bellville.

St Johannes Lutheran Church, Kelvin, Overview, 2011. Johannesburg: ELCSA N-T.

Kreuzkirchengemeindbrief, Kruiskerk Nuusbrief, 12/2007, 01/ 2008, 2007. Bellville: Evangelical Lutheran Church Bellville.

Liturgical Practices in our Parish, 2010. Durban: Durban Central Parish, ELCSA.

Lutheran Church Bellville, Kalender, Februar 2011–Maart 2011, 2011. Cape Town: Lutheran Church Bellville.

The Lutheran Church in the Cape, n.d. Cape Town: ELCSA Cape Church.

Lüdemann, Joe, 2012, *Durban Central Parish Report 2011*. Durban: Durban Central Parish, ELCSA.

Marimba Mass, St Thomas' Anglican Church, 09h45 Family Mass, n.d., Johannesburg: St Thomas' Anglican Church Linden.

Message of the Church Council to the congregations on the instruction of the General Synod, "Christ is our Hope", 1986. Cape Town: UELCSA.

Music at St Thomas', n.d., Leaflet about music in St Thomas' Anglican Church Linden. Johannesburg: St Thomas' Anglican Church Linden.

New German Lutheran Church, 2011, ELCSA N-T, Johannesburg: ELCSA N-T.

Objectives for Christian Education in ELCSA, 1984. Johannesburg: ELCSA.

Overview of the Durban Parish, n.d., ELCSA N-T. Johannesburg: ELCSA N-T.

St Peter Claver Catholic Church, Pimville, 1928–2008, 80th Anniversary, 2008. Pimville: St Peter Claver Catholic Church.

St Peter's by the Lake Lutheran Church, Overview, 2011. Johannesburg: ELCSA N-T.

St Peter's Congregation, Pretoria, Overview, 2011. Johannesburg: ELCSA N-T.

Prins. D., *Athlone Methodist Church, Sixteen Years Down Memory Lane 1977–1993*, c.a. 1993.

Rubow, Hürgen, 2011, *Bericht des Kirchenvorstandes: 27 Februar 2011, Evangelisch-Lutherische Kreuzkirche, Bellville*. Cape Town: Bellville Lutheran Church.

St Thomas' Anglican Church Linden, Parish Profile, 5th March 2011, 2011. Johannesburg: St Thomas' Anglican Church Linden.

St Thomas' Treble Choir, n.d., Leaflet about music young singers in St Thomas' Anglican Church Linden. Johannesburg: St Thomas' Anglican Church Linden.

The St Thomas's Magazine, April 2010, 2010. Johannesburg: St Thomas' Anglican Church Linden.

The St Thomas's Magazine, April 2011, 2011. Johannesburg: St Thomas' Anglican Church Linden.

The St Thomas's Magazine, August 2010, 2010. Johannesburg: St Thomas' Anglican Church Linden.

The St Thomas's Magazine, January & February 2011, 2011. Johannesburg: St Thomas' Anglican Church Linden.

The St Thomas's Magazine, January/February 2010, 2010. Johannesburg: St Thomas' Anglican Church Linden.

The St Thomas's Magazine, January 2014, 2014. Johannesburg: St Thomas' Anglican Church Linden.

The St Thomas's Magazine, March 2011, 2011. Johannesburg: St Thomas' Anglican Church Linden.

The St Thomas's Magazine, May 2011, 2011. Johannesburg: St Thomas' Anglican Church Linden.

The St Thomas's Magazine, November & December 2010, 2010. Johannesburg: St Thomas' Anglican Church Linden.

"The Turning Point", The history of St. Olav Lutheran Church, From 1980–2002 and into the 21st Century as the St Olav Church, 2002. Durban: St Olav Church.

Welcome to St Thomas' Anglican Church, Linden, 2011, Johannesburg: St Thomas' Anglican Church Linden.

West Rand Lutheran Community Church, Overview, 2011. Johannesburg: ELCSA N-T.

Websites

Anglican Church of Southern Africa, Diocese of Johannesburg, Archdeaconries, 2014. [online] Johannesburg: Anglican Church of Southern Africa, Diocese of Johannesburg. Available at: <http://www.anglicanjoburg.org.za/archdeaconries.aspx> <http://www.anglicanjoburg.org.za/region3/Region3.aspx> [Accessed 2014-04-01].

Athlone School for the Blind, History, 2014. [online] Cape Town: Athlone School For the Blind. Available at: <http://www.athloneschoolfortheblind.org.za/history.php> [Accessed 2014-05-05].

St Charles Borromeo Roman Catholic Parish, Holy Masses, 2013. [online] Johannesburg: St. Charles Borromeo Roman Catholic Parish. Available at: <http://saintcharles.co.za/holy-masses/> [Accessed 2013-12-10].

City Harvest Ministries, Good News to the young generation, 2013. [online] Pyra Labs. Available: <http://cityharvestministries.blogspot.com/2011/12/good-news-to-young-generation.html> [Accessed 2013-12-19].

City Harvest Ministries, The life of City Harvest Ministries, 2013. [online] Pyra Labs. Available: <http://cityharvestministries.blogspot.com/2011/12/v-behaviorurldefaultvmlo.html> [Accessed 2013-12-19].

City Harvest Ministries, The Notice Board of C.H.M., 2013. [online] Pyra Labs. Available: <http://cityharvestministries.blogspot.com/2011/12/notice-boradof-chm.html> [Accessed 2013-12-19].

City Harvest Ministries, Year Plan for the year 2012, 2013. [online] Pyra Labs. Available: <http://cityharvestministries.blogspot.com/2011/12/year-plan-for-year-2012.html> [Accessed 2013-12-19].

Day, Katie, 2009. The Curious Conversion of Adriaan Vlok. *Journal of Religion, Conflict, and Peace.* [e-journal] Vol. 2, Issue 2, Spring 2009. Goshen, Ind.: Plowshares. Available at: <http://www.religionconflictpeace.org/volume-2-issue-2-spring-2009/curious-conversion-adriaan-vlok> [Accessed 2015-10-01].

Deutscher Kindergarten, Bellville, Fees, 2014. [online] Cape Town: Deutscher Kindergarten, Bellville. Available: <http://en.deutscher-kindergarten.co.za/homepage/fees/?id=231> [Accessed 2014-04-21].

Durban Central Parish, Leadership team, 2014. [online] Durban: Durban Central Parish. Available:
<http://www.elcsadurban.co.za/Home/About_us_-_Leadership_team.html>
<http://www.elcsadurban.co.za/Home/About_us_-_Rev._Dr._Joe_Ludemann.html>
<http://www.elcsadurban.co.za/Home/About_us_-_Rev._Sybil_Chetty.html>
<http://www.elcsadurban.co.za/Home/About_us_-_Rev._Sabelo_G._Mkhathini.html>
<http://www.elcsadurban.co.za/Home/About_us_-_Rev._Fred_von_Fintel.html> [Accessed 2014-02-17].

Durban Central Parish, Leagues and Organisations, Abasizikazi, Amadoda, Abasha, iMbokodo, Youthe Adult League, Sunday School, ELCSASO, ELCSAMO, 2011. [online] Durban: Durban Central Parish. Available:
<http://www.elcsadurban.co.za/Home/Leagues.html>
<http://www.elcsadurban.co.za/Home/Leagues_-_Abasizikazi_-_Prayer_Womens_League.html>
<http://www.elcsadurban.co.za/Home/Leagues_-_Amadoda_-_Prayer_Mens_League.html>
<http://www.elcsadurban.co.za/Home/Leagues_-_Abasha_-_Youth_League.html>
<http://www.elcsadurban.co.za/Home/Leagues_-_iMbokodo.html>
<http://www.elcsadurban.co.za/Home/Leagues_-_Young_Adult_League.html>
<http://www.elcsadurban.co.za/Home/Leagues_-_Sunday_School.html>
<http://www.elcsadurban.co.za/Home/Leagues_-_ELCSASO.html>
<http://www.elcsadurban.co.za/Home/Leagues_-_ELCSAMO.html> [Accessed 2011-06-17].

Durban Central Parish, Projects, Inner-City Outreach, The P.U.S.H. Project, Lutheran Uniting in Action, 2011. [online] Durban: Durban Central Parish. Available:
<http://www.elcsadurban.co.za/Home/Projects.html>
<http://www.elcsadurban.co.za/Home/Projects_-_Inner-City_Outreach.html>
<http://www.elcsadurban.co.za/Home/Projects_-_The_P.U.S.H._Project.html>
<http://www.elcsadurban.co.za/Home/Projects_-_Lutherans_Uniting_in_Action.html> [Accessed 2011-06-17].

Durban Central Parish, Short history of the congregations, 2014. [online] Durban: Durban Central Parish. Available: <http://www.elcsadurban.co.za/Home/About_us_-_History.html> [Accessed 2014-02-11].

Durban Central Parish, Who are we?, Congregations, St Michael's, 2011. [online] Durban: Durban Central Parish. Available
<http://www.elcsadurban.co.za/Home/About_us.html>
<http://www.elcsadurban.co.za/Home/Congregations.html>
<http://www.elcsadurban.co.za/Home/Congregations_-_St._Michaels.html> [Accessed 2011-06-17].

H.E.L.P. Ministries International Trust, 2014. [online] Cape Town: Help Trust Ministries. Available: <http://www.help-trust.org.za/home.htm> [Accessed 2014-04-14].

St Johannis Heim in Bellville, Sponsors, 2014. [online] Cape Town: St Johannis Heim in Bellville. Available: <http://stjohannisheim.co.za/who-we-are/sponsors/?lang=en> [Accessed 2014-04-21].

Linden St Thomas, Normal Schedule of Services, 2011. [online] Johannesburg: Anglican Church of Southern Africa, Diocese of Johannesburg. Available at: <http://anglicanjoburg.org.za/linden/LindenStTomas/DetailsofServices.aspx> [Accessed 2011-09-03].

Linden St Thomas, Our Outreach Project, 2011. [online] Johannesburg: Anglican Church of Southern Africa, Diocese of Johannesburg. Available at: <http://anglicanjoburg.org.za/linden/LindenStTomas/Outreach.aspx> [Accessed 2011-09-03].

Linden St Thomas, Welcome to St Thomas Linden, 2011. [online] Johannesburg: Anglican Church of Southern Africa, Diocese of Johannesburg. Available at: <http://anglicanjoburg.org.za/linden/LindenStTomas.aspx> [Accessed 2011-09-03].

Lutheran Church Bellville, Activities, 2011. [online] Cape Town: Lutheran Church Bellville. Available at: <http://www.kreuzkirche.co.za/pages/activities.html> [Accessed 2011-08-17].

Lutheran Church Bellville, Who Are We?, 2011. [online] Cape Town: Lutheran Church Bellville. Available at: <http://www.kreuzkirche.co.za/pages/about.html> [Accessed 2011-08-17].

Lutheran Church Bellville, Worship Services, 2011. [online] Cape Town: Lutheran Church Bellville. Available: <http://www.kreuzkirche.co.za/pages/services.html> [Accessed 2011-08-17].

The Methodist Church of Southern Africa, Circuits and Societies in the Cape of Good Hope District, 2014. [online] Johannesburg: The Methodist Church of Southern Africa. Available at: <http://www.methodist.org.za/societies/cape-of-good-hope> [Accessed 2014-04-14].

St Peter Claver Parish, Pimville, Soweto, 2011. [online] Johannesburg: St Peter Claver Catholic Church, Pimville. Available at: <http://www.stpeterclaver.co.za> [Accessed 2011-12-11].

SACC Member Churches, 2013. [online] Johannesburg: SACC. Available: <http://www.sacc.org.za/pages/member.html> [Accessed 2013-10-02].

Van der Riet, Louis, 2014. Truth and Reconciliation – A Matter of Faith?. *IJR Connect*, Vol. 5, Issue 5, 2014. [online] Cape Town: IJR. Available at: <http://www.ijr.org.za/news-and-events.php?nid=203&type=news> [Accessed 2015-09-29].

WCC Membership Churches and Organisations in South Africa, 2013. [online] Geneva: WCC. Available: <http://www.oikoumene.org/en/member-churches/africa/south-africa> [Accessed 2013-10-02].

Census 2011 Downloads

Statistics South Africa. Population Census 2011 [database]. Version 1. Pretoria: Statistics South Africa [producer and distributor], 2013. Available at: <http://interactive.statssa.gov.za/superweb/login.do> [Accessed 2013-12-19].

Census 2011, Athlone. Statistic South Africa.

Census 2011, Avondstil. Statistic South Africa.

Census 2011, Bellville. Statistic South Africa.

Census 2011, Bellville Central. Statistic South Africa.

Census 2011, Bosmont. Statistic South Africa.

Census 2011, Chatsworth. Statistic South Africa.

Census 2011, Chrismar. Statistic South Africa.

Census 2011, City of Cape Town Metropolitan Municipality. Statistic South Africa.

Census 2011, City of Johannesburg Metropolitan Municipality. Statistic South Africa.
Census 2011, Durban Central. Statistic South Africa.
Census 2011, eThekwini Metropolitan Municipality. Statistic South Africa.
Census 2011, Eversdale Ext 21. Statistic South Africa.
Census 2011, Harry De Villiers. Statistic South Africa.
Census 2011, Hillrise. Statistic South Africa.
Census 2011, Kempenville. Statistic South Africa.
Census 2011, Kingston. Statistic South Africa.
Census 2011, Klipspruit. Statistic South Africa.
Census 2011, Kliptown. Statistic South Africa.
Census 2011, Lenasia. Statistic South Africa.
Census 2011, Linden. Statistic South Africa.
Census 2011, Newland East. Statistic South Africa.
Census 2011, North Beach. Statistic South Africa.
Census 2011, Ntuzuma. Statistic South Africa.
Census 2011, Oakdale. Statistic South Africa.
Census 2011, Pimville Zone 1-8, Klipspruit and Kliptown. Statistic South Africa.
Census 2011, Randburg. Statistic South Africa.
Census 2011, Rylands. Statistic South Africa.
Census 2011, South Beach. Statistic South Africa.
Census 2011, Soweto. Statistic South Africa.
Census 2011, Sunkist. Statistic South Africa.
Census 2011, Wentworth. Statistic South Africa.

Submissions and Materials from the Truth and Reconciliation Commission's Faith Communities Hearing in East London 17-19 November 1997

Available at South African History Archive (SAHA), William Cullen Library, University of the Witwatersrand, Collection no: AL 3066_1.1-1.55, Documents Relating to the TRC Faith Hearing.

Apostolic Faith Mission.
   Submission, 4 August 1997, signed by President I.S. Burger.

Church of the Province of Southern Africa.
Submission, 30 June 1997, signed by Archbishop Njongonkulu Ndungane.

Lutheran Church of Southern Africa Natal-Transvaal.
Submission, 19 March 1998, signed by Bishop D.R. Lilje on behalf of the Church Council of the ELCSA N-T.

Methodist Church of Southern Africa.
Submission, August 1997, signed by Presiding Bishop of the Methodist Church of Southern Africa H. Mvume Dandala.

The programme for the three days of hearing (with the names of the panelists), 1997. Johannesburg: TRC.

Roman Catholic Church.
Submission, 15 August 1997, unsigned.

Audiovisual Productions

The Truth and Reconciliation Commission's Faith Communities Hearing in East London 17–19 November 1997. Recordings made by SABC. Accessible at the Department of Government Communication and Information System in Pretoria and National Archives, Pretoria.

TRC Special Hearing: Religion Tape 3, East London, Church of England, Methodist, Catholic, Presbyterian, (TRC0357 – 19971117). 1997 [DVD] Pretoria: Department of Government Communication and Information System, Republic of South Africa.

TRC Special Hearing: Religion Tape 11, East London, Apostolic Faith Mission, United Reformed Church, NG Kerk, (TRC0366 – 19971119). 1997. [DVD] Pretoria: Department of Government Communication and Information System, Republic of South Africa.

Published Sources and Literature

Abraham, Garth, 1989. *The Catholic Church and Apartheid: The Response of the Catholic Church in South Africa to the First Decade of Nationalist Rule, 1948–1957*, Braamfontein: Ravan Press (Pty) Ltd.

Acting Against Poverty, 2005. Pretoria: SACBC / Justice & Peace Department.

Adhikari, Mohamed, 2009. *Burdened by Race: Coloured identities in southern Africa*. Cape Town: UCT Press.

An African Challenge to the Church in the 21st Century, 1997. Eds. Guma, Mongezi & Milton, A. Leslie Milton. Marshalltown, Johannesburg: South African Council of Churches.

Altaarboek Evangelies-Lutherse Kerk in Suidelike Afrika, 1995. Bonaero Park: ELCSA.

Altar Book Evangelical Lutheran Church in Southern Africa, 1995. Bonaero Park: ELCSA.

Alvesson, Mats, & Sköldberg, Kaj, 2008. *Tolkning och reflektion: vetenskapsfilosofi och kvalitativ metod*. Lund: Studentlitteratur.

Anderson, Allan H., & Pillay, Gerald J., 1997. The Segregated Spirit: The Pentecostals. In: Elphick, Richard & Davenport, Rodney, eds. 1997. *Christianity in South Africa*. Berkeley, Calif.: University of California Press. Ch. 13.

Andrew, Daniël Nicolaas, 2005. *From vision to structure: Assessing the Apostolic Faith Mission of South Africa in the light of the one, holy, catholic and apostolic church*. Cape Town: UWC. DTh.

An Anglican Prayer Book, 1989. London: Collins Liturgical Publications; Claremont [SA].

'n Anglikaanse gebedeboek, 1989. London: Collins Liturgical Publications; Claremont [SA].

Badcock, Gary D., 2009. *The House Where Good Lives*. Grand Rapids, Michigan: Wm. B. Eerdmans Publishing Co.

Banks, Marcus, 1996. *Ethnicity: Anthropological constructions*. London: Routledge.

Baptism, Eucharist and Ministry, 1982. Faith and Order Paper No. 111. Geneva: World Council of Churches.

Bass, Dorothy C., & Dykstra, Craig, 2010. *Practicing our Faith*. San Francisco: Jossey-Bass.

Bassham, Gregory, & Hamilton, Mark, 2007. Hardwood Dojos: What Basketball Can Teach Us about Character and Success. In: Walls, Jerry L., & Bassham, Gregory, eds. 2007. *Basketball and Philosophy: Thinking Outside the Paint*. Lexington, Ky.: University Press of Kentucky. pp. 44–56.

Being the Church in South Africa Today, 1995, Eds. Pityana, Barney N., & Villa-Vicencio, Charles. Johannesburg: South African Council of Churches.

Berggren, Erik, 2005. Pieces in the Puzzle: A Local Study of Denominationalism and Ethnicity towards Unity in South Africa. *SMT Swedish Missiological Theme*. Vol. 93, No. 1. Uppsala: Swedish Institute of Mission Research. pp. 87–113.

Bernard, H. Russell, 2002. *Research Methods in Anthropology: Qualitative and Quantitative Approaches*. 3rd ed. Walnut Creek: AltaMira Press.

Bickford-Smith, Vivian, & Van Heyningen, Elizabeth, & Worden, Nigel, 2000. *Cape Town in the Twentieth Century: An Illustrated Social History*. Cape Town: David Philip.

Black Priest due in white African Parishes, 1977, *Bakersfield Californian*. Sat Feb, 12, 1977. Bakersfield, CA: The Bakersfield Californian. p. 3.

Boraine, Alex, 2000, *A country unmasked: Inside South Africa's Truth and Reconciliation Commission*. Oxford: Oxford University Press.

Bosch, David J., 1991. Churches Perspectives on the Future of South Africa. In: Alberts, Louw, & Chikane, Frank, eds. 1991. *The Road to Rustenburg*. Cape Town: Struik Christian Books Ltd. pp. 129–139.

Bosch, David, 1993. Nothing but heresy. In: De Gruchy J. & Villa-Vicencio, C., eds. 1993. *Apartheid is a heresy*. Grand Rapids, Mich.: W.B. Eerdmans Publishing Co., 1983. pp. 24–38.

Brain, Joy, 1997. Moving from the Margins to the Mainstream: The Roman Catholic Church. In: Elphick, Richard & Davenport, Rodney, eds. 1997. *Christianity in South Africa*. Berkeley, Calif.: University of California Press. Ch. 11.

Brantlinger, Patrick, 1985. Victorians and Africans: The Genealogy of the Myth of the Dark Continent. *Critical Inquiry*, Vol. 12, No. 1 (1985). Chicago: University of Chicago Press. pp. 166–203.

Breaking Barriers: Nairobi 1975: The Official Report of the Fifth Assembly of the World Council of Churches, 23 November–10 December, 1975, 1976. Ed. Paton, David M. London: SPCK; cop.

Brodd, Sven-Erik, 2006. Theme in Operative Ecclesiology. *International Journal for the Study of the Christian Church*, Vol 6 No 2, 2006. Chichester: Routledge. pp. 124–125.

Brodd, Sven-Erik, 2008. Theological Focus: Ecclesiological Elements in Understanding 'Church' in the HIV and AIDS Pandemic. In: Ward, Edwina, & Leonard, Gary, eds. *A Theology of HIV and AIDS on Africa's East Coast*. Uppsala: Swedish Institute of Mission Research. pp. xvi–xl.

Bryman, Alan, 2012. *Social Research Methods*. 4th ed. Oxford: Oxford University Press.

Burger, Isak, & Nel, Marius, 2008. *The Fire Falls in Africa: A History of the Apostolic Faith Mission of South Africa*. Vereeniging: Christian Art Publishers.

Butler, Jon, 2008. *New World Faith: Religion in Colonial America*. Oxford; New York: Oxford University Press.

Called to One Hope – The Gospel in Diverse Cultures, 1998. Duraisingh, Christopher. ed. Geneva: WCC Publications.

The Cambridge Encyclopedia, 1994. 2nd ed. Cambridge: Cambridge University Press.

Cantle, Ted, 2012. *Interculturalism: The New Era of Cohesion and Diversity*. Basingstoke, Hampshire; New York: Palgrave Macmillan.

Cape Town Consultation Proposal for Action, 1991. In: PCR information. *From Cottesloe to Cape Town, The WCC visit to South Africa, October 1991, Challenges for the Church in post-apartheid South Africa*. PCR information; 1991/ no. 30, Geneva: World Council of Churches, Programme to Combat Racism. pp. 103–108.

Cawood, Lesley, 1964. *The Churches and Race Relations in South Africa*. Johannesburg: South African Institute of Race Relations.

Census 2001: Primary tables South Africa Census '96 and 2001 compared Statistics South Africa, Report No. 03-02-04 (2001), 2004. Pretoria: Statistics South Africa.

Census 2011, Census in Brief, Report No. 03-01-41, 2012. Pretoria: Statistics South Africa.

Chen, Yiya, & Downing, Laura J., 2011. All Depressors are not alike: A comparison of Shanghai Chinese and Zulu. In: Elordieta, Gorka, & Frota, Sonia & Prieto, Pilar, eds. 2011. *Prosodic Categories: Production, Perception and Comprehension*. Dordrecht: Springer. pp. 243–266.

Chikane, Frank & Alberts, Louw, 1991. Foreword, Introduction. In: Chikane, Frank & Alberts, Louw, eds. 1991. *The Road to Rustenburg*. Cape Town: Struik Christian Books Ltd. pp. 9–11.

Christerson, Brad, & Edwards, Korie L., & Emerson, Michael O., 2005. *Against all Odds: The Struggle for Racial Integration in Religious Organisations*. New York & London: New York University Press.

Christian Perspectives on Theological Anthropology, 2005. Faith and Order paper No. 199. Geneva: WCC.

The Church and Racism: Towards a more Fraternal Society, 1989. Pretoria: SACBC.

Church and World: The Unity of the Church and the Renewal of Human Community: A Faith and Order Study Document, 1990. Geneva: WCC Publications.

The Church – Towards a common vision, 2012. Doc. No. GEN 06. Geneva: WCC.

Civil Union Act No. 17 of 2006, 2006, Government Gazette, 30 November 2006, 2006. Pretoria: Government Printer.

Clements, Keith, 1995. *Learning to Speak: The Church's Voice in Public Affairs*. Edinburgh: T & T Clark.

Cochrane, James R. & de Gruchy, John W. & Martin, Stephen, 1999. *Facing the truth: South African faith communities and the Truth & Reconciliation Commission*. Athens: Ohio University Press.

Coertze, Roelof D., 2007. 'Racism and ethnicity': Reflection on the debatable permanence of terminology. *Anthropology Southern Africa*, Vol. 30 No. 1&2. Pretoria: Bureau for Scientific Publ. pp. 11–19.

Community Serving Humanity, 1989. Pretoria: Southern African Catholics Bishops' Conference.

Confessing the One Faith: An Ecumenical Explication of the Apostolic Faith as it is Confessed in the Nicene-Constantinopolitan Creed (381), 1991. Faith and Order Paper no. 153. Geneva: WCC Publications.

Congar, Yves M.-J.,1966. L'"Ecclesia" ou communauté chrétienne, sujet intégral de l'action liturgique. In: Congar, Yves M.-J. & Jossua, Jean-Pierre. eds. 1967. *La liturgie après Vatican II: bilans, études, prospective.* – (Unam Sanctam; 66). Paris: Les Éditions du Cerf. pp. 242–282.

Constitution and Canons of the Anglican Church of Southern Africa, 2012. Westhoven: The Publishing Committee, Anglican Church of Southern Africa.

Constitution of the Apostolic Faith Mission of South Africa, 2010. Centurion: AFM.

Constitution of the Evangelical Lutheran Church in Southern Africa, 2009. Bonaero Park, Johannesburg: ELCSA.

Constitution of the Lutheran world Federation (as adopted by the LWF Eighth Assembly, Curitiba, Brazil, 1990, including amendments adopted by the LWF Ninth Assembly, Hong Kong, 1997 and by the LWF Eleventh Assembly, Stuttgart, 2010), 2010. Geneva: LWF.

The Constitution of the Republic of South Africa, 1996. Adopted on 8 May and amended on 11 October 1996 by the Constitutional Assembly. Pretoria: South African Government Information.

Convention on the Rights of the Child, 1990, United Nation: UN.

Cook, G. P., 1991. Cape Town. In: Lemon, Anthony, ed. 1991. *Homes and Apart; South Africa's Segregated Cities*. London: Chapman.

Cyril of Jerusalem & Nemesius of Emesa, 1955. *Cyril of Jerusalem and Nemesius of Emesa*. The Library of Christian Classics Volume IV, ed. Telfer, William. London: SCM Press.

Davenport, Rodney, 1997. Settlement, Conquest, and Theological Controversy: The Churches of Nineteenth-century European Immigrants. In: Elphick, Richard & Davenport, Rodney, eds. 1997. *Christianity in South Africa*. Berkeley, Calif.: University of California Press. Ch. 3.

Davies, R. J., 1991. Durban. In: Lemon, Anthony, ed. 1991. *Homes and Apart; South Africa's Segregated Cities*. London: Chapman.

Day, Katie, 2009. The Curious Conversion of Adriaan Vlok. *Journal of Religion, Conflict, and Peace*. [e-journal] Vol. 2, Issue 2, Spring 2009. Goshen, Ind.: Plowshares. Available at: <http://www.religionconflictpeace.org/volume-2-issue-2-spring-2009/curious-conversion-adriaan-vlok> [Accessed 2015-10-01].

De Beer, Frik C., 1989. Ethnicity in Nation States with Reference to South Africa. *Suid-Africaanse Tydskrif vir Etnologie*. No 1 1989. Johannesburg: Vereniging van Afrikaanse Volkekundiges. pp. 32–39.

De Beer, Jan Mathys, 2008. *Die missionêre waarde van die Belhar Belydenis vir die NG Kerk: instrument tot inheemswording*. Ph.D. Pretoria: University of Pretoria.

Declaration of Commitment on Social Justice and Race Relations Within the Church; SACBC Plenary Session, February 1977, 1997. Pretoria: SACBC.

Declaration of Intention Concerning Church Unity by the Convocation of Pastors of ELCSA (Cape Church). Cape Town, 19th August 1982. Cape Town: ELCSA (Cape Church).

Degenaar, Johan J., 1990. *Nation and Nationalism: The Myth of the South African Nation*. Occasional Paper No. 40. Mowbray: IDASA.

De Gruchy, John, 1991. Understanding the Church Situation and Obstacles to Christian Witness in South Africa. In: Chikane, Frank & Alberts, Louw, eds. *The Road to Rustenburg*. Cape Town: Struik Christian Books Ltd. Ch 12.

De Gruchy, John W., 1995. Becoming the Ecumenical Church. In: Pityana, Barney N., & Villa-Vicencio, Charles, eds. 1995. *Being the Church in South Africa Today*. Johannesburg: South African Council of Churches. pp. 12–24.

De Gruchy, John W., 1997. Grappling with a Colonial Heritage: The English-speaking Churches under Imperialism and Apartheid. In: Elphich, Richard, & Davenport, Rodney, eds. 1997. *Christianity in South Africa*. Claremont: David Philip Publishers (Pty) Ltd. Ch 9.

De Gruchy, John & de Gruchy, Steve, 2005. *The Church Struggle in South Africa*. Minneapolis: Fortress Press.

De Gruchy, John, 2009. *Christianity and the modernisation of South Africa*. Pretoria: UNISA Press.

De los Reyes, Paulina & Mulinari, Diana, 2005. *Intersektionalitet: kritiska reflektioner över (o)jämlikhetens landskap*. Malmö: Liber.

DeYoung, Curtiss, & Emerson, Michael O., & Yancey, George, & Chai Kim, Karen, 2003. *United by Faith: The Multicultural Congregation as an Answer to the Problem of Race*. Oxford: Oxford University Press.

Documentary History of Faith and Order, 1963–1993, 1993. Faith and Order Paper no. 159. Ed. Gassmann, Günther. Geneva: WCC Publications, 1993.

Dulles, Avery, 1985. *The Catholicity of the Church*. Oxford: Clarendon Press.

Du Preez, Hannetjie, 2009. Genadendal's Historical Context and Project Set-up. In: du Preez, Hannetjie, & Van Oers, Ron, & Roos, Job, & Verhoef, Leo, eds. 2009. *The Challenge of Genadendal*. Amsterdam: IOS Press. pp. 11–20.

Durand, J. J. F., 1961. *Una sancta Catholica in Sedingperspektief: 'n analise van die probleme rondom kerklike pluriformiteit en ekumenisiteit in die sending*. Amsterdam: W ten Have. PhD.

Dykstra, Craig, 1991 (1997). Preconceiving Practice in Theological Inquiry and Education. In: Murphy, Nancey C., & Kallenberg, Brad J., & Nation, Mark, eds. 1997. *Virtues & Practices in the Christian Tradition, Christian Ethics after MacIntyre*. Valley Forge, PA: Trinity Press International. pp. 161–184.

Ecclesial Practices: Journal of Ecclesiology and Ethnography, 2014, Vol. 1, No 1. Ed. Ward, Peter. Leiden: Brill.

Ecclesiology and Ethics: Ecumenical Ethical Engagement, Moral Formation and the Nature of the Church, 1997. Eds. Best, Thomas F. & Robra, Martin. Geneva: WCC.

Edgardh, Ninna, 2001, *Feminism och liturgi: – en ecklesiologisk studie*. Stockholm: Verbums Förlag AB.

Edwards, Korie L., 2008. *The Elusive Dream: The Power of Race in Intercultural Churches*. New York: Oxford University Press.

Ekenberg, Anders, 1996. *Låt oss be och bekänna*. Örebro: Libris.

ELCSA Almanac 2011, 2011, Johannesburg: ELCSA.

Emerson, Michael O., & Smith, Christian, 2000. *Divided by Faith: Evangelical Religion and the Problem of Race in America*. Oxford; New York: Oxford University Press.

Employment Equity Act, No. 55 Of 1998, 1998. Republic of South Africa. Pretoria: Department of Labour.

Empty Hands, 1980. Geneva: WCC.

Encyclopedia of Race, Ethnicity, and Society, 2008. Schaefer, Richard T. ed. Los Angeles: SAGE Publications.

Encyclopedia of South Africa, 2011. Boulder, Colo.: Lynne Rienner Publishers, Inc.

Engdahl, Hans S. A., 2006. *Theology in Conflict – Readings in Afrikaner Theology*. Th.D. Frankfurt am Main: Peter Lang.

English Hymn Book, 1980. Evangelical Lutheran Church in Malaysia and Singapore.

Entre Nous, 1995. Rustenburg: The Southern African Council of Priests.

European Convention on Human Rights, 2010. Strasbourg: European Court of Human Rights Council of Europe.

Evangelisches Gesangbuch (Niedersachsen, Bremen), 1994. Bremen: Evangelische Gesangbuch Niedersachen.

The Evanston Report: The Second Assembly of the World Council of Churches 1954, 1955. Ed. Visser't Hooft, W.A. London: SCM Press.

Fahlgren, Sune, 2006. *Predikantskap och församling: sex fallstudier av en ecklesial baspraktik inom svensk frikyrklighet fram till 1960-talet*. Th.D. Uppsala: Uppsala universitet.

Farisani, Elelwani Bethuel, 2008. The Challenges Facing Lutherans in South Africa. In: Aageson, James W. & Jacobson, Arland Dean, eds. 2008. *The Future of Lutheranism in a Global Context*. Minneapolis, MN: Augsburg Fortress. pp. 37–45.

Fiddes, Paul S., 2012. Ecclesiology and Ethnography: Two Disciplines, Two Worlds?. In: Ward, Peter, ed. 2012. *Perspectives on Ecclesiology and Ethnography*. Grand Rapids, Mich.: W.B. Eerdmans Pub. Co. Ch. 1.

The First Assembly of the World Council of Churches, held at Amsterdam, August 22nd to September 4th, 1948, 1949. Ed. Willem Adolph Visser 't Hooft. London: SCM Press.

Fish, Jennifer N., 2006. Engendering Democracy: Domestic Labour and Coalition-Building in South Africa. *Journal of Southern African Studies*. Vol. 32, No. 1. Abingdon: Taylor & Francis, Ltd. pp. 107–127.

Florin, Hans, Wilhelm, 1967. *Lutherans in South Africa*. Durban: Lutheran Publishing Co.

Florin, Hans Wilhelm, 1999. 'Out of Solidarity with the Victims' – the South African Apartheid Regime, the New Democratic South Africa and the Policy of the World Council of Churches. In: Besier, Gerhard, ed. 1999. *The Churches, Southern Africa and the Political Context*. Atlanta; London: Minerva. Ch. 5.

Forskningsetiska principer inom humanistisk-samhällsvetenskaplig forskning, 2002. Stockholm: Vetenskapsrådet.

Fosseus, Helge, 1974. *Mission blir kyrka*. Stockholm: Verbum.

The Fourth World Conference on Faith and Order, Montreal 1963: The Report, 1964. Eds. Rodger, Patrick C., & Vischer, Lukas. London: SCM Press.

Fuchs, Lorelei F., 2008. *Koinonia and the Quest for an Ecumenical Ecclesiology*. Grand Rapids, Mich.: William B. Eerdmans Pub. Co.

Fuerth, Patrick W., 1973. *The concept of catholicity in the documents of the World Council of Churches, 1948-1968: A historical study with systematic-theological reflections*. Roma: Ed. Anselmiana.

Gaitskell, Deborah, 2002. Whose Heartland and Which Periphery? Christian Women Crossing South Africa's Racial Divide in the Twentieth Century. *Women's History Review*, Vol. 11, No. 3. Wallingford, Oxford, U.K.: Triangle Journals. pp. 375–394.

Gaitskell, Deborah, 2004. Crossing Boundaries and Building Bridges: The Anglican Women's Fellowship in Post-Apartheid South Africa. *Journal of Religion in Africa*, Vol. 34, Fasc. 3. Leiden: Brill. pp. 266-297.

Gaitskell, Deborah, & Kimble, Judy, & Maconachie, Moira, & Unterhalter, Elaine, 1983. Class, Race and Gender: Domestic Workers in South Africa. *Review of African Political Economy*, No. 27/28, Women, Oppression and Liberation. London: Oryx Press. pp. 86-108.

Gastrow, Peter & Shaw, Mark, 2001. In Search of Safety: Police Transformation and Public Responses in South Africa. *Daedalus*, Vol. 130, No. 1. Cambridge, Mass.: American Academy of Arts and Sciences. pp. 259-275.

Gathered for Life: Official Report, VI Assembly World Council of Churches, Vancouver, Canada 24 July-10 August 1983, 1983. Geneva: World Council of Churches.

Gibaut, St-Helier, John, 2011. Catholicity, Faith and Order, and the Unity of the Church. *The Ecumenical Review*, Vol. 63, Issue 2, July 2011. Oxford: Blackwell Publishing. pp. 177-185.

Gibson, James L., 2004. *Overcoming Apartheid: Can Truth Reconcile a Divided Nation?*. New York: Russell Sage Foundation.

Giddens, Anthony, & Sutton, Philip W., 2013. *Sociology*. 7th ed. Cambridge: Polity, 2013.

God, in your grace ...: Official Report of the Ninth Assembly of the World Council of Churches, 2007. Geneva: WCC.

Groome, Thomas H., 1998. *Education for Life: A Spiritual Vision for Every Teacher and Parent*. Allen, Tex.: T. More.

Grundlingh, Albert, 1989. From Feverish Festival to Repetitative Ritual. *Suid-Afrikaanse Historiese Joernaal*, No. 21, 1989. Pretoria: SAHJ. pp. 19-37.

Guma, Mongezi & Milton, A. Leslie, eds., 1997. *An African Challenge to the Church in the 21st Century*. Marshalltown, Johannesburg: South African Council of Churches.

Göranzon, Anders, 2011, *The Prophetic Voice of the South African Council of Churches after 1990 - Searching for a Renewed Kairos*. Ph.D. Uppsala: SIM.

Hagen Agøy, Berit, 2000. The Freedom Struggle in South Africa. In: Linné Eriksen, Tore, ed. 2000. *Norway and National Liberation in Southern Africa*. Uppsala Nordic Africa Institute. Ch. 7.

Harshe, Rajen, 1993. Understanding Transition towards Post-Apartheid South Africa. *Economic and Political Weekly*, Vol. 28, No. 38 (Sep. 18, 1993). Bombay: Sameeksha Trust. pp. 1980-1983.

Healy, Nicholas M., 2000, *Church, World and Christian Life: Practical-prophetic Ecclesiology*, New York: Cambridge University Press.

Healy, Nicholas M., 2003. Practices and the New Ecclesiology: Misplaced Concreteness?. *International Journal of Systematic Theology*, Vol. 5 No. 3 (2003). Oxford: Blackwell Publishing Ltd. pp. 287–308.

Healy, Nicholas M., 2004. Ecclesiology and Communion. *Perspectives in Religious Studies*. Vol. 3, No. 3. Waco, TX: NABPR. pp. 273–290.

Hodgson, Janet, 1997. A Battle for Sacred Power: Christian Beginnings among the Xhosa. In: Elphick, Richard & Davenport, Rodney, eds. 1997. *Christianity in South Africa*. Berkeley, Calif.: University of California Press. Ch. 4.

Household Questionnaire A, Demographics, Census 2011, 2010. Pretoria: Statistics South Africa.

How to get zero: Faster, Smarter, Better: UNAIDS World AIDS Day Report 2011, 2011. Geneva: Joint United Nations program on HIV/AIDS (UNAIDS).

Hylland Eriksen, Thomas, 2010. *Ethnicity and Nationalism: Anthropological Perspectives*. 3rd ed. London: Pluto Press.

Ideström, Jonas, 2009. *Lokal kyrklig identitet: en studie av implicit ecklesiologi med exemplet Svenska kyrkan i Flemingsberg*. Th.D. Skellefteå: Artos & Norma.

"In Christ – Hope for the World", 1985. LWF Report No. 19/20 Mau, Jr., Carl H., ed. Geneva: Lutheran World Federation.

In Christ – a new community: the proceedings of the sixth assembly of the Lutheran World Federation, Dar-es-Salaam, Tanzania, June 13–25, 1977, 1977. Ed. Sovik, Arne. Geneva: LWF.

Incwadi Yamamisa Ngamasonto, 1983, Mariannhill: Mariannhill Mission Institute.

Incwadi Yase Altare Ye-Evangelical Lutheran Church in Southern Africa, 1995. Bonaero Park: ELCSA.

Incwadi yenkonzo, kunye neminye imithandazo, nezingoma, emiselwe libandla Lamamethodisi aseningizimu Neafrika: Ibalwe ngesizulu, 1938. Cape Town: Methodist Book Depot and Pub. House.

Incwadi Yokuhlabelela yeBandla lamaLuthere, 2008. Durban: Lutheran Publishing House.

Inter-Diocesan Consultation 2012; Southern African Catholics Bishops' Conference; Phase I, 2011. Pretoria: Southern African Catholics Bishops' Conference.

Incwadi yokukhuleka yasetshetshi, 1989. London: Collins Liturgical Publications; Claremont, SA.

Jackelén, Antje, 1999. Response to Nicholas Healy: A Different Kind of Church-talk Ecclesiology for a Pilgrim Church, *Tro & Liv*, No 2 (1999). Stockholm: Tro & Liv. pp. 15-19.

Jamison, Christopher, 2012. Compass in the Catholic Church: Finding a Path to Vocation Discernment. In: Simmonds, Gemma, ed. 2012. *A Future Full of Hope?* Blackrock, Co Dublin: The Columba Press. Ch. 5.

Jonker, Willie, 1991. Understanding the Church Situation and Obstacles to Christian Witness in South Africa. In: Chikane, Frank & Alberts, Louw, eds. 1991. *The Road to Rustenburg*. Cape Town: Struik Christian Books Ltd. Ch. 9.

Jonker, Willie D., 1992. Catholicity, Unity, and Truth. In: Schrotenboer, Paul, G., ed. 1992. *Catholicity and Secession, a Dilemma?*. Kampen: J.H. Kok Pub. pp. 16-27.

The Kairos Document, 1985. Braamfontein: Skotaville Publishers.

Kamwangamalu, Nkonko M., et al., 2000. *International Journal of the Sociology of Language*. Berlin: De Gruyter Mouton.

Kamwangamalu, Nkonko M., 2003. Social Change and Language Shift: South Africa. *Annual Review of Applied Linguistics*, Vol. 23 / mars 2003. Cambridge; New York: Cambridge University Press. pp. 225-242.

Kamwangamalu, Nkonko M., 2006. Religion, Social History, and Language Maintenance; African Language in Post-apartheid South Africa. In: Omoniyi, Tope, & Fishman, Joshua A., eds. 2006. *Explorations in the Sociology of Language and Religion*. Amsterdam, NLD: John Benjamins Publishing Company. Ch. 8.

Kaufmann, Larry, 1985. Towards an Ecclesiology for South Africa. *Grace & Truth*, No. 1, 1985. Cedara: SJTI, St. Joseph's Theological Institute. pp. 6-23.

Kearney, Paddy. 2009. *Guardians of the Light - Denis Hurley: Renewing the Church, Opposing Apartheid*. New York: Continuum International.

Khoza, Mgojo, 1995. The Church in History: Struggle and Challenge. In: Pityana, Barney N., & Villa-Vicencio, Charles, eds. 1995. *Being the Church in South Africa Today*. Johannesburg: South African Council of Churches. pp. 3-11.

Kimber Buell, Denise, 2005. *Why This New Race, Ethnic Reasoning in Early Christianity*. New York: Columbia University Press.

Kinghorn, Johann, 1990. On the theology of Church and society in the DRC. *Journal of Theology for Southern Africa*. No. 70, March 1990. Braamfontein: SACC. pp. 21-36.

Kingdon, John W., 1995. *Agendas, Alternatives, and Public Policies*. New York: Longman.

Kruger, Pieter, 2008. *'n Dowwe spieël? 'n Kerkhistoriese ondersoek na die resente stand van die Nederduitse Gereformeerde Kerk, 1990–2006.* MA. Pretoria: University of Pretoria.

Käßmann, Margot 1992. *Die eucharistische Vision: Armut und Reichtum als Anfrage an die Einheit der Kirche in der Diskussion des Ökumenischen Rates.* München: Kaiser; Mainz: Grünewald. PhD.

LaPorta, Japie, 1999. Unity or Division: A Case Study of the Apostolic Faith Mission of South Africa. In: Dempster, Murray W., & Klaus, Byron D., & Petersen, Douglas, eds. 1999. *The Globalization of Pentecostalism.* Oxford, UK; Irvine, Calif.: Regnum Books Intl. Ch. 7.

Laudate: gesangboek van die Verenigde Evangelies-Lutherse Kerk in Suider-Afrika, 1982. Genadendal: Uitgawe vir die Verenigde Evangelies-Lutherse Kerk in Suider-Afrika van die Gesangboek van die Federasie van Evangelies-Lutherse Kerk in Suider-Afrika.

The Laws and Discipline of the Methodist Church of Southern Africa; Eleventh Edition, 2007. Woodstock: Salty Print.

Lemon, Anthony, 1991. The apartheid city. In: Lemon, Anthony, ed. 1991. *Homes and Apart; South Africa's Segregated Cities.* London: Chapman.

Lindekleiv, Heidi Marie, 2008 a. Sjømannskirkene som forsvant. *Vårt Land*, 2008-05-31, p. 12–13. Oslo: Vårt Land.

Lindekleiv, Heidi Marie, 2008 b. "– Skamplett å selge kirken i Durban". *Vårt Land*, 2008-06-03, p. 12. Oslo: Vårt Land.

List of Participants of the Cape Town Consultation, 1991. In: PCR information. *From Cottesloe to Cape Town, The WCC visit to South Africa, October 1991, Challenges for the Church in post-apartheid South Africa.* PCR information; 1991/no. 30, Geneva: World Council of Churches, Programme to Combat Racism. pp. 109–112.

Liturgy of Reconciliation, Unity and Equality, 2008. Johannesburg: South African Council of Churches.

Lodberg, Peter, 1988. *Apartheid og de lutherske kirker.* Århus: Anis.

The Local Government Handbook: South Africa: A Complete Guide to Municipalities in South Africa 2014, 2014. 4th ed. Cape Town: Yes! Media.

Lutheran Churches in the World: a Handbook, 1989. Eds. Bachmann, Ernest Theodore & Bachmann, Mercia Brenne. Minneapolis: Augsburg.

Lutheran Hymnal with Supplement, 1989. Adelaide: Lutheran Pub. House.

Mabuza, Wesley Madonda, 2009. *Kairos Revisited: Investigating the Relevance of Kairos Document for Christian-State Relations Within a Democratic South Africa.* Ph.D. University of Pretoria.

Macazoma, Saki Charles, 1995. Challenges Facing the Government of National Unity. In: Pityana, Barney N., & Villa-Vicencio, Charles, eds. 1995. *Being the Church in South Africa Today*. Johannesburg: South African Council of Churches. pp. 54–56.

MacIntyre, Alasdair, 1984. *After Virtue, A study in Moral Theory*. Notre Dame, Indiana: University of Notre Dame Press.

Mangcu, Xolela, 2003. The state of race relations in post-apartheid South Africa. In: Daniel, John, & Habib, Adam, & Southall, Roger, eds. 2003. *State of the Nation: South Africa, 2003–2004*. Cape Town: HSRC Press. pp. 105–117.

Masisukumeni, Let's Stand Up, 2004. Pretoria: SACBC / Justice & Peace Department.

McCann, Dennis P., & Brownsberger, M. L., 1995. Management as a Social Practice: Rethinking Business Ethics after MacIntyre. In: Stackhouse, Max L., ed. 1995. *On Moral Business: Classical and Contemporary Resources for Ethnics in Economic Life*. Grand Rapids, Mich.: W.B. Eerdmans Pub. pp. 508–513.

McCullum, Hugh, 2004. Racism and Ethnicity. In: Briggs, John, & Ambo Oduyoye, Mercy, & Tsetsis, Georges, eds. *History of the Ecumenical Movement Vol. 3 1968–2000*. Geneva: World Council of Churches. pp. 345–372.

Meierkord, Christiane, 2007. Lingua franca communication in multiethnic contexts. In: Kotthoff, Helga, & Spencer-Oatey, Helen, eds. 2007. *Handbook of Intercultural Communication*. Berlin; New York: Mount de Gruyter. Ch. 10.

Die Metodiste-gesangboek, 1987, Kaapstad: Methodist Publishing House.

Methodist Worship, 1999. Peterborough: Methodist Publishing.

Metzler, David G., 1973. *The Concept of Catholicity in the Faith and Order Movement, 1910–1968*. Boston: Boston University School of Theology.

Meyer, Harding, 1991, Reconciled Diversity. *Dictionary of the Ecumenical Movement*. Geneva: WCC Publications; Grand Rapids, Mich.: Eerdmans.

Mgojo, Khoza, 1995. The Church in History: Struggle and Challenge. In Pityana, Barney N., & Villa-Vicencio, Charles, eds. 1995. *Being the Church in South Africa Today*. Johannesburg: South African Council of Churches. pp. 3–11.

Minutes of the Seventy-Fifth Annual Conference of the Methodist Church of South Africa, 1958. Cape Town: Methodist Publishing House and Book Depot.

Missale Romanum ex decreto sacrosancti Œcumenici Concilii Vaticani II instauratum auctoritate Pauli PP. VI promulgatum: ordo missæ, 1969. Vaticanus: Typis Polyglottis Vaticanis.

Mtyala, Quinton, & Serrao, Angelique, & Davis, Gaye, & Williams, Murray, 2011. You're a racist, Jimmy; Manuel hits out at spin doctor over views on coloured people. *The Star*, 2011-03-02, p. 1. Johannesburg: The Star.

Mufamadi, Thembeka Doris, 2011. *The World Council of Churches and its Programme to Combat Racism: The Evolution and Development of their Fight against Apartheid, 1969-1994.* Ph.D. Pretoria: UNISA.

Munck, Ronaldo, 2005. *Globalization and Social Exclusion: A Transformationalist Perspective.* Bloomfield, CT: Kumarian Press.

Mutambirwa, James, 1991. Introduction. In: PCR information. *From Cottesloe to Cape Town, The WCC visit to South Africa, October 1991, Challenges for the Church in post-apartheid South Africa.* PCR information; 1991/no. 30, Geneva: World Council of Churches, Programme to Combat Racism. pp. 7-9.

Myburgh, D.W., 1998, Urban settlement in the Tygerberg, 1945-1995. In: du Plessis, Neil M. ed., 1998. *The Tygerberg: The Story of the Tygerberg Hills and the town of Parow, Bellville and Durbanville.* Cape Town: Tafelberg. Ch. 4.

The Nature and Mission of the Church: A stage on the Way to a Common Statement, 2005, Faith and Order Paper 189. Geneva: WCC.

The Nature and Purpose of the Church: A stage on the way to a common statement, 1998. Faith and Order paper No. 181. Geneva: WCC.

Naudé, Beyers, 1991. Oom Bey Today. *Challenge,* Dec 1991, No. 2. Johannesburg: Challenge. pp. 2-4.

The New Encyclopædia Britannica, Vol. 6, 1986. Chicago: Encyclopædia Britannica.

The New Delhi Report: The Third Assembly of the World Council of Churches 1961, 1962. London: SCM Press.

New Keywords: A Revised Vocabulary of Culture and Society, 2005. Ed. Bennett, Tony, & Grossberg, Lawrence, & Morris, Meaghan. Malden, Mass.: Blackwell Publishing.

Nicol, Willem, 2004. Accompanying the Flock: The Development of the Dutch Reformed Church 1974-1990. In: Weisse, Wolfram, & Anthonissen, C. A., eds. 2004. *Maintaining Apartheid or Promoting Change?* Münster: Waxmann. pp. 115-122.

Nodal Economic Development Profile (INK) Inanda, Ntuzuma and KwaMashu KwaZulu Natal, 2007. Gauteng: Department of Provincial and Local Government, Business Trust.

Nolan, Albert, 1995. Church and State in a Changing Context. In: Pityana, Barney N., & Villa-Vicencio, Charles, eds. 1995. *Being the Church in South Africa Today.* Johannesburg: South African Council of Churches. pp. 151-156.

Nordenbrock, William A., 2011. *Beyond Accompaniment: Guiding a Fractured Community to Wholeness.* Collegeville, Minn.: Liturgical Press.

The St. Olav Lutheran Church 1880-1980, 1980, Ed. Lear, M.F. Durban: Unity Publications.

One Baptism: Towards Mutual Recognition, 2011. Faith and Order Paper No. 210, Geneva: WCC.

On the Way to Fuller Koinonia, 1994. Eds. Best, Thomas, F. & Gassmann, Gunther. Faith and Order Paper no. 166. Geneva: WCC.

Orman, Jon, 2009. *Language Policy and Nation-Building in Post-Apartheid South Africa*. Dordrecht; London: Springer.

Orobator, Agbonkhianmeghe, E., 2005. *From Crisis to Kairos*. Limúru: Paulines Publications Africa.

Osborne, Kenan B., 2007. *The Permanent Diaconate: Its History and Place in the Sacrament of Orders*. New York: Paulist Press.

Osborne, Kenan B., 2009. *Theology of the Church for the Third Millennium*. Leiden: Brill.

Ospino, Hoffman, 2008. Rethinking the Urban Parish in the Light of the New Catholicity. *New Theology Review*, Vol. 21, No. 1, 2008. pp. 63-72.

Ottermann, Reino, 1995. *The Centenary of the Synod 1895-1995*. Cape Town: The Evangelical Lutheran Church in Southern Africa (Cape Church).

Pacyga, Dominic A., 1991. Polish Immigrants and Industrial Chicago. Columbus: Ohio State University Press.

Parnell, S. M. & Pirie, G. H., 1991. Johannesburg. In: Lemon, Anthony, ed. 1991. *Homes and Apart; South Africa's Segregated Cities*. London: Chapman. pp. 129-145.

Participating in God's Mission of Reconciliation: A Resource for Churches in Situations of Conflict, 2006. Faith and Order Paper No. 201. Geneva: WCC.

Pityana, Barney N., & Villa-Vicencio, Charles, eds., 1995. *Being the Church in South Africa Today*. Johannesburg: SACC.

Plaatjies, Mary-Anne, & Vosloo, Robert. eds., 2013. *Reformed Churches in South Africa and the Struggle for Justice: Remembering 1960-1990*. Stellenbosch: SunMedia.

Plaatjies-Van Huffel, Mary-Anne, 2008. *Die Doleansiekerkreg en die kerkreg en kerkregering van die Nederduitse Gereformeerde Sendingkerke en die Verenigende Gereformeerde Kerk in Suider-Afrika*. Ph.D. Pretoria: University of Pretoria.

Population Registration Act No 30 of 1950, 1950. Cape Town: Parliament of South Africa.

Post-synodal apostolic exhortation Ecclesia in Africa of the Holy Father John Paul II to the bishops, priests and deacons, men and women religious and all the church in Africa and its evangelizing mission towards the year 2000, 1995. Vatican City: Vatican.

Priest, Robert J., & Nieves, Alvaro L., eds, 2007. *This Side of Heaven*. Oxford; New York: Oxford University Press.

Program of Action – Preamble, 1995. In: Pityana, Barney N., & Villa-Vicencio, Charles, eds. 1995. *Being the Church in South Africa Today*. Johannesburg: South African Council of Churches. pp. 170–171.

Race Relations and the Catholic Church in South Africa: A Decade After Apartheid, 2005. Pretoria: SACBC Justice and Peace Department.

Racism in Theology – Theology Against Racism, Document III. 12, 1975. In: Gassmann, Günther ed. 1993. *Documentary History of Faith and Order, 1963–1993*. Faith and Order paper, no. 159. Geneva: WCC Publications. pp. 148–1952.

Rembe, Symphorosa Wilibald, 2005, *The Politics of Transformation in South Africa*. Grahamstown: Rhodes University.

Report of the Second World Conference on Faith and Order: (Edinburgh, August 3-18, 1937), 1937. London: Student Christian Movement Press.

Reports of the World Conference on Faith and Order, Lausanne, Switzerland, August 3 to 21, 1927, 1927. Boston, Mass.: The Secretariat.

Rite of reconciliation, 1996. Johannesburg: South African Council of Churches.

Ruiters, Michele, 2009. Collaboration, assimilation and contestation: emerging constructions of coloured identity in post-apartheid South Africa. In: Adhikari, Mohamed, ed. 2009. *Burdened by Race: Coloured identities in southern Africa*. Cape Town: UCT Press. Ch. 5.

The Rustenburg Declaration, 1990. In: Chikane, Frank & Alberts, Louw, eds. 1991. *The Road to Rustenburg*. Cape Town: Struik Christian Books Ltd. pp. 275–286.

SACBC Statement on Unscriptural Racial Policies (8/6/82), 1982. Pretoria: SACBC.

The Sacramentary, 1998. Washington, D.C.: International Commission on English in the Liturgy.

Sacrosanctum Concilium, 1963. Vatican City: Roman Catholic Church.

Sanjek, Roger, 1990. *Fieldnotes*. Ithaca & London: Cornell University Press.

Die Sakramentarium, 1989. Kaapstad: Katolieke Kerk, Sakramentarium Subkomitee.

Schoedel, William R., 1985. *Ignatius of Antioch: A Commentary on the Letters of Ignatius of Antioch*. Ed. Koester, Helmut. Philadelphia: Fortress Press.

Scott, Peter, 1955. Cape Town: A Multi-Racial City. *The Geographical Journal*, Vol. 121, No, 2. London: Royal Geographical Society. pp. 149–157.

Scriba, George & Lislerud, Gunnar, 1997. Lutheran Mission and Churches in South Africa. In: Elphick, Richard & Davenport, Rodney, eds. 1997. *Christianity in South Africa*. Berkeley, Calif.: University of California Press. Ch. 10.

Senn, Frank C., 1997. *Christian Liturgy: Catholic and Evangelical*. Minneapolis: Fortress Press.

Signs of the Spirit: Official Report, Seventh Assembly: Canberra, Australia, 7–20 February 1991, 1991. Geneva: WCC.

Sing Together: A Multi-Lingual Hymnbook. 1992, Cape Town: Methodist Publishing House.

Smith, Nico, 1972. Die planting van afsonderlike kerke vir nie-blanke bevolkingsgroepe deur die Nederduitse Gereformeerde Kerk in Suid-Afrika: 'n histories-missiologiese analise en ekklesiologiese beoordeling. Pretoria: Universiteit van Pretoria. D.D.

Smit, Johannes A., 1999. *The Dancing Dwarf from the Land of Spirit*. Durban: CSSALL.

Snowden, Jr., Frank M., 1970, *Blacks in Antiquity: Ethiopians in the Greco-Roman Experience*. Cambridge, Mass.: The Belknap Press of Harvard Univ.

South Africa & Apartheid, 1971. Peterson, Robert W. ed. New York: Facts on title.

Southern African Catholic Bishops' Conference Pastoral Letter, February 1960. Pretoria: SACBC.

Southern African Catholic Bishops' Conference Statement on Race Relations, June 1952. Pretoria: SACBC.

Staff, Grant, 1994. The Changing Face of the South African City: From Urban Apartheid to the Deracialization of Space. *International Journal of Urban and Regional Research*, Vol. 18, Issue 3, September 1994. Chichester: John Wiley & Sons, Ltd. pp. 377–391.

Standard Encyclopaedia of Southern Africa, Vol. 4, 1971. Cape Town: Nasou Limited.

Standard Encyclopaedia of Southern Africa, Vol. 6, 1972. Cape Town: Nasou Limited.

Standard Encyclopaedia of Southern Africa, Vol. 9, 1973. Cape Town: Nasou Limited.

Standard Encyclopaedia of Southern Africa, Vol. 10, 1974. Cape Town: Nasou Limited.

Statement issued by the Cape Town Consultation, 1991. In: *From Cottesloe to Cape Town, The WCC visit to South Africa, October 1991, Challenges for the Church in post-apartheid South Africa*. PCR information; 1991/no. 30. Geneva: World Council of Churches, Programme to Combat Racism. pp. 97–101.

Statement on Reconstructing and Renewing the Church in South Africa, 1995. In: Pityana, Barney N., & Villa-Vicencio, Charles, eds. 1995. *Being the Church in South Africa Today*. Johannesburg: South African Council of Churches. pp. 163–168.

Statement on the History of the Berliner Mission in South Africa, 2000. Berlin: Berliner Missionswerk.

Steyn, Melissa, 2001, *Whiteness Just Isn't What It Used To Be, White Identity in a Changing South Africa*. Albany: State University of New York Press.

Swakopmund – Appeal/FELCSA 1975, Appeal to Lutheran Christians in Southern Africa Concerning the Unity and the Witness of Lutheran Churches and their Members in Southern Africa, 1975. Johannesburg: FELCSA.

Tayob, Abdulkader, 1999. Managing Cultural Diversity in a Democratic South Africa: Is there a Surplus Value to the National Project?. In: Tayob, Abdulkader, & Weisse, Wolfram, eds. 1999. *Religion and Politics in South Africa: From Apartheid to Democracy*. Münster; New York: Waxmann.

Terreblanche, Sampie, 2002. *A History of Inequality in South Africa, 1652–2002*. Pietermaritzburg: University of Natal Press; Sandton: KMM Review Pub.

Theological Refection, 2005. Pretoria: SACBC / Justice & Peace Department.

Theron, P. F., 1978. *Die ekklesia as kosmies-eskatologiese teken. Die eenheid van die kerk as 'profesie' van die eskatologiese vrede*. Pretoria: N.G. Kerkboekhandel.

Theron, P. F., 1979. Die kerk as eskatologiese teken van eenheid. In: Meiring, P. G. J., & Lederle, H. I., eds. 1979. *Die eenheid van die kerk*. Kaapstad: Tafelberg. pp. 6–13.

Theron, P. F. 1986. Kerklike eenheid en natuurlike verskeidenheid. In: Kinghorn, J. ed. 1986. *Die NG Kerk en apartheid*. Johannesburg: Macmillan.

Thiessen, Gesa E., 2009. Seeking Unity: Reflecting on Methods in Contemporary Ecumenical Dialogue. In: Thiessen, Gesa E., & Hogan, Linda, eds. 2009. *Ecumenical Ecclesiology*. London; New York: T & T Clark. Ch. 2.

The Third World Conference on Faith and Order: Held at Lund August 15th to 28th, 1952, 1953. London: S.C.M. Press.

Thompson, Leonard, 2001. *A History of South Africa*. New Haven; London: Yale University Press.

Titlestad, Peter, 1996. English, the Constitution and South Africa's Language Future. In: De Klerk, Vivian, ed. 1996. *Focus on South Africa*. Amsterdam; Philadelphia: John Benjamins Pub. Co. pp. 163–173.

Together on the way: Official Report of the Eighth Assembly of the World Council of Churches, 1999. Geneva: WCC.

The Toronto Statement on "The Church, the Churches, and the World Council of Churches", 1950. Received by the WCC Central Committee in Toronto in 1950. Geneva: WCC.

Towards Sharing the One Faith: A study guide for discussion groups, 1996. Faith and Order paper No. 173. Geneva: WCC.

Township Renewal: INK Case Study, 2009. Johannesburg: South African Cities Network.

A Treasure in Earthly Vessels: An instrument for an ecumenical reflection on hermeneutics, 1998. Faith and Order paper No. 182. Geneva: WCC.

Tronêt, Jakob, 2014. *Förverkligad katolicitet: Max Thurians syn på vägar till Kyrkans enhet*. Skellefteå: Artos & Norma bokförlag.

Truth and Reconciliation Commission of South Africa Report, Vol. 1, 1998. Cape Town: The Commission.

Truth and Reconciliation Commission of South Africa Report, Vol. 4, 1998, Cape Town: The Commission.

Truth and Reconciliation Commission of South Africa Report, Vol. 5, 1998, Cape Town: The Commission.

Tutu, Desmond, 1991. Opening Worship. In: Alberts, Louw, & Chikane, Frank, eds. 1991. *The Road to Rustenburg*. Cape Town: Struik Christian Books Ltd. Ch. 1.

Tutu, Desmond, 1999. *No Future Without Forgiveness*. New York: Doubleday.

United Nations Universal Declaration of Human Rights 1948, 1948. United Nation: UN.

The Unity of the Church: Gift and Calling – The Canberra Statement, 1991. Geneva: WCC.

The Uppsala Report 1968: Official Report of the Fourth Assembly of the World Council of Churches, Uppsala July 4–20, 1968. Ed. Goodall, Norman. Geneva: World Council of Churches.

UKZN Pioneers the Introduction of isiZulu in Undergraduate Degrees, Media Release UKZN 2013-05-15. Durban: University of KwaZulu-Natal.

Van der Borght, E. A. J. G., 2012. In: Doyle, Dennis M., & Furry, Timothy J., & Bazzell, Pascal D., eds. 2012. *Ecclesiology and Exclusion: Boundaries of Being and Belonging in Postmodern Times*. Maryknoll, N.Y.: Orbis Books. pp. 317–324.

Van der Linde, Hugo Hendrik, 2002. *'n Kerkhistoriese en kerkregtelike studie van die kerkverenigingsproses in die NG Kerkfamilie* Pretoria: Universiteit van Pretoria.

Van der Merwe, Barend Jacobus, 2010. *Historiese Perspektiewe op die Verhouding Tussen die Nederduitse Gereformeerde Kerk van Suid-Afika en Apartheid, 1980–1990*. MA. Bloemfontein: University of the Free State.

Van der Merwe, Hugo, 2003. The Role of the Church in Promoting Reconciliation in Post-TRC South Africa. In: Chapman, A., & Spong, B., eds. 2003. *Religion and Reconciliation in South Africa.* Philadelphia: Templeton Foundation Press. pp. 269-281.

Van der Merwe, Hugo, & Chapman, Audrey R., 2008. Did the TRC Deliver?. In: Chapman, Audrey R., Chapman & Van der Merwe, Hugo, eds. 2008. *Truth and Reconciliation in South Africa.* Philadelphia, Pa.: University of Pennsylvania Press. Ch. 10.

Van der Merwe, J.M., 1990. *"Ras Volk en Nasie" en "Kerk en Samelewing" as beleidstukke van die Ned Geref Kerk - 'n Kerkhistoriese studie.* Ongepubliseerde DD. Pretoria: Universiteit van Pretoria.

Villa-Vicencio, Charles, 1995. Freedom is Forever Unfinished: The Incomplete Theological Agenda. In: Pityana, Barney N., & Villa-Vicencio, Charles, eds. 1995. *Being the Church in South Africa Today.* Johannesburg: South African Council of Churches. pp. 57-72.

Vischer, Lucas, 1963. The Meaning of Catholicity. *The Ecumenical Review*, Vol. 16, Issue 1, October 1963. Geneva: WCC. pp. 24-32.

Volf, Miroslav, 1998. *After our likeness: The Church as the Image of the Trinity.* Grand Rapids, Mich.: William B. Eerdmans.

Volf, Miroslav, & Bass, Dorothy C. eds., 2002. *Practicing Theology: Beliefs and Practices in Christian Life.* Grand Rapids, Mich: W.B. Eerdmans.

Vorster, Koos, 1991. Understanding the South African Reality. In: Chikane, Frank & Alberts, Louw, eds. 1991. *The Road to Rustenburg.* Cape Town: Struik Christian Books Ltd. Ch. 5.

Walshe, Peter, 1995. Christianity and Democratisation in South Africa: The Prophetic Voice within Phlegmatic Churches. In: Gifford, Paul, ed. 1995. *The Christian Churches and the Democratisation of Africa.* Leiden: Brill. Co. Ch. 5.

Ward, Peter, ed., 2012. *Perspectives on Ecclesiology and Ethnography.* Grand Rapids, Mich.: W.B. Eerdmans Pub.

Wepener, Cas, 2009. *From fast to feast: A ritual-liturgical exploration of reconciliation in South African cultural contexts.* Leuven: Peeters.

Wesson, Alf, 1998, The Tygerberg Hills 1652 to 1945. In: du Plessis, Neil M. ed., 1998. *The Tygerberg: The Story of the Tygerberg Hills and the town of Parow, Bellville and Durbanville.* Cape Town: Tafelberg. Ch. 3.

Williams, Catrin, 2005. An Introduction to the Study. In: Best, Thomas F., ed. 2005. *Faith and Order at the Crossroads: Kuala Lumpur 2004: The Plenary Commission Meeting.* Geneva: WCC.

Winkler, Harald, E., 1989. *The Divided Roots of Lutheranism in South Africa.* Cape Town: University of Cape Town.

Woods, Anya, 2004. *Medium or Message?: Language and Faith in Ethnic Churches.* Clevedon: Multilingual Matters Limited.

A Word of Hope in the Present Situation in South Africa by the council of the Evangelical Lutheran Church in Southern Africa (Natal-Transvaal), 1987. Johannesburg: ELCSA N-T.

World Values Survey (2010-2014) - South-Africa 2013, WV6-Results South-Africa 2013 Technical record. Alcobendas, Spain: Data Archive WVS.

Worsnip, Michael, 1991. *Between The Two Fires: The Anglican Church and Apartheid 1948-1957.* Pietermaritzburg: University of Natal Press.

Yancey, George, 2003. *One Body One Spirit: Principles of Successful Multicultural Churches.* Downers Grove, Ill.: InterVarsity Press.

1997 Year Book of the Methodist Church of Southern Africa, 1997. Cape Town: Methodist Publishing House and Book Depot.

1998 Year Book of the Methodist Church of Southern Africa, 1998. Cape Town: Methodist Publishing House and Book Depot.

2000/2001 Yearbook of the Methodist Church of Southern Africa, 2001. Cape Town: Methodist Publishing House and Book Depot.

2002 Yearbook of the Methodist Church of Southern Africa, 2002. Cape Town: Methodist Publishing House and Book Depot.

2003 Yearbook of the Methodist Church of Southern Africa, 2003. Cape Town: Methodist Publishing House and Book Depot.

2005 Yearbook of the Methodist Church of Southern Africa, 2005. Cape Town: Methodist Publishing House and Book Depot.

2006 Yearbook of the Methodist Church of Southern Africa, 2006. Cape Town: Methodist Publishing House and Book Depot.

2008 Yearbook of the Methodist Church of Southern Africa, 2008. Cape Town: Methodist Publishing House and Book Depot.

2009 Yearbook of the Methodist Church of Southern Africa, 2009. Cape Town: Methodist Publishing House and Book Depot.

2010 Yearbook of the Methodist Church of Southern Africa, 2010. Cape Town: Methodist Publishing House and Book Depot.

2011 Yearbook of the Methodist Church of Southern Africa, 2011, Cape Town: Methodist Publishing House.

2014 Yearbook, The Methodist Church of Southern Africa, 2014. Cape Town: Methodist Publishing House.

Yong, Amos, & Attanasi, Katy, 2012. *Pentecostalism and Prosperity: The Socio-Economics of the Global Charismatic Movement.* New York: Palgrave Macmillan.

Abbreviations

ABET	Adult Basic Education and Training
ACSA	Anglican Church of Southern Africa
AFM	Apostolic Faith Mission of South Africa
AGS	Apostolise Geloof Sending van Suid-Afrika (the same as AFM)
AIC	African Indigenous / Independent / Initiated Churches
ANC	African National Congress
BEE	Black Economic Empowerment
BEM	Baptism, Eucharist and Ministry (Faith and Order Paper No. 111)
BMW	Berliner Missionswerk (Berlin Mission Society)
CESA	Church of England in South Africa (Also operating as REACH-SA)
CPSA	Church of the Province of Southern Africa (in 2006 renamed: Anglican Church of Southern Africa, ACSA)
CWME	World Council of Churches' Commission on World Mission and Evangelism
DiVA	Digital Academic Archive (Digitala Vetenskapliga Arkivet) at Uppsala University
EKD	Evangelische Kirche in Deutschland (Evangelical Church in Germany)
ELCIN	Evangelical Lutheran Church in Namibia
ELCSA	Evangelical Lutheran Church in Southern Africa
ELCSA-Cape	Evangelical Lutheran Church in Southern Africa-Cape Church
ELCIN-GELC	Evangelical Lutheran Church in Namibia – German Evangelical Lutheran Church
ELCSA N-T	Evangelical Lutheran Church in Southern Africa Natal-Transvaal
ELM	Evangelisch-lutherischen Missionswerkes in Niedersachsen (Evangelical-Lutheran Mission in Lower Saxony)
FCH	TRC's Faith Communities Hearing in East London 1997
FELCSA	Federation of Evangelical Lutheran Churches in Southern Africa (This organisation became LUCSA in 1991)
F&O	World Council of Churches' Commission on Faith and Order
GEAR	Growth, Employment and Redistribution

GK	Gereformeerde Kerk (Reformed Church, sister church to NGK and NHKA)
IMC	International Missionary Council (merged with the WCC in 1961 and became CWME)
INK	Common name for the Inanda, Ntuzuma and KwaMashu townships in eThekwini Municipality
LUA	Lutherans United in Action
LUCSA	Lutheran Communion in Southern Africa
LWF	Lutheran World Federation
MCSA	Methodist Church of Southern Africa
NGK	Nederduits Gereformeerde Kerk (Dutch Reformed Church, sister church to NHKA and GK)
NHKA	Nederduitsch Hervormde Kerk van Afrika (Netherdutch Reformed Church of Africa, sister church to NGK and GK)
NMS	Norwegian Mission Society (Det Norske Misjonsselskap)
OMI	Missionary Oblates of Mary Immaculate
PCR	Programme to Combat Racism
RCC	Roman Catholic Church
RDP	Reconstruction and Development Programme
SACBC	Southern African Catholic Bishops' Conference
SACC	South African Council of Churches
SJ	Society of Jesus (Jesuits)
Stats SA	Statistics South Africa
TRC	Truth and Reconciliation Commission
UCT	University of Cape Town
UELCSA	United Evangelical Lutheran Church in Southern Africa (ELCSA-Cape, ELCSA N-T, ELCIN-GELC)
URCSA	Uniting Reformed Church in Southern Africa (Verenigende Gereformeerde Kerk in Suider Afrika)
VOC	Vereenigde Oostindische Compagnie (The Dutch East India Company)
WCC	World Council of Churches